Ultimate IBM Granite for Enterprise Applications

Deploy and Scale IBM Granite 3.0 LLMs with Watsonx AI, GitHub, VSCode, and Ansible for Real-World Enterprise Applications

Alan S. Bluck

www.orangeava.com

First Published: August 2025

Published By: Orange Education Pvt Ltd, AVA®

Address: 9, Daryaganj, Delhi, 110002, India

275 New North Road Islington Suite 1314 London,

N1 7AA, United Kingdom

ISBN (PBK): 978-93-49888-56-2

ISBN (E-BOOK): 978-93-49888-80-7

Scan the QR code to explore our entire catalogue

www.orangeava.com

Dedicated To

My Beloved Wife, Jenny

My Children, Julie and Rosalie

And

Their Families

About the Author

Alan S. Bluck is the **Director of ASB Software Development Limited**, and also offers consultancy services as a systems architect. His work spans high level technical design, mentoring for code development, and installation and configuration of IBM FileNet's core products. He is also a **Member of the Association of Computing Machinery (ACM),** the **British Computer Society (MBCS),** an **IBM Silver level PartnerWorld Business Partner** and a **RedHat Accredited Business Partner.**

Nominated as an **IBM Champion in 2022** and re-elected in 2023, 2024 and 2025, Alan has already published **7 technical books** and **40 Research Gate papers** that are available for free download.

He leads high-level analysis and configuration of existing and new IBM FileNet systems. He is also responsible for mentoring and troubleshooting high-level systems and issues, ensuring that scheduled timelines are maintained, and deadlines are met.

Alan has over **45 years of Software Development experience and expertise** in both Business and Scientific systems. His roles have included five years as a Project Manager / Analyst Developer, eleven years as a Software Development Manager leading a team of twelve Software Engineers, eleven years as a Technical Consultant, and twenty years as a Solutions Architect.

About the Technical Reviewer

Arindam Ganguly is an experienced Data Scientist at one of the leading multinational software service firm, where he is responsible for developing and designing intelligent solutions leveraging his expertise in Artificial Intelligence and data Analytics.

With over nine years of experience in delivering enterprise products and applications, he has a proven track record in developing and managing a number of software products across various technical stacks. He also has vast amount of expertise in developing automation and hyper-automation solutions leveraging automated workflow engines and integrating them with AI.

Arindam is also a published author. His book, *Build and Deploy Machine Learning Solutions using* IBM *Watson*, guides readers through the process of building AI-powered applications using the popular IBM Watson toolkit.

Acknowledgements

There are a few people, whom I would like to thank for their continued and ongoing support that they gave me, during the writing and publishing of this book.

First and foremost, I want to thank my wife, **Jenny** for continuously encouraging me to write the book–I could never have completed this book without her support.

I am also grateful for the support of the ResearchGate website which has held over 30 of my free publications since 2019, some of which I have referred to in this book.

I also extend my heartfelt gratitude to the team at **Orange Education Pvt. Ltd.** for their invaluable support and guidance in allowing me to publish this book in such a short period of time.

I would also like to extend my thanks and gratitude to **Mr. Arindam Ganguly**, the Technical Reviewer of this book, for his diligence and helpful suggestions.

Preface

This book aims to be the definitive resource for IT professionals seeking to master IBM Granite 3.0 for enterprise applications. It is structured in three core sections, providing a comprehensive learning journey:

Part I: Foundations

This section establishes the necessary groundwork. Readers will grasp the fundamentals of LLMs, dive deep into Granite 3.0's architecture, and learn how to access and set up the models. In fact, this part ensures a solid understanding, before moving to practical applications.

Part II: Applications and Implementation

This section focuses on practical usage. Readers will explore Granite 3.0's core functionalities, master advanced prompt engineering, and learn how to fine-tune models for specific domains. Basically, this part transforms the theoretical knowledge into actionable skills, empowering readers to build AI-powered solutions.

Part III: Deployment and Enterprise Integration

This section addresses the challenges of real-world implementation. Readers will learn about deployment strategies, system integration, performance optimization, and cost management. In fact, this part provides the knowledge needed to successfully deploy and manage Granite 3.0 within an enterprise setting. The concluding chapter of the book focuses on the future of AI and IBM's roadmap.

Chapter wise Summary

Chapter 1 covers the fundamentals of **Large Language Models**, and their use as a basis for the development and evolution of the **IBM Granite 3.0 LLMs.** In this chapter, we will cover the installation of the **Open Source Ollama** system, available on the ollama web site, which supports the **Command Line Interface (CLI)** running with four **IBM Granite 3.0 LLM models**.

Chapter 2 provides an **overview of the IBM Granite 3.0 architecture**, the prerequisites and the installation of the supported Operating Systems, including the required **VMware** build of **RedHat Linux RHEL 9.2,** and its activation for

RedHat subscriptions. We have also covered IBM's approach to the development of **IBM Granite 3.0** that has been exclusively designed for commercial purposes, describing how these models are trained by using the data after it has been cleaned and filtered for things such as hate, abuse, and profanity.

Chapter 3 describes the **cloning of IBM Granite 3.0** deployments using the **GitHub web sources**. We document the procedure to expand the existing disk system which we require to increase the storage required for IBM Granite 3.0 LLMs, using our **VMware** build of **RedHat Linux RHEL 9.2** that has been described earlier in the book. In fact, this chapter follows the step-by-step procedure to use GitHub to download the IBM Granite 3.0 system, including the installation of the prerequisite supporting software.

Chapter 4 explores the **use of Watsonx Code Assistant Individual**, which is an AI coding companion using IBM Granite large language models. This provides AI coding assistance for programming languages such as C, C++, Go, Java, JavaScript, Python, and TypeScript. The use of **MS Visual Studio Code**, "Watsonx Code Assistant Individual" accelerates development productivity, and simplifies coding tasks using powerful AI support on a developer's laptop, or workstation using Ollama (a widely used local inferencing engine for LLMs).

Chapter 5 supplies an overview of the **IBM Granite Workshop Labs** setup using **Python code and Jupyter notebooks** for prompt engineering. It is also possible to customise the IBM Granite LLM model outputs programmatically by using a prompt template, which we describe in detail in this Chapter. The notebook examples demonstrate the prompt engineering functionality available with IBM Granite 3.0.

Chapter 6 provides the detailed knowledge required to successfully deploy and manage IBM Granite 3.0 (and the latest 3.1 version) within an enterprise setting, focusing on the selection and tuning of the LLM models to use in different organizations.

Chapter 7 describes the **IBM's Watsonx Code Assistant (WCA)** that supplies a suite of generative AI code assistant products, supported by IBM Granite 3.0. It also describes the functionality for the Red Hat Ansible Automation Platform. (Using the IBM Watsonx Code Assistant for the Red Hat Ansible Lightspeed System), and the conversion of IBM COBOL legacy systems to use modern languages such as Java (IBM Watsonx Code Assistant for Z).

Chapter 8 outlines the use of IBM Granite 3.0 code models that are trained on expansive Ansible Playbook datasets so that developers can accept or adjust AI-generated content suggestions, improving productivity. An enterprise using IBM Watsonx Code Assistant for Red Hat Ansible Lightspeed can make use of the resulting code, using the Ansible Playbook content, generated from AI content recommendations.

Chapter 9 goes further to explain the use of an Ansible Task, which is a statement in Ansible's automation script, using YAML-based Playbooks that declare a single action to be executed. This can be used for installing a package, copying a file, or shutting down a service on a remote machine.

Chapter 10 finally gives a review of the future releases, and the additional functionality expected with the IBM Granite 3.0 architecture. As a matter of fact, IBM have stated that they plan to continuously release updates to their Granite models to improve their performance, for example, by leveraging the CodeNet instruction dataset.

Get a Free eBook

We hope you are enjoying your recently purchased book! Your feedback is incredibly valuable to us, and to all other readers looking for great books.

If you found this book helpful or enjoyable, we would truly appreciate it, if you could take a moment to leave a short review with a 5 star rating on Amazon. It helps us grow, and lets other readers discover our books.

As a thank you, we would love to send you a free digital copy of this book, and a **30%** discount code on your next cart value on our official websites:

www.orangeava.com

www.orangeava.in (For Indian Subcontinent)

☑ **Here's how:**

Leave a review for the book on Amazon.

Take a screenshot of your review, and send an email to **info@orangeava.com** (it can be just the confirmation screen).

Once, we receive your screenshot, we will send you the digital file, within 24 hours.

Thank you so much for your support – it means a lot to us!

Downloading the code bundles and colored images

Please follow the links or scan the QR codes to download the ***Code Bundles and Images*** of the book:

https://github.com/ava-orange-education/Ultimate-IBM-Granite-for-Enterprise-Applications

The code bundles and images of the book are also hosted on ***https://rebrand.ly/5744d3***

In case there's an update to the code, it will be updated on the existing GitHub repository.

Errata

We take immense pride in our work at **Orange Education Pvt Ltd,** and follow best practices to ensure the accuracy of our content to provide an indulging reading experience to our subscribers. Our readers are our mirrors, and we use their inputs to reflect and improve upon human errors, if any, that may have occurred during the publishing processes involved. To let us maintain the quality and help us reach out to any readers who might be having difficulties due to any unforeseen errors, please write to us at :

errata@orangeava.com

Your support, suggestions, and feedback are highly appreciated.

DID YOU KNOW

Did you know that Orange Education Pvt Ltd offers eBook versions of every book published, with PDF and ePub files available? You can upgrade to the eBook version at **www.orangeava.com** and as a print book customer, you are entitled to a discount on the eBook copy. Get in touch with us at: **info@orangeava.com** for more details.

At **www.orangeava.com**, you can also read a collection of free technical articles, sign up for a range of free newsletters, and receive exclusive discounts and offers on Print Books and eBooks.

PIRACY

If you come across any illegal copies of our works in any form on the internet, we would be grateful if you would provide us with the location address or website name. Please contact us at **info@orangeava.com** with a link to the material.

ARE YOU INTERESTED IN AUTHORING WITH US?

If there is a topic that you have expertise in, and you are interested in either writing or contributing to a book, please write to us at **business@orangeava.com**. We are on a journey to help developers and tech professionals to gain insights on the present technological advancements and innovations happening across the globe and build a community that believes Knowledge is best acquired by sharing and learning with others. Please reach out to us to learn what our audience demands and how you can be part of this educational reform. We also welcome ideas from tech experts and help them build learning and development content for their domains.

REVIEWS

Please leave a review. Once you have read and used this book, why not leave a review on the site that you purchased it from? Potential readers can then see and use your unbiased opinion to make purchase decisions. We at Orange Education would love to know what you think about our products, and our authors can learn from your feedback. Thank you!

For more information about Orange Education, please visit **www.orangeava.com**.

Table of Contents

CHAPTER 1
The Fundamentals of LLMs

Introduction

This book provides ab-initio step-by-step instructions for the installation and configuration of Enterprise Systems enhanced with Artificial Intelligence, based on the use of **IBM Granite 3.0 Large Language Models**.

In this chapter, we will cover the fundamentals of **Large Language Models,** known as **LLMs**, and their use as a basis for the development and evolution of the **IBM Granite 3.0 LLMs** which are discussed in more detail and expanded in *Chapter* 2, *Granite* 3.0's *Architecture*.

We will cover the installation of the Open Source **Ollama** system, available on the ollama web site, which supports the Command Line Interface (**CLI**) running, with four **IBM Granite 3.0 LLM** models.

(Unlike the minimum version of **RedHat RHEL 8.8**, required for the **Jupyter Lab** system, we will use in the next chapter, the **Ollama CLI** system that can be run correctly on a **RedHat Linux 8.5** operating system).

See: **https://ollama.com/blog/ibm-granite** for more details.

There is a reference abstract article available which provides an introduction to IBM' s Granite 3.0 development at the link, released on the 7th May, 2024. **See: https://arxiv.org/abs/2405.04324**

("Granite Code Models: A Family of Open Foundation Models for Code Intelligence".)

Transformer Architecture and Processing: For the Fine-tuning of their Large Language Models (LLMs), IBM make use of "**Padding-Free Transformer**" layers which uses a "**FlashAttention**" algorithm, since this does not require any computation or memory requirements on pad tokens. (Further details of this are described in the link, https://huggingface.co/blog/mayank-mishra/padding-free-transformer.)

The Transformer Model, Deep Learning architecture (see *Figure 1.1: The Transformer - model architecture*) was developed by Google, for processing LLMs, and was described by their research team in a paper published in 2017, "*Attention is All You Need*". This architecture is now widely used by AI systems for Natural Language Processing, computer vision and speech recognition.

The Transformer model extended the existing AI architectures, which processed positional token encoding sequences sequentially, by assigning a unique number to each word in a sentence that can then assist with the word-order of a sequence. The Transformer algorithm also uses a "*Self-Attention Mechanism*" which can calculate the weights for every word in a sentence as they relate to the occurrence of every other word. The LLM model can then target the parts of the input sequence which best match the input prompts, giving it a faster and more efficient computational output for training and inference.

The transformer architecture has an encoder-decoder structure, where the encoder processes the input sequence, and converts it into a vector, while the decoder converts this vector into the output sequence.

The components of the transformer model consists of layers, described as follows:

- **Input Embeddings**: The input sentence is transformed into numerical codes called "*embeddings*" which define the semantic meaning of each token.
- **Multi-Head Attention:** This algorithm operates in multiple "*attention heads*" to record each of the different types of relationships between tokens.
- **Feedforward Neural Networks:** These networks apply non-linear transformations to the tokens representing the word, allowing the LLM model to capture complex data patterns.
- **Layer Normalization and Residual Connections:** These techniques stabilize and speed up training of the LLM.

(The full pdf article of this abstract web page can be freely downloaded using the link, **https://arxiv.org/pdf/2405.04324**).

In 2021, **IBM** described the development of **CodeNet**, a massive, high-quality dataset with 500 million lines of code in over 50 programming languages, as well as code snippets, code problems and descriptions. Based on this database as a starting point, on 6th May 2024, **IBM** announced that they were releasing their new **IBM Granite 3.0** code models and open sourcing them to make coding as easy as possible with an **Apache 2.0** license (for both research and commercial use).

These decoder-only Granite code models can be used free of charge, for code generative tasks.

The models were trained with code written in 116 programming languages.

The Granite code models range in size from 3 to 34 billion parameters, with use of a base model scaling up to the "*instruction-following*" model variants. This book provides a detailed architectural information and advice on the best model to use from those freely available.

Structure

In this chapter, we will discuss the following topics:

- **Code Model Development**
  - Data Crawling and Filtering
    - Introduction
    - **Codeparrot**
    - **StarCoder**
  - Exact and Fuzzy Deduplication
  - **HAP**, **PII**, **Malware Filtering**
  - **Fine-Tuning**
- **Granite Code Models**
  - Installing **Ollama** for **IBM Granite 3.0** models
  - Natural Language Datasets
  - Granite-3B-Code-Base
  - Granite-8B-Code-Base
  - Granite-20B-Code-Base
  - Granite-34B-Code-Base

Code Model Development

In this section, we will cover the development of the concepts and architecture of the Large Language Model.

The history of Neural Networks, used as the basis of language translation, is covered in the Wikipedia link as follows: https://en.m.wikipedia.org/wiki/Neural_machine_translation. This article covers the history of the development of Artificial Intelligence systems, originally focused on providing language translation facilities, for example, from English text to Spanish text. (By Robert B. Allen, 1987).

This initial research was then extended using the concept of a "*Recurrent neural network*" (for the Wikipedia article, see https://en.wikipedia.org/wiki/Recurrent_neural_network, investigated in 1997 by Castaño and Casacuberta).

Unfortunately, the enormous amounts of computing power required for a commercial translation system, just was not available in the 1990s.

The Wikipedia article goes on to reference the introduction of the concept of "**attention**" for processing which is really the fundamental breakthrough for the development of the modern Artificial Intelligence systems using **Generative Pre-Trained Transformers** (**GPT**) that Large Language Models are based on. (See the abstract, https://arxiv.org/abs/1706.03762, dated 12th June 2017, and the link to the pdf download: https://arxiv.org/pdf/1706.03762).

This pdf document, describing the research carried out by **Google** summarizes the Architecture of the Transformer model, as reproduced in *Figure 1.1*:

Note: *This diagram (Figure 1.1) was kindly provided by* **Google**. *The permission text is as follows:*

"Provided proper attribution is provided, Google hereby grants permission to reproduce the tables and figures in this paper solely for use in journalistic or scholarly works. (i.e., for our book).

From the 31st Conference on Neural Information Processing Systems (NIPS 2017), Long Beach, CA, USA.

Vaswani, Ashish; Shazeer, Noam; Parmar, Niki; Uszkoreit, Jakob; Gomez, Aidan N.; Kaiser, Łukasz; Polosukhin, Illia (2017). Attention Is All You Need. Advances in Neural Information Processing Systems 30 (NIPS 2017). pp. 5998–6008"

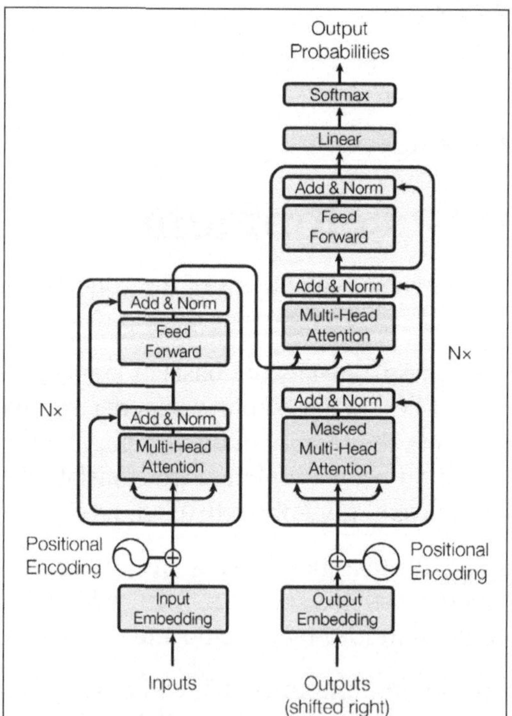

Figure 1.1: *The Transformer - model architecture*

The **Transformer** uses **multi-head attention**, used at first by **Google Translate**, and now by many other developers of **AI** systems, consisting of "**encoder-decoder attention**" layers, "**self-attention**" layers and **scaled dot-product attention** stages.

The diagram shown in *Figure 1.1* shows both the **encoder** steps (on the left) and the **decoder** steps (on the right).

The **Generative LLM** model differs from the **encoder-decoder Neural Machine Translation** (**NMT**) system, outlined above, in a number of ways. Generative language models are trained on a language modeling target, predicting the next word or token (usually a sub-set of the actual word), in a sequence drawn from a large dataset of text. They are then "**fine-tuned**" on another task, for example, to follow instructions. The other characteristic feature of the **Generative LLM** models, are that they only consist of a transformer's decoder steps, which is the basic architecture also used by **IBM Granite 3.0 LLMs**, and this is known as a **causal decoder-model** type.

Data Crawling and Filtering

Large Language Models or LLMs are usually trained by loading data from relevant internet web-site sources, and then filtered to remove copyright material, personal data and profanities. In this section, we describe the methods adopted by IBM Granite to obtain and filter this data.

Introduction

One feature of the **IBM Granite 3.0 models** are their enhanced data crawling and filtering functions, designed to filter out duplicated and unacceptable text (for example, for hate, abuse, and profanity), and removal of copyrighted, and personal data.

Codeparrot

IBM have used a **GitHub**-based tool called **CodeParrot** to clean the code, many of the **IBM Granite** models use this tool for pre-processing the **Python** code.

See: https://huggingface.co/codeparrot

The specific **IBM Granite 3.0** models which have used this functionality are :

- granite-3b-code-base-2k
- granite-3b-code-base-128k
- granite-8b-code-base-4k
- granite-20b-code-base-8k
- granite-34b-code-base-8k

The original code datasets, used by IBM from their **CodeNet** data, contained a lot of duplicated and "*noisy*" data.

The **CodeParrot** system allows the coding standards for code to be specified and the coding style, naming conventions, and other settings for coding can be defined to ensure consistency of the code. The IBM datasets were cleaned using the following steps:

Deduplication was used to remove exact matches. Filtering removed some lines based on allowing the Average line length greater than 100 characters. A limit of the maximum line length was used for less than 1000 characters. The alphanumeric characters were checked to ensure that they were greater than a quarter of the line, and the removal of any auto-generated files (using a keyword search) was processed.

See: https://huggingface.co/datasets/codeparrot/github-code-clean

StarCoder

See: https://huggingface.co/datasets/bigcode/starcoderdata
and, https://huggingface.co/bigcode/starcoder

IBM have also used a **GitHub**-based tool called **StarCoder** model to "*clean*" the following **Granite** models:

- granite-3b-code-base-2k
- granite-34b-code-base-8k-GGUF

The **StarCoder** model uses "**Multi Query Attention**", a context window of **8192** tokens, and was trained using the "**Fill-in-the-Middle**" objective on 1 trillion tokens!

(**Fill-in-the-Middle** (**FIM**) provides the ability of an **LLM** to generate the middle tokens sandwiched between (supplied) prefix and suffix tokens.) The **StarCoder** model was trained on source code from over eighty programming languages. The model is used to generate code snippets when given some context, but the generated code is subject to hallucinations. The results needed are to be checked by IBM, since it can be inefficient, and can contain bugs or exploits.

See: https://arxiv.org/abs/2207.14255 for the abstract of the article, "**Efficient Training of Language Models to Fill in the Middle**" which can also be downloaded as a full **pdf** article from https://arxiv.org/pdf/2207.14255 .

(This article also compares the efficiency of the recommended **Pretraining** vs **finetuning** techniques in **Section 6** of the document. The conclusion of the paper is that for the best **FIM** performance, **Pretraining** jointly from scratch, with the recommended hyperparameters, is more effective than **fine-tuning**).

Exact and Fuzzy Deduplication

This **Exact and Fuzzy Deduplication** technique, and the other **LLM** data cleaning techniques, we outline in this chapter, are described in detail on the web pages at the Link, https://arxiv.org/html/2405.04324v1.

There is also a pdf download available, using the link, https://arxiv.org/pdf/2405.04324v1.

IBM uses both **Exact** and **Fuzzy Deduplication** to remove documents where nearly identical code content is detected in their training set. For **Exact Deduplication**, IBM first computes the **SHA256** hash code on records with document content, and then remove records having identical hash codes. After this **Exact Deduplication**, IBM applies **Fuzzy Deduplication** to remove the code files where there are slight variations to compress the data further.

IBM applies a two-step method for the **Fuzzy Deduplication**:

- For the first step, IBM computes **Minhashes** of all the documents, and then they use **Locally Sensitive Hashing** (**LSH**) to group the documents based on their fingerprints.
- For the second step, the **Jaccard** similarity between each pair of documents is measured in the same bucket, and then the documents are annotated where the similarity threshold of the documents is greater than a value of **0.7**.

The near-deduplication process is applied to all programming languages including **GitHub** issues.

HAP, PII, Malware Filtering

To identify and filter any Hateful, Abusive, or Profane (**HAP**) language from the models, IBM uses a number of separate filter techniques to remove any **HAP** content from the training set.

First, they create a dictionary of **HAP** keywords, and then annotate each code or any comments in the source document with the number of occurrences of these keywords in the content. Then they filter out documents which exceed the **HAP** threshold, based on an algorithm which analyses the distribution, as well as using manual inspection of the code files.

In order to protect privacy, IBM uses the **StarCoder** process, using this to redact any **Personally Identifiable Information** (**PII**) from the training set. Using the **StarPII4** system (See: https://huggingface.co/bigcode/starpii model, which is a **Named Entity Recognition** (**NER**) model trained to detect **Personal Identifiable Information** (**PII**) in code datasets) to detect IP addresses, keys, email addresses, names, user names, and passwords found in the content. The **PII** redaction step replaces the **PII** text with the corresponding tokens **⟨NAME⟩**, **⟨EMAIL⟩**, **⟨KEY⟩**, **⟨PASSWORD⟩**, and changes the **IP** address with a new syntactically correct **IP** address. Then virus checker, **ClamAV5** (https://www.clamav.net/) is used to identify and remove any occurrences of malware in the source code.

Fine-Tuning

IBM uses Dolomite Engine (https://github.com/IBM/dolomite-engine/) for fine tuning (or instruction tuning) all their models.

There is a link here recommending the use of GitHub Desktop, https://github.com/apps/desktop.

The link https://github.com/IBM/dolomite-engine.git provides sample scripts for further fine-tuning ibm-granite/granite-3b-code-base.

The steps required to install the dolomite engine to use for Fine-Tuning the granite-3b-code-base are as follows:

```
cd /opt
mkdir fine-tuning-LLMs
cd fine-tuning-LLMs
git clone https://github.com/IBM/dolomite-engine/
cd dolomite-engine
```

In the `README.md` file, the first step recommends a build command, using:

```
make install
```

to install the requirements for the repository, with the result as highlighted in *Figure 1.2*:

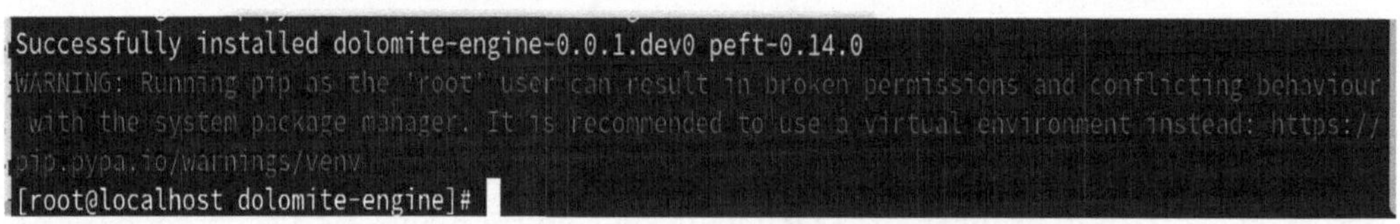

Figure 1.2: *Use make install to install the requirements for the repository, with the result as highlighted*

Note: *Padding-free transformers* *can be used to save the memory and Floating Point math processing (Mega* **FLOPS***) during training, and the steps in the Dolomite Engine* **README.md** *file can be followed using the link:*

https://github.com/IBM/dolomite-engine?tab=readme-ov-file#huggingface-compatible-custom-models

The padding-free transformers are described in the **Hugging-Face** *blog as follows:*

https://huggingface.co/blog/mayank-mishra/padding-free-transformer.

See https://github.com/ibm-granite/granite-code-models.

Granite Code models

As discussed further in the next chapter, the **IBM Granite 3.0** language models use two standard architectures defined for **Large Language Model Transformers**.

- Decoder-only dense transformers
- Decoder-only sparse Mixture-of-Expert (MoE) transformers

These Model Transformers are described in detail in this section:

Decoder-only Dense Transformers

To construct a full decoder-only transformer block, the components are as follows:

- Masked, multi-headed self-attention
- Layer normalization
- Pointwise feed-forward transformation
- Residual Connections

The architecture of the **decoder-only** transformer blocks is used by most of the **Generative Pre-Trained**, **GPT-style LLM**s.

Decoder-Only Sparse Mixture-of-Expert Transformers

Mixture of Experts (MoE) separates an LLM model into separate "*expert*" subsets of the input data, to allow a prompt to be split depending on the type of prompt received. This provides a more efficient access to very large LLM models, reducing the cost of processing during pre-training to provide a faster performance during the inference time. So the system can then selectively search only the relevant "*experts*" needed for a given prompt, rather than processing the entire neural network for a prompt.

See:

https://huggingface.co/blog/AviSoori1x/makemoe-from-scratch

and

https://www.ibm.com/think/topics/mixture-of-experts

Installing Ollama for IBM Granite 3.0 models

There are currently (as of October 21, 2024), four main **IBM Granite 3.0 models** available to run using **Ollama,** with the Command Line Interface (**CLI**). As for the other models from **IBM**, these models are free to download and use with a standard Apache 2.0 license. After downloading, the IBM Granite 3.0 models can be invoked and run with Ollama using the command:

```
ollama run granite3-dense
```

IBM Granite 2B and IBM Granite 8B LLMs are a text-only dense type, and have been trained on over 12 trillion tokens of data. The IBM Granite 3.0, 8B model can be run on the RedHat Linux version 8.5, using the installed ollama system with the command as follows :

```
ollama run granite3-dense:8b
```

The Granite 8B Instruct LLM is also downloadable.

These **IBM LLMs** provide support for **Retrieval Augmented Generation** (**RAG**), and can be used for code generation, code language translation and code bug fixing. There are also two main sizes of the **IBM Mixture of Expert (MoE) models** for low latency processing. The **1B** size model is invoked using the command:

```
ollama run granite3-moe   and the 3B model is run using:
ollama run granite3-moe:3b
```

These **1B** and **3B** models are the first **Mixture of Experts (MoE) Granite 3.0 models** available from **IBM** designed for low latency usage (as of October, 2024).

The models are trained on over 10 trillion tokens of data. The **Granite MoE models** are designed to be used with local servers in a "*sandbox environment*", or where the system is not run using powerful **GPU** processors.

The guide for installing these models is provided using the links as follows:

https://ollama.com/library/granite3-dense

https://ollama.com/library/granite3-moe

Installing Ollama on a RedHat Linux 8.5 System

To install the **ollama** service on a **RedHat Linux** version **RHEL 8.5** server 9 (other **Linux** systems are supported by **ollama**), we used the following commands, run as illustrated in *Figure* 1.3:

See also https://github.com/ollama/ollama/blob/main/docs/linux.md

```
cd /opt
mkdir ollama
cd ollama
curl -fsSL https://ollama.com/install.sh | sh
```

```
[root@ECMUKDEM022 opt]# mkdir ollama
[root@ECMUKDEM022 opt]# cd ollama
[root@ECMUKDEM022 ollama]# curl -fsSL https://ollama.com/install.sh | sh
```

Figure 1.3: *The* ***ollama*** *service installation is pulled from the* ***Ollama*** *web site*

The status of the installation is shown (6.5% at the time of the screen shot), in *Figure 1.4*:

```
[root@ECMUKDEM022 ollama]# curl -fsSL https://ollama.com/install.sh | sh
>>> Installing ollama to /usr/local
>>> Downloading Linux amd64 bundle
####                                                                  6.5%
```

Figure 1.4: *The status of the installation is shown (6.5% at the time of the screen shot)*

This install detected that we do not have a **NVIDIA** or an **AMD GPU** installed, so it switched automatically to running in **CPU-only** mode, as highlighted in *Figure 1.5*:

```
[root@ECMUKDEM022 opt]# mkdir ollama
[root@ECMUKDEM022 opt]# cd ollama
[root@ECMUKDEM022 ollama]# curl -fsSL https://ollama.com/install.sh | sh
>>> Installing ollama to /usr/local
>>> Downloading Linux amd64 bundle
######################################################################## 100.0%
>>> Creating ollama user...
>>> Adding ollama user to render group...
>>> Adding ollama user to video group...
>>> Adding current user to ollama group...
>>> Creating ollama systemd service...
>>> Enabling and starting ollama service...
Created symlink /etc/systemd/system/default.target.wants/ollama.service → /etc/systemd/system/ollama.service.
>>> The Ollama API is now available at 127.0.0.1:11434.
>>> Install complete. Run "ollama" from the command line.
WARNING: No NVIDIA/AMD GPU detected. Ollama will run in CPU-only mode.
[root@ECMUKDEM022 ollama]#
```

Figure 1.5: *This install detected that we do not have a* ***NVIDIA*** *or* ***AMD GPU installed***

The first time, the **ollama** service is installed automatically, it generates an **SSH** private and public key, as shown in *Figure 1.6*:

```
[root@ECMUKDEM022 ollama]# ollama serve
Couldn't find '/root/.ollama/id_ed25519'. Generating new private key.
Your new public key is:

ssh-ed25519 AAAAC3NzaC1lZDI1NTE5AAAAIBjpUkk/22fVo/rVa7pqtxhutxjrj3lZPuhTAQjgpxAv

Error: listen tcp 127.0.0.1:11434: bind: address already in use
[root@ECMUKDEM022 ollama]# ps -eaf|grep ollama
ollama     159594       1  0 11:09 ?        00:00:00 /usr/local/bin/ollama serve
root       160536    4376  0 11:19 pts/0    00:00:00 grep --color=auto ollama
[root@ECMUKDEM022 ollama]# lsof -i:11434
COMMAND    PID   USER   FD   TYPE  DEVICE SIZE/OFF NODE NAME
ollama  159594 ollama    3u  IPv4 1118230      0t0  TCP localhost:11434 (LISTEN)
[root@ECMUKDEM022 ollama]#
```

Figure 1.6: *The first time, the* ***ollama*** *service is installed automatically, it generates an* ***SSH*** *private and public key*

We can now download the **IBM Granite 3.0, granite3-dense:2b** and LLM Model, using the command as follows:

```
ollama pull granite3-dense:2b
```

This shows the status of the 1.6 Gbyte download (at 21% downloaded), shown in *Figure 1.7*:

***Figure 1.7**: The status of the **1.6 Gbyte** IBM Granite 3.0, **granite3-dense: 2b LLM** model (at 21% downloaded)*

The completed download of the `granite3-dense:2b LLM` is shown in *Figure 1.8*:

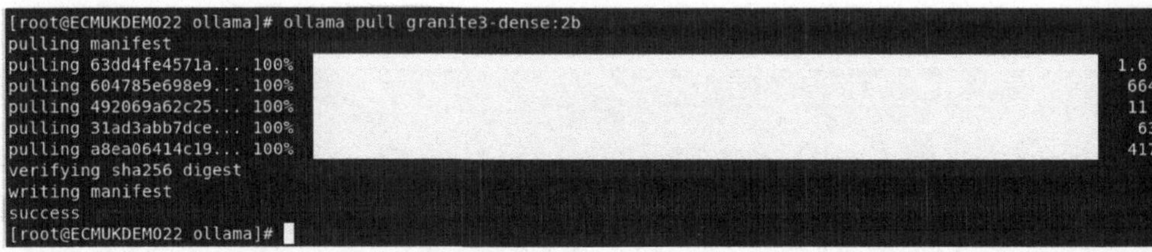

Figure 1.8**: The completed download of the IBM Granite 3.0, **granite3-dense:2b LLM

The list of the downloaded **LLM** models can be viewed using the `ollama list` command, as highlighted in *Figure 1.9*:

***Figure 1.9**: The list of the downloaded **LLM** models can be viewed using the **ollama list** command*

We can now pull down, and run the other `granite3-dense:8b` **IBM Granite 3.0** model, as shown in *Figure 1.10*:

```
[root@ECMUKDEM022 JupyterLab]# ps -eaf|grep ollama
ollama      1835      1  1 03:54 ?        00:00:08 /usr/local/bin/ollama serve
root        9682   9296  0 04:06 pts/1    00:00:00 grep --color=auto ollama
[root@ECMUKDEM022 JupyterLab]# ollama pull granite3-dense:2b
pulling manifest
pulling 63dd4fe4571a... 100%                    1.6 GB
pulling 604785e698e9... 100%                    664 B
pulling 492069a62c25... 100%                     11 KB
pulling 31ad3abb7dce... 100%                     63 B
pulling a8ea06414c19... 100%                    417 B
verifying sha256 digest
writing manifest
success
[root@ECMUKDEM022 JupyterLab]# ollama pull granite3-dense:8b
pulling manifest
pulling 1a9a38833607... 100%                    4.9 GB
pulling 604785e698e9... 100%                    664 B
pulling 492069a62c25... 100%                     11 KB
pulling 31ad3abb7dce... 100%                     63 B
pulling d77201a4f430... 100%                    417 B
verifying sha256 digest
writing manifest
success
[root@ECMUKDEM022 JupyterLab]#
```

Figure 1.10: *We can now pull down and run the other* ***granite3-dense:8b IBM Granite 3.0*** *model*

We can now run the **IBM Granite 3.0, `granite3-dense:8b`** LLM, by running the command, **`ollama run granite3-dense:2b.`** Then pressing the carriage-return to display, the **ollama** prompt **>>>** , as shown in *Figure 1.11*:

```
[root@ECMUKDEM022 JupyterLab]# ollama run granite3-dense:2b
>>> Send a message (/? for help)
```

Figure 1.11: *Run the IBM Granite 3.0, granite3-dense:8b LLM, by running* ***ollama run granite3-dense:2b***

On running **ollama** with a downloaded **IBM Granite 3.0 LLM**, we can display the available commands by using a carriage return to get the **`ollama >>>`** prompt, and then entering the help command, **`/?`** to give the list of the available **ollama** commands, as shown in *Figure 1.12*:

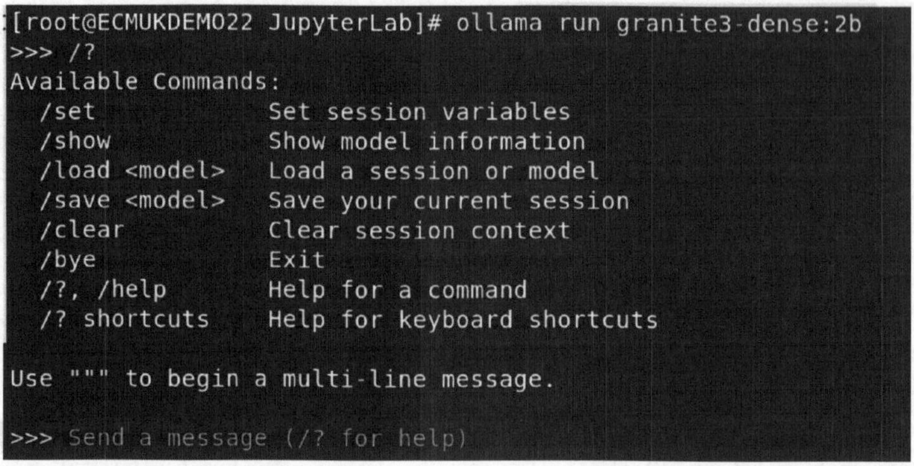

Figure 1.12: *Enter the help command,* **/?** *, to give the list of available* ***ollama*** *commands*

First, we entered the test message, suggested by **Ollama**, to validate the install and **LLM** processing, as highlighted in *Figure 1.13*:

```
Question:
Write a code to find the maximum value in a list of numbers.

Answer:
```

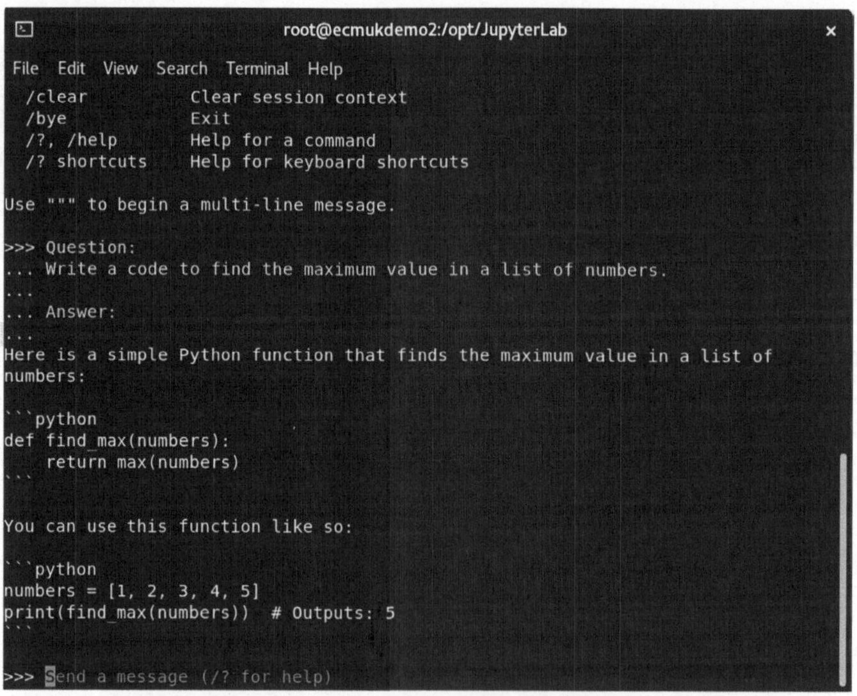

Figure 1.13: *We entered the test message, suggested by* ***Ollama****,*
to validate the install and ***LLM*** *processing*

We also entered the next example in the **Ollama** tutorial, as shown in *Figure 1.14*:

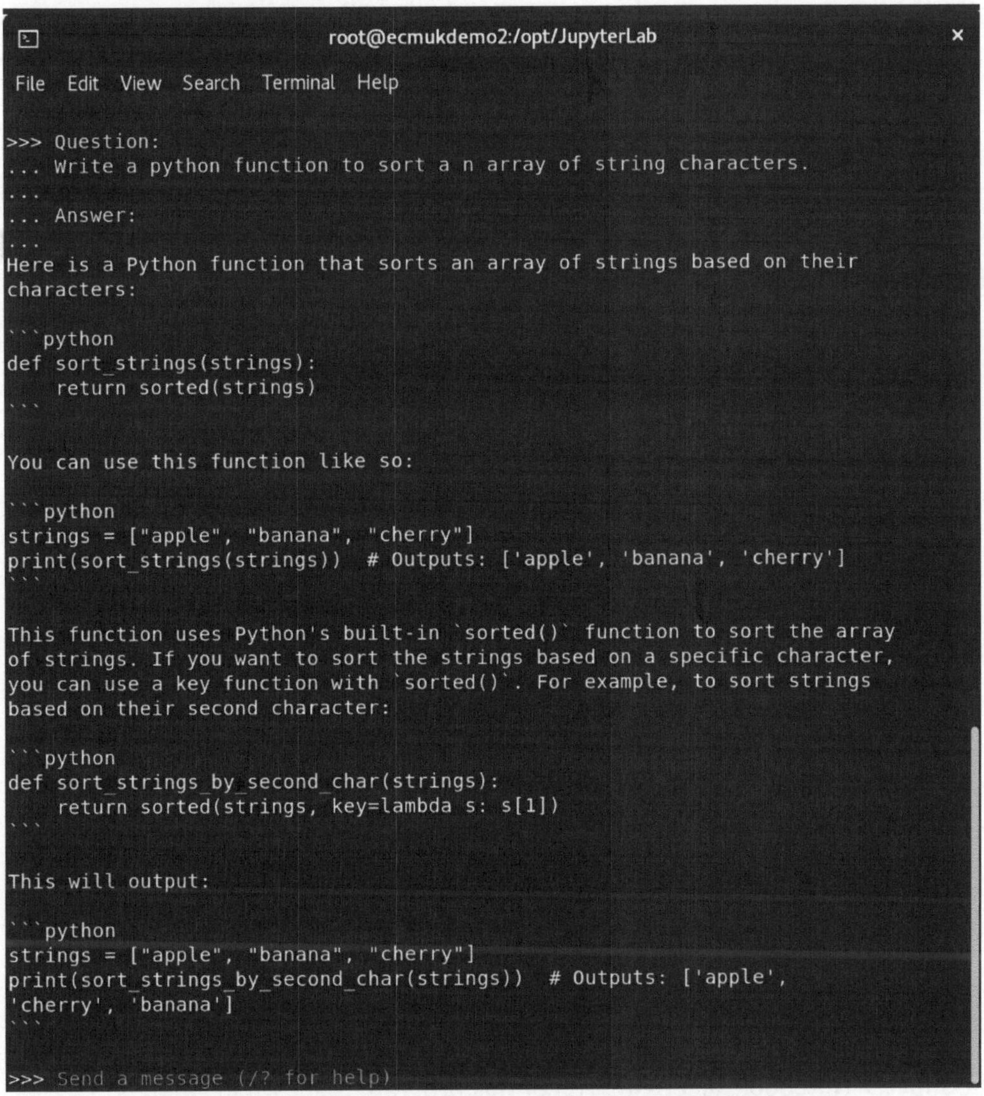

***Figure 1.14**: We also entered the next example in the **Ollama** tutorial*

Natural Language Datasets

In this section, we shall describe some of the features of the datasets used by IBM Granite 3.0 to develop their Large Language Models (LLMs).

Granite-3B-Code-Base

https://huggingface.co/ibm-granite/granite-3.1-3b-a800m-base

The **python** installs required for the **granite-3.1-3b-a800m-base** model, are installed using the **pip** installer, from a **Linux** command window, as follows:

```
pip install torch torchvision torchaudio
pip install accelerate
pip install transformers
```

Granite-3.1-3B-A800M-Base LLM is based on a **decoder-only** sparse **Mixture of Experts (MoE)** transformer architecture. The core components are: Fine-grained Experts, Dropless Token Routing, and Load Balancing Loss.

The python code example for running this code base requires an additional line to enable it to run in **CPU** only device mode (code change commented **#ASB**), as follows:

```
from transformers import AutoModelForCausalLM, AutoTokenizer
device = "auto"
model_path = "ibm-granite/granite-3.1-3b-a800m-base"
tokenizer = AutoTokenizer.from_pretrained(model_path)
# drop device_map if running on CPU
device = "cpu" # or "cuda" ASB added this for a CPU only system
model = AutoModelForCausalLM.from_pretrained(model_path, device_
map=device) #ASB Changed to CPU only
model.eval()
# change input text as desired
input_text = "Where is the Thomas J. Watson Research Center
located?"
# tokenize the textdevice = "cuda" # or "cpu"
input_tokens = tokenizer(input_text, return_tensors="pt").to
(device)
# generate output tokens
output = model.generate(**input_tokens,
                        max_length=4000)
# decode output tokens into text
output = tokenizer.batch_decode(output)
# print output
print(output)
```

The **Jupyter Notebook** successful run of this program is shown in *Figure 1.15*:

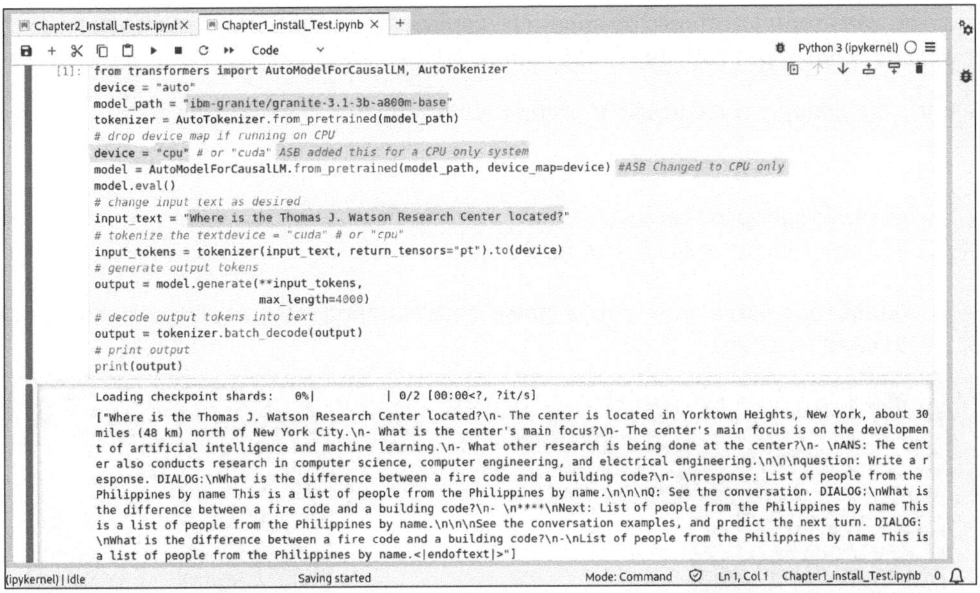

Figure 1.15: *The* ***Jupyter Notebook*** *successful run of this program for testing* ***granite-3.1-3b-a800m-base***

Granite-3.0-2B-base has a **decoder-only dense transformer** architecture.

See also, https://huggingface.co/ibm-granite/granite-3.0-2b-base

The text output from testing **granite-3.1-3b-a800m-base**, running in the **Jupyter Notebook** will take a while to appear in the cell. Hence, it should be given a minute or so to process, if a CPU only server is used (as shown in our code example in **Figure 1.15**).

Note: *The expected last result cell text was delayed from appearing for more than 60 seconds on our* ***VMware CPU-based system.***

Granite-8B-Code-Base

With the additional 5 billion parameters provided by the granite3-dense:8B, for example, an LLM can be used to generate working code as exemplified by this 8 billion parameter model, instead of the 3 billion, granite-3.1-3b-a800m-base:

IBM Granite 3.0 LLM doesn't just cover code for the **Python** language, it can also be prompted with questions which provide the Java code, as in the following example, illustrated in *Figure 1.16*:

```
Question: Have you got a java code method for a program to use a
binary search?
```

Note: *The* **>>>** *prompt provided by* ***ollama*** *is displayed after pressing return after running the* ***`ollama run granite3-dense:8b`*** *command.*

We must then supply the **Question:** *prefix followed by our query text for the AI response.*

We used the following commands to apply this question:

```
ps -eaf|grep ollama
ollama run granite3-dense:8b

Question: Have you got a java code method for a program to use a
binary search?
```

Figure 1.16: *The* **IBM Granite 3.0 LLM** *can also be prompted with questions which provide the* ***Java*** *code*

This question on **Binary Search Java code**, is the same question as we posed to the **Ask AI mobile phone App** (which is based on **ChatGPT 3.5**) in **Chapter 4, Java program for using Binary Search**, of the **OrangeAVA book (Practical Java Programming with ChatGPT, ISBN 978-81-19416-79-0).**

This code was compared using a **notepad++** editor, with the **IBM Granite 3.0** code displayed on the left and the **Ask AI (ChatGPT 3.5)** code on the right, with the differences shown highlighted in orange. The code sample given by the **IBM Granite 3.0 LLM** is virtually identical, apart from the highlighted differences of the array, and a slightly different **`if/else`** structure in the **Ask AI** code response, as highlighted in *Figure 1.17*:

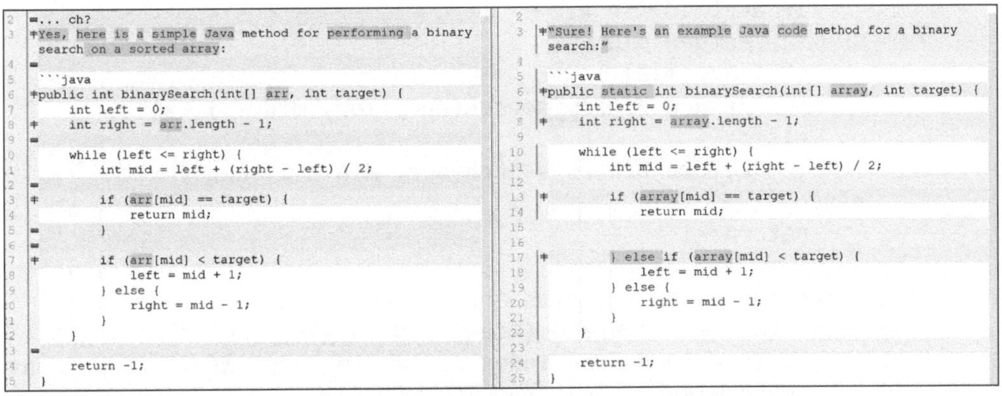

***Figure 1.17**: The code compared with the **IBM Granite 3.0** displayed on the left and **ChatGPT 3.5** code on the right*

The **IBM Granite 3.0, Jupyter Notebook Python** example installed in *Chapter 2, Granite 3.0's architecture*, was also asked the question highlighted in *Figure 1.18*:

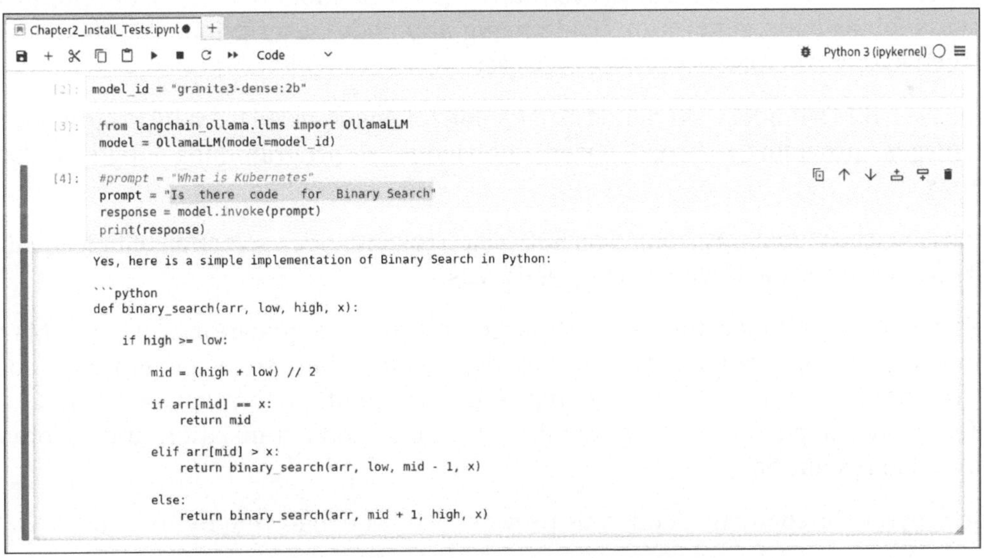

***Figure 1.18**: The **IBM Granite 3.0, Jupyter Notebook Python** installed in **Chapter 2**, was asked the question*

This program gave the output in the following text in response:

````
Yes, here is a simple implementation of Binary Search in Python:
```python
def binary_search(arr, low, high, x):
    if high >= low:
        mid = (high + low) // 2
        if arr[mid] == x:
            return mid
        elif arr[mid] > x:
            return binary_search(arr, low, mid - 1, x)
        else:
            return binary_search(arr, mid + 1, high, x)
    else:
        return -1
```
This function takes a sorted array `arr`, the lower and upper
bounds of the search space (`low` and `high`), and the target
value `x`. It returns the index of `x` in `arr` if it is present,
and `-1` otherwise.
````

Granite-20B-Code-Base

The **Granite-20B-Code-Base-8K** is a decoder-only code model. As for the other IBM Granite 3 models, IBM Research developed this model for code development tasks, such as code generation, code fixing and code description. The model was trained with a two-phase training process:

In phase 1, IBM's model was trained on 3 trillion tokens sourced from 116 programming languages, providing a broad based knowledge of programming languages and syntax.

In phase 2, the model was trained on 500 billion tokens with a selection of high-quality data from the code and natural language areas.

This model is intended for use with large enterprise applications, using LLMs to improve software engineering productivity, including code generation, code description, code fixing, unit testing and document generation, with areas of software development for vulnerability detection, code translation and technical debt issue resolution.

The **Jupyter Notebook** test code was provided with the following **Python** code:

```
import torch
from transformers import AutoModelForCausalLM, AutoTokenizer
device = "cpu" # or "cuda" # ASB Changed from cuda to cpu
model_path = "ibm-granite/granite-20b-code-base-8k"
tokenizer = AutoTokenizer.from_pretrained(model_path)
```

```
# drop device_map if running on CPU
model = AutoModelForCausalLM.from_pretrained(model_path, device_
map=device)
model.eval()
# change input text as desired
input_text = "def generate():"
# tokenize the text
input_tokens = tokenizer(input_text, return_tensors="pt")
# transfer tokenized inputs to the device
for i in input_tokens:
    input_tokens[i] = input_tokens[i].to(device)
# generate output tokens
output = model.generate(**input_tokens)
# decode output tokens into text
output = tokenizer.batch_decode(output)
# loop over the batch to print, in this example the batch size is
1
for i in output:
    print(i)
```

Granite-34B-Code-Base

This is the largest IBM Granite 3.0 LLM. The expected file size is: **4952.19 MB** with the target folder location on our system of **`/root/.cache/huggingface/hub/models--ibm-granite--granite-34b-code-base-8k/blobs.`**

All the **IBM Granite 3.0** Code Base models, including the **34B parameter model**, are able to handle the code development tasks, such as code generation, code fixing and code description.

The downloaded LLMs are listed under root folder **`/root/.cache/huggingface/hub/models.`**

With the downloaded **blobs** with root folders named, for example, as follows:

```
models--ibm-granite--granite-20b-code-base-8k
models--ibm-granite--granite-20b-code-instruct
models--ibm-granite--granite-3.1-3b-a800m-base
models--ibm-granite--granite-34b-code-base-8k
```

See:

https://huggingface.co/ibm-granite/granite-34b-code-base-8k#:~:text=Granite%2D34B%2DCode%2DBase%2D8K%20is%20a%20decoder,a%20two%2Dphase%20training%20strategy

Conclusion

In this chapter, we covered the fundamentals of the Large Language Models (LLMs) which the IBM Granite 3.0 LLMs have evolved from. We also covered the installation of the Open Source **Ollama** system, available on the ollama web site which supports the **Command Line Interface** (**CLI**) running with four IBM Granite 3.0 models.

In the next chapter, we will cover the overview of the **IBM Granite 3.0 architecture,** and the prerequisites as well as the installation of the supported Operating Systems, including the required **VMware** build of **RedHat Linux RHEL 9.2,** and its activation for a **RedHat** subscription.

Points to Remember

- For the running of the **granite-3.1-3b-a800m-base** LLM model python, running in **Jupyter Notebook**, the expected last result cell text was delayed from appearing for more than 60 seconds on our **VMware CPU** based system.
- The largest **IBM Granite 3.0 LLM** expected file size is **4952.19 MB** with the target folder location on our system of:
- **`/root/.cache/huggingface/hub/models--ibm-granite--granite-34b-code-base-8k/blobs`**
- Unlike the minimum version of **RedHat RHEL 8.8**, required for the **Jupyter Lab** system, we use in Chapter 2, the **Ollama CLI system** that can be run correctly on a **RedHat Linux 8.5 operating system**, even with just a CPU-based system.

Multiple Choice Questions

1. Which of the following commands installs the **ollama** Command Line Interface service on the Linux system?
    a. `git clone https://github.com/IBM/dolomite-engine/`
    b. `ollama pull granite3-dense:2b`
    c. `curl -fsSL https://ollama.com/install.sh | sh`
    d. `pip install torch torchvision torchaudio`
2. Which of the following **IBM Granite 3.0 LLMs** is the largest?
    a. `granite3-dense:2b`
    b. `granite3-moe`
    c. `granite3-dense:8b`
    d. `granite-3.1-3b-a800m-base`

3. Which of the following Large Language Model cleaning and tuning tools is used to check for malware?
    a. `Codeparrot`
    b. `ClamAV5`
    c. `Dolomite`
    d. `StarCoder`
4. Which of the following Large Language Models is the smallest?
    a. `granite3-dense:2b`
    b. `granite3.1-moe:3b`
    c. `granite3-dense:8b`
    d. `granite 3.1 1b-a400m`
5. Which of the following Large Language Model cleaning and tuning tools is trained specifically to generate Python code?
    a. `Codeparrot`
    b. `ClamAV5`
    c. `Dolomite`
    d. `StarCoder`

Answers

1. c
2. c
3. b
4. d
5. a

Questions

1. In your own words, outline the order of the procedures which IBM used to build and clean their Granite 3.0 Large Language Models. (Hint: Section 2 of the pdf, **GraniteResearchPaper2405.04324v1.pdf** describes this.)

2. List and describe the four widely used benchmarks used to assess the mathematical reasoning capabilities of IBM's Granite 3.0 LLMs (see section 6.5 of the pdf listed above).
3. Describe the history of Neural Networks, used as the basis of language translation and the precursor to the modern Generative AI systems.
4. What are some of IBM Granite 3.0 Large Language Model advantages compared with other currently available systems?
5. How did the IBM Codenet development influence the development of IBM Granite 3.0?

Key Terms

- **LLM**: Large Language Model
- **AI**: Artificial Intelligence Software that mimics the responses you might expect to questions supplied by a human operator.
- **HAP**: **H**ateful, **A**busive, or **P**rofane language, filtered out as part of the cleaning process on the source text used to build the IBM Granite 3.0 LLMs.
- **PII**: Personal Identifiable Information in code datasets, is the reference name for personal IP addresses, keys, email addresses, names, user names, and passwords found in the content used for the text input for training the IBM Granite 3.0 LLMs.
- **RAG:** Retrievement Augmented Generation, provides an enhanced AI response by merging the output from the pre-trained Large Language Models with external data to enhance the response from the AI system.
- **FLOPS:** Floating-Point Operations Per Second, is a unit measuring a computer's computing power for mathematical calculations performed by the Arithmetic Logic Unit (ALU) section of the CPU.
- **GPU:** These are hardware Graphics Processing Units, providing a high-speed processing resource. Using their high performance capabilities, they are ideal for developing and using AI Large Language Models.
- **RHEL:** RedHat Enterprise Linux. A commercial version of the Linux Operating system, now owned by **IBM**.
- **CUDA:** This stands for Compute Unified Device Architecture, and it is a parallel computing platform and Application Programming Interface (API) model created by NVIDIA.

  The **CUDA** system is used for general computing on **GPUs**.

References

There are a number of useful links which provide some background reading to the **IBM Granite 3.0 system**, categorized as follows:

- **GitHub Activity:**
  - **For the IBM Granite community**

    https://github.com/ibm-granite-community
  - **For the base CodeNet database:**

    https://github.com/IBM/Project_CodeNet

  and

    https://rebrand.ly/a1lw80s
  - **For Granite 3.0**

    https://ibm.github.io/granite-workshop/pre-work/ ,

    https://github.com/ibm-granite/granite-code-models ,

    and https://github.com/ibm-granite
  - **Associated Watsonx AI:**

    https://github.com/ibm-granite/watsonx-code-assistant-individual
- **Stackoverflow Activity:**
  - **HuggingFace:**

    https://stackoverflow.com/questions/79019770/huggingface-model-downloads-are-not-counted
  - **Watsonx AI**

    https://stackoverflow.com/questions/77641146/extract-response-data-from-custom-llm-in-langchain-through-callbacks

  and

    https://stackoverflow.blog/2023/12/06/behind-the-scenes-building-ibm-watsonx-an-ai-and-data-platform/
- **Relevant YouTube Links:**

    https://www.youtube.com/watch?v=PoA3VG6EneQ

    "IBM Unveils Granite 3.0 - Open Source Family of Small Models!"

(Authored by Mathew Berman)

This very informative 12 minute video describes the overview of **IBM Granite 3.0,** and compares the model to competing LLM Benchmarks as well as their use in Enterprise systems.

This has the Link: "**Try Granite 3.0 free here**:" https://ibm.biz/BdanLV (currently dated, October 25th , 2024).

This video describes the distinguishing features of **IBM Granite 3.0 LLMs** covering their ability to include Corporate and private Enterprise Data, which can be trained with the inclusion of the IBM base LLM's as a starting point, to enhance the AI capability, and improve the relevance to the organization.

IBM Granite 3.0 has also been incorporated into the **IBM Watsonx** Coding Assistant which now also includes **CrewAI.** See: https://www.ibm.com/new/announcements/announcing-new-crewai-integration-with-watsonx-ai-to-build-and-streamline-workflows-with-multiple-ai-agents

The video also covers the **IBM Granite 3.0** extensions using IBM's **InstructLab** (which is also released as an open source tool, available through **GitHub**). The video explains how this provides a "middle ground" functionality, combining the existing **LLM** development features of **Retrievement Augmented Generation (RAG)** and **"Fine-Tuning".** This also includes a description of IBM's **InstructLab** as an alignment technique to add further training data. So this system enables new data to be added to the base **IBM Granite 3.0 LLMs**, as described earlier.

The spin-off features of **IBM Granite 3.0** for **IBM Granite Guardian** for **AI-**based security for **Guardrails** and **Safety** is also outlined.

https://www.youtube.com/watch?v=5-xMSQZ9xx0

This 37-minute video discusses the **IBM Granite 3.0** release and other AI related systems. Hosted by Tim Hwang, he asks questions for Kate Soule, Kush Varshney and Petros Zerfos for IBM TechXchange week. These experts describe how the team created the **IBM Granite 3.0** models.

https://www.youtube.com/watch?v=kZlGG4_DLjE

This 3-minute video covers the **IBM Granite 3.0** updates from **IBM TechXchange**. It introduces the new Large Language Models (LLMs) that use the Mixture of Experts feature (**Granite-3.0-3B-A800M-Instruct** and **Granite-3.0-3B-A800M-Instruct** released under the APACHE2 License). The video also outlines the IBM Watsonx code assistant, supporting the Python, Java, C, C++, GO, JavaScript, Typescript and many other languages.

- **User Downloads**:

  https://developer.ibm.com/data/project-codenet/ which is available to download from the link: https://codait%2Dcos%2Ddax.s3.us.cloud%2Dobject%2Dstorage.appdomain.cloud/dax%2Dproject%2Dcodenet/1.0.0/Project_CodeNet.tar.gz

  (This **7.8 GByte** file can be unpacked using: `tar -zxvf Project_CodeNet_full.tar.gz`).

- *Overview and* IBM *Granite trial links:*

  https://www.ibm.com/granite

  There is also a new links for **IBM Granite 3.1** as follows:

  https://www.ibm.com/granite/docs/

  Free pdf document Downloads are listed in *Table* 1.1:

ISBN/IBM	Title	Publisher(s)	Date
IBM	Granite Code Models: A Family of Open Foundation Models for Code Intelligence	IBM https://arxiv.org/pdf/2405.04324	7th May 2024
IBM	GRANITE 3.0 LANGUAGE MODELS	https://github.com/ibm-granite/granite-3.0-language-models/blob/main/paper.pdf	9th November 2024
Google	Attention Is All You Need	Google https://arxiv.org/pdf/1706.03762	12th June, 2017 Updated 2nd August, 2023
OpenAI	Efficient Training of Language Models to Fill in the Middle	OpenAI https://arxiv.org/pdf/2207.14255	28th July 2022
Universidad Pontificia Comillas, Madrid, Spain	ChatGPT is not all you need. A State of the Art Review of large Generative AI models	Universidad Pontificia Comillas https://arxiv.org/pdf/2301.04655	11th January, 2023

Table 1.1: *Free pdf document Downloads are listed*

CHAPTER 2
Granite 3.0's Architecture

Introduction

This chapter covers an overview of the **IBM Granite 3.0** architecture, the prerequisites and the installation of supported Operating Systems, including the required **VMware** build of **RedHat Linux RHEL 9.2,** and its activation for a **RedHat** subscription.

IBM describes their approach to the development of **IBM Granite 3.0** as a model designed for commercial use. The models are trained by using the data after it has been cleaned and filtered for things like hate, abuse, and profanity.

With generative AI systems built on **IBM Granite 3.0 LLMs** (Large Language Models), developers can translate legacy systems written in **COBOL** into more modern languages like **Java.**

IBM have also endeavored to provide free access to the LLM models, they obtained from the process, by licensing of these models with an Apache 2.0 License.

IBM's Conclusion in the GitHub paper their research team produced, states:

"*We present Granite 3.0, an openly available family of lightweight generative language models that are highly versatile in their ability to accomplish a wide range of enterprise tasks. We release four sizes of models across two different architectures (dense and mixture-of-experts), and provide both base and instruct checkpoints. Aligned with IBM's commitment to transparent and responsible AI, we present descriptions of training data, pre-processing steps, data mixture, training details, energy consumption, and evaluation methodologies used throughout the model development lifecycle. Granite 3.0 language models demonstrate strong performance across a battery of academic benchmarks for language understanding, reasoning, coding, function calling, and safety. Our experience and results demonstrate that Granite 3.0 language models have a proven ability to better handle different enterprise tasks such as RAG, cybersecurity and function calling among others.* ***We release all our Granite 3.0 language models under an Apache 2.0 license for***

***both research and commercial use.** We plan to continuously release updates to these models to improve their performance with safety in mind, for example, improving multilinguality and coding, including long-context model variants"*

The full IBM Research Paper, "GRANITE 3.0 LANGUAGE MODELS" is available as a free download from the GitHub URL link, as follows:

https://github.com/ibm-granite/granite-3.0-language-models/blob/main/paper.pdf

Structure

In this chapter, we will discuss the following topics:

- **The Architecture of the Models**
  - Decoder-only Dense transformers
  - Decoder-only Sparse Mixture-of-Expert transformers
  - Ollama Architecture
- **Hardware and Software Requirements**
  - Requirements for RedHat Linux
  - Version Requirements for Python
  - Python Libraries For running Ollama
  - Developing the Granite-3B-Code-Base
  - Developing the Granite-8B-Code-Base
  - Developing the Granite-20B-Code-Base
  - Developing the Granite-34B-Code-Base

The Architecture of the Models

The **IBM Granite 3.0** language models use two standard architectures defined for Large Language Model Transformers (as described in detail in *Chapter 1, The Fundamentals of LLMs*):

- Decoder-only dense transformers
- Decoder-only sparse Mixture-of-Expert (MoE) transformers.

The Granite models were trained on 12 trillion tokens of data, across multiple languages as well as the code data.

Decoder-only Dense Transformers

There is an in-depth article which describes this architecture in great detail. See https://cameronrwolfe.substack.com/p/decoder-only-transformers-the-workhorse.

The link describes the **Decoder-only** transformer architecture, which IBM have used, in great detail, using comprehensive examples.

From this article, there is Python code available from the GitHub links:

https://gist.github.com/wolfecameron/26863dbbc322b15d2e224a2569868256/raw/21a836285584d6437e477f035a26c39efdc5f442/**causal_self_attention.py**

and

https://gist.githubusercontent.com/wolfecameron/f9cb6645dc87a165ce3a7fae980610a4/raw/dbd72de3ef5e3714d68afb467c29b1446cf24f82/**exploding_activations.py**

and

https://gist.githubusercontent.com/wolfecameron/3ed9274a0297aab403b5e2d2254ee0ac/raw/70535fc537da3bddb776b05665815646cdd07d6b/**transformer_ffnn.py**

To construct a full decoder-only transformer block, the components are as follows:

- Masked, multi-headed self-attention
- Layer normalization
- Pointwise feed-forward transformation
- Residual Connections

The architecture of the decoder-only transformer blocks is used by most Generative PreTrained, GPT-style LLMs. The example Python code for this decoder-only transformer block is implemented in PyTorch as shown in the following code sample:

(See https://github.com/karpathy/nanoGPT/)

The prerequisites for this are satisfied using:

```
pip install torch numpy transformers datasets tiktoken wandb tqdm
```

on a **RedHat Linux version RHEL 9.2** system installed as **root**, as shown in *Figure 2.1*:

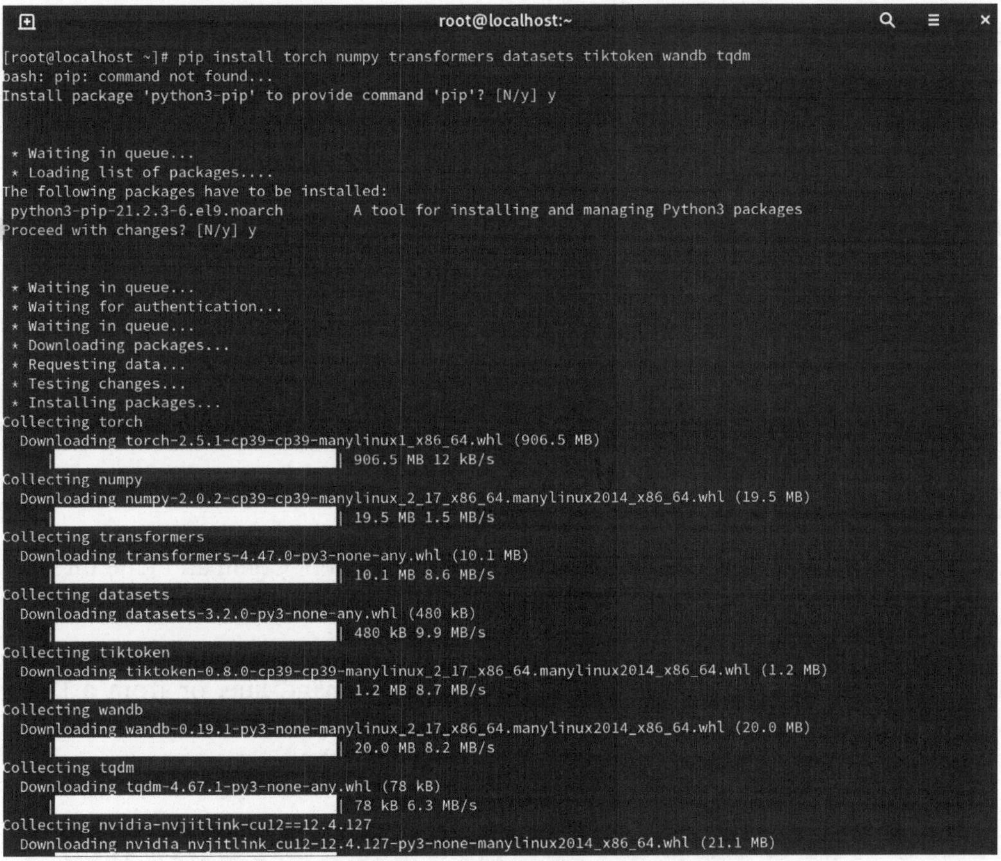

Figure 2.1:** Using the command:* ***pip install torch numpy transformers datasets tiktoken wandb tqdm

Dependencies

The Python language library name dependencies for the **decoder-only transformer** blocks are listed as follows:

- **pytorch** <3 from https://pytorch.org/
- **numpy** <3 from https://numpy.org/install/
- **transformers** for huggingface transformers <3 (to load GPT-2 checkpoints)
- **datasets** for huggingface datasets <3
- **tiktoken** for OpenAI's fast BPE code <3 from https://github.com/mvitlov/tiktoken
- **wandb** for optional logging <3
- **tqdm** for progress bars <3

Decoder-only Sparse Mixture-of-Expert Transformers

In the following blog link, Multi-head self attention and sparse mixture of experts are combined to form a sparse mixture of experts transformer block. Skip connections are added to ensure that the training is stable. This blog also describes how layer normalization is employed to stabilize the learning process.

See: https://huggingface.co/blog/AviSoori1x/makemoe-from-scratch

IBM has also documented this transformer architecture in their link:

https://www.ibm.com/think/topics/mixture-of-experts

Ollama Architecture

Ollama uses a Client-Server architecture using a CLI, Client Command Line Interface, which allows the user to enter questions that the ollama CLI processes, and then displays an answer.

The Server on Linux can be started by using a command line, or from a Docker container. Ollama runs locally on a sandboxed server, as an AI coding assistant, ensuring that maximum possible security can be established.

Hardware and Software Requirements

The **IBM Granite 3.0** language models are supported on several Operating System platforms for development testing:

- **Microsoft Windows version 10** or later versions
- **RedHat Linux RHEL Version 8.8** and **RHEL Version 9.2**

The standard supported hardware configuration to deploy custom foundation models are as follows:

- **NVIDIA A100** with 80 GB of GPU memory
- **NVIDIA H100** with 80 GB of GPU memory
- **NVIDIA L40S** with 48 GB of GPU memory

Requirements for RedHat Linux

Having tried unsuccessfully to use an existing RedHat Linux RHEL 8.5 version on **VMware,** we downloaded and installed a new version of **RedHat Linux, RHEL version**

9.2, as recommended by IBM, from a RedHat developer account, and installed it on VMware as follows:

To register for a RedHat account, use the link:

https://www.redhat.com/wapps/ugc/register.html?_flowId=register-flow&_flowExecutionKey=e1s1

For a personal or corporate account setup

Or

https://developers.redhat.com/articles/faqs-no-cost-red-hat-enterprise-linux

for the instructions to create a free to download RedHat Enterprise Linux zipped tar file to install on VMware using

https://www.redhat.com/en/technologies/linux-platforms/enterprise-linux

select

https://console.redhat.com/insights/image-builder/imagewizard?source=RHD#SIDs=&tags=

A RedHat developers account can then be used to access the **Activation Key** site, which RedHat now uses to set up their Subscription service access (replacing the previous Redhat subscription manager system tool that was transitioned in April, 2024 and finally withdrawn on 25th of October 2024.)

See: https://shorturl.at/xxrVA

As illustrated in *Figure* 2.2, we select the **`Bare metal - Installer (.iso)`** option, and click **Next** on the wizard page.

Next, we selected the Activation Keys link on the next page.

https://console.redhat.com/insights/connector/activation-keys#SIDs=&tags=

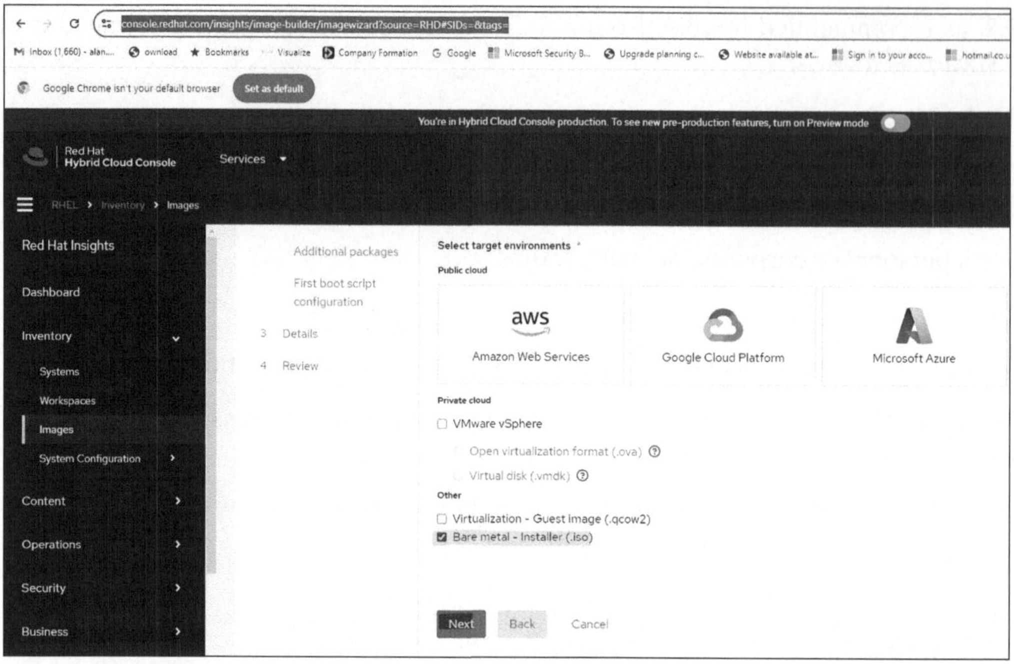

Figure 2.2**: We select the **Bare metal – Installer (.iso)** option and click **Next

The following link is required to create the **RedHat Activation Key**, which we will use later during the bare metal iso disk image installation for **RHEL 9.2**, and this registers the operating system allowing the download of additional libraries that also allows incremental upgrades for the system. We select the **Create activation key** command button, to add a new machine to our existing **ECMUKDEMO22** key, as illustrated in *Figure 2.3*:

https://console.redhat.com/insights/connector/activation-keys#SIDs=&tags=

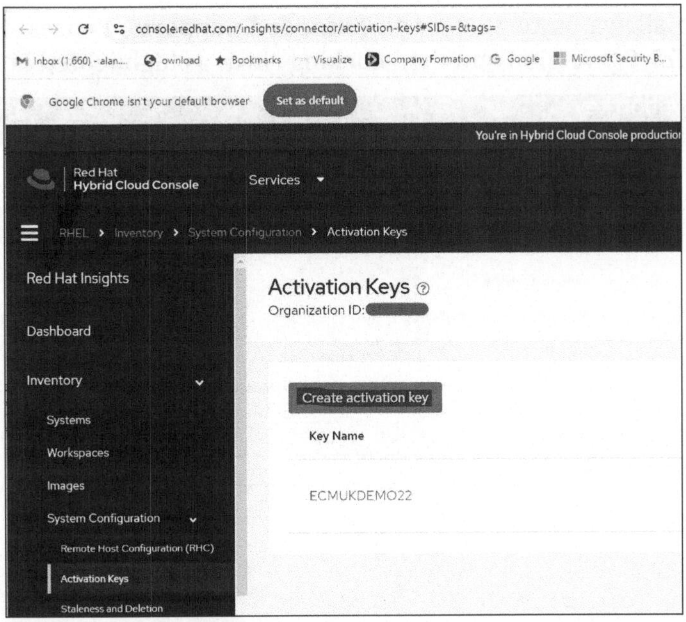

***Figure 2.3**: Select the **Create activation key** command button, to add a new machine*

This action will generate a link as follows:

https://console.redhat.com/insights/connector/activation-keys/ECMUKDEMO2025

We enter the **ECMUKDEMO2025** key name and description as shown in *Figure 2.4*:

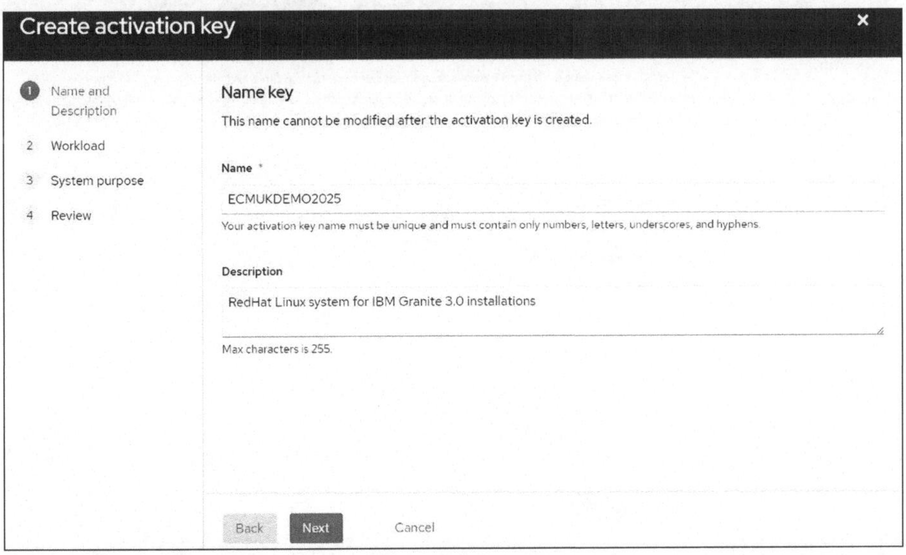

***Figure 2.4**: We enter the **ECMUKDEMO2025** key name and description, and select the **Next** command*

The **`Next`** step allows us to select the **Extended support releases** option, and we choose the **RHEL 9.2** version and then clicking Next, as highlighted in *Figure 2.5*:

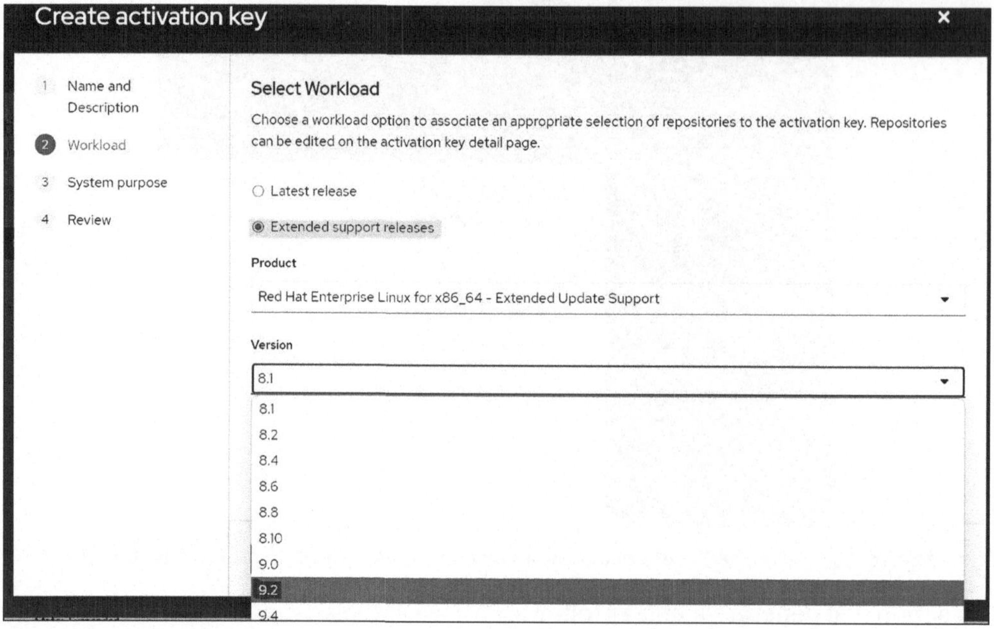

Figure 2.5: *Select the* **Extended support releases** *option, and choose the* **RHEL 9.2** *Linux version*

The **System purpose** wizard step screen is shown next, as illustrated in *Figure 2.6*:

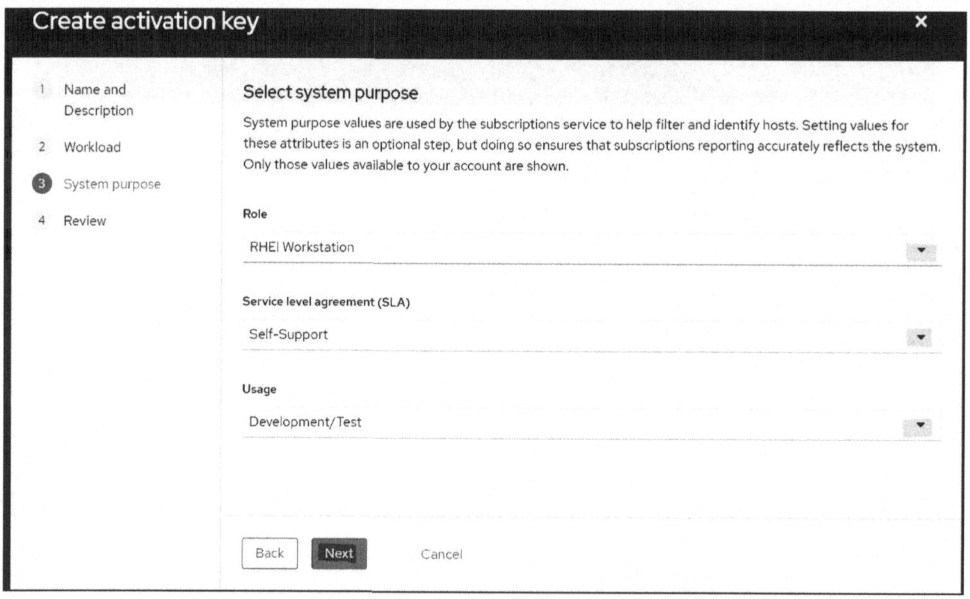

Figure 2.6: *The* **System purpose** *wizard step screen is shown to allow the entry of the main system usage*

After the **Next** command button is selected, the Review of the entries, we have made is shown. We can then select the **Create** button or go back using the **Back** button, if we need to change anything displayed, as illustrated in *Figure 2.7*:

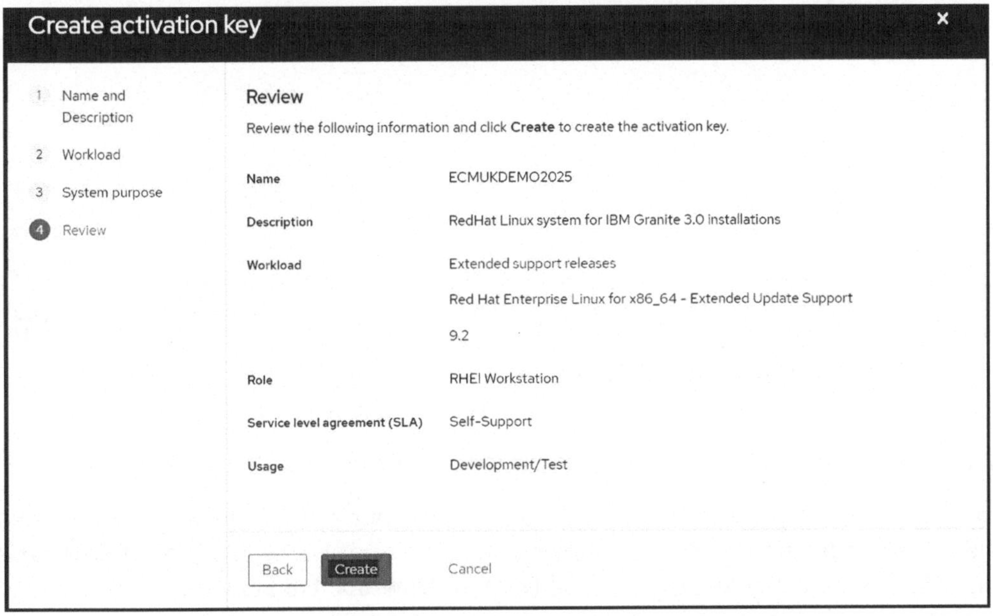

***Figure 2.7**: The Review of the entries, we have made is shown, and we can then select the **Create** button*

We can now View the activation key we have created, as illustrated in *Figure 2.8*:

***Figure 2.8**: We can now View the activation key, we have created*

The View activation key command button allows us to add additional repositories, if required, using the `Add repositories` command button as shown in *Figure 2.9*:

Figure 2.9: *The View activation key command button allows us to add additional repositories (if required)*

(There were no additional repositories added for our RedHat RHEL 9.2 system.)

From the link https://developers.redhat.com/products/rhel/download#rhelforsap896, we scroll down to the section shown as follows, and choose the **RedHat Enterprise Linux 9.2** as well as select the x86_64 DVD iso **Download (8.94 GB)** command button as highlighted in *Figure 2.10*:

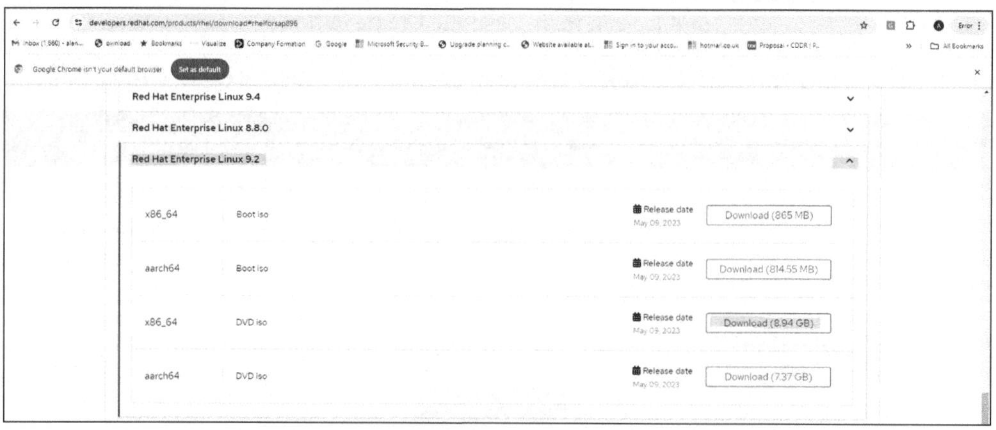

Figure 2.10: *Choose the RedHat Enterprise Linux 9.2, and select the x86_64 DVD iso* ***Download (8.94 GB)*** *command*

The **rhel-9.2-x86_64-dvd.iso** disk image file download file folder can now be selected as shown in *Figure 2.11* (there should be at least 9 GByte of free space on the disk for this file).

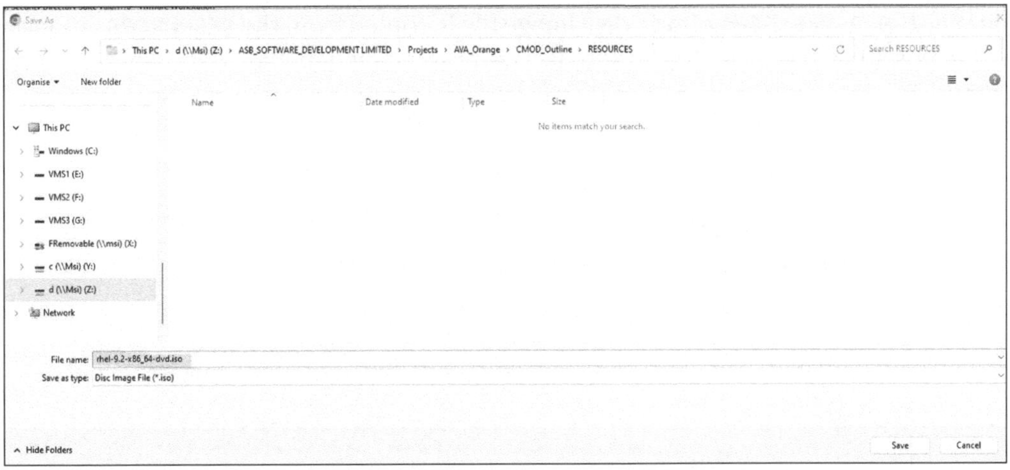

***Figure 2.11**: The **rhel-9.2-x86_64-dvd.iso** disk image file download file folder can now be selected*

The **direct link** URL is shown in *Figure* 2.12 to the download page, in case of any issues:

https://access.cdn.redhat.com/content/origin/files/sha256/a1/a18bf014e2cb5b6b9cee3ea09ccfd7bc2a84e68e09487bb119a98aa0e3563ac2/rhel-9.2-x86_64-dvd.iso?_auth_=1734100596_**XXXXXXXXXXXXXXXXXXXXXXXXX**3fcbe28

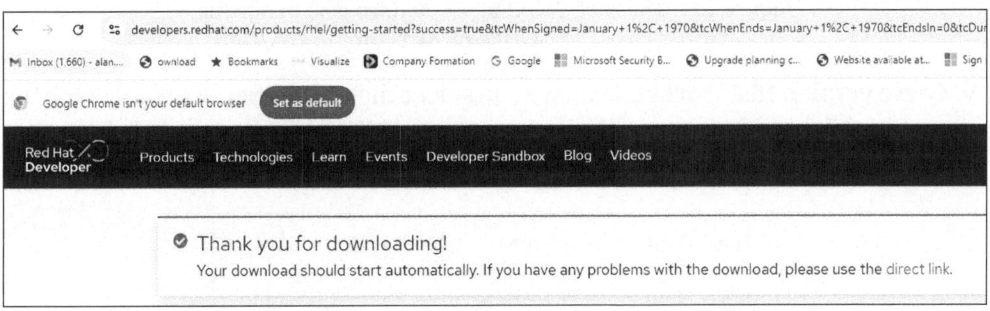

***Figure 2.12**: The **direct link** URL is available to the download page as shown*

The highlighted icon in the browser window can be selected to observe the progress of the download, as shown in *Figure* 2.13:

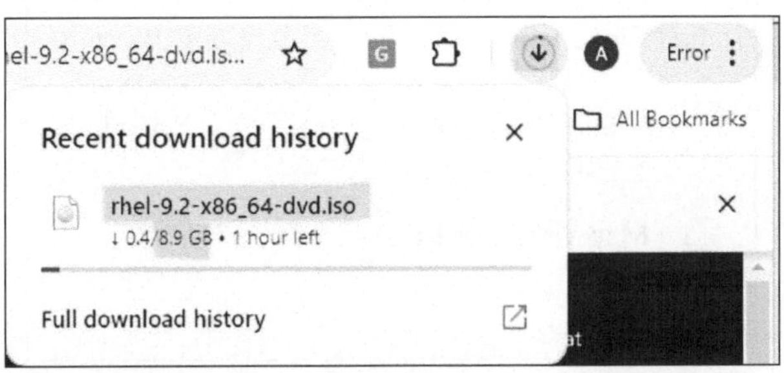

***Figure 2.13**: The highlighted icon in the browser window can be selected to observer the progress of the download*

This **`rhel-9.2-x86_64-dvd.iso`** disk image file is copied from the **`RESOURCES`** directory to our Windows 11 server **G:\VMS** folder, we created (which had **1 TByte** of free space available).

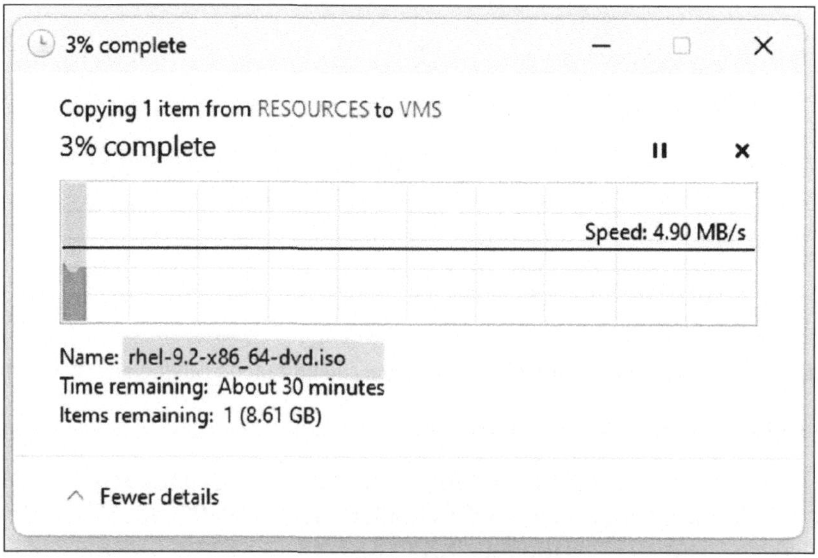

Figure 2.14**: The **rhel-9.2-x86_64-dvd.iso** disk image file is copied from the RESOURCES directory to **G:\VMS

In **VMware version 16.2 Workstation,** we can select the **`File-> New Virtual Machine`**... option as highlighted in *Figure 2.15*:

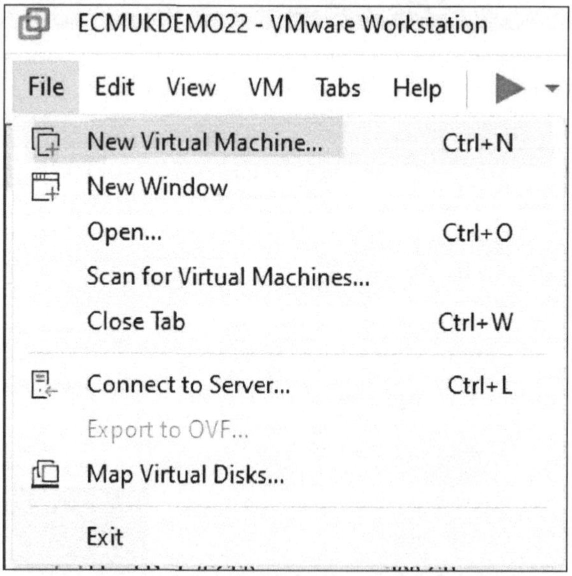

***Figure 2.15:** In **VMware** version 16.2 Workstation, we can select the **File-> New Virtual Machine...** option*

We use the default Custom (advanced) option, and select the **`Next>`** command as highlighted in *Figure 2.16*:

***Figure 2.16**: We use the default **Custom (advanced)** option, and select the **Next>** command*

The latest VMware **Workstation 16.2.x** default option is selected for Hardware compatibility, and the **`Next>`** command is selected, as shown in *Figure 2.17*:

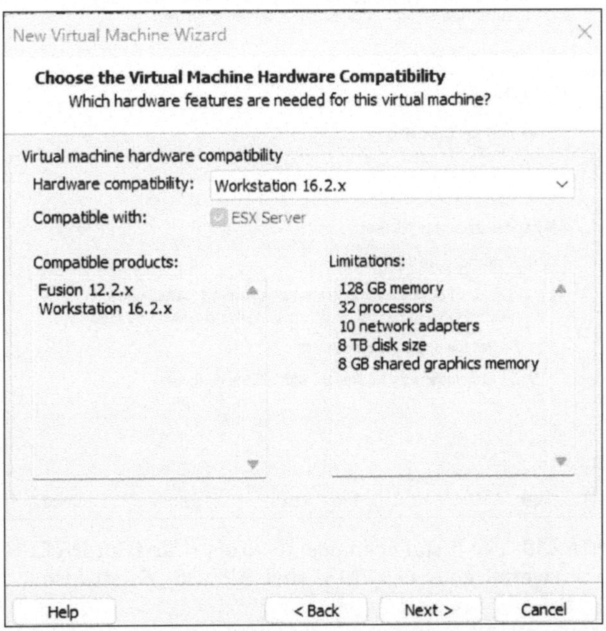

***Figure 2.17:** The **Workstation 16.2.x** default option is selected for Hardware, and the **Next>** command is selected*

The **`Browse`** command is used in the next screen to select the DVD iso **`image rhel-9.2-x86_64-dvd.iso`** disk image file location, as highlighted in *Figure* 2.18:

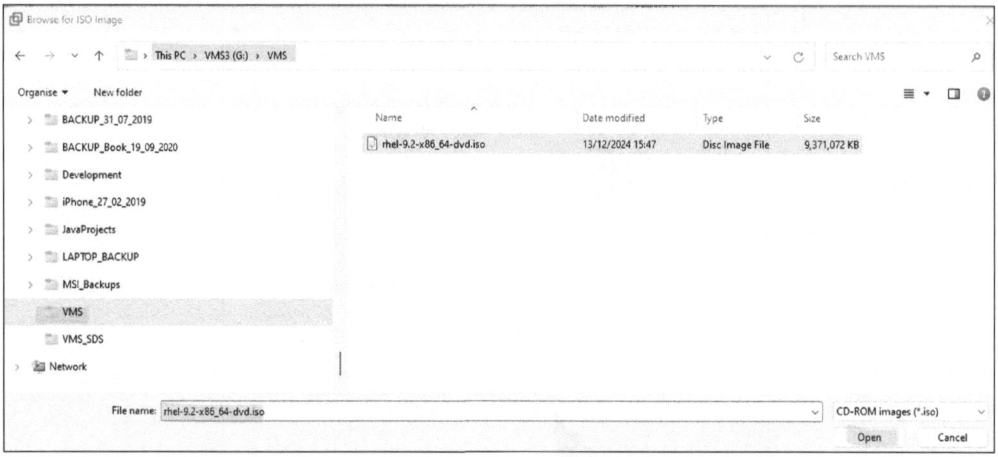

***Figure* 2.18:** *The Browse command is used to select the DVD iso image rhel-9.2-x86_64-dvd.iso disk image file*

The **Installer disc image file (iso)** for **RedHat RHEL 9.2** is now referenced at **`G:\VMS\rhel-9.2-x86_64-dvd.iso`**, as highlighted in *Figure* 2.19, and we can now select **`Next>`**.

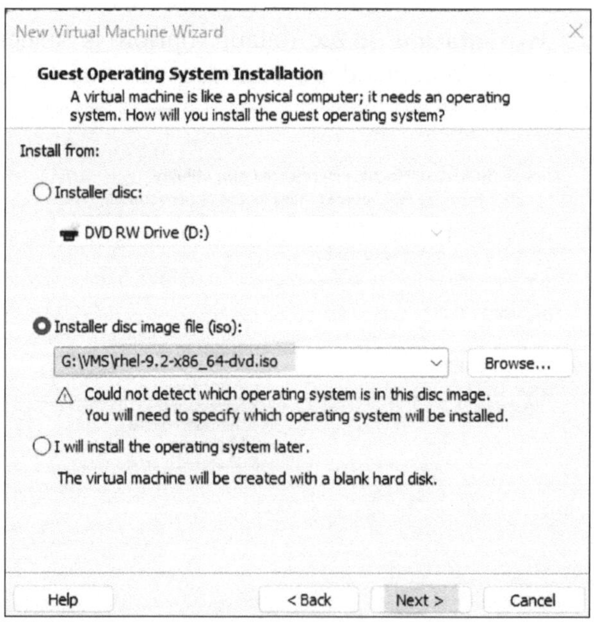

Figure* 2.19:** *The Installer image file (iso) for* ***RedHat RHEL 9.2 *is referenced at* ***G:\VMS\rhel-9.2-x86_64-dvd.iso***

The operating system option is selected as **Linux**, and we use the **Red Hat Enterprise Linux 8 64-bit** option (as this is the latest available). This did not affect the installation or running of the **RedHat RHEL 9.2** version in **VMware**. The **`Next>`** command is selected, as illustrated in *Figure 2.20*:

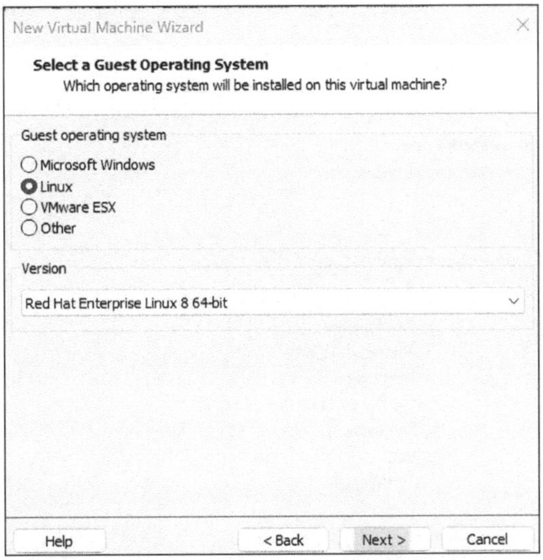

***Figure 2.20:** The **Next>** command is selected*

The **Virtual machine name** text box is entered with **`RedHat Enterpise Linux 9 64-bit,`** and the **`Browse...`** button is used to select the **`G:\VMS`** folder, and then the **`Make New Folder`** command is selected to create a subfolder, as highlighted in *Figure 2.21*:

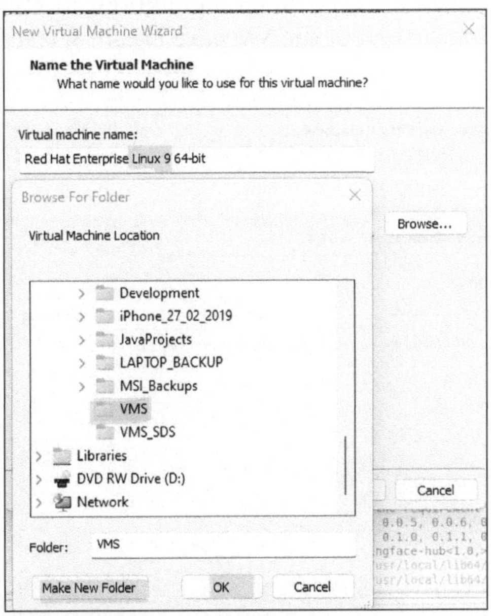

Figure 2.21:** The **Make New Folder** command is selected to create a new subfolder, **Granite3**, under **G:\VMS

The **OK** command is then used to confirm the new folder location, **G:\VMS\Granite3**, as illustrated in *Figure 2.22*:

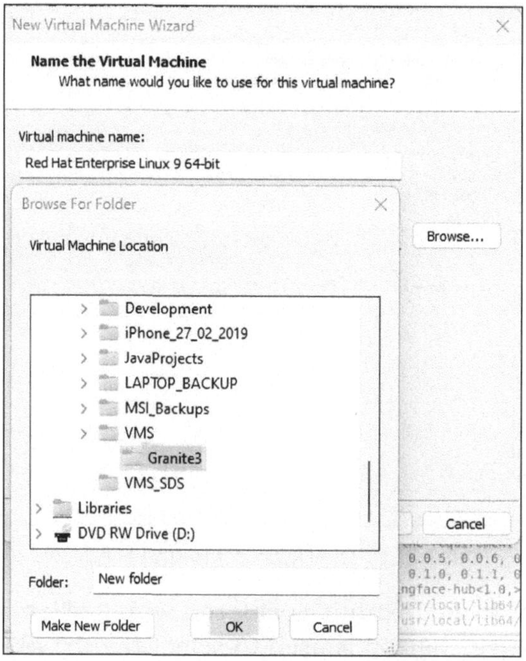

Figure 2.22:** The **OK** command is used to confirm the new folder location, **G:\VMS\Granite3

The **Next>** command can now be used, as highlighted in *Figure 2.23*, to display the **Processor Configuration** screen of the VMware create wizard.

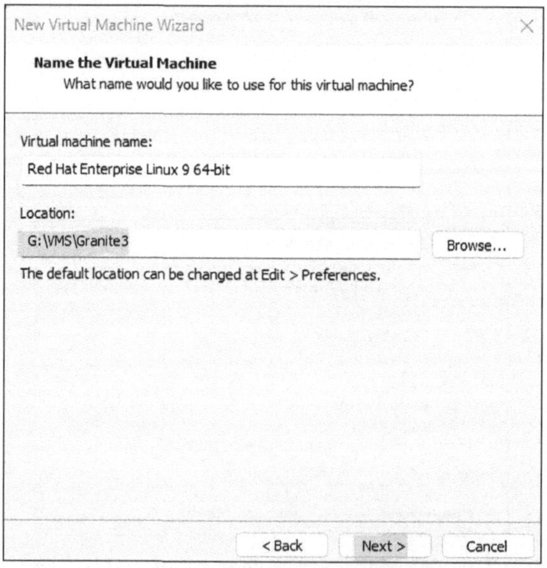

***Figure 2.23:** The **Next>** command can now be used to display the **Processor Configuration** screen*

Since this **Linux** server has to perform a number of **CPU** intensive functions to support the **IBM Granite 3.0** AI system, we allocated 10 processors, of 1 core each, and selected the **`Next>`** command as highlighted in *Figure 2.24*:

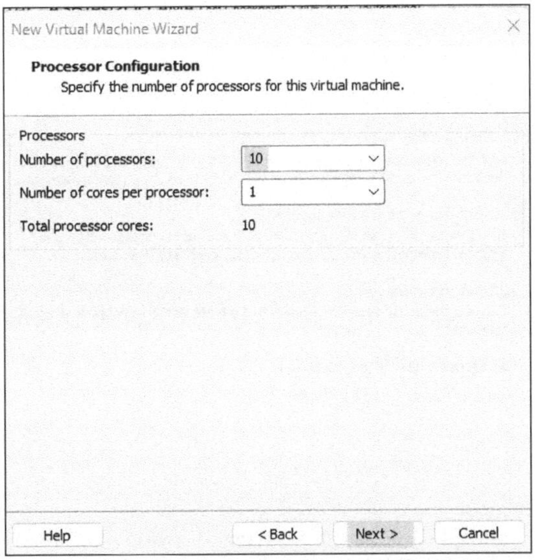

***Figure 2.24:** We allocated 10 processors, of 1 core each, and selected the **Next>** command*

The virtual **Linux** server on our **VMWare** system was allocated **32 GByte** of memory (32768 Mbytes, the Windows 11 host server has 64 Gbyte of memory available), as shown in *Figure 2.25*:

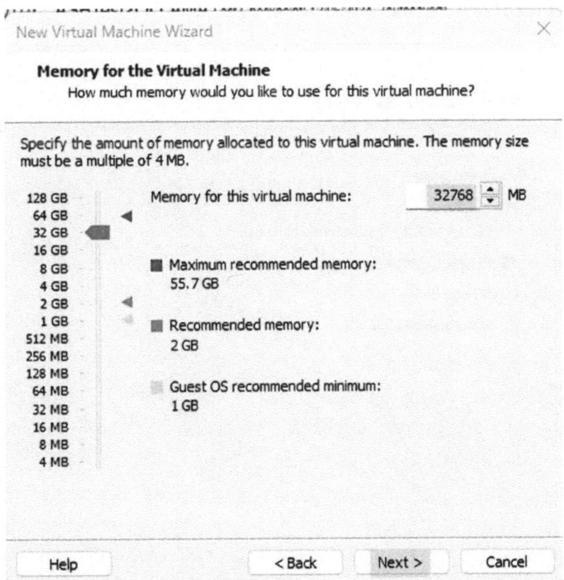

***Figure 2.25:** The virtual **Linux** server on our **VMWare** system was allocated **32 GByte** of memory (**32768** Mbytes)*

The **Next>** command displays the screen which allows us to select a **NAT** Network Card (for Network Address Transalation), as illustrated in *Figure 2.26*:

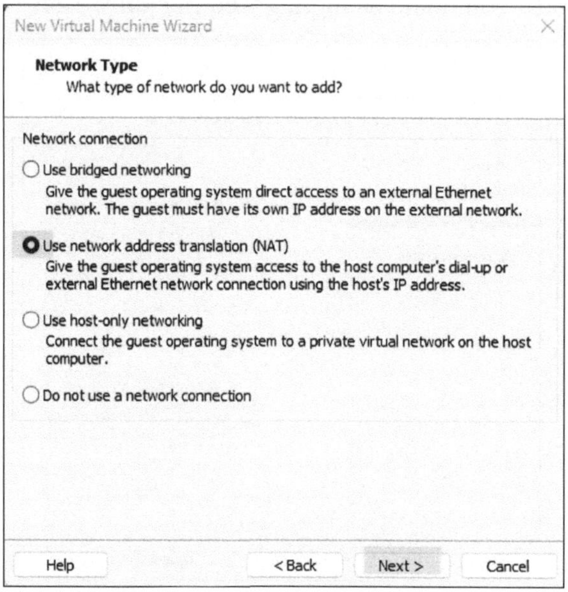

Figure 2.26: *This is the screen which allows us to select a* ***NAT Network Card*** *(for Network Address Translation)*

After selecting the **NAT Network Card** and the **Next>** command for the network card, we select the **LSI Logic, SCSI Controller**, as recommended by **VMware,** and select the **Next>** command as highlighted in *Figure 2.27*:

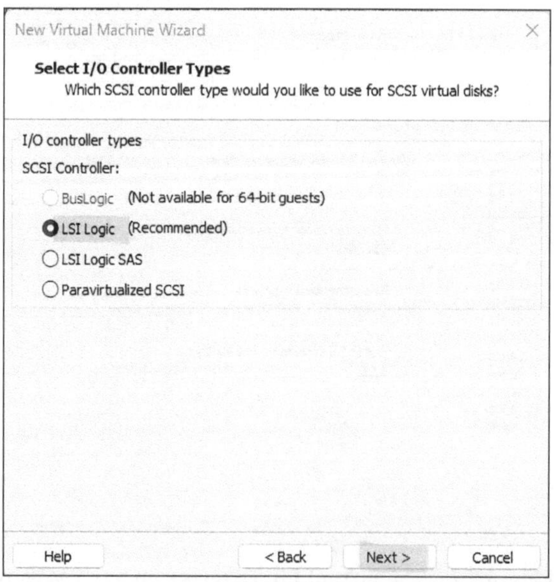

Figure 2.27: *We select the* ***LSI Logic*****,** ***SCSI Controller*** *and select the* ***Next>*** *command*

We can now select the Disk type, which we select as a **SCSI** disk, as shown in *Figure 2.28*:

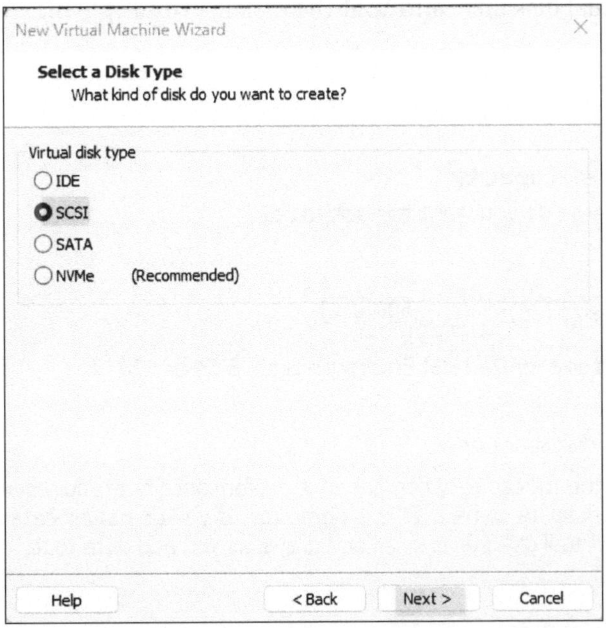

Figure 2.28: *We can now select the Disk type, which we choose as a* **SCSI** *disk*

We select the option to **`Create a new virtual disk`**, as highlighted in *Figure 2.29*:

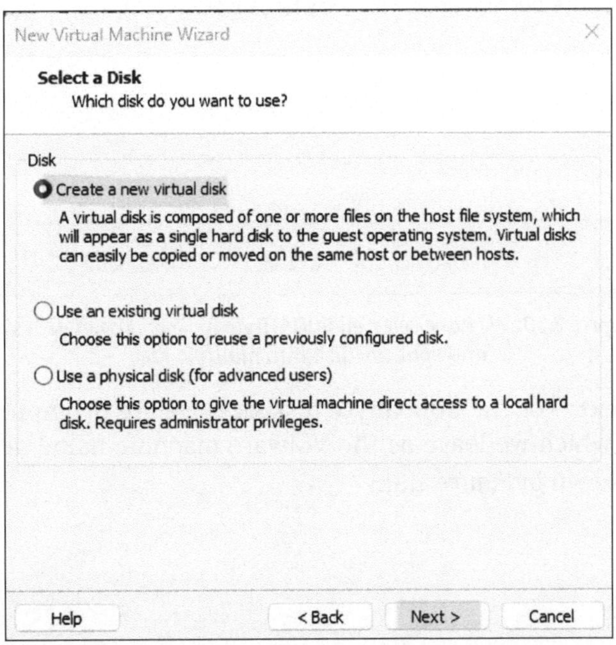

Figure 2.29: *We select the option to* ***Create a new virtual disk***

For **IBM Granite 3.0** installations, IBM recommends at least **250 GByte** and ideally **500 GByte** disk size, depending on the **LLM** model selected. We have selected **500 GByte** for our virtual disk size, and split the disk into multiple files, as shown in *Figure 2.30*:

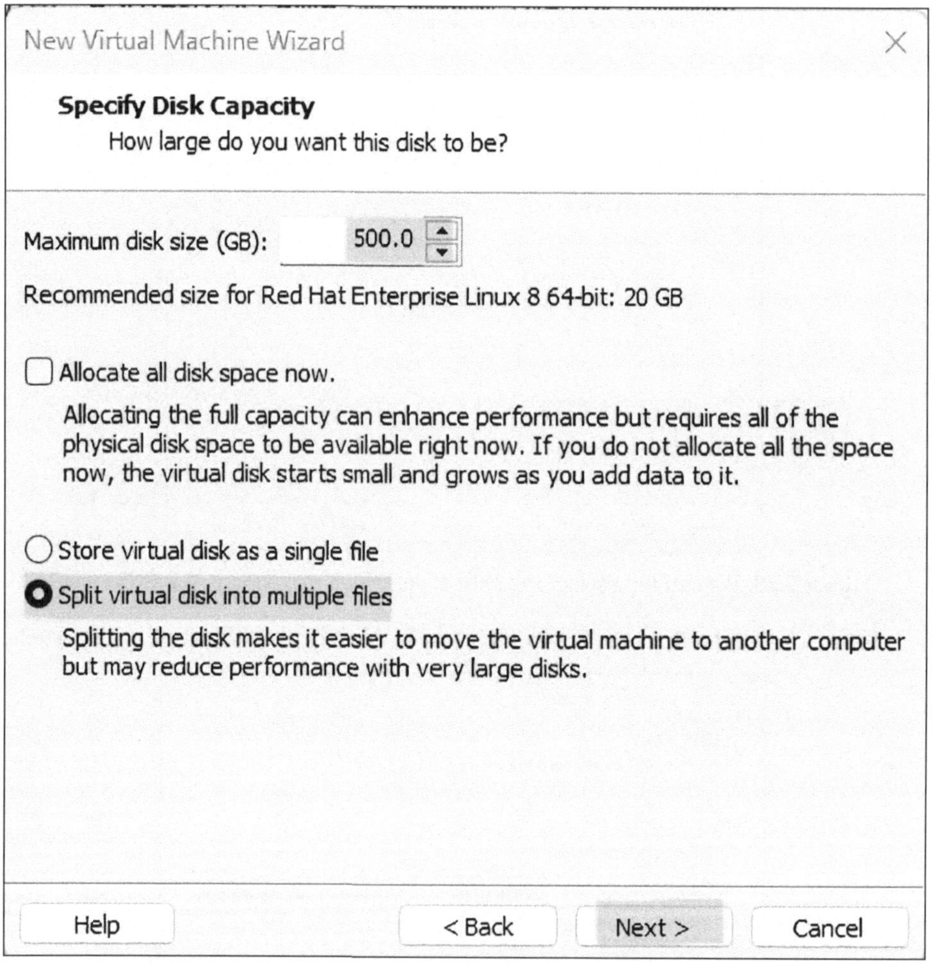

Figure 2.30*: We have selected* ***500 GByte*** *for our virtual disk size, and split the disk into multiple files*

After selecting **`Next>`** for the **500 Gbyte** disk size, we are prompted for the generic file .vmdk name, which we leave as the VMware machine name default option, and select **`Next>`** as shown in *Figure 2.31*:

Figure 2.31: *We are prompted for the generic .vmdk file name, which we leave as the default option*

On selecting the **`Next>`** command, we are presented with the wizard review page, which allows us to add a second network card, using the **`Customize Hardware...`** command button, as highlighted in *Figure 2.32*:

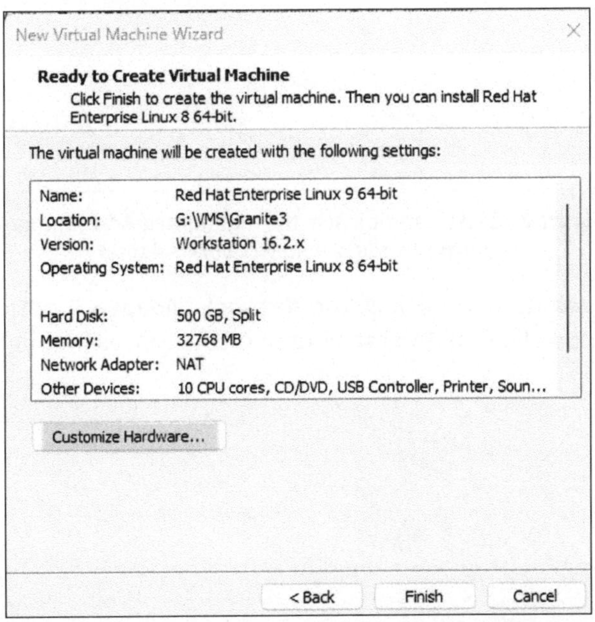

Figure 2.32: *Add a second network card, using the* **Customize Hardware...** *command button*

We can now use the highlighted **`Add`** command button to add a new **`Network Adapter`**, as highlighted in *Figure 2.33*:

Figure 2.33**: We can now use the highlighted **Add** command button to add a new **Network Adapter

From the pop-up window, we select the **`Network Adapter`** option from the list of Hardware types, then click the **`Finish`** command button, as highlighted in *Figure 2.34*:

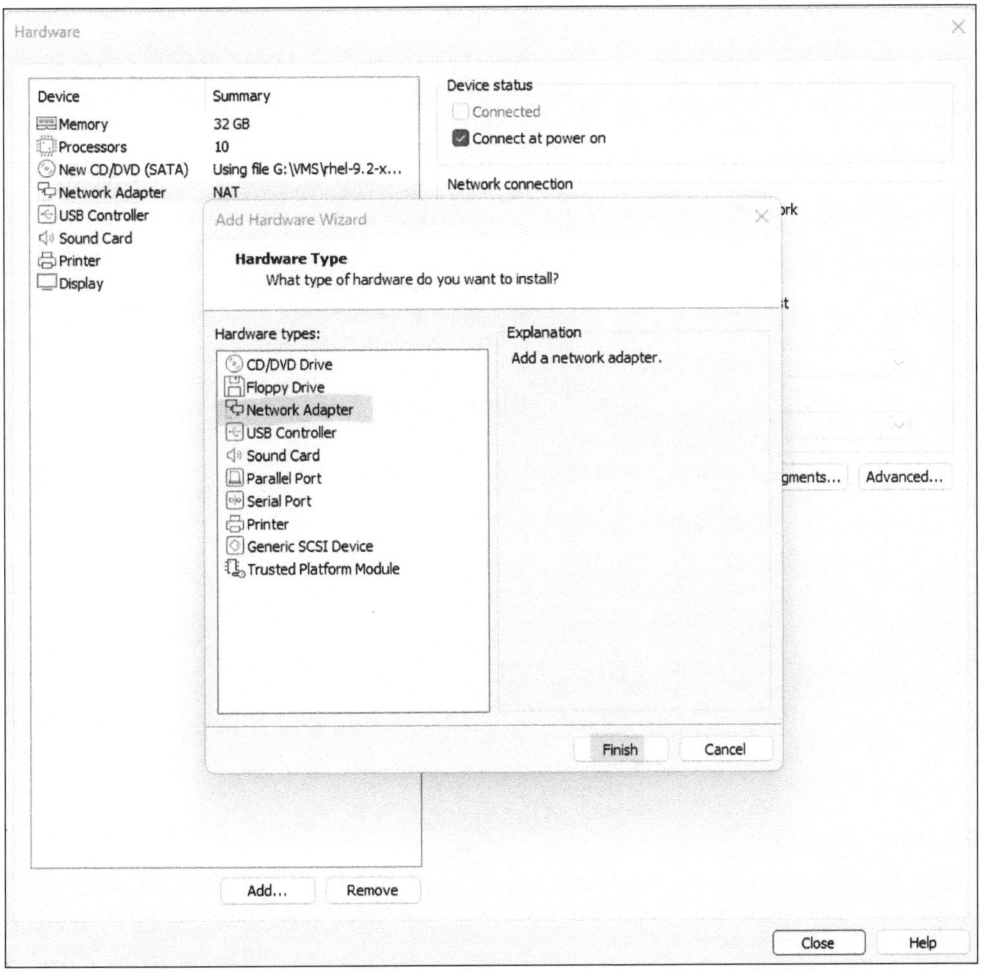

***Figure 2.34**: Select the **Network Adapter** from the list of Hardware, and then the pop-up window, **Finish** command*

The second **`Network Adapter`** card is used to provide a link to the **`Host Server`** network which enables the virtual Linux server to communicate with the Host machine. We can now set this second **`Network Adapter`** card as **`Host-only`**, and confirm this selection using the **`Close`** command button, as shown in *Figure 2.35*:

Figure 2.35**: We can now set this second Network Adapter card as **Host-only**, and confirm this with **Close

We can start the build of our new virtual **`RedHat Linux RHEL Version 9.2`** server by selecting the **`Finish`** command as highlighted in *Figure 2.36*:

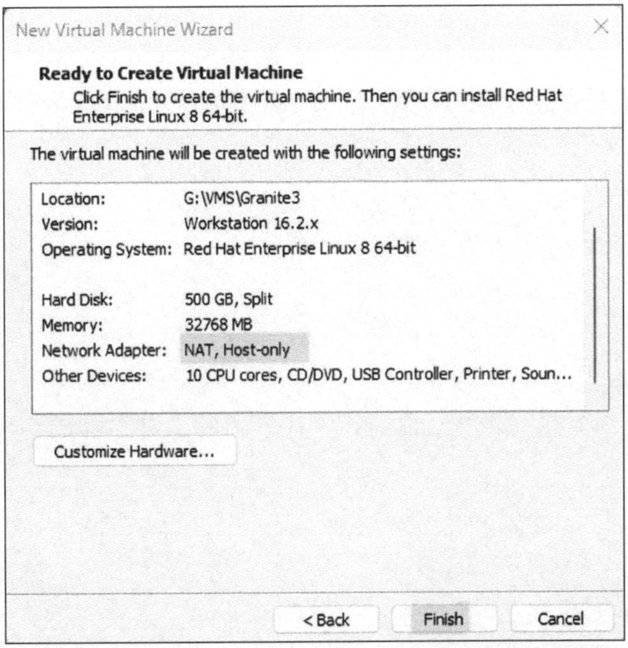

Figure 2.36: *We can start the build of the virtual* **RedHat Linux RHEL Version 9.2** *server using* **Finish**

The RedHat Linux version **RHEL 9.2** is now built by VMware, and we can run the new operating system by selecting the highlighted green arrow start icon, as highlighted in *Figure 2.37*:

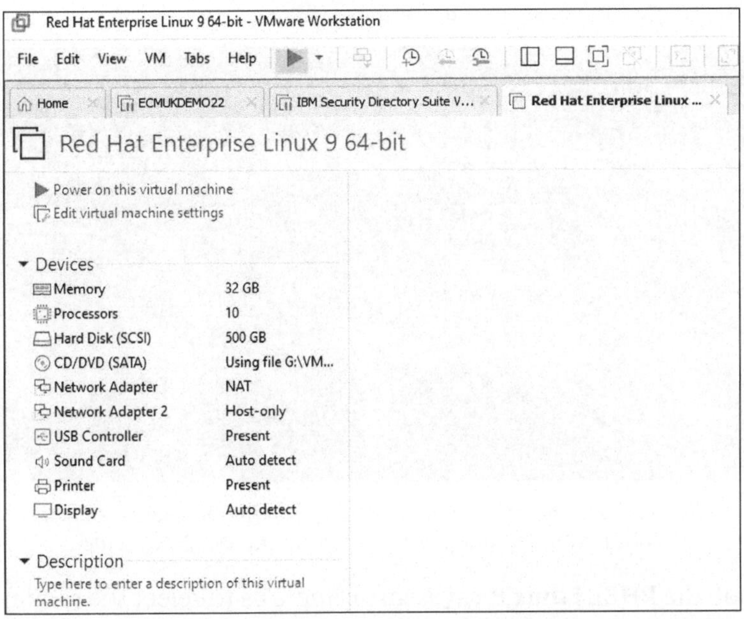

Figure 2.37: *Run the new operating system by selecting the highlighted green arrow start icon*

The splash screen appears to provide the details of the system, and has a 1 minute count-down to start the initial boot process, as illustrated in *Figure* 2.38:

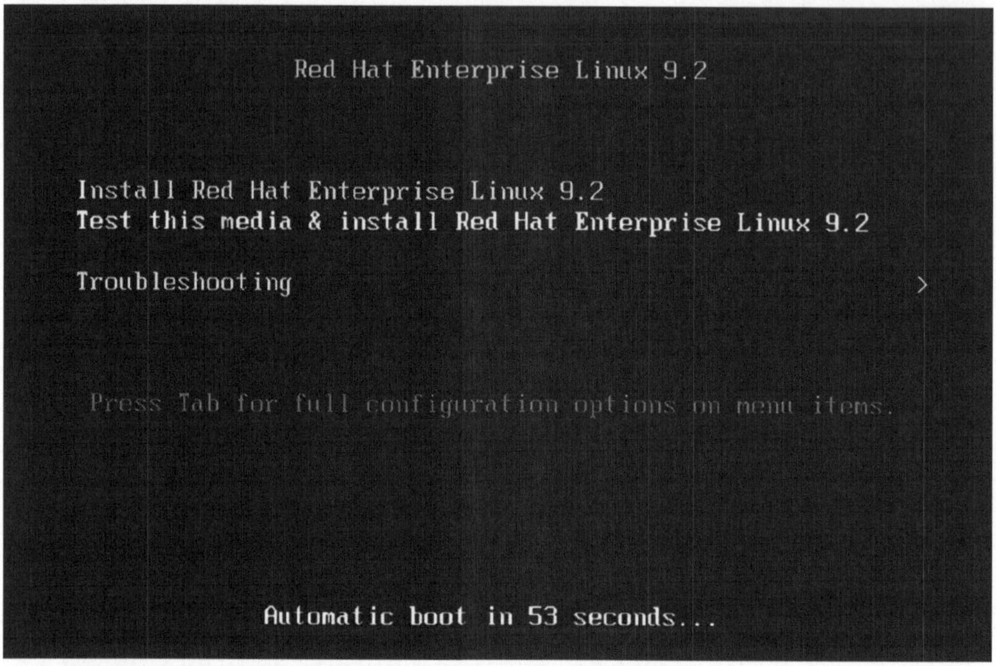

***Figure* 2.38:** *The system has a 1 minute count-down to start the initial boot process*

The initial boot starts a checking process to ensure that we are loading a secure copy of the iso Disk image file, as shown in *Figure* 2.39:

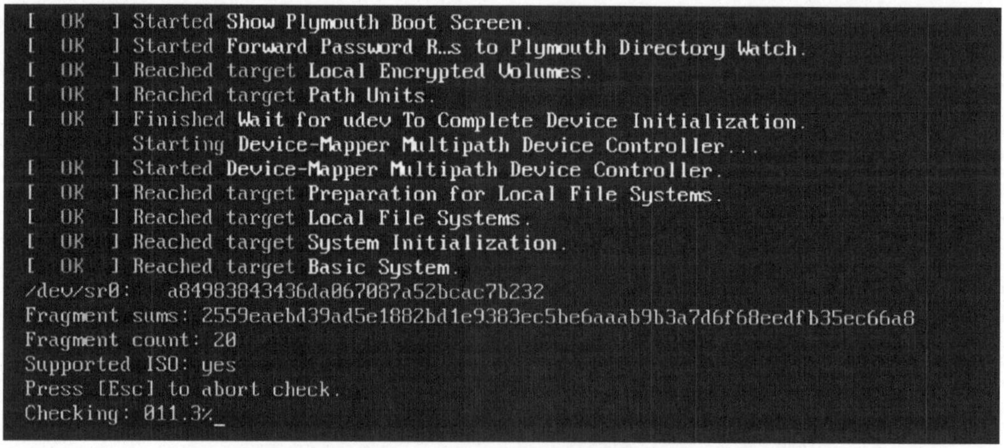

***Figure* 2.39:** *The initial boot starts a checking process to ensure that we are loading a secure copy of the iso Disk image*

On initial boot, the **RHEL Linux 9.2** system prompts us to select the required Language from the list given, as illustrated in *Figure* 2.40:

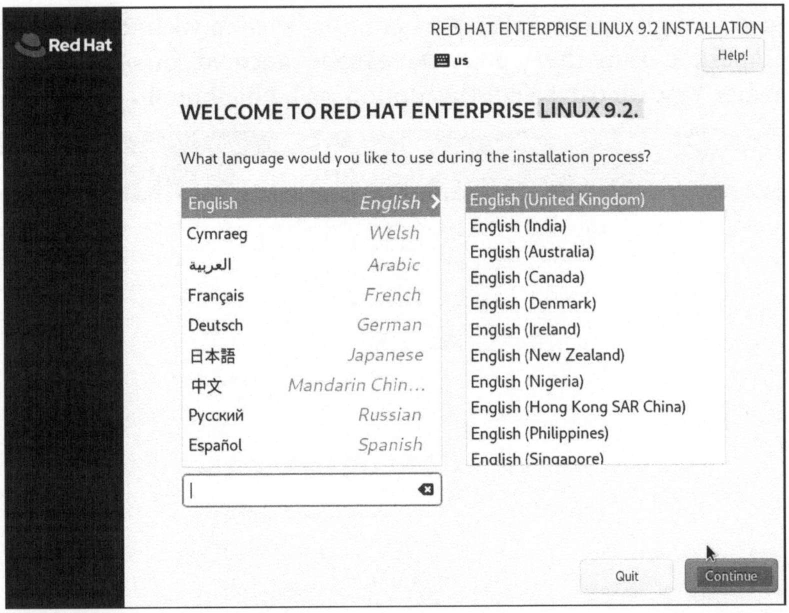

Figure 2.40: *On initial boot, the* **RHEL Linux 9.2** *system prompts us to select a Language*

After the **`Continue`** command is selected, we are shown the keyboard layout. We selected the **`English (UK)`** default, and then selected the **Done** command as highlighted in *Figure 2.41*:

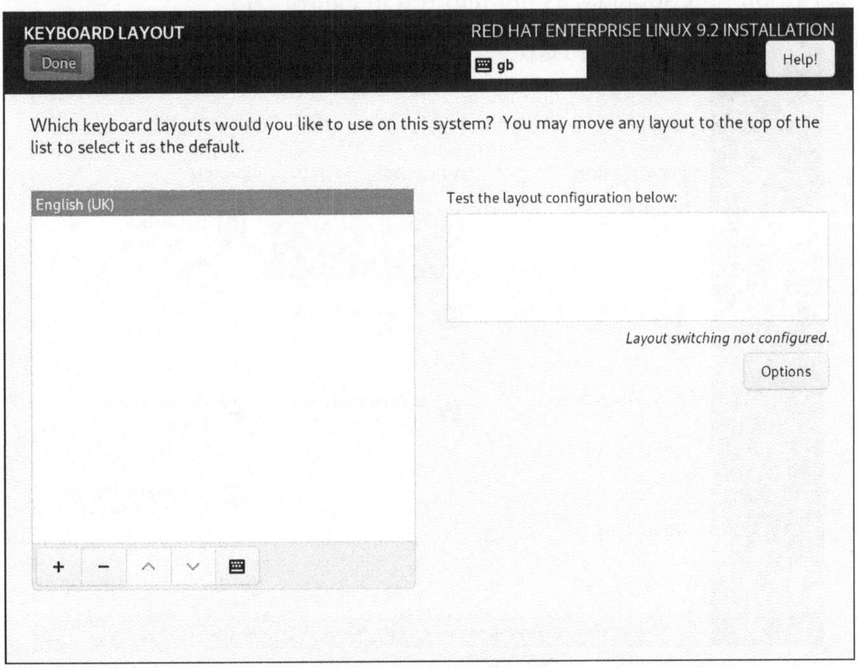

Figure 2.41: *We selected the* **English (UK)** *default, and then selected the* **Done** *command*

Next, we need to register the **RHEL 9.2** operating system with **RedHat** which can be either accomplished using the **`RedHat Developer Account`**, or since we have created our **`Activation Key`**, we can select this option, as highlighted in *Figure 2.42*:

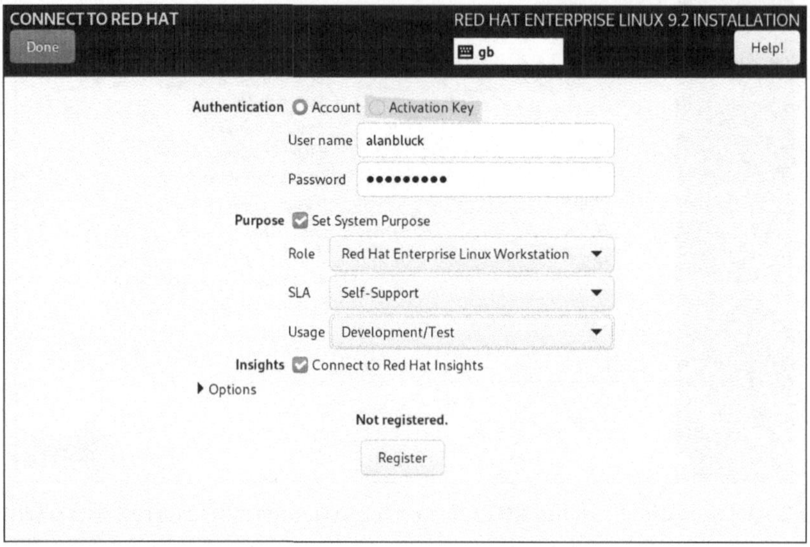

***Figure 2.42:** Since we have created our **Activation Key**, we can select this option*

The highlighted **`Connect to Red Hat`** is selected to choose the Red Hat **`Activation Key`** Subscription functionality, as highlighted in *Figure 2.43*:

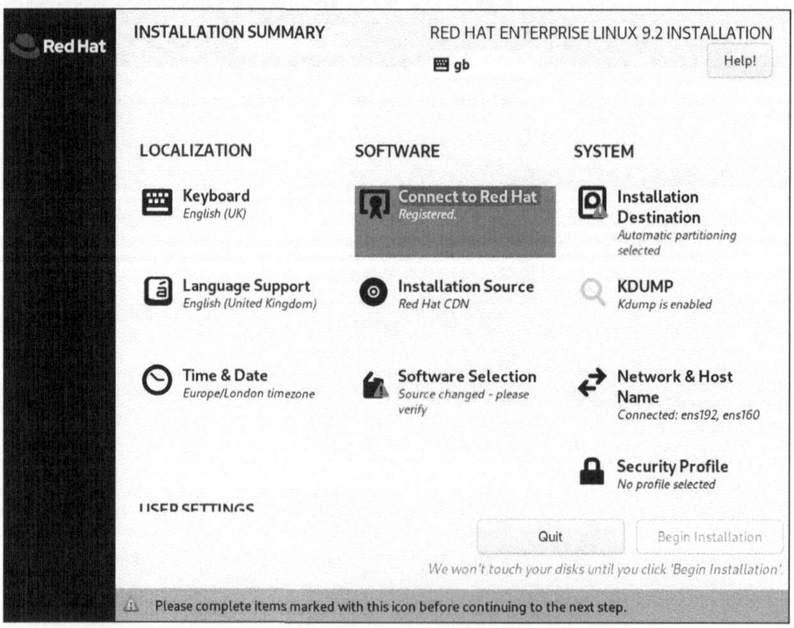

***Figure 2.43:** The highlighted **Connect to Red Hat** link is selected for the Red Hat **Activation Key** Subscription.*

Now, we can select the **`Activation Key`** option, and we must then enter our **Organization** ID as well as the **`ECMUKDEMO2025 Activation Key,`** we created earlier, and then the **`Purpose`** and **`Insights`** options are selected with the details set from the **Drop-downs** as shown in *Figure 2.44*. Then to confirm the registration, the highlighted **`Register`** command must be set.

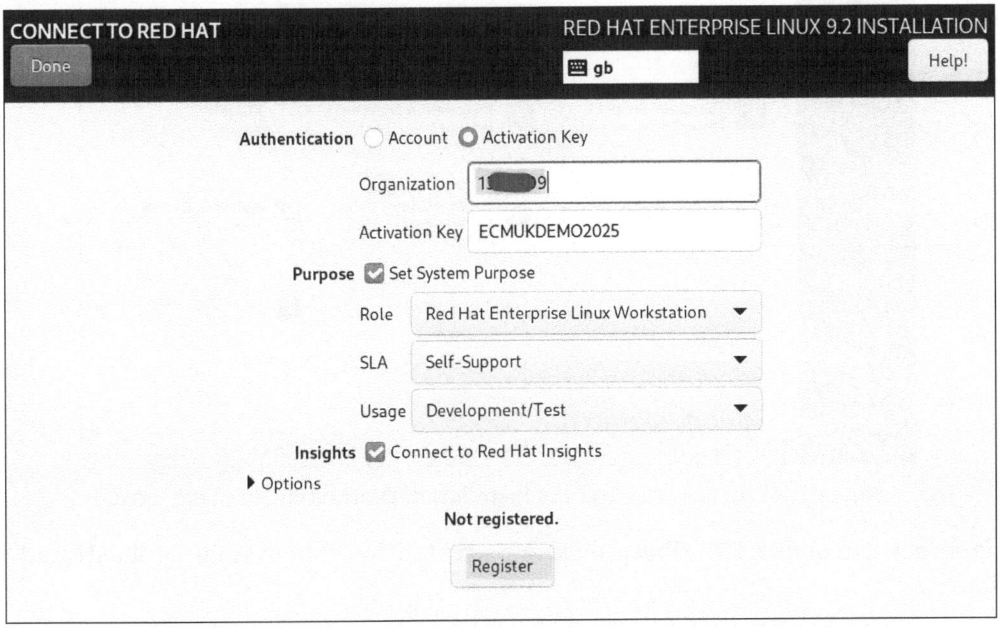

***Figure 2.44:** Enter our **Organization** ID and the **ECMUKDEMO2025 Activation Key,** we created earlier*

On selecting the **`Register`** command, the **`Subscription`** registration status is shown, as illustrated in *Figure 2.45*:

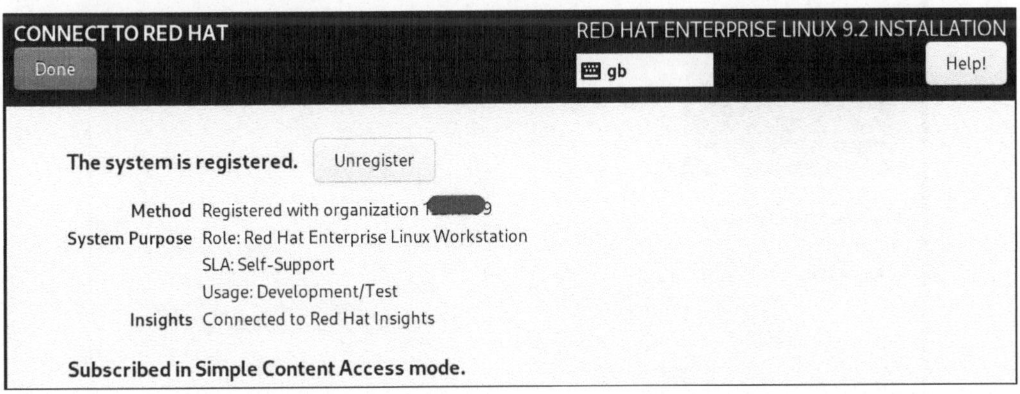

***Figure 2.45:** On selecting the **Register** command, the **Subscription Registration** status is shown*

After selecting **`Done`**, in the top-right of the **`Subscription Registration`** status page, we need to select the **`Installation Destination`**, as highlighted in *Figure 2.46*:

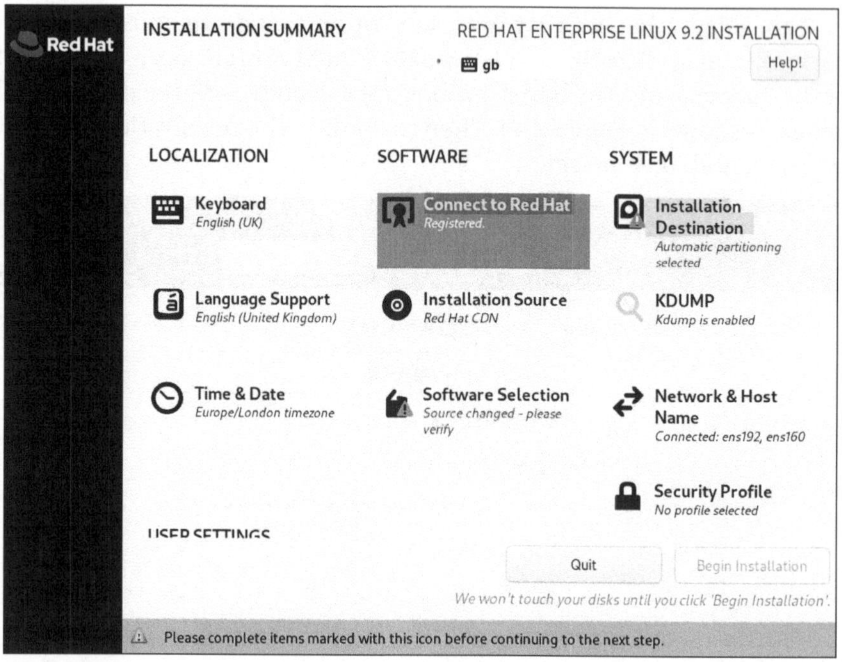

Figure 2.46: *We need to select the* ***Installation Destination****, as highlighted*

We select the single **500 Gbyte** disk, we created for this system as illustrated in *Figure 2.47*:

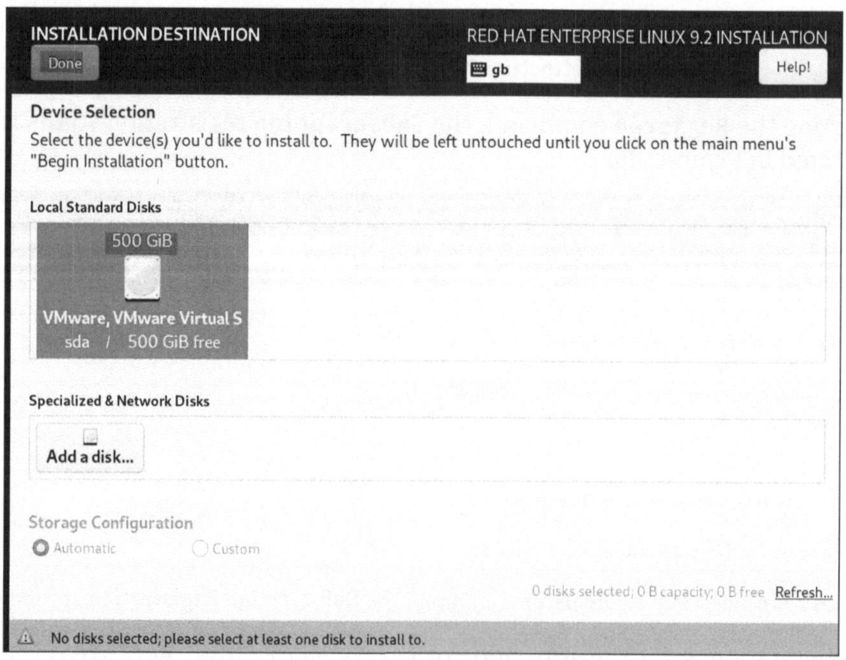

Figure 2.47: *We select the single* ***500 GByte*** *disk which we created for this system*

The selected disk is then shown in a pop-up window which allows us to review the selection, and then select the highlighted **`Close`** command, as shown in *Figure* 2.48:

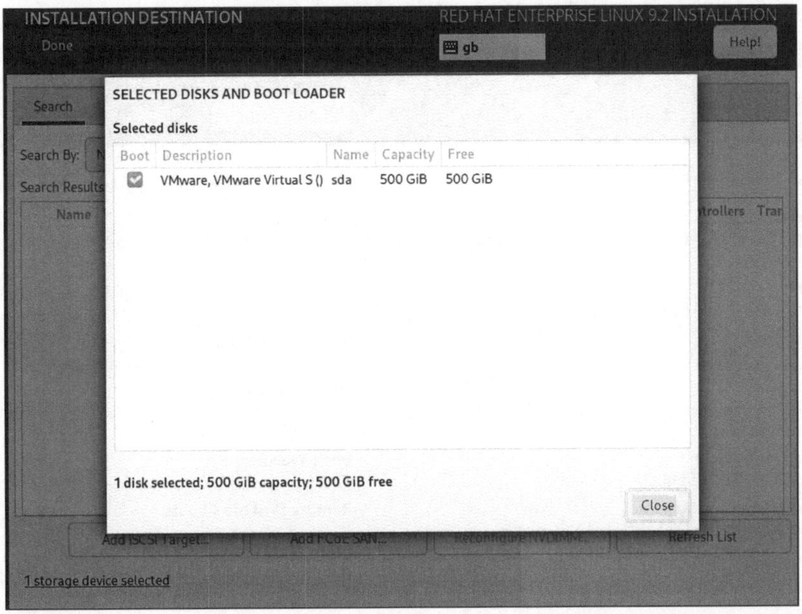

Figure 2.48: *We review the selection, and then select the highlighted Close command*

Now, we select the **`Software Selection`** option as highlighted in *Figure* 2.49:

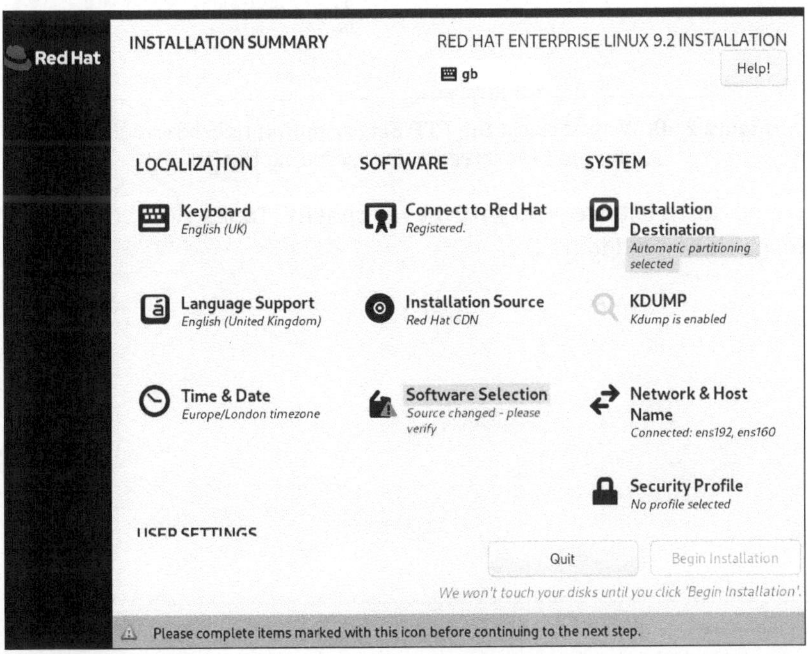

Figure 2.49: *We select the highlighted* ***Software Selection*** *option*

The **`Software Selection`** option has a scrollable tick-box list from which we just select the **`FTP Server`** option, highlighted in *Figure* 2.50 on the first screen, and then scroll down to view a second page of options.

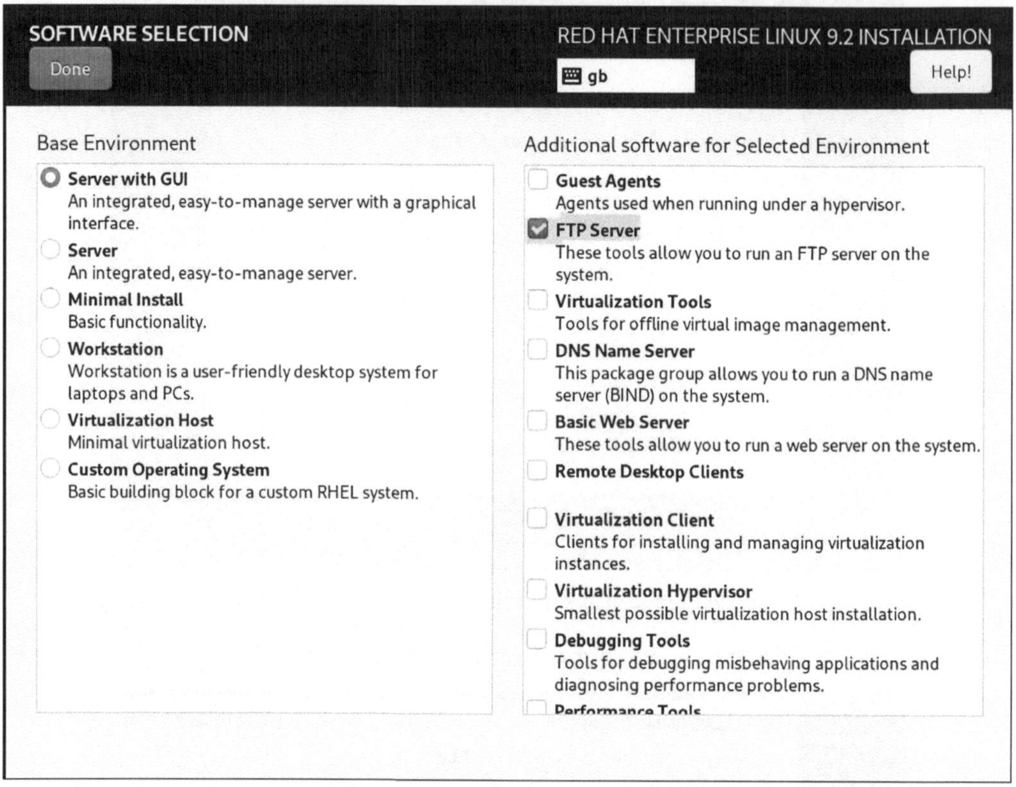

Figure 2.50: *We just select the* ***FTP Server*** *option tick-box, highlighted on the first screen before scrolling the list.*

On the scrolled down list, we select the **`Development Tools`** tick-box option, and then select **Done**, as shown in *Figure* 2.51:

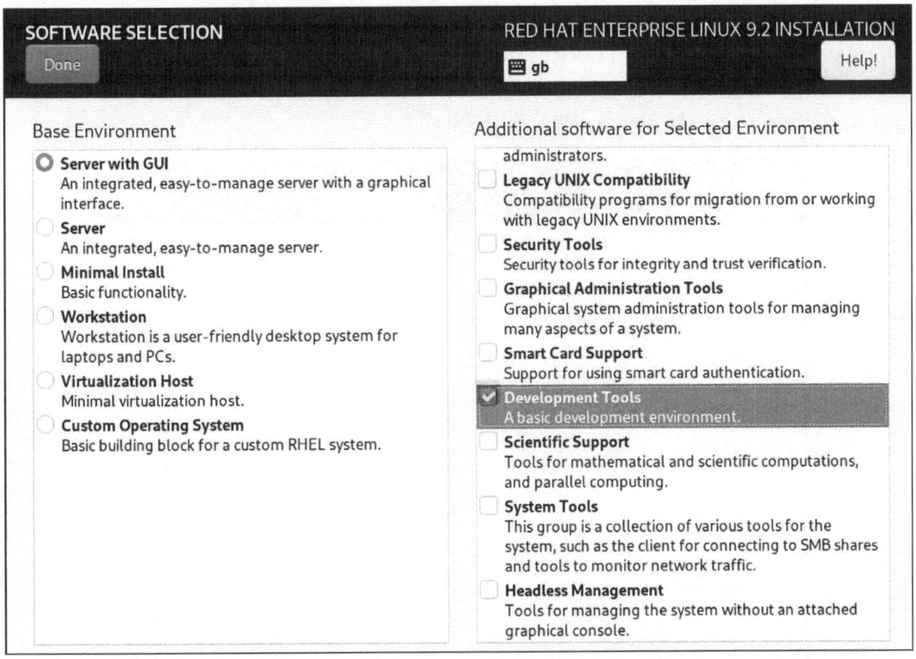

Figure 2.51: *On the scrolled down list, we select the* ***Development Tools*** *tick-box option, and then select* ***Done***

Now we can select the **Root Password** command, as highlighted in *Figure* 2.52:

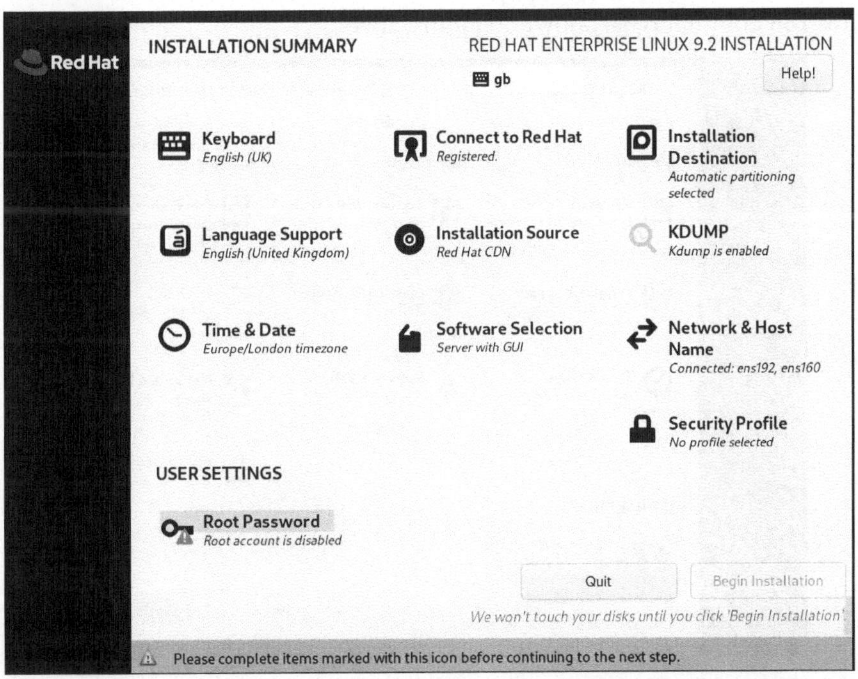

Figure 2.52: *We can select the highlighted* ***Root Password*** *command*

The **Root Password** is entered, and then re-entered to **Confirm** it. Because we chose a short password found in a Dictionary validation check, we have to select the **Done** command twice to allow it to be used (not recommended in a production system)! The warning message is as shown in *Figure 2.53*:

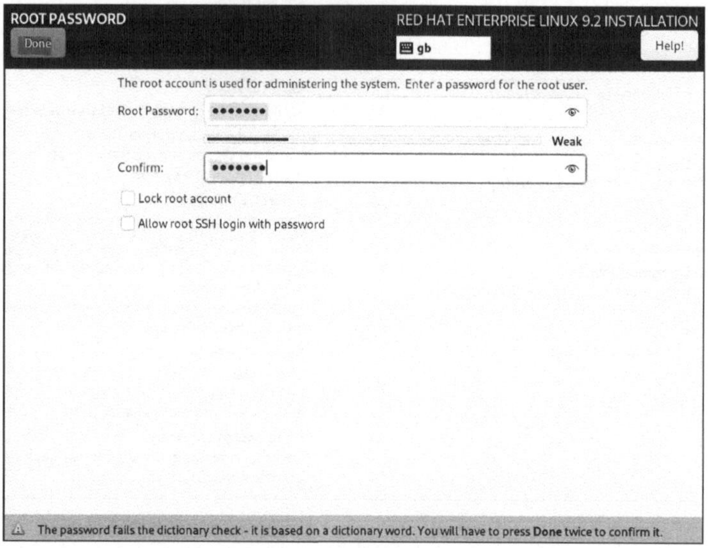

Figure 2.53: *The* ***Root Password*** *is entered and then re-entered to* ***Confirm*** *it*

Having updated all the flagged options, we are now able to select the **Begin Installation** command, as shown in *Figure 2.54*:

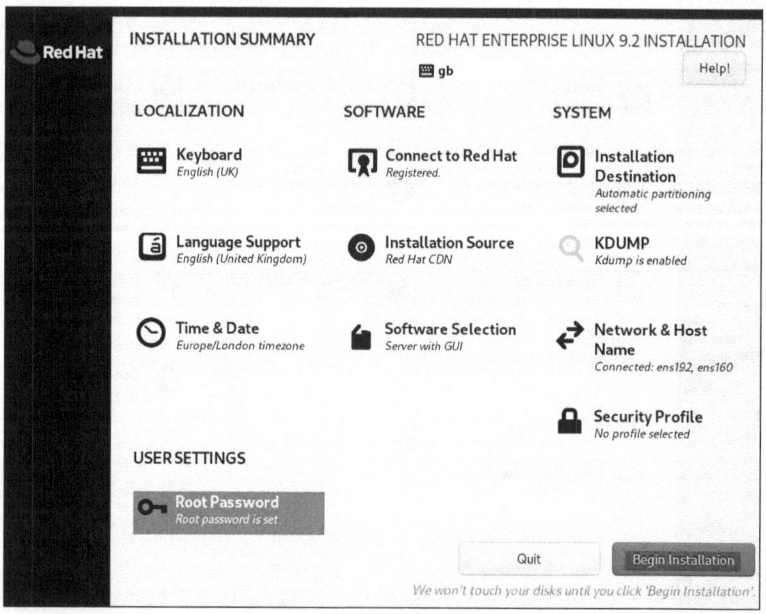

Figure 2.54: *We are now able to select the* ***Begin Installation*** *command*

The **INSTALLATION PROGRESS** status window is now displayed, as illustrated in *Figure 2.55*:

***Figure** 2.55: The **INSTALLATION PROGRESS** status window is now displayed*

At the bottom of the **VMware** window, we can now view the status bar which has a message and a referenced command button, as shown in *Figure 2.56*:

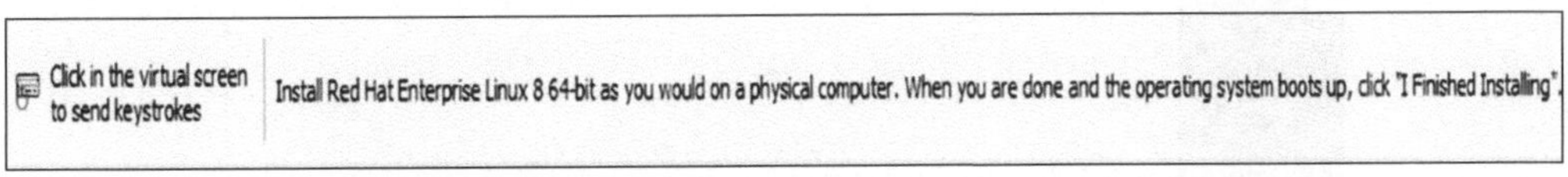

***Figure 2.56**: We can now view the status bar which has a message and a referenced command button*

The **I Finished Installing** command is highlighted in the bottom right-hand corner of the VMWare window, as highlighted in *Figure 2.57*:

***Figure 2.57**: The **I Finished Installing** command is in the bottom right-hand corner of the **VMWare** window*

Towards the end of the Installation process, we can see the **RedHat Subscription**, which is configured, as highlighted in *Figure* 2.58:

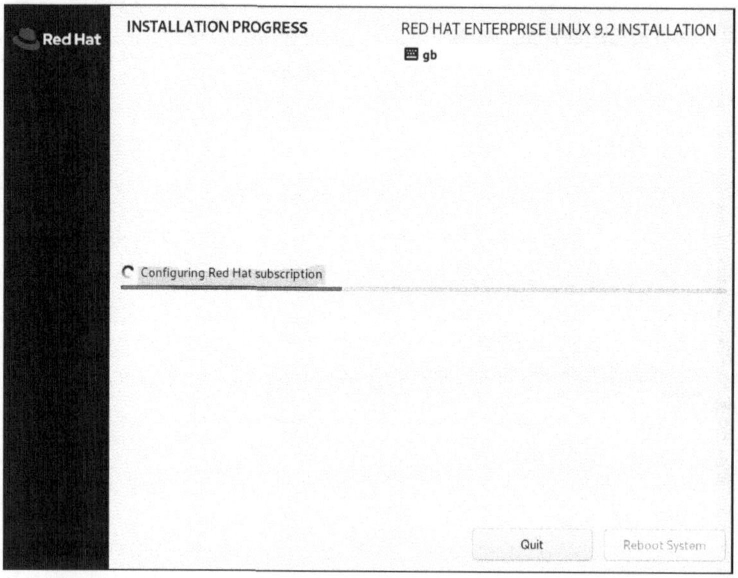

Figure 2.58: *Towards the end of the Installation process, we can see the* ***RedHat Subscription,*** *which is configured*

The **INSTALLATION PROGRESS** window indicates that the installation is successfully completed, and we can select the **Reboot System** command, as illustrated in *Figure* 2.59:

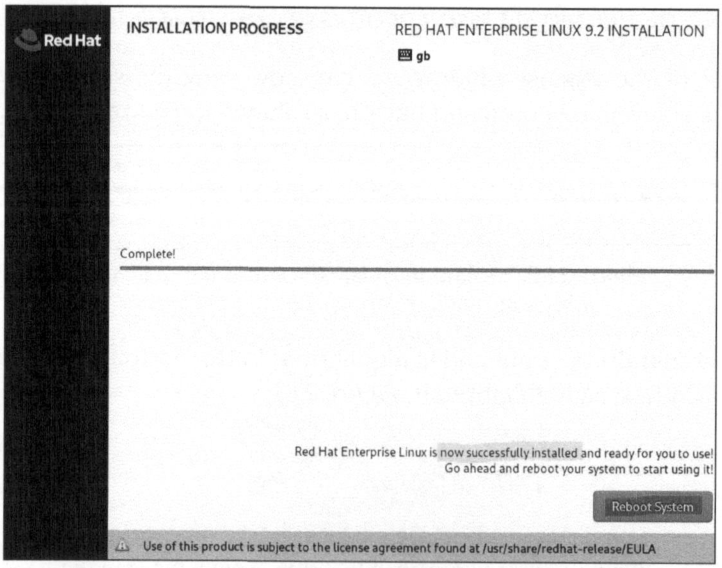

Figure 2.59: *The* **INSTALLATION PROGRESS** *window indicates that the install is successfully completed*

We can now select the **Start Setup** command to begin the final configuration steps, as illustrated in *Figure 2.60*:

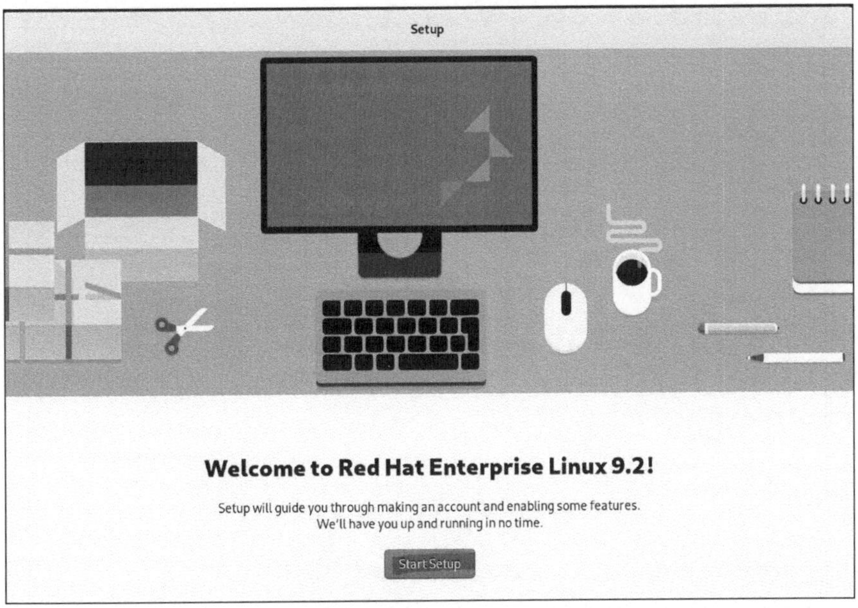

***Figure 2.60**: We can now select the **Start Setup** command to begin the final configuration steps*

We select the **Next** command on the **Privacy** page, as shown in *Figure 2.61*:

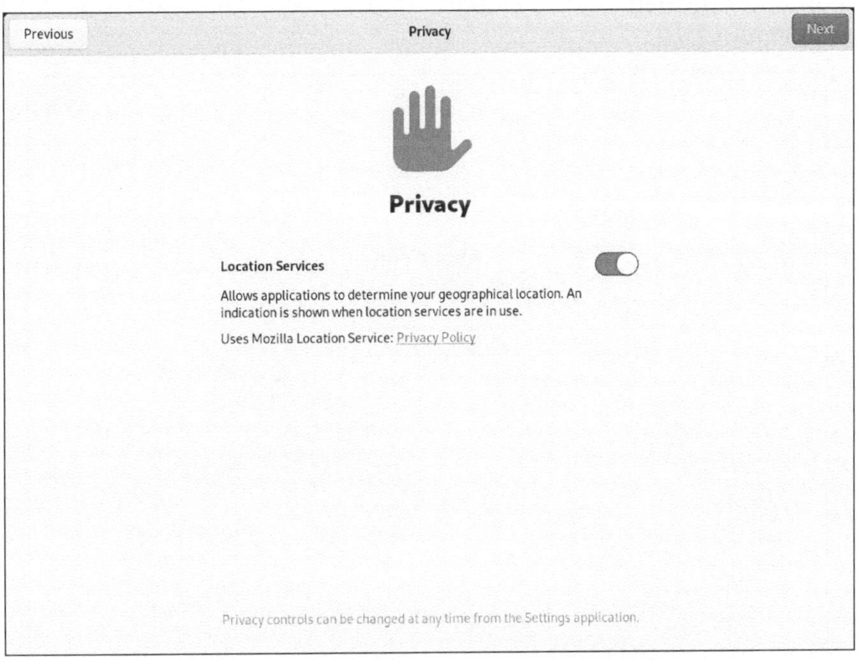

***Figure 2.61**: We select the **Next** command on the Privacy page*

Next, we selected the highlighted **`Skip`** command on the **`Connect Your Online Accounts`** page, as shown in *Figure 2.62*:

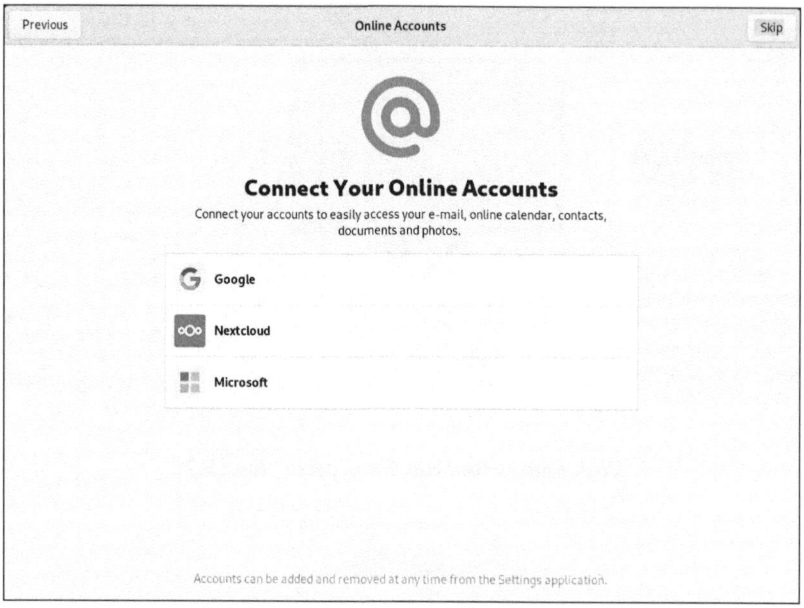

***Figure 2.62**: Next, we selected the highlighted **Skip** command on the **Connect Your Online Accounts** page*

We can now enter the details of a personal Linux account, and select **`Next`**, highlighted as shown in *Figure 2.63*:

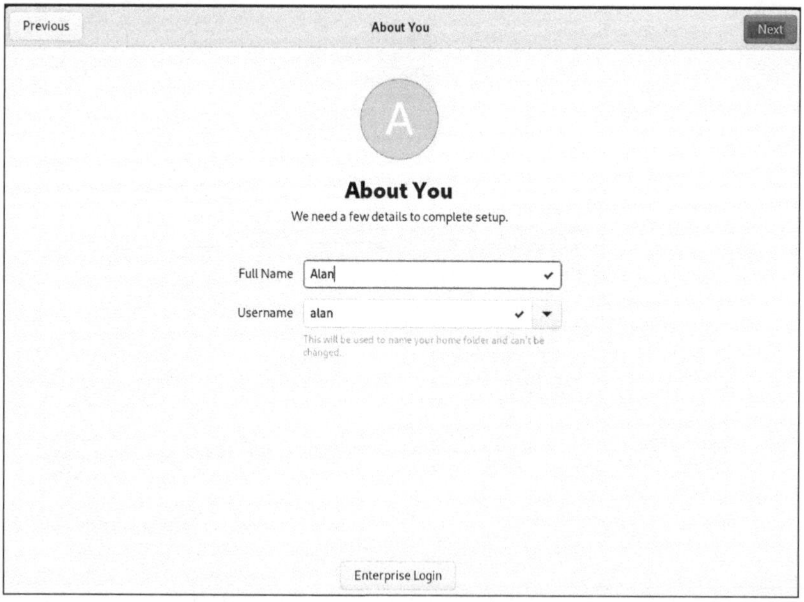

Figure 2.63**: We can now enter the details of a personal Linux account, and select **Next

We must enter the account **Password** and **Confirm**, as highlighted in *Figure* 2.64:

Figure 2.64**: We must enter the account **Password** and **Confirm

We have now completed the basic **RedHat RHEL 9.2** system configuration, and we can select the **Start Using Red Hat Enterprise Linux** command, as highlighted in *Figure* 2.65:

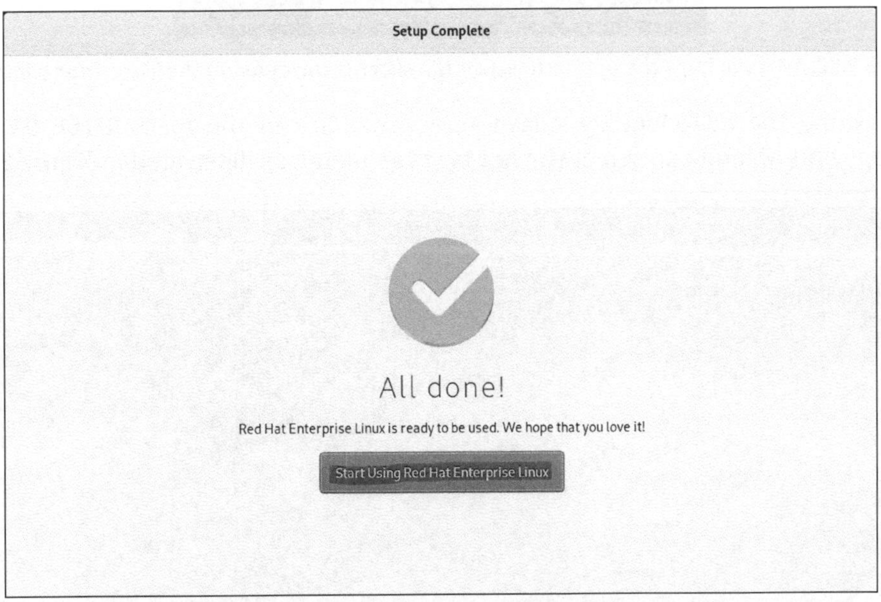

***Figure 2.65:** We can select the **Start Using Red Hat Enterprise Linux** command*

We now have the option to select the short tutorial using the **Take Tour** command, in the introductory splash screen, as highlighted in *Figure* 2.66:

Figure 2.66: *We now have the option to select the short tutorial using the* ***Take Tour*** *command*

After exiting the introductory splash screen, we are in the main **RHEL 9.2** Linux desktop window, and can select the **`Activities`** menu, as illustrated in *Figure 2.67*:

Figure 2.67: *After exiting the introductory splash screen, we are in the main* **RHEL 9.2** *Linux desktop*

The **Activities** menu can be used to select the **Linux Command** window icon, as highlighted in *Figure 2.68*:

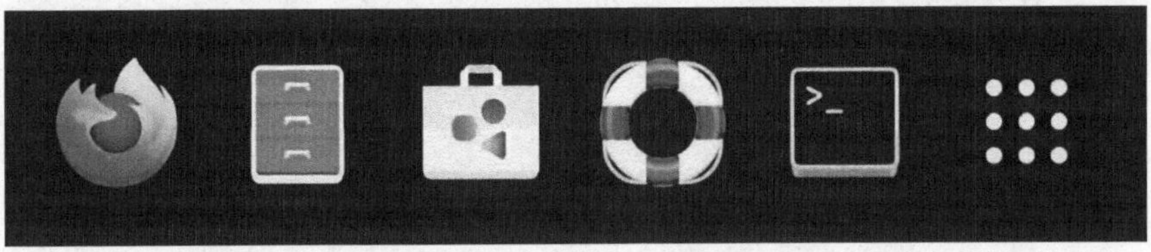

Figure 2.68: *The **Activities** menu can be used to select the **Linux Command** window icon*

We can also confirm that our **ECMUKDEMO2025 Activation key** is listed using the RedHat URL link:

https://console.redhat.com/insights/connector/activation-keys

(Activation Keys - System Configuration | RHEL)

This page now has the details of our key, **ECMUKDEMO2025,** as highlighted in *Figure 2.69*:

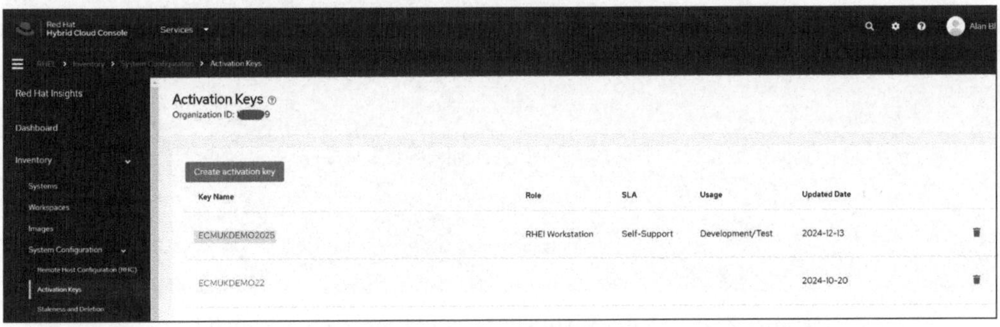

Figure 2.69: *We display the details of our Subscription Activation key,* **ECMUKDEMO2025**

The following Linux commands are required, run as the **root** user, for installing the supporting libraries and software languages on RedHat Linux (using the Python 3.11 version):

```
su - root
dnf install gcc gcc-c++ make git python3.11 python3.11-devel
```

The result of using this installation command are shown in *Figure 2.70*:

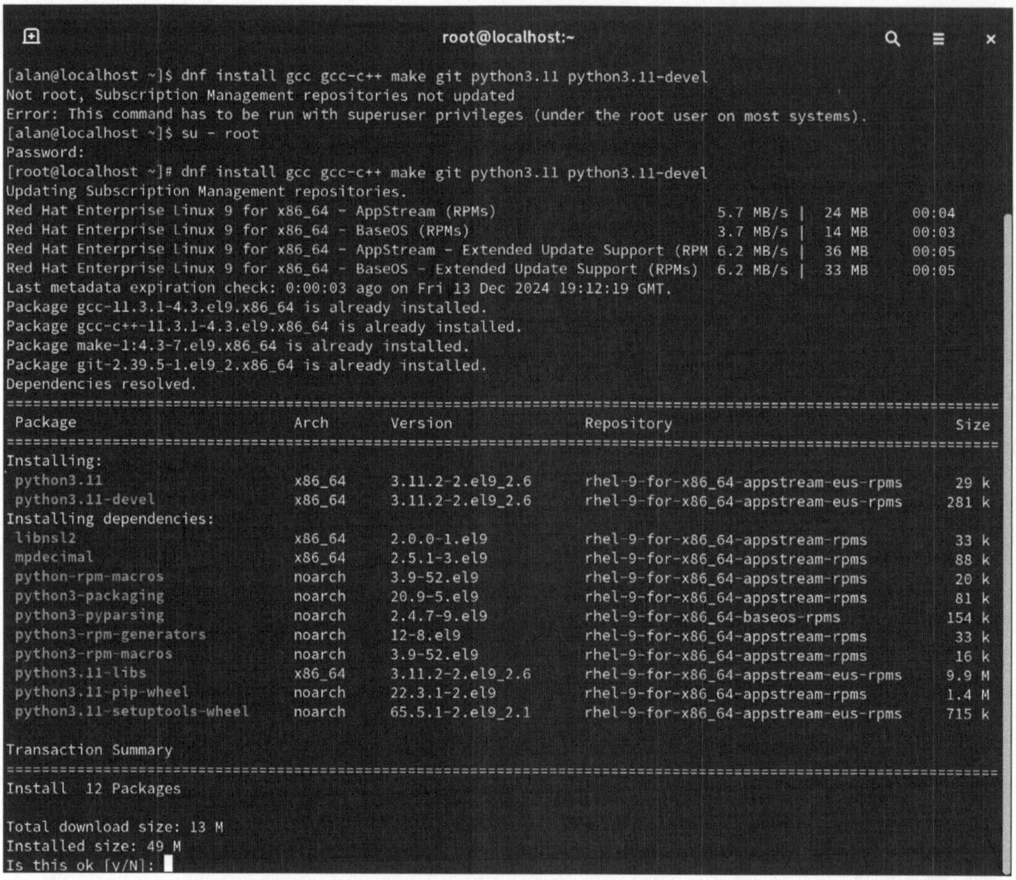

Figure 2.70: *The* ***dnf install gcc gcc-c++ make git python3.11 python3.11-devel*** *install command is run from* **root**

To install the packages, we need to enter **y** to confirm the installation, as shown in *Figure 2.71*:

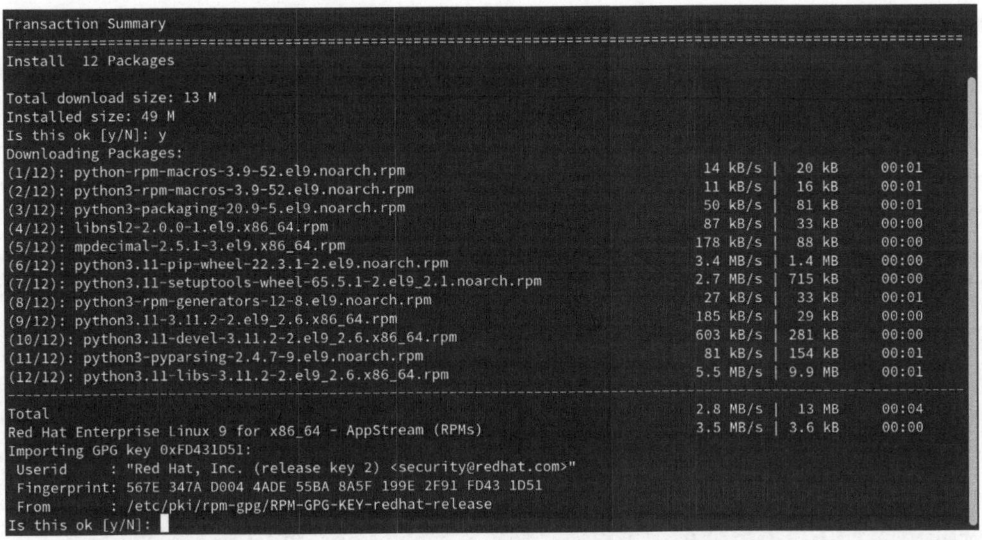

Figure 2.71: *To install the packages, we need to enter* **y** *to confirm the installation*

The list of installed **Python** library packages, essential for using **IBM Granite 3.0** are displayed, as shown in *Figure 2.72*:

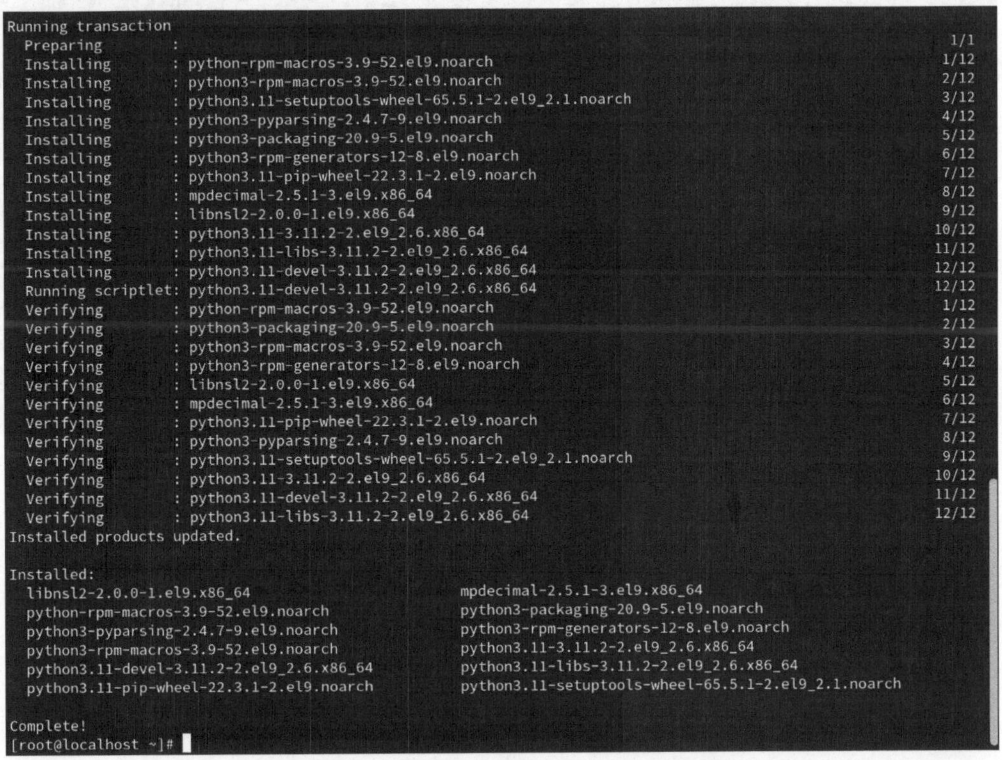

Figure 2.72: *The list of installed* **Python** *library packages, essential for using* **IBM Granite 3.0** *are displayed*

Then, we install the supporting **Python AI** libraries:

```
pip install torch numpy transformers datasets tiktoken wandb tqdm
```

As shown in *Figure* 2.73, the system first detects that the **pip** installer is not installed, but prompts for it to be installed as part of the original command entered (this enhanced response would not have been the response in earlier RedHat Linux systems)!

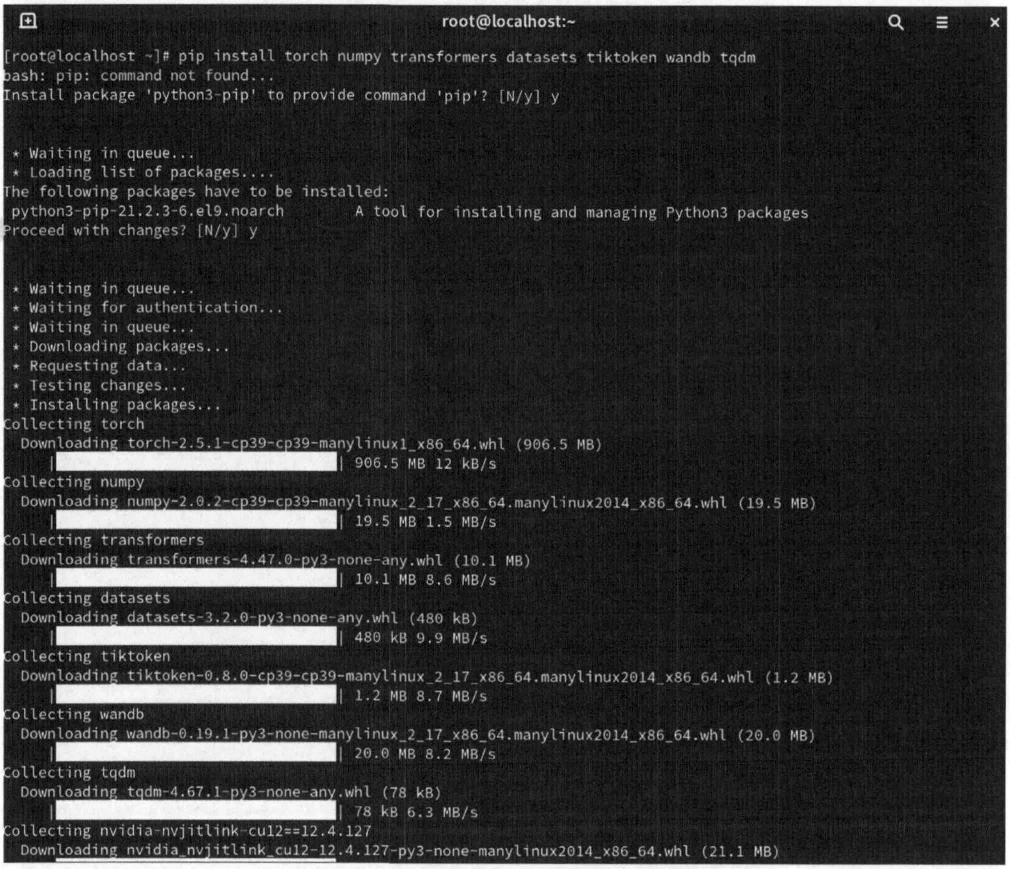

Figure 2.73: *The system first detects that the* **pip** *installer is not installed*

As shown in *Figure* 2.74, the complete list of libraries required are installed:

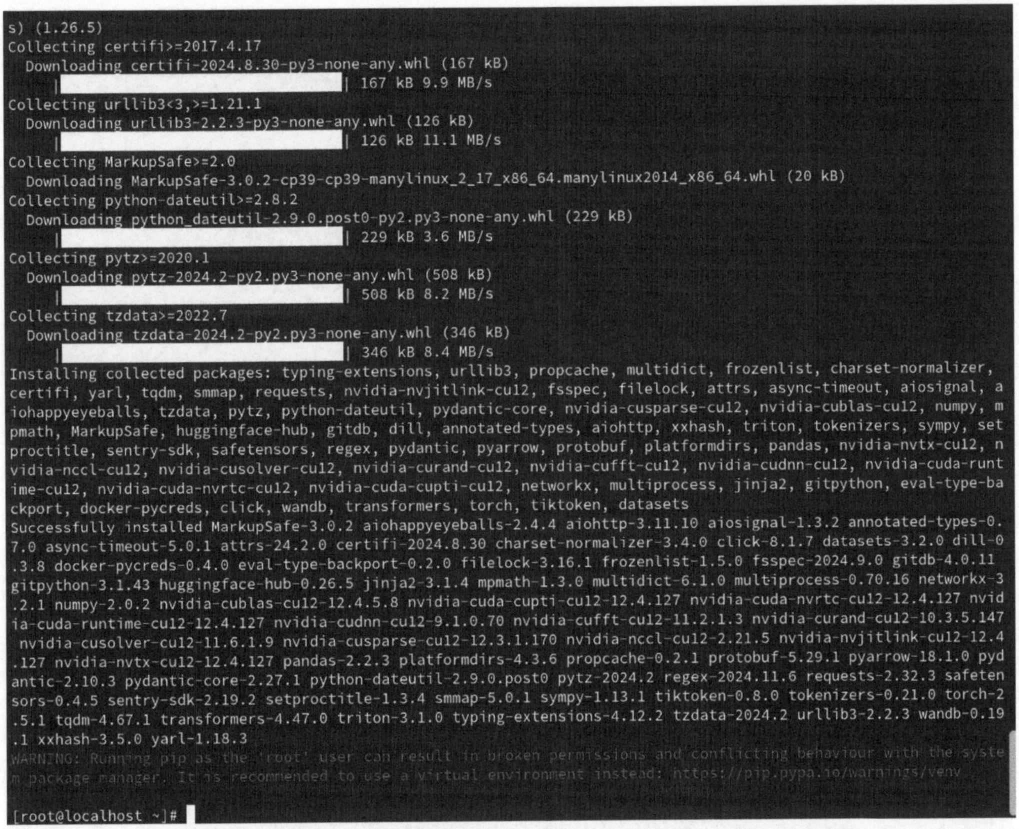

Figure 2.74: *The complete list of libraries required are installed*

Installing Jupyter Lab

The **`pip install jupyterlab`** Linux command is entered, as shown in *Figure 2.75*:

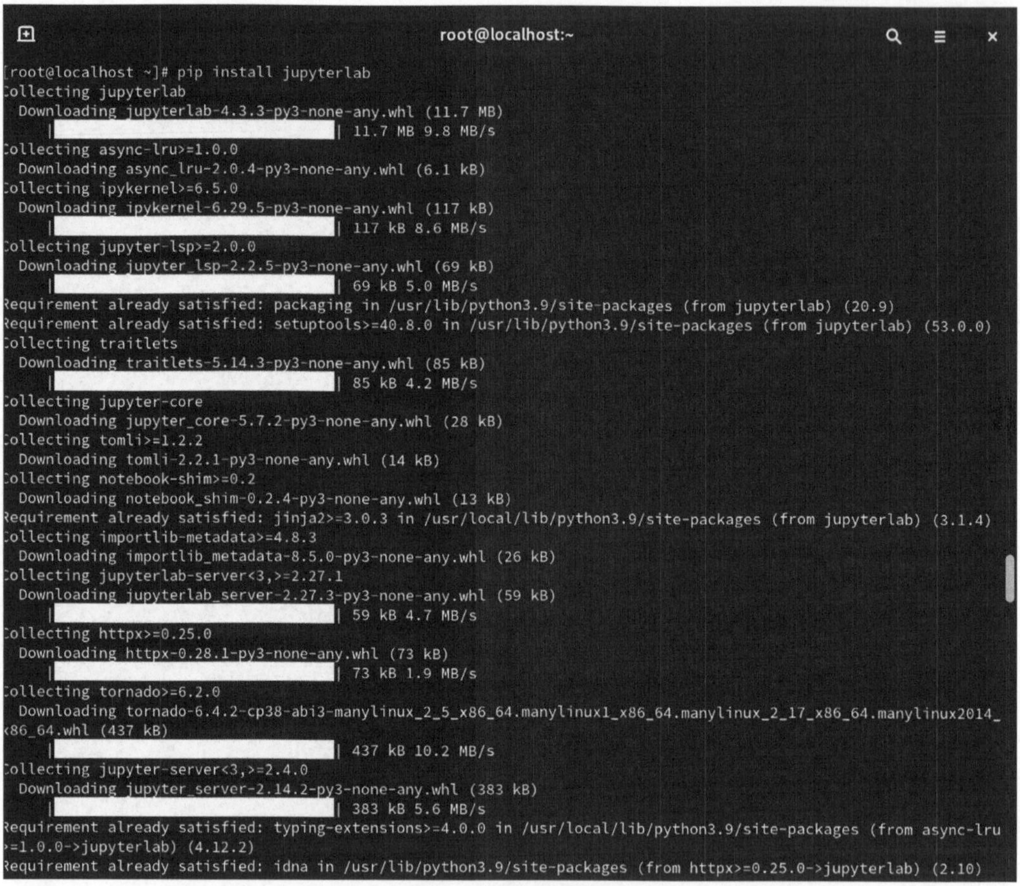

Figure 2.75: *The* ***pip install jupyterlab*** *Linux command is entered*

The **`pip install jupyterlab`** Linux command is shown successfully completed in *Figure 2.76*:

***Figure 2.76**: The **pip install jupyterlab** Linux command is shown successfully completed.*

Version Requirements for Python

The example, Python Language code in this book for IBM Granite 3.0, requires Python 3.10 or Python 3.11 versions to be installed. (We have used Python version 3.11, as this is the only fully working version on RedHat Linux RHEL 9.2 as of 14th December, 2024.)

Note: *As of November 8th, 2024,* **Python 3.10** *is not available in* **RedHat RHEL 9** *and* **RedHat RHEL 8**. **Python 3.12** *is currently not supported for the* **GitHub** *examples, as some dependencies don't work on* **Python 3.12**, *as of December 2024.*

The Jupyter Lab IDE is available for the development of IBM Granite 3.0 Large Language Models, using the command as follows (if running as the root user):

```
jupyter lab --allow-root
```

Check the installation using the link:

https://developer.ibm.com/tutorials/awb-accessing-llms-jupyter-notebook-ollama/

The initial Jupyter Lab web page can now be accessed, and the highlighted launcher selected as highlighted in *Figure 2.77*:

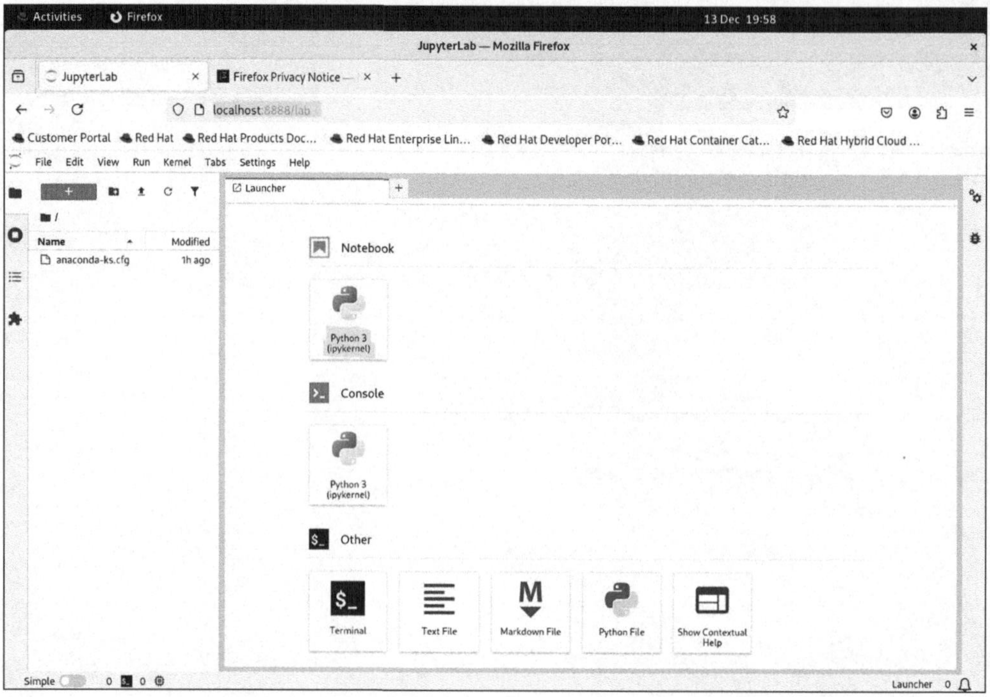

Figure 2.77: *The initial* **Jupyter Lab** *web page can now be accessed, and the highlighted launcher selected.*

Python Libraries for running Ollama

Install the Ollama system, using the following link:

https://ollama.com/download?utm_source=ibm_developer&utm_content=in_content_link&utm_id=tutorials_awb-accessing-llms-jupyter-notebook-ollama

This link displays the following download screen, as shown in *Figure* 2.78 (the web page automatically detects the operating system where the browser is run from, so this highlighted the Windows download command button, when we tried it initially.)

Figure 2.78: *The Ollama download web page running using a Windows browser*

On Linux, we used the command as follows, as shown running in *Figure 2.79*:

```
curl -fsSL https://ollama.com/install.sh | sh
```

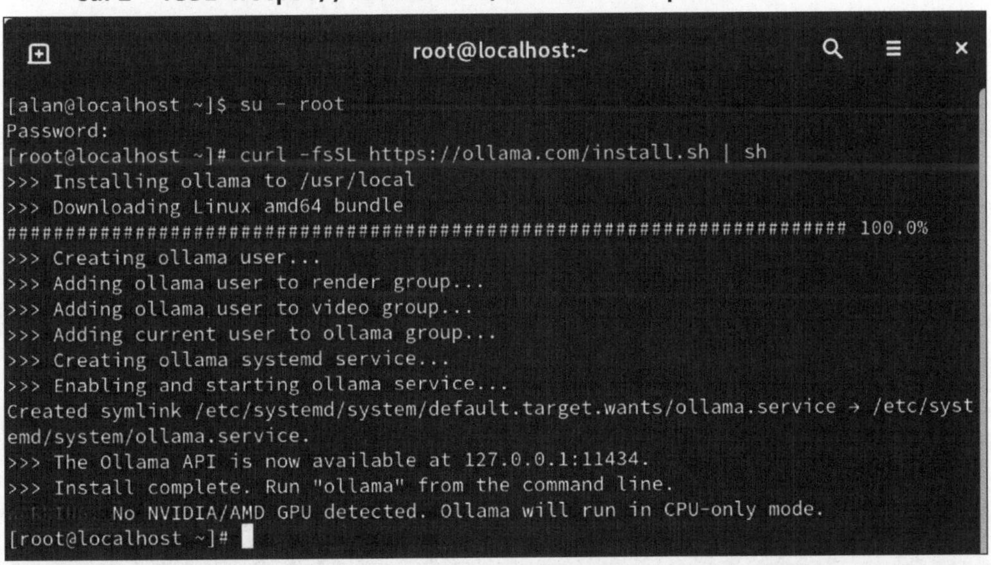

Figure 2.79: *The Ollama installation using* **curl -fsSL https://ollama.com/install.sh | sh**

This Linux command, used above, was copied from the following web page displayed from the FireFox browser running on Linux, using the highlighted icon illustrated in *Figure 2.80*:

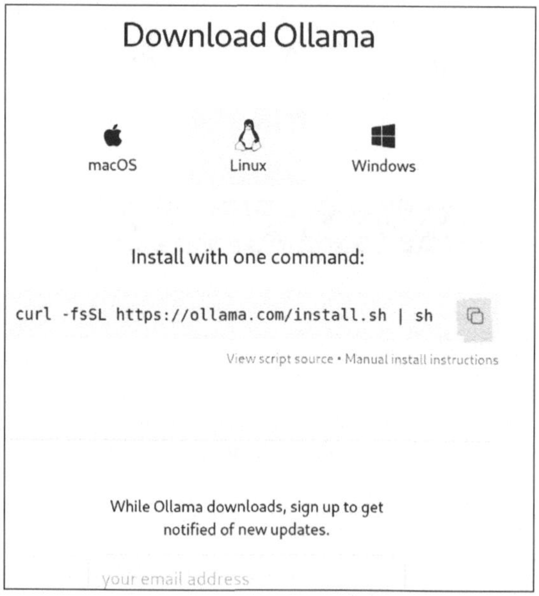

Figure 2.80: *The Linux command displayed from the FireFox browser running on Linux*

On RedHat Linux, a minimum of 250GB disk space is required. Approximately 500GB disk space is recommended for the entire InstructLab end-to-end process. (We set the VMware to use 500 GByte.)

Download of the IBM Granite 3.0 LLMs is shown using ollama, as shown in *Figure 2.81*:

```
ollama pull granite3-dense:2b
```

Start the app (if required, as it should start automatically after installation): **ollama server**

Check to see if this is in memory already using: **`ps -eaf|grep ollama`**

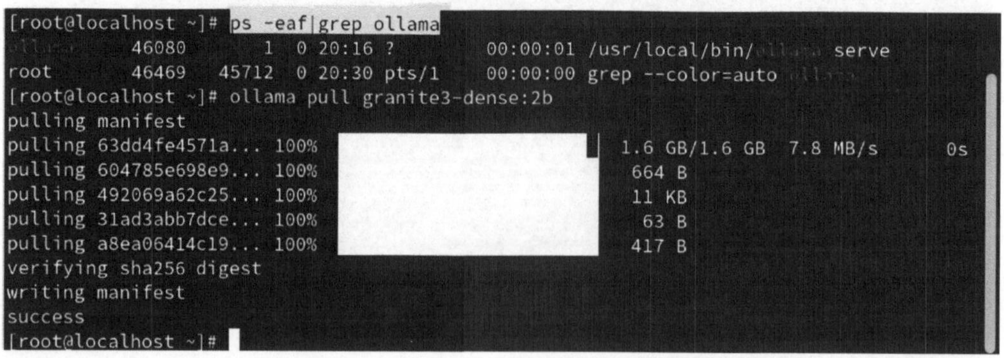

Figure 2.81: *Download of the IBM Granite 3.0 LLM and* ***granite3-dense:2b****, is shown using ollama*

The list of LLMs downloaded can be shown using the command: **`ollama list`** as illustrated in *Figure 2.82*:

```
[root@localhost ~]# ollama list
NAME                 ID              SIZE      MODIFIED
granite3-dense:2b    5c2e6f3112f4    1.6 GB    2 minutes ago
[root@localhost ~]#
```

Figure 2.82:** The list of LLMs downloaded can be shown using the command **ollama list

The following **Python** source code can be used to validate that the system is correctly installed, as shown in *Figure 2.83*:

See here:

https://developer.ibm.com/tutorials/awb-accessing-llms-jupyter-notebook-ollama/

(Accessing IBM Granite LLMs in Jupyter Notebook through Ollama - IBM Developer.)

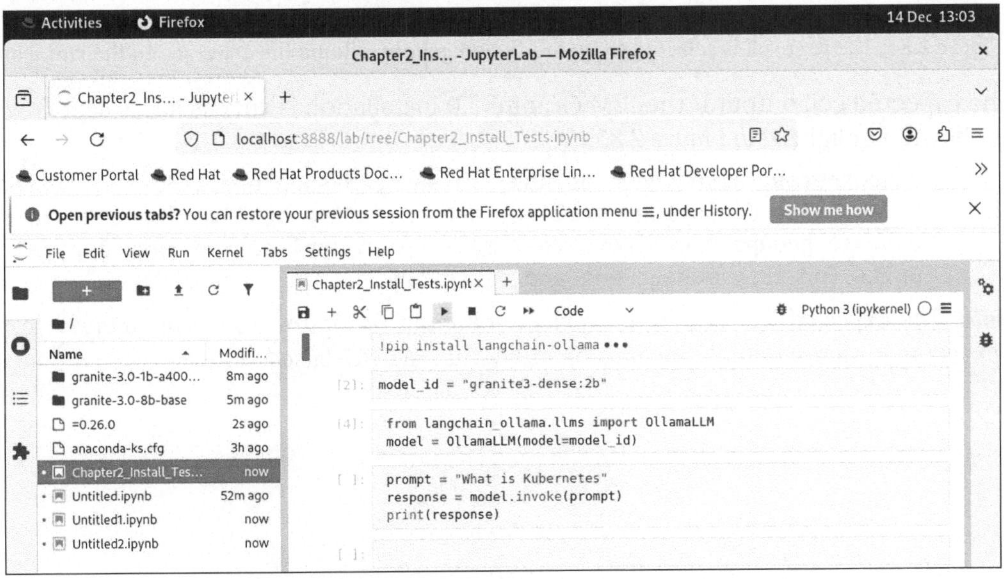

***Figure 2.83:** The following **Python** source code can be used to validate that the system is correctly installed*

The first cell is selected to install the **`langchain-ollama`** libraries, using the **`run`** icon, highlighted in *Figure 2.84*:

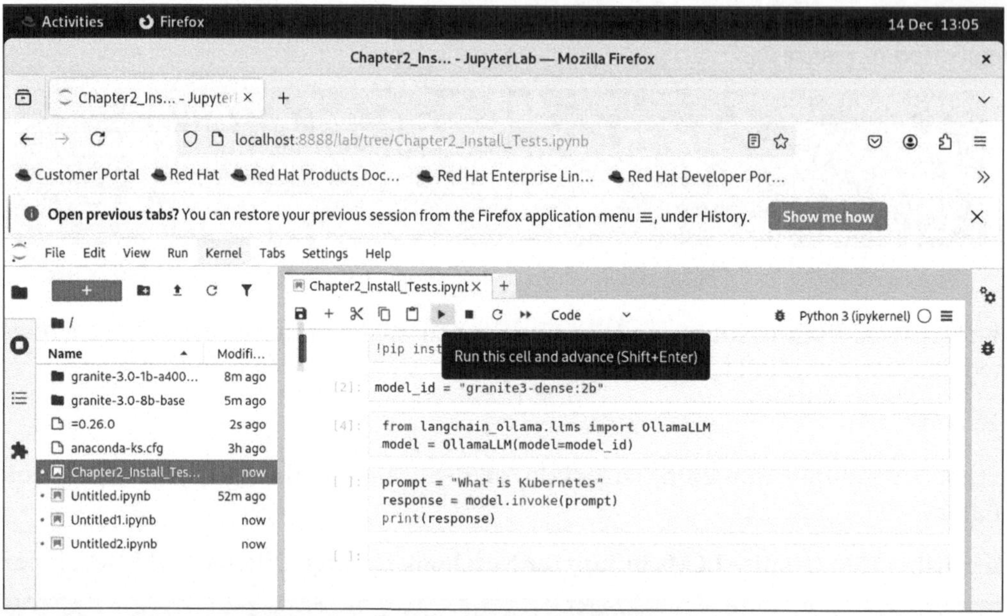

***Figure 2.84:** The first cell is selected to install the **langchain-ollama** libraries, using the run icon*

The expected cell output if the IBM Granite 3.0 installation is successful is as follows, as shown highlighted in *Figure* 2.85:

```
"Kubernetes, also known as K8s, is an open-source platform designed to automate deploying, scaling, and operating application containers. It groups containers that make up an application into logical units for easy management and discovery."
```

Note: *The expected last result cell text (highlighted in Figure 2.85) was delayed from appearing for more than 20 seconds on our VMware CPU-based system.*

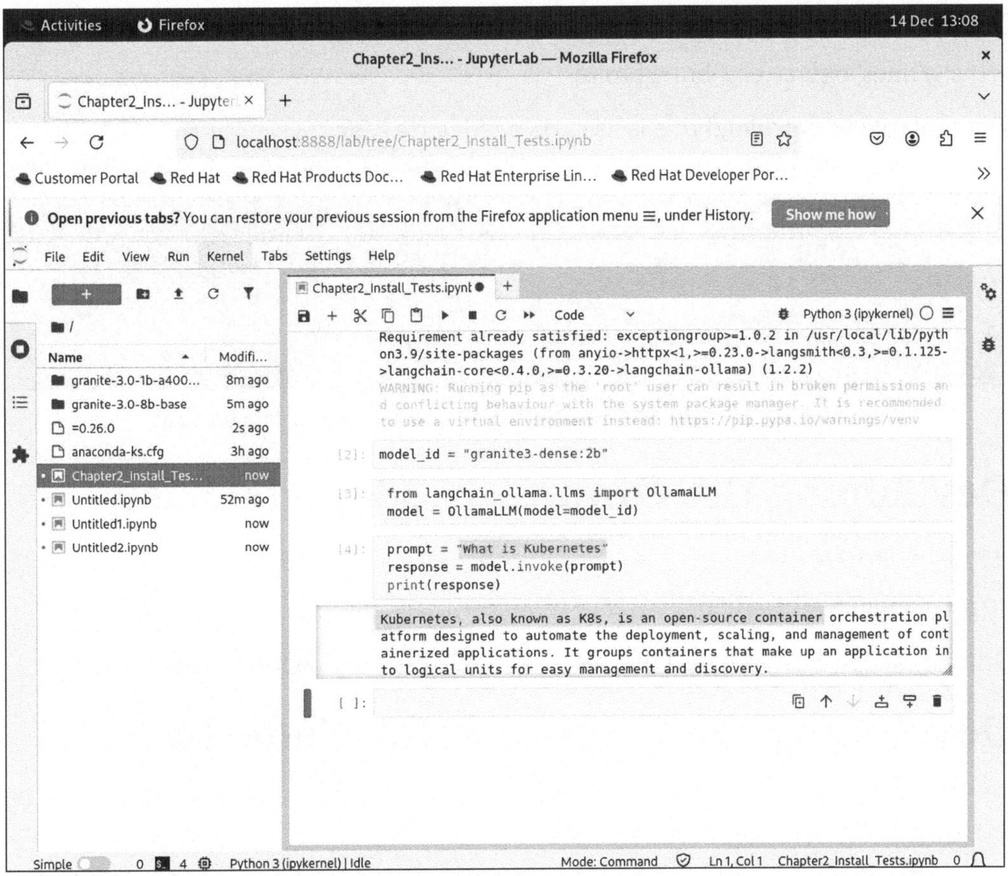

Figure 2.85: *The expected cell output if the IBM Granite 3.0 installation is successful*

For other IBM Granite 3.0 LLMs, See:

https://github.com/ibm-granite/granite-3.0-language-models

To use any of the IBM models, the **`model_path`** can be selected from the list as follows:

- **`ibm-granite/granite-3.0-2b-base`**
- **`ibm-granite/granite-3.0-2b-instruct`**
- **`ibm-granite/granite-3.0-8b-base`**
- **`ibm-granite/granite-3.0-8b-instruct`**
- **`ibm-granite/granite-3.0-1b-a400m-base`**
- **`ibm-granite/granite-3.0-1b-a400m-instruct`**
- **`ibm-granite/granite-3.0-3b-a800m-base`**
- **`ibm-granite/granite-3.0-3b-a800m-instruct`**

or

https://huggingface.co/ibm-granite

The example to download this is as shown in *Figure* 2.86:

`git clone https://hu ggingface.co/ibm-granite/granite-3.0-1b-a400m-base`

```
[root@localhost ~]# git clone https://huggingface.co/ibm-granite/granite-3.0-1b-a400m-base
Cloning into 'granite-3.0-1b-a400m-base'...
remote: Enumerating objects: 65, done.
remote: Counting objects: 100% (61/61), done.
remote: Compressing objects: 100% (61/61), done.
remote: Total 65 (delta 32), reused 0 (delta 0), pack-reused 4 (from 1)
Unpacking objects: 100% (65/65), 624.72 KiB | 2.66 MiB/s, done.
[root@localhost ~]#
```

Figure 2.86: The LLM ***granite-3.0-1b-a400m-base*** *is downloaded*

Developing the Granite-3-2B-Code-Base

See the following link:

https://huggingface.co/ibm-granite/granite-3.0-2b-base

Granite-3.0-2B-Base is based on a decoder-only dense transformer architecture.

Developing the Granite-3-8B-Code-Base

The following Linux command can be used to download the LLM **`granite-3.0-8b-base`**, as shown running in *Figure* 2.87:

`git clone https://huggingface.co/ibm-granite/granite-3.0-8b-base`

```
[root@localhost ~]# git clone https://huggingface.co/ibm-granite/granite-3.0-8b-base
Cloning into 'granite-3.0-8b-base'...
remote: Enumerating objects: 73, done.
remote: Counting objects: 100% (69/69), done.
remote: Compressing objects: 100% (69/69), done.
remote: Total 73 (delta 33), reused 0 (delta 0), pack-reused 4 (from 1)
Unpacking objects: 100% (73/73), 627.22 KiB | 2.08 MiB/s, done.
[root@localhost ~]#
```

Figure 2.87**: The following Linux command can be used to download the LLM* ***`granite-3.0-8b-base`

Developing the Granite-20B-Code-Base

See:

https://www.ibm.com/docs/en/watsonx/w-and-w/2.1.x?topic=models-granite-20b-code-instruct-model-card

Developing the Granite-34B-Code-Base

See: https://huggingface.co/ibm-granite/granite-34b-code-base-8k

Conclusion

This chapter outlined the **IBM Granite 3.0** architecture, and provided a step-by-step example for installing the prerequisites and the installation of the supported Operating Systems, including the required **VMware** build of **RedHat Linux RHEL 9.2,** and its activation for a **RedHat** subscription.

We then covered the installation of the **Python** language libraries, **torch, numpy, transformers, datasets, tiktoken, wandb** and **tqdm.** Also the install for **Jupyter lab** and the **ollama** service.

In the next **Chapter 3**, "**Setting up Granite 3.0 from GitHub**", we cover the procedure to expand the existing disk system and the IBM Granite 3.0 deployments using the GitHub web sources. We describe the step-by-step procedure to use GitHub to download the **IBM Granite 3.0** system, including the installation of the prerequisite supporting software.

Points to Remember

- As of November 8th, 2024, **Python 3.10** is not available in **RedHat RHEL 9** and **RedHat RHEL 8. Python 3.12** is currently not supported for the **GitHub** examples, as some dependencies don't work on **Python 3.12**, as of December 2024.
- The **RedHat Activation Key** web site, must be used for RedHat Subscription service access. As of 25th October, 2024, the subscription manager command is no longer available.
- IBM recommends that the **IBM Granite 3.0 LLMs** are installed on a system with at least 250 GBytes of disk space to run.

Multiple Choice Questions

1. Which of the following RedHat RHEL versions are supported for **IBM Granite 3.0**?
   a. `RHEL Version 8.5 and RHEL Version 9.0`
   b. `RHEL Version 8.8 and RHEL Version 9.2`
   c. `RHEL Version 8.7 and RHEL Version 9.1`
   d. `RHEL Version 8.0 and RHEL Version 9.0`
2. Which of the following RedHat RHEL commands install the **Python** system?
   a. `curl -fsSL https://ollama.com/install.sh | sh`
   b. `dnf install gcc gcc-c++ make git python3.11 python3.11-devel`

    c. **pip install torch numpy transformers datasets tiktoken wandb tqdm**

    d. **pip install jupyterlab**

3. Which one of the following RedHat RHEL disk image types do we use for the VMware Workstation installation download?

    a. **Open virtualization format (.ova)**

    b. **Virtual disk (.vmdk)**

    c. **Bare metal - Installer (.iso)**

    d. **Virtualization - Guest image (.qcow2)**

Answers

1. b
2. b
3. c

Questions

1. Outline the procedure which must be used to provide a RedHat subscription for the RedHat Enterprise Linux developer operating system.
2. List the names and the main versions of the supporting software systems which are required by the **IBM Granite 3.0** Large Language Models.

Key Terms

- **LLM**: Large Language Model
- **AI**: Artificial Intelligence Software that mimics the responses, you might expect to questions supplied by a human operator.
- **COBOL:** Common Business-Oriented Language - a business language, derived from FLOW-MATIC a language developed by Dr. Grace Hopper. See https://www.ibm.com/topics/cobol.
- **NVIDIA GPU:** are hardware graphics processing unit, providing a high speed processing resource. Using their high performance capabilities, they are ideal for developing and using AI Large Language Models.
- **RHEL:** RedHat Enterprise Linux. A commercial version of the Linux Operating system, now owned by **IBM**.

CHAPTER 3
Setting up Granite 3.0 from GitHub

Introduction

This chapter covers the cloning of **IBM Granite 3.0** deployments using the **GitHub** web sources. First, we describe the procedure to expand the existing disk system which we require to increase the storage required for **IBM Granite 3.0 LLMs**, using our **VMware** build of **RedHat Linux RHEL 9.2**, which we described in *Chapter 2, Granite 3.0's Architecture.*

This chapter follows the step-by-step procedure to use **GitHub** to download the **IBM Granite 3.0** system, including the installation of the prerequisite supporting software.

Structure

In this chapter, we will discuss the following topics:

- Expanding the VMWare Disk Space
- Base Models Available
    - Time Series Foundation Models
    - Direct Forecasting Models
    - Retrieval-Augmented Generation Models
    - Granite Embedding Models
- Downloading IBM's Models
    - Downloading Time Series Foundation Models
- Using IBM's Models
    - Direct Forecasting Example
    - Security: Guardian Models
    - Granite Embedding Models
    - Agentic RAG Model

Expanding the VMWare Disk Space

We decided to increase the Linux **VMware** disk space. As shown in *Figure* 3.1, the two LLMs, we downloaded used most of the **`root`** users partition:

```
[root@localhost ~]# df -k
Filesystem              1K-blocks       Used  Available Use% Mounted on
devtmpfs                     4096          0       4096   0% /dev
tmpfs                    16289792         12   16289780   1% /dev/shm
tmpfs                     6515920      18720    6497200   1% /run
/dev/mapper/rhel-root    73364480   71773340    1591140  98% /
/dev/mapper/rhel-home   433132920    3057444  430075476   1% /home
/dev/sda1                 1038336     300852     737484  29% /boot
tmpfs                     3257956        124    3257832   1% /run/user/1000
vmhgfs-fuse            1953497084 1008998444  944498640  52% /mnt/hgfs
[root@localhost ~]# ollama list
NAME                  ID              SIZE      MODIFIED
granite3-dense:8b     199456d876ee    4.9 GB    9 days ago
granite3-dense:2b     5c2e6f3112f4    1.6 GB    2 weeks ago
[root@localhost ~]#
```

***Figure 3.1**: Chapter 2, Granite 3.0's Architecture, VMware build reached 98% on the root mount point*

After shutting down the **VMware** workstation, **RHEL 9.2 Linux** server, we can select the current **`500 GB`** disk and expand it, selecting **`Hard Disk (SCSI)`**, as highlighted in *Figure* 3.2:

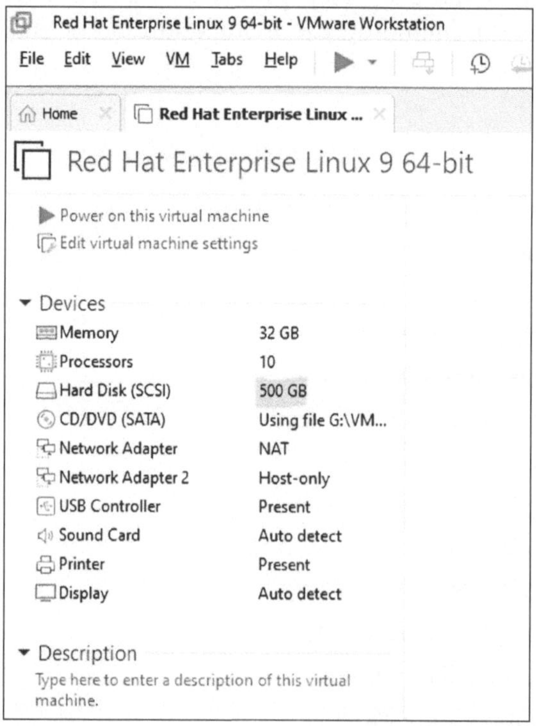

***Figure 3.2**: From the **RHEL 9.2 Linux** server we can select the current **500 GB** disk and expand it*

We can see from **`MS Windows VMware Host`**, and the **`File Explorer`**, that the **G Drive,** we are using has **`932 GB`** of its **`1.81 TB`** capacity free for use by our virtual Linux server, as highlighted in *Figure* 3.3:

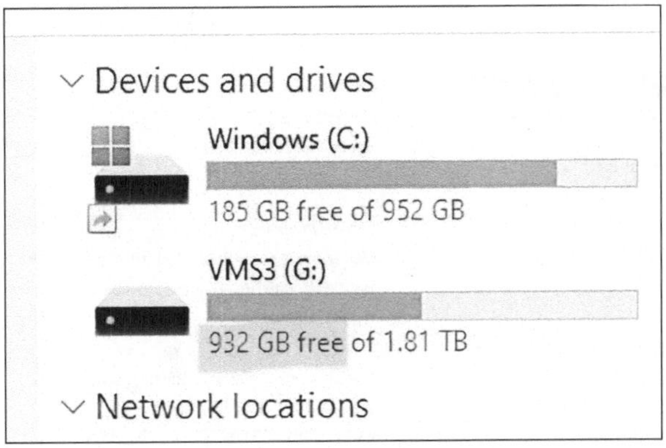

***Figure* 3.3**: *The* **G Drive,** *we are using has* **932 GB** *of its* **1.81 TB** *capacity free*

First, we make a backup copy of the RHEL 9.2 Linux VMware folder deployment to a 4 TB Western Digital portable USB drive, as shown in *Figure* 3.4:

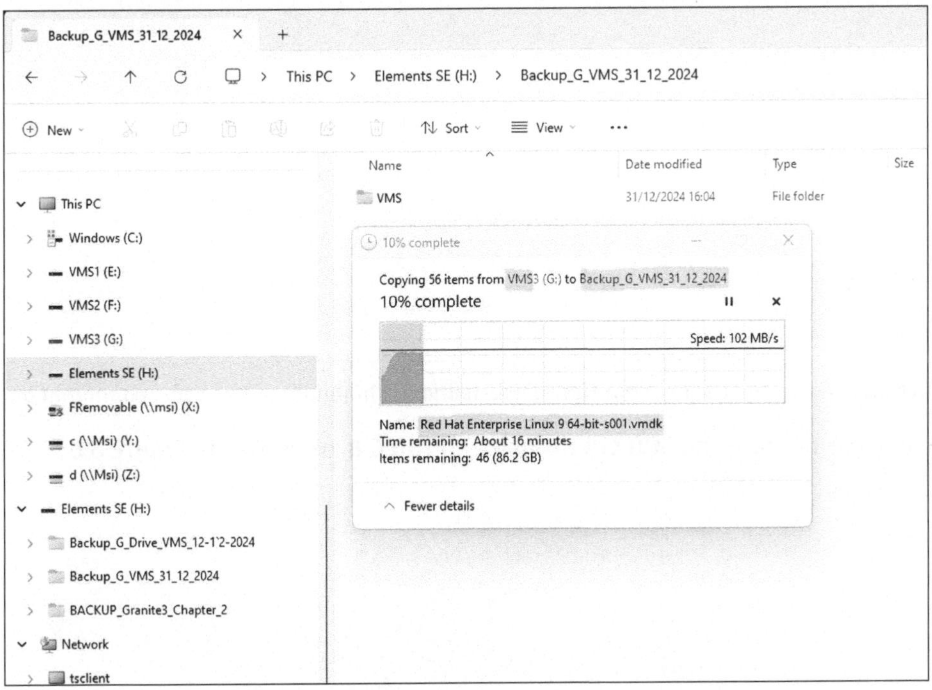

***Figure* 3.4**: *We make a backup copy of the RHEL 9.2 Linux VMware folder deployment to a 4 TB USB Drive*

We can now safely expand the existing Hard Disk, using the highlighted **Expand...** command button, as highlighted in *Figure* 3.5:

Figure 3.5: *We expand the existing Hard Disk, using the highlighted Expand... command button*

We can now increase the **500 GB** disk size to **750 GB**, as shown in *Figure 3.6*:

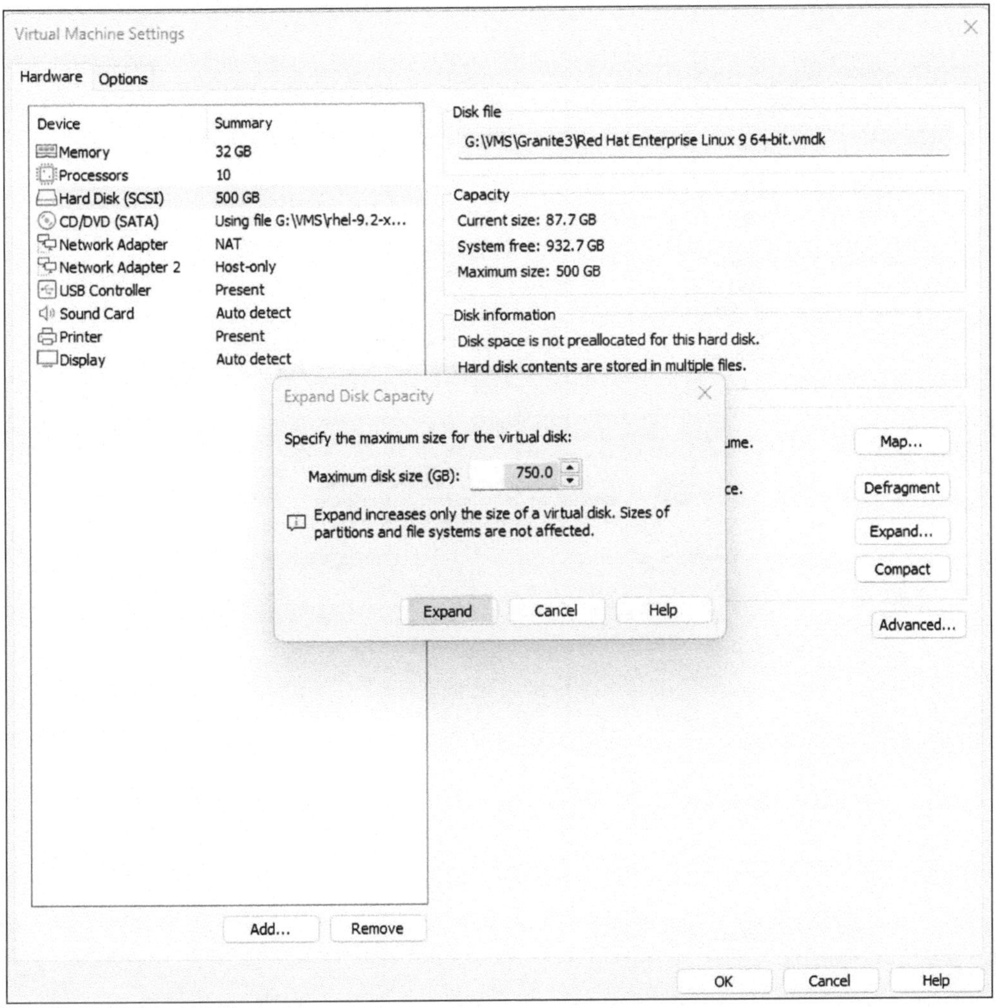

Figure 3.6: *We can now increase the 500 GB disk size to 750 GB*

The increased disk size operation is shown to be successful, as highlighted in *Figure 3.7*:

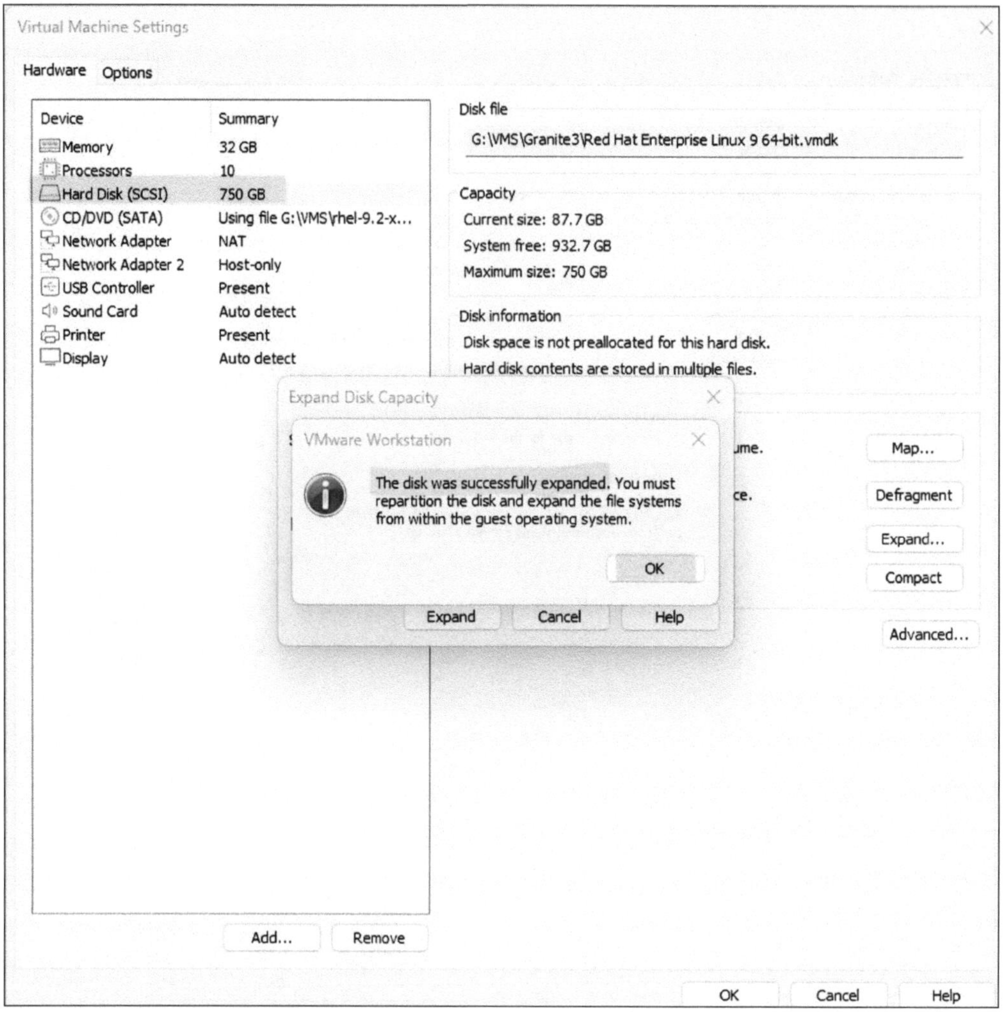

***Figure 3.7**: The increased disk size operation is shown to be successful*

The **fdisk -l /dev/sda** command shows the increased disk capacity on VMware power-up, as highlighted in *Figure* 3.8:

```
root@localhost:~

[root@localhost ~]# fdisk -l /dev/sda
Disk /dev/sda: 750 GiB, 805306368000 bytes, 1572864000 sectors
Disk model: VMware Virtual S
Units: sectors of 1 * 512 = 512 bytes
Sector size (logical/physical): 512 bytes / 512 bytes
I/O size (minimum/optimal): 512 bytes / 512 bytes
Disklabel type: dos
Disk identifier: 0x4c75a38d

Device     Boot   Start        End    Sectors  Size Id Type
/dev/sda1  *       2048    2099199    2097152    1G 83 Linux
/dev/sda2       2099200 1048575999 1046476800  499G 8e Linux LVM
[root@localhost ~]#
```

Figure 3.8: *The fdisk -l /dev/sda command shows the increased disk capacity*

The LVM utility allows the management of logical volumes within X windows or graphically. It is run using the following command as the root user:

To install the **Logical Volume Manager** (**LVM**) graphical user interface (**GUI**) on **Red Hat 9.2**, you can type **`yum install lvm2`**, as shown in *Figure* 3.9:

To extend the **LVM** partition use:

```
lvextend -L +250G /dev/mapper/rhel-root
```

```
[root@localhost ~]# yum install lvm2
Updating Subscription Management repositories.
Last metadata expiration check: 0:18:57 ago on Tue 31 Dec 2024 16:56:16 GMT.
Package lvm2-9:2.03.17-7.el9.x86_64 is already installed.
Dependencies resolved.
Nothing to do.
Complete!
[root@localhost ~]#
```

Figure 3.9: *To install the Logical Volume Manager (LVM) GUI on Red Hat 9.2, you can type yum install lvm2*

The graphical Disk utility can be accessed from the Linux Desktop icon, as shown in *Figure* 3.10:

Figure 3.10: *The graphical Disk utility can be accessed from the highlighted Linux Desktop icon*

The highlighted **Utilities** icon can then be selected, as shown in *Figure 3.11*:

***Figure 3.11**: The highlighted Utilities icon can then be selected*

This then shows the **Disks** utility we require, as highlighted in *Figure 3.12*:

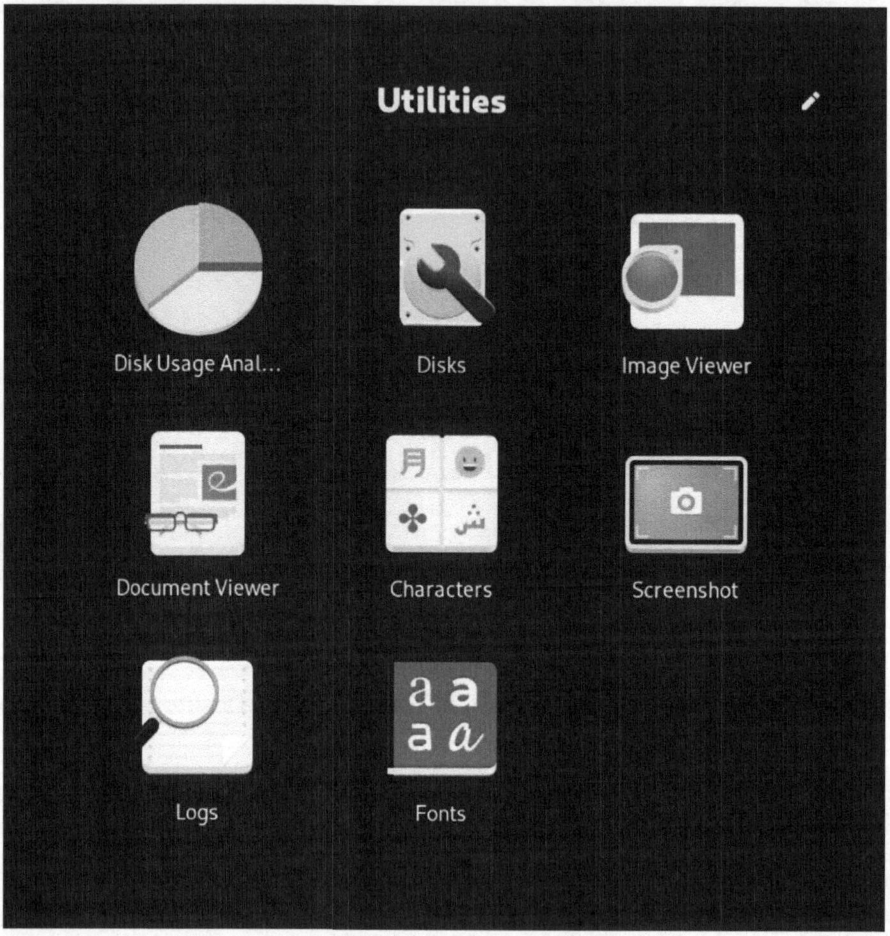

***Figure 3.12**: This then shows the **Disks** utility we require*

The **Disks** utility can then be used to **Resize...** any required partition, as shown in *Figure 3.13*:

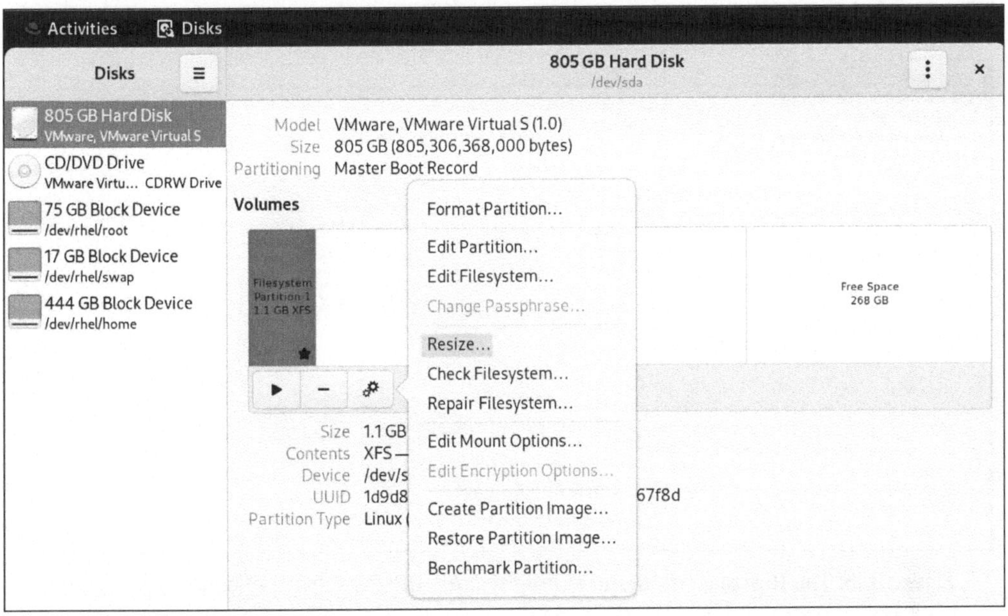

Figure 3.13: *The Disks utility can then be used to Resize... any required partition*

Next, we selected the **`/dev/sda2 Linux LVM`** device type, as shown in *Figure 3.14*:

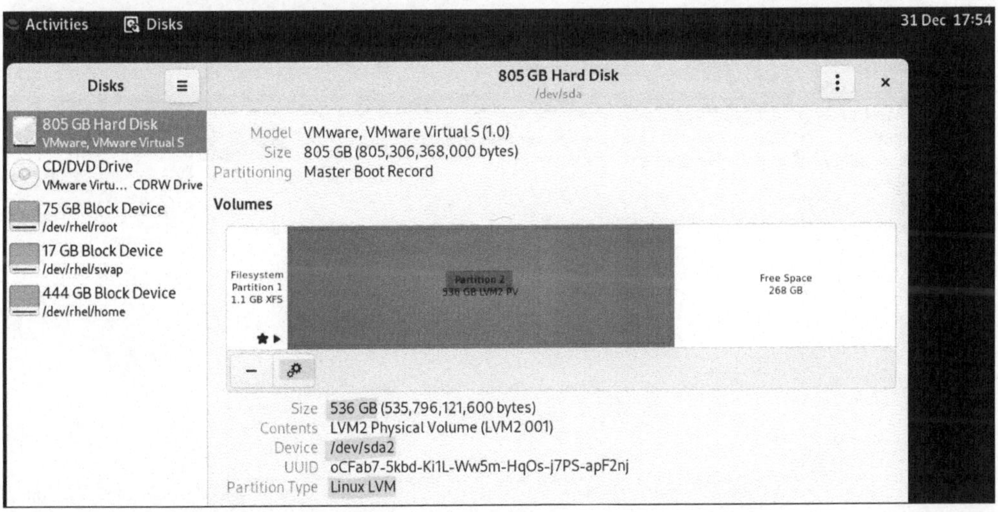

Figure 3.14: *We selected the /dev/sda2 Linux LVM device type*

The **`Resize...`** command is used to start the **`Free Space`** allocation procedure, as highlighted in *Figure 3.15*:

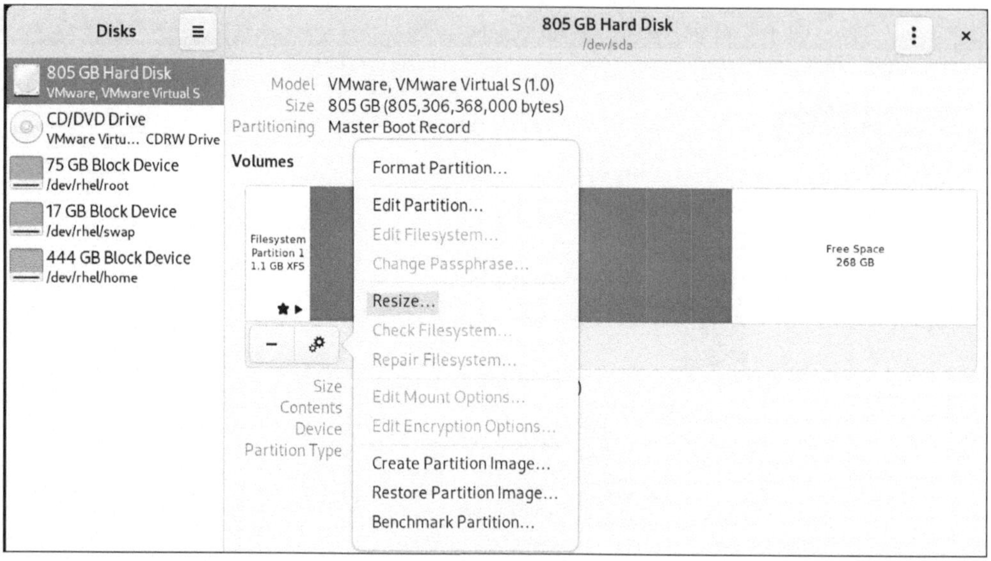

***Figure 3.15**: The **Resize...** command is used to start the Free Space allocation procedure*

The Partition size is increased to **`800 GB`**, as shown in *Figure 3.16*:

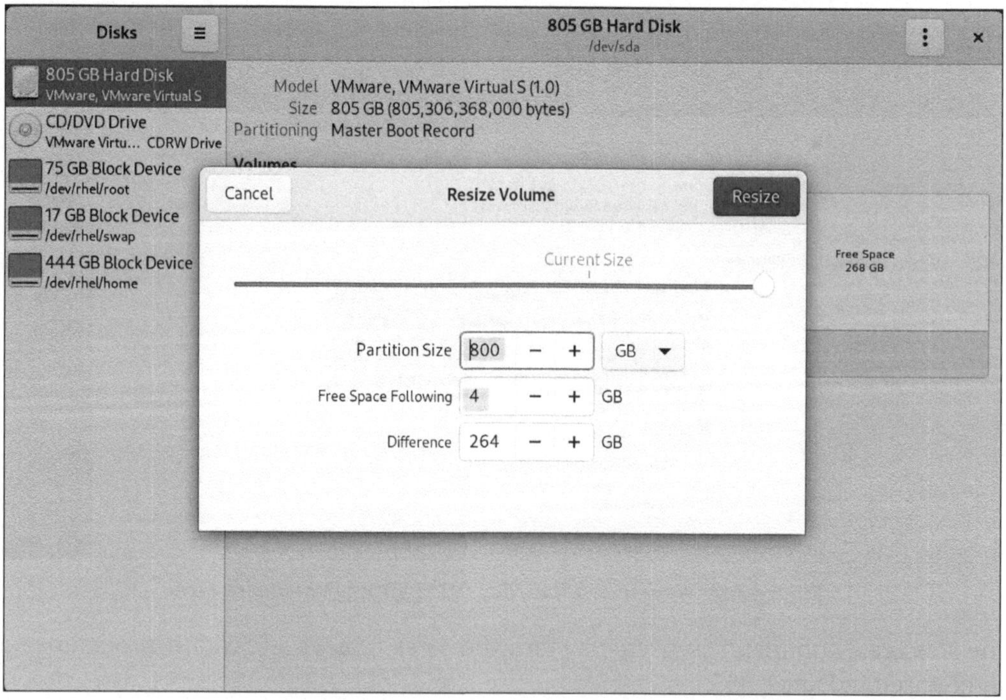

***Figure 3.16**: The Partition size is increased to 800 GB*

The **`Partition`** is now shown with the additional disk space allocated, leaving **`4.2 GB`** of **`Free Space`**, as shown in *Figure 3.17*:

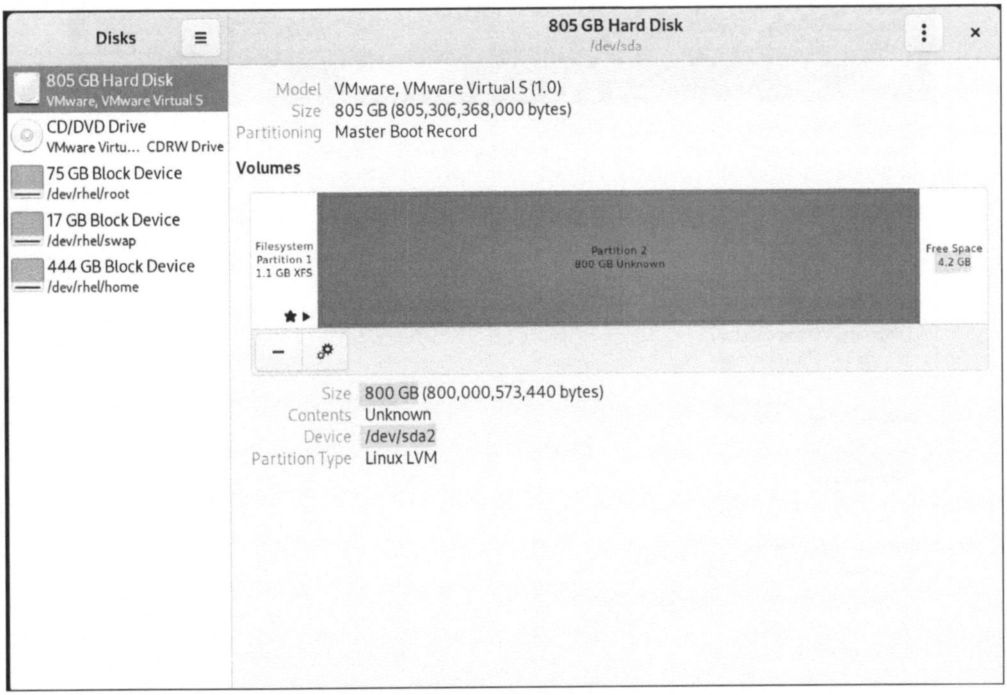

Figure 3.17: *The Partition is now shown with the additional disk space allocated, leaving 4.2 GB of Free Space*

The system is now rebooted (which reruns the connected **RHEL 9.2** iso installation disk), using the commands, as shown in *Figure* 3.18:

```
su - root
reboot
```

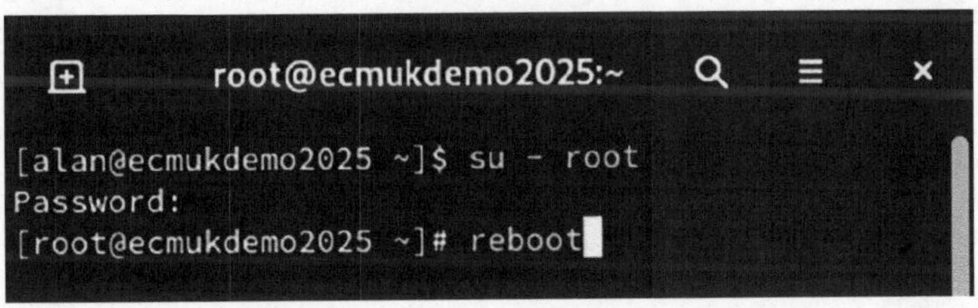

Figure 3.18: *The system is now rebooted (which reruns the connected RHEL 9.2 iso installation disk)*

The reboot installation now highlights the **750 GB** sda disk, as shown in *Figure* 3.19:

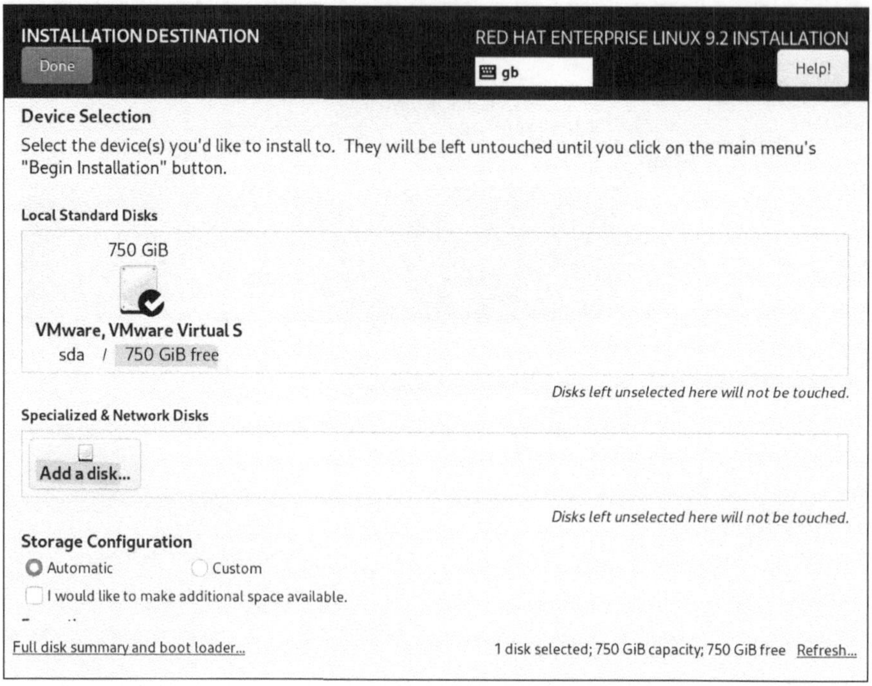

Figure 3.19: *The reboot installation now highlights the 750 GB sda disk*

The **`Add a disk...`** command allows us to select the disk for use, as shown in *Figure* 3.20:

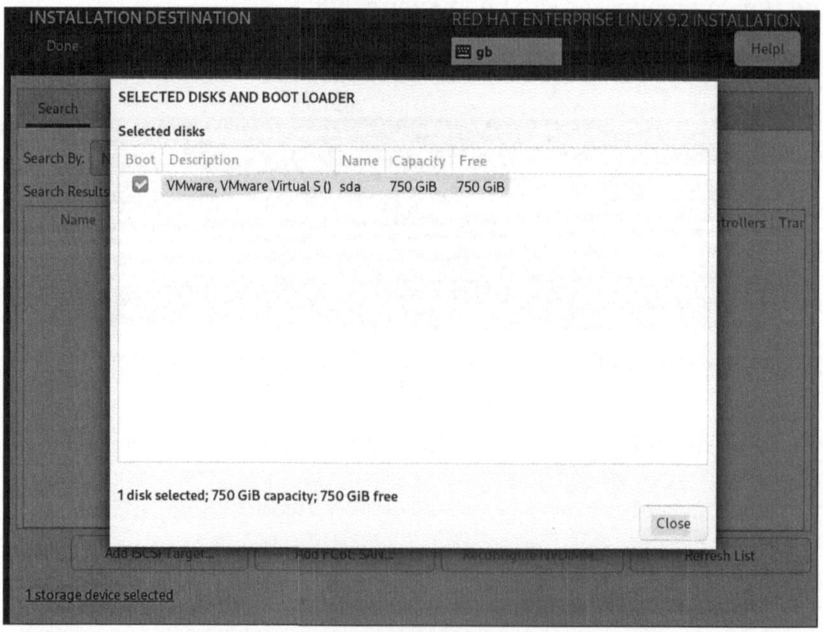

Figure 3.20: *The* **Add a disk...** *command allows us to select the disk for use*

We have to recreate the **root** password, as highlighted in *Figure 3.21*:

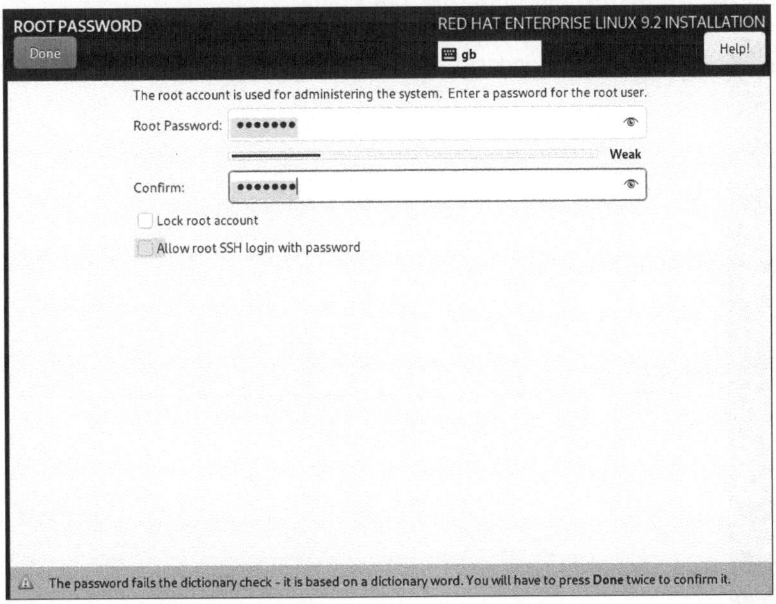

***Figure 3.21**: We have to recreate the root password*

We can now select the **Begin Installation** command button, as highlighted in *Figure 3.22*:

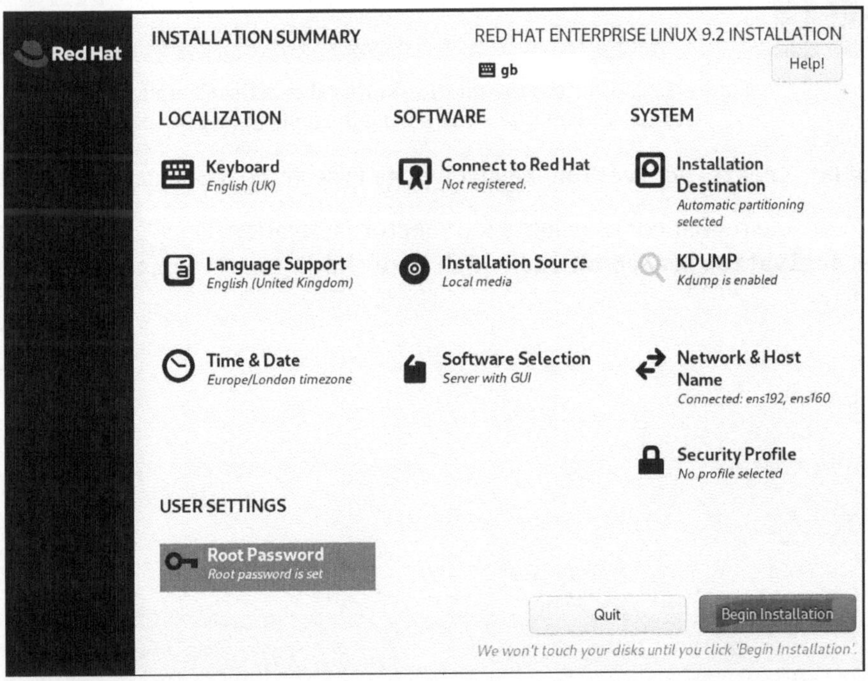

***Figure 3.22**: We can now select the **Begin Installation** command button*

After the Installation status, shows the **`Complete!`** status, and then, we can select the **`Reboot System`** command, as highlighted in *Figure* 3.23:

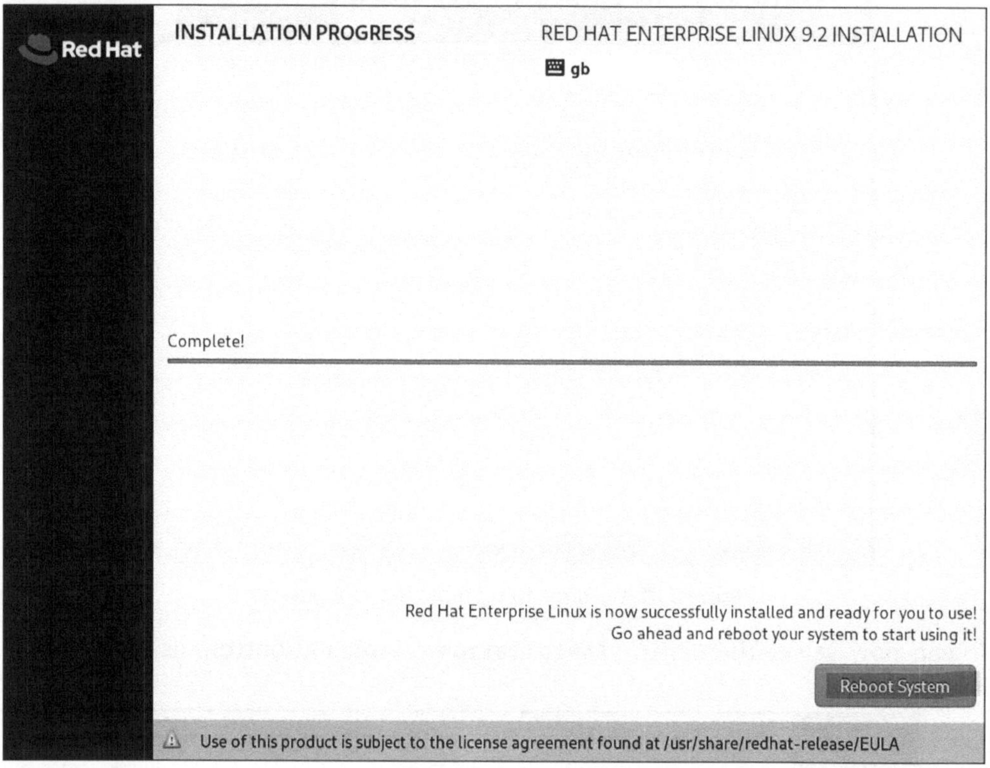

***Figure 3.23**: After the Installation status shows the Complete! status, we can select the Reboot System command*

The **`RedHat Create activation key`** web page is selected **`Next`**, using the URL:

https://console.redhat.com/insights/connector/activation-keys . This shows the **`Create activation key` command** which then shows the screen, as shown in *Figure* 3.24:

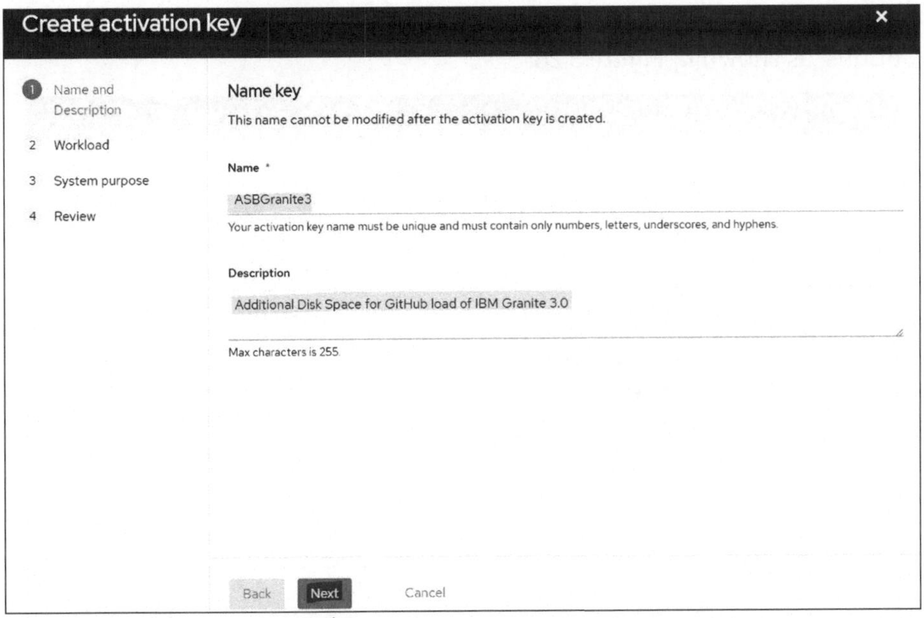

***Figure 3.24**: The RedHat Create activation key web page is selected next, using the URL: https://console.redhat.com/insights/connector/activation-keys*

The **`Next`** command shows the **`Workload`** page of the wizard where we set the **`Extended support releases`**, and select the **RHEL 9.2** version, using the dropdowns as highlighted in *Figure 3.25*:

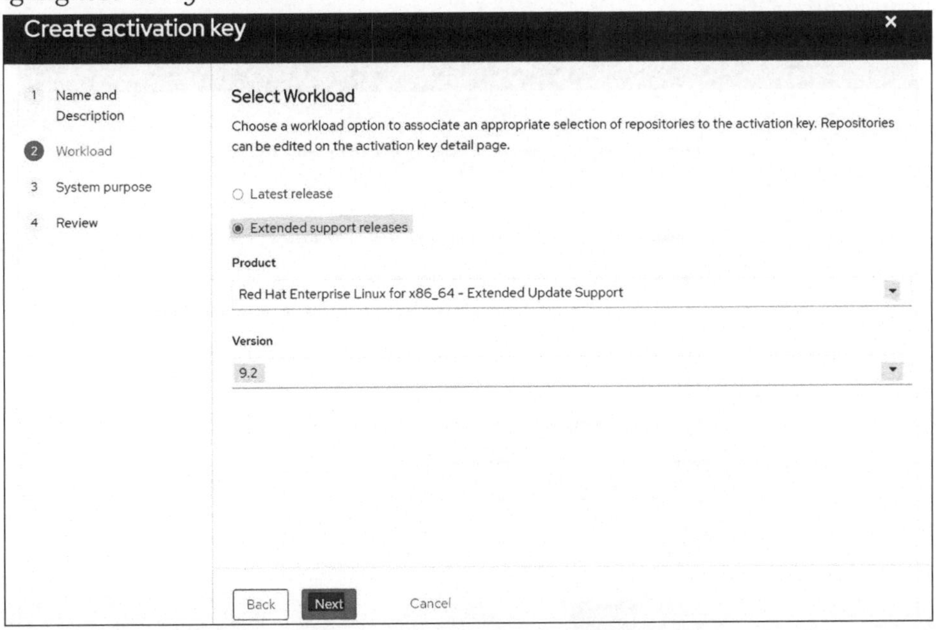

***Figure 3.25**: The **Next** command shows the Workload page of the wizard. We set the Extended support releases*

The **`Next`** command then gives us the **`System purpose`** page, for which we select the field options, as shown in *Figure 3.26*:

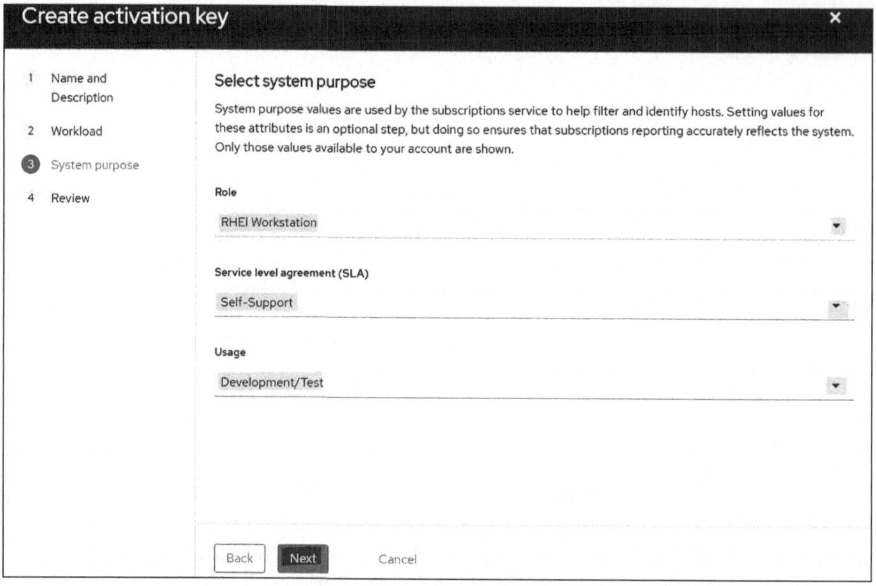

Figure 3.26: *The Next command then gives us the System purpose page, for which we select the field options*

On the last **`Review`** page, we confirm the settings, and select the **`Create`** command, as shown in *Figure 3.27*:

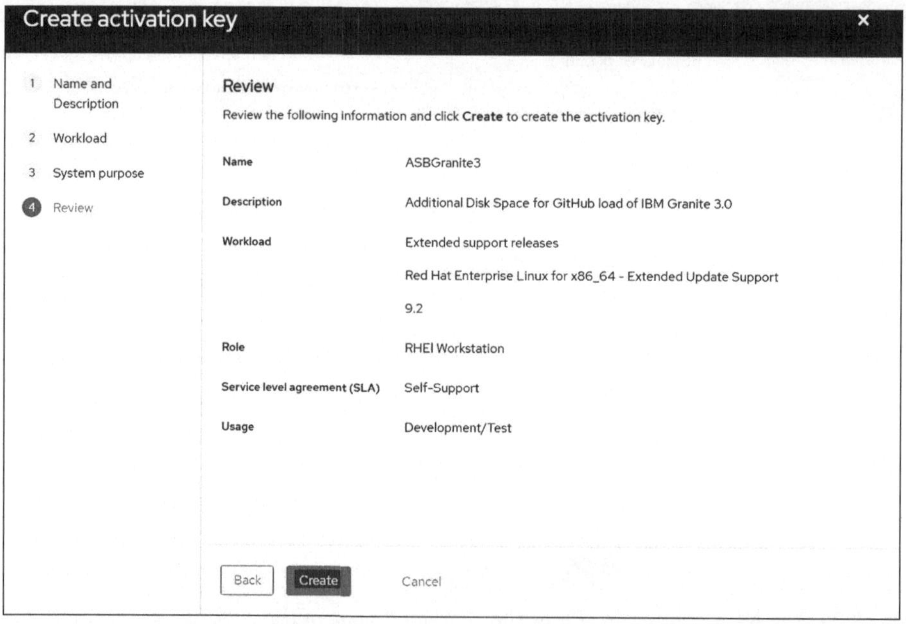

Figure 3.27: *On the last Review page we confirm the settings and select the* **Create** *command*

The pop-up status window shows we have created an **`Active Activation key`**, as shown in *Figure 3.28*:

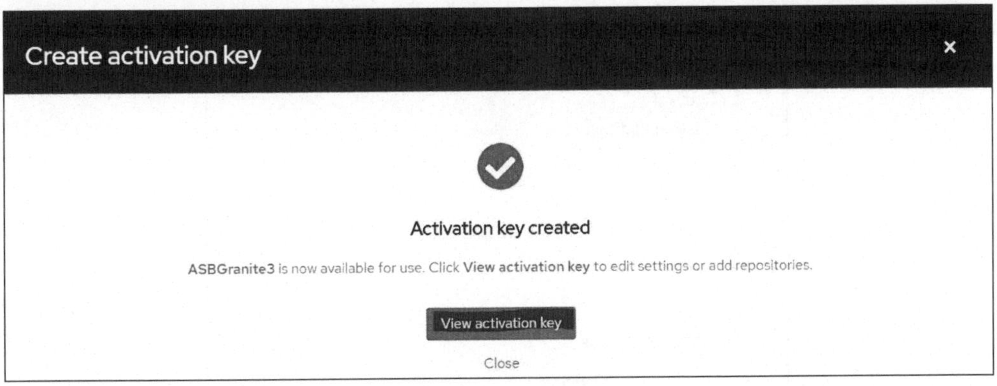

Figure 3.28: *The pop-up status window shows we have created an Active Activation key*

The **`ASBGranite3`** Activation key is now created, as shown in *Figure 3.29*:

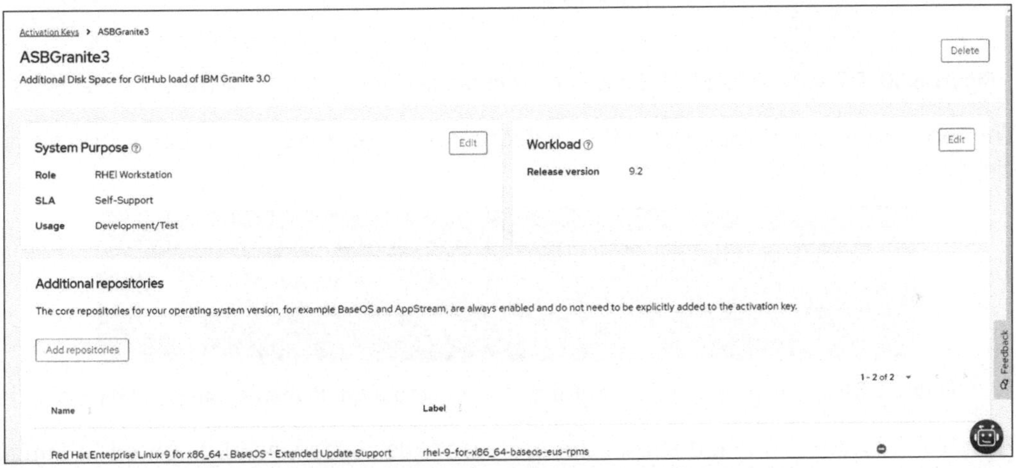

Figure 3.29: *The ASBGranite3 Activation Key is now created*

This time, on running the Installation during the **RHEL 9.2** disk size expansion, we get prompted to **`Register`** the system. We selected the **`Red Hat Account`** option, which requires the settings to be entered, as shown in *Figure 3.30*:

***Figure 3.30**: We selected the Red Hat Account option, which requires the settings to be entered*

The pop-up window appears after selecting the **`Register`** command button as displayed in *Figure 3.31*:

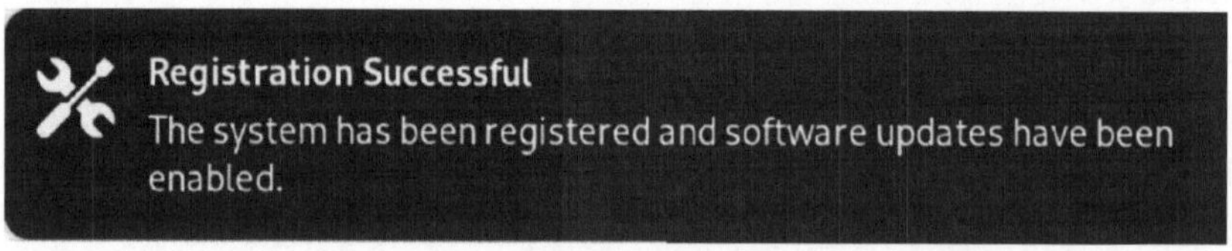

***Figure 3.31**: The pop-up window appears after selecting the **Register** command button*

The **`df -k`** Linux command shows the increased disk space, as highlighted in *Figure 3.32*:

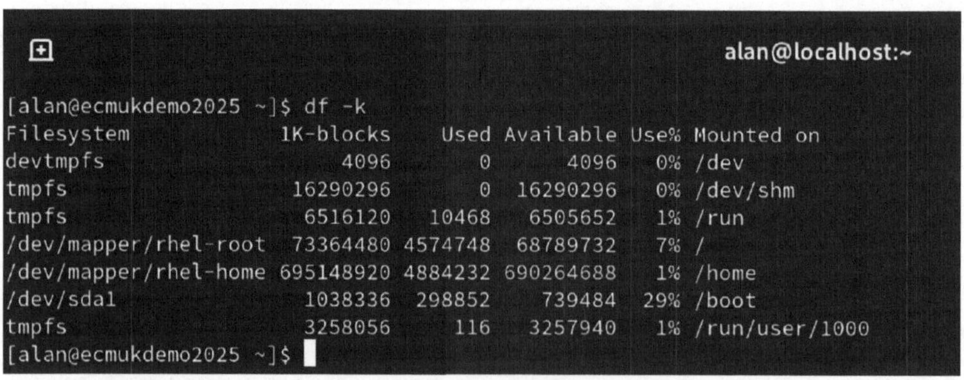

***Figure 3.32**: The df -k Linux command shows the increased disk space*

The **`fdisk -l`** command displays the full list of new disk space values, as shown in *Figure 3.33*:

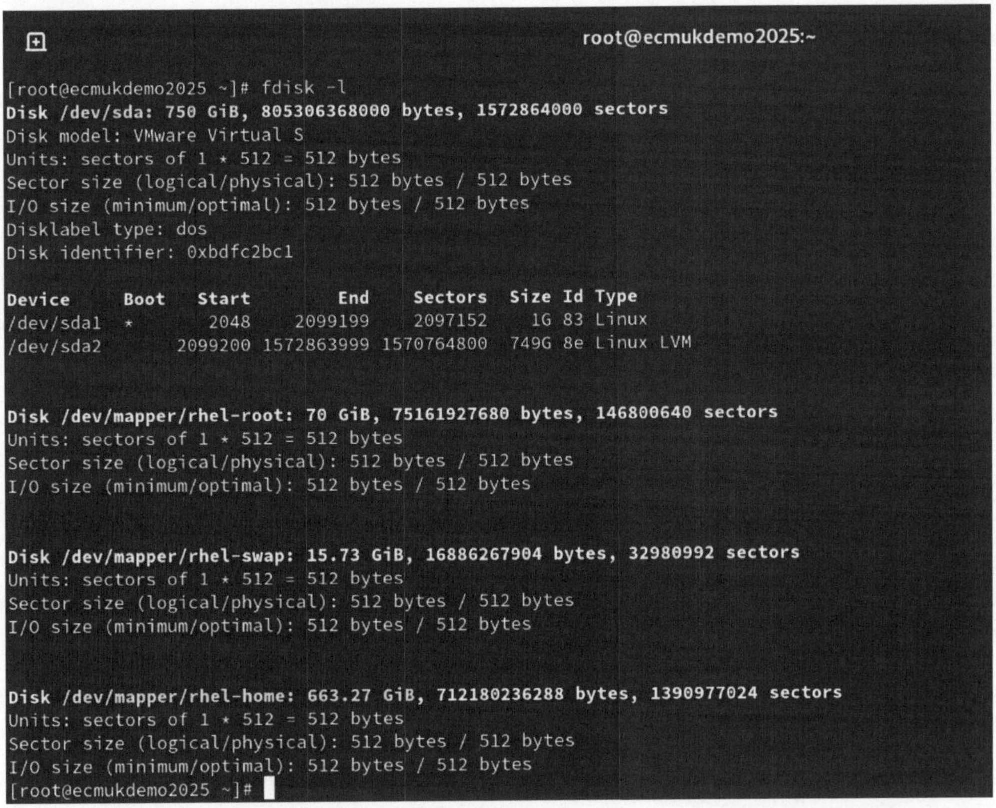

Figure 3.33: *The **fdisk -l** command displays the full list of new disk space values*

Now, we need to deselect the CD/DVD RHEL 9.2 iso image disk so that a **`reboot`** does not re-install a fresh kernel of the **RedHat 9.2** operating system to our virtual Linux server, as shown in *Figure 3.34*:

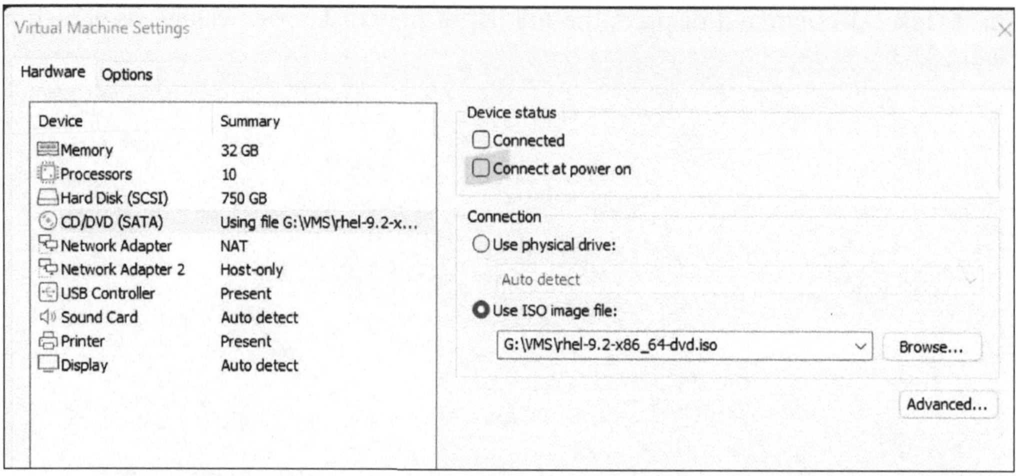

Figure 3.34: *Now, we need to deselect the CD/DVD RHEL 9.2 iso image disk*

Base Models Available

There are a number of **GitHub** entries for models developed by **IBM Research** and available as Open Source downloads from **GitHub**, described in the following sub-sections.

For this, first, we need to install the **Linux git** system, using the **root** user, as follows. Also highlighted in *Figure* 3.35:

As **root** run:

```
su - root
yum install git
```

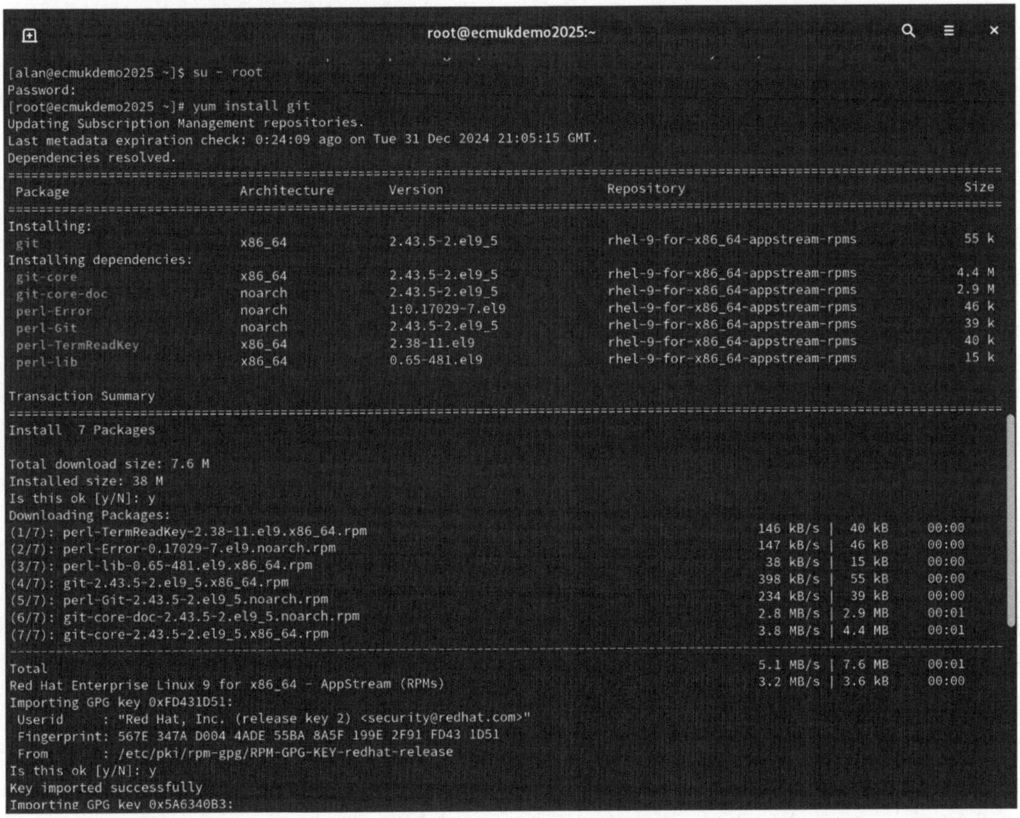

Figure 3.35: *We need to install the Linux git system, using the root user*

Time Series Foundation Models

Time Series Forecasting has been successfully used for financial applications, sales forecasting, long term weather forecasts, and for medical applications. Time series forecasting can be applied to process any historical datasets which record changing values over a time period, allowing the prediction of future values of a sequence of data points that are recorded at regular intervals, over time. IBM's **Tiny Time Mixers (TTM)** algorithms are trained on historical time series data to learn patterns and relationships, enabling them to make predictions about future values.

IBM recommends the **TTMs** approach, which they are planning to extend to other **AI** applications because using the very small pre-trained model for multivariate time-series forecasting is very efficient, when compared with earlier versions of **LLMs**. The **TTM LLM** is much smaller, and so gives faster results with pre-training and fine-tuning workflows.

Thus, the results, obtained in benchmarks by **IBM**, prove that the **TTM** procedure is very efficient for pre-training on diverse datasets despite its small model size. It produces very competitive output in zero/few-shot forecasting with a minimum **CPU/GPU** processing load, enabling the capture of cross-channel relationships and external variables, a feature missing in other standard methods. **TTM** is also relatively easy to use because it supports both **CPU** and **GPU** deployments.

The details for these models can be downloaded from the pdf authored by IBM Research, http://arxiv.org/pdf/2401.03955 ("*Tiny Time Mixers (TTMs): Fast Pre-trained Models for Enhanced Zero/Few-Shot Forecasting of Multivariate Time Series*", dated 7th November, 2024).

The current Python versions supported by TSFM are 3.9, 3.10, 3.11, 3.12.

The default installed Python version on our RHEL 9.2 Linux system was checked using

```
[alan@ecmukdemo2025 ~]$ python -V
Python 3.9.16
[alan@ecmukdemo2025 ~]$
```

Note: *The current Python versions supported are 3.9, 3.10, 3.11, and 3.12, but as of November 8th, 2024,* **Python 3.10** *is not available in* **RedHat RHEL 9** *and* **RedHat RHEL 8**. **Python 3.12** *is currently not supported for the* **GitHub** *examples as some dependencies do not work on* **Python 3.12**, *as of December 2024.*

Direct Forecasting Models

Tiny Time Mixers (TTMs) uses gated attention, a mechanism that selectively controls simple perceptron blocks to link time series variables. This new approach uses much less **CPU** power during training and fine-tuning, resulting in smaller models which are focused on time series tasks.

The Fine-tuning process follows the steps to prepare data, load the model, evaluate the data model, and then fine-tune and reassess.

The **Beijing Air Quality** dataset is a real-world test case illustrating the **TTM**'s ability to forecast PM2.5 air pollution levels using historical data values. The example uses the data available from the link,

https://archive.ics.uci.edu/dataset/381/beijing+pm2+5+data?utm_source=ibm_developer&utm_content=in_content_link&utm_id=tutorials_awb-foundation-model-time-series-forecasting

With the csv file, `PRSA_data_2010.1.1-2014.12.31.csv`, this application demonstrates the model's application for environmental monitoring and urban planning.

Granite Embedding Models

These models generate embedding responses for text inputs, such as queries, passages, and documents. They were developed using retrieval-oriented pre-training, contrastive fine-tuning, knowledge distillation, and model merging.

The IBM Granite Embedding models provide high benchmark performance using benchmarks such as BEIR, and IBM have demonstrated that they can outperform models of the same size for many enterprise use cases.

Retrieval-Augmented Generation Models

Retrieval-Augmented Generation (RAG), uses Natural Language Processing (**NLP**) to combine information retrieval and **GPT**, and Generative Pre-Trained Transformer data models to produce responses which include the latest up-to-date information.

Usually, Large Language Models (**LLMs**) construct responses based on the users' prompt, for example, for use with chatbots. For pre-built **LLM** models, the available information will be out of date, but the **RAG** concept allows the basic trained information to be augmented from more recent online data, in real-time.

RAG also enables company specific data to be incorporated to enhance LLMs with enterprise data. So, as an example, chatbots can be powered by LLMs with replies that reflect the enterprise specific datasets. RAG allows the development of LLMs from the data from company standard operating manuals, product literature and support documents.

RAG processing requires an enterprise to collect the relevant data for the LLM to access. This data can come from text sources, such as word documents, PDFs, video clips, emails, presentation slides and tabular data from appropriate sources, including spreadsheets and even internet sources. **RAG** also supports "*multimodal*" AI solutions, so a combination of multiple AI models can be used to process data of any modality, including sound, images, and video.

The RAG based models were developed to meet enterprise-grade expectations, and they are offered under the **Apache 2.0 license**, for both research and commercial developments.

Downloading IBM's Models

In this section we cover the download and running of the IBM Granite 3.0 Python language, Jupyter Lab notebook examples for the **TSFM**, Time Series Foundation and the **Granite-Guardian** models, which are used for data filtering and security.

Downloading Time Series Foundation Models

As the created user (we used Alan), exit the root user, if required and run, as shown in *Figure* 3.36:

```
git clone "https://github.com/ibm-granite/granite-tsfm.git"
cd granite-tsfm
```

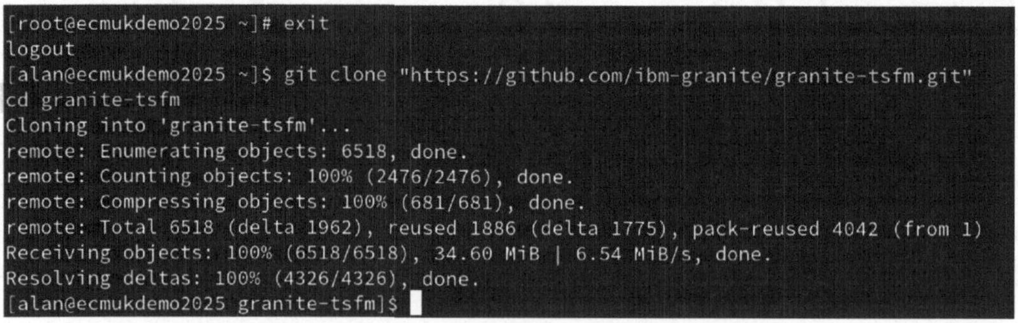

Figure 3.36: *As the created user, exit root and run git clone https://github.com/ibm-granite/granite-tsfm.git*

Several notebooks are provided in the notebooks folder which can be installed with the following command, as shown in *Figure* 3.37.

```
pip install ".[notebooks]"
```

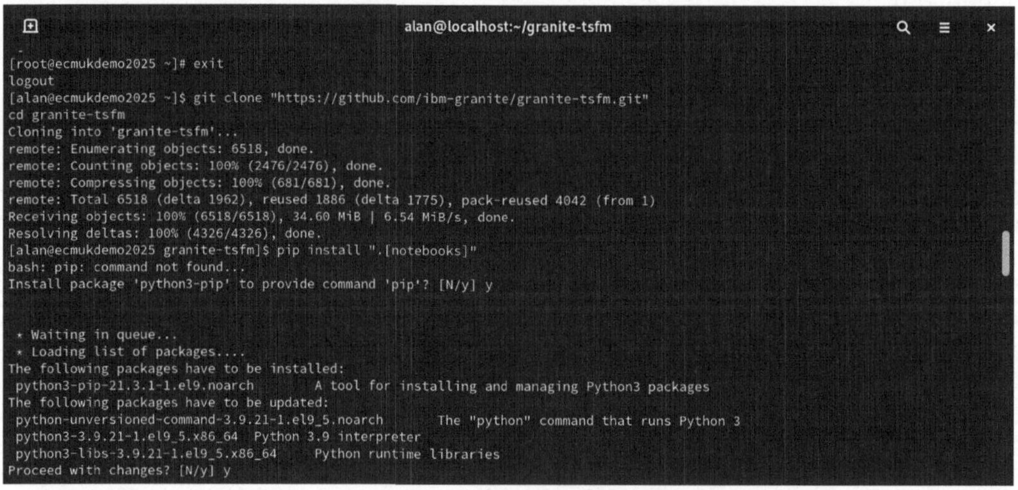

Figure 3.37: *Several notebooks are provided in the notebooks folder which can be installed*

These notebooks support pre-training and fine-tuning on the IBM Granite TSFM models.

This install should load a large number of libraries as shown in *Figure* 3.38:

Figure 3.38: *This install should load a large number of libraries*

You can also run the **IBM TTM** tutorial in **Google Colab**, to build a demo forecasting application with the pre-trained **TSFM** models.

From the default user (**Alan**), we can install **`Jupyter lab`**, as shown in *Figure* 3.39:

```
pip install Jupyter lab
```

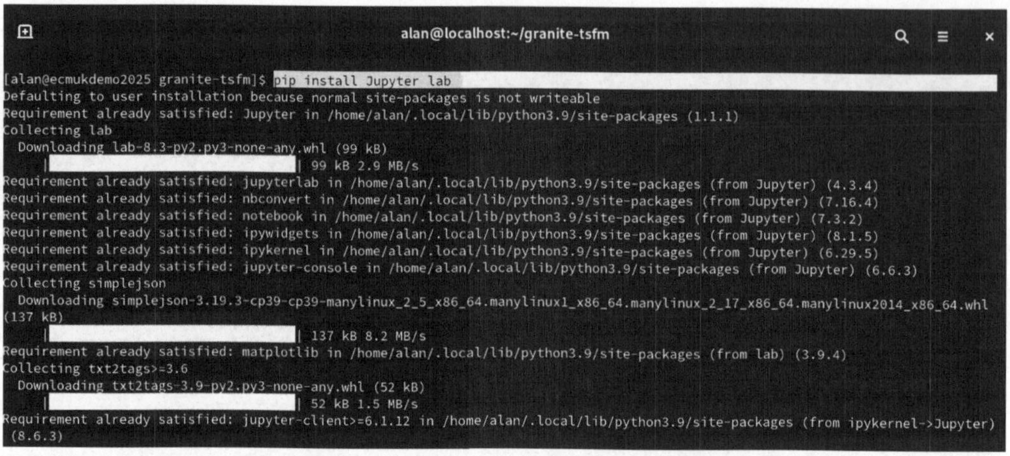

***Figure 3.39**: From the default user (Alan) we can install Jupyter lab*

Using IBM's Models

In the **`README.md`** file (in the install directory, **`/home/alan/granite-tsfm`**), we have the links listed as follows: **Links to the notebooks:**

- **Getting started with `PatchTSMixer`**

  https://github.com/ibm-granite/granite-tsfm/blob/main/notebooks/hfdemo/patch_tsmixer_getting_started.ipynb

- **Transfer learning with `PatchTSMixer`** https://github.com/ibm-granite/granite-tsfm/blob/main/notebooks/hfdemo/patch_tsmixer_transfer.ipynb

- **Transfer learning with `PatchTST`** https://github.com/ibm-granite/granite-tsfm/blob/main/notebooks/hfdemo/patch_tst_transfer.ipynb

- **Getting started with `TinyTimeMixer (TTM)`** https://github.com/ibm-granite/granite-tsfm/blob/main/notebooks/hfdemo/ttm_getting_started.ipynb

- **`TTM` full benchmarking scripts** and results are available at https://github.com/ibm-granite/granite-tsfm/tree/main/notebooks/hfdemo/tinytimemixer/full_benchmarking

- **Google Colab Tutorials**

  Run the **TTM** tutorial in Google Colab to build a forecasting application with the pre-trained TSFM models.

- **TTM Colab Tutorial** https://colab.research.google.com/github/ibm-granite/granite-tsfm/blob/main/notebooks/hfdemo/ttm_getting_started.ipynb

We can now load the examples from our **git clone** download by running Jupyter Notebooks, using the **Jupyter Lab** command, as shown in *Figure 3.40*:

```
jupyter lab
```

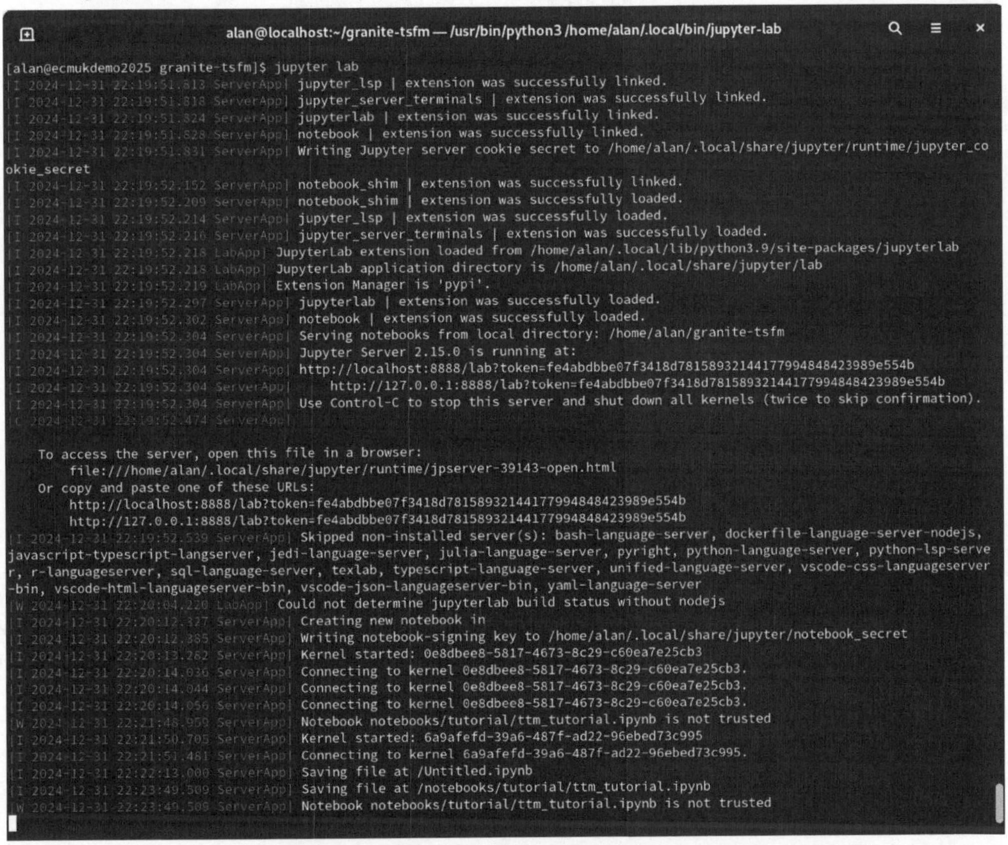

Figure 3.40: *We can now load the examples from our git clone download by running Jupyter Notebooks*

This automatically loads the **Firefox** browser web page, as shown in *Figure 3.41*:

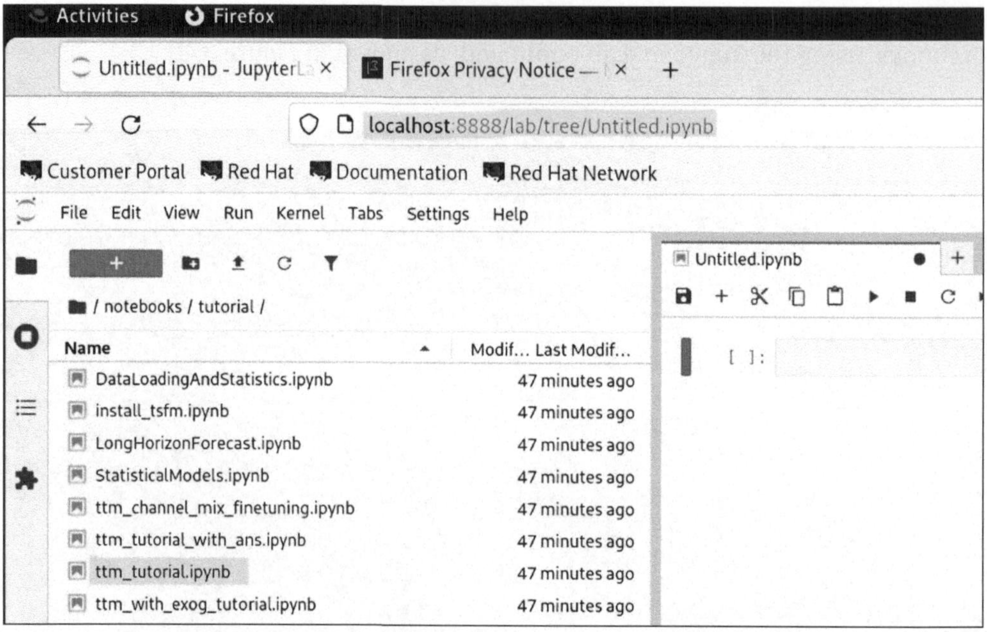

***Figure 3.41**: This automatically loads the Firefox browser web page*

On the web page, we can load the **Python** option, and browse to the **`./notebooks/tutorial`** which displays the list of notebook files for the **IBM Granite 3.0 TTM** tutorials, and we can then select the highlighted Notebook, **`ttm_tutorial.ipynb`**, as shown loaded in *Figure 3.42*:

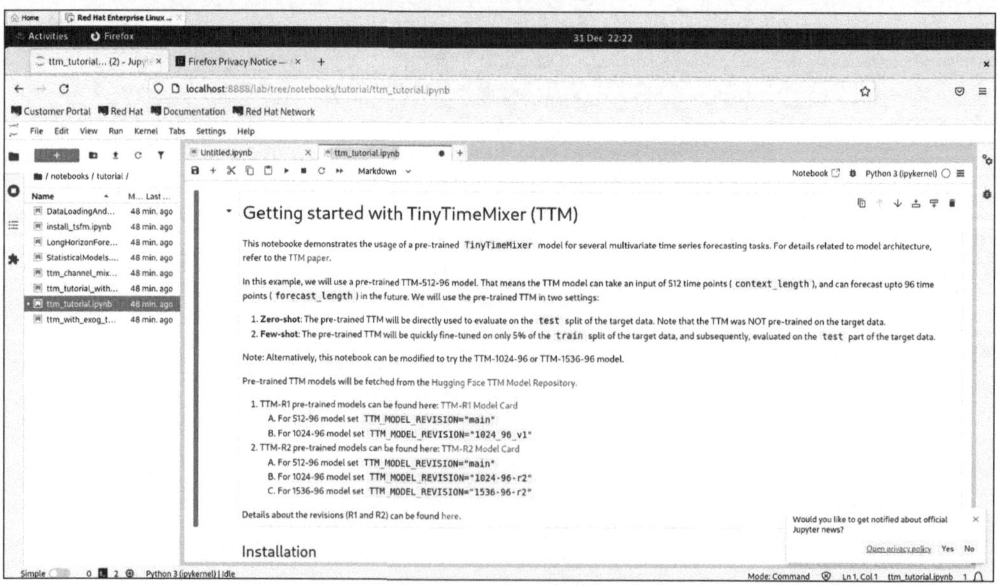

***Figure 3.42**: We can then select the highlighted Notebook, ttm_tutorial.ipynb*

In conclusion for this section, we can show that there is plenty of additional space on the **/dev/rhel/home** mount point, which was a **444 GB** Block Device, as shown in *Figure 3.43*:

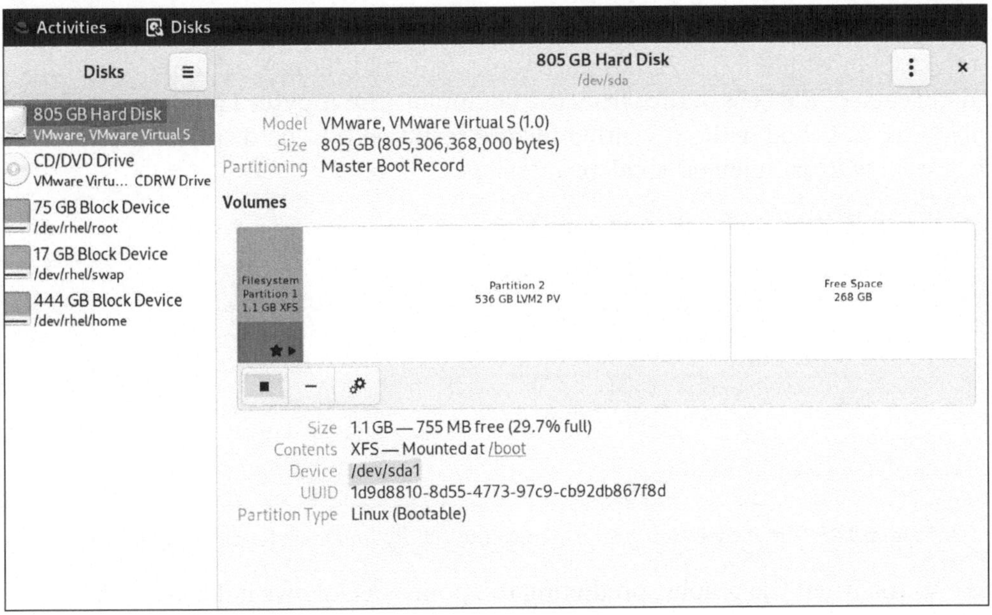

Figure 3.43: *The original disk allocation of* 444 GB

The resized **/dev/rhel/home** mount point has now been expanded to a **712 GB Block Device**, as shown in *Figure 3.44*:

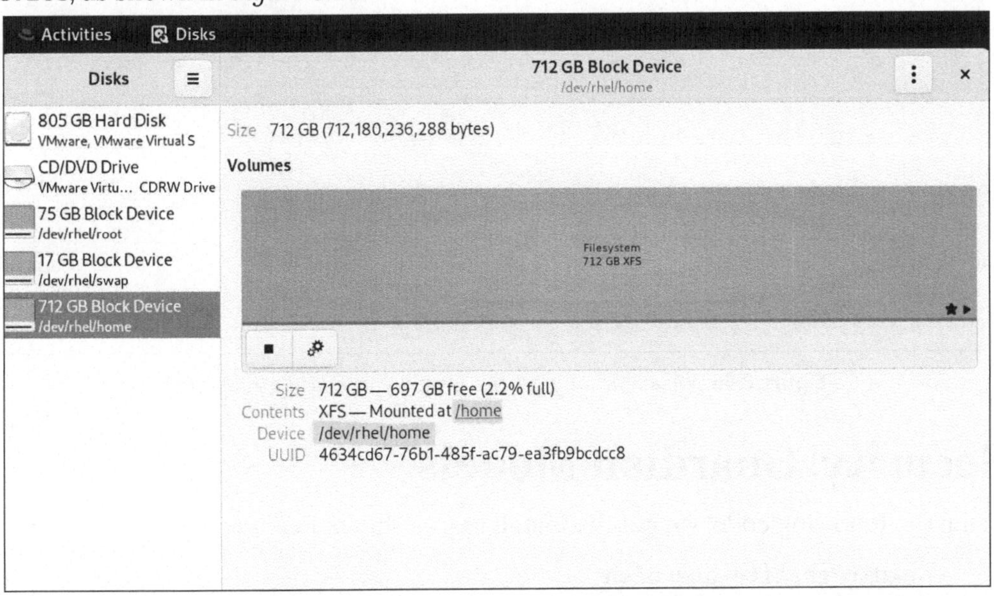

Figure 3.44: *The new disk allocation of* 712 GB

Direct Forecasting Example

From the **`LongHorizonForecast.ipynb`** Jupyter Lab example shown in *Figure 3.41*, we loaded the Notebook:

http://localhost:8888/lab/tree/notebooks/tutorial/LongHorizonForecast.ipynb, and ran each of the cells in turn from the beginning (the **Jupyter Lab** allows each of the cells to be launched without waiting for the result cells to be displayed). The Jupyter lab system will just queue the cell processing.

For the cell **Python** code, as shown in *Figure 3.45*:

```
[10]: random_indices = np.random.default_rng(1).choice(len(testY), N_SAMPLE_TO_PLOT, replace=False)

      fig, axs = plt.subplots(N_SAMPLE_TO_PLOT, 1, sharex="col", sharey=True, figsize=(20, 2 * N_SAMPLE_TO_PLOT))

      for i, index in enumerate(random_indices):
          n_history = min(PAST_WINDOW, CONTEXT_LENGTH)
          y_true = np.concatenate([testX[index, -n_history:], testY[index]])
          y_pred = np.concatenate([testX[index, -n_history:], predictY[index]])
          axs[i].plot(y_true, color="green", linestyle="dashed", linewidth=1, label="actual")
          axs[i].plot(y_pred, color="orange", linewidth=1, label="predicted")
          for s in ["top", "right"]:
              axs[i].spines[s].set_visible(False)
          axs[i].plot([n_history - 1, n_history - 1], [0, 15], linewidth=2, linestyle="dotted", color="gray")
          axs[i].legend()
```

***Figure 3.45**: The Jupyter lab system shows the cell Python code for the output graphs*

We eventually get the graphs, predicting the points, as follows in *Figure 3.46*:

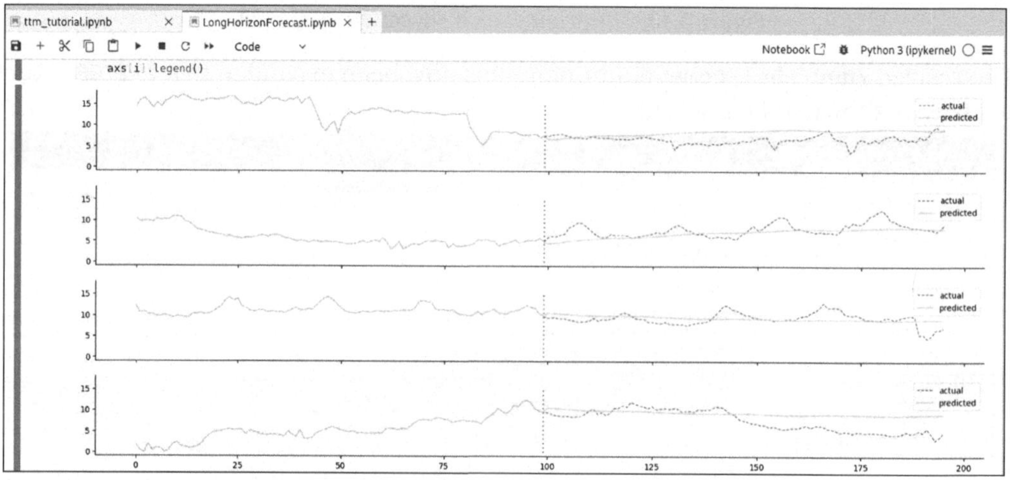

***Figure 3.46**: We eventually get the graphs, predicting the points*

Security: Guardian Models

Using the following code, we get the install log, as shown in *Figure 3.47*:

```
mkdir granite-guardian
git clone "https://github.com/ibm-granite/granite-guardian.git"
```

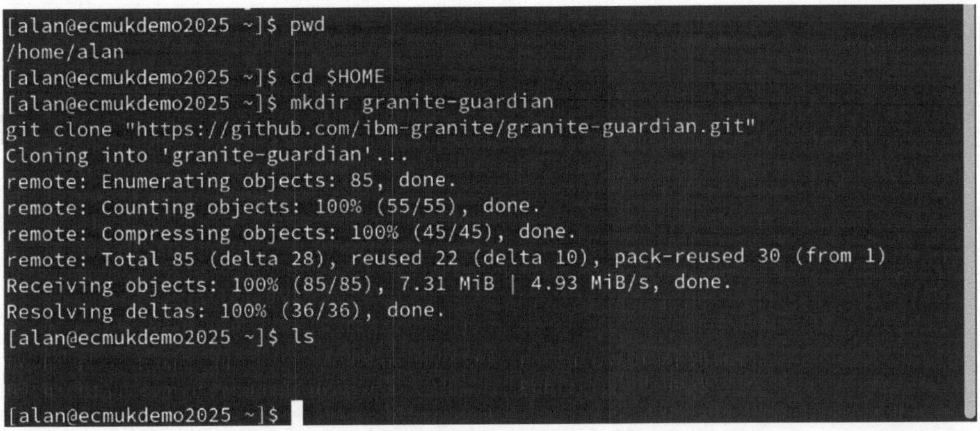

Figure 3.47: *Using the following git clone, https://github.com/ibm-granite/granite-guardian.git*

Next, we launched the Jupyter Lab notebook by moving to the path, we cloned:

`/home/alan/granite-guardian/cookbooks/granite-guardian-3.1`

Launching the notebook, as shown in *Figure* 3.48:

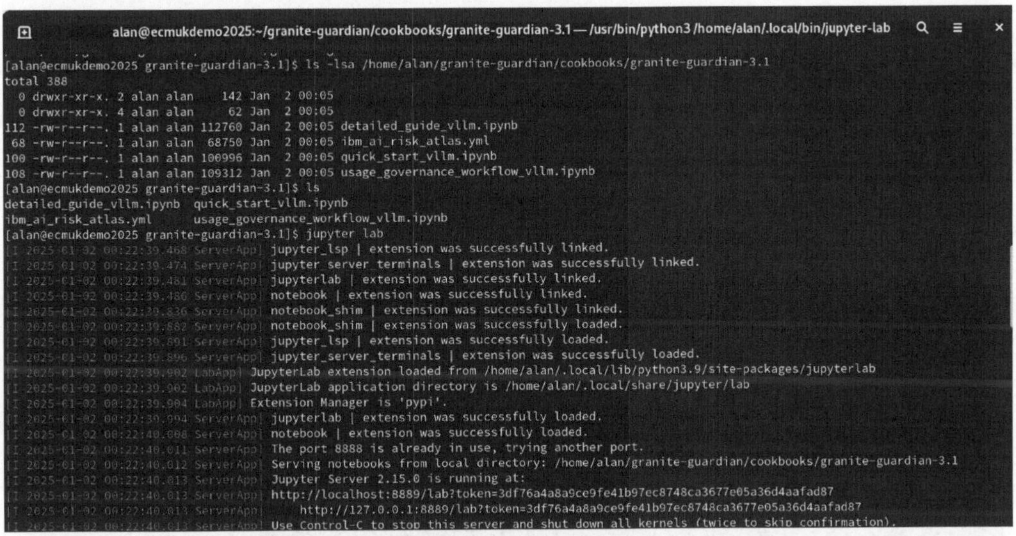

Figure 3.48: *We launched the Jupyter Lab notebook*

After selecting the **`Python`** language icon, the Firefox browser web page lists the **`IBM Granite Guardian 3.1 Python`** language notebook example files, as shown in *Figure* 3.49:

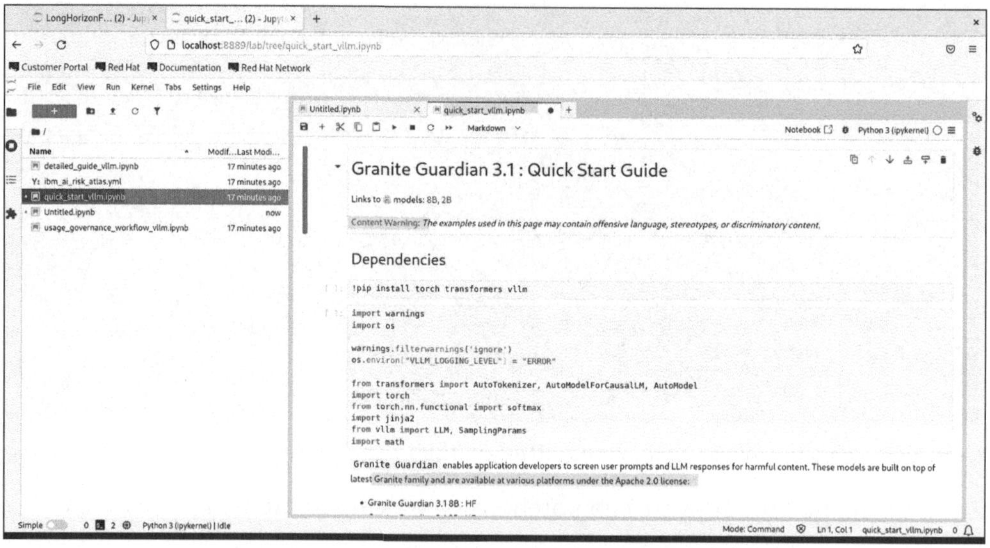

Figure 3.49: *The Firefox browser web page lists the IBM Granite Guardian 3.1 Python language notebook files*

Agentic RAG model

This can be installed from **GitHub** using the commands:

```
mkdir granite-snack-cookbook
git clone https://rebrand.ly/fas54gl
```

The output is shown in *Figure 3.50*:

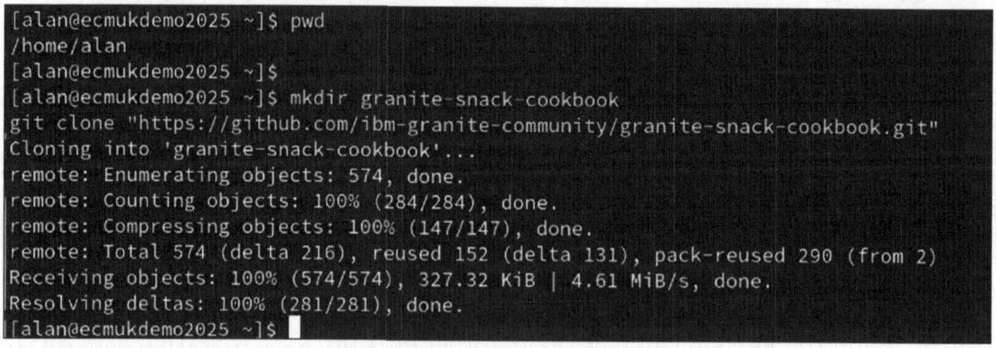

Figure 3.50: *The git clone https://github.com/ibm-granite-community/granite-snack-cookbook.git command*

In the **/home/alan/granite-snack-cookbook/README.md** file the IBM License conditions are defined, and summarized as follows:

"*The Granite Snack Cookbook's base license is* CC BY 4.0.

Code in this repository, including in notebook cells, is licensed under Apache 2.0.

Any example datasets committed to this repository are licensed under CDLA Permissive 2.0."

Jupyter lab can now be launched, using the Python language icon, to give the web screen, with a list of Notebook folders as follows, in *Figure 3.51*:

```
cd /home/alan/granite-snack-cookbook/recipes
jupyter lab
```

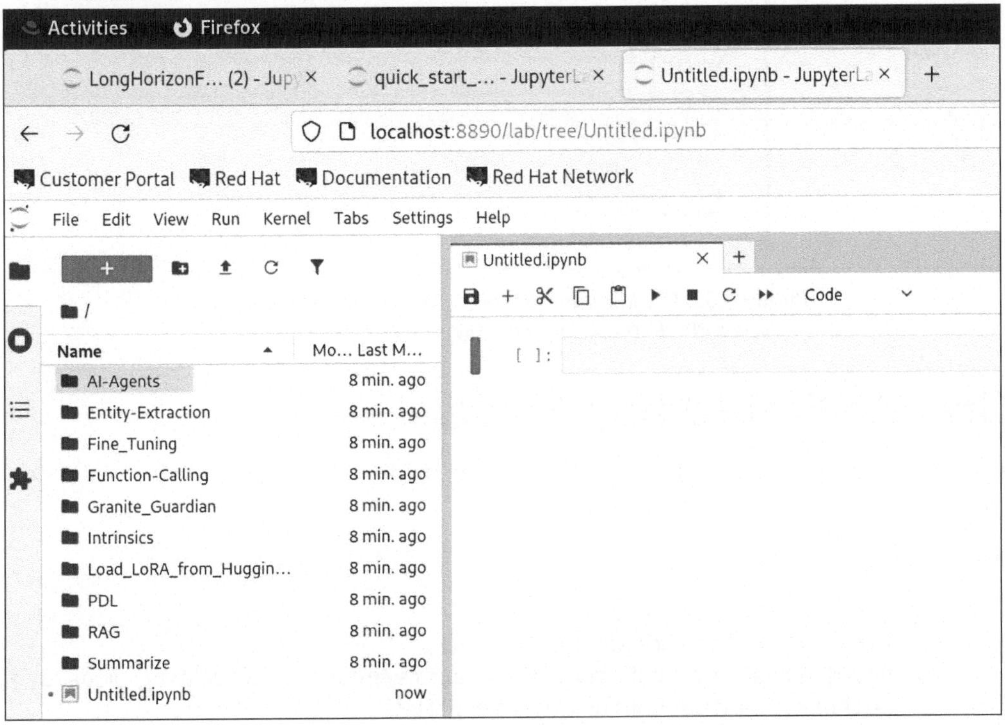

Figure 3.51: *Jupyter lab can now be launched, using the Python language icon*

Clicking the top folder, **`AI-Agents`**, we can then select the Python language file, **`Agentic_RAG.ipynb`**, as shown in *Figure 3.52*:

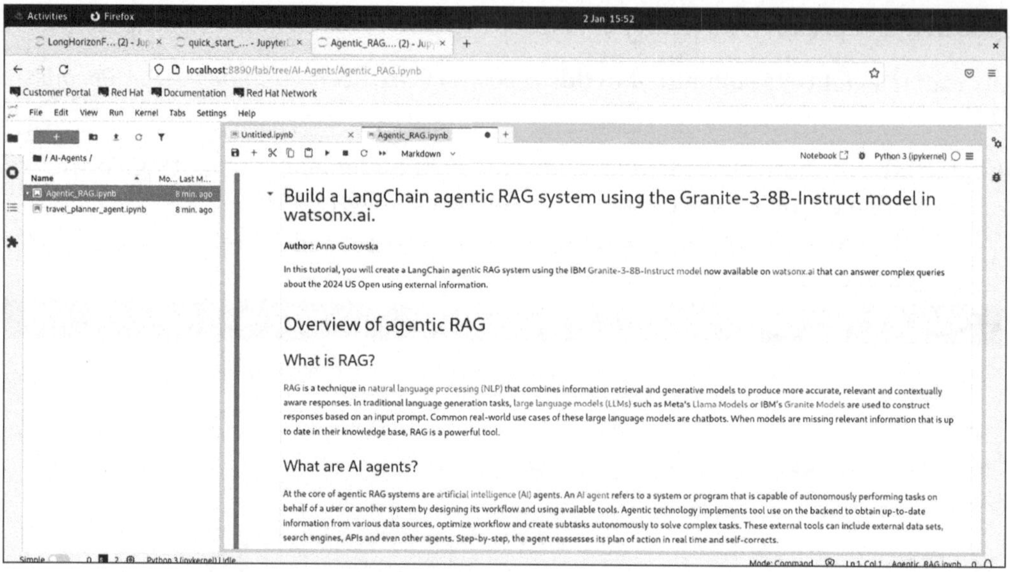

***Figure 3.52:** Clicking the top folder, AI-Agents, we can then select the Python language file, Agentic_RAG.ipynb*

Granite Embedding Models

The **IBM Granite 3.0 Embedding** collection provides sentence-transformer models used for retrieval-based applications.

Users finding these models useful are asked to include the following text:

```
@misc{granite2024embedding,
  title={Granite Embedding Models},
  url={https://github.com/ibm-granite/granite-embedding-models/},
  author={Granite Embedding Team, IBM},
  month={December},
  year={2024}
}
```

The Granite Embedding lineup includes four different models of varying sizes:

- **`granite-embedding-30m-english`**: English-only model producing embedding vectors, size 384.
- **`granite-embedding-125m-english`**: English-only model producing embedding vectors, size 768.
- **`granite-embedding-107m-multilingual`**: Multilingual embedding, with vectors with a size 384.
- **`granite-embedding-278m-multilingual`**: Multilingual embedding, with vectors with a size 768.

The following commands were used to download the IBM Granite 3.0 embedding models which are used for embedding responses for text inputs: **`mkdir granite-embedding`**

`"git clone https://github.com/ibm-granite/granite-embedding-models.git"`

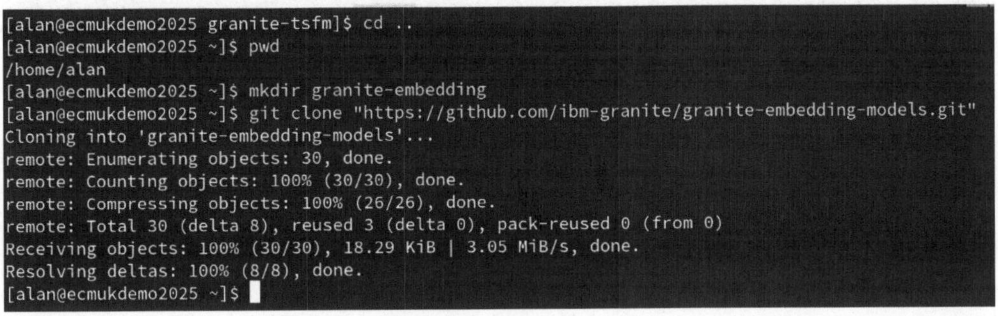

***Figure 3.53**: The commands used to download IBM Granite 3.0 embedding models, used for embedding responses*

The **`README.md`** file contains a **Python** language example, as shown in *Figure 3.54*:

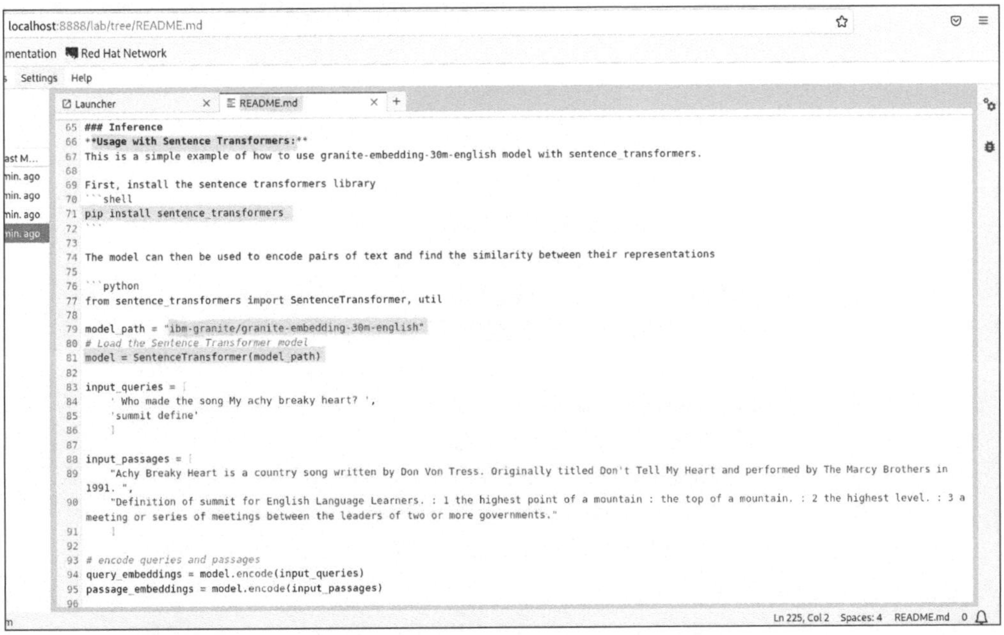

***Figure 3.54**: The README.md file contains a Python language example*

We just install the recommended **`sentence_transformers`**, using:

```
pip install sentence_transformers
```

This is shown in *Figure* 3.55:

***Figure 3.55**: We just install the recommended sentence_transformers, using: pip install sentence_transformers*

Next, we run the section of the **Python** code from lines 77 to 98 of the **`README.md`** file, as shown in *Figure* 3.56:

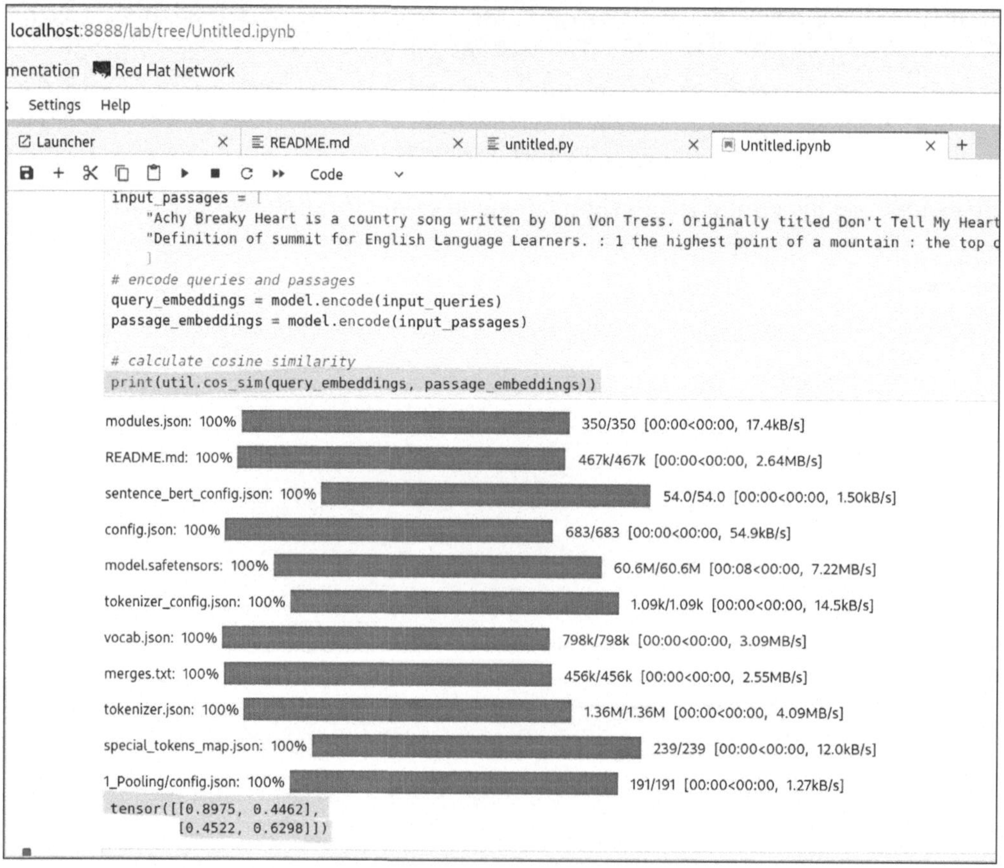

***Figure 3.56:** We run the section of the Python code from lines 77 to 98 of the README.md file*

Conclusion

This chapter outlined the **IBM Granite 3.0 GitHub** downloads available, and provided step-by-step examples for installing the prerequisites, and the installation of supported operating system libraries. It also covered the **VMware** disk size expansion for our **RedHat Linux RHEL 9.2** VMware server and its activation for a **RedHat** subscription.

In the next chapter, we describe the use of **Watsonx Code Assistant Individual**, which is an **AI** coding companion using **IBM Granite** large language models. This provides **AI** coding assistance for programming languages, such as **C, C++, Go, Java, JavaScript, Python,** and **TypeScript**. Using **MS Visual Studio Code**, "**Watsonx Code Assistant Individual**" accelerates development productivity, and simplifies coding tasks using powerful **AI** support on a developer's laptop or workstation using **ollama** (a widely used local inferencing engine for **LLMs**).

Points to Remember

- We need to deselect the VMware **CD/DVD RHEL 9.2** iso image disk so that a reboot does not re-install a fresh kernel of the **RedHat 9.2** operating system to our virtual **Linux** server.
- We need to install the **Linux git** system, using the **root** user in order to clone the IBM Granite 3.x Python Notebook examples.
- The current Python versions supported are **3.9, 3.10, 3.11, and 3.12**, but as of November 8th, 2024, Python **3.10** is not available in RedHat RHEL 9 and RedHat RHEL 8. Python **3.12** is currently not supported for the **GitHub** examples as some dependencies do not work on Python **3.12**, as of December 2024.
- You can also run the **IBM TTM** tutorial in **Google Colab**, to build a demo forecasting application with the pre-trained **TSFM** models.
- See https://colab.research.google.com/github/ibm-granite/granite-tsfm/blob/main/notebooks/hfdemo/ttm_getting_started.ipynb
- Multiple **Jupyter lab** commands can be run in different folder paths, at the same time. Each resulting Jupyter web service then gets a separate port, starting with port **8888**. We had three open web services running with URL links as follows:

  http://localhost:8888/lab/tree/notebooks/tutorial/LongHorizonForecast.ipynb

  http://localhost:8889/lab/tree/quick_start_vlim.ipynb

  http://localhost:8890/lab/tree/AI-Agents/Agentic_RAG.ipynb

Multiple Choice Questions

1. Which of the following **RedHat RHEL** commands installs the **Logical Volume Manager** system?
   a. `yum install git`
   b. `pip install ".[notebooks]"`
   c. `yum install lvm2`
   d. `pip install Jupyter lab`
2. Which of the following **IBM Granite 3.0** model **GitHub** clone commands is used for the **Agentic RAG** model?
   a. `git clone "https://github.com/ibm-granite/granite-tsfm.git"`
   b. `git clone "https://github.com/ibm-granite/granite-guardian.git"`
   c. `git clone https://rebrand.ly/989553`
   d. `git clone https://github.com/ibm-granite/granite-embedding-models.git`
3. Which of the following **RedHat RHEL** commands installs the **Jupyter** system supporting libraries for the IBM Granite TSFM models?
   a. `yum install git`
   b. `pip install ".[notebooks]"`
   c. `yum install lvm2`
   d. `pip install Jupyter lab`
4. Which of the following **RedHat RHEL** directories has the `README.md` file for the **IBM Granite 3.0** Time Series Foundation models?
   a. `/home/alan/granite-tsfm/`
   b. `/home/alan/granite-snack-cookbook/`
   c. `/home/alan/granite-snack-cookbook/recipes`
   d. `/home/alan/granite-guardian/cookbooks/granite-guardian-3.1`

5. Which models are designed to detect risks in prompts and responses?
    a. IBM Granite Agentic RAG
    b. IBM Granite TSFM Foundation
    c. IBM Granite Embedding
    d. IBM Granite Guardian

Answers

1. c
2. c
3. b
4. a
5. d

Questions

1. Outline the procedure which must be used to expand the Disk space for a RedHat Linux virtual server on a VMware Workstation.
2. List the names and the primary use of the model types which are available for the **IBM Granite 3.0** Large Language Models.

Key Terms

- **LLMs**: Large Language Models are created by processing large volumes of data and analysing the word positions, weighting each word in a sequence to understand and generate human language for AI systems. They are trained on vast amounts of text data retrieved from internet sources and utilise deep learning processes to perform a wide range of natural language processing (NLP) tasks.
- **GitHub:** It is an open-source, web-based version control system, which signed-up users can use to create, store, and change files or code in a repository of code files and documents.

  This allows a team of developers to work on a project at the same time, and they can access the most recent version in real-time.
- **TSFM:** Time Series Foundation Models are used by AI systems to provide accurate forecasts for assisting business decisions based on analysing real

time series data points, collected previously, which can then be used for pre-training LLMs.

See: https://github.com/ibm-granite/granite-tsfm

- **RAG Models:** Models that use Natural Language Processing (**NLP**) to combine information retrieval and GPT, Generative Pre-trained Transformer data models are called RAG Models.
- **GPT**: Generative Pre-Trained Transformer data models
- **NLP:** Natural Language Processing is used by artificial intelligence (AI) programs to enable a computer system to interpret, and generate output of relevant English and other human languages from the input of text or voice prompts.
- **TTM:** Tiny Time Mixers: The details for these models can be downloaded from the pdf authored by IBM Research, http://arxiv.org/pdf/2401.03955.

References

- The procedure to expand an existing VMware Workstation Pro 16, disk system for **RedHat Linux RHEL 9.2**:

  https://docs.vmware.com/en/VMware-Workstation-Pro/16.0/workstation-pro-16-user-guide.pdf

- The installation of the prerequisite supporting software for the **IBM Granite 3.0** system:

  https://github.com/ibm-granite and https://github.com/ibm-granite/granite-3.0-language-models)

- For further details of Time Series:

  https://developer.ibm.com/tutorials/awb-foundation-model-time-series-forecasting/ and https://www.ibm.com/blog/time-series-forecasting/

- For the **IBM Granite 3.0 Embedding Models** details:

  https://github.com/ibm-granite/granite-embedding-models

- For downloading the IBM Granite 3.0 TSFM Foundation Models:

  https://github.com/ibm-granite/granite-tsfm

- You can also run the **IBM TTM** tutorial in **Google Colab**, to build a demo forecasting application with the pre-trained **TSFM** models. Refer to:

  https://colab.research.google.com/github/ibm-granite/granite-tsfm/blob/main/notebooks/hfdemo/ttm_getting_started.ipynb

- The example code for IBM Granite Guardian is available at:

  https://github.com/ibm-granite/granite-guardian.

  (This code was updated in December 2024.)

- There is an **IBM YouTube** video available to help with the prerequisite setup, for the Python language used to demonstrate the **IBM Agentic RAG LLM** Model as follows:

  https://www.youtube.com/watch?v=3sav6vUG_XQ.

  See also, the direct web link for the file:

  https://github.com/ibm-granite-community/granite-snack-cookbook/blob/main/recipes/AI-Agents/Agentic_RAG.ipynb

  and, the main GitHub web page:

  https://github.com/ibm-granite-community/granite-snack-cookbook/tree/main.

CHAPTER 4
Granite 3.0's Core Functionalities

Introduction

This chapter covers the use of **Watsonx Code Assistant Individual**, which is an **AI** coding companion using **IBM Granite** large language models. This provides **AI** coding assistance for programming languages, such as **C, C++, Go, Java**, **JavaScript, Python,** and **TypeScript**. Using **MS Visual Studio Code**, **"Watsonx Code Assistant Individual"** accelerates development productivity, and simplifies coding tasks using powerful **AI** support on a developer's laptop or workstation, using **ollama** (a widely used local inferencing engine for **LLMs**).
See: https://github.com/ibm-granite/granite-3.0-language-models and https://ibm.github.io/granite-workshop/pre-work/
For the list of functionality sections see:
https://github.com/ibm-granite/

Structure

In this chapter, we will discuss the following topics:

- IBM Watsonx Code Assistant Individual
- Granite Guardian
- TSFM: Time Series Foundation Models
- Geospatial Biomass

IBM Watsonx Code Assistant Individual

Watsonx Code Assistant Individual is an **AI** coding companion using **Granite** large language models. This provides AI coding assistance for programming languages, such as C, C++, Go, Java, JavaScript, Python, and TypeScript. Using **MS Visual Studio Code**, **"Watsonx Code Assistant Individual"** accelerates development productivity and simplifies coding tasks using powerful **AI** support on a developer's laptop or workstation using **Ollama** (a widely used local inferencing engine for **LLMs**). By default, **IBM watsonx Code Assistant** uses the **granite-code:8b** model for both chat and code completion. The link for downloading this **AI** coding companion software is as follows:

https://marketplace.visualstudio.com/items?itemName=IBM.wca-core.

"Note for IBM Granite.Code users: *IBM Granite.Code is now IBM watsonx Code Assistant Individual. For individual users, you can continue to use Ollama to access a local IBM Granite model. For increased performance and new features, provision a trial of watsonx Code Assistant on IBM Cloud*." Also, IBM state the following:

'Free for individual use on a personal laptop, use **IBM watsonx Code Assistant Individual** to access a local model through Ollama, (https://ollama.com/) which is a local inferencing engine for LLMs. **Ollama** wraps the underlying model-serving project, **llama.cpp** (https://github.com/ggerganov/llama.cpp)'."

See: https://github.com/ibm-granite/watsonx-code-assistant-individual.

Installing Ollama

There is an overview of the **Ollama** system described in *Chapter 1, The Fundamentals of LLMs.*

For MacOS, Linux, Windows: Download and run the **ollama** installer (from https://ollama.com/download).

Note: *If you wish to change the default model file location, for the* **IBM Granite 3.0** *model downloads, using* **ollama**, *you can do so by setting the* **OLLAMA_MODELS** *environment variable to the desired directory. This is particularly useful if you want to store models on a different drive, or in a specific folder for space issues. To change this, edit the* ***/etc/systemd/system/ollama.service*** *file*

And append the text in bold, as an example, under the : ***[Service]*** *heading Environment="PATH=/home/alan/.local/bin:/home/alan/bin:/usr/local/bin:/usr/local/sbin:/usr/bin:/usr/sbin",***"OLLAMA_MODELS=/home/alan/IBMGranite3"***

See: https://developer.ibm.com/tutorials/awb-local-ai-copilot-ibm-granite-code-ollama-continue/

The service will need to be restarted before use, using:

- **`systemctl daemon-reload`**
- **`systemctl restart ollama`**

To verify that Ollama is using the new model file location, run the command as follows:

```
ollama list
```

The following **IBM Granite** code based models can be downloaded

Parameter Sizes are as follows:

34B Parameters:

```
ollama pull granite-code:34b
```

20B Parameters :

```
ollama pull granite-code:20b
```

8B Parameters (with 128K context window):

```
ollama pull granite-code:8b
```

3B Parameters (with 128K context window):

```
ollama pull granite-code:3b
```

30M - English only for code generation

```
ollama pull granite-embedding:30m
```

278M - Multilingual use cases for code generation

(Supporting English, German, Spanish, French, Japanese, Portuguese, Arabic, Czech, Italian, Korean, Dutch, Chinese (Simplified))

```
ollama pull granite-embedding:278m
```

To pull each of the **IBM Granite 3.0** models (released on October 21st, 2024) available for **ollama**, the commands can be used as follows:

```
ollama pull granite3-dense:2b
ollama pull granite3-dense:8b
ollama pull granite3-moe:1b
ollama pull granite3-moe:3b
```

See: https://ollama.com/blog/ibm-granite.

After downloading the models, using the `ollama pull` command, they can then be run using a command such as:

```
ollama run granite3-dense:8b
```

Then wait for `ollama` to display the prompt `>>>`. The install commands and the question-and-answer text was entered as shown, and highlighted in yellow in the *Figure 4.1*:

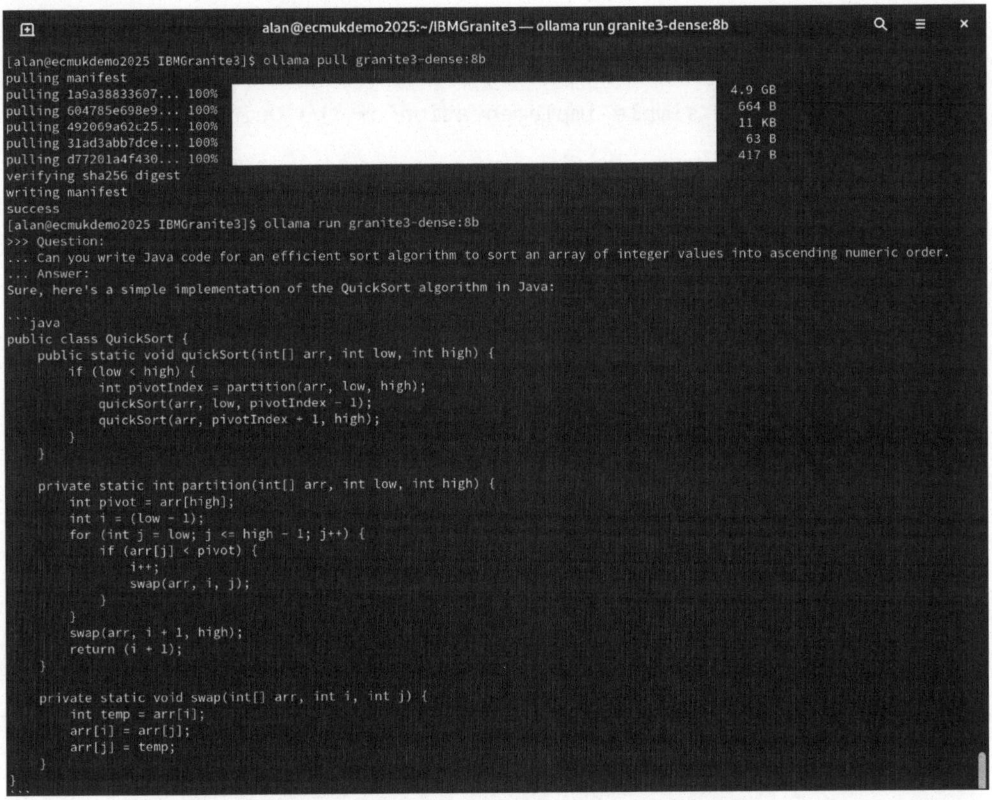

Figure 4.1: *The install commands, and question and answer text, entered by us, is highlighted in yellow*

The full process of download, then running a question-and-response interaction (our entry text is in bold, italics), is as follows:

```
[alan@ecmukdemo2025 IBMGranite3]$ ollama pull granite3-dense:8b
pulling manifest
pulling 1a9a38833607... 100% ████████████████████
████████████████████ 4.9 GB
pulling 604785e698e9... 100% ████████████████████
████████████████████ 664 B
pulling 492069a62c25... 100% ████████████████████
████████████████████  11 KB
pulling 31ad3abb7dce....100% ████████████████████
████████████████████   63 B
pulling d77201a4f430... 100% ████████████████████
████████████████████  417 B
verifying sha256 digest
writing manifest
success
[alan@ecmukdemo2025 IBMGranite3]$ ollama run granite3-dense:8b
>>> Question:
```

~~~~
... Can you write Java code for an efficient sort algorithm to sort
an array of integer values into ascending numeric order.
... Answer:
Sure, here's a simple implementation of the QuickSort algorithm
in Java:

```java
public class QuickSort {
    public static void quickSort(int[] arr, int low, int high) {
        if (low < high) {
            int pivotIndex = partition(arr, low, high);
            quickSort(arr, low, pivotIndex - 1);
            quickSort(arr, pivotIndex + 1, high);
        }
    }

    private static int partition(int[] arr, int low, int high) {
        int pivot = arr[high];
        int i = (low - 1);
        for (int j = low; j <= high - 1; j++) {
            if (arr[j] < pivot) {
                i++;
                swap(arr, i, j);
            }
        }
        swap(arr, i + 1, high);
        return (i + 1);
    }

    private static void swap(int[] arr, int i, int j) {
        int temp = arr[i];
        arr[i] = arr[j];
        arr[j] = temp;
    }
}
```

This code sorts an array of integers using the QuickSort algo-
rithm. The `quickSort` method is a recursive method that
partitions the array and then sorts the two resulting sub-arrays.
The `partition` method selects a pivot element from the
array and rearranges the array so that all elements less than the
pivot are to its left and all elements greater than the
pivot are to its right. The `swap` method is a helper method used
to swap two elements in the array.

>>> Send a message (/? for help)
~~~~

We can download several **IBM Granite LLM Models**, as required and shown in *Figure 4.2*:

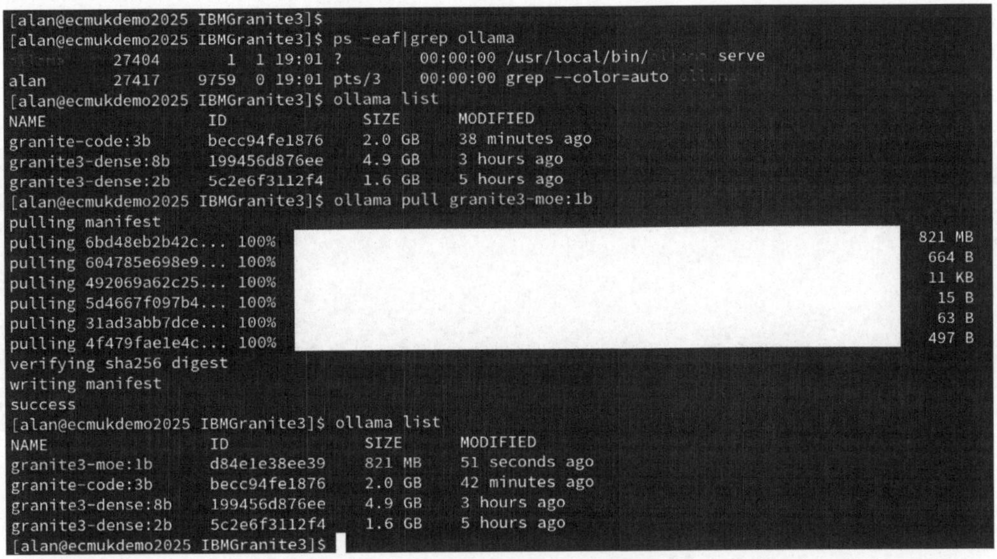

Figure 4.2: *The* ***`ollama pull granite3-moe:1b`*** *is added to our list of available models*

The **`/?`** Ollama server Entry gives the help command list as follows:

```
>>> /?
Available Commands:
  /set            Set session variables
  /show           Show model information
  /load <model>   Load a session or model
  /save <model>   Save your current session
  /clear          Clear session context
  /bye            Exit
  /?, /help       Help for a command
  /? shortcuts    Help for keyboard shortcuts

Use """ to begin a multi-line message.

>>> Send a message (/? for help)
```

Ollama can also be run from a Docker image, see the blog URL here:

`https://ollama.com/blog/ollama-is-now-available-as-an-official-docker-image`

You can set this up using the command as follows (for our "CPU *only*" system):

First, ensure that Docker is installed by running the following command:

```
su - root
Password:
yum install docker
```

This gave the following confirmation on our system, as shown in *Figure 4.3*:

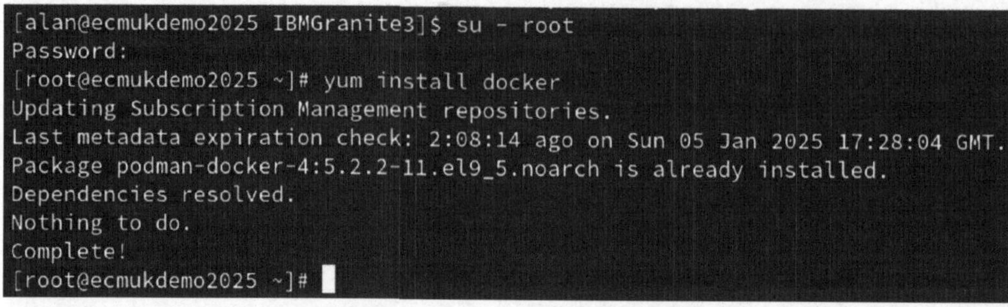

Figure 4.3: *The command, yum install docker gave the following confirmation on our system*

We have to stop the ollama system service on the main Linux system first, using:

```
systemctl stop ollama
```

We also have to upgrade the **crun** package, as illustrated in *Figure 4.4*, using

```
dnf install crun
```

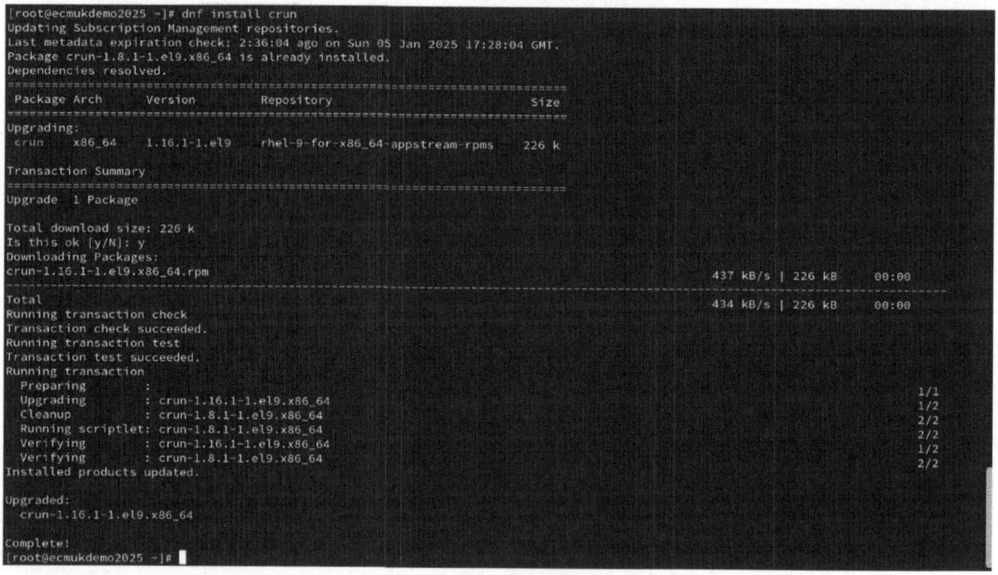

Figure 4.4: *We upgrade the* ***crun*** *package using* ***dnf install crun***

This will allow the ollama container to use the **11434** port, so we can now run, as shown in *Figure* 4.5:

```
docker run -d -v ollama:/root/.ollama -p 11434:11434 --name
ollama ollama/ollama
```

```
[alan@ecmukdemo2025 IBMGranite3]$ docker run -d -v ollama:/root/.ollama -p 11434:11434 --name ollama ollama/ollama
Emulate Docker CLI using podman. Create /etc/containers/nodocker to quiet msg.
Resolved "ollama/ollama" as an alias (/home/alan/.cache/containers/short-name-aliases.conf)
Trying to pull docker.io/ollama/ollama:latest...
Getting image source signatures
Copying blob 9423a26b200c done   |
Copying blob 00b71e3f044c done   |
Copying blob 6414378b6477 done   |
Copying blob 629da9618c4f done   |
Copying config 325786c469 done   |
Writing manifest to image destination
b547336148d6e2aafa8d6793bd947510af070162502aed7b680f15b3cad34d69
[alan@ecmukdemo2025 IBMGranite3]$
```

Figure 4.5: *We can now run:* ***docker run -d -v ollama:/root/.ollama -p 11434:11434 --name ollama ollama/ollama***

Note: *To delete all the existing docker images for a clean start use:*

```
docker rmi $(docker images -q).
```

Nvidia GPU

Install the **Nvidia** container toolkit, if you have access to an **Nvidia GPU**.

Run Ollama inside a Docker container:

```
docker run -d --gpus=all -v ollama:/root/.ollama -p 11434:11434
--name ollama ollama/ollama
```

Run a Model

Now, we run our model IBM **granite3-moe:1b** inside the container, as shown in *Figure* 4.6.

```
docker exec -it ollama ollama run granite3-moe:1b
```

(Using just the CPU version.)

```
[alan@ecmukdemo2025 IBMGranite3]$ docker exec -it ollama ollama run granite3-moe:1b
Emulate Docker CLI using podman. Create /etc/containers/nodocker to quiet msg.
pulling manifest
pulling 6bd48eb2b42c... 100%   821 MB
pulling 604785e698e9... 100%   664 B
pulling 492069a62c25... 100%    11 KB
pulling 5d4667f097b4... 100%    15 B
pulling 31ad3abb7dce... 100%    63 B
pulling 4f479fae1e4c... 100%   497 B
verifying sha256 digest
writing manifest
success
>>> Send a message (/? for help)
```

Figure 4.6: *We run our model IBM* ***granite3-moe:1b*** *inside the container*

We then pasted the following text at the **>>>** prompt:

```
Question:
... Can you write Java code for an efficient binary search
algorithm return the position of a string value from an array of
string values sorted in ascending order.
... Answer:
```

We were presented with the required Java code, as expected, in just a few seconds, as shown in *Figure 4.7*:

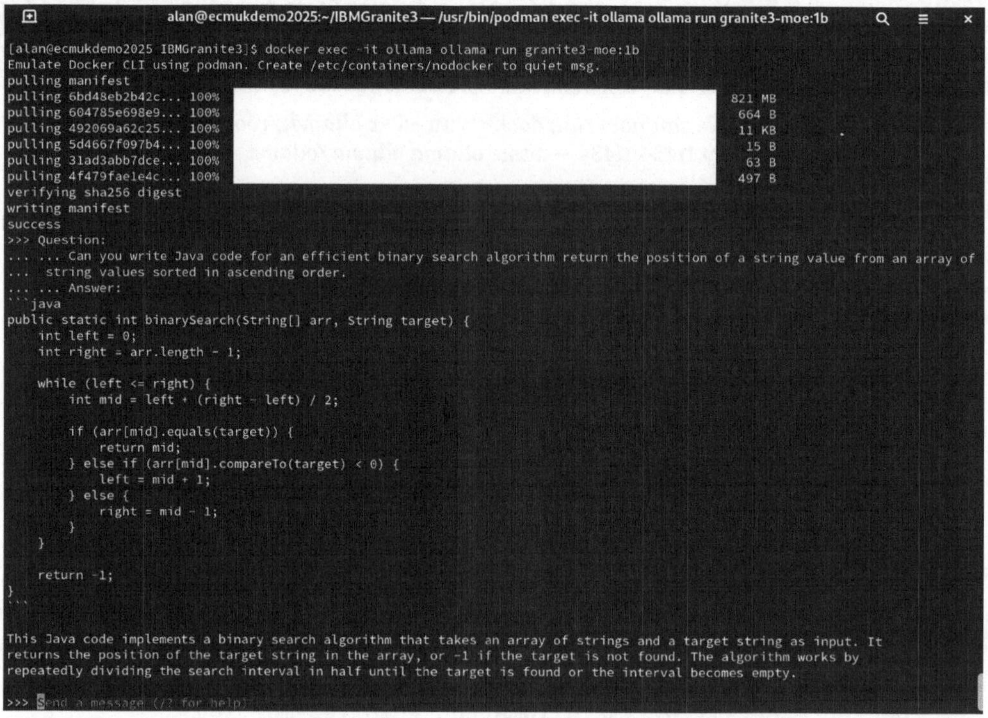

***Figure 4.7:** We ask the question: Can you write Java code for an efficient binary search algorithm?*

We can also run other **ollama** commands, as shown in *Figure 4.8*:

```
docker exec -it ollama ollama list
```

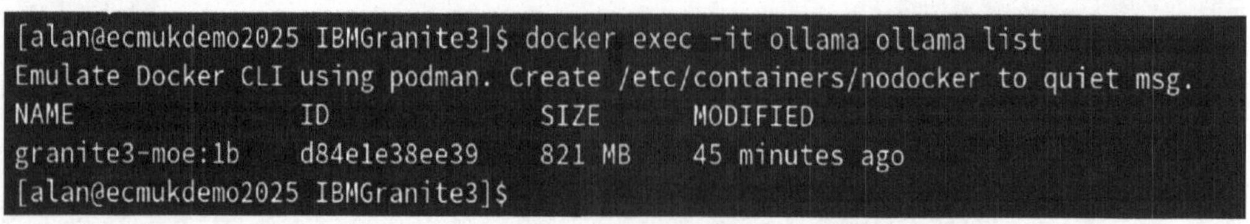

Figure 4.8: *We can also run the list command:* **docker exec -it ollama ollama list**

Install VS Code on a RedHat Linux Server

https://code.visualstudio.com/

Using FireFox browser, we selected the **RedHat/Fedora** command, as illustrated in *Figure 4.9*:

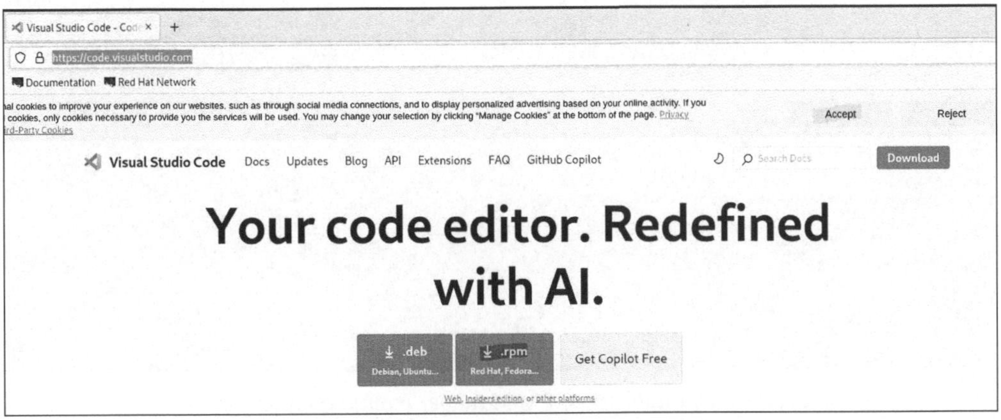

***Figure 4.9**: Using **FireFox** browser, we selected the **RedHat/Fedora** command*

This **.rpm** command button then lists the required scripts to be run on a Linux command line, as shown in *Figure 4.10*:

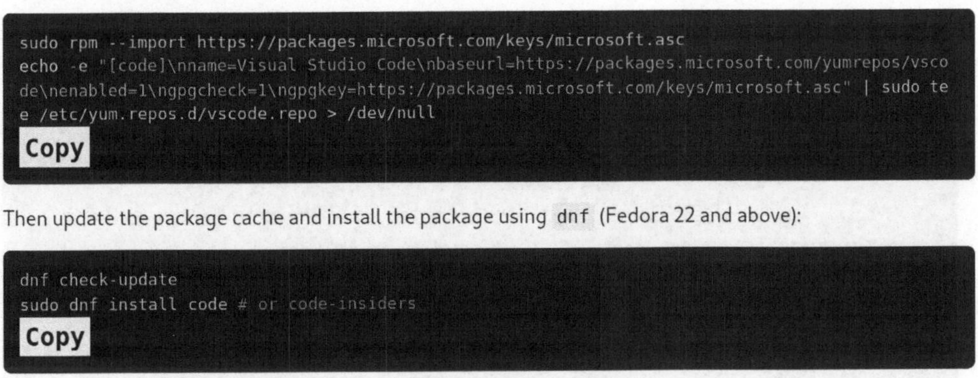

***Figure 4.10**: This **.rpm** command button then lists the required install scripts to be run on a Linux command line*

```
sudo rpm --import https://packages.microsoft.com/keys/microsoft.
asc
echo -e "[code]\nname=Visual Studio Code\nbaseurl=https://pack-
ages.microsoft.com/yumrepos/vscode\nenabled=1\ngpgcheck=1\ngp-
gkey=https://packages.microsoft.com/keys/microsoft.asc" | sudo
tee /etc/yum.repos.d/vscode.repo > /dev/null
```

The above script runs the rpm to enable the RedHat Package Manager (rpm) repository file, in the location **`/etc/yum.repos.d/vscode.repo`** for installation of **VS Code** using the **`dnf`** command, running as shown in *Figure 4.11*:

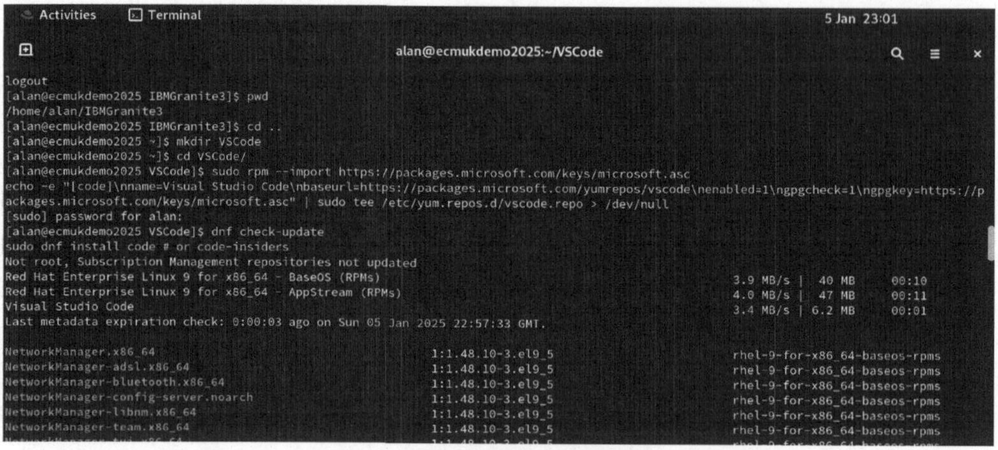

Figure 4.11:** Enable the RPM Manager (rpm) repository file, in the location **/etc/yum.repos.d/vscode.repo

We also copy the **dnf** command used for the installation of the **VS Code** on our RedHat **`RHEL 9.2`** Linux server, **`ECMUKDEMO2025`**:

```
dnf check-update
sudo dnf install code # or code-insiders
```

The **VS Code** is installed ready for use, as listed in *Figure 4.12*:

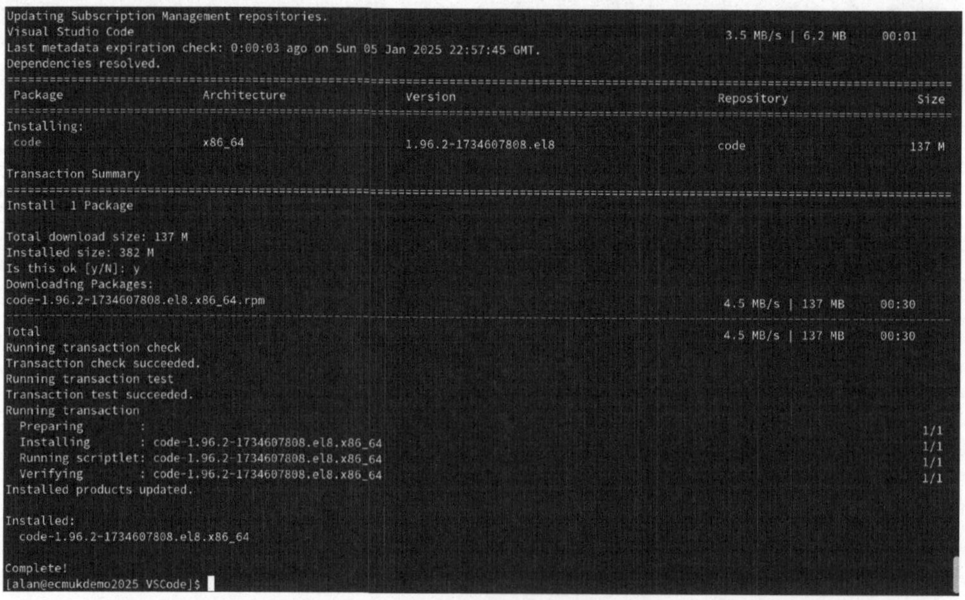

Figure 4.12:** The **VS code** is installed ready for use with **sudo dnf install code

If all is installed correctly, just typing in **code** on the command line will launch an **X-Windows** based **IDE** interface, as shown in *Figure* 4.13:

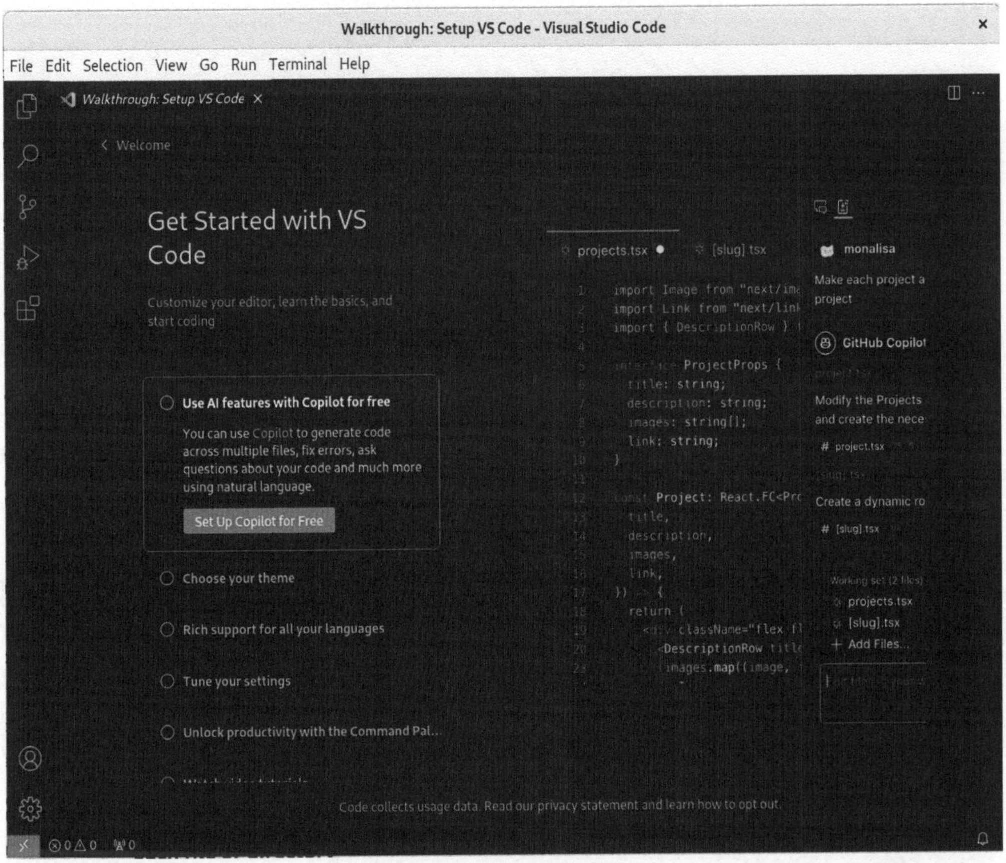

Figure 4.13: *Typing in* **code** *on the command line will launch an* **X-Windows** *based* **IDE** *interface*

The details to install **IBM Granite 3.0** as a code assistant are described in full at:

https://developer.ibm.com/tutorials/awb-local-ai-copilot-ibm-granite-code-ollama-continue/

As a first step, we just use the newly installed code to create a folder, under the users Home folder, as shown in *Figure* 4.14:

Figure 4.14: *First, we just use the newly installed code to create a folder, under the users Home folder*

Now, we have the **VS Code IDE** installed, we need to add the following prerequisite:

With the **IBM Granite** models available and **ollama** running, we can start using them in the **code** editor. We need to install **`Continue`** into the installed **Visual Studio Code**. This can be done with the command line, as highlighted in *Figure 4.15*:

```
code --install-extension continue.continue
```

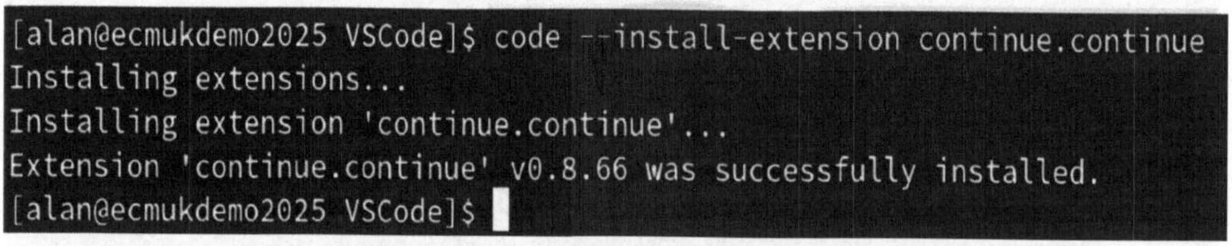

Figure 4.15: *Install* **Continue** *for the* **VS Code IDE**, *with the command:* ***code --install-extension continue.continue***

1. After running the code from the command line window, the **X-Windows VS Code IDE** is loaded, and we can select **`Continue`** from the new highlighted **VS Code** icon, as shown in *Figure 4.16*:

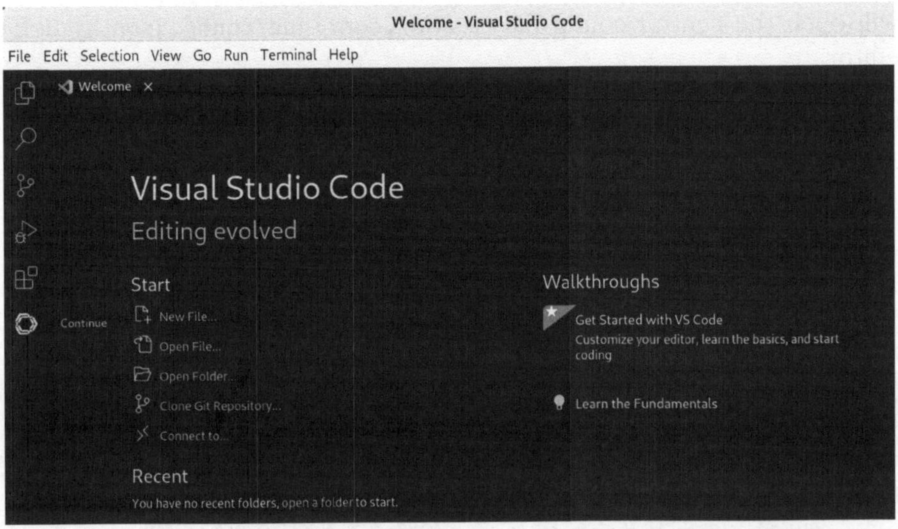

Figure 4.16: *We can select Continue from the new highlighted* **VS Code** *icon*

2. After selecting **`Continue`**, we can open the **`config.json`** text file in the **VS Code** editor, by selecting the **`Local`** tab, and then clicking the highlighted **`config file`** link, as shown in *Figure* 4.17:

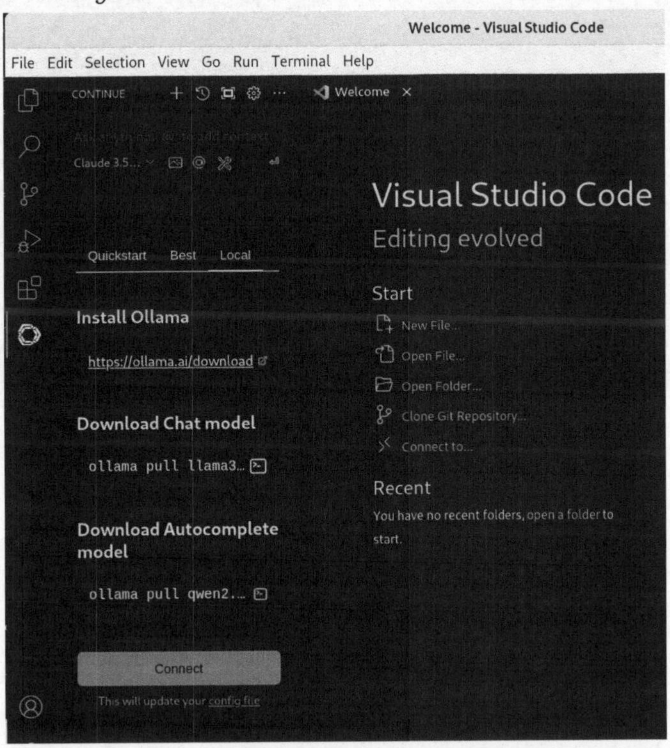

Figure 4.17: *We open the* **config.json** *text file with the Local tab by clicking on the highlighted* **config file** *link*

This will open the central config file (**`$HOME/.continue/config.json`** by default) in your editor.

3. To enable the **ollama Granite** models, we need to edit the following sections, as shown in *Figure 4.18:*
   - **models**: This will set up the model to use for chat and long-form prompts (for example, explain)
   - We replaced the existing one, set as the default:

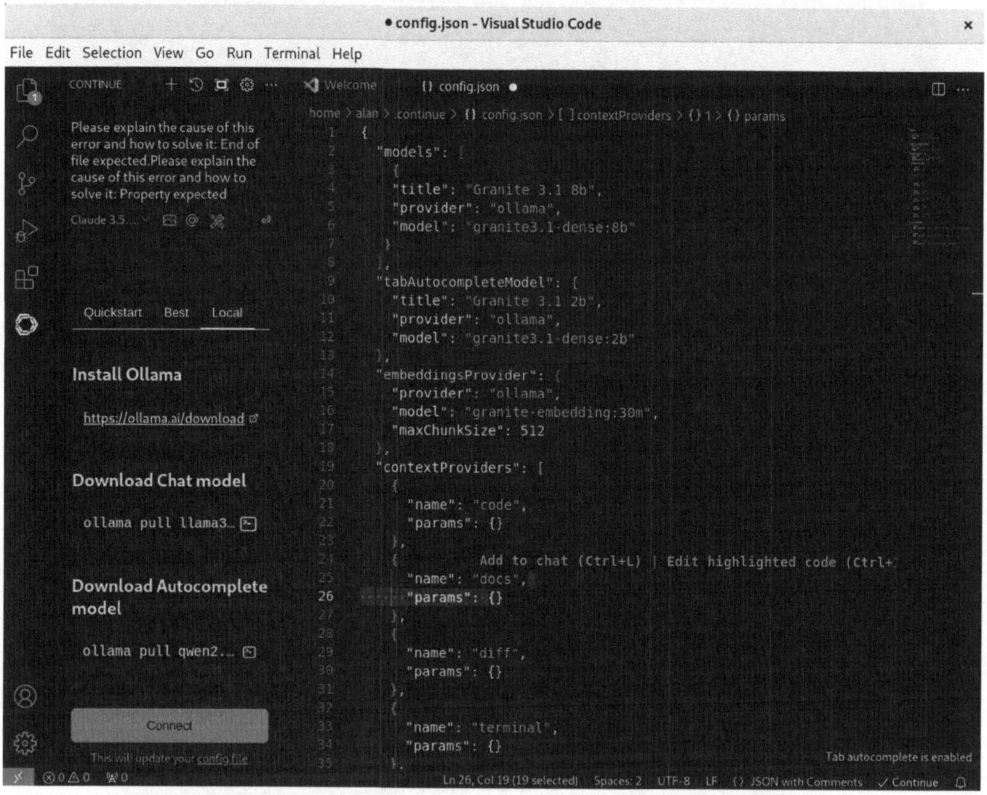

Figure 4.18: *To enable the* **ollama** *Granite models, we need to edit the highlighted sections*

```
"models": [
  {

    "model": "claude-3-5-sonnet-latest",
    "provider": "anthropic",
    "apiKey": "",
    "title": "Claude 3.5 Sonnet"
  }
],
```

With the following **JSON** text:

```
"models": [
  {
    "title": "Granite 3.1 8b",
    "provider": "ollama",
    "model": "granite3.1-dense:8b"
  }
],
```

4. For the **tabAutocompleteModel:** which sets up the model to use for inline completions, we replaced the existing default one:

```
"tabAutocompleteModel": {
  "title": "Codestral",
  "provider": "mistral",
  "model": "codestral-latest",
  "apiKey": ""
},
```

With

```
"tabAutocompleteModel": {
  "title": "Granite 3.1 2b",
  "provider": "ollama",
  "model": "granite3.1-dense:2b"
},
```

5. For the **embeddingsProvider:** which sets up the embedding model to use for indexing our code, we added the following to the end of the list:

```
"embeddingsProvider": {
    "provider": "ollama",
    "model": "granite-embedding:30m",
    "maxChunkSize": 512
},
```

6. We can now use the **File-> Save** command to update our **config.json** file, as shown in *Figure 4.19*:

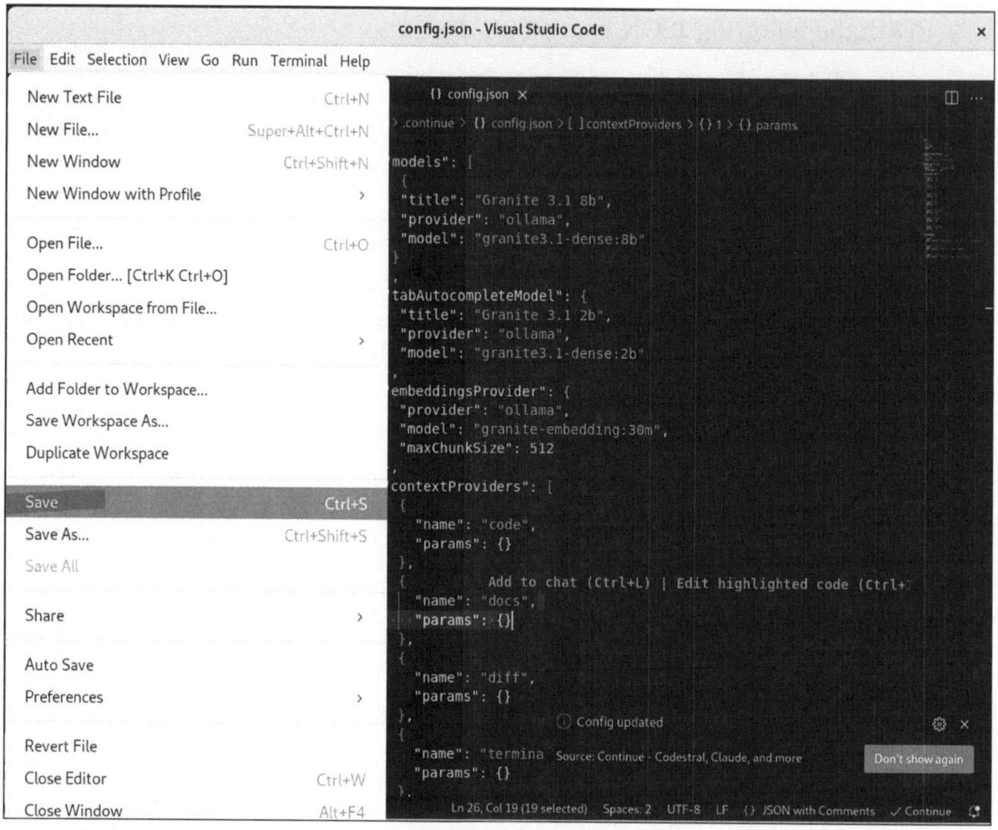

Figure 4.19: *We can now use the* **File-> Save** *command to update our* **config.json** *file*

7. With **`Continue`** installed and **IBM Granite** running, everything should now be installed to run the local **AI co-pilot**. First, we selected the new **`continue`** icon in the sidebar, and select to start the download of an **LLM** model, as shown in *Figure 4.20*:

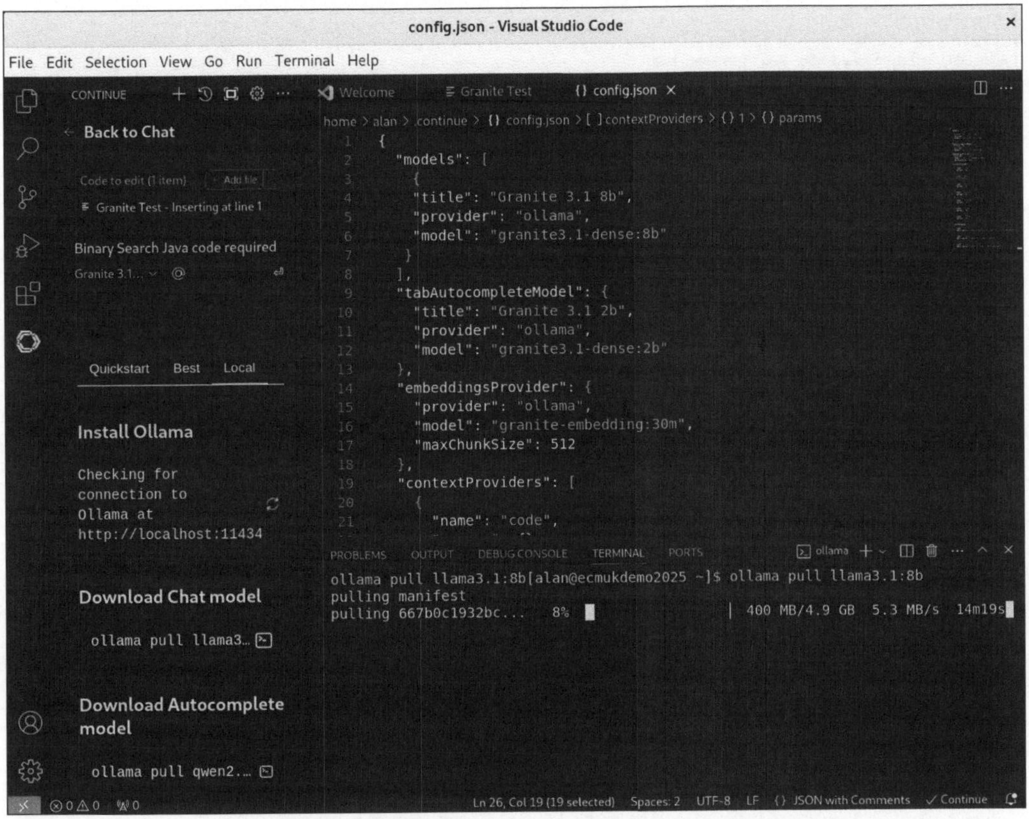

Figure 4.20: *We select the new* **continue** *icon in the sidebar, and select to start the download of an* **LLM** *model*

The model is downloaded successfully, as shown in *Figure 4.21*:

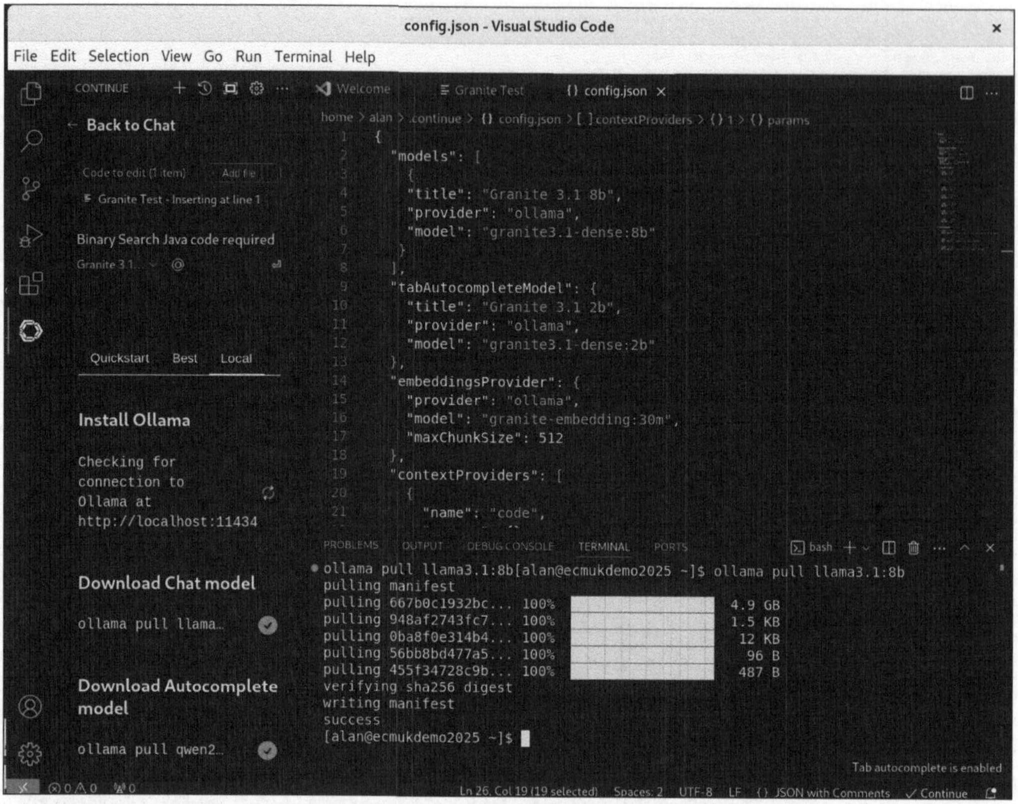

***Figure 4.21:** The **llama3.1:8b** model is downloaded successfully*

The full usage guidelines are in the documentation link: https://docs.continue.dev/intro?utm_source=ibm_developer&utm_content=in_content_link&utm_id=tutorials_awb-local-ai-copilot-ibm-granite-code-ollama-continue.

Thus, to install the **Java JDK** for **VS Code,** we are first prompted by the IDE to install the **`Extension Pack for Java`**, as highlighted in *Figure 4.22*:

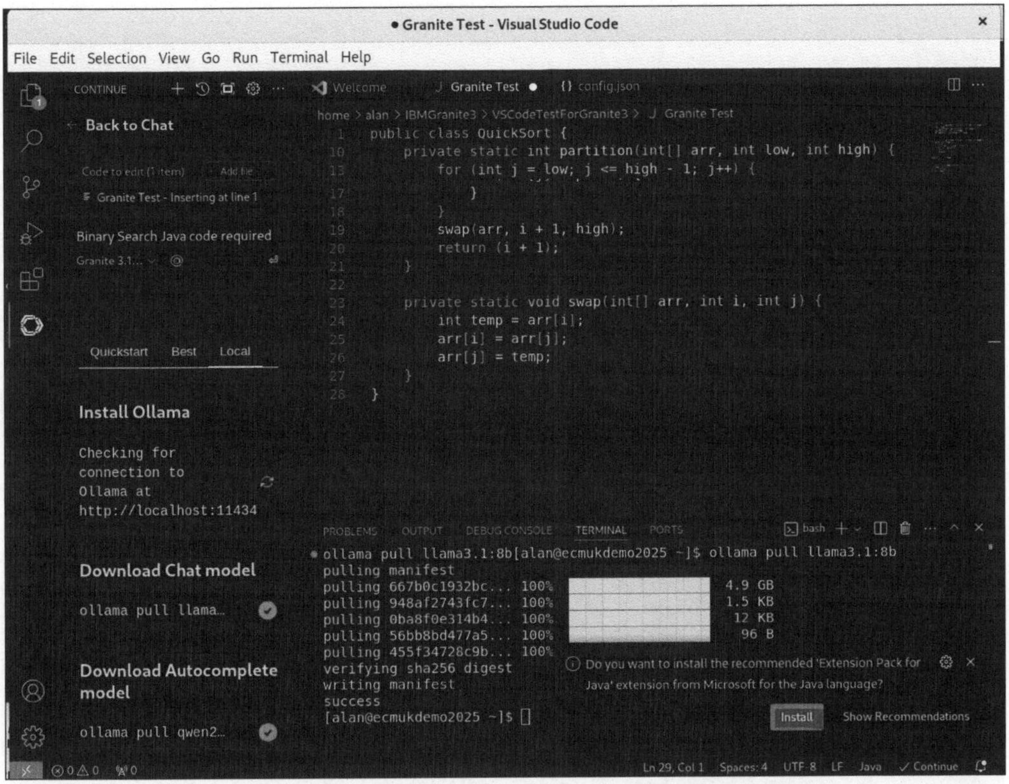

Figure 4.22: *Install the* **Java JDK** *for* **VS Code**, *which is prompted by the* **IDE**, *for installing the Java Extension Pack*

The **`Java Extension Pack`** is shown installing, in *Figure 4.23*:

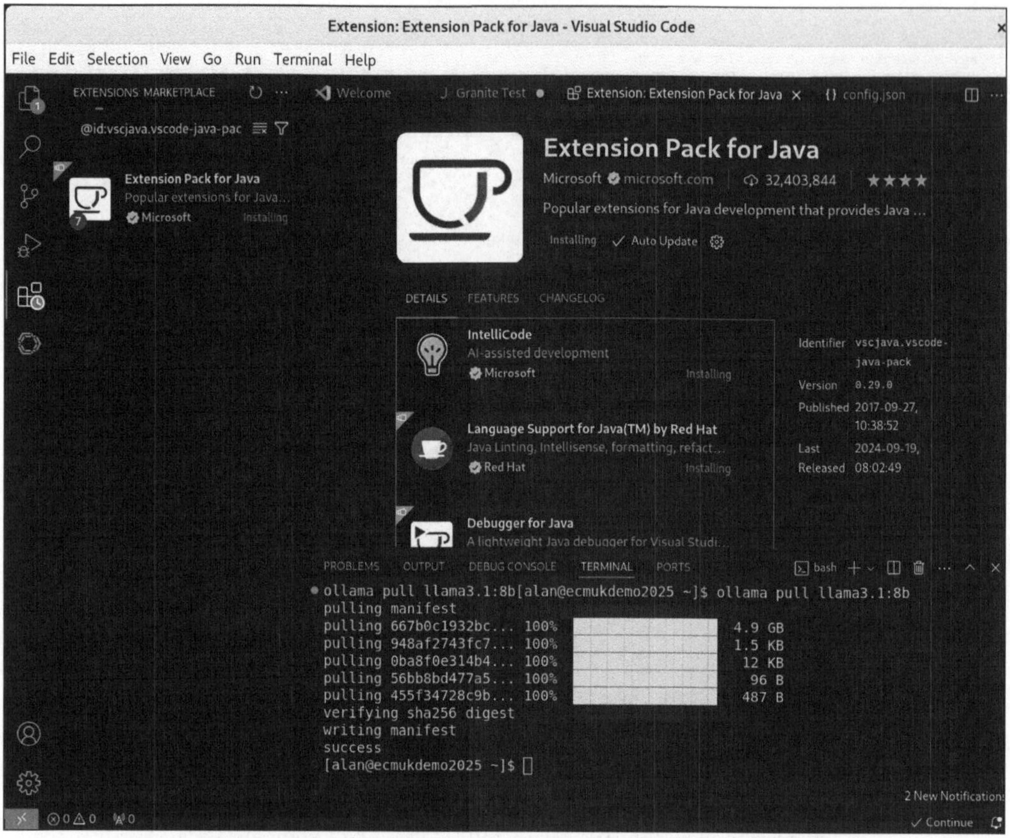

Figure 4.23: *The Java Extension Pack is shown installing*

Next, we are prompted by **VS Code**, to install the **JDK**, as shown in *Figure* 4.24:

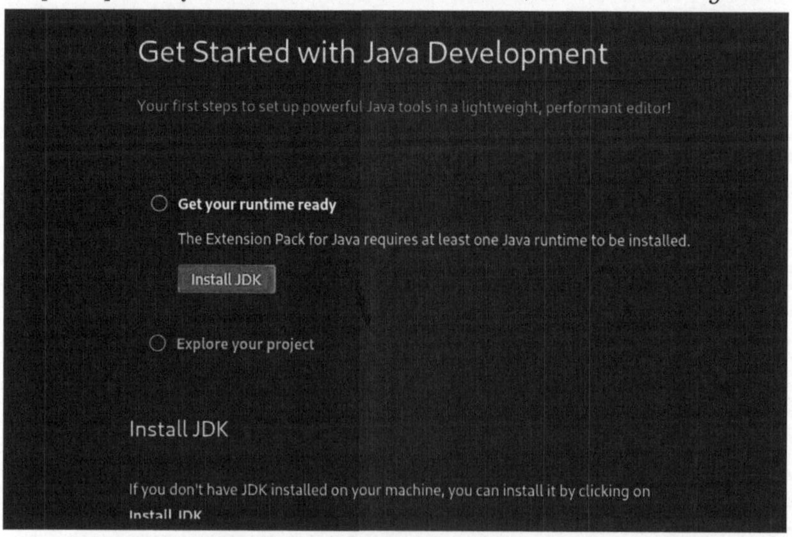

Figure 4.24: *We are prompted by* **VS Code**, *to install the* **JDK**

The **VS Code** prompts for the version option for installation (we choose the latest, 21), and then we select the highlighted **`Download`** command button, as shown in *Figure 4.25*:

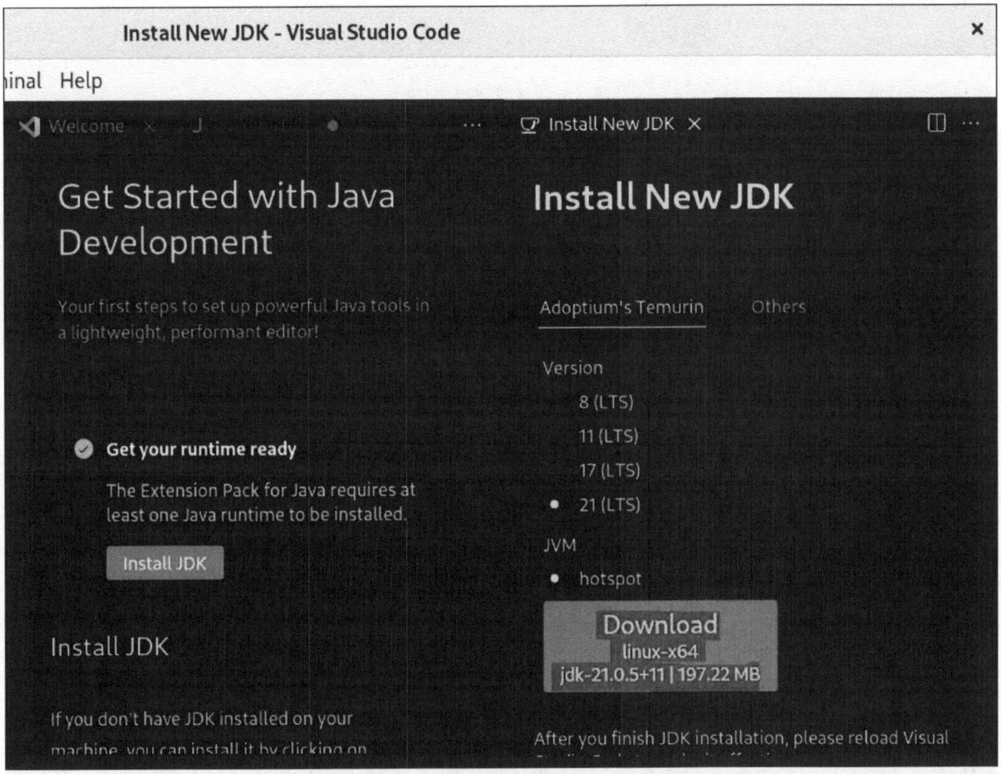

***Figure 4.25:** The **VS Code** prompts for the **JDK** version option for installation (we choose the latest, **21**)*

The FireFox web browser indicates that the JDK has been downloaded, as shown in *Figure 4.26*:

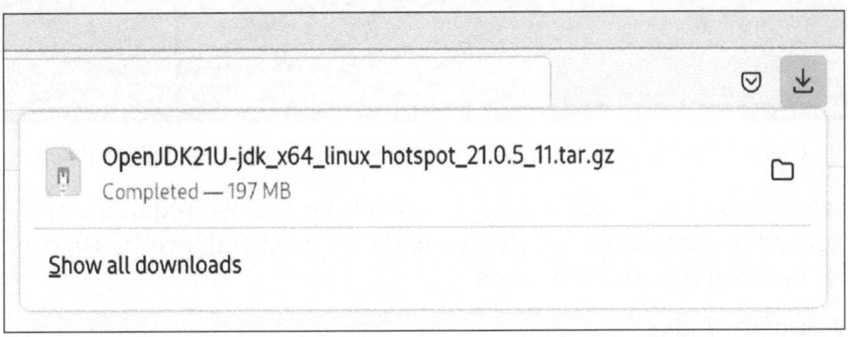

***Figure 4.26:** The **FireFox** web browser indicates that the **JDK** has been downloaded*

The downloaded gzipped tar file is extracted as shown in *Figure 4.27*:

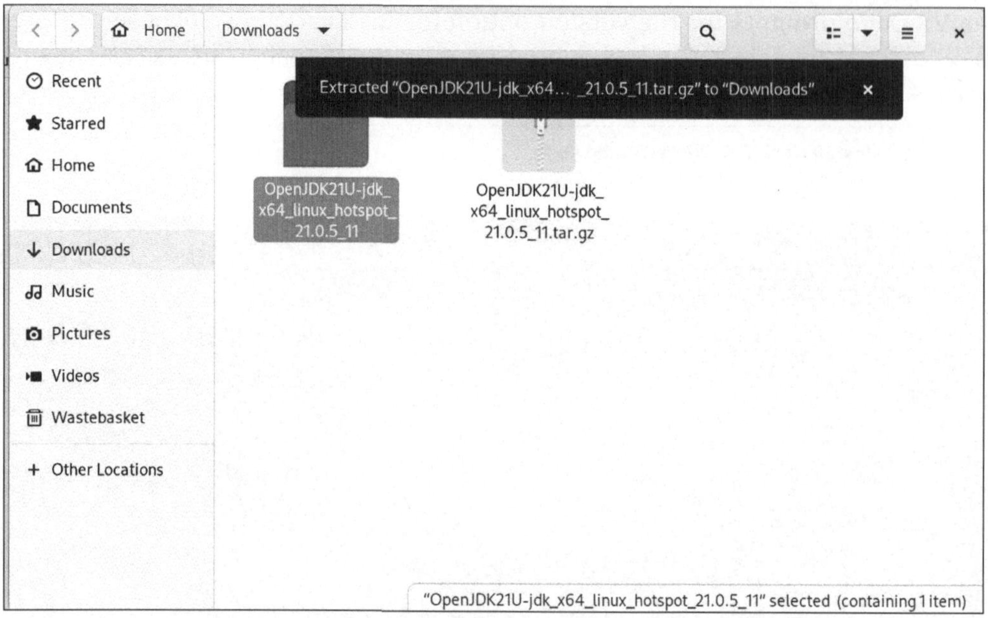

Figure 4.27: *The downloaded gzipped tar file is extracted*

Alternatively, we can use the command line to install a JDK (this one is version 17):

```
sudo yum install java-17-openjdk
$ java -version
```

The installation libraries are shown in *Figure 4.28*:

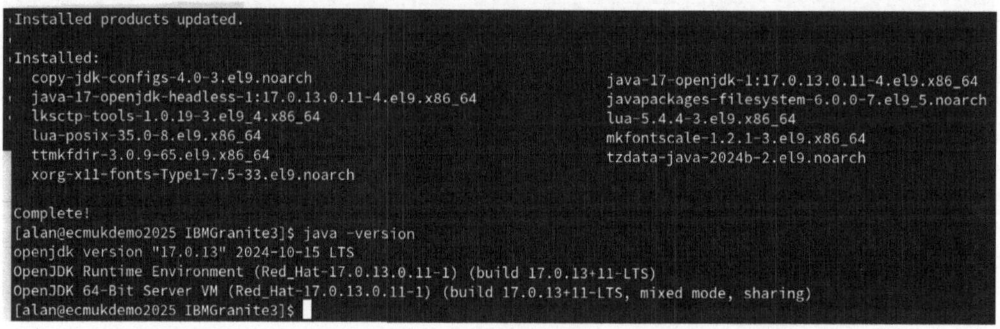

Figure 4.28: *The* **JDK** *installation libraries which were installed are listed*

Or, we can use the link, as follows to download the JDK we require: https://access.redhat.com/jbossnetwork/restricted/listSoftware.html?product=core.service.openjdk&downloadType=distributions

```
$ mkdir ~/jdks
$ cd ~/jdks
$ tar -xf java-17-openjdk-17.0.5.0.8-2.portable.jre.el7.x86_64.
tar.xz -C ~/jdks
```

```
$ ln -s ~/jdks/java-17-openjdk-17.0.5.0.8-2.portable.jdk.el7.
x86_64 ~/jdks/java-17
$ export JAVA_HOME=~/jdks/java-17
```

The default **`Autocomplete`** model, **`qwen2.5-coder:1.5b`**, is downloaded through the **`ollama`** link, as shown in *Figure 4.29*:

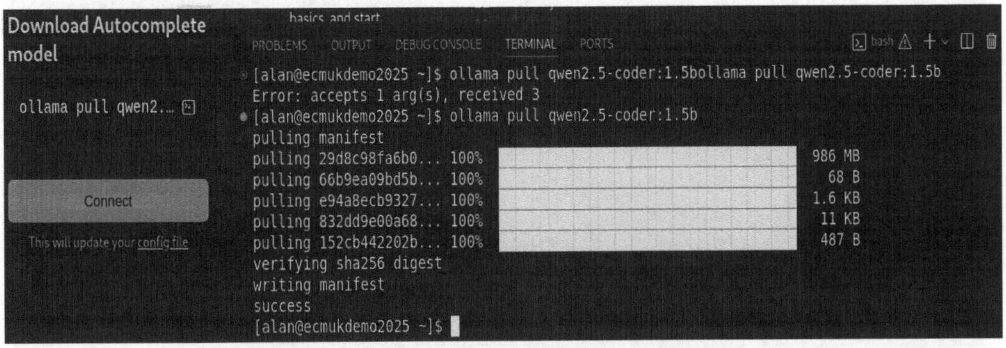

***Figure 4.29:** The default **Autocomplete** model, **qwen2.5-coder:1.5b**, is downloaded through the **ollama** link*

The **`App.java`** default **VS Code IDE** code is ready to be run, to test the **Java** extension, as shown in *Figure 4.30*:

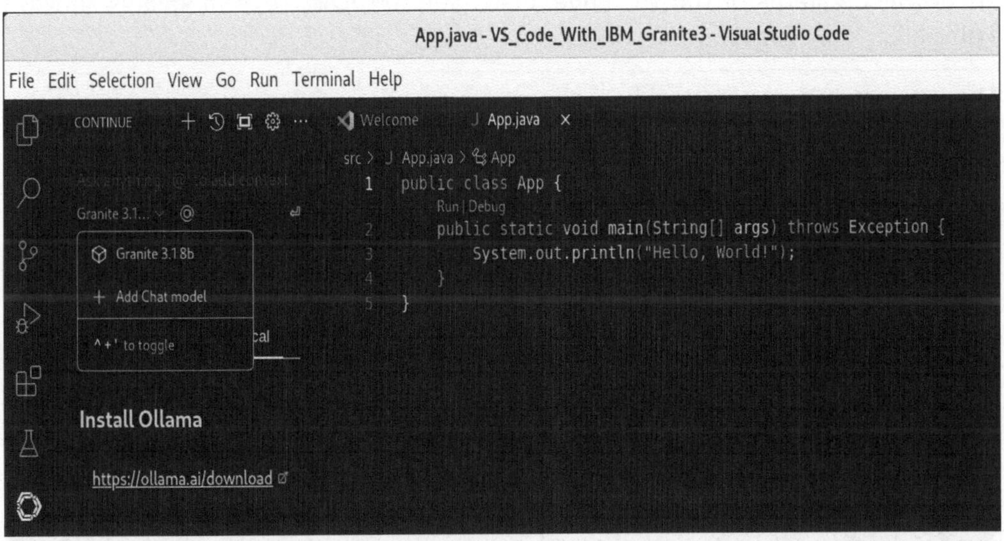

***Figure 4.30:** The **App.java** default **VS Code IDE** code is ready to be run, to test the **Java** extension*

We can **`Download`** the default **`VS Code Chat`** model, using the highlighted command button, as shown in *Figure 4.31*:

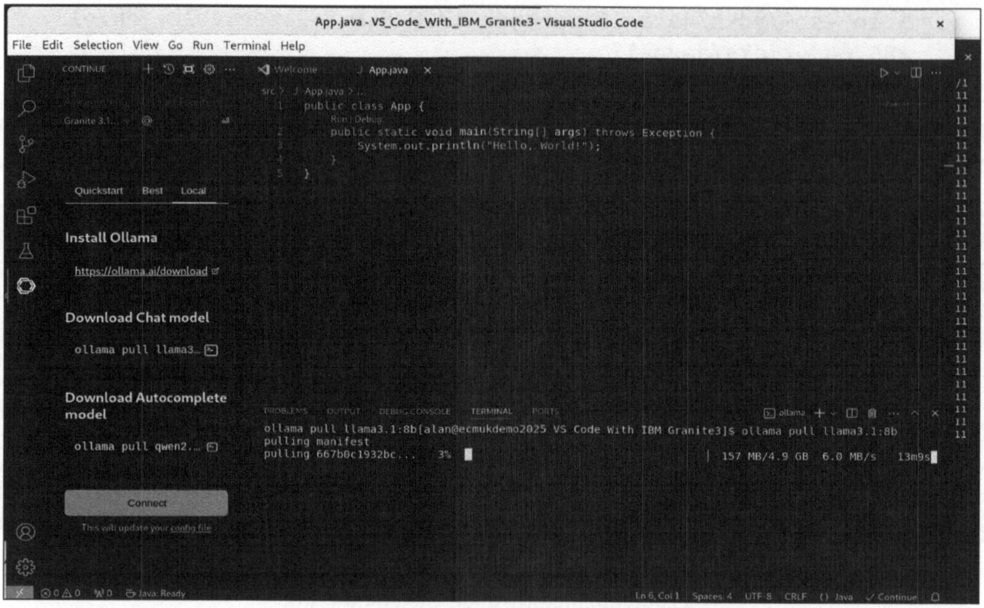

***Figure 4.31:** We can **Download** the default **VS Code Chat** model, using the highlighted command button*

The download status of the **`VS Code`**, **`Chat`**, and **`Autocomplete`** models is shown in *Figure 4.32:*

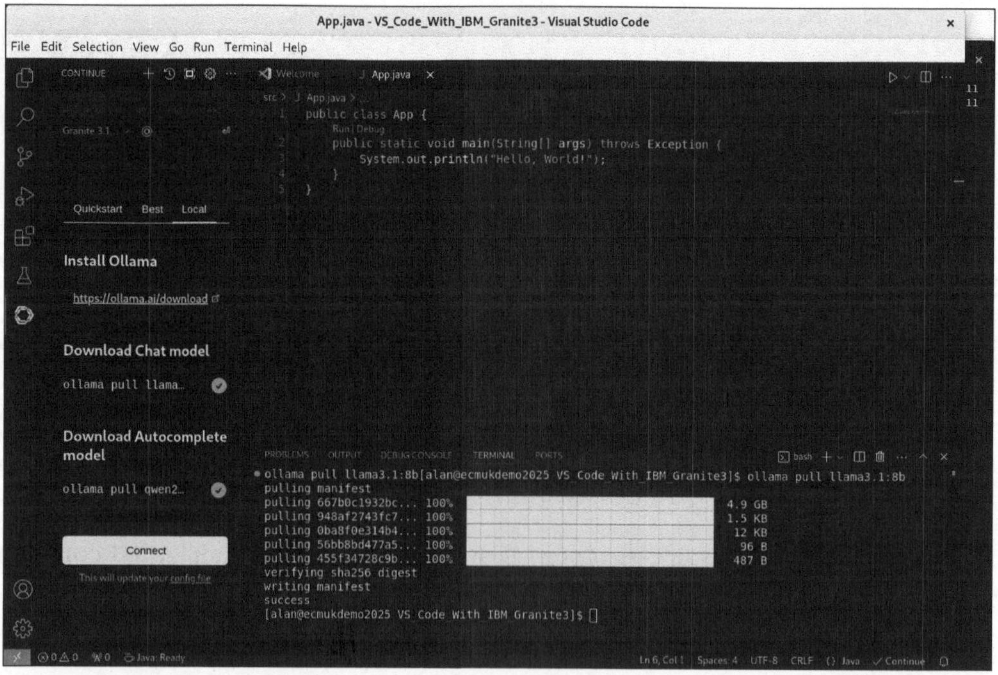

***Figure 4.32:** The download status of the **VS Code, Chat** and **Autocomplete** models*

We can now run the **Java** initial program to check the updates we made, using the **`Run Without Debugging`**, as shown in *Figure 4.33*:

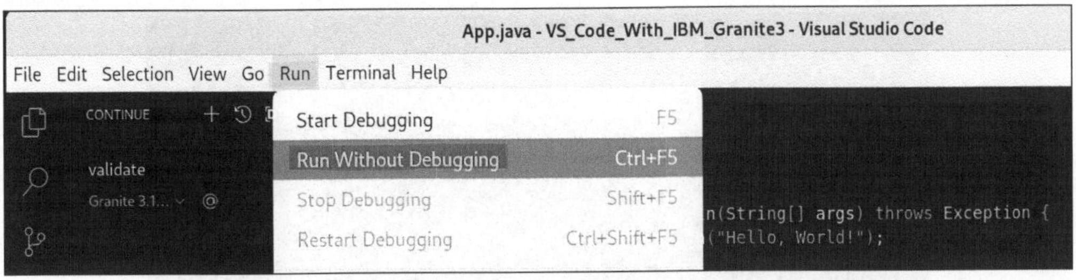

Figure 4.33:** We run the **Java** initial program to check the downloaded updates, with **Run Without Debugging

The program runs without errors in the **`VS Code TERMINAL`** output, where the **`app.java`** executes successfully using our installed Java JDK version 17, as illustrated in *Figure 4.34*:

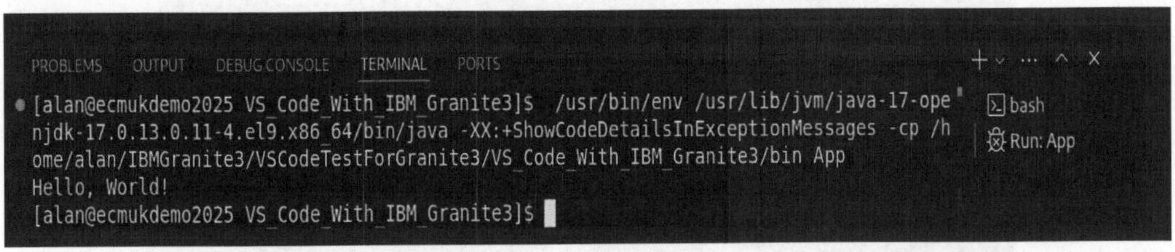

***Figure 4.34:** The program runs without errors in the **VS Code TERMINAL** output*

We have now updated the **VS Code config.json** file to include the following **IBM Granite 3.0** models, recommended by **IBM** to be used with **VS Code**, as shown in *Figure 4.35*:

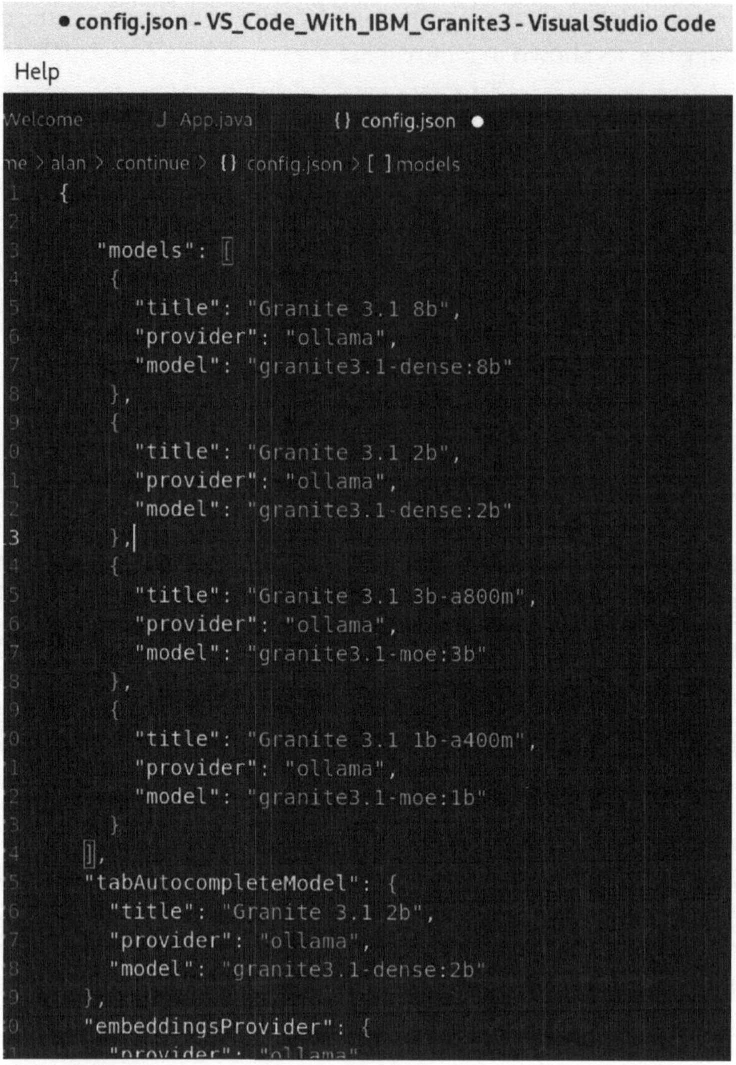

Figure 4.35: *The* ***VS Code config.json*** *file includes the* ***IBM Granite 3.0*** *models, recommended by* ***IBM*** *to be used*

We can now load the example **`Continue`** python code from the file **`continue_tutorial.py`**, which triggers the **`VS Code`** for us to run the **`VS Code 'Python'`** extension, using the highlighted **Install** command button, as shown in *Figure* 4.36:

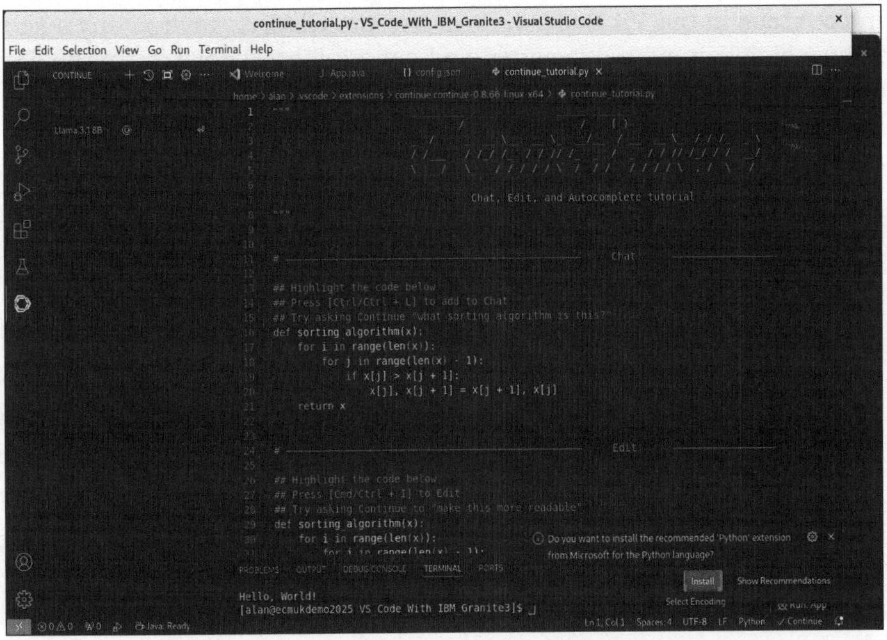

Figure 4.36: *We can now load the example* **Continue** *python code, from the file* **continue_tutorial.py**

The Python extension is now installed, and we select our **`continue_tutorial.py`** file to try the AI support, as highlighted in *Figure 4.37*:

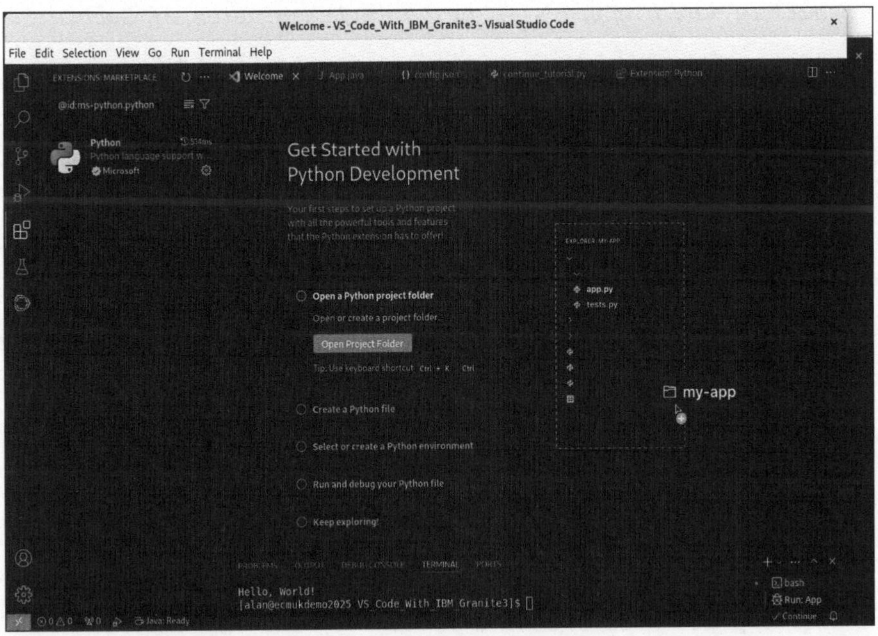

Figure 4.37: *The* **Python** *extension is installed, and we select the* **continue_tutorial.py** *file to try the* **AI** *support*

Now, in **`Continue`** in the **VS Code**, we can use the CTRL/L key to copy a section of the code we highlight, with a question and get a full breakdown from the **Granite 3** embedded models as illustrated in *Figure 4.38*:

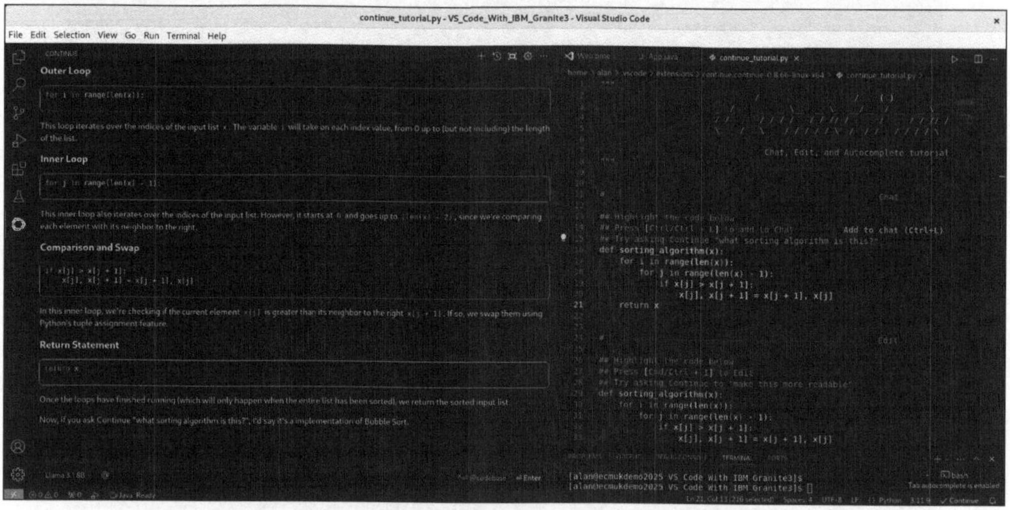

Figure 4.38: *In Continue in the* **VS Code**, *we can use the* **CTRL/L** *key to copy a section of the code, we highlight*

The **AI** response text from this question is italicized, as listed:

````
"It Looks Like you're asking me to analyze the `sorting_algorithm`
function, which appears to be an implementation of Bubble Sort.

Here's a breakdown of what this code does:"

### Function Signature

```python
def sorting_algorithm(x):
```

This defines a function named `sorting_algorithm` that takes one
input argument `x`.

### Outer Loop

```python
for i in range(len(x)):
```

This Loop iterates over the indices of the input List `x`. The
variable `i` will take on each index value, from 0 up to (but not
including) the Length of the List.
````

````
### Inner Loop

```python
for j in range(len(x) - 1):
```

This inner loop also iterates over the indices of the input list.
However, it starts at `0` and goes up to `(len(x) - 2)`, since
we're comparing each element with its neighbor to the right.

### Comparison and Swap

```python
if x[j] > x[j + 1]:
    x[j], x[j + 1] = x[j + 1], x[j]
```

In this inner loop, we're checking if the current element `x[j]`
is greater than its neighbor to the right `x[j + 1]`. If so, we
swap them using Python's tuple assignment feature.

### Return Statement

```python
return x
```

Once the loops have finished running (which will only happen when
the entire list has been sorted), we return the sorted input
list.

Now, if you ask Continue "what sorting algorithm is this?", I'd
say it's a implementation of Bubble Sort.
````

Our updates to the **JSON** in the `VS Code config.json` file, we entered earlier, as shown in *Figure* 4.35, can be seen to be available to select from a list, as illustrated in *Figure* 4.39:

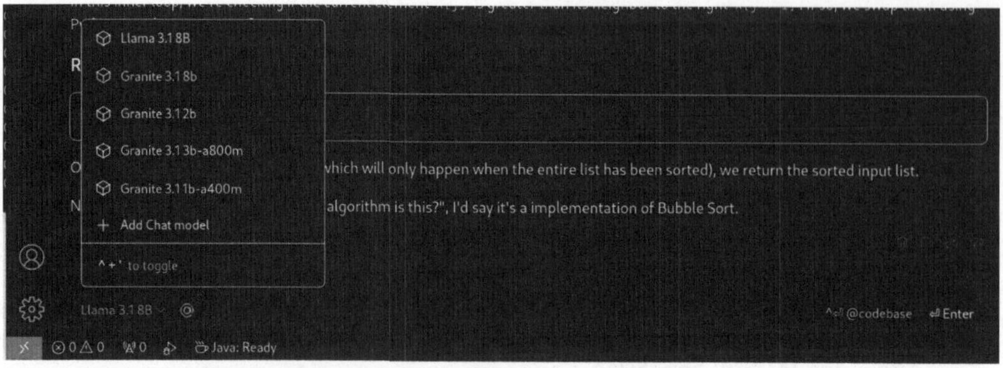

Figure 4.39: *Updates to the **JSON** in the **VS Code config.json** file we entered, can be seen to be available to select*

We try the second example in the tutorial, using CTRL/L after highlighting the code, as shown in *Figure* 4.40, to provide a more readable code listing, with additional comments added by the **AI** model.

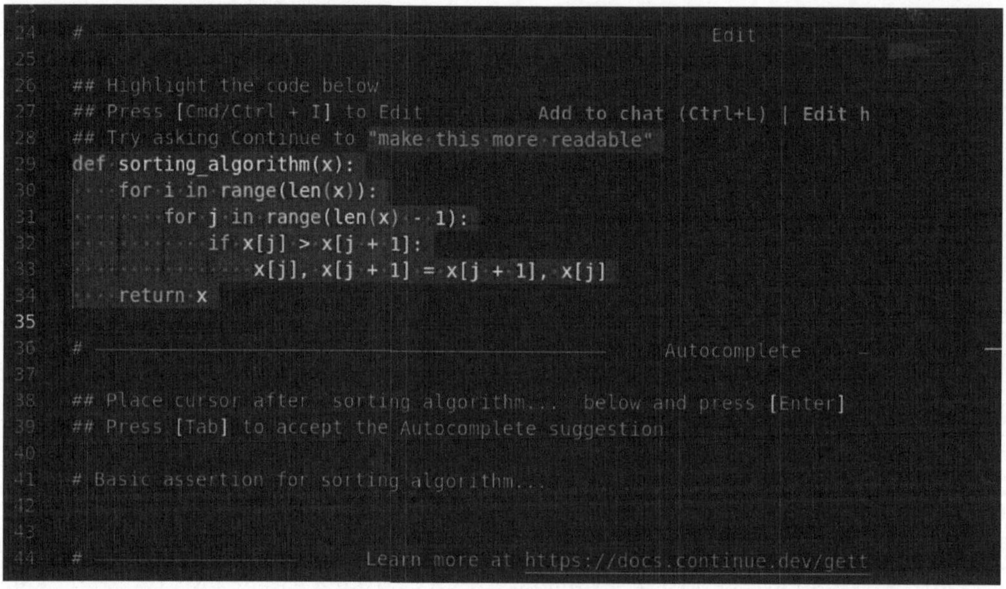

Figure 4.40: *We try the second example in the tutorial, using **CTRL/L** after highlighting the code*

The code for analysis is copied to the **`CONTINUE`** window, and we can start the **AI** code improvement analysis by selecting the highlighted *Enter* key, shown in *Figure* 4.41:

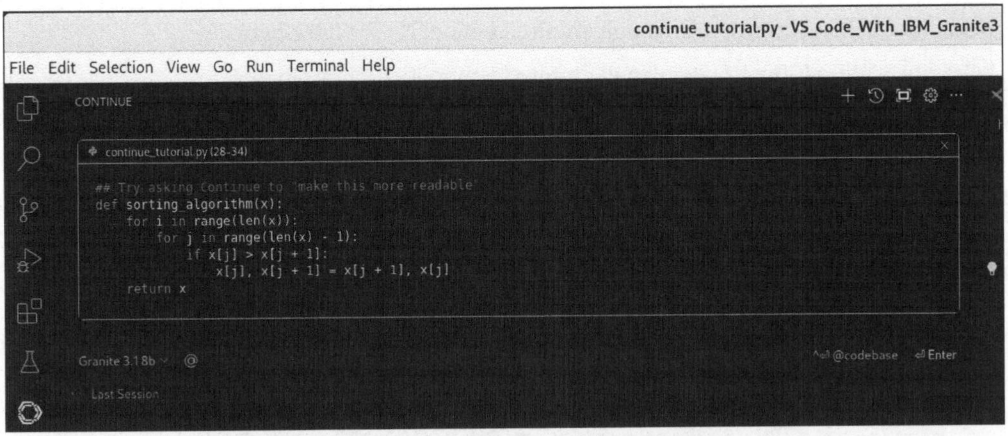

Figure 4.41: *The code is copied to the* **CONTINUE** *window, and we can start the AI code improvement analysis*

The **AI** updated code is displayed in the **`CONTINUE`** window, as shown in *Figure 4.42*:

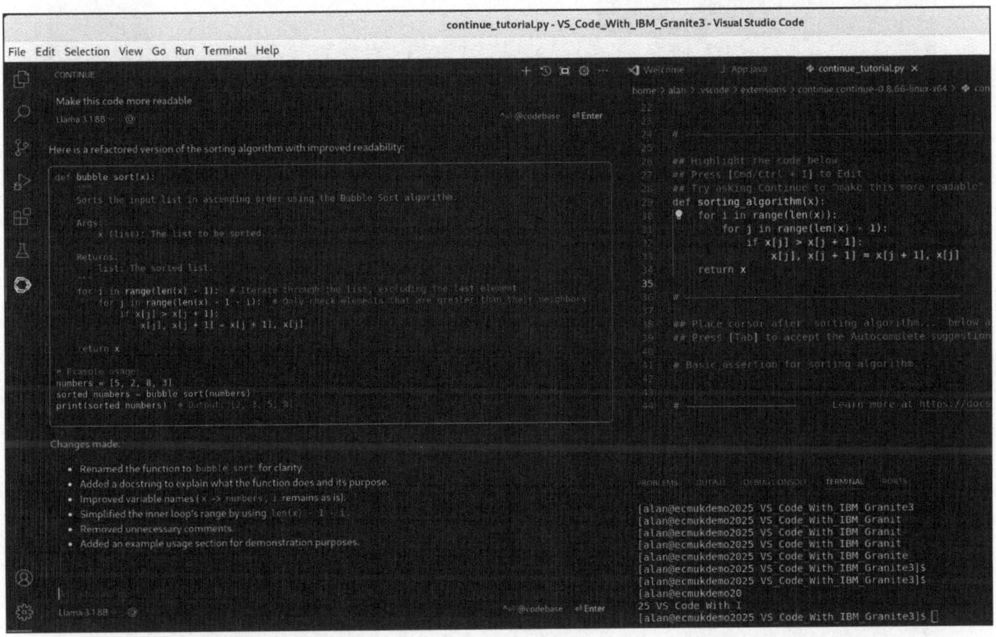

Figure 4.42: *The* **AI** *updated code is displayed in the* **CONTINUE** *window*

We have to use the **ollama** command to pull down the additional **IBM LLM models,** we referenced in the **VS Code config.json** file, using the following *Table 4.1*:

Display Name	Pull Command	Size
Granite 3.1 8b	ollama pull granite3.1-dense:8b	4.9 Gbytes
Granite 3.1 2b	ollama pull granite3.1-dense:2b	1.5 Gbytes

Granite 3.1 3b-a800m	ollama pull granite3.1-moe:3b	2.0 Gbytes
Granite 3.1 1b-a400m	ollama pull granite3.1-moe:1b	1.4 Gbytes

***Table 4.1:** The additional **IBM LLM** models, we referenced in the **VS Code config.json** file are listed*

The **`ollama pull`** commands were run in our Linux command window as shown in *Figure 4.43:*

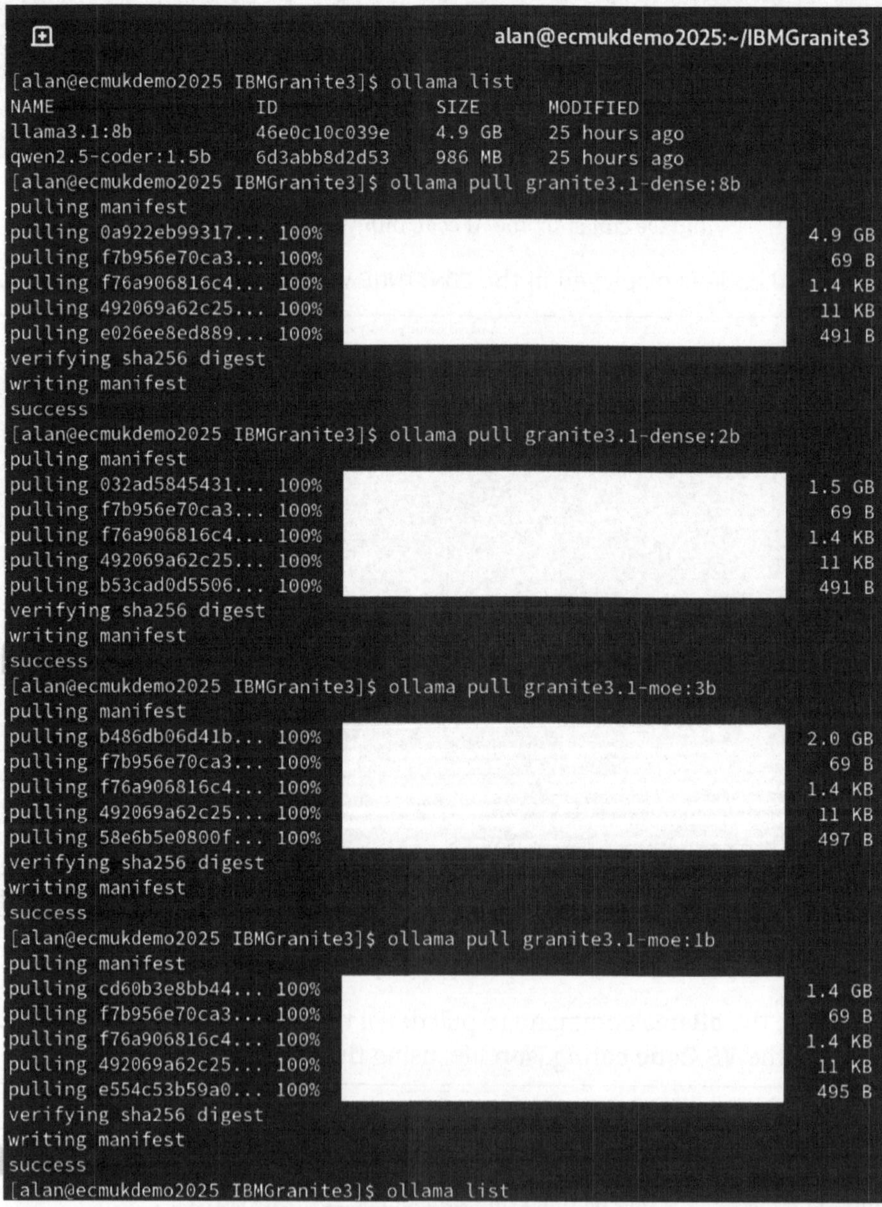

***Figure 4.43:** The **ollama pull** commands were run in our **Linux** command window*

The **`ollama list`** command can be used to display all the available models, downloaded, as shown in *Figure 4.44*:

```
[alan@ecmukdemo2025 IBMGranite3]$ ollama list
NAME                    ID              SIZE      MODIFIED
granite3.1-moe:1b       3269ce3e31ea    1.4 GB    15 seconds ago
granite3.1-moe:3b       df6f6578dba8    2.0 GB    4 minutes ago
granite3.1-dense:2b     34a5cc3ccb39    1.5 GB    11 minutes ago
granite3.1-dense:8b     86ac4cf0cb84    4.9 GB    14 minutes ago
llama3.1:8b             46e0c10c039e    4.9 GB    25 hours ago
qwen2.5-coder:1.5b      6d3abb8d2d53    986 MB    25 hours ago
[alan@ecmukdemo2025 IBMGranite3]$
```

***Figure 4.44:** The **ollama list** command can be used to display all the available models*

We can now go back to our **`app.java`** program, and select the **IBM Granite 3.1** or **Granite 3.1 8b LLM** model that we previously downloaded. Next, we highlight our "**`Hello World`**" java code and re-enter the prompt, "**`Make this code more readable`**" for the **AI** to improve our basic test code, as shown in *Figure 4.45*:

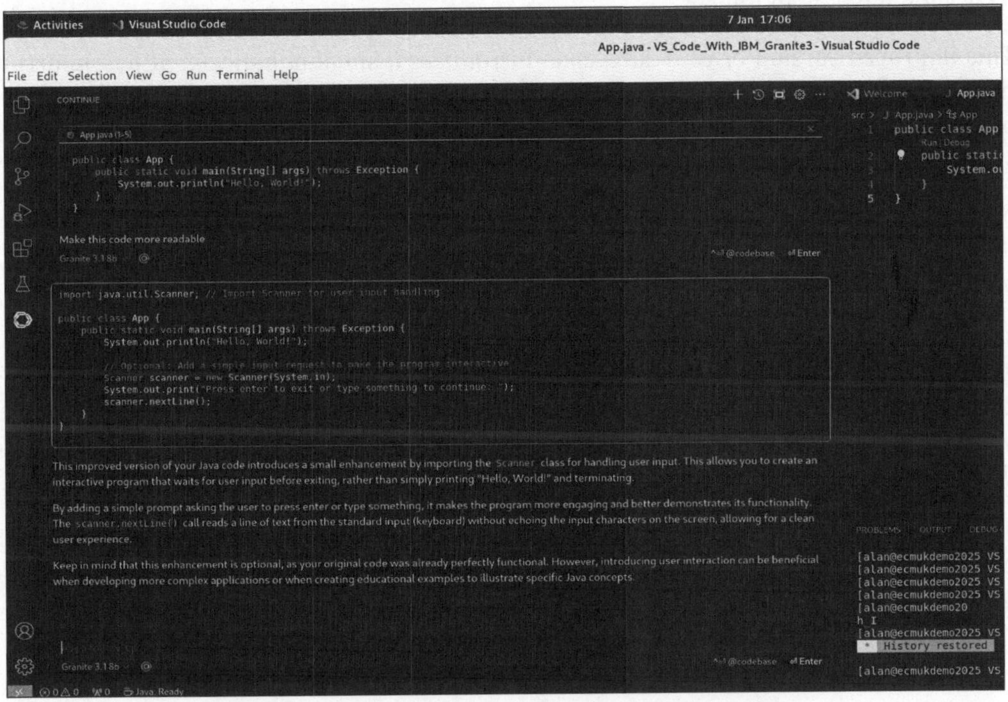

***Figure 4.45:** We highlight our "**Hello World**" java code, and repeat the question, "**Make this code more readable**"*

The improved **app.java** code is listed as follows:

```
import java.util.Scanner; // Import Scanner for user input handling

public class App {
    public static void main(String[] args) throws Exception {
        System.out.println("Hello, World!");

        // Optional: Add a simple input request to make the
program interactive
        Scanner scanner = new Scanner(System.in);
        System.out.print("Press enter to exit or type something
to continue: ");
        scanner.nextLine();
    }
}
```

The text description generated by the **IBM Granite 3.1 LLM,** using the **ollama** engine **AI** is shown below in italics:

*This improved version of your Java code introduces a small enhancement by importing the **Scanner** class for handling user input. This allows you to create an interactive program that waits for user input before exiting, rather than simply printing "Hello, World!" and terminating.*

*By adding a simple prompt asking the user to press enter or type something, it makes the program more engaging and better demonstrates its functionality. The **scanner.nextLine()** call reads a line of text from the standard input (keyboard) without echoing the input characters on the screen, allowing for a clean user experience.*

Keep in mind that this enhancement is optional, as your original code was already perfectly functional. However, introducing user interaction can be beneficial when developing more complex applications or when creating educational examples to illustrate specific Java concepts.

The details of a downloaded **ollama** model can be displayed using the **ollama show** command, for example, **ollama show granite3.1-dense:8b** as illustrated in *Figure 4.46*:

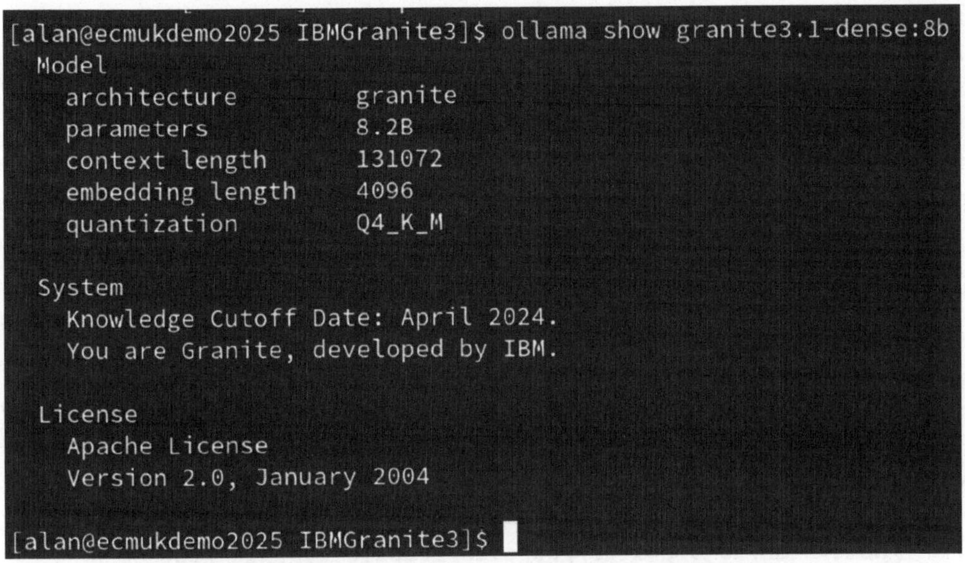

***Figure 4.46:** The details of a downloaded **ollama** model can be displayed using the **ollama show** command*

Granite Guardian

Granite Guardian is useful for risk detection use-cases, such as detecting harm-related risks within prompt text or model response; The **RAG** (retrieval-augmented generation) use-case where the guardian model assesses three key issues: Context relevance (whether the retrieved context is relevant to the query), groundedness (whether the response is accurate and faithful to the provided context), and answer relevance (whether the response directly addresses the user's query).

See https://github.com/ibm-granite/granite-guardian, which expands on IBM's statement that "*These models are trained on unique data comprising human annotations from socioeconomically diverse people and synthetic data informed by internal red-teaming.*"

The Risk list, covered for filtering data, is categorized into sections where the content is listed as "**`Harm`**", "**`Social Bias`**", "**`Profanity`**", "**`Sexual Content`**", "**`Unethical Behavior`**", "**`Violence`**", "**`Harm Engagement`**", "**`Evasiveness`**", "**`Jailbreaking`**" (deliberate attempts to circumnavigate AI safeguards), "RAG Safety" and "Hallucination" (where the AI response returned is false).

A QuickStart example is available at the link: https://www.ibm.com/granite/docs/models/guardian/ which covers the IBM Granite Guardian 3.2 version, overview and example Python code.

and

https://ibm.github.io/watsonx-prompt-lab/lab-2/ which covers the IBM watsonx-prompt-lab RAG LLM's capability for the retrieval of data from an external source.

and

https://www.ibm.com/think/tutorials/agentic-rag, which provides guidance for building a LangChain agentic RAG system, using Granite-3.0-8B-Instruct in watsonx.ai, including a Python code example.

We need to download the **Jupyter Notebook**, we found on the web in the **GitHub** path:

```
cookbooks/granite-guardian-3.1/quick_start_vllm.ipynb
```

Using:

```
git clone https://github.com/ibm-granite/granite-guardian.git
```

This creates the path and files as follows:

```
[alan@ecmukdemo2025 granite-guardian-3.1]$ pwd
/home/alan/IBMGranite3/guardian/granite-guardian/cookbooks/
granite-guardian-3.1
[alan@ecmukdemo2025 granite-guardian-3.1]$ ls
detailed_guide_vllm.ipynb  ibm_ai_risk_atlas.yml  quick_start_
vllm.ipynb  usage_governance_workflow_vllm.ipynb
```

The **Jupyter Lab .ipynb** files can be loaded using **jupyter lab** giving the web page in FireFox, as shown in *Figure 4.47*:

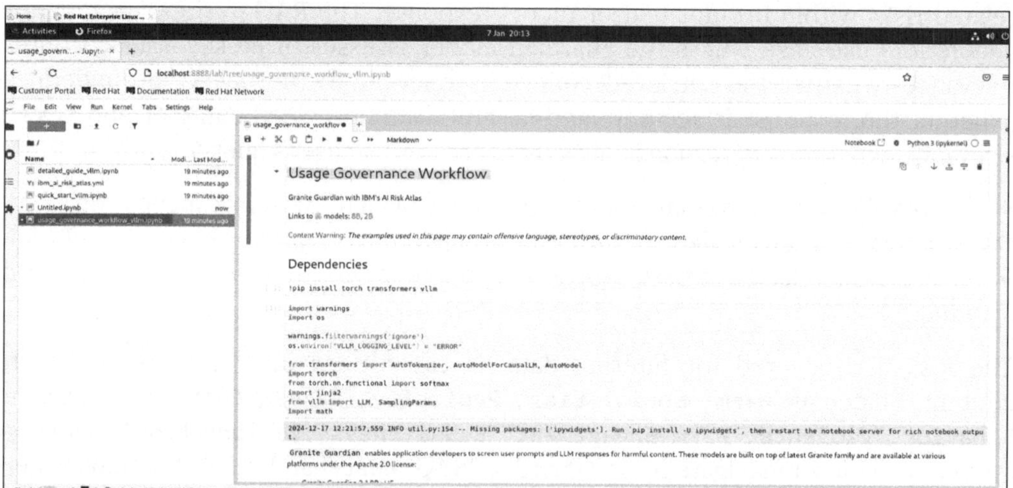

Figure 4.47: *The* **Jupyter Lab.ipynb** *files can be loaded using:* **jupyter lab** *giving a web page in* **FireFox**

Time Series Foundation Models (TSFM)

A time series model is a set of data points ordered in time, used in forecasting the future, for example, the weather or Financial Marketing trends.

See https://github.com/ibm-granite/granite-tsfm

The following URL link provides a long list of references: https://github.com/ibm-granite/granite-tsfm/wiki.

We have covered the use of this model in detail in the section entitled, "**Using IBM's Models**" of *Chapter 3, Setting up Granite 3.0 from GitHub.*

Geospatial Biomass

Geospatial biomass is the use of geospatial technology to assess and map biomass which is the living and dead plant material on the Earth's surface. The **IBM Granite Geospatial Biomass** uses an **AI** model trained on optical satellite imagery to predict the above ground biomass. This model can help estimate crop yields, monitor forest timber production, and track carbon sequestered by nature.

See:

https://github.com/ibm-granite/granite-geospatial-biomass

This has a link https://github.com/ibm-granite/granite-geospatial-biomass/blob/main/notebooks/agb_getting_started.ipynb

to Load a Python Language Jupyter Notebook to run working python code examples.

We used the commands, with the output, as illustrated in *Figure* 4.48:

```
mkdir granite-geospatial-biomass
git clone https://github.com/ibm-granite/granite-geospatial-bio-
mass.git
```

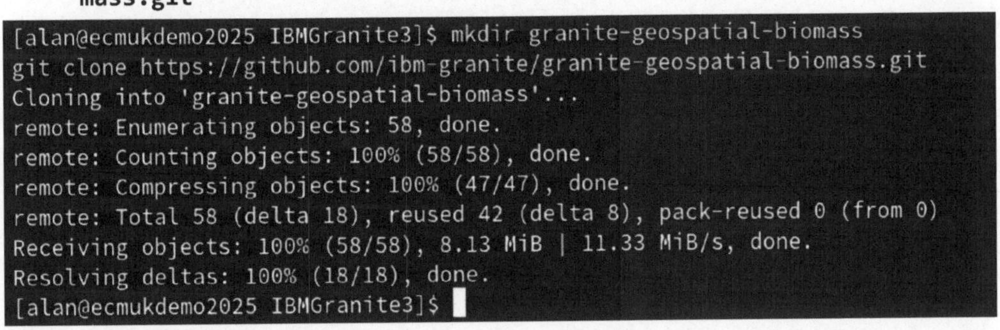

Figure 4.48: *We used the commands,* ***mkdir granite-geospatial-biomass*** *and* ***git clone https://github.com/ibm-granite/granite-geospatial-biomass.git***

From the **README.md** file we run:

```
cd /home/alan/IBMGranite3/granite-geospatial-biomass
pip install -e .
```

To install all necessary dependencies to run the notebook, using

```
cd /home/alan/IBMGranite3/granite-geospatial-biomass/notebooks
jupyter lab
```

After running the **tar.gz** file which downloads, as shown in *Figure 4.49*:

```
[5]: # Download dataset from Zenodo
     dataset_path = '../granite-geospatial-biomass-datasets.tar.gz'
     !wget "https://zenodo.org/records/12356481/files/granite-geospatial-biomass-datasets.tar.gz?download=1" -O {dataset_path}

     --2025-01-07 22:33:37--  https://zenodo.org/records/12356481/files/granite-geospatial-biomass-datasets.tar.gz?download=1
     Resolving zenodo.org (zenodo.org)... 188.185.48.194, 188.185.43.25, 188.185.45.92, ...
     connected. to zenodo.org (zenodo.org)|188.185.48.194|:443...
     HTTP request sent, awaiting response... 200 OK
     Length: 8151007565 (7.6G) [application/octet-stream]
     Saving to: '../granite-geospatial-biomass-datasets.tar.gz'

     ../granite-geospati 100%[===================>]   7.59G  7.56MB/s    in 12m 56s

     2025-01-07 22:46:33 (10.0 MB/s) - '../granite-geospatial-biomass-datasets.tar.gz' saved [8151007565/8151007565]

[6]: # Unpack compressed dataset
     target_directory = '../'
     !tar -xf {dataset_path} --directory {target_directory}
```

Figure 4.49: *Install the dependencies for notebook, extracting file* ***granite-geospatial-biomass-datasets.tar.gz***

In a terminal window, we can unpack the file using:

```
cd /home/alan/IBMGranite3/granite-geospatial-biomass/notebooks/
granite-geospatial-biomass
tar -xvf granite-geospatial-biomass-datasets.tar.gz
```

See also:

https://ibm.github.io/terratorch/quick_start/

The above URL recommends that the python versions should be 3.10 <= Python <= 3.12.

Also to get started, PyTorch should be preinstalled.

Since we were currently using **Python 3.9.21** (checked using **python -V**), we did not attempt to run this model, as there are known dependencies that require **Python 3.11**. However, there are useful descriptions of the graphical processing which can be used with an **AI** model in the notebook, **agb_getting_started.ipynb**.

Conclusion

This chapter covered the use of **Watsonx Code Assistant Individual**, with the **MS VS Code–an AI** coding companion using **IBM Granite** large language models. The **AI** coding assistant for programming languages was demonstrated with examples of Java and Python code.

In the next *Chapter 5, Advanced Prompt Engineering*, we cover IBM Granite Workshop labs setup using **Python code** within **Jupyter notebooks**. These notebooks can be run on a local workstation, or remotely using the **Google Colab** service, and this is used to demonstrate the prompt engineering functionality available with **IBM Granite 3.0**.

Points to Remember

- **IBM Granite.Code** is now renamed as **IBM watsonx Code Assistant Individual**. For individual users, it is still available with **Ollama**, using the **MS VS Code IDE**.
- If you wish to change the default model file location, for the **IBM Granite 3.0** model downloads, using **ollama**, you can do so by setting the `OLLAMA_MODELS` environment variable to the desired directory.
- To delete all the existing docker images for a clean start use:
  `docker rmi $(docker images -q). .`

Multiple Choice Questions

1. Which one of the following **IBM Granite Model** versions are recommended for **MS VS Code** use?
   a. `ollama pull granite-code:34b`
   b. `ollama pull granite3.1-dense:8b`
   c. `ollama pull granite-code:3b`
   d. `ollama pull granite-embedding:30m`
2. Which of the following Linux commands installs the **code** system?
   a. `pip install -e .`
   b. `sudo yum install java-17-openjdk`
   c. `sudo dnf install code`
   d. `code --install-extension continue.continue`

3. Which one of the following IBM Granite 3.1 models is the largest?
    a. Granite 3.1 2b (`ollama pull granite3.1-dense:2b`)
    b. Granite 3.1 3b-a800m (`ollama pull granite3.1-moe:3b`)
    c. Granite 3.1 8 (`ollama pull granite3.1-dense:8b`)
    d. Granite 3.1 1b-a400m (`ollama pull granite3.1-moe:1b`)
4. Which of the following IBM Granite models would be most useful as the basis of a ChatBot for a sales website?
    a. IBM Granite for Language
    b. IBM Granite for Code
    c. IBM Granite for Time Series
    d. IBM Granite for GeoSpatial
5. Which one of the following IBM Granite models would be most useful for forecasting energy demands?
    a. IBM Granite for Language
    b. IBM Granite for Code
    c. IBM Granite for Time Series
    d. IBM Granite for GeoSpatial

Answers

1. b
2. c
3. c
4. a
5. c

Questions

1. Outline the procedure which must be used to download and install the Continue AI helper system add-on into the Microsoft VS Code IDE program.
2. Describe the installation of the prerequisite software systems which are required by the **docker (podman)** container system for the download and running of the container based Ollama system.

3. What docker command would you use to display the details of the installed `granite3-moe:1b` model?
4. What are the advantages of using the latest Mixture of Expert (MoE) LLM models?
5. In what areas of AI processing would you employ the IBM Granite 3.0 Guardian LLM models?

Key Terms

- **LLM**: Large Language Model
- **AI**: Artificial Intelligence Software that mimics the responses, you might expect to the questions supplied by a human operator.
- **Python:** A high-level, object-oriented programming language, with many libraries freely available for supporting mathematic, graphical and AI development functions.
- **NVIDIA GPU:** A hardware graphics processing unit, providing a high-speed processing resource. Using their high performance capabilities, they are ideal for developing and using AI Large Language Models.
- **RHEL:** RedHat Enterprise Linux. A commercial version of the Linux Operating System, now owned by **IBM**.
- **VS Code: Visual Studio Code**, is a free **IDE** system, developed by Microsoft, and available as Open Source, on the main operating system platforms of Linux, macOS, and MS Windows.

  There is a Microsoft License, at https://code.visualstudio.com/License (basically giving the user full free access, but with no express warranties, guarantees or conditions for its use).

CHAPTER 5
Advanced Prompt Engineering

Introduction

This chapter covers an overview of the **IBM Granite Workshop** labs setup using **Python** code and **Jupyter** notebooks for prompt engineering. It is also possible to customise the **IBM Granite LLM** model outputs programmatically by using a prompt template which we describe in detail in this Chapter.

The notebooks can be run on a local workstation or remotely using the **Google Colab** service to demonstrate the prompt engineering functionality available with **IBM Granite 3.0**.

In December 2024, IBM released the **IBM Granite 3.1 version**– the latest update to their Granite series of open source language models, with significant performance improvements and new features.

Starting with **IBM Granite 3.1**, the context windows have been increased to 128K for all models.

IBM have also added a new function to identify hallucination detection, so users have more control over **Agentic AI** workflows. There are also four additional IBM Granite embedding models offering multilingual support for 12 different languages.

IBM Granite 3.1 represents IBM's third generation of large language models, released as open source, under an **Apache 2.0** license and matching top performance on general, enterprise, and safety benchmarks. Among other features, **IBM Granite 3.1** models provide a better way to handle **RAG** and function-calling tasks. **IBM Granite 3.1** instruction models are fine-tuned from **IBM Granite-3.1** base models using a combination of open source instruction datasets with permissive license and internally collected synthetic datasets tailored for solving long context problems. The **IBM Granite 3.1** language model family includes:

- **Granite Dense:** High performance "*workhorse*" models designed for enterprise AI.

- **Granite MoE**: Inference-efficient Mixture of Experts (**MoE**) models ideal for local server applications or **CPU**-based deployments.
- **Granite Accelerator:** Speculative decoding companion model for increased inference speed and lower latency.

Structure

In this chapter, we will discuss the following topics:

- Connecting to `watsonx.ai`
    - Creating a sandbox Project in `watsonx.ai`
- Prompt Engineering
- Adjusting the **LLM** Model's Behavior
    - Transfer Learning by Combining Two Pre-trained **LLM** Datasets
    - Developing a Local Server **agentic RAG System** using **IBM Granite 3.1**
- IBM Cloud Pak for Data -`Watsonx`

Connecting to `watsonx.ai`

The **IBM Granite 3.0** language models can be accessed through **IBM Watsonx.ai** at their **GitHub** location.

(See https://github.com/ibm-granite-community/granite-snack-cookbook/blob/main/recipes/AI-Agents/Agentic_RAG.ipynb)

After using the clone command:

```
git clone https://github.com/ibm-granite-community/granite
-snack-cookbook.git
```

We can launch the Notebook example as follows:

```
[alan@ecmukdemo2025]$ cd /home/alan/granite-snack-cookbook/
recipes/AI-Agents
[alan@ecmukdemo2025 AI-Agents]$ ls
Agentic_RAG.ipynb  travel_planner_agent.ipynb
[alan@ecmukdemo2025 AI-Agents]$ jupyter lab.
```

From this, we select the `Agentic_RAG.ipynb` notebook file, double clicking it from the launched **FireFox** Jupyter web page file list panel.

(Or we can use the link directly in FireFox using:
`http://localhost:8888/lab/tree/Agentic_RAG.ipynb )`

Creating a sandbox Project in `watsonx.ai`

First, we created an IBM account, and then used it to log into **IBM Watsonx** using https://dataplatform.cloud.ibm.com/login , as shown in *Figure* 5.1:

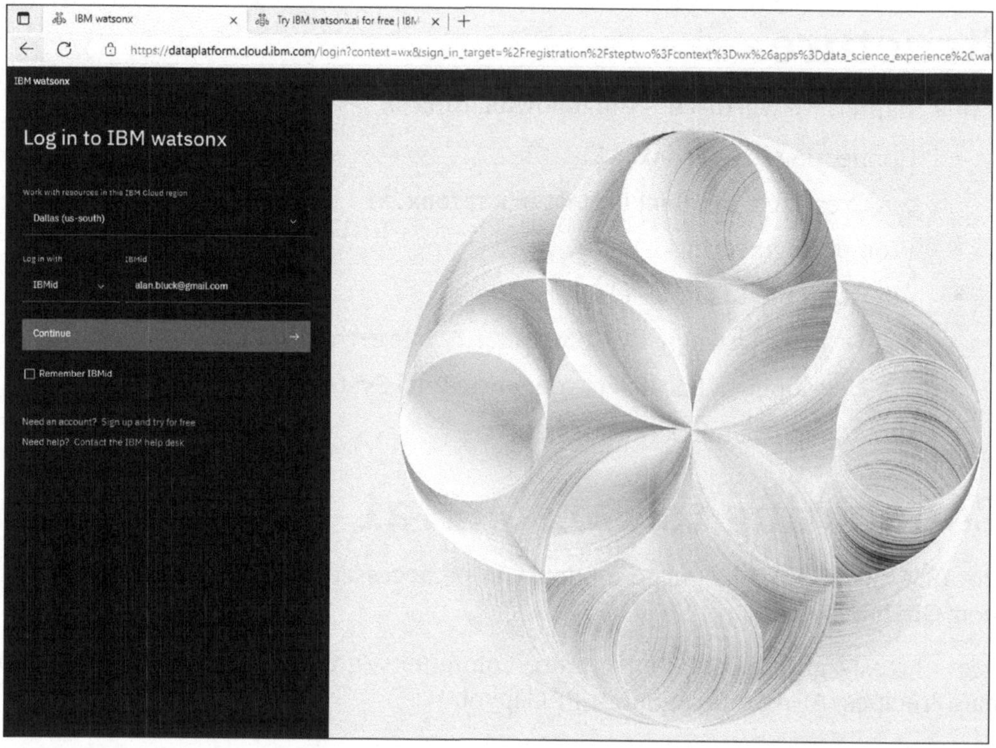

Figure 5.1: *First, we created an IBM account and then used it to log into* **IBM Watsonx**

A free trial is also available at

https://dataplatform.cloud.ibm.com/registration/stepone?context=wx

For the terms of service link on login page displays the IBM Terms text, which is available in 17 languages (including French).

```
https://www.ibm.com/support/customer/csol/terms/?id=i126-9640&l-
c=en#detail-document
```

As of March, 2025, a typical Watsonx AI basic monthly cost in the UK for the required components are:

```
Block Storage for VPC - General Purpose Tier Gen2
(eu-gb) GIGABYTE_HOURS   £  1.10 + VAT
Image Service for VPC - Standard Gen2 -          (eu-gb)
GIGABYTE_HOURS   £  0.06 + VAT
Virtual Server for VPC - Gen3 GPU  gx3-64x320x4l4 (eu-gb)
```

```
Instance Hours    £237.23 + VAT
Floating IP for VPC - Standard Gen2 -                 (eu-gb)
INSTANCES         £  0.75 + VAT
Cloud Object Storage - Standard -                     (eu-gb) Standard
storage  £  0.02 + VAT
```

The link provides a description page for the use of **IBM Watsonx,** entitled, **IBM Watsonx as a Service,** as shown in *Figure 5.2*:

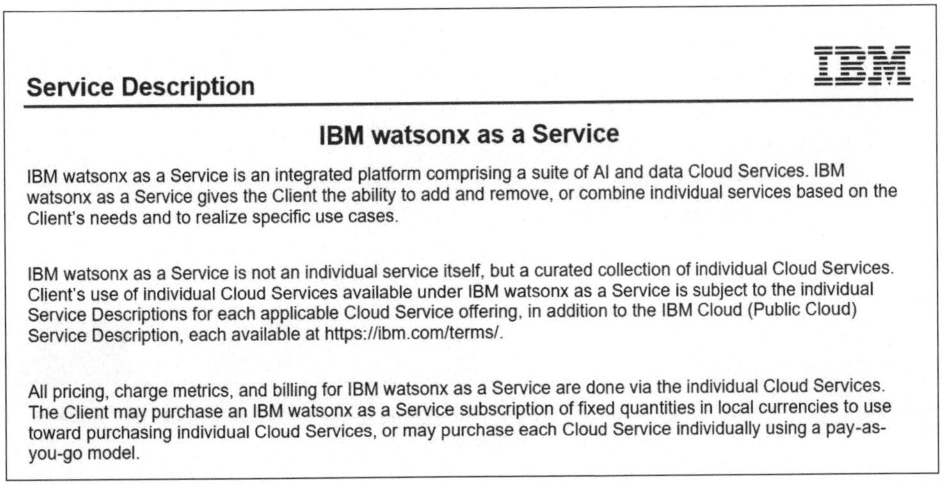

Service Description

IBM

IBM watsonx as a Service

IBM watsonx as a Service is an integrated platform comprising a suite of AI and data Cloud Services. IBM watsonx as a Service gives the Client the ability to add and remove, or combine individual services based on the Client's needs and to realize specific use cases.

IBM watsonx as a Service is not an individual service itself, but a curated collection of individual Cloud Services. Client's use of individual Cloud Services available under IBM watsonx as a Service is subject to the individual Service Descriptions for each applicable Cloud Service offering, in addition to the IBM Cloud (Public Cloud) Service Description, each available at https://ibm.com/terms/.

All pricing, charge metrics, and billing for IBM watsonx as a Service are done via the individual Cloud Services. The Client may purchase an IBM watsonx as a Service subscription of fixed quantities in local currencies to use toward purchasing individual Cloud Services, or may purchase each Cloud Service individually using a pay-as-you-go model.

***Figure 5.2:** The IBM terms of service using the link on login page displays the IBM Terms text*

We can then select the tick-box to agree to the **`terms`**, the **`Date Use Policy`** and the **`Cookie Use`**, as shown in *Figure 5.3*:

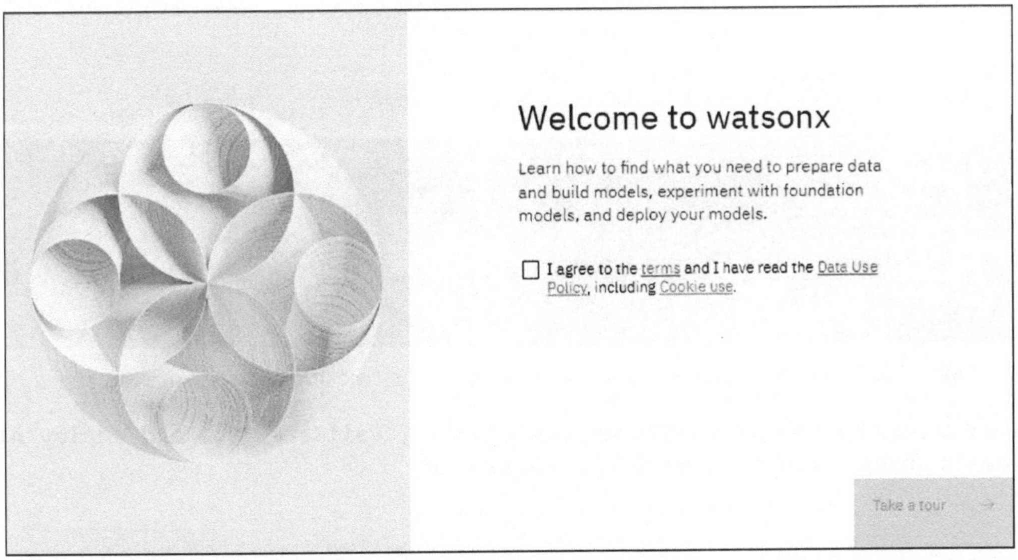

Figure 5.3:** We can then select the tick-box to agree to the **terms**, the **Date Use Policy** and the **Cookie Use

After ticking the box to agree to all the terms of use, we can select the "**`Take a tour`**" command in the bottom left of the screen, as shown in *Figure* 5.4:

Figure 5.4: *After ticking the box to agree to all the terms of use, we can select the "**Take a tour**" command*

This prompts us to select a task based on the type of process, we are interested in, as illustrated in *Figure* 5.5:

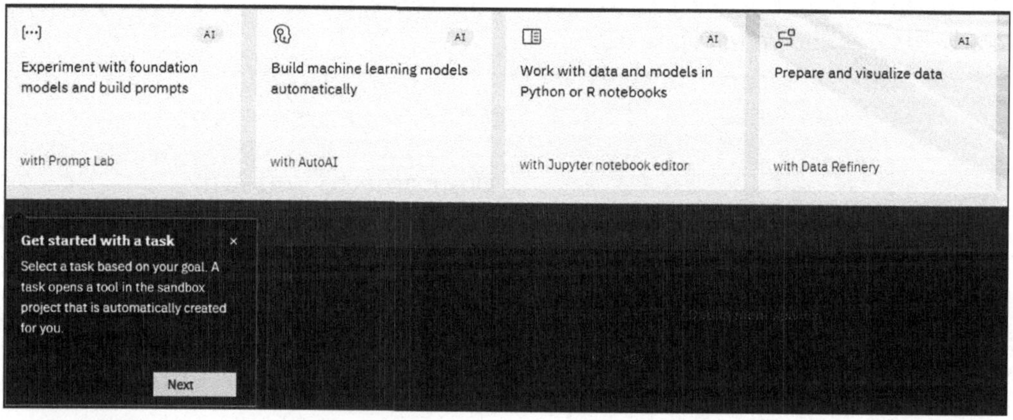

Figure 5.5: *We are prompted to select a task based on the type of process, we are interested*

We can select a number of tasks, such as to "**`Train, validate tune and deploy AI models`**" (using Prompt Lab) as shown in *Figure* 5.6:

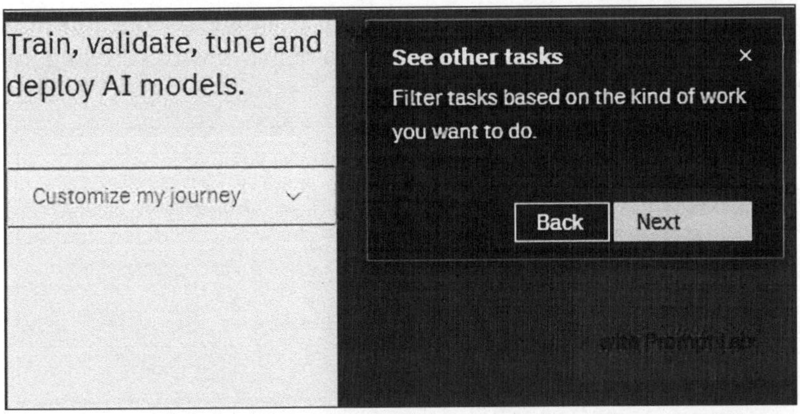

Figure 5.6: *We can select a number of tasks, such as to "**Train, validate tune and deploy AI models**"*

As a test example, we then created a structured prompt to ask the question:

Have you got a java code method for a binary search program?

This initially provided the text as follows:

```
Yes, here is a Java program for a binary search:

    public static int binarySearch(int[] arr, int target) {
        int left = 0;
        int right = arr.length - 1;

        while (left <= right) {
            int mid = left + (right - left) / 2;

            if (arr[mid] == target) {
                return mid; // target found
            }

            if (arr[mid] < target) {
                left = mid + 1; // search in the right half
            } else {
                right = mid - 1; // search in the left half
            }
        }

        return -1; // target not found
    }
```

This can then be trained for further responses. For example, the question and response can be entered, using the **Freeform** mode which displays with scrolling, the result in *Figure 5.7*:

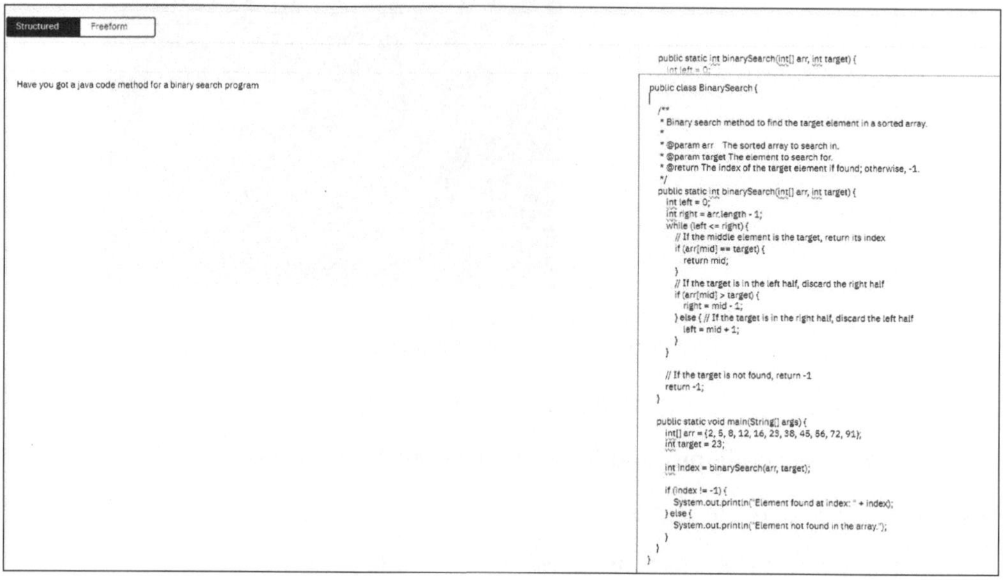

Figure 5.7: *Using the Freeform option displays a more complete response*

Note: *There are also* **Jupyter NoteBook Python** *language for AI and Data resource examples (over 460 scrollable panels) on the Resources link available,* "**`Resource hub | IBM Cloud Pak for Data`**", *at:*

https://eu-gb.dataplatform.cloud.ibm.com/gallery?context=cpdaas .

We go on to select the Work with data panel, as shown in *Figure 5.8*:

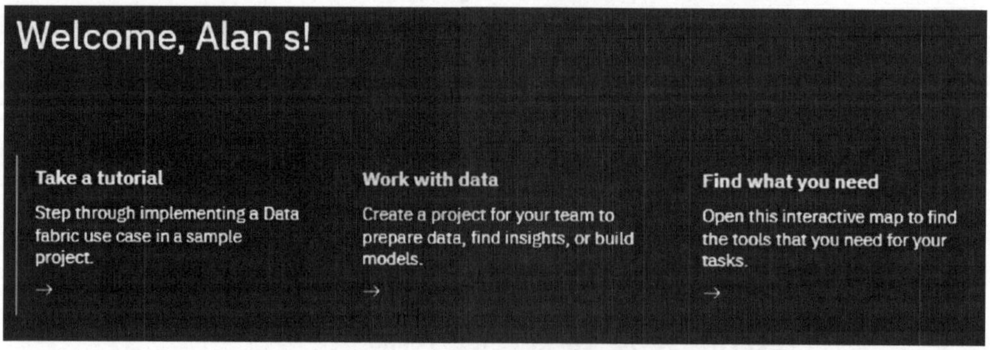

Figure 5.8: *We go on to select the Work with data link*

We selected the **Create a project** link, which is highlighted to show the Project creation web page, as shown in *Figure 5.9*:

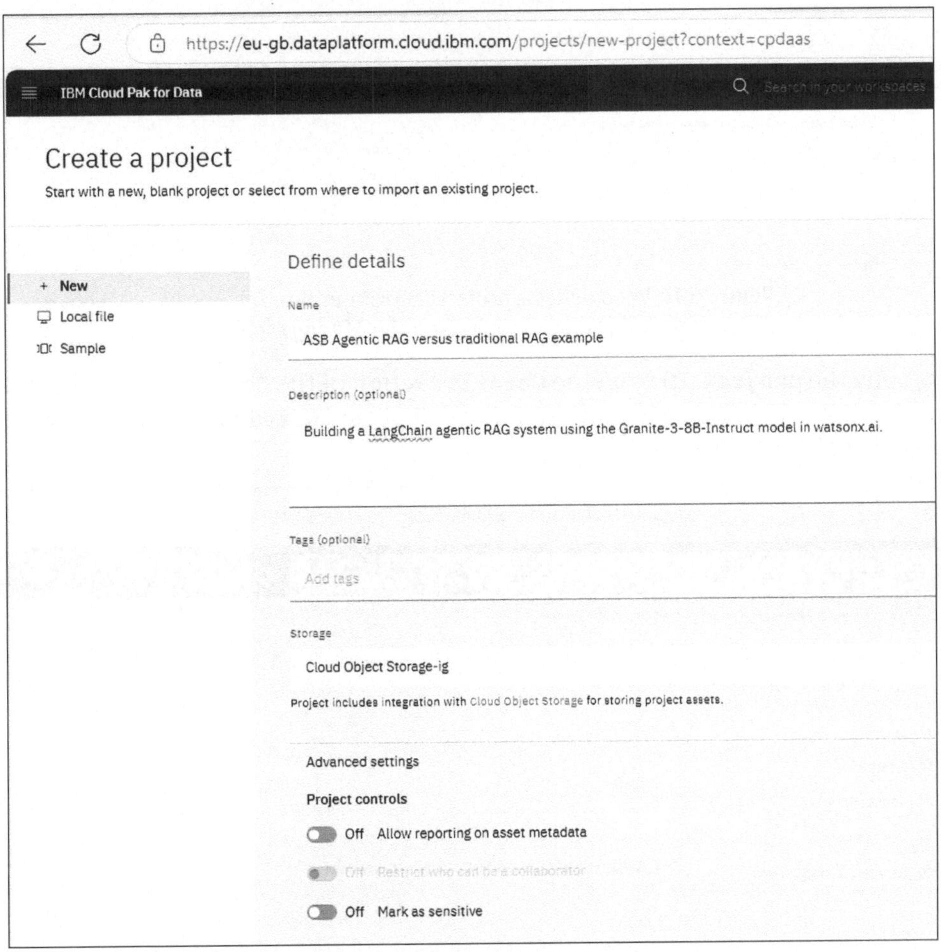

Figure 5.9: *We selected the Create a project link, highlighted to show the Project creation web page*

We, then select the bottom left **Create** command, as shown in *Figure 5.10*:

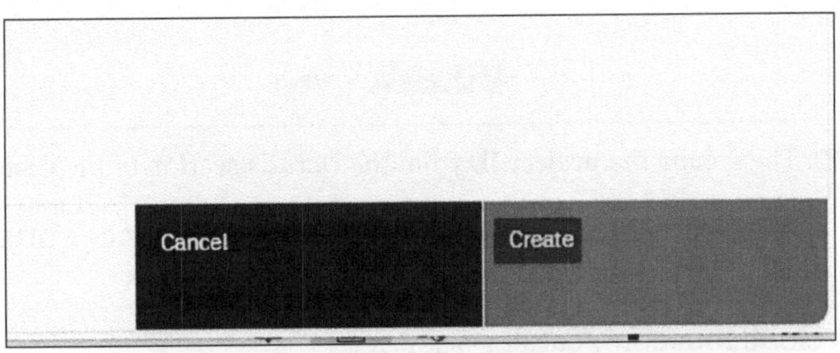

Figure 5.10: *We select the bottom left* ***Create*** *command*

We can get a project ID from within the newly created project by selecting the **Manage** tab, as shown in *Figure 5.11*.

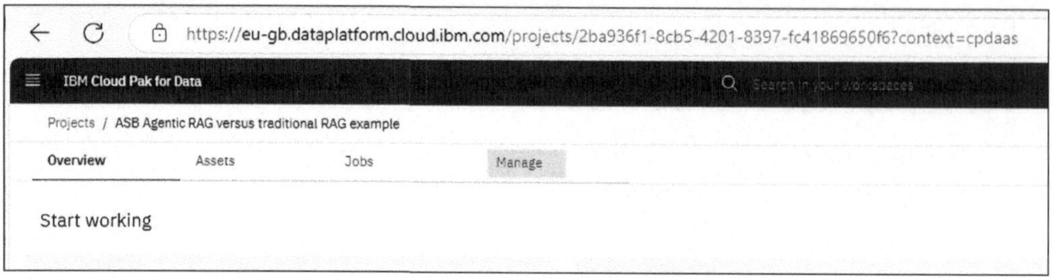

Figure 5.11: *We can get a project ID from within the newly created project by selecting the* **Manage** *tab*

Then, copy the **project ID** from the **Details** section of the **General** page, as shown in *Figure 5.12*. You need this **project ID** for the **Jupyter NoteBook** tutorial (**2ba936f1-8cbX-XXX-XXXX-XX41869650f6**).

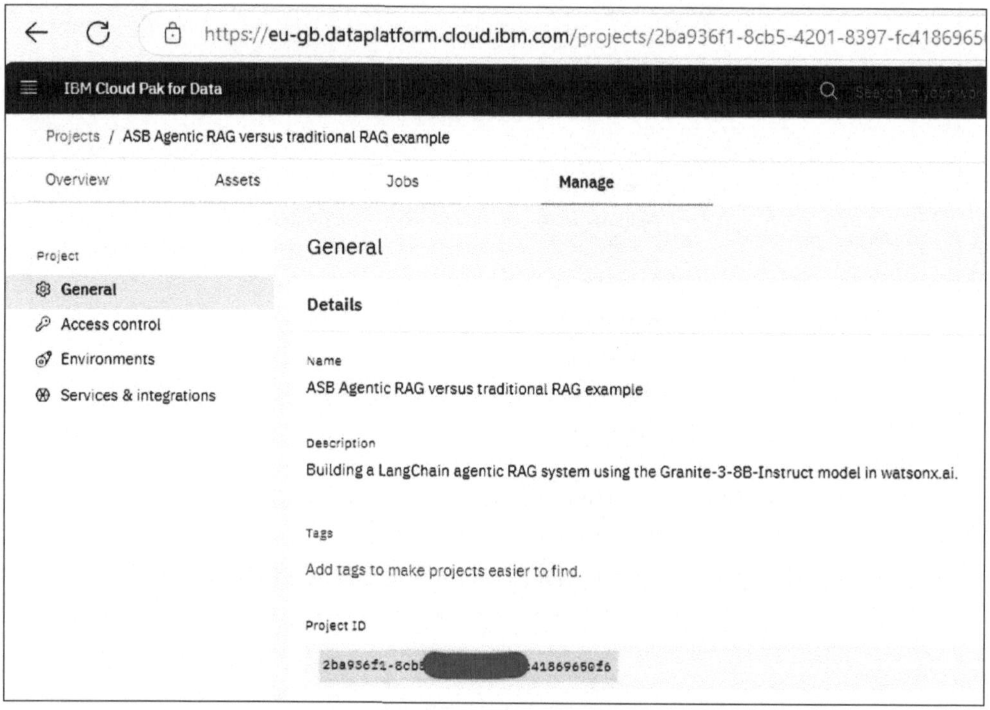

Figure 5.12: *Then, copy the* **project ID** *from the* **Details** *section of the* **General** *page*

1. Create a **Watsonx Machine Learning** service instance. https://cloud.ibm.com/catalog/services/watson-machine-learning

   https://cloud.ibm.com/catalog#services

   Scroll down to select the service highlighted in *Figure 5.13*:

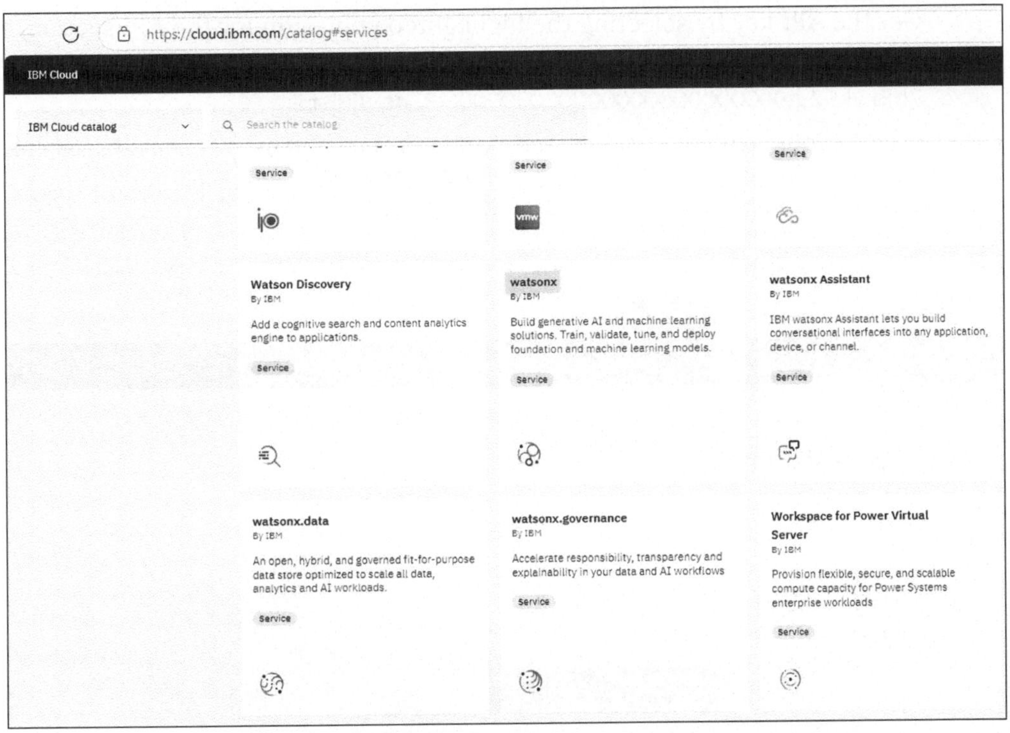

Figure 5.13: *Create a* **Watsonx Machine Learning** *service instance*

2. Select the appropriate region, and choose the **`Lite`** plan, which is a free instance, as highlighted in *Figure 5.14*:

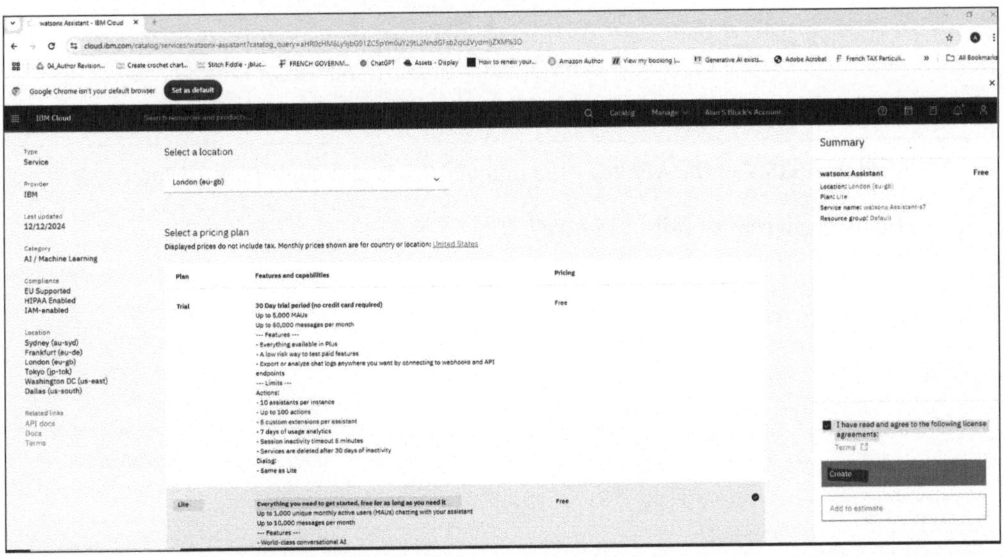

Figure 5.14: *Select the appropriate region, and choose the* **Lite** *plan, which is a free instance*

Get the **API** key by selecting the highlighted copy icon for the **API** section, as shown in *Figure* 5.15:

`7hFxvk92ueXXXXXXXXXXXXXXXXXXXXXXX-R3dqvCHBmi`

(The unique URL is also copied for later use: https://api.eu-gb.assistant.watson.cloud.ibm.com/instances/1f4fdXXXXXXXXX-be45-eaXXXXXX0a)

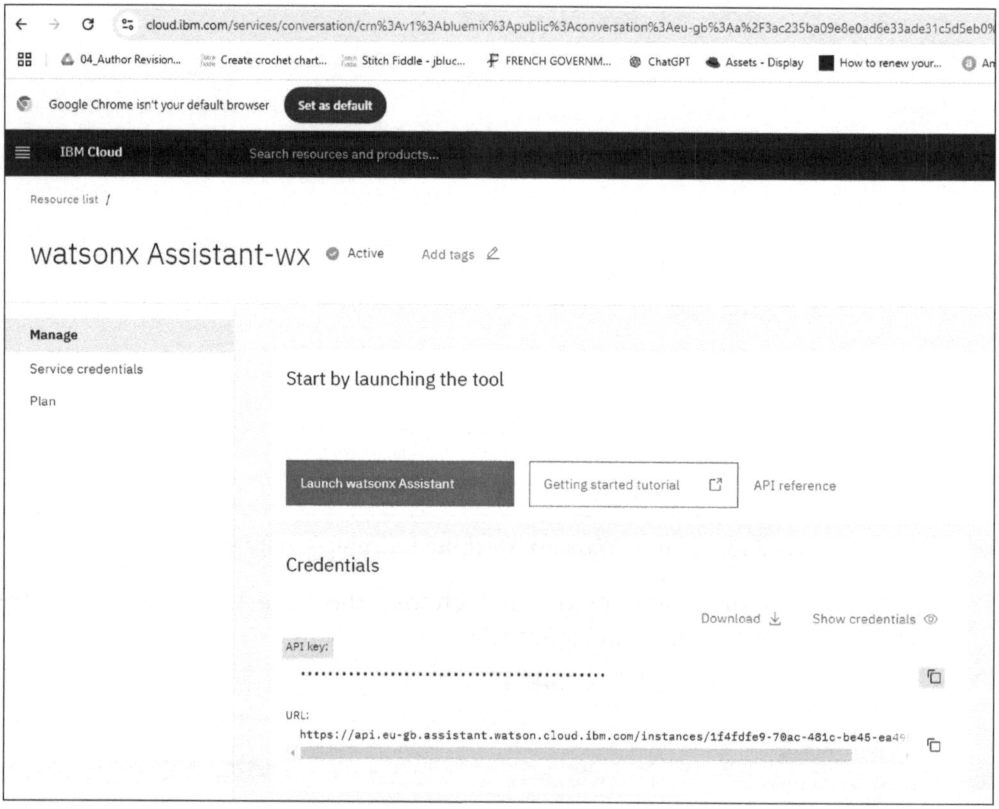

***Figure* 5.15:** *Get the* **API** *key - the unique* **URL** *is also copied for use later*

3. This is shown in detail in *Figure* 5.16:

Figure 5.16: *The* **URL** *and* **API Key** *copy icons are shown in detail*

Dependencies

We have to associate the **API key** we created with the **Project Key**, which we copied after creating a new IBM Cloud project, following the procedure available in the link:

https://dataplatform.cloud.ibm.com/docs/content/wsj/getting-started/assoc-services.html?context=cpdaas

Then, using our **`Admin`** user role in the project to add an associated service, we select the project URL link that we displayed earlier:

https://eu-gb.dataplatform.cloud.ibm.com/projects/2ba93XX-XXX-XXX-XXX-fc41869650f6

Then, we can add the **`API service`** to the project using the following steps:

1. Go to the project's **`Manage`** tab, and select the **`Services and integrations`** menu from the left panel to show the page.

   (This initially displays **`No Services`**, in the middle of the web page because we have to associate the **`API service,`** we created.)

2. In the **`IBM Services`** section, click **`Associate Service`**.

3. Select the service instance, tick-box (named **`watsonx Assistant-wx`**), we created earlier, and click **`Associate`**.

This then updates the Tab heading to **`IBM Services(1)`** for our project.

Next, we followed the steps to create a new notebook in our project:

1. In the project, on the **`Assets`** tab, click **`New asset`** > **`Work with data and models in Python or R notebooks`**.
2. Optionally, type a name and description.
3. Select a runtime environment for the notebook.
    a. To run Decision Optimization models, we need a deployment space that is associated with our project's Machine Learning service.
    b. We, then select the command, **`Add a Machine Learning service.`**
4. We also need to create a storage space for our Decision-making example.
5. Next, we follow the tutorial, which we cover in the last section of this chapter, *IBM Cloud Pak for Data - Watsonx.*

Prompt Engineering

Prompt engineering is the way to structure the prompts for an AI instruction to achieve the best possible response from a Large Language Model (LLM). One method of obtaining a useful response from an AI is to use Chain-of-Thought (CoT) prompting. This technique, introduced by Google Research, allows LLMs to resolve a problem by using a series of intermediate prompt steps, submitted to the AI before it provides the final answer. (Google found that simply appending the words "*Let's think step-by-step*" was sufficient to improve the AI response).

Another emerging feature of the currently released LLMs is the use of In-context learning, which allows a model to temporarily learn from prompts.

The **IBM Granite 3.0** models can be used for general questions, using two prompting methods locally, on our **`RedHat Linux RHEL 9.2`** server, through the **Ollama AI** support system:

1. Using the **API REST** interface, as shown in *Figure* 5.17:

```
curl http://localhost:11434/api/generate -d '{
  "model": "granite3-moe:1b",
  "prompt": "Why is the sky blue?"
}'
```

Figure 5.17: *Using the* **API REST** *interface*

This provides a response with the breakdown of each token processed, which we have highlighted, and the statistics, as shown in *Figure* 5.18:

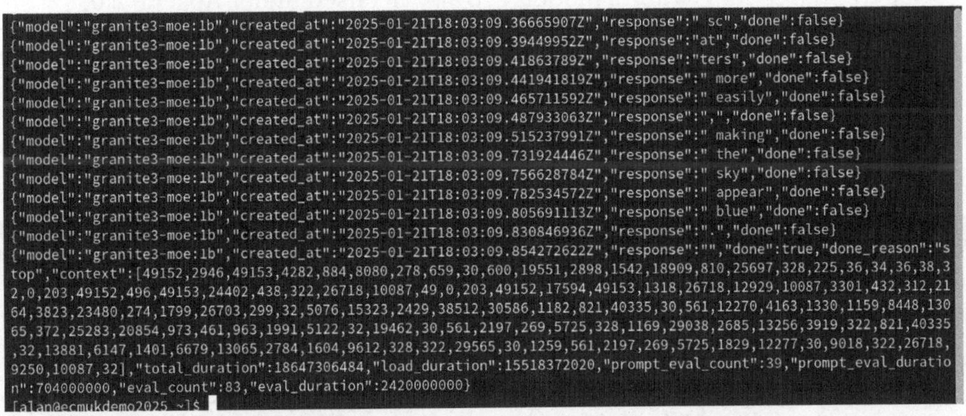

Figure 5.18: *The response statistics are displayed*

2. The same question can, alternatively, be prompted directly by using the **`ollama run`** command, which provides the response unwrapped, as shown in *Figure* 5.19:

```
ollama run granite3-moe:1b
```

This is always entered after the **>>> Ollama AI** prompt, in the form:

```
Question:
Why is the sky blue?

Answer:
```

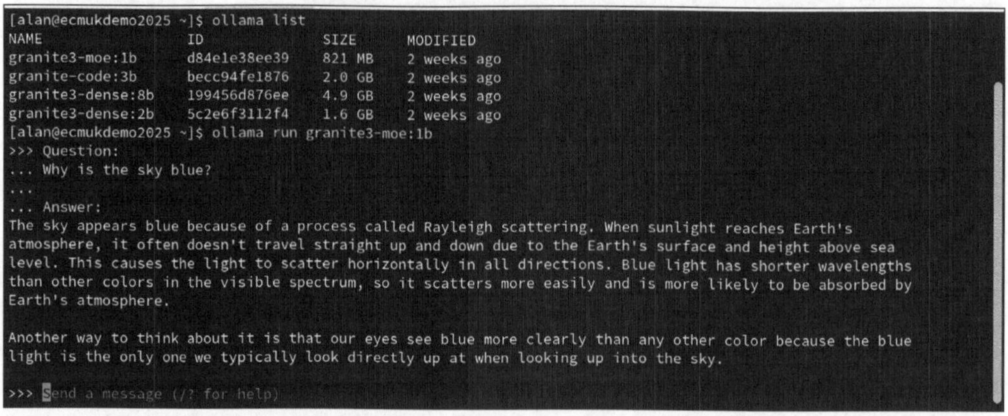

Figure 5.19: *The response, unwrapped by the* ***Ollama AI*** *is output to the* ***Linux*** *command window*

Adjusting the LLM Model's Behavior

The latest (released on December 2024) **IBM Granite 3.1** models were trained with 12 trillion tokens, using 12 modern foreign languages and 116 programming languages. These open-source IBM Granite models are also licensed under **Apache 2.0**.

The latest of these models (updated January 18th, 2025) was loaded down to the **Ollama AI** using

```
ollama run granite3.1-dense:8b-instruct-q4_0
```

This download is illustrated in *Figure* 5.20:

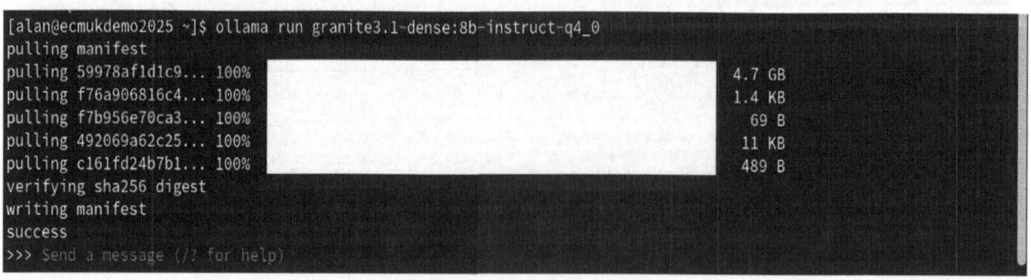

Figure 5.20: *The latest of these models (updated on January 18th, 2025) was loaded down to the Ollama AI*

(see https://ollama.com/library/granite3.1-dense:8b-instruct-q4_0)

IBM recommend (See: https://www.ibm.com/granite/docs/models/granite/) the system prompt for **IBM Granite 3.1** models as follows.

For Multi-turn conversation prompts:

```
<|start_of_role|>system<|end_of_role|>Knowledge Cutoff Date: April
2024.
Today's Date: January 22, 2025.
You are Granite, developed by IBM. You are a helpful AI assistant.
<|end_of_text|>
<|start_of_role|>user<|end_of_role|>Please list an IBM Research
laboratory located in the United States.<|end_of_text|>
<|start_of_role|>assistant<|end_of_role|>
```

Important: *Prompts built via transformers library using the* ***apply_chate_template*** *function, will automatically include the recommended system prompt, as long as users do not specify a custom system prompt.*

- IBM *recommends the use of this system prompt to obtain the best performance from the* **IBM Granite 3.1** *models.*
- *Even though* IBM *does not restrict defining custom system prompts, using a non-default system prompt may have unexpected results.*

IBM also recommends using a specific system prompt for function-calling tasks.

It recommends that users use this prompt to obtain the best performance.

The turn type for the list of tools has changed from **available_tools** (**IBM Granite 3.0**) to just **tools** (**IBM Granite 3.1**).

IBM slightly changed the schema to define the list of tools for **IBM Granite 3.1** models (similar to the concepts used by **Agentic AI** which uses a mix of technologies, including Machine Learning (ML), Large Language Models (LLMs), and Natural Language Processing (NLP)). Tools are now an array of dictionaries with a structure that includes the tool name, description, and the required arguments.

The format of the assistant responses containing function calls also changed for **IBM Granite 3.1 models.** The tool call is now pre-pended by a **<tool_call>** token.

The following is the IBM test example (updated with the current run date) of how a function-calling prompt with **IBM Granite 3.1 models** should be formatted.

```
<|start_of_role|>system<|end_of_role|>Knowledge Cutoff Date: April
2024.
Today's Date: January 22, 2025.
You are Granite, developed by IBM. You are a helpful AI assistant
with access to the following tools. When a tool is required to
answer the user's query, respond with <|tool_call|> followed by a
JSON list of tools used. If a tool does not exist in the provided
```

```
list of tools, notify the user that you do not have the ability
to fulfill the request.<|end_of_text|>
<|start_of_role|>tools<|end_of_role|>[
    {
        "name": "get_current_weather",
        "description": "Get the current weather",
        "arguments": {
            "location": {
                "description": "The city and state, e.g. San
Francisco, CA"
            }
        }
    },
    {
        "name": "get_stock_price",
        "description": "Retrieves the current stock price for a
given ticker symbol. The ticker symbol must be a valid symbol for
a publicly traded company on a major US stock exchange like NYSE
or NASDAQ. The tool will return the latest trade price in USD.
It should be used when the user asks about the current or most
recent price of a specific stock. It will not provide any other
information about the stock or company.",
        "arguments": {
            "ticker": {
                "description": "The stock ticker symbol, e.g.
AAPL for Apple Inc."
            }
        }
    }
]<|end_of_text|>
<|start_of_role|>user<|end_of_role|>What's the current weather in
New York?<|end_of_text|>
<|start_of_role|>assistant<|end_of_role|>
```

IBM state that this should give the response as follows, which it does, as also highlighted in *Figure 5.21*:

```
<tool_call>[{"name": "get_current_weather", "arguments":
{"location": "New York"}}]<|end_of_text|>
```

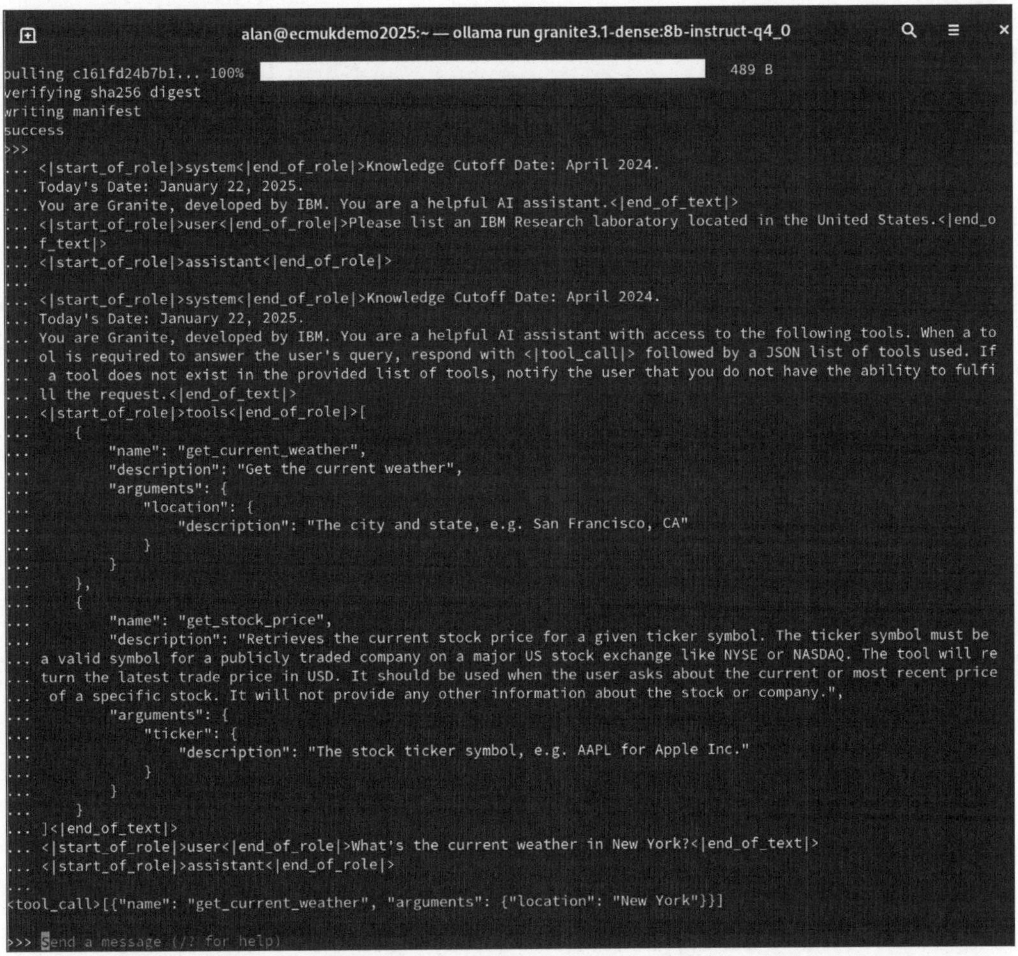

Figure 5.21: *The expected response for the prompt setup text is highlighted*

For IBM's **Retrieval Augmented Generation** (**RAG**) models, the **RAG** generation tasks, have the following updates:

IBM recommends that users use the official system prompt for **RAG** generation tasks with **IBM Granite 3.1** models.

IBM Granite 3.1 models provide a much easier way to handle documents. Documents are no longer required to be included in the user query. Instead, the turn type of **documents** can be used to provide the list of documents, the model should process. Inside the list of documents, a header of **Document 0, Document 1, ..., Document N** signals the beginning of the document, and a line break signals the end.

IBM Granite 3.1 models also provide a better way to handle questions which are independent of the documents provided. The AI assistant returns a default message if the question cannot be answered with the documents provided.

The following IBM example to illustrate this, shows the format for **RAG** inference with **IBM Granite 3.1** models.

```
<|start_of_role|>system<|end_of_role|>Knowledge Cutoff Date: April
2024.
Today's Date: January 22, 2025.
You are Granite, developed by IBM. Write the response to the
user's input by strictly aligning with the facts in the provided
documents. If the information needed to answer the question is
not available in the documents, inform the user that the question
cannot be answered based on the available data.<|end_of_text|>
<|start_of_role|>documents<|end_of_role|>Document 0
Bridget Jones is a binge drinking and chain smoking thirty-some-
thing British woman trying to keep her love life in order while
also dealing with her job as a publisher. When she attends a
Christmas party with her parents, they try to set her up with
their neighbours' son, Mark. After being snubbed by Mark, she
starts to fall for her boss Daniel, a handsome man who begins to
send her suggestive e-mails that leads to a dinner date. Daniel
 reveals that he and Mark attended college together, in that time
Mark had an affair with his fiancée. Bridget decides to get a new
job as a TV presenter after finding Daniel being frisky with a
colleague. At a dinner party, she runs into Mark who expresses
his affection for her, Daniel claims he wants Bridget back, the
two fight over her and Bridget must make a decision who she wants
to be with.

Document 1
Bridget is currently living a happy life with her lawyer boy-
friend Mark Darcy, however not only does she start to become
threatened and jealous of Mark's new young intern, she is angered
by the fact Mark is a Conservative voter. With so many issues
already at hand, things get worse for Bridget as her ex-lover,
Daniel Cleaver, re-enters her life; the only help she has are her
friends and her reliable diary.,

Document 2
Bridget Jones is struggling with her current state of life,
including her break up with her love Mark Darcy. As she pushes
 forward and works hard to find fulfilment in her life seems to do
wonders until she meets a dashing and handsome American named
Jack Quant. Things from then on go great, until she discovers
that she is pregnant but the biggest twist of all, she does not
know if Mark or Jack is the father of her child.<|end_of_text|>
<|start_of_role|>user<|end_of_role|>Could you please tell me what
the first Bridget Jones's movie is about?, please be brief in your
response.<|end_of_text|>
```

```
<|start_of_role|>assistant<|end_of_role|>Bridget Jones's first
movie revolves around a thirty-something British woman, Bridget,
who is a binge drinker and chain smoker. She's a publisher trying
to balance her love life and career. The story unfolds when her
parents set her up with Mark, her boss Daniel starts sending
suggestive emails, and Bridget must decide between Mark and Dan-
iel after they both express interest in her.<|end_of_text|>
<|start_of_role|>user<|end_of_role|>What's the current weather in
New York?<|end_of_text|>
<|start_of_role|>assistant<|end_of_role|>
<tool_call>[{"name": "get_current_weather", "arguments":
{"location": "New York"}}]

(Note: The actual weather query would be handled by an external
weather API, but this is just a placeholder.)

>>> Send a message (/? for help)
```

The above response is highlighted in *Figure* 5.22:

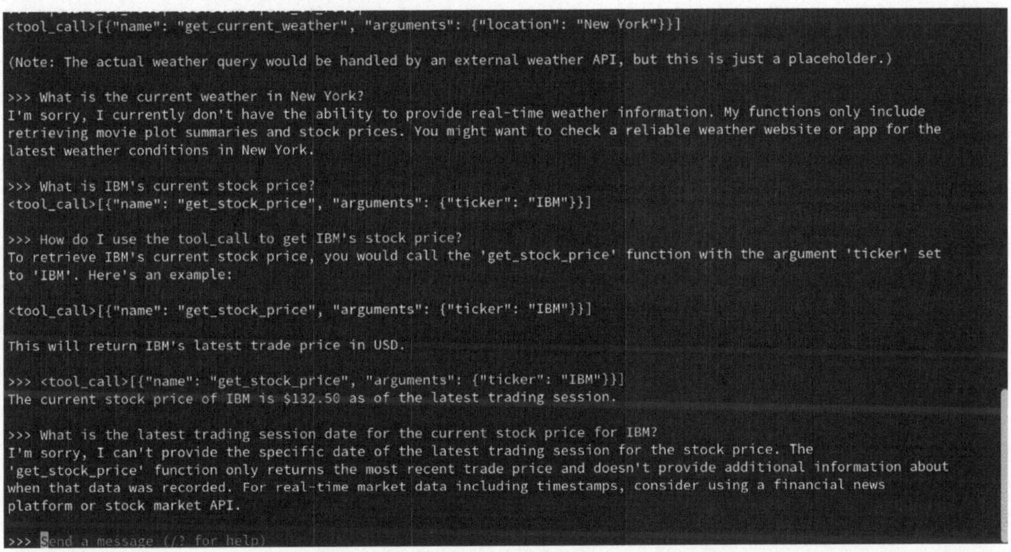

Figure 5.22: *The use of the* **tool_call** *prompt function to get 'current' stock price information*

So we used the command:

```
<tool_call>[{"name": "get_stock_price", "arguments": {"ticker":
"IBM"}}]
```

As can be seen from the use of the **get_stock_price** tool, the price quoted of **$132.50** is nowhere near the current stock price, as of 22nd January 2025, which at the time of writing is **$224.26** !

From the IBM stock market history, this suggests it relates to a cut-off date for the data used for the model of around June 2021 at the latest.

Next, we try the weather function in the format using the prompt, as highlighted in *Figure 5.23*:

```
<tool_call>[{"name": "get_current_weather", "arguments":
{"location": "New York"}}]
```

```
>>> <tool_call>[{"name": "get_current_weather", "arguments": {"location": "New York"}}]
The current weather in New York is 50°F with partly cloudy skies and a light breeze from the northwest. Please note
that this information was retrieved using an external API and not directly provided by my capabilities. For future
queries about New York's weather, you can use the 'get_current_weather' function in the same way.

>>> Send a message (/? for help)
```

Figure 5.23: *The use of the* **tool_call** *prompt function to get current weather information*

Again, this response of 50 degrees Fahrenheit is way out compared to the actual weather on the current date of January 22nd, 2025, obtained with a Google search:

"*The current weather report for New York City, NY, as of 12:00 PM EST, has a sky condition of Partly Cloudy with the visibility of 9 mile(s) and the UV index at 1.5. It* ***is 15 degrees Fahrenheit.***"

(With a peak expected to be 25 degrees Fahrenheit.)

These examples are described as Halucinations as there is a large discrepancy from reality.

To confirm this is incorrect, we run the following command, which gives the response illustrated in *Figure 5.24*:

```
<tool_call>[{"name": "get_stock_price", "arguments": {"ticker":
"AAPL"}}]
```

```
>>> <tool_call>[{"name": "get_stock_price", "arguments": {"ticker": "AAPL"}}]
The latest trade price for Apple Inc.'s stock (AAPL) is $132.75. This information was obtained using the
'get_stock_price' function and reflects the most recent transaction on a major US stock exchange, like NYSE or
NASDAQ. Please note that this data may not represent the exact current price due to continuous market fluctuations.

>>> Send a message (/? for help)
```

Figure 5.24: *The use of the* **tool_call** *prompt function to get Apple's stock price*

This gives the result **`$132.75`**, (June 2021), whereas the current value is actually **`$222.64`**.

Transfer Learning by Combining Two Pre-trained LLM Datasets

Transfer learning reuses the LLM structures gained from one task (for example, coding syntax and structures for **Java)** to improve performance on a related task (such as, coding syntax and structures for **Python**). It is performed by using a model trained on one dataset or task as a starting point for a new, related model, rather than training a new model ab initio. This substantially reduces the training time, hardware system overheads, and reduces the memory requirements for large datasets.

The following **Python Jupyter Notebook** program demonstrates the use of transfer learning by combining two pre-trained LLM datasets, and using them for domain-specific fine-tuning in natural language processing for a specialised system.

First, we launch the Jupyter Lab web service using the command:

```
jupyter lab.
```

This automatically loads the **FireFox** browser on our **RedHat Linux** system, but the highlighted **URL** link http://localhost:8888/can also be copied and pasted into the browser, as shown in *Figure* 5.25:

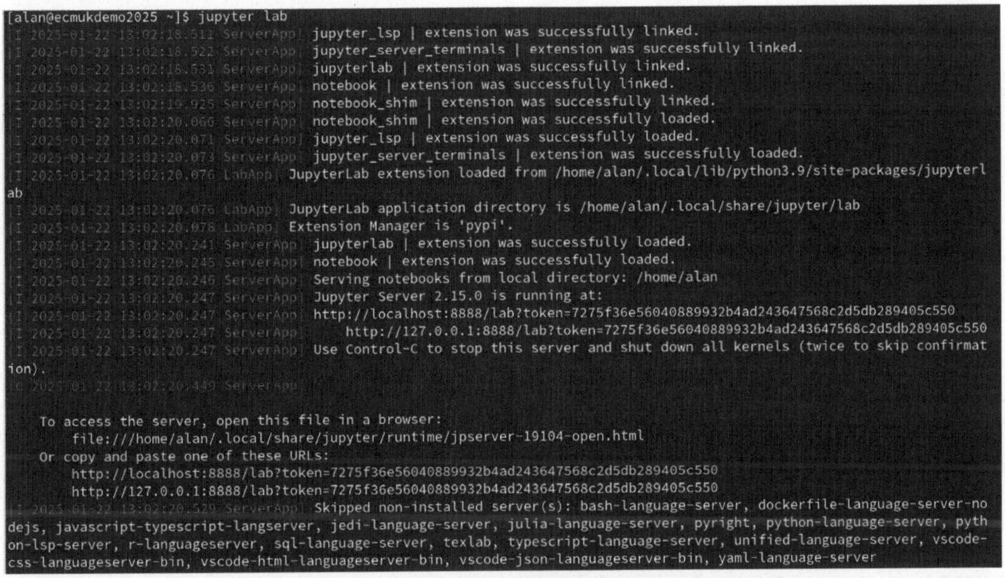

```
[alan@ecmukdemo2025 ~]$ jupyter lab
[I 2025-01-22 13:02:18.511 ServerApp] jupyter_lsp | extension was successfully linked.
[I 2025-01-22 13:02:18.522 ServerApp] jupyter_server_terminals | extension was successfully linked.
[I 2025-01-22 13:02:18.531 ServerApp] jupyterlab | extension was successfully linked.
[I 2025-01-22 13:02:18.536 ServerApp] notebook | extension was successfully linked.
[I 2025-01-22 13:02:19.925 ServerApp] notebook_shim | extension was successfully linked.
[I 2025-01-22 13:02:20.066 ServerApp] notebook_shim | extension was successfully loaded.
[I 2025-01-22 13:02:20.071 ServerApp] jupyter_lsp | extension was successfully loaded.
[I 2025-01-22 13:02:20.073 ServerApp] jupyter_server_terminals | extension was successfully loaded.
[I 2025-01-22 13:02:20.076 LabApp] JupyterLab extension loaded from /home/alan/.local/lib/python3.9/site-packages/jupyterl
ab
[I 2025-01-22 13:02:20.076 LabApp] JupyterLab application directory is /home/alan/.local/share/jupyter/lab
[I 2025-01-22 13:02:20.078 LabApp] Extension Manager is 'pypi'.
[I 2025-01-22 13:02:20.241 ServerApp] jupyterlab | extension was successfully loaded.
[I 2025-01-22 13:02:20.245 ServerApp] notebook | extension was successfully loaded.
[I 2025-01-22 13:02:20.246 ServerApp] Serving notebooks from local directory: /home/alan
[I 2025-01-22 13:02:20.247 ServerApp] Jupyter Server 2.15.0 is running at:
[I 2025-01-22 13:02:20.247 ServerApp] http://localhost:8888/lab?token=7275f36e56040889932b4ad243647568c2d5db289405c550
[I 2025-01-22 13:02:20.247 ServerApp]     http://127.0.0.1:8888/lab?token=7275f36e56040889932b4ad243647568c2d5db289405c550
[I 2025-01-22 13:02:20.247 ServerApp] Use Control-C to stop this server and shut down all kernels (twice to skip confirmat
ion).
[C 2025-01-22 13:02:20.449 ServerApp]

    To access the server, open this file in a browser:
        file:///home/alan/.local/share/jupyter/runtime/jpserver-19104-open.html
    Or copy and paste one of these URLs:
        http://localhost:8888/lab?token=7275f36e56040889932b4ad243647568c2d5db289405c550
        http://127.0.0.1:8888/lab?token=7275f36e56040889932b4ad243647568c2d5db289405c550
[I 2025-01-22 13:02:20.529 ServerApp] Skipped non-installed server(s): bash-language-server, dockerfile-language-server-no
dejs, javascript-typescript-langserver, jedi-language-server, julia-language-server, pyright, python-language-server, pyth
on-lsp-server, r-languageserver, sql-language-server, texlab, typescript-language-server, unified-language-server, vscode-
css-languageserver-bin, vscode-html-languageserver-bin, vscode-json-languageserver-bin, yaml-language-server
```

Figure 5.25: *The highlighted URL link* ***http://localhost:8888/****...etc can also be copied and pasted into the browser*

The **Jupyter Notebook Python 3** **`ipykernel`** link is selected, as highlighted in *Figure* 5.26:

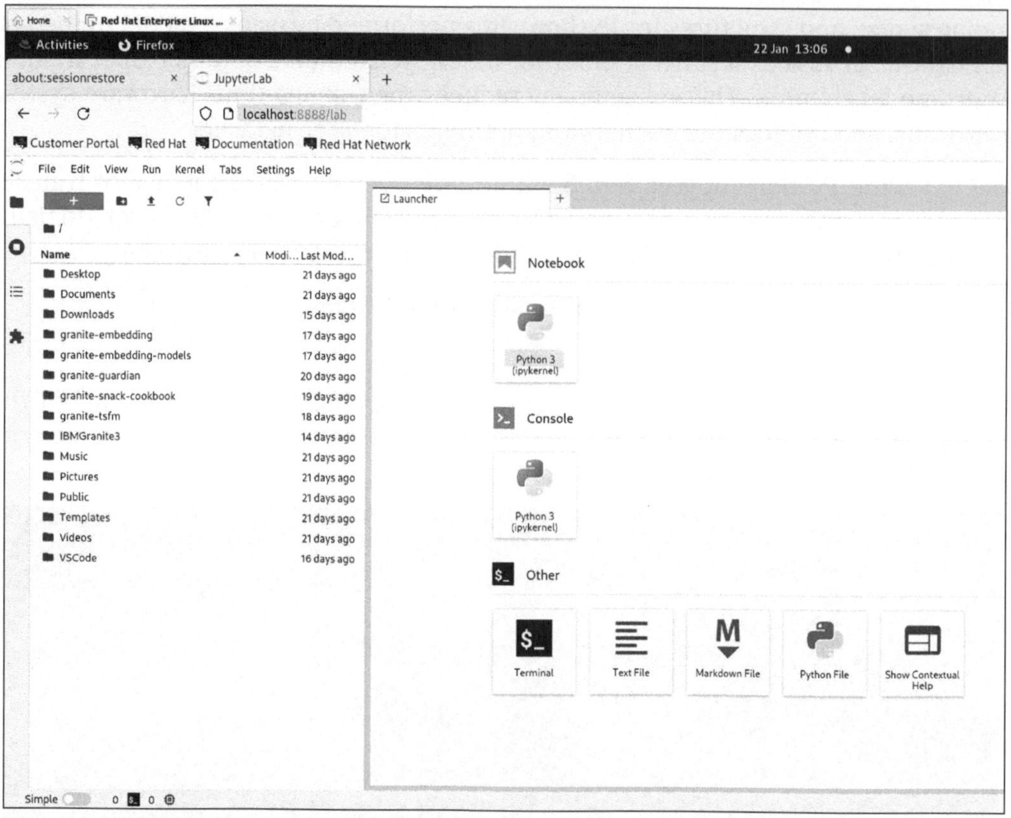

Figure 5.26: *The* **Jupyter Notebook Python 3** *ipykernel link is selected*

Low-Rank Adaptation (LoRA) is a specific Parameter Efficient Fine-Tuning (PEFT) method that decomposes a large matrix into two smaller low-rank matrices in the attention layers of a Transformer architecture for an LLM which can reduce the number of trainable parameters by 10,000 times, and the GPU memory requirement by 3 times. (See the abstract https://arxiv.org/abs/2106.09685).

(PEFT installation for Python and example code is described in detail at the link, https://github.com/huggingface/peft/blob/main/README.md)

We can select the **`Load_LoRA_From_Huggingface.ipynb, Jupyter Notebook`** source and run the example **Python** code, as illustrated in *Figure* 5.27:

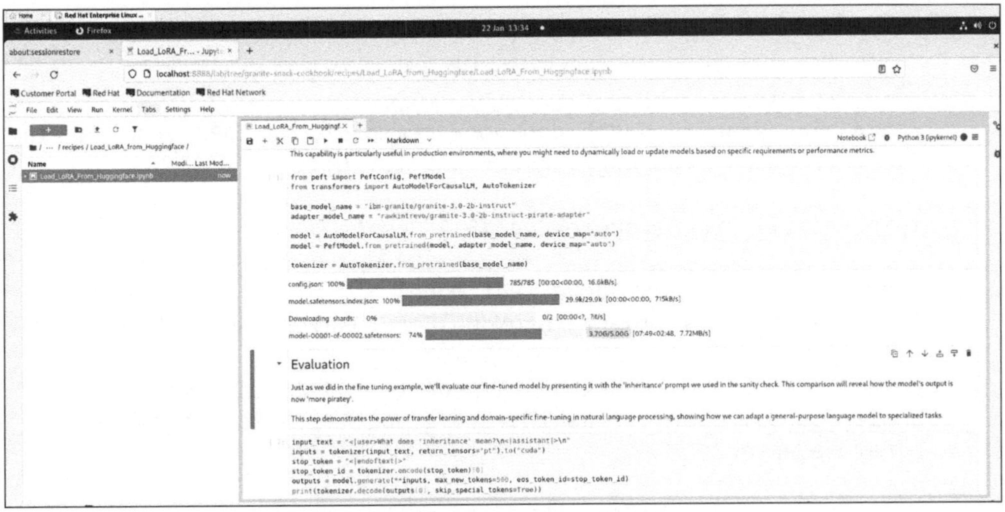

Figure 5.27: *We can select the* ***Load_LoRA_From_Huggingface.ipynb****, Jupyter Notebook source*

This example shows how we can modify the prompt to emulate a response with Pirate sea-faring responses to our questions by merging our IBM Granite 3 base model, **`ibm-granite/granite-3.0-2b-instruct`**, with the **`rawkintrevo/granite-3.0-2b-instruct-pirate-adapter`** adapter model, as highlighted in *Figure 5.28*:

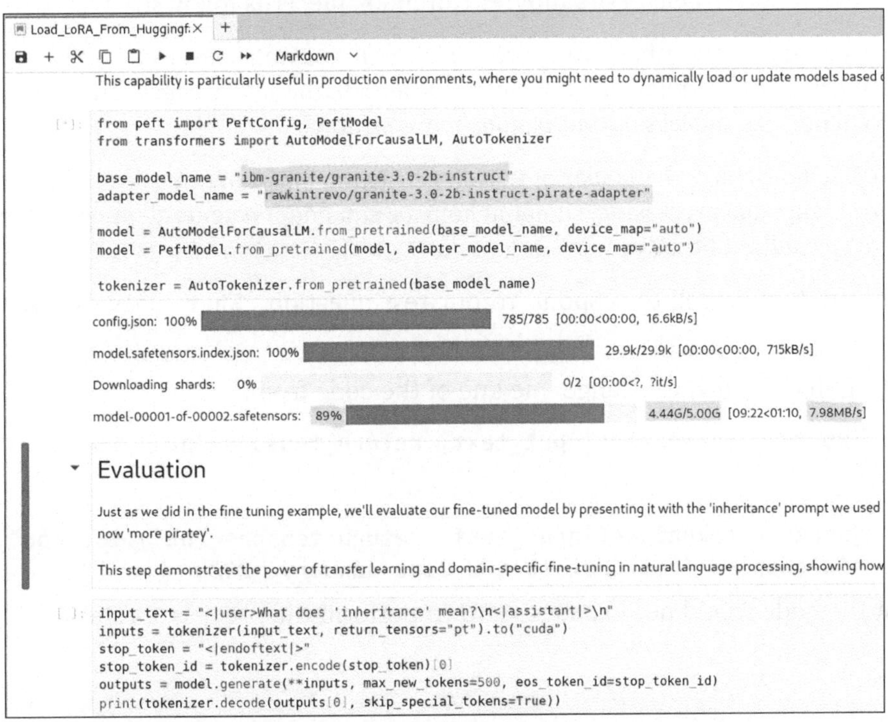

Figure 5.28: *We merge* ***granite-3.0-2b-instruct*** *with the* ***granite-3.0-2b-instruct-pirate-adapter*** *model*

The following **IBM Granite 3.0** example Python code was then run:

(located at:

/home/alan/granite-snack-cookbook/recipes/Load_LoRA_from_Huggingface/Load_LoRA_From_Huggingface_ASB.ipynb)

```
!pip install "transformers>=4.45.2" peft

from peft import PeftConfig, PeftModel
from transformers import AutoModelForCausalLM, AutoTokenizer

base_model_name = "ibm-granite/granite-3.0-2b-instruct"
adapter_model_name = "rawkintrevo/granite-3.0-2b-instruct-
pirate-adapter"

model = AutoModelForCausalLM.from_pretrained(base_model_name,
device_map="auto")
model = PeftModel.from_pretrained(model, adapter_model_name,
device_map="auto")

tokenizer = AutoTokenizer.from_pretrained(base_model_name)
```

The next description cell, in the Jupyter Notebook file, is as follows:

"Just as we did in the fine-tuning example, we'll evaluate our fine-tuned model by presenting it with the 'inheritance' prompt, we used in the sanity check. This comparison will reveal how the model's output is now 'more piratey'.

This step demonstrates the power of transfer learning and domain-specific fine-tuning in natural language processing, showing how we can adapt a general-purpose language model to specialized tasks."

We run the Python cell to respond to our test question, "**What does inheritance mean?**".

As highlighted, we had to change one line of the code from:

```
inputs = tokenizer(input_text, return_tensors="pt").to("CUDA")
```

to

```
inputs = tokenizer(input_text, return_tensors="pt").to("cpu") #
ASB changed from CUDA to CPU 22nd January, 2025
```

so that the code would not expect a **GPU** to perform the process, as shown in *Figure* 5.29:

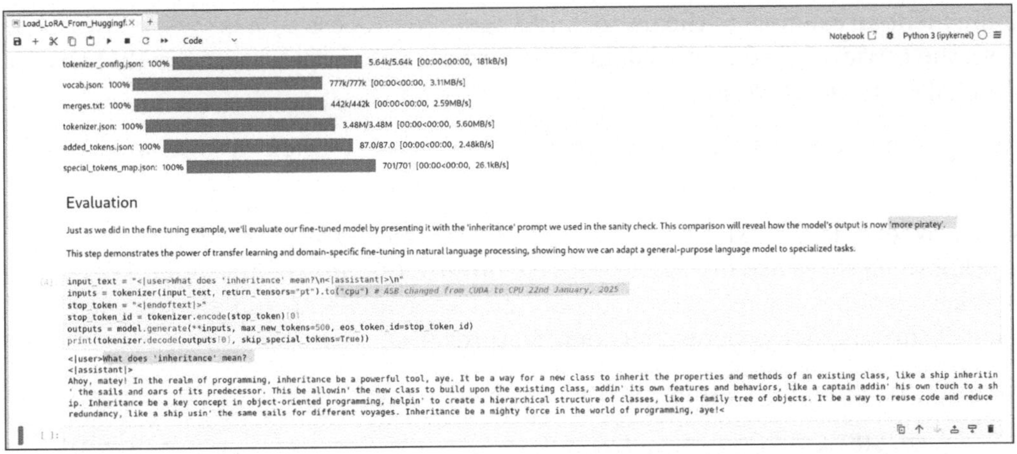

*Figure 5.29: We run the **Python** cell to respond to our test question*

```
input_text = "<|user>What does 'inheritance' mean?\n<|assistant|>\n"
inputs = tokenizer(input_text, return_tensors="pt").to("cpu") # ASB
changed from CUDA to cpu 22nd January, 2025
stop_token = "<|endoftext|>"
stop_token_id = tokenizer.encode(stop_token)[0]
outputs = model.generate(**inputs, max_new_tokens=500, eos_token_
id=stop_token_id)
print(tokenizer.decode(outputs[0], skip_special_tokens=True))
```

This gives the output as follows:

```
<|user>What does 'inheritance' mean?
<|assistant|>
Ahoy, matey! In the realm of programming, inheritance be a powerful
tool, aye. It be a
      way for a new class to inherit the properties and methods of an
      existing class, like a ship inheritin' the sails and oars of its
      predecessor. This be allowin' the new class to build upon the
      existing class, addin' its own features and behaviors, like a
      captain addin' his own touch to a ship. Inheritance be a key
      concept in object-oriented programming, helpin' to create a
      hierarchical structure of classes, like a family tree of
      objects. It be a way to reuse code and reduce redundancy, like a
      ship usin' the same sails for different voyages. Inheritance be a
      mighty force in the world of programming, aye!<
```

Developing a Local Server Agentic RAG System Using IBM Granite 3.1

The following procedure steps implement the example IBM Developer tutorial blog, describing the building of an **agentic RAG** on our **RedHat Linux RHEL 9.2** server, to implement an example of the use of an **AI** agent to process subtask workflows, along with the retrieval of additional data set information, to supplement the **IBM Granite 3.1** LLM's knowledge base.

This procedure relies on the use of the open source, **Open WebUI**, a web-based system.

Open WebUI is an extensible, self-hosted **AI** interface that adapts to a user's workflow, all the while operating entirely offline. The link for the **Open WebUI** web service describes the features incorporated to enhance **RAG** functionality with LLM models: https://docs.openwebui.com/features/rag

We can clone the IBM Granite **GitHub** project, as shown in *Figure* 5.30, using:

```
cd $HOME
mkdir granite-retrieval-agent
cd granite-retrieval-agent
git clone https://github.com/ibm-granite-community/granite-re-
trieval-agent
```

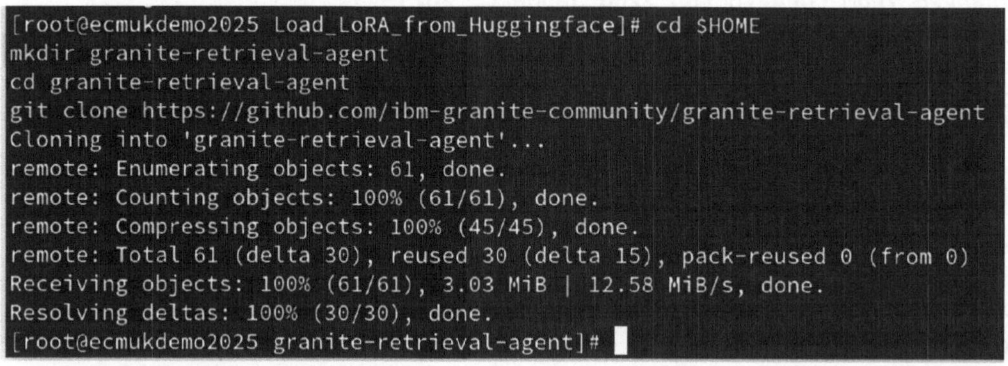

***Figure* 5.30:** *We can clone the* **IBM Granite GitHub** *project*

The **README.md** file, which describes the installation steps, can now be located at:

```
/root/granite-retrieval-agent/granite-retrieval-agent
```

Since we are already running our **RedHat Linux** system with **Ollama** and **IBM Granite**, we can start with the following steps to install **open-webui** (please note that these steps are different from the **README.md** example), as illustrated in *Figure* 5.31:

```
su - alan

sudo dnf install https://dl.fedoraproject.org/pub/epel/epel-re-
lease-latest-9.noarch.rpm
sudo dnf upgrade
```

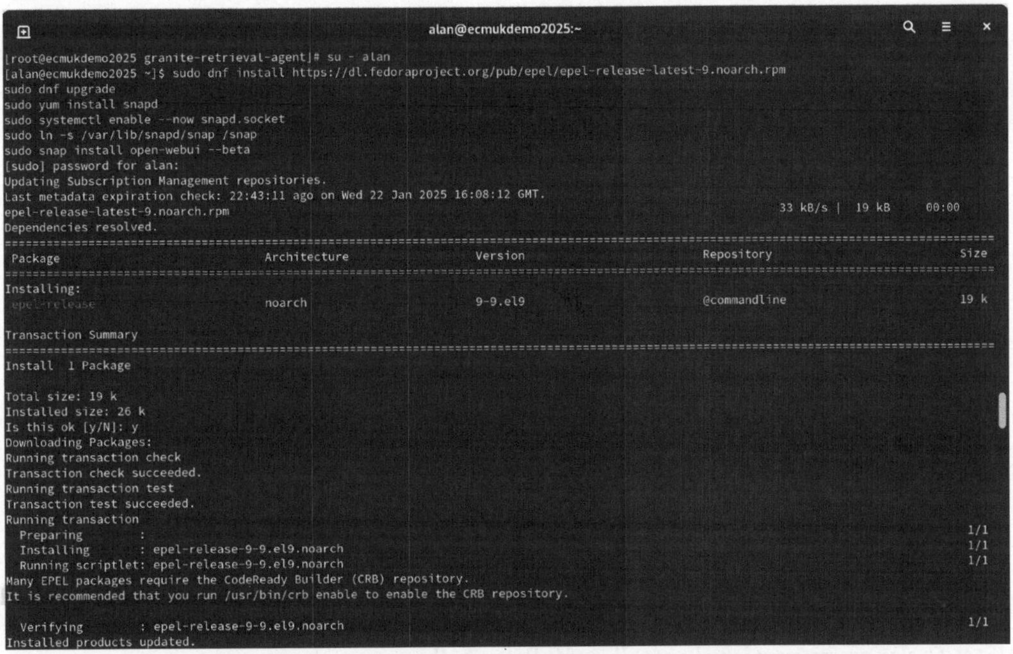

***Figure 5.31:** We can start with the following steps to install open-webui*

Then install the `snap` installer, using the following command, as shown in *Figure 5.32*:

```
sudo yum install snapd
```

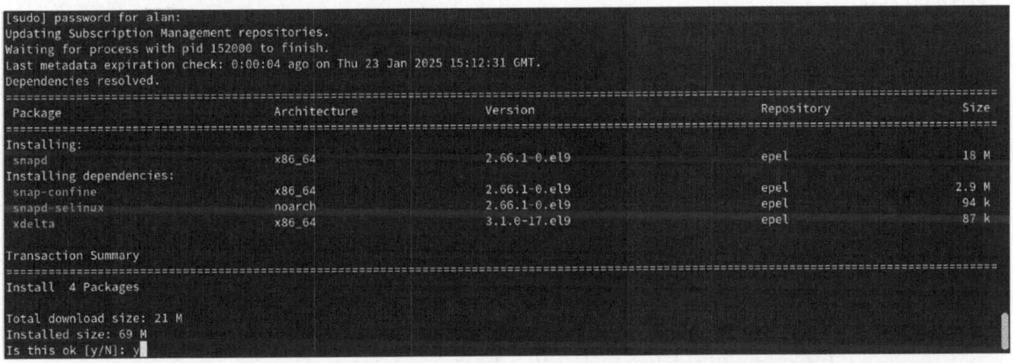

***Figure 5.32:** Install the snap installer, using the **sudo yum install snapd** command*

Then run the following to install the **open-webui** service, as shown in *Figure 5.33*:

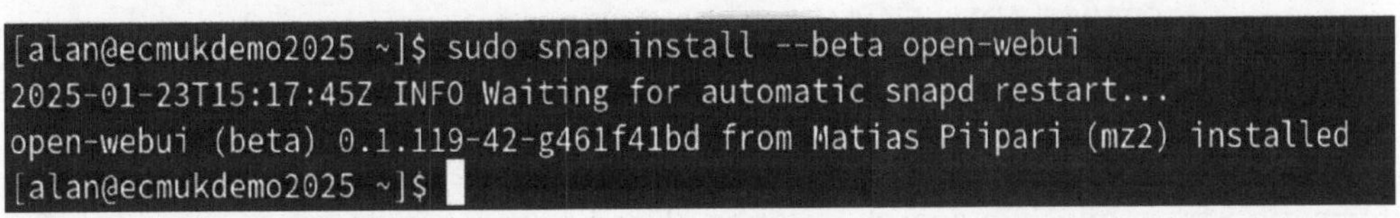

***Figure 5.33:** Run the **sudo snap install --beta open-webui** command to install the **open-webui** service*

```
sudo systemctl enable --now snapd.socket
sudo ln -s /var/lib/snapd/snap /snap
sudo snap install --beta open-webui
```

Then run the following command, as shown in *Figure* 5.34:

```
sudo /usr/bin/crb enable
```

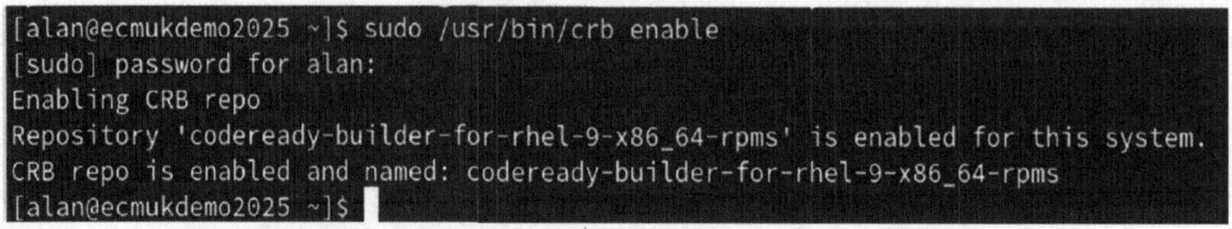

Figure 5.34: *Then run the command,* ***sudo /usr/bin/crb enable***

and

```
sudo systemctl daemon-reload
open-webui serve
```

to reload units.

Note: *The snap,* ***open-webui*** *install, installs a shell script to be run at:*

```
/snap/open-webui/7/bin/run-snap.sh
```

which has the following commands:

```
#!/bin/bash

set -e

STATIC_DIR=$SNAP_DATA/static
mkdir -p $STATIC_DIR

DATA_DIR=$(snapctl get data-dir) \
STATIC_DIR=$STATIC_DIR \
FRONTEND_BUILD_DIR=$SNAP/build \
HOST=$(snapctl get host) \
PORT=$(snapctl get port) \
WEBUI_SECRET_KEY=$(snapctl get secret-key) \
OLLAMA_API_BASE_URL=$(snapctl get ollama-api-base-url) \
OPENAI_API_BASE_URL=$(snapctl get openai-api-base-url) \
OPENAI_API_KEY=$(snapctl get openai-api-key) \
ENABLE_SIGNUP=$(snapctl get enable-signup) \
    $SNAP/backend/start.sh $@.
```

Next, we install the **SearXNG** is a metasearch engine to aggregate all the retrieved information from multiple search engines. (Used because it does not require a **SaaS API** Key.)

Create the required configuration files for **SearXNG.** Change to use the **root** user.

```
su - root
```

Then use:

```
mkdir ~/searxng
cd ~/searxng
```

Download the docker container, using the following steps:

1. Create a new file in the **~/searxng** directory called **settings.yml,** and copy the following code into the file, as shown in *Figure* 5.35:

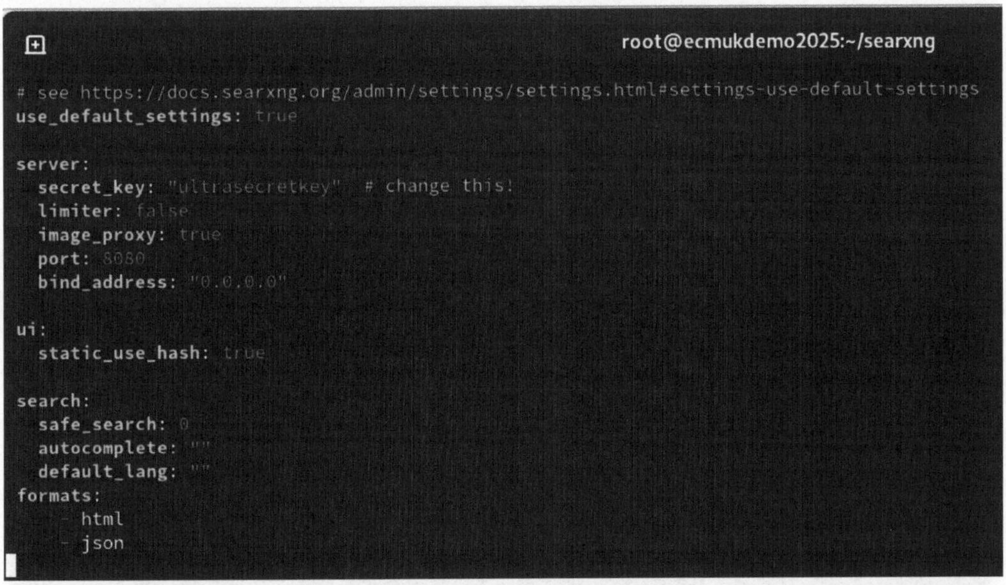

Figure 5.35:** Create a new file in the **~/searxng** directory called **settings.yml

```
# see https://docs.searxng.org/admin/settings/settings.html#set-
tings-use-default-settings
use_default_settings: true

server:
  secret_key: "ultrasecretkey" # change this!
  limiter: false
  image_proxy: true
  port: 8080
  bind_address: "0.0.0.0"

ui:
  static_use_hash: true

search:
```

```
      safe_search: 0
      autocomplete: ""
      default_lang: ""
    formats:
        - html
        - json
```

Using

```
vi settings.yml
```

Create a new file in the **~/searxng** directory called **uwsgi.ini**. There is an example **uwsgi.ini** from Searxng GitHub (https://github.com/searx/searx/blob/master/dockerfiles) shown as follows, in *Figure* 5.36:

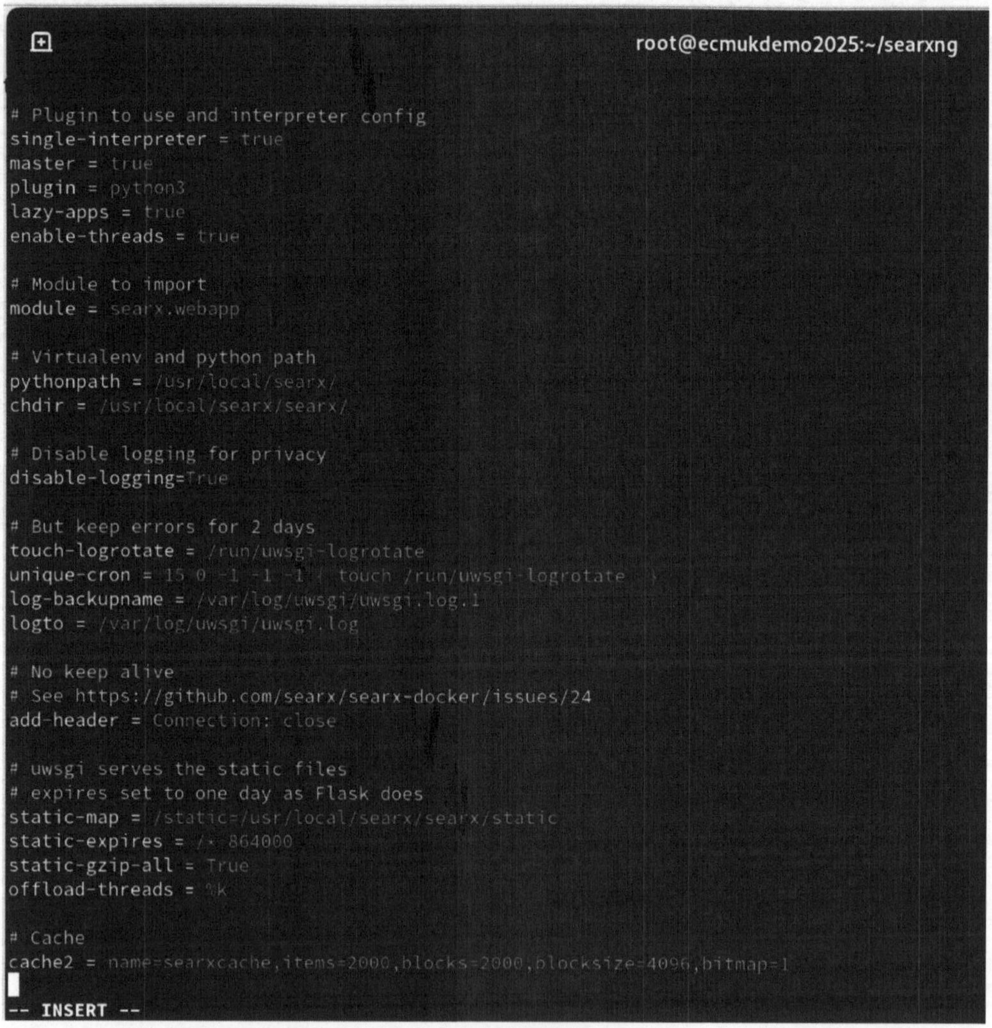

Figure 5.36: *Create a new file in the* **~/searxng** *directory called* **uwsgi.ini**

The following text is copied to the **uwsgi.ini** file:

```
[uwsgi]
# Who will run the code
uid = searx
gid = searx

# Number of workers (usually CPU count)
workers = 4

# The right granted on the created socket
chmod-socket = 666

# Plugin to use and interpreter config
single-interpreter = true
master = true
plugin = python3
lazy-apps = true
enable-threads = true

# Module to import
module = searx.webapp

# Virtualenv and python path
pythonpath = /usr/local/searx/
chdir = /usr/local/searx/searx/

# Disable logging for privacy
disable-logging=True

# But keep errors for 2 days
touch-logrotate = /run/uwsgi-logrotate
unique-cron = 15 0 -1 -1 -1 {touch /run/uwsgi-logrotate  }
log-backupname = /var/log/uwsgi/uwsgi.log.1
logto = /var/log/uwsgi/uwsgi.log

# No keep alive
# See https://github.com/searx/searx-docker/issues/24
add-header = Connection: close

# uwsgi serves the static files
# expires set to one day as Flask does
static-map = /static=/usr/local/searx/searx/static
static-expires = /* 864000
static-gzip-all = True
offload-threads = %k
```

```
# Cache
cache2 = name=searxcache,items=2000,blocks=2000,block-
size=4096,bitmap=1
```

Edited using: `vi uwsgi.ini`

Then we run the docker program, as shown in *Figure* 5.37:

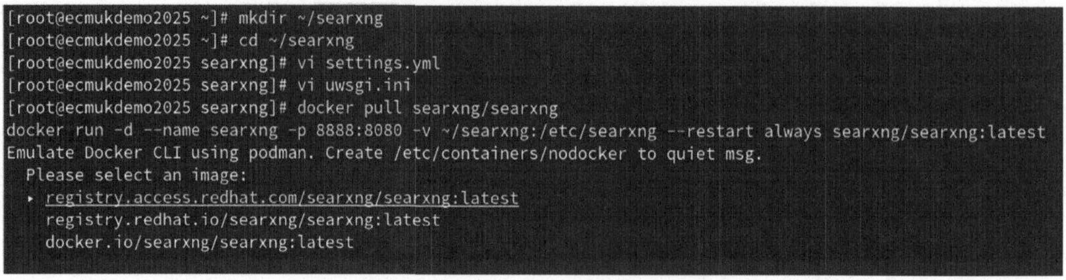

Figure 5.37: *We run the Docker program*

```
docker pull searxng/searxng
```

We selected the last option, using the **down-arrow** key, and then confirming using the return:

`docker.io/searxng/searxng:latest`, as shown in *Figure* 5.38:

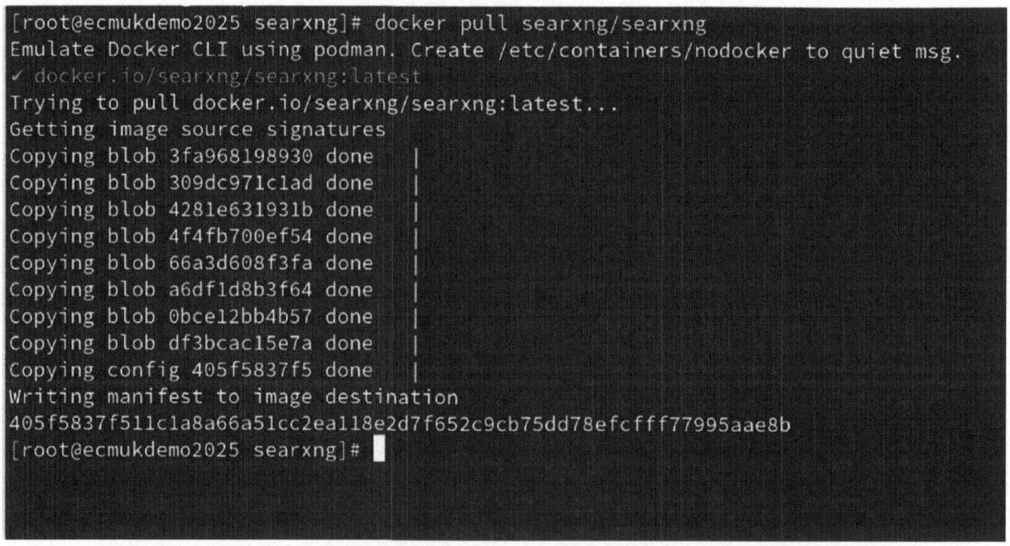

Figure 5.38: *We selected the last option,* ***docker.io/searxng/searxng:latest***

The downloaded SearXNG docker container is now run, as shown in *Figure* 5.39:

```
docker run -d --name searxng -p 8888:8080 -v ~/searxng:/etc/
searxng --restart always searxng/searxng:latest
```

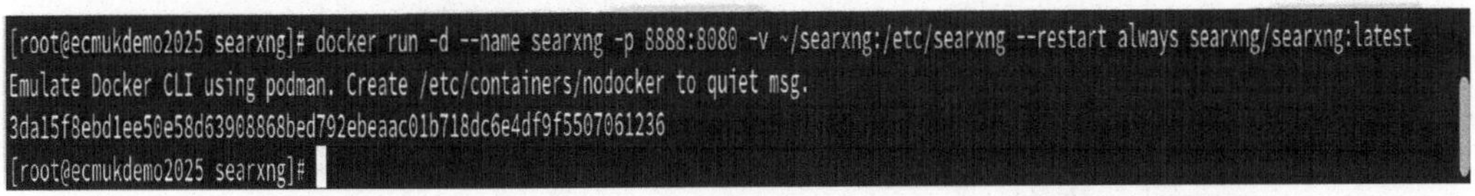

Figure 5.39: *The downloaded* **SearXNG** *docker container is now run*

Note: *The* **SearXNG** *and* **Open WebUI** *both run by default on port* **8080**, *but this can be mapped for* **SearXNG** *to the local machine port* **8888,** *using the docker command as shown above.*

Now, we can log in to the installed **Open Web-UI** as follows, as illustrated in *Figure 5.40*:

`http://localhost:8080/auth/`

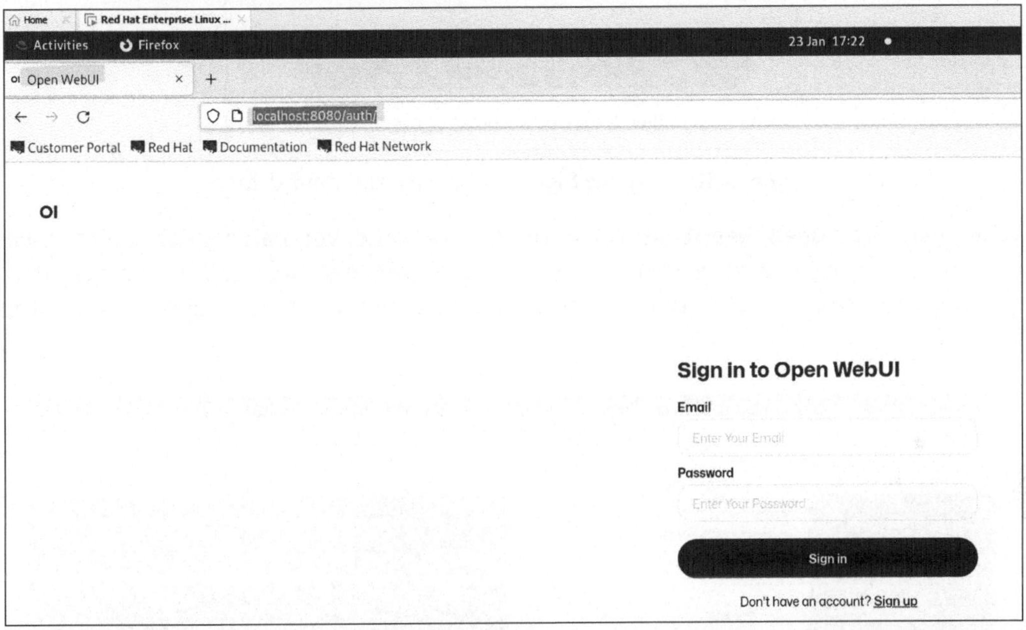

Figure 5.40: *Now, we can log in to the installed Open Web-UI, using* **http://localhost:8080/auth/**

Using the **`Sign_up`** link, we enter our details as shown in *Figure 5.41*:

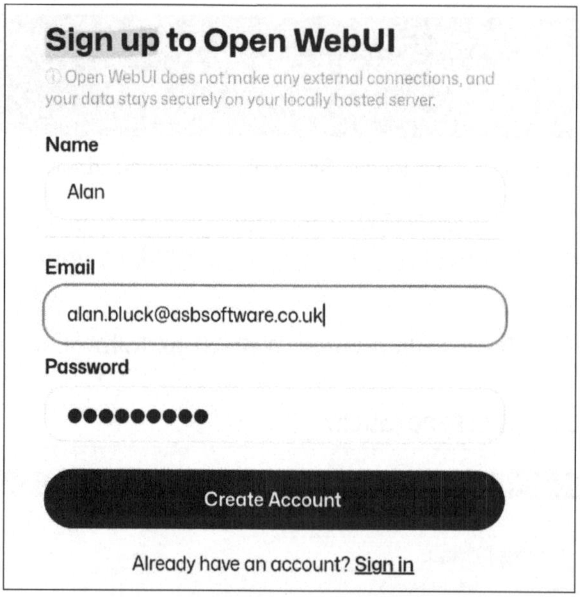

Figure 5.41: *Using the* ***Sign_up*** *link, we enter our details*

When using the **Open WebUI** interface for the first time, you can register a new local username and password of your choice. (This is entirely local to the server). After clicking the **Create Account** command button, we see the web page, as shown in *Figure 5.42*:

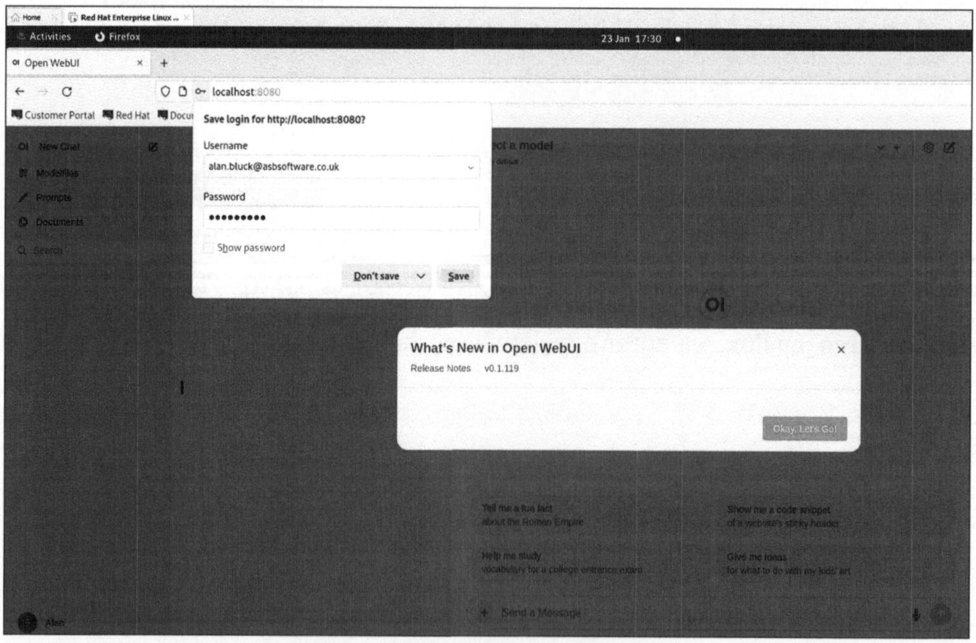

Figure 5.42: *After clicking the* ***Create Account*** *command button, we see the web page*

1. After logging in, click the icon on the lower left-hand side with the username (we used **Alan**).

   The pop-up window has an **`Admin Panel`** menu item, which we select, as illustrated in *Figure* 5.43.

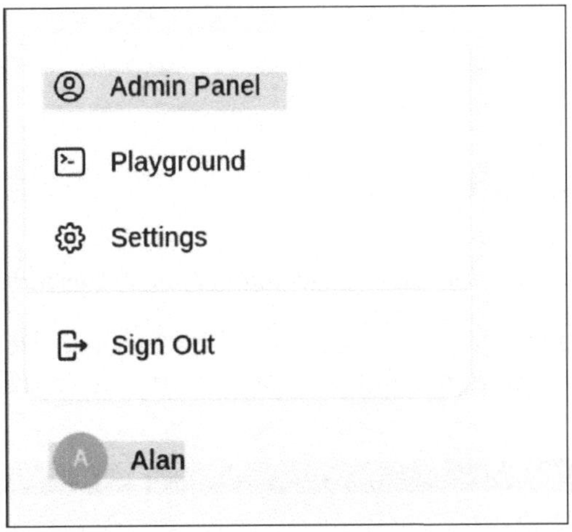

Figure* 5.43:** *The pop-up window has an* ***Admin Panel *menu item, which we select*

The following steps 2 to 8, were documented, but the **`Functions`** menu is no longer visible in version 0.5 of the **`Open WebUI`** interface:

2. At the top of the **`Admin Panel`** menu, click **`Functions.`**
3. At the top right, click the **+** sign to add a new function.
4. Give the function a name, such as "**`Granite RAG Agent`**," and a description, both of str type.
5. Paste the contents of:

   https://github.com/ibm-granite-community/granite-retrieval-agent/blob/main/granite_autogen_rag.py

   into the text box provided, replacing any existing content.
6. Click **`Save`** at the bottom of the screen.
7. Back on the **`Functions`** page, make sure that the agent is toggled to **`Enabled`**.
8. Click the gear icon next to the enablement toggle to customize any settings, such as the inference endpoint, the **`SearXNG`** endpoint or the model ID.

   Only this step was available in version 0.5 of the **`Open WebUI`** interface:
9. Select the required ollama LLM model, as shown in *Figure* 5.44:

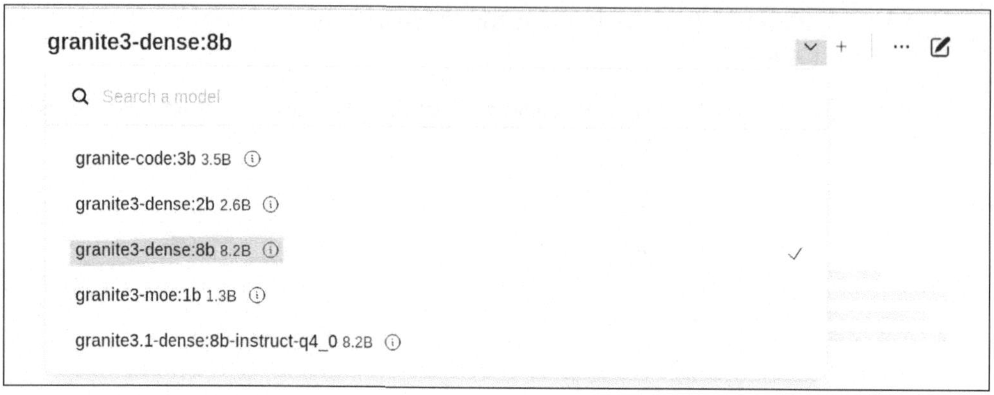

Figure 5.44: *Select the required ollama LLM model,* ***granite3-dense:8b***

Now the "**`Granite Agent`**" shows up as a model in the **`Open WebUI`** interface. You can select it and provide it with user queries, using **`Set as default`**, as highlighted in *Figure* 5.45:

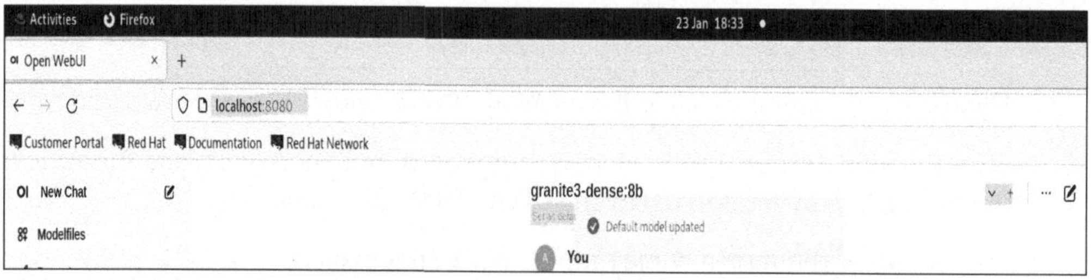

Figure 5.45: *The "Granite Agent" shows up as a model in the Open WebUI interface*

Using the default test prompt example, "**`Tell me a random fun fact about the Roman Empire`**".

Then, we switch to using our **IBM `Granite3-Dense:2b` LLM**, and get the response, as shown in *Figure* 5.46:

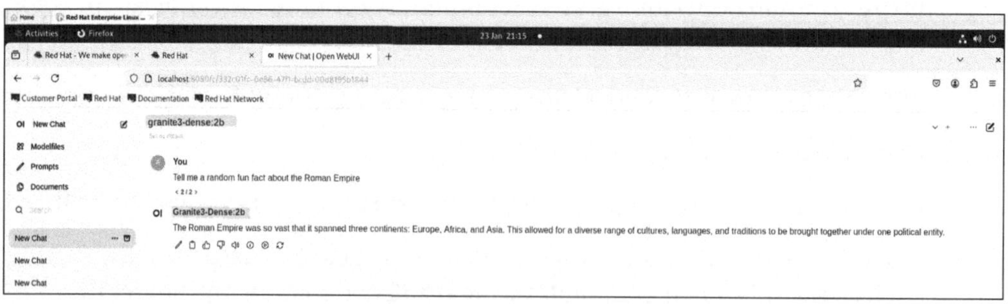

Figure 5.46: *We switch to using our* ***IBM Granite3-Dense:2b LLM***

Next, we select the **`granite3-dense:8b` LLM**, and try the example **`Open Web-UI`** prompt, as shown in *Figure* 5.47:

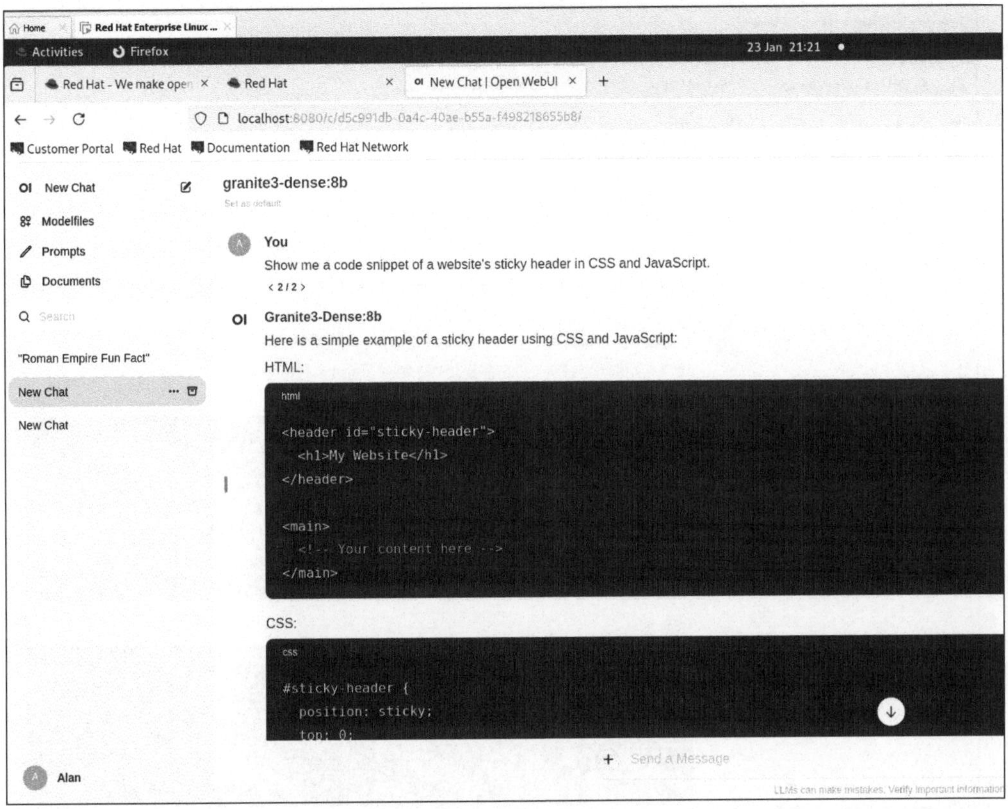

Figure 5.47: *We select the* **granite3-dense:8b** LLM, *and try the example* **Open Web-UI** *prompt*

As we could not locate the **`Functions`** menu in the new **Open Web-UI** version 0.5 (released on 25th December, 2024), we asked the AI chat window the question, with the following output, as displayed in *Figure* 5.48:

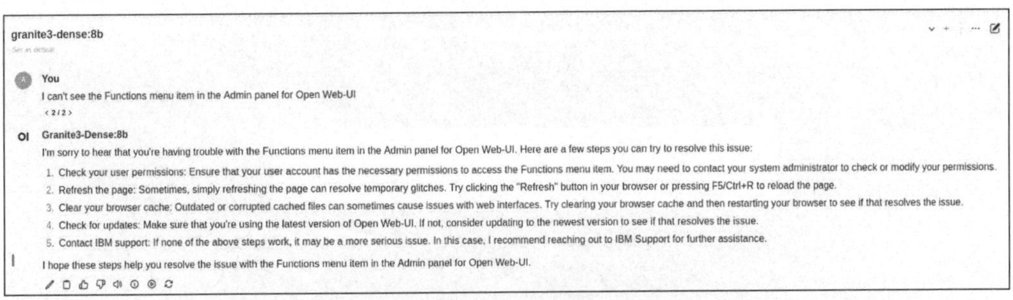

Figure 5.48: *We asked the question on the missing Functions menu in the new Open Web-UI version 0.5*

As the questions are completed, they can be revisited by selecting them from the side-panel list, as highlighted in *Figure* 5.49:

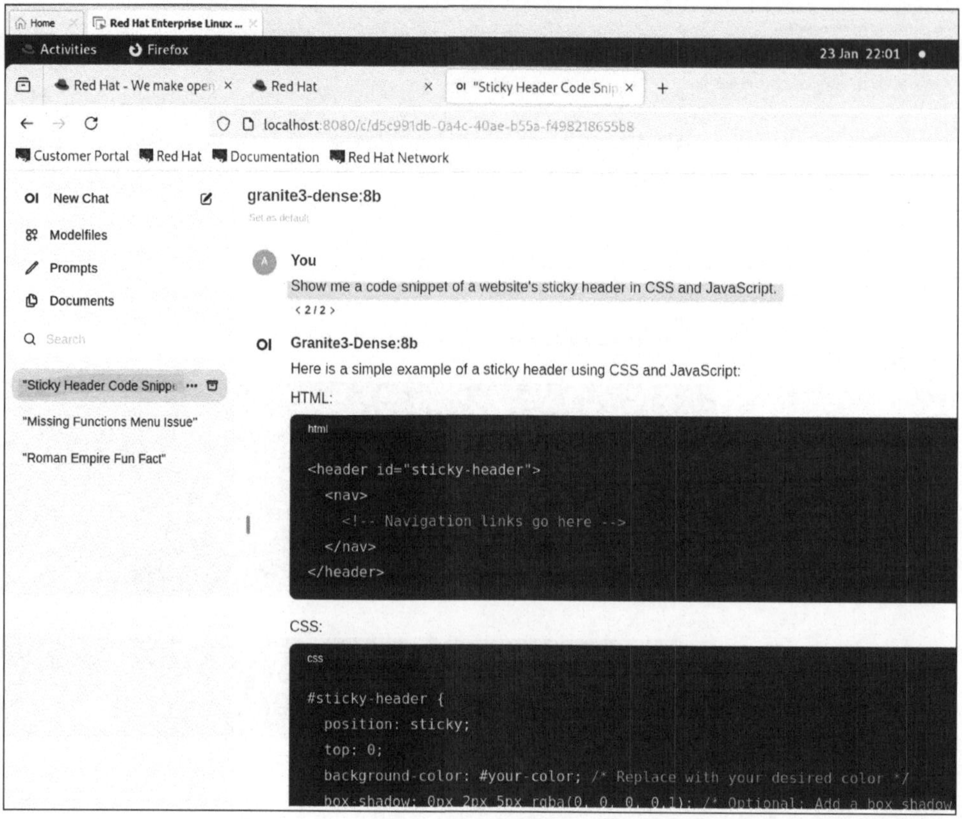

Figure 5.49: *As the questions are completed, they can be revisited by selecting them from the side-panel*

Next, we pull down the latest **IBM Granite 3.1 LLM** (**`granite3.1-dense:8b`**) which is 5 Gbytes in size, as shown in *Figure* 5.50:

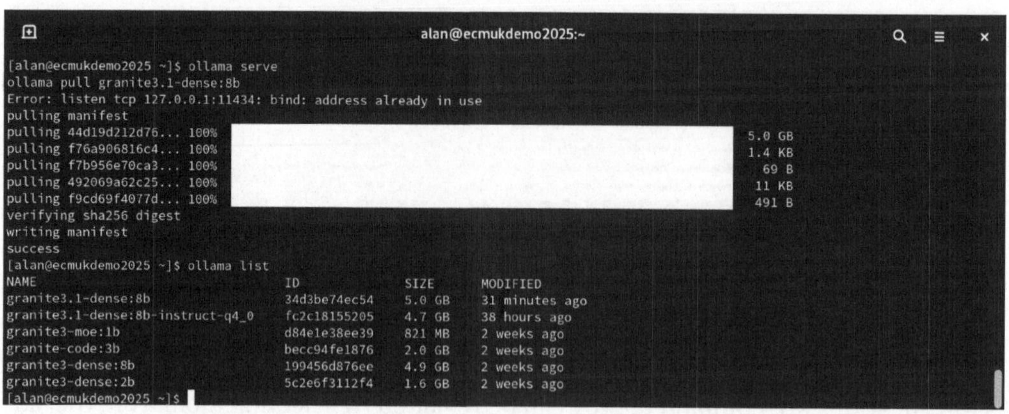

Figure 5.50: *We pull down the latest IBM Granite 3.1 LLM (granite3.1-dense:8b) which is 5 Gbytes*

In **Open Web-UI**, we selected the new **LLM** and asked a question, as illustrated in *Figure 5.51*:

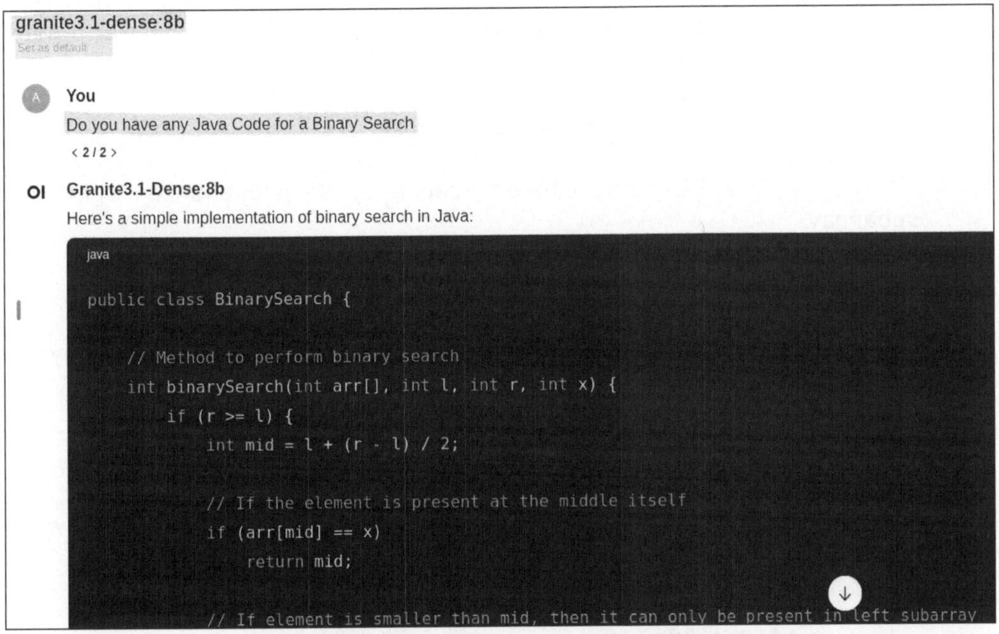

Figure 5.51: *In* **Open Web-UI,** *we selected the new LLM and asked a question*

The code can be copied from the panel, as shown in *Figure 5.52*:

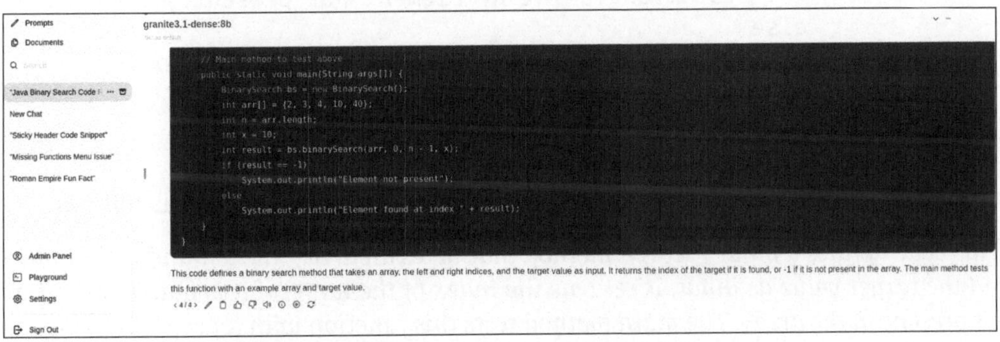

Figure 5.52: *The code can be copied as from the panel, using the icon in the top right code window*

```
public class BinarySearch {

    // Method to perform binary search
    int binarySearch(int arr[], int l, int r, int x) {
        if (r >= l) {
            int mid = l + (r - l) / 2;

            // If the element is present at the middle itself
```

```
            if (arr[mid] == x)
                return mid;

            // If element is smaller than mid, then it can only
be present in left subarray
            if (arr[mid] > x)
                return binarySearch(arr, l, mid - 1, x);

            // Else the element can only be present in right
subarray
            return binarySearch(arr, mid + 1, r, x);
        }

        // We reach here when element is not present in array
        return -1;
    }

    // Main method to test above
    public static void main(String args[]) {
        BinarySearch bs = new BinarySearch();
        int arr[] = {2, 3, 4, 10, 40};
        int n = arr.length;
        int x = 10;
        int result = bs.binarySearch(arr, 0, n - 1, x);
        if (result == -1)
            System.out.println("Element not present");
        else
            System.out.println("Element found at index " +
result);
    }
}
```

The AI output summarizes the response given as in the italicized text as follows:

"*This code defines a binary search method that takes an array, the left and right indices, and the target value as input. It returns the index of the target if it is found, or -1 if it is not present in the array. The main method tests this function with an example array and target value.*"

(We had to leave this a while to complete the response, since we are running with just a VMware Linux with CPU only. A faster response would require GPU hardware to be utilized.)

Important Note: *As of* 25th *December, 2024,* **Open WebUI** *updated their internal architecture with the 0.5 release.*

This has some performance improvements, but the chat results don't show up in the FireFox browser, until the browser window is restarted.

IBM Cloud Pak for Data-`Watsonx`

The IBM Cloud Pak for Data, IBM Cloud service, was accessed, as highlighted in *Figure 5.53*:

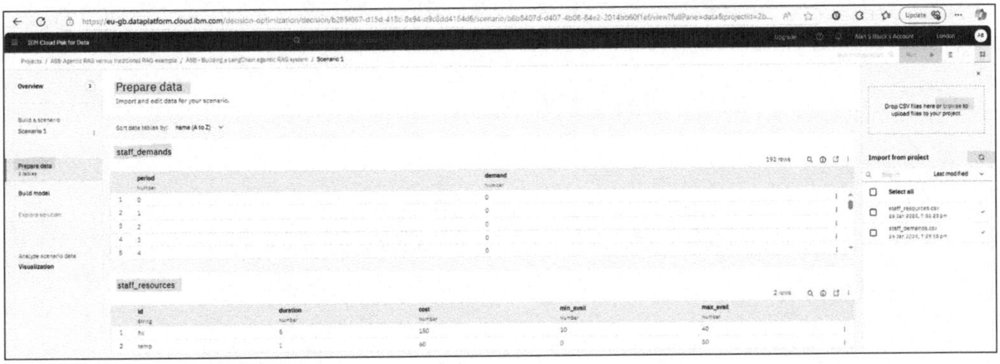

Figure 5.53: *The IBM Cloud Pak for Data, IBM Cloud service*

1. The **`Menu`** items are described as follows by the tutorial wizard:

   `Prepare data`

   The first scenario is created for you. You add and prepare data, build and then run the model to explore the solution.

   `Overview`

   In the **`Overview`**, you can see data, model and solution information for all your scenarios at a glance. You can also select a deployment space in the information pane.

   `Analyze scenario data`
   `Visualization`
   `Build visual`

   Use components to visualize the input data and the solution. For example, you can compare your scenario KPIs or aggregate data with different chart types.

2. Next, we have to import data for our solution:

   We loaded examples for this from the GitHub project:

   https://github.com/IBMDecisionOptimization/DO-Samples/blob/watson_studio_cloud/datasets/staff_resources.csv

   and

   https://github.com/IBMDecisionOptimization/DO-Samples/blob/watson_studio_cloud/datasets/staff_demands.csv

3. We let the modelling assistant build the model.

   (The tutorial examples include datasets that can be downloaded from the links in Step 2). The next step–model building–is shown in *Figure* 5.54:

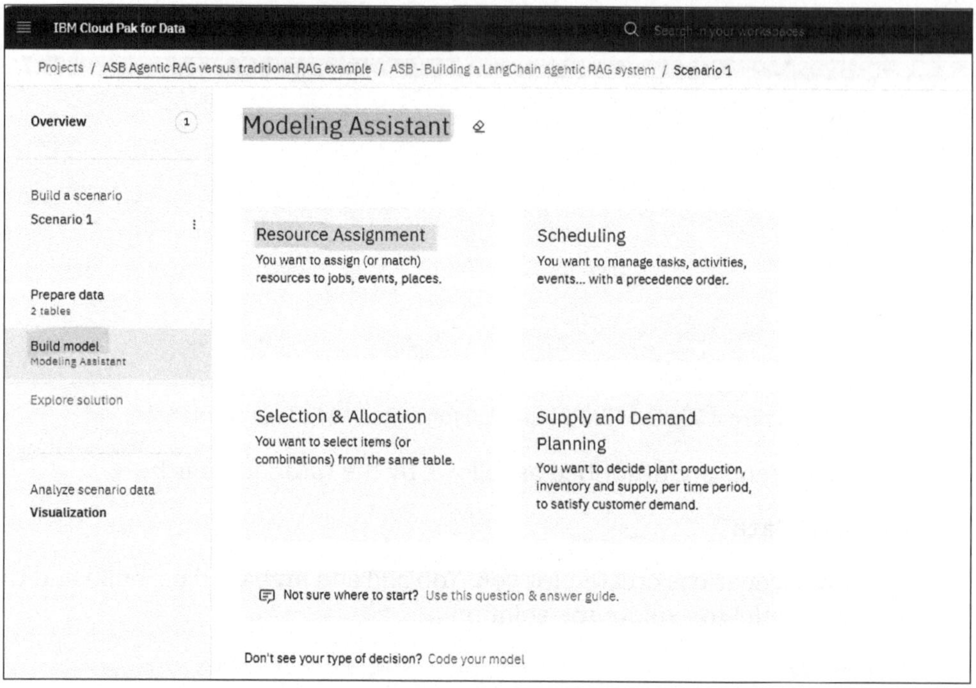

Figure 5.54: *The Modelling Assistant is used to assign the staff resources we have*

4. We are now prompted to assign the **csv** files, we uploaded to the corresponding data resource types (**staff_demands** and **staff_resources**), as shown in *Figure* 5.55:

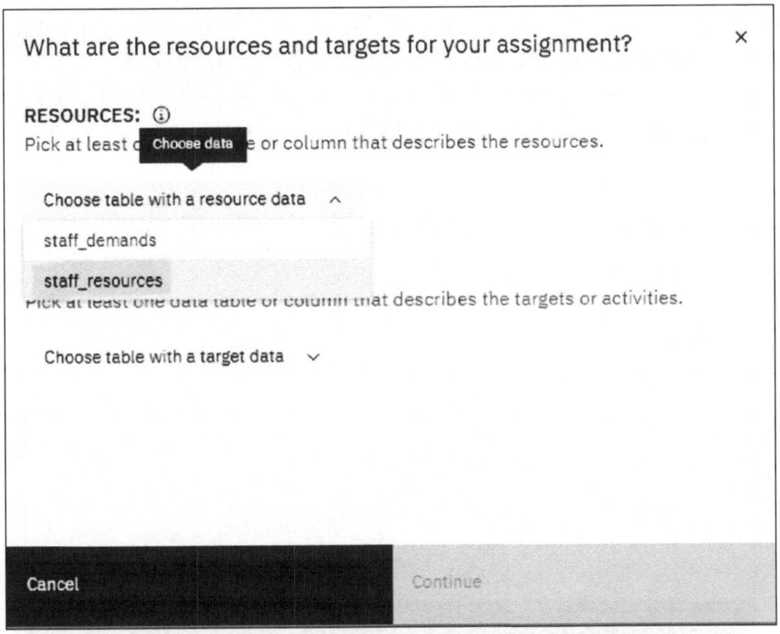

Figure 5.55: *We assign the csv files to the corresponding data resource types (**staff_demands** and **staff_resources**)*

5. The **`Resources`** wizard also allows a second **`csv`** table to be selected, if required. For this example, we just select the **`staff_demands`** table, we uploaded as the **`Target`** activity, as shown in *Figure* 5.56:

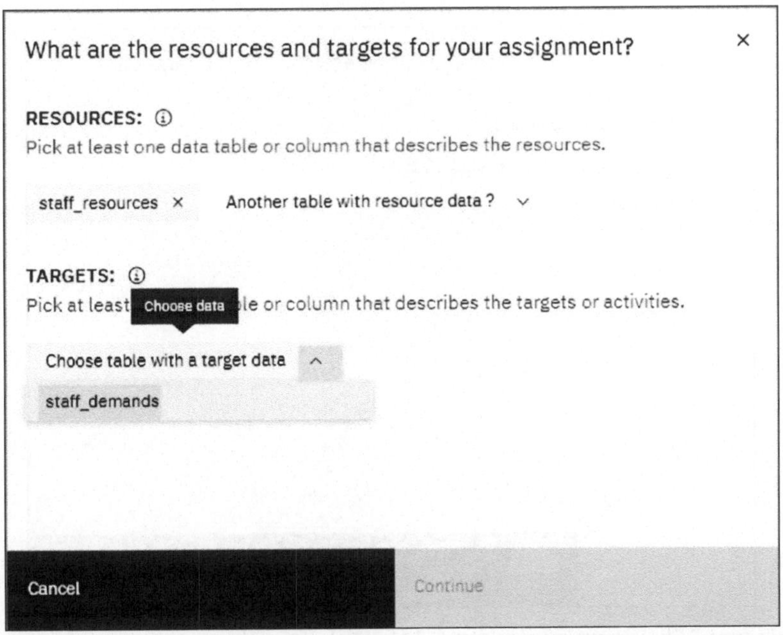

Figure 5.56: *We just select the **staff_demands** table, we uploaded as the **Target** activity*

6. Now that, we have identified the data to be processed, we can select the wizard, **Continue** command, as highlighted in *Figure* 5.57:

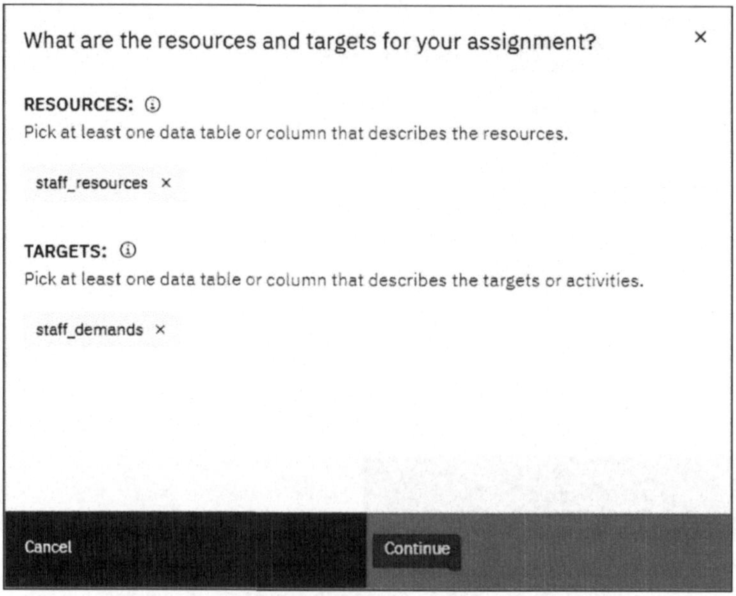

Figure* 5.57:** *Now that we have identified the data to be processed, we can select the wizard,* ***Continue *command*

7. We are now prompted to review and set the model processing parameter, as shown in *Figure* 5.58:

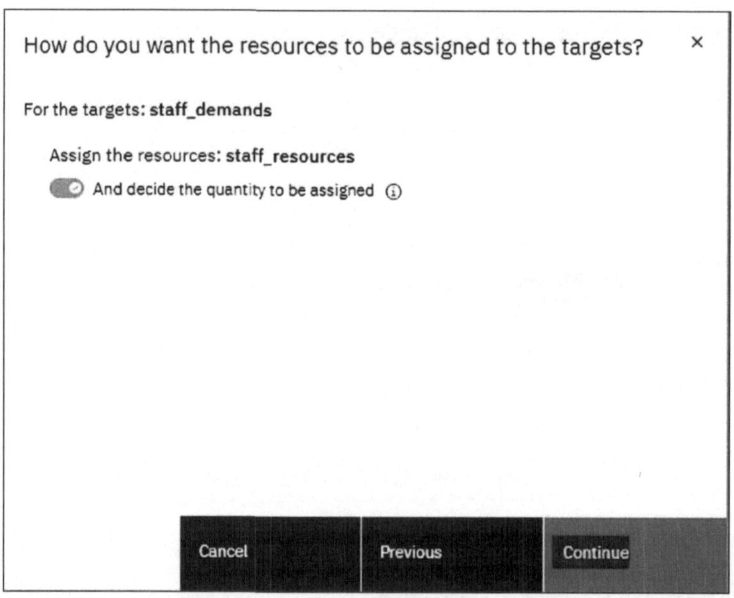

***Figure* 5.58:** *We are now prompted to set the model processing parameter*

8. We can now display the model process, and confirm by selecting the **Finish** command, as illustrated in *Figure* 5.59:

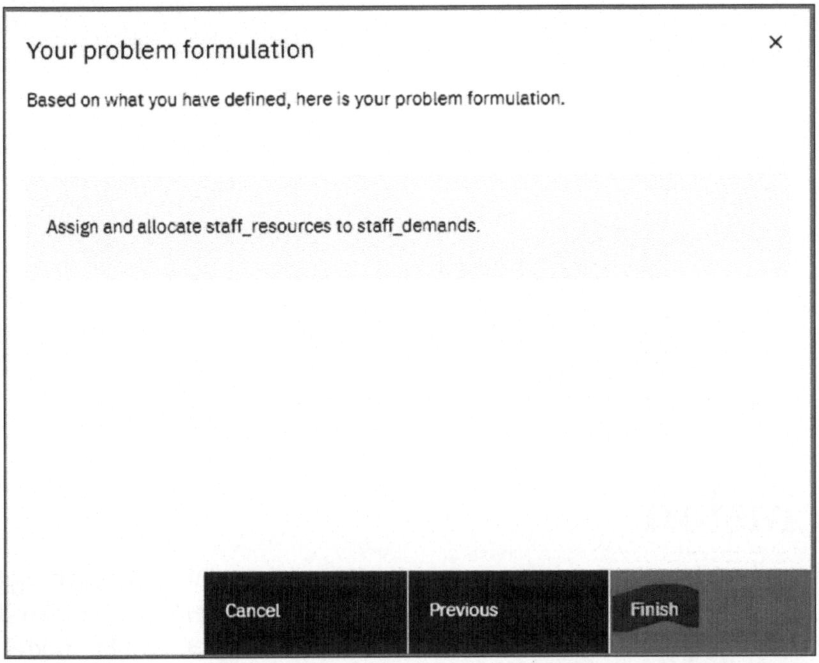

Figure* 5.59:** *We can now display the model process, and confirm by selecting the* ***Finish *command*

9. The modelling assistant suggests a number of possible analysis scenarios and objectives, which can be given weights, as highlighted in *Figure* 5.60:

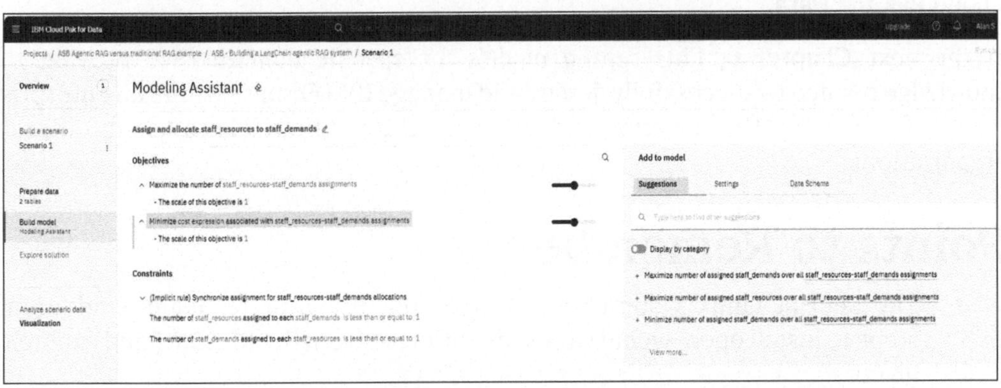

***Figure* 5.60:** *The modelling assistant suggests a number of possible analysis scenarios and objectives*

10. Finally, we select the Visualization using a Vega Chart displayed from columns select from our uploaded table data, staff demands, plotted against the period, as shown in *Figure* 5.61:

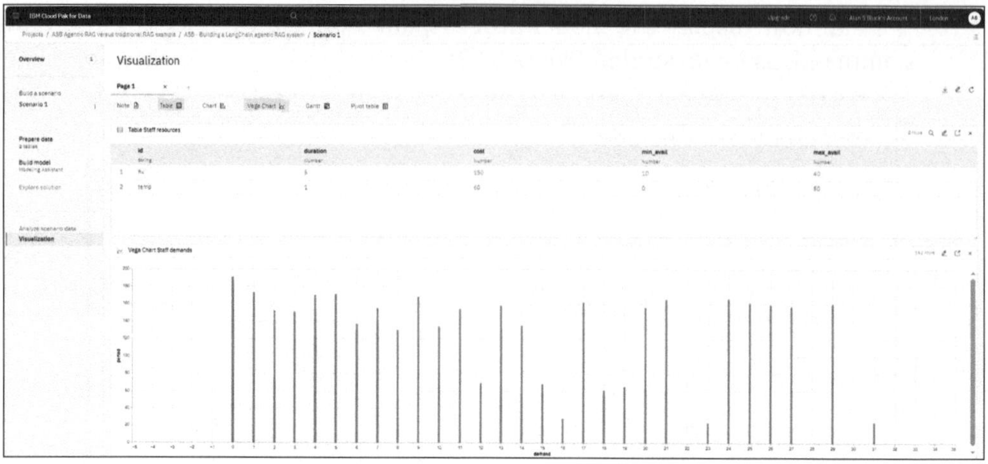

Figure 5.61: *Finally, we select the* **Visualization** *using a* **Vega Chart** *displayed from columns from our uploaded data*

Conclusion

In this chapter, we covered an overview of the IBM Granite Workshop labs setup using python code, using Jupyter Notebooks for prompt engineering. We also described the procedure required to customize the **IBM Granite 3.0 LLM model outputs** programmatically by using a prompt template.

The procedure described how to download **LLM** models from the recently released, **IBM Granite 3.1 version**. Finally, we covered the use of **IBM Watsonx** run with **IBM CLoud Pak for Data**.

In the next Chapter 6, *Fine-tuning models for specific domains*, we provide the knowledge needed to successfully deploy and manage IBM Granite within an enterprise setting, focusing on the selection and tuning of the LLM models to use in different organizations.

Points to Remember

- The RedHat Linux system with Ollama and IBM Granite requires additional steps to install open-webui which are different from the README.md examples given.
- There are Jupyter NoteBook Python language for AI and Data resource examples with over 460 scrollable panels on the Resources link available at:

  https://eu-gb.dataplatform.cloud.ibm.com/gallery?context=cpdaas
- Prompts built via the transformers library using the **apply_chate_template** function, will automatically include the recommended system prompt as long

as users do not specify a custom system prompt. IBM recommend the use of this system prompt to obtain the best performance from the IBM Granite 3.1 models.

- The snap, `open-webui install`, installs a shell script to be run at:

  `/snap/open-webui/7/bin/run-snap.sh`

- The **SearXNG** and **Open WebUI** both run by default on port **8080**, but this can be mapped for **SearXNG** to the local machine port **8888** using a Docker command.
- As of 25th December, 2024, Open WebUI updated their internal architecture with the 0.5 release. This has some performance improvements, but the chat results don't show up in the FireFox browser until the browser window is restarted.

Multiple Choice Questions

1. Which of the following commands is used to create a symbolic link for the snap system?

   a. **`sudo yum install snapd`**

   b. **`sudo systemctl enable --now snapd.socket`**

   c. **`sudo ln -s /var/lib/snapd/snap /snap`**

   d. **`sudo snap install --beta open-webui`**

2. Which of the following commands is used to download the **SearXNG** container image?

   a. **`docker.io/searxng/searxng:latest`**

   b. **`vi uwsgi.ini`**

   c. **`docker pull searxng/searxng`**

   d. **`docker run -d --name searxng -p 8888:8080 -v ~/searxng:/etc/searxng --restart always searxng/searxng:latest`**

3. Which of the following LLM models is the largest?

   a. **`granite3-moe:1b`**

   b. **`granite-code:3b`**

   c. **`granite3-dense:8b`**

   d. **`granite3-dense:2b`**

4. Which of the following LLM models is the smallest?
    a. **`granite3-moe:1b`**
    b. **`granite-code:3b`**
    c. **`granite3-dense:8b`**
    d. **`granite3-dense:2b`**
5. Which of the following LLM models is the latest to be released?
    a. **`granite3-moe:1b`**
    b. **`granite3.1-dense:8b-instruct-q4_0`**
    c. **`granite3.1-dense:8b`**
    d. **`granite-code:3b`**

Answers

1. c
2. c
3. c
4. a
5. b

Questions

1. Outline the procedure which must be used to create an **IBM Cloud** account for use with **IBM API** calls.
2. List the **LLMs** and their sizes available with **IBM Granite 3.1**.
3. Outline the **Python** code which could be used to provide an alternative response style for an **LLM** model.
4. Describe the use of Open Web-UI for managing prompts and its advantages over using the **`ollama`** command line interface.
5. Which of the IBM Granite LLM model classes would be ideal for use on a local server application or where a **CPU**-based deployment is required?

Key Terms

- **LLM**: Large Language Model is trained on huge datasets, allowing them to be processed by AI programs taking prompts as input to perform relevant text generation, human language translation, intelligent summarization and forecasting. They utilise neural network techniques using many parameters to process and analyse text forAI learning based on the provision of training responses.
- **AI**: Artificial Intelligence Software that mimics the responses, you might expect to questions supplied by a human operator.
- **API**: Application Program Interface is a set of callable functions which allow the use of communications between a client and a server system, or a server to server platform used to transmit and process data in a defined format.
- **CUDA**: Compute Unified Device Architecture is a software platform and **API** interface that accelerates the performance of Graphics Processing Units (**GPUs**) which can then be used for general-purpose processing, especially useful for AI applications.
- **REST**: Representational State Transfer is a web client/server API software architecture that defines how APIs communicate.
- **GPU:** These are hardware graphics processing units, providing a high speed processing resource. Using their high performance capabilities, they are ideal for developing and using AI Large Language Models.
- **RHEL:** RedHat Enterprise Linux is a commercial version of the Linux Operating system, now owned by **IBM.**
- **RAG: Retrieval-Augmented Generation** provides an existing LLM with datasets from additional data sources, without the need for any further fine-tuning.

  (See: https://research.ibm.com/blog/retrieval-augmented-generation-RAG)

References

1. There is a Granite Notebooks section describing how to set up the Python notebooks.

   See:
   https://ibm.github.io/granite-workshop/pre-work/
   and
   https://ibm.github.io/watsonx-prompt-lab/pre-work/
   https://ibm.github.io/watsonx-prompt-lab/lab-1/
2. For prompt Exercises, see https://ibm.github.io/watsonx-prompt-lab/lab-3/
3. For examples based on the IBM documentation entitled

"Programmatically inferencing a foundation model by using a prompt template - IBM Documentation", see:
https://www.ibm.com/docs/en/watsonx/saas?topic=library-inferencing-prompt-template

4. The following link, https://www.ibm.com/new/announcements/ibm-granite-3-1-powerful-performance-long-context-and-more describes the deep-dive into the improvements, additions and new IBM Granite 3.1 capabilities for IBM Granite 3.1.

5. The link https://www.ibm.com/granite now provides more information on the new IBM Granite 3.1 version, and its open source enterprise LLMs.

   See: https://www.ibm.com/granite/docs/models/granite/ for the Home page for the new IBM Granite 3.1 release.

6. The IBM Granite 3.1 models are available to run Locally with Ollama:

   https://ollama.com/library/granite3.1-dense:8b

7. IBM Granite playground provides a web page to try out the IBM Granite 3.1 capabilities by entering questions directly:

   https://www.ibm.com/granite/playground

8. The IBM Granite 3.1 models are also available on Hugging Face: https://huggingface.co/ibm-granite/granite-3.1-8b-instruct

9. The following link provides examples of the prompts required for the new IBM Granite 3.1 models.

   https://www.ibm.com/docs/en/watsonx/saas?topic=library-inferencing-prompt-template

10. Installation of **ibm-watsonx-ai** Python library is publicly available on PyPI: https://pypi.org/project/ibm-watsonx-ai/.

11. The package can be installed with pip, see further details on:

    https://ibm.github.io/watsonx-ai-python-sdk/install.html

12. The following link is for a tutorial describing the building of an **agentic RAG** to implement an example of the use of an **AI** agent to process subtask workflows, along with the retrieval of additional data set information, to supplement the **IBM Granite 3.1** LLM's knowledge base.

    https://developer.ibm.com/tutorials/awb-build-agentic-rag-system-granite/

    There is also a GitHub link as follows:

    https://github.com/ibm-granite-community/granite-retrieval-agent

CHAPTER 6
Fine-Tune Models for Specific Domains

Introduction

This chapter provides the knowledge needed to successfully deploy and manage **IBM Granite 3.0** (and the latest **3.1 version**) within an enterprise setting, focusing on the selection and tuning of the **LLM** models to use in different organisations.
(See https://www.ibm.com/granite/docs/how-to/fine-tuning/granite/
And
https://github.com/ibm-granite-community/granite-snack-cookbook/blob/main/recipes/Fine_Tuning/Finetuning_Granite_Pirate_Style.ipynb)

Structure

In this chapter, we will discuss the following topics:

- Fine-Tuning an Instruction LLM Model
- Dataset Preparation
- Model Loading and Quantization
- Text Generation Dataset Preparation
- Checking the Tuned LLM Model
- Training Setup
- Training Process
- Saving the Fine-tuned Model

Fine-Tuning an Instruction LLM Model

There is an IBM Notebook (**`Finetuning_Granite_Pirate_Style.ipynb`**) which we can use to demonstrate how an **LLM** can be Fine-tuned which follows the process of adapting a pre-trained model to a new domain. As described in detail, in the last *Chapter*

5, *Advanced Prompt Engineering*, the domain-specific terms (such as '*inheritance*') can shift based on the training data.

This Notebook covers the following steps, with background information in the URL links:

https://github.com/ibm-granite-community/granite-retrieval-agent

and

https://www.ibm.com/think/tutorials/chunking-strategies-for-rag-with-langchain-watsonx-ai , ("**Implementing RAG chunking strategies with LangChain and watsonx.ai**")

As explained in the second link, "*chunking*" is the process of breaking large pieces of text into smaller text segments or chunks. The chunking process is used by **RAG** for Natural Language Processing (**NLP**) to allow the merging of current internet data with pre-trained Large Language Models (**LLMs**), so that supplemental datasets can be used to optimize the quality of the LLM's output.

For the processing of large documents, chunking can be used to split the text into smaller token sets of meaningful chunks. These text token chunks can then be embedded and stored in a vector database through the use of an embedding model.

The **RAG** system can then use semantic search to retrieve only the most relevant chunks.

For this, smaller chunks usually outperform the larger chunks, since they tend to be easier to process for models with smaller token context window sizes.

The link, https://huggingface.co/ibm-granite/granite-guardian-3.1-8b, provides another example, which describes the use of **IBM Granite Guardian 3.1 8B** which is a fine-tuned Instruct model designed to detect risks in prompts and responses.

As another example we follow a **GitHub** tutorial for fine-tuning a Code Instruction Model for Legal Tasks.

We will be using the model:

https://github.com/ibm-granite-community/granite-code-cookbook/blob/main/recipes/Fine_Tuning_Granite/Finetuning_Granite.ipynb

We can clone the IBM GitHub **`granite-code-cookbook`** using:

```
df -k /home/alan
mkdir QnAChatbot
```

The following three commands can be used each time, we create a default command window for the user. This sets up our Python environment, ready for the Jupyter Lab load:

```
cd QnAChatbot/
python3 -m venv venv
source venv/bin/activate
```

We have to install the Python libraries we need for the Notebooks, as follows:

Install dependencies:

```
vi requirements.txt
```

And enter the following list:

```
pydantic==2.9.1
pydantic_core==2.23.3
requests==2.32.3
streamlit==1.38.0
urllib3==2.2.2
python-dotenv==1.0.1
```

Then run the following command:

```
pip install -r requirements.txt
```

Shown as follows:

```
(venv) [alan@ecmukdemo2025 QnAChatbot]$ vi requirements.txt
(venv) [alan@ecmukdemo2025 QnAChatbot]$ pip install -r
requirements.txt
Collecting pydantic==2.9.1
  Downloading pydantic-2.9.1-py3-none-any.whl (434 kB)
     |████████████████████████████████| 434 kB 2.0 MB/s
Collecting pydantic_core==2.23.3
  Downloading pydantic_core-2.23.3-cp39-cp39-manylinux_2_17_
x86_64.manylinux2014_x86_64.whl (2.1 MB)
Etc…
Etc…
Installing collected packages: typing-extensions, rpds-py, attrs,
referencing, smmap, six, mdurl, MarkupSafe, jsonschema-specifica-
tions, urllib3, tzdata, pytz, python-dateutil, pygments, packag-
ing, numpy, narwhals, markdown-it-py, jsonschema, jinja2, idna,
gitdb, charset-normalizer, certifi, watchdog, tornado, toml, te-
nacity, rich, requests, pydeck, pydantic-core, pyarrow, protobuf,
pillow, pandas, gitpython, click, cachetools, blinker, annotat-
ed-types, altair, streamlit, python-dotenv, pydantic
Successfully installed MarkupSafe-3.0.2 altair-5.5.0 annotat-
ed-types-0.7.0 attrs-25.1.0 blinker-1.9.0 cachetools-5.5.1 cer-
tifi-2024.12.14 charset-normalizer-3.4.1 click-8.1.8 gitdb-4.0.12
```

```
gitpython-3.1.44 idna-3.10 jinja2-3.1.5 jsonschema-4.23.0
jsonschema-specifications-2024.10.1 markdown-it-py-3.0.0
mdurl-0.1.2 narwhals-1.23.0 numpy-2.0.2 packaging-24.2 pan-
das-2.2.3 pillow-10.4.0 protobuf-5.29.3 pyarrow-19.0.0 pydan-
tic-2.9.1 pydantic-core-2.23.3 pydeck-0.9.1 pygments-2.19.1
python-dateutil-2.9.0.post0 python-dotenv-1.0.1 pytz-2024.2
referencing-0.36.2 requests-2.32.3 rich-13.9.4 rpds-py-0.22.3
six-1.17.0 smmap-5.0.2 streamlit-1.38.0 tenacity-8.5.0 toml-
0.10.2 tornado-6.4.2 typing-extensions-4.12.2 tzdata-2025.1
urllib3-2.2.2 watchdog-4.0.2
(venv) [alan@ecmukdemo2025 QnAChatbot]$
```

Now, we set up the **IBM Granite 3.0 GitHub** clone, which downloads the environment for our example **Jupiter lab Notebook** files, as illustrated in *Figure 6.1*:

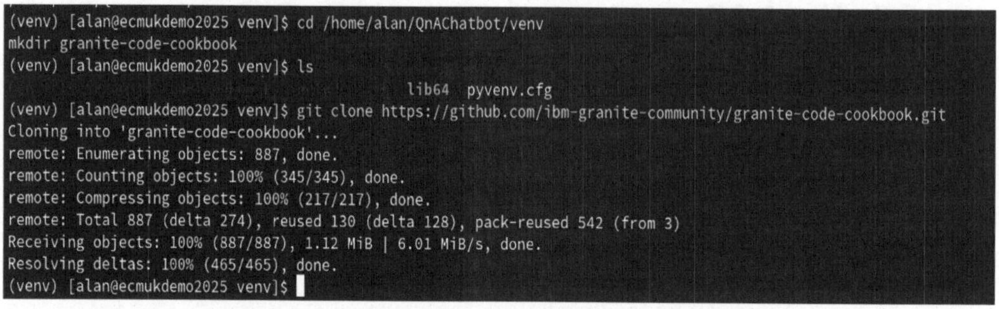

Figure 6.1: *We clone examples for IBM Granite 3.0 GitHub to download the example,* ***Jupiter Lab*** *Notebook files*

```
cd /home/alan/QnAChatbot/venv
mkdir granite-code-cookbook
git clone https://github.com/ibm-granite-community/gran-
ite-code-cookbook.git
```

Finally, we move to the **granite-code-cookbook** top directory and launch **Jupyter lab(venv).**

```
 [alan@ecmukdemo2025 venv]$ cd /home/alan/QnAChatbot/venv/gran-
ite-code-cookbook
(venv) [alan@ecmukdemo2025 granite-code-cookbook]$ jupyter lab
```

Installing Necessary Dependencies

We installed the necessary **Python AI** libraries as follows:

First, we have to install the **Python 3.11.9** version using the **dnf** installer command:

```
(venv) [alan@ecmukdemo2025 granite-code-cookbook]$ sudo dnf
install python3.11
```

Next, we use the **pip3.11** installer to load supporting libraries, as follows:

```
pip3.11 install "transformers>=4.45.2" datasets accelerate bit-
sandbytes peft trl
```

And upgraded **pip**:

Then, we have to install the **ipykernel** module for **python 3.11** on the system and activate it for **jupyter**:

As can be demonstrated as follows, we can have multiple versions of python installed, and set the version we use for Jupyter Lab by selecting the required **Python** kernel from the **IDE** web page.

```
(venv) [alan@ecmukdemo2025 granite-code-cookbook]$ python -V
Python 3.9.21
(venv) [alan@ecmukdemo2025 granite-code-cookbook]$ python3.11 -V
Python 3.11.9
```

We achieve this, after installing **Python** version **3.11.9**, by using the **pip3.11** python installer, to install a Jupyter **ipykernel**, as shown:

```
(venv) [alan@ecmukdemo2025 granite-code-cookbook]$ pip3.11
install ipykernel
```

Then install the **Jupyter lab** kernel

```
(venv) [alan@ecmukdemo2025 granite-code-cookbook]$ python3.11 -m
ipykernel install --user
```

We also needed to install the Python **ipywidgets** libraries:

```
(venv) [alan@ecmukdemo2025 granite-code-cookbook]$ pip3.11 in-
stall ipywidgets
```

Also we included the **GCC** shared object libraries:

```
[alan@ecmukdemo2025 ~]$ su - root
```

Password:

```
[root@ecmukdemo2025 ~]# yum install libstdc++
```

For the Jupyter Notebook, **Finetuning_Granite.ipynb**, loaded first as shown in *Figure 6.2*:

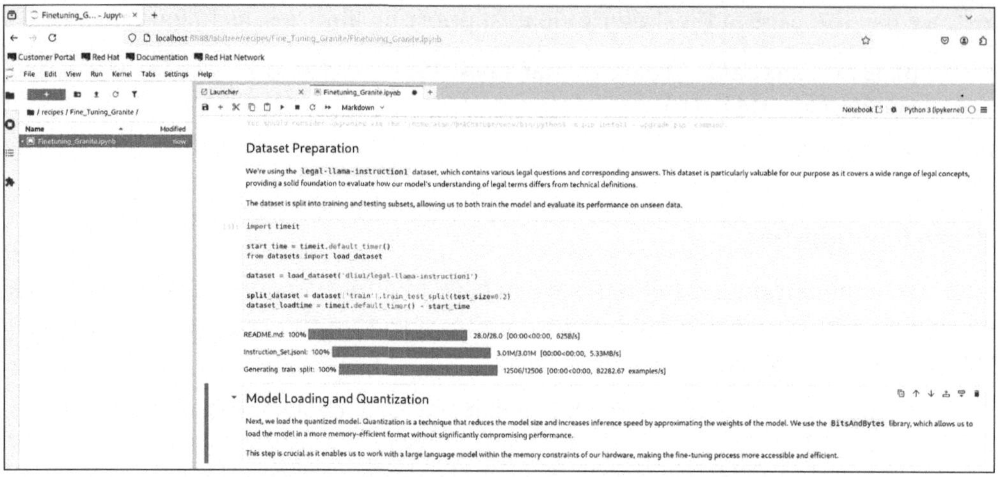

Figure 6.2: The Jupyter Notebook, **Finetuning_Granite.ipynb**

The first cell runs correctly, as shown in *Figure* 6.3:

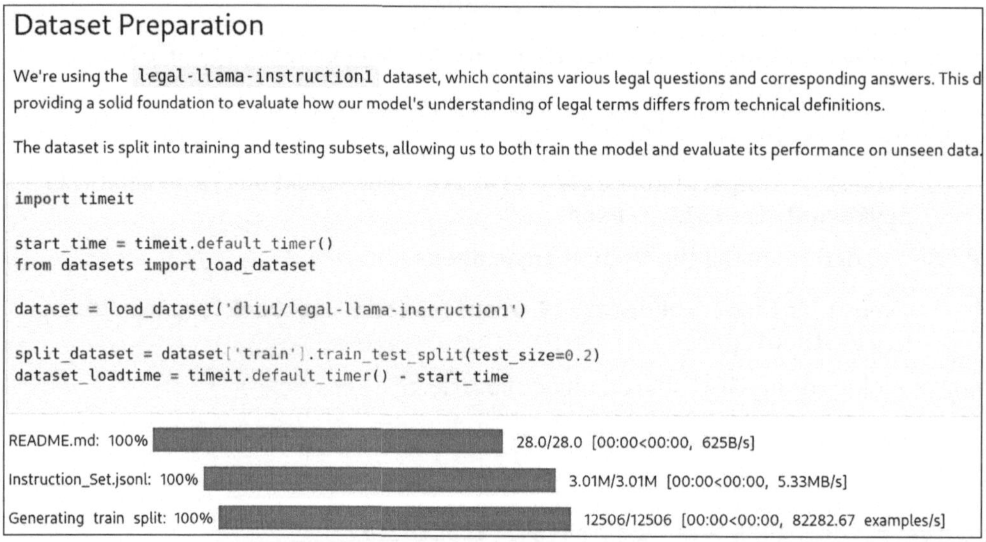

Figure 6.3: *The first cell of the Jupyter Notebook,* **Finetuning_Granite.ipynb** *works correctly*

We needed to update the **Python pip** installer version we are using, to **pip-25.0**, using the command:

```
/home/alan/QnAChatbot/venv/bin/python3 -m pip install --upgrade
pip
```

As shown in *Figure 6.4*:

```
(venv) [alan@ecmukdemo2025 granite-code-cookbook]$ /home/alan/QnAChatbot/venv/bin/python3 -m pip install --upgrade pip
Requirement already satisfied: pip in /home/alan/QnAChatbot/venv/lib/python3.9/site-packages (21.3.1)
Collecting pip
  Downloading pip-25.0-py3-none-any.whl (1.8 MB)
     |████████████████████████████████| 1.8 MB 3.9 MB/s
Installing collected packages: pip
  Attempting uninstall: pip
    Found existing installation: pip 21.3.1
    Uninstalling pip-21.3.1:
      Successfully uninstalled pip-21.3.1
Successfully installed pip-25.0
(venv) [alan@ecmukdemo2025 granite-code-cookbook]$
```

Figure 6.4: *We needed to update the Python pip installer version we are using, to pip-25.0*

Next, we updated the version of the Jupyter lab **`ipykernel`** we are using, as illustrated in *Figure 6.5*:

```
alan@ecmukdemo2025:~/QnAChatbot/venv/granite-code-cookbook

(venv) [alan@ecmukdemo2025 granite-code-cookbook]$ python3.11 -V
Python 3.11.9
(venv) [alan@ecmukdemo2025 granite-code-cookbook]$ pip3.11 install ipykernel
bash: pip3.11: command not found...
Install package 'python3.11-pip' to provide command 'pip3.11'? [N/y] y


 * Waiting in queue...
 * Loading list of packages....
The following packages have to be installed:
 python3.11-pip-22.3.1-5.el9.noarch     A tool for installing and managing Python packages
 python3.11-setuptools-65.5.1-3.el9.noarch      Easily build and distribute Python packages
Proceed with changes? [N/y] y


 * Waiting in queue...
 * Waiting for authentication...
 * Waiting in queue...
 * Downloading packages...
 * Requesting data...
 * Testing changes...
 * Installing packages...
Defaulting to user installation because normal site-packages is not writeable
Collecting ipykernel
  Using cached ipykernel-6.29.5-py3-none-any.whl (117 kB)
Collecting comm>=0.1.1
  Using cached comm-0.2.2-py3-none-any.whl (7.2 kB)
```

Figure 6.5: *We updated the version of the Jupyter lab* ***ipykernel,*** *we are using*

This downloaded **`ipykernel`** version needs to be installed, using the command:

```
python3.11 -m ipykernel install --user
```

This is shown in *Figure 6.6*:

```
Collecting pure-eval
  Using cached pure_eval-0.2.3-py3-none-any.whl (11 kB)
Installing collected packages: wcwidth, pure-eval, ptyprocess, typing_extensions, traitlets, tornado, six, pyzmq, pygments, psutil
, prompt_toolkit, platformdirs, pexpect, parso, packaging, nest-asyncio, executing, decorator, debugpy, asttokens, stack_data, pyt
hon-dateutil, matplotlib-inline, jupyter-core, jedi, comm, jupyter-client, ipython, ipykernel
Successfully installed asttokens-3.0.0 comm-0.2.2 debugpy-1.8.12 decorator-5.1.1 executing-2.2.0 ipykernel-6.29.5 ipython-8.31.0 j
edi-0.19.2 jupyter-client-8.6.3 jupyter-core-5.7.2 matplotlib-inline-0.1.7 nest-asyncio-1.6.0 packaging-24.2 parso-0.8.4 pexpect-4
.9.0 platformdirs-4.3.6 prompt_toolkit-3.0.50 psutil-6.1.1 ptyprocess-0.7.0 pure-eval-0.2.3 pygments-2.19.1 python-dateutil-2.9.0.
post0 pyzmq-26.2.0 six-1.17.0 stack_data-0.6.3 tornado-6.4.2 traitlets-5.14.3 typing_extensions-4.12.2 wcwidth-0.2.13

(venv) [alan@ecmukdemo2025 granite-code-cookbook]$ python3.11 -m ipykernel install --user
Installed kernelspec python3 in /home/alan/.local/share/jupyter/kernels/python3
(venv) [alan@ecmukdemo2025 granite-code-cookbook]$
```

Figure 6.6: *The downloaded* ***ipykernel*** *version needs to be installed*

We made some progress by using **`Finetuning_Granite.ipynb`** by adding additional lines, as shown:

1. To check the version of the Jupyter lab **`ipykernel`** we are using, we added the cell with lines:

   ```
   import sys
   print(sys.version)
   ```

   This displays the **Python** version (**3.11.9**) and the library version of **GCC**:

   3.11.9 (main, Dec 9 2024, 00:00:00) [GCC 11.5.0 20240719 (Red Hat 11.5.0-2)], as shown in *Figure* 6.7:

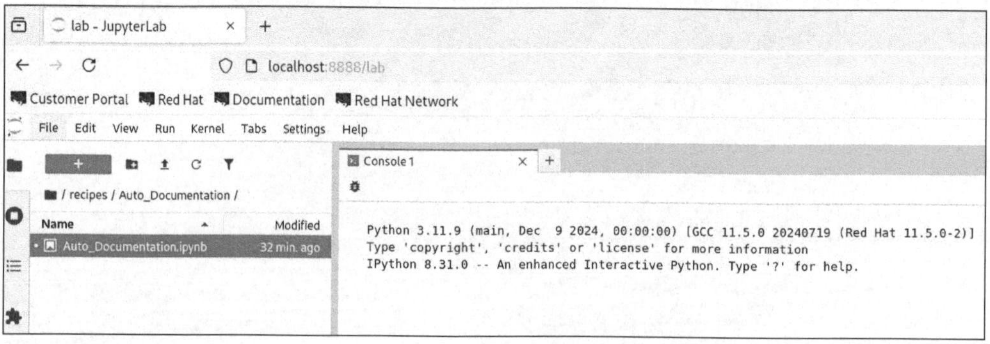

Figure 6.7: *The* ***python print(sys.version)*** *command shows the Python version (3.11.9), and the library version of GCC in the Console window*

The widget libraries were also installed with versions, as illustrated in *Figure* 6.8:

```
Installing collected packages: widgetsnbextension, jupyterlab-widgets, ipywidgets
Successfully installed ipywidgets-8.1.5 jupyterlab-widgets-3.0.13 widgetsnbextension-4.0.13
(venv) [alan@ecmukdemo2025 granite-code-cookbook]$
```

Figure 6.8: *The widget libraries were also installed with the required versions*

2. Then we added:

   ```
   device = 'cuda' if torch.cuda.is_available() else 'cpu' #ASB Add-
   ed for our CPU system with no GPU
   ```

   An attempt was made to switch to **CPU**-only mode; however, a dependent library appears to rely on the use of a **GPU** processor, which wasn't installed on our server.

   CUDA, developed by **NVIDIA** for its **GPU**s, stands for Compute Unified Device Architecture, and drives **NVIDIA**s parallel computing platform, **GPU** system (Graphical Processing Units) and the **NVIDIA** programming model. It provides an application programming interface supporting developers using **NVIDIA GPU**s for general-purpose computing, providing **AI** processing functionality rather than just graphics processing. **CUDA** enables programmers to use the power of **GPU**s for tasks such as artificial intelligence, deep learning, and mathematical programming by utilizing a **GPU**'s parallel processing functionality.

3. The symbolic link command was made to correct an issue with access to the library:

   (With an error message as follows: "`lib/x86_64-linux-gnu/libstdc++ so 6 version glibcxx_3 4.32 not found on RedHat Linux`")

   ```
   #ASB added for resolving shared object libraries
   !ln -sf /usr/lib64/libstdc++.so.6
   ```

This worked to correct this error but, unfortunately the **`autotuner.py`** library (line 368) sets a parameter to **`use_cuda_graph`** which we think implies a dependency on a **GPU** processor, wasn't available on our system.

For the Notebook, **`code_summarization.ipynb`** (Using **CLDK** to explain **Java** methods) we ran this successfully by using the **python 3.11** version in our **Jupyter lab** environment.

The following prerequisites were specified:

- **Python 3.11** or later
- **Java 11** or later
- **Maven 3.9** or later
- **Ollama 0.3.4** or later
- IBM Granite code models (The **`granite-code:3b`** model was used).

And then we found that the **Python pip** command line install cells defined in the GitHub copy of the Jupyter lab NoteBook file, **`code_summarization.ipynb`**, had to be changed from:

```
!pip install ollama
to
!pip3.11 install ollama #ASB Changed from !pip to !pip3.11
```

```
And:
!pip install cldk==0.1.4
to
!pip3.11 install cldk==0.1.4 #ASB Changed from !pip to !pip3.11
```

For the tutorial file, **code_summarization.ipynb,** IBM use **CLDK** to generate a summary explanation for a **Java** method. **CLDK** performs program analysis, building an **LLM**-based code summarizer. On completing the tutorial, we implemented the tool and generated a summary for a Java method.

We edited, created and ran the cells for a working version of the NoteBook, saved as the file, **code_summarization_ASB.ipynb** which runs in our **RedHat Linux RHEL 9.2 VMware** server.

The following question was posed for a section of **Java** code in **Cell 10** of the **Python**:

```
def format_inst(code, focal_method, focal_class, language):
    """
    Format the instruction for the given focal method and class.
    """
    inst = f"Question: Can you write a brief summary for the
method `{focal_method}` in the class `{focal_class}` below?\n"

    inst += "\n"
    inst += f"```{language}\n"
    inst += code
    inst += "```" if code.endswith("\n") else "\n```"
    inst += "\n"
    return inst
```

This Jupyter Lab Notebook gives the following output cell on a successful run:

````
Class: org.apache.commons.cli.GnuParser
Instruction:
Question: Can you write a brief summary for the method `protected
String[] flatten(final Options, final String[] arguments, final
boolean stopAtNonOption)` in the class `GnuParser` below?

```java
package org.apache.commons.cli;

import java.util.ArrayList;
import java.util.List;

@Deprecated
public class GnuParser extends Parser {

    @Override
````
````

```
    protected String[] flatten(final Options options, final String[]
arguments, final boolean stopAtNonOption) {
        final List<String> tokens = new ArrayList<>();
        boolean eatTheRest = false;
        for (int i = 0; i < arguments.length; i++) {
            final String arg = arguments[i];
            if ("--".equals(arg)) {
                eatTheRest = true;
                tokens.add("--");
            } else if ("-".equals(arg)) {
                tokens.add("-");
            } else if (arg.startsWith("-")) {
                final String opt = Util.stripLeadingHyphens(arg);
                if (options.hasOption(opt)) {
                    tokens.add(arg);
                } else {
                    final int equalPos = DefaultParser.index-
                    OfEqual(opt);
                    if (equalPos != -1 && options.hasOption(opt.
                    substring(0, equalPos))) {
                        tokens.add(arg.substring(0, arg.index-
                        Of(Char.EQUAL))); // --foo
                        tokens.add(arg.substring(arg.index-
                        Of(Char.EQUAL) + 1)); // value
                    } else if (options.hasOption(arg.substring(0,
                    2))) {
                        tokens.add(arg.substring(0, 2)); // -D
                        tokens.add(arg.substring(2)); // proper-
                        ty=value
                    } else {
                        eatTheRest = stopAtNonOption;
                        tokens.add(arg);
                    }
                }
            } else {
                tokens.add(arg);
            }

            if (eatTheRest) {
                for (i++; i < arguments.length; i++) { // NOPMD
                    tokens.add(arguments[i]);
                }
            }
        }

        return tokens.toArray(Util.EMPTY_STRING_ARRAY);
    }
```

```
}
```

```
Generating code summary and it will take few minutes (or even
seconds) based on where the model has been hosted...
```

We have shown the **LLM Java** code **AI** analysis output we had returned for our **`code_summarization_ASB.ipynb`**, Jupyter lab Notebook **Python**, in italics:

```
LLM Output:
"The `flatten` method is responsible for parsing command-line options and arguments in the Apache Commons CLI library. It takes three parameters: `options`, which is an instance of the `Options` class representing the available command-line options; `arguments`, which is an array of strings containing the command-line arguments; and `stopAtNonOption`, a boolean value indicating whether to stop parsing at non-option arguments.

The method uses a loop to iterate through each argument in the `arguments` array. If the argument is a double dash (`--`), it sets the `eatTheRest` flag to true, indicating that the rest of the arguments should be added to the result. If the argument is a single dash (`-`), it adds the dash itself to the result.

If the argument starts with a dash (`-`), the method checks if the option exists in the `options` instance using the `hasOption` method. If the option exists, the argument is added to the result. Otherwise, the method checks for an equal sign (`=`) in the option and, if found, checks if the option exists with the value specified after the equal sign. If both conditions are met, the option and its value are added to the result.

If none of the above conditions are met, the `eatTheRest` flag is set to the value of the `stopAtNonOption` parameter, indicating whether to stop parsing at non-option arguments. The argument is then added to the result.

Finally, if the `eatTheRest` flag is true, the method adds any remaining arguments after the current one to the result. The resulting list of tokens is converted to an array and returned."
```

Loading and Exploring the Dataset

We outline the functionality of the fine-tuning examples provided by IBM in this section.

Note: *This section uses code from "Fine-tuning Guide for IBM Granite 3.0 – IBM Granite"*

https://www.ibm.com/granite/docs/how-to/fine-tuning/granite/

and

https://github.com/ibm-granite-community/granite-snack-cookbook/blob/main/recipes/Fine_Tuning/Finetuning_Granite_Pirate_Style.ipynb

IBM use the **alespalla/chatbot_instruction_prompts** dataset, which contains various chat prompts and responses. This dataset is used to create the pirate talk data set, so all the **LLM** responses will be spoken like a pirate (see *Chapter 5, Advanced Prompt Engineering*, in the section: "*Transfer learning by combining two pretrained LLM datasets*" for the complete procedure used to run the **Load_LoRA_From_Huggingface_ASB.ipynb** Jupyter Notebook).

The **qLoRA** (Quantized Low-Rank Adaptation) technique is described further as follows.

This **alespalla/chatbot_instruction_prompts** dataset is split into training and testing subsets, so that the model can be trained, and the model performance can be validated on the unseen data.

Setting up the Quantized Model

In this section, the Python code is described for each cell in the Jupiter Notebook cell examples:

We can run the following python code to download the datasets required:

```
!pip3.11 install "transformers>=4.45.2" datasets accelerate bit-
sandbytes peft trl
```

Then, we set the timer to record the processing time for the code, and load the dataset, **'alespalla/chatbot_instruction_prompts'** example, as shown in the following Python code:

```
import timeit

start_time = timeit.default_timer()
from datasets import load_dataset

dataset = load_dataset('alespalla/chatbot_instruction_prompts')

# split_dataset = dataset['train'].train_test_split(test_
size=0.2)
dataset_loadtime = timeit.default_timer() - start_time
```

Next, the quantized model is loaded, as shown in the following listing. This uses a technique called quantization that reduces the model size and increases the inference speed by approximating the weights of the model. The **BitsAndBytes** library is used to load the model in a memory-efficient format. (This code can only be run on a system with a **GPU**). The **BitsAndBytes** library step is critical to enable the program to work with the **LLM** given the limitations of the hardware memory available.

```
start_time = timeit.default_timer()
import torch
from transformers import AutoTokenizer, AutoModelForCausalLM,
TrainingArguments, BitsAndBytesConfig
from peft import LoraConfig
from trl import SFTTrainer

model_checkpoint = "ibm-granite/granite-3.0-2b-instruct"
tokenizer = AutoTokenizer.from_pretrained(model_checkpoint)

BitsAndBytesConfig

bnb_config = BitsAndBytesConfig(
    load_in_4bit=True,
    bnb_4bit_quant_type="nf4",
    bnb_4bit_use_double_quant=True,
    bnb_4bit_compute_dtype=torch.float16 # if not set will throw a
warning about slow speeds when training
)

model = AutoModelForCausalLM.from_pretrained(
  model_checkpoint,
  quantization_config=bnb_config,
  device_map="auto"

)

model_loadtime = timeit.default_timer() - start_time
```

The Key functionality used by the software listing is described by IBM as follows:

- **Filtering**: The **filter_long_examples** function removes examples with more than 50 prompt tokens or 200 response tokens, ensuring manageable input lengths for the model.
- **Pirate text generation**: The **pirateify** function performs the following steps:
    - Tokenizes input prompts with a transformer tokenizer

    - Generates pirate-like responses using a transformer model (configured for GPU acceleration in the original, but we changed the code to use our CPU using:
      `inputs = tokenizer(prompts, return_tensors="pt", padding=True, truncation=True).to('cpu') #ASB Changed from 'cuda' to 'cpu'`
    - Decodes generated tokens back into text
    - Applies batch processing for efficiency (batch size: 64)
- **Dataset preparation:**
    - Selects subsets of the original train and test datasets (6000 and 500 examples)
    - Applies filtering and pirate text generation to these subsets (resulting in 1500 and 250 examples)
    - Combines the transformed sets into a new **`DatasetDict`** named **`pirate_dataset`**

```
from transformers import pipeline
import datasets

def pirateify(batch):
  prompts = [f"make it sound like a pirate said this, do not
include any preamble or explanation only piratify the following:
{response}" for response in batch['response']]
  # Tokenize the inputs in batch and move them to GPU
  inputs = tokenizer(prompts, return_tensors="pt", padding=True,
truncation=True).to('cpu') #ASB Changed from 'cuda' to 'cpu'
  # Generate the pirate-like responses in batch
  outputs = model.generate(**inputs, max_new_tokens=256, do_sam-
ple=True, top_p=0.95, temperature=0.7)
  # Decode the generated tokens into text for each output in the
batch
  pirate_responses = []
  for output in outputs:
    pr = tokenizer.decode(output, skip_special_tokens=True)
    if '\n\n' in pr:
      pirate_responses.append(pr.split('\n\n')[-1])
    else:
      pirate_responses.append(pr)

  # Move the outputs back to CPU (to free up GPU memory)
  inputs = inputs.to('cpu')
  outputs = outputs.to('cpu')
  # Clear the GPU cache to release any unused memory
  torch.cuda.empty_cache()
  return {
```

```
        'prompt': batch['prompt'],  # The original prompts (already
a batch)
        'response': pirate_responses  # The pirate responses,
generated in batch
    }


def filter_long_examples(example):
    prompt_tokens = tokenizer.tokenize(example['prompt'])
    response_tokens = tokenizer.tokenize(example['response'])  #
Tokenize the response
    return len(response_tokens) <= 200 and len(prompt_tokens) <=
50

# Apply the filter to both train and test splits
train_filtered = dataset['train'].select(range(6000)).filter
(filter_long_examples)
test_filtered = dataset['test'].select(range(500)).filter(filter_
long_examples)

print(f"train_filtered: {len(train_filtered)} observations\ntest_
filtered: {len(test_filtered)} observations")
pirate_train = train_filtered.select(range(1500)).map(pirateify,
batched=True, batch_size=64)
pirate_test = test_filtered.select(range(250)).map(pirateify,
batched=True, batch_size=64)

# Save the new dataset
pirate_dataset = datasets.DatasetDict({
    'train': pirate_train,
    'test': pirate_test
})
```

The following code can then be run to train the Large Language Model:

```
pirate_dataset['train'].to_pandas().head()
import torch
torch.cuda.empty_cache()
```

Performing a Sanity Check

The next section of Python code is used to provide a sanity check for our new merged **LLM**, before the Fine-Tuning stage, by feeding it an example prompt about 'inheritance' which **IBM** recommends "*To ensure it produces intelligible and contextually appropriate responses*".

At this stage, we expect the model to interpret 'inheritance' in a programming context, explaining how classes inherit properties and methods from one another.

We can use this output as an initial baseline, for comparison on how the model's understanding shifts after fine-tuning on legal data. The output produced will be truncated because of the setting, **max_new_tokens=100.**

```
start_time = timeit.default_timer()
input_text = "<|user>What does 'inheritance' mean?\n<|assis-
tant|>\n"

inputs = tokenizer(input_text, return_tensors="pt")

outputs = model.generate(**inputs, max_new_tokens=100)
print(tokenizer.decode(outputs[0], skip_special_tokens=True))

model_check_loadtime = timeit.default_timer() - start_time
```

We expect the output obtained to be as follows (shown in italic font):

```
Output
Inheritance is a mechanism by which one class acquires the prop-
erties and behaviors of another class. In object-oriented pro-
gramming, inheritance allows a new class to inherit the proper-
ties and methods of an existing class, known as the parent or
base class. This can be useful for code reuse and creating a
hierarchy of classes.

For example, let's say we have a base class called "Vehicle" that
has properties like "make" and "model". We can create a subclass
called "Car" that
```

Configuring and Executing the Training Process

A model is created which has learned to give all answers as if it were a pirate, illustrating the method of transfer learning in Natural Language Processing.

This model is run (successfully) as already demonstrated in the previous chapter, using the Python Code in the Jupyter Lab Notebook file, **Load_LoRA_From_Huggingface_ASB.ipynb.**

Dataset Preparation

The following Jupyter Notebook, **Auto_Documentation.ipynb**, using the IBM Granite LLM, **granite-8B-Code-instruct-128k**, entitled "**Auto-generating Documentation: A Long Document Summarization Approach**" can be run to automatically generate documentation.

This is run on our **RedHat Linux version RHEL 9.2** system installed as **root**.

Dependencies

First, a Replicate API token is required from the web site: https://replicate.com/.

This is a costed service, with the prices shown in the link:

https://replicate.com/pricing.

Model Loading and Quantization

We see the description cell (in **`Auto_Documentation.ipynb`**) that covers an overview of the process. It describes the use of the **`granite-8B-Code-instruct-128k`** model, which has a context window of 128,000 tokens. This context window includes both the input (the example code used) and the output (the generated documentation). Because Tokenization can vary between models, the code used the specific tokenizer for the chosen model. If the input is too large, this can be split into smaller chunks, or it can be summarized.

Text Generation Dataset Preparation

For new users, there is a (temporary) **`free option`**.

The terms of service are located at https://replicate.com/terms.

From this, clause 6 states:

1. You can try "**`featured models`**" (see https://replicate.com/explore#featured-models) out on "Replicate for free", but some features are only available to customers with billing set up. See Section 4 for clauses related to fees.

   This notebook demonstrates an innovative application of long document summarization techniques to automatically generate documentation for Python code.

   We commented out the non-working line:

   a. `!python -upgrade`

2. We created the required API token from the Replicate web-site, which is then entered as shown in *Figure* 6.9:

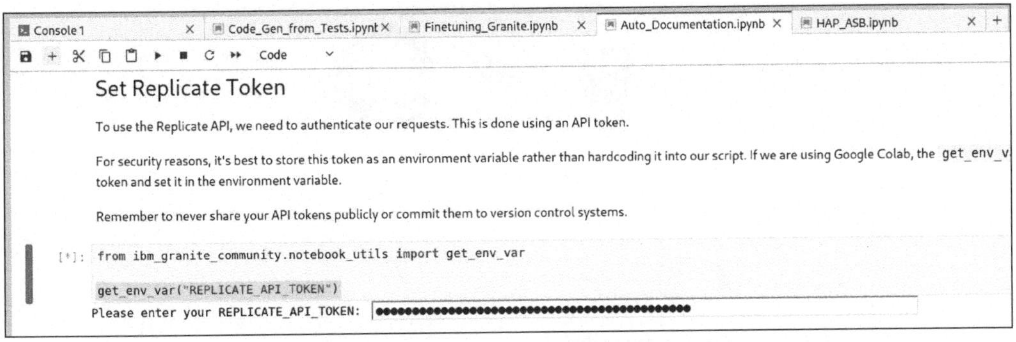

Figure 6.9: *We created the required API token from the Replicate web-site*

First, we create a Replicate account, based on our GitHub account, as shown in *Figure 6.10*:

Figure 6.10: *First, we created a Replicate account, based on our GitHub account*

3. We can use an existing **GitHub** account to authorize the **Replicate** site to access our **GitHub** system, as illustrated in *Figure 6.11*:

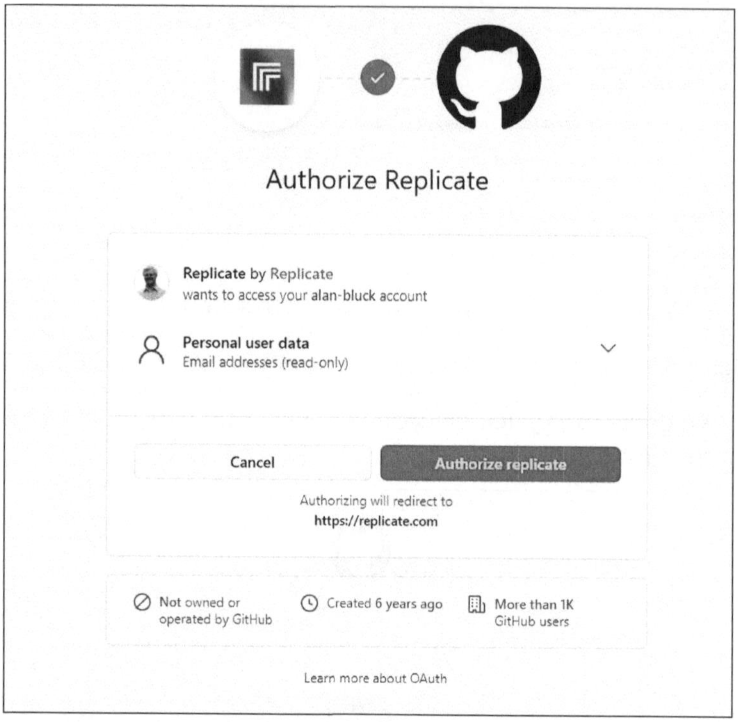

Figure 6.11: *We can use an existing* **GitHub** *account to authorize the* **Replicate** *site*

4. We need to enter an email address for **`Replicate`** to use:

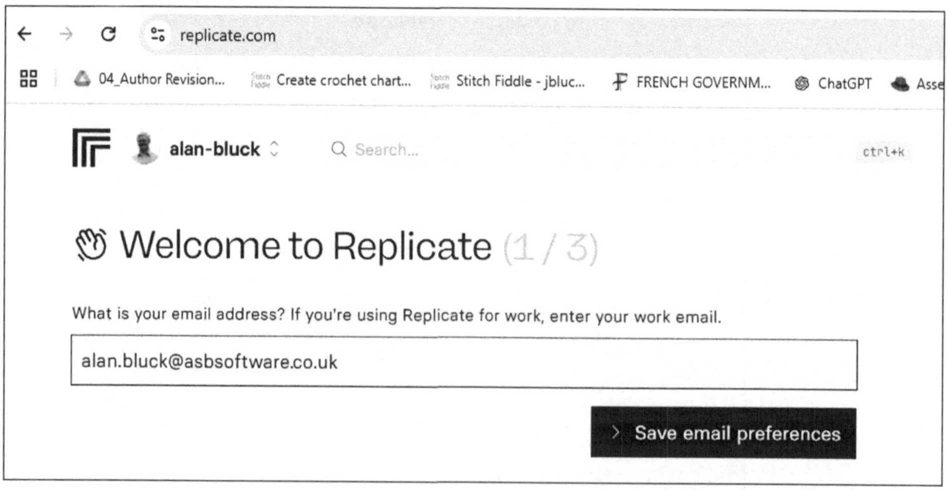

Figure 6.12: *We need to enter an email address for* **Replicate** *to use*

5. The details of the user preferences are entered, as highlighted in *Figure 6.13*:

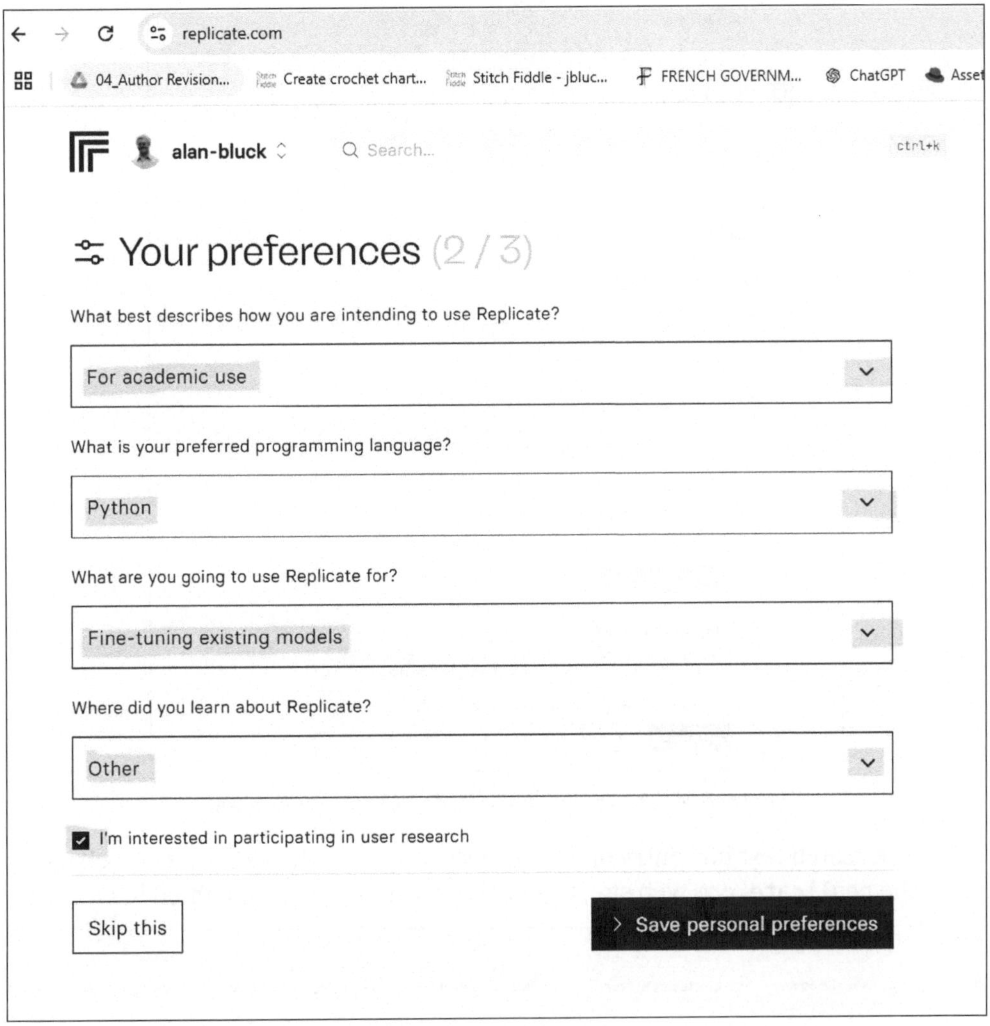

Figure 6.13: *The details of the user preferences are entered as highlighted*

6. After the **`Save personal preferences`** command is selected, the option is ticked to **`Create an account`**, as shown in *Figure 6.14*:

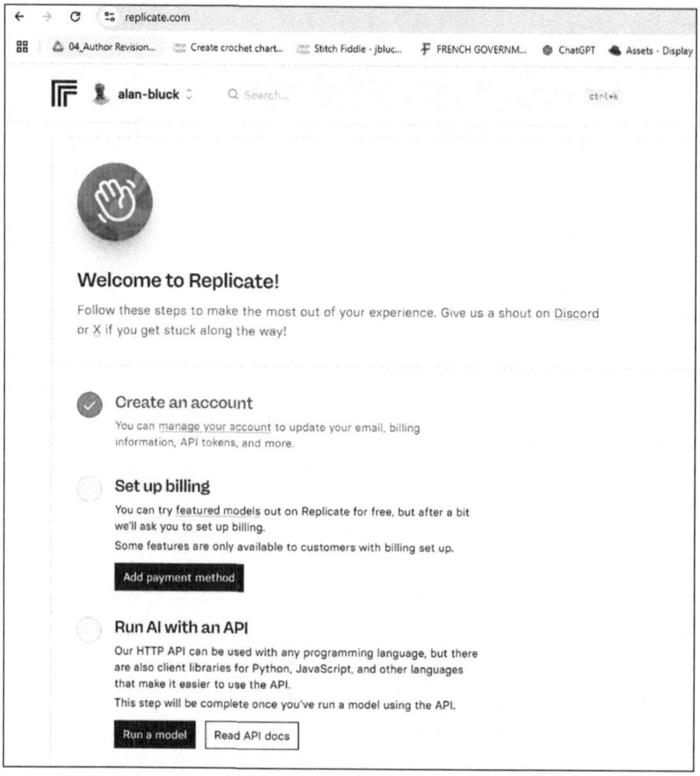

Figure 6.14:** The option is selected to **Create an account

7. The search text box entry of "**AP**" allows us to select the **API Tokens** web page on the **replicate.com** web site, **Pages** dropdown box, as highlighted in *Figure 6.15*:

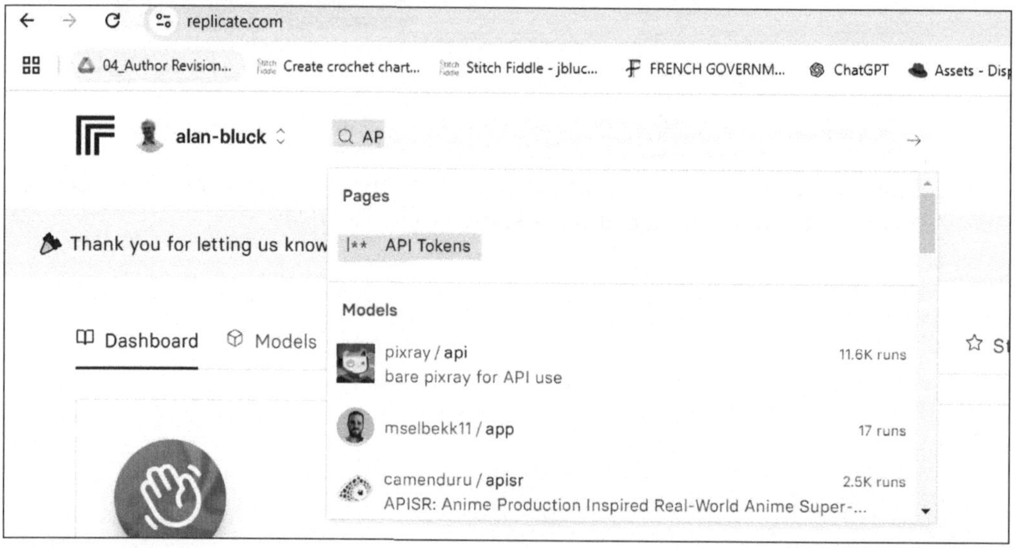

***Figure 6.15:** The search text box entry of AP allows us to select the API Tokens web page*

8. We are prompted to enter an **`API`** token name to use, which we enter in the **`Text Box`** shown in *Figure 6.16*:

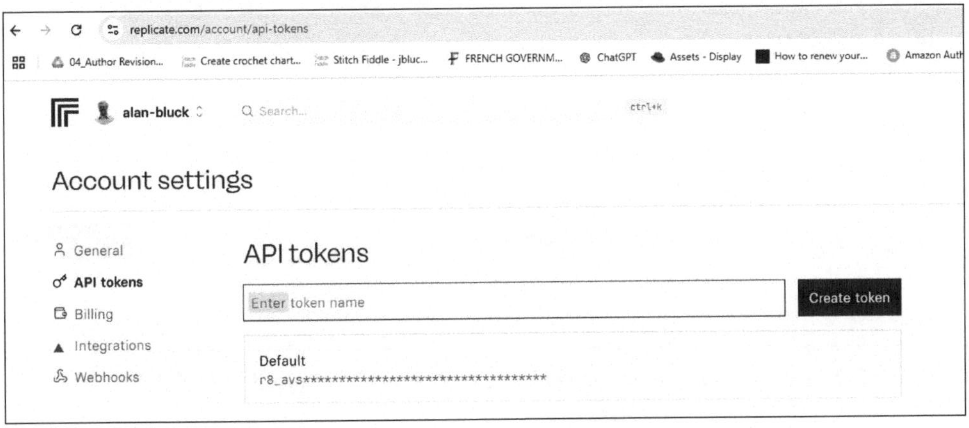

Figure 6.16: *We are prompted to enter an* **API** *token name to use*

9. We enter the reference name for the **`API Token,`** we require **`IBM Autogenerate Token ASB Test 1`**, as shown in *Figure 6.17*:

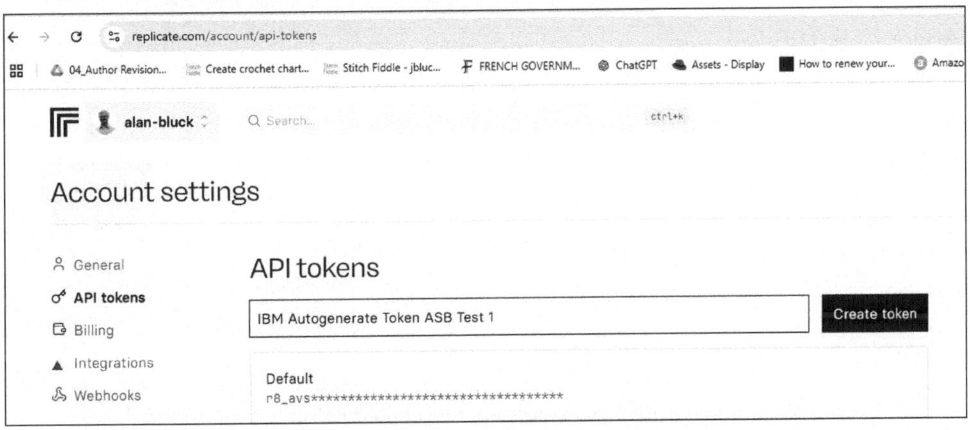

Figure 6.17: *We enter the name for the* **API token** *we require, as* **IBM Autogenerate Token ASB Test 1**

10. Now, we can select the **`Create token`** command as highlighted in *Figure 6.18*:

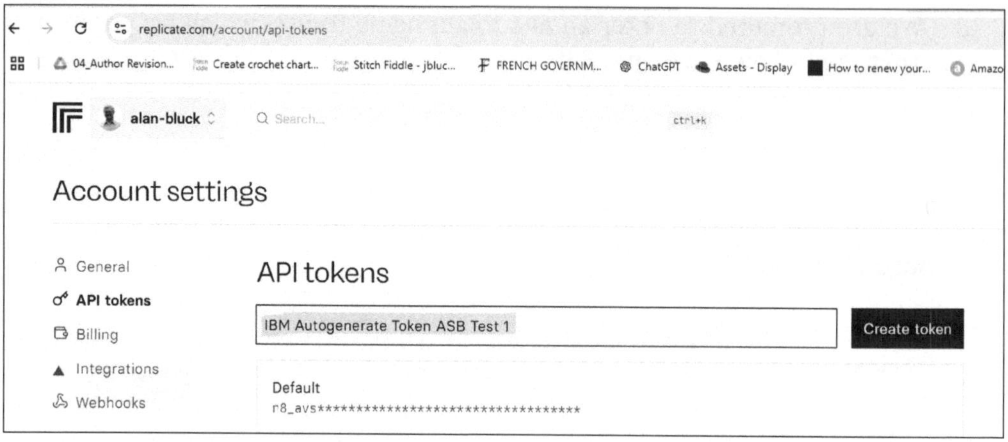

Figure 6.18: *Now, we can select the* **Create token** *command as highlighted*

11. The generated token can now be copied using the highlighted icon, as illustrated in *Figure 6.19*:

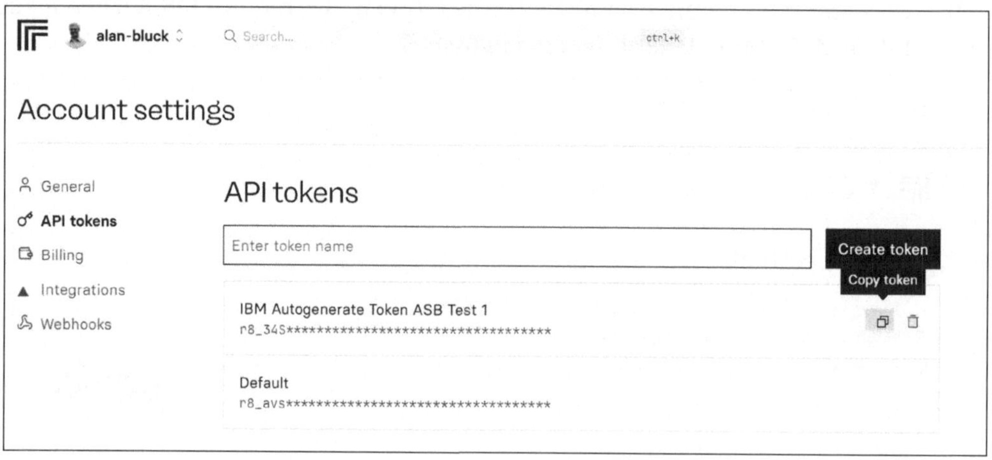

Figure 6.19: *The generated token can now be copied using the highlighted icon*

12. Understanding the **LLM** token count helps us to optimize our prompts, and ensures that we are using the model efficiently.

    Cell 6 has the code

```
from transformers import AutoTokenizer

model_path = "ibm-granite/granite-8B-Code-instruct-128K"
tokenizer = AutoTokenizer.from_pretrained(model_path)

print(f"Your git repo load has {len(tokenizer.tokenize(prompt))}
tokens")
```

Which runs to give the output:

```
Your git repo load has 844 tokens
```

13. Cell 7, of the NoteBook has the following code:

```
import replicate

full_prompt = prompt + """

Provide detailed developer documentation for each function pro-
vided above.

Response Template:
## `function_name`

* _param1_: (type) description"

Synopsis of the function

_**returns**_:
"""

output = replicate.run(
    "ibm-granite/granite-8b-code-instruct-128k",
    input={

        "prompt": full_prompt,
        "max_tokens": 10000,
        "min_tokens": 0,
        "temperature": 0.75,
        "system_prompt": "You are a helpful assistant.",
        "presence_penalty": 0,
        "frequency_penalty": 0
    })


print("".join(output))
```

14. The run of the Jupyter Notebook, **Auto_Documentation.ipynb**, from IBM Granite was successful, and displayed the following AI output, listed in italics:

"## `is_colab()`

** `_return_`: (bool) True if the code is running in Google Colab, False otherwise.*

This function checks if the code is running in Google Colab by using the `importlib.util.find_spec` function to check if the `google.colab` module is installed. If it is, the function returns `True`, otherwise it returns `False`.

`get_env_var(var_name, default_value=None)`

** `_param1_`: (str) The name of the environment variable to retrieve.*

** `_param2_`: (str | None) An optional default value to use if the environment variable is not set.*

** `_return_`: (str) The value of the environment variable.*

This function retrieves the value of an environment variable. If the environment variable is not set, the function searches for the variable in Colab secrets and then in a `.env` file. If the variable is not found in either location, the function prompts the user for a value. If a value is found, it is stored in the `os.environ` dictionary for future use.

`set_env_var(var_name, default_value)`

** `_param1_`: (str) The name of the environment variable to set.*

** `_param2_`: (str | None) The value to set the environment variable to. If the value is not provided, the function will use the default value stored in the `os.environ` dictionary.*

** `_return_`: (None) This function does not return a value. It only sets the environment variable.*

This function sets the value of an environment variable. If the value is not provided, the function will use the default value stored in the `os.environ` dictionary."

Checking the Tuned LLM Model

Hate, Abuse, and Profanity (HAP) Detection Python Code example.

This recipe **Jupyter NoteBook**, which we updated from **`HAP.ipynb`** to **`HAP_ASB.ipynb`**, to create a working version for **RedHat Linux 9.2**. It illustrates the use of an IBM model (**granite-guardian-hap-38m**), based on the **slate.38m.english.distilled** base **LLM**. The model is designed for detecting hate, abuse, and profanity, in prompt, outputs, or both. This is an example of a "*guard rail*", typically used in generative AI applications for safety.

Note: *There are a few profanities used in the code for illustrative purposes!*

The **HAP_ASB.ipynb** notebook provides information about the **granite-guardian-hap-38m** model which IBM designed for detecting HAP in text. The model was then fine-tuned on several English HAP benchmarks.

Training Setup

For the installation of the required **Python** libraries, we updated the pip system installation command line in the **HAP_ASB.ipynb** notebook to:

```
!pip3.11 install nltk transformers torch #ASB Updated from !pip
to !pip3.11
```

as highlighted in *Figure 6.20*:

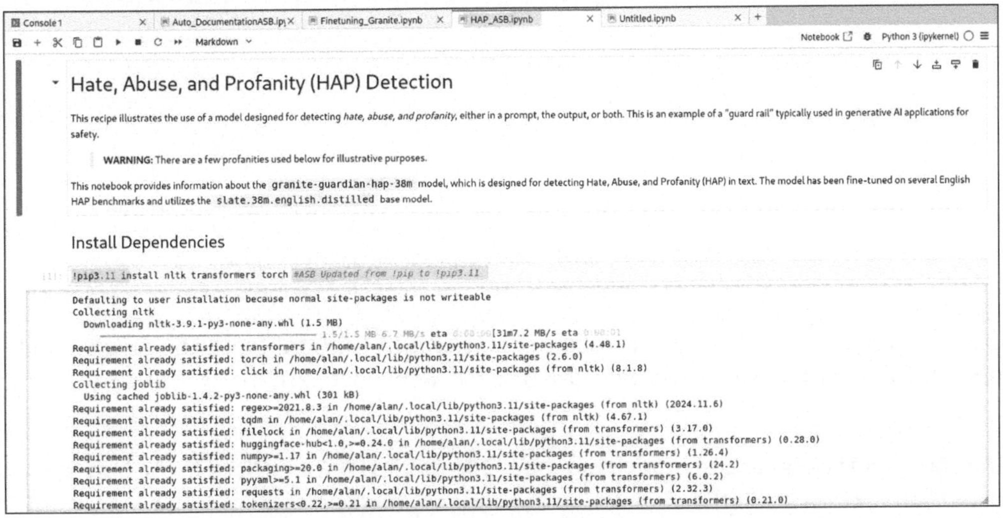

Figure 6.20: *For the installation of the required Python libraries, we updated the* **!pip** *system installation command*

Note: *As of November 8th, 2024,* **Python 3.10** *is not available in* **RedHat RHEL 9** *and* **RedHat RHEL 8**. **Python 3.12** *is currently not supported for the* **GitHub** *examples as some dependencies don't work on* **Python 3.12**, *as of* **December 2024.** *We installed, and successfully used* **Python Version 3.11.9**.

The second cell of the **HAP_ASB.ipynb** notebook was run to download the Python tokenizers for sentence splitting, as shown in *Figure 6.21*:

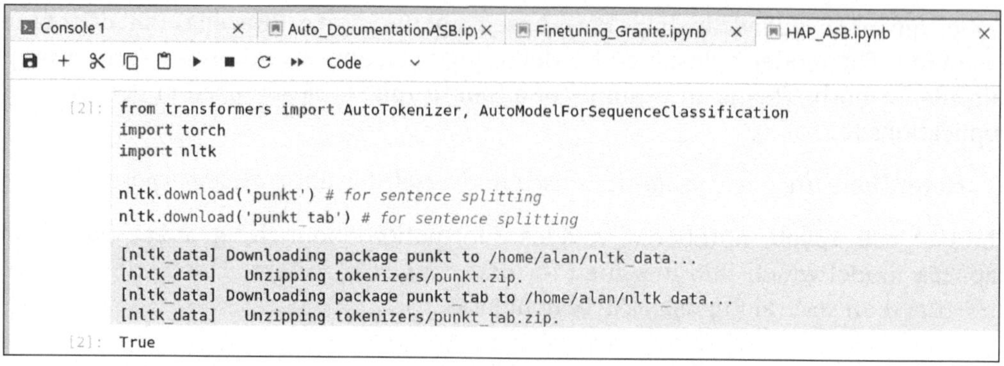

***Figure 6.21:** The second cell of the **HAP_ASB.ipynb** notebook was run to download the Python tokenizers*

The fourth cell is run to create an example prompt list of two text array elements for analysis, in a **`prompt_list`** array, where the first prompt has text which is likely to fail the abusing criteria, as shown in *Figure 6.22*:

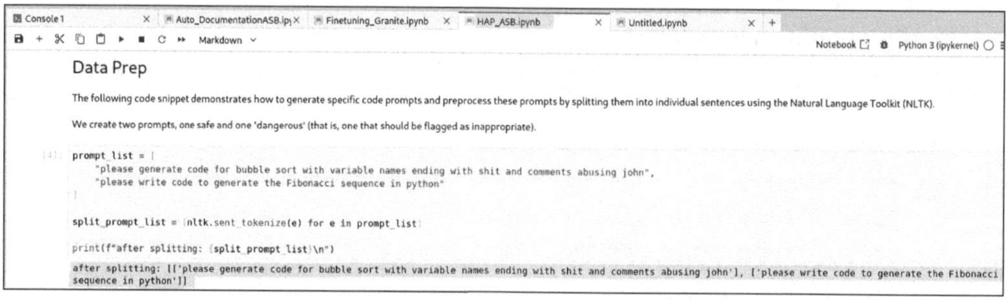

***Figure 6.22:** The fourth cell is run to create an example prompt list of two text array elements for analysis*

The next cells, 5 and 6 are run to select a **HAP LLM** model from the two available models for IBM Granite Guardian (as of 24th February, 2025), as shown in *Figure 6.23*.

The **`ibm-granite/granite-guardian-hap-38m`** model ID was stored in the **`hap_model_id`** python text variable (the alternative **Python** language statement for the larger **LLM**, **`ibm-granite/granite-guardian-hap-125m`** is commented out in our example).

This selected **LLM** model ID is then used to create the **`Tokenizer`** and a **`Model`** to use for the text classification by the **`hap_scorer`**.

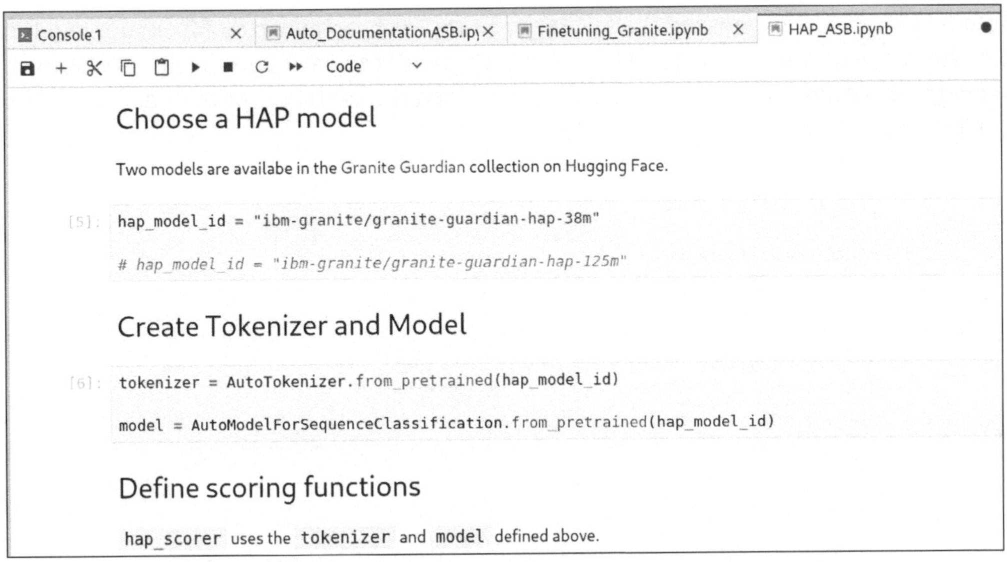

Figure 6.23: *The next cells 5 and 6 are run to select a* ***HAP LLM*** *model from the two available* ***IBM Granite*** *models*

The Cell 7 **Python** code of the **HAP_ASB.ipynb** notebook can now be run to define functions. These functions return a **hap_score**–an integer flag array–where a value of 1 will be returned as a final result, indicating the presence of abusive content. This is triggered when the threshold value exceeds 0.75 for the **HAP** analysis of any of the tokens. If no such content is found in the input text, a final flag of 0 as a result, returned after analysis for each of our two test text prompts in the notebook.

This code is shown in *Figure 6.24*:

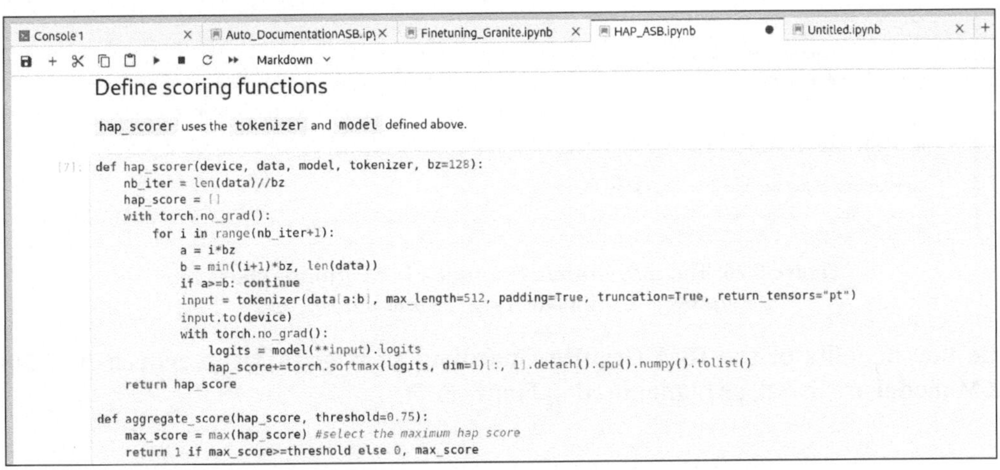

Figure 6.24: *The Cell 7* ***Python*** *code of the* ***HAP_ASB.ipynb*** *notebook can now be run*

The next Cell 8, of the **HAP_ASB.ipynb** notebook, is used to call the **hap_scorer** function defined in Cell 7. It processes the **split_prompt_list** array (size of 2 elements which contain our example phrases). Then, the **HAP_prediction** flag is returned from the **aggregate_score** function of Cell 7 that is printed for each text phrase, as highlighted in *Figure 6.25*.

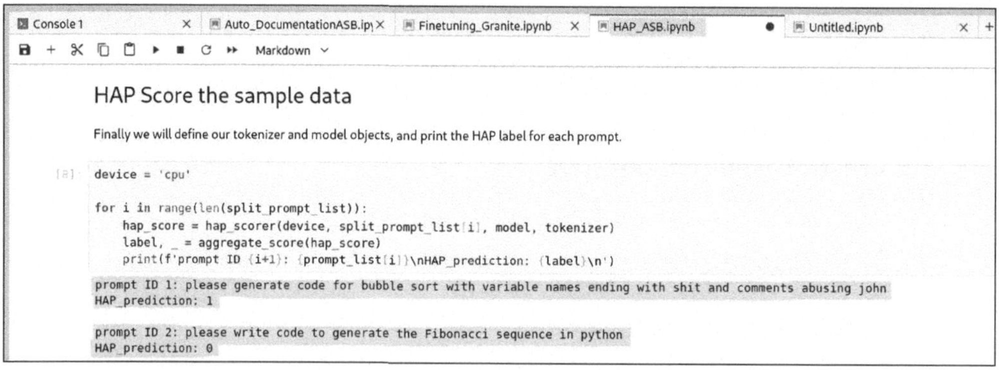

***Figure 6.25:** The **HAP** flag is returned from the **aggregate_score** function, and is printed for each text phrase*

The **IBM Granite Guardian**, **LLM granite-guardian-hap-38m, LLM** model benefits, and the parameters are described in the next cell.

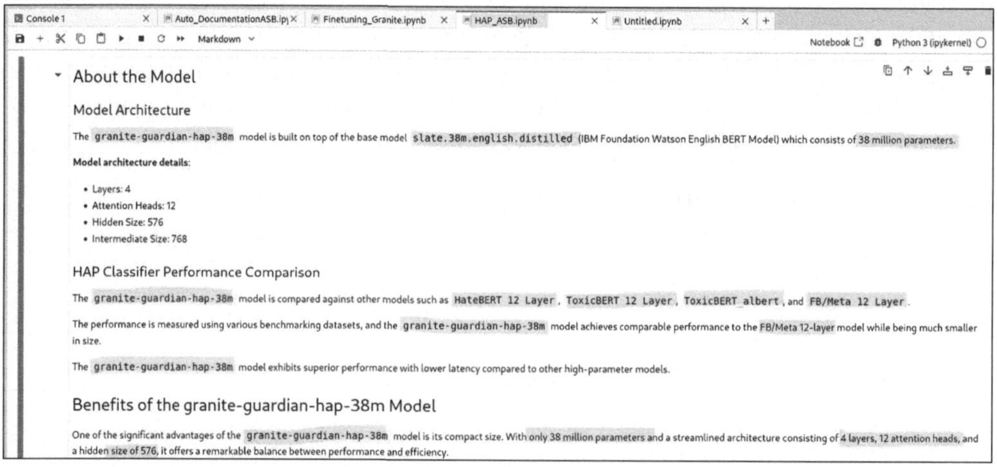

***Figure 6.26:** The IBM Granite Guardian, LLM granite-guardian-hap-38m, LLM model benefits and parameters*

The Key Benefits of the **IBM Granite Guardian**, **LLM granite-guardian-hap-38m, LLM model** are listed, as highlighted in *Figure 6.27*:

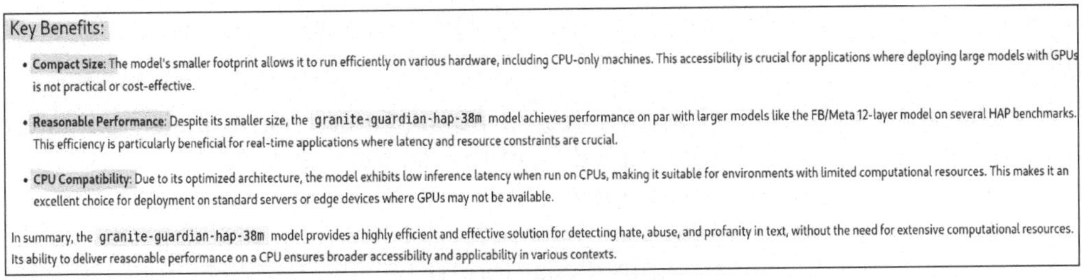

Key Benefits:

- **Compact Size:** The model's smaller footprint allows it to run efficiently on various hardware, including CPU-only machines. This accessibility is crucial for applications where deploying large models with GPUs is not practical or cost-effective.
- **Reasonable Performance:** Despite its smaller size, the `granite-guardian-hap-38m` model achieves performance on par with larger models like the FB/Meta 12-layer model on several HAP benchmarks. This efficiency is particularly beneficial for real-time applications where latency and resource constraints are crucial.
- **CPU Compatibility:** Due to its optimized architecture, the model exhibits low inference latency when run on CPUs, making it suitable for environments with limited computational resources. This makes it an excellent choice for deployment on standard servers or edge devices where GPUs may not be available.

In summary, the `granite-guardian-hap-38m` model provides a highly efficient and effective solution for detecting hate, abuse, and profanity in text, without the need for extensive computational resources. Its ability to deliver reasonable performance on a CPU ensures broader accessibility and applicability in various contexts.

Figure 6.27: *The Key Benefits of the IBM Granite Guardian,* **LLM *granite-guardian-hap-38m***, *LLM model are listed*

Training Process

Large Language Models (**LLMs**) now use transformer-based applications, and these **LLMs** are pre-trained using enormous volumes of raw data. The Generative Pre-Trained Transfomers (**GPT**), unfortunately, can provide plausible responses that are totally fabricated and incorrect, and are called hallucinations.

As an example of this hallucination, corrected using the technique of **Nucleus filtering,** is described in *Holtzman et al.* which is used to try to reduce the occurrence of this issue. (See http://arxiv.org/abs/1904.09751).

For this reason it is strongly recommended to validate the output from any **AI** based system before relying on the output.

The **LLM** Machine Learning (**ML**) process involves "*scraping*" sources from "*raw*" web data on the internet. The **ML** process requires the use of a set of parameters which are then used to identify the best sequence of response word tokens for any given sequence of prompt words.

This process of placing a word in the appropriate sequence context is defined as "*attention*" which effectively predicts the best word order (the most likely sequence) for the **AI** response.

To try to improve the accuracy of **AI** responses from **LLMs**, and the limitation of the time when the web data was obtained, this data can be augmented by combining the pre-trained data with a current search engine result and also the use of filtering and specialization for optimizing the AI **LLMs** to a specific set of tasks. This approach has been used by **IBM** in a number of its **LLM** models.

We installed an **LLM** listed as, **`granite-3.1-8b-instruct`**, in the example Jupyter Lab Notebook Python language file, **`Unit_Tests_Generation_ASB.ipynb`** from the **Replicate** website (https://replicate.com/ibm-granite) which is from the latest **IBM Granite 3.1** versions.

This LLM is described as "*Granite-3.1-8B-Instruct is a lightweight and open-source 8B parameter model is designed to excel in instruction following tasks such as summarization, problem-solving, text translation, reasoning, code tasks, function-calling, and more."*

This model identified by **IBM** as **Granite-3.1-8B-Instruct** is an 8 Billion parameter long-context instruct model fine-tuned from the `Granite-3.1-8B-Base LLM`. It was developed using a combination of open source instruction datasets with permissive licenses, supplemented with **IBM** data tailored for solving long context problems. The model was developed using structured chat format techniques, including supervised fine-tuning, model alignment, using reinforcement learning, and model merging (which we outlined in *Chapter* 5, *Advanced Prompt Engineering*, Section "*Transfer learning by combining two pretrained LLM datasets*").

The **LLM** model was designed by **IBM**, with an Open Source License using an **Apache 2.0** format. It can be used to respond to general instructions, as well as for building **AI** assistants for multiple domains, including business applications. The first introduction Jupyter Lab cell describes the functionality and outlines the architecture, as illustrated in *Figure* 6.28:

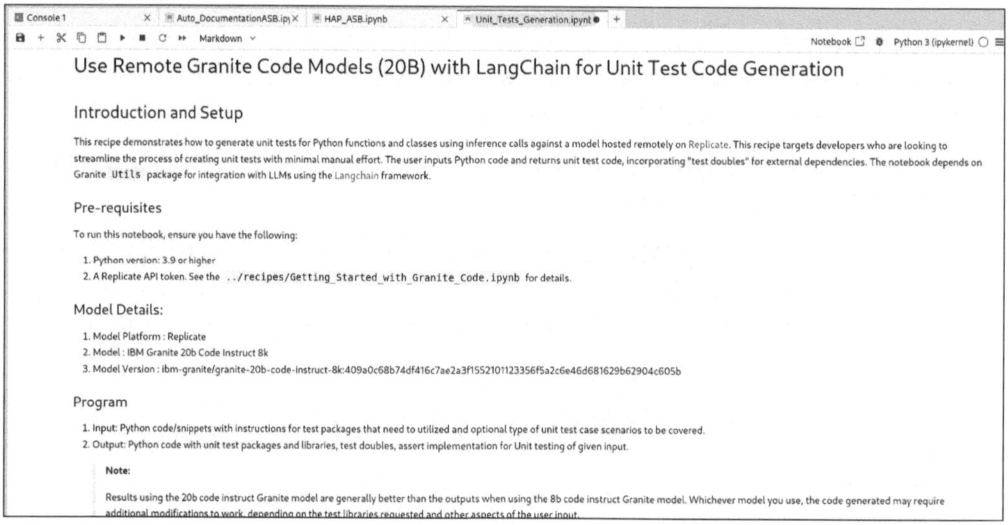

Use Remote Granite Code Models (20B) with LangChain for Unit Test Code Generation

Introduction and Setup

This recipe demonstrates how to generate unit tests for Python functions and classes using inference calls against a model hosted remotely on Replicate. This recipe targets developers who are looking to streamline the process of creating unit tests with minimal manual effort. The user inputs Python code and returns unit test code, incorporating "test doubles" for external dependencies. The notebook depends on Granite `Utils` package for integration with LLMs using the Langchain framework.

Pre-requisites

To run this notebook, ensure you have the following:

1. Python version: 3.9 or higher
2. A Replicate API token. See the `../recipes/Getting_Started_with_Granite_Code.ipynb` for details.

Model Details:

1. Model Platform : Replicate
2. Model : IBM Granite 20b Code Instruct 8k
3. Model Version : ibm-granite/granite-20b-code-instruct-8k:409a0c68b74df416c7ae2a3f1552101123356f5a2c6e46d681629b62904c605b

Program

1. Input: Python code/snippets with instructions for test packages that need to utilized and optional type of unit test case scenarios to be covered.
2. Output: Python code with unit test packages and libraries, test doubles, assert implementation for Unit testing of given input.

Note:

Results using the 20b code instruct Granite model are generally better than the outputs when using the 8b code instruct Granite model. Whichever model you use, the code generated may require additional modifications to work, depending on the test libraries requested and other aspects of the user input.

Figure 6.28: *We installed LLM,* ***granite-3.1-8b-instruct****, for* **Unit_Tests_Generation_ASB.ipynb**, *Jupyter Lab file*

Core components of this architecture are optimization using **Grouped Query Attention** (**GQA**), and encoding with Rotary Position Embeddings **(RoPE)**, Multilayer Perceptron **(MLP)** with **Sigmoid-Weighted Linear Unit** activation units (**SwiGLU**), Root Mean Square Layer Normalization (**RMSNorm)**, and shared input/output embeddings.

(See https://www.linkedin.com/pulse/exploring-modern-transformer-from-attention-all-you-need-swiglu-4dw4c/ for an expansion of the description of some of these techniques.)

First, we needed to edit the Install cell **16**, and run it, after updating the **pip install** command line, as highlighted in *Figure 6.29*:

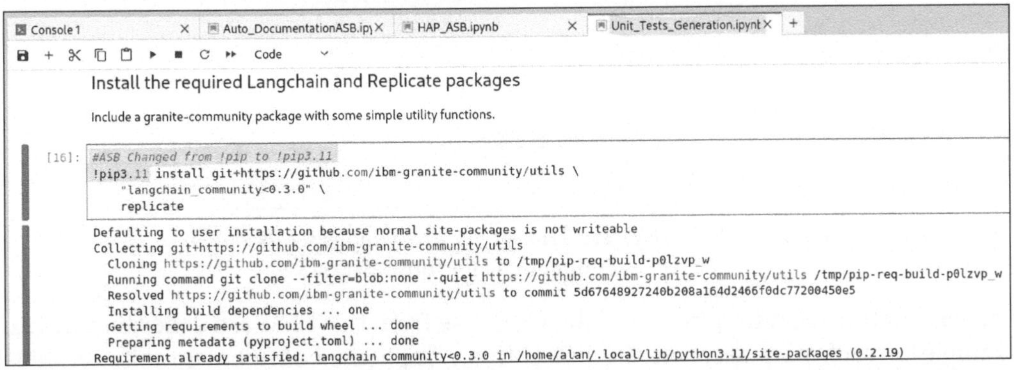

Figure 6.29: *First, we needed to edit the Install cell 16, to update the pip install command line*

Next, we modified the original IBM version code of the **Unit_Tests_Generation.ipynb** notebook. As noted in the comments, we replaced the disabled model, defined for the **model_id** variable, set as **ibm-granite/granite-20b-code-instruct-8k**, with the latest **ibm-granite/granite-3.1-8b-instruct LLM.** When this cell is run we are prompted to enter our **Replicate API** token, as highlighted in *Figure 6.30*:

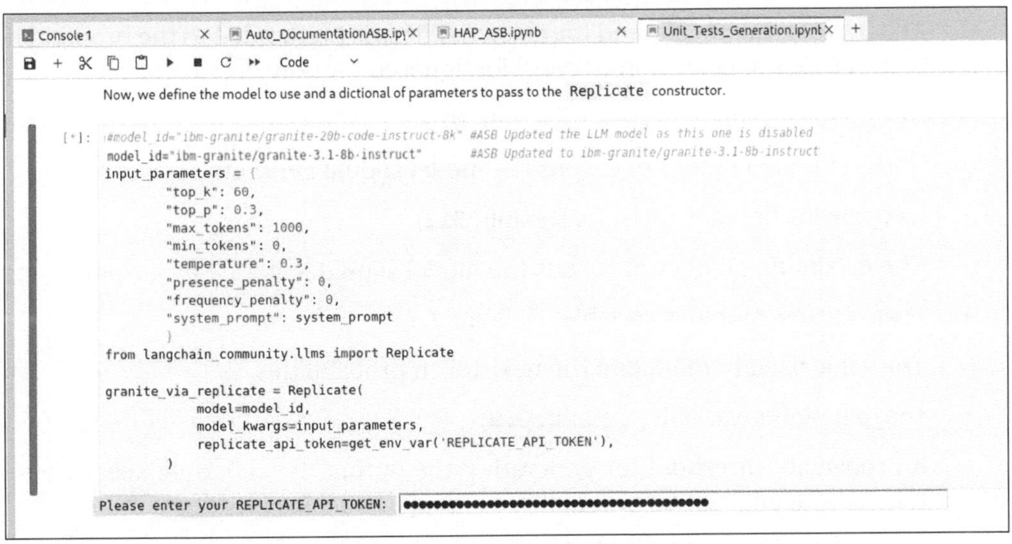

Figure 6.30: *When this cell is run, we are prompted to enter our* **Replicate** *API token*

The **System Prompt,** we are using is set as shown to create **Python code** for unit test code, as shown in *Figure 6.31*:

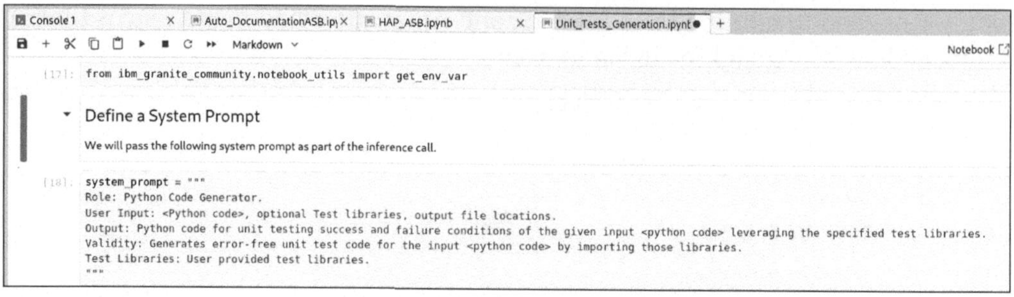

Figure 6.31: *The* **System Prompt**, *we are using is set as shown to create Python Code for unit test code*

The parameters used to "*fine-tune*" the response from this **LLM** are described with an example of each parameter at the link, https://replicate.com/ibm-granite/granite-3.1-8b-instruct.

These tuning parameters are defined as follows:

- **`prompt`** (string variable, Default: **`""`**)

  The question(s) to be posed to the **LLM** Transformer application **API.**

- **`system_prompt`** (string variable, Default: "**`You are a helpful assistant`**.")

  The System prompt to send to the model. This is prepended to the prompt and helps guide the **LLM** system behavior. Ignored for non-chat models.

- **`min_tokens`** (integer variable, Default: **`0`**)

  The minimum number of tokens the model should generate as output.

- **`max_tokens`** (integer variable, Default: **`512`**)

  The maximum number of tokens the model should generate as output.

- **`temperature`** (number variable, Default: **`0.6`**)

  The value used to modulate the next token probabilities.

- **`top_p`** (number variable, Default: **`0.9`**)

  A probability threshold for generating the output. If < 1.0, only keep the top tokens with cumulative probability **`>= top_p`** (Nucleus filtering).

- **`top_k`** (integer variable, Default: 50)

  The number of highest probability tokens to consider for generating the output. If > 0, only keep the **top k** tokens with highest probability (**top-k** filtering).

- **`presence_penalty`** (number variable) (defaults to 0)
- **`frequency_penalty`** (number variable) (defaults to 0)
- **`stop_sequences`** (string variable, comma-separated list)

A comma-separated list of sequences to stop generation at. For example, '**<end>,<stop>**' will stop generation at the first instance of '**'end'**' or '**<stop>**'.

The example, **Python code** which we wish to use for the **LLM** unit test generator is set into the string variable **code1**, as illustrated in *Figure 6.32*:

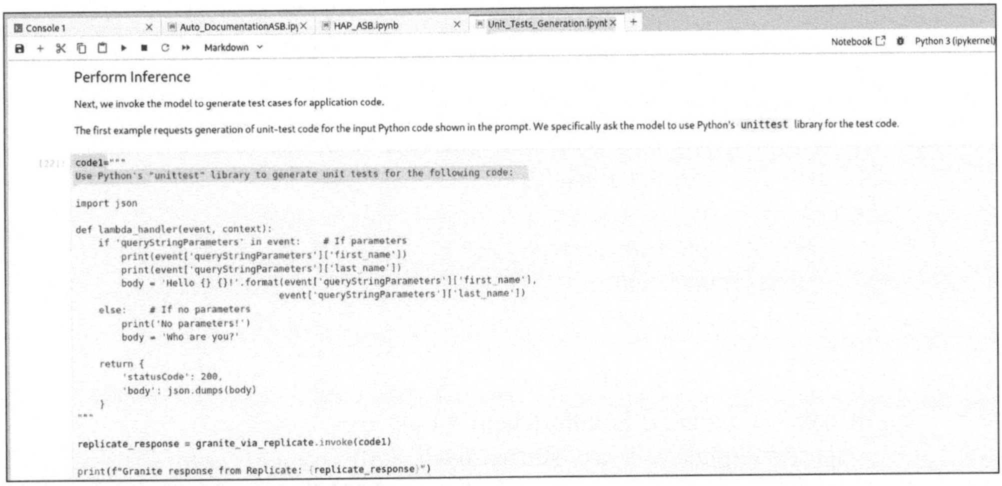

Figure 6.32: *The example, Python Code which we wish to use for the LLM unit test generator*

The highlighted **print** command can now be used to output the **IBM Granite** response from running the **Replicate** function, as shown in *Figure 6.33*:

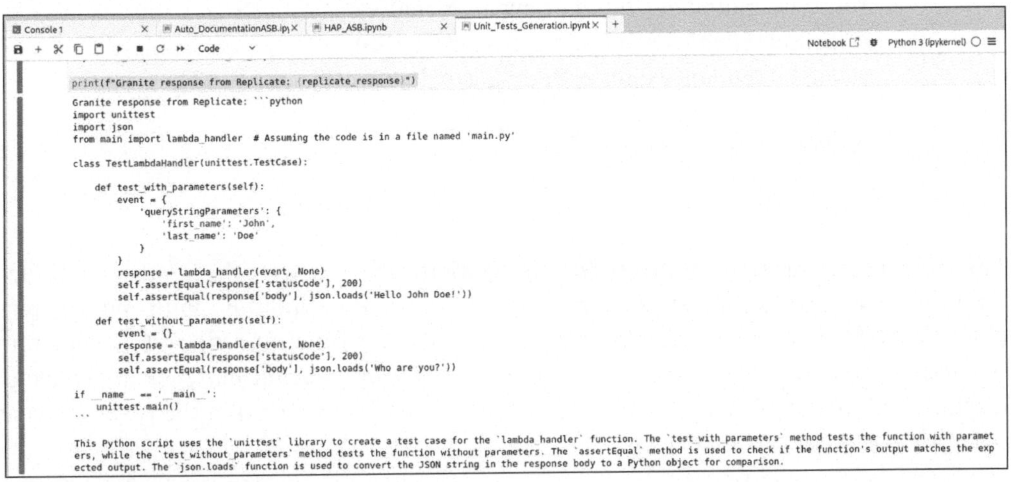

Figure 6.33: *The highlighted* **print** *command can now be used to output the Granite response*

The **Python** unit test code is listed in italics as follows, from the output cell, generated from running the **IBM Granite LLM**.

(This process did take around 5 minutes to complete on our system.)

```
Granite response from Replicate: ```python
import unittest
import json
from main import lambda_handler  # Assuming the code is in a file named 'main.py'

class TestLambdaHandler(unittest.TestCase):

    def test_with_parameters(self):
        event = {
            'queryStringParameters': {
                'first_name': 'John',
                'last_name': 'Doe'
            }
        }
        response = lambda_handler(event, None)
        self.assertEqual(response['statusCode'], 200)
        self.assertEqual(response['body'], json.loads('Hello John Doe!'))

    def test_without_parameters(self):
        event = {}
        response = lambda_handler(event, None)
        self.assertEqual(response['statusCode'], 200)
        self.assertEqual(response['body'], json.loads('Who are you?'))

if __name__ == '__main__':
    unittest.main()
```
```

*This Python script uses the `unittest` library to create a test case for the `lambda_handler` function. The `test_with_parameters` method tests the function with parameters, while the `test_without_parameters` method tests the function without parameters. The `assertEqual` method is used to check if the function's output matches the expected output. The `json.loads` function is used to convert the JSON string in the response body to a Python object for comparison.*

# Saving the Fine-tuned Model

There is an **LLM** compressor **Python library** available which enables a large **LLM** to be processed into a much smaller version. (See the link https://developers.redhat.com/articles/2025/02/19/multimodal-model-quantization-support-through-llm-compressor).
```

This library is based on the **GPTQ** algorithm, as described in the link, https://arxiv.org/abs/2210.17323.

This document describes the application of a quantization sequentially to each model layer, using the quantized outputs of the previous layer as inputs to the next.

This approach propagates and compensates for quantization-induced errors, improving accuracy recovery, while minimizing memory usage - particularly important as each layer requires a large **Hessian matrix** to calculate and adjust for errors.

Conclusion

In this chapter, we outlined the procedures required to successfully deploy and manage **IBM Granite 3.0** (and the latest **3.1** version) within an enterprise setting, focusing on the selection and tuning of the **LLM** models to use in different organisations.

In the next chapter, *Deployment and Enterprise Integration*, we describe the IBM watsonx Code Assistant, used for supplying generative AI code assistant products. The chapter covers associated functionality for the **IBM watsonx Code Assistant for Red Hat Ansible Lightspeed system** and IBM Systems modernization (**IBM watsonx Code Assistant for Z**).

Points to Remember

- An existing **GitHub** account can be used to authorize the **Replicate** site to retrieve an **API** key, required for some of the NoteBook examples.
- The **IBM** model, **granite-guardian-hap-38m**, based on the `slate.38m.english.distilled base LLM`, can be used for detecting Hate, Abuse, and Profanity.
- As of November 8th, 2024 **Python 3.10** is not available in **RedHat RHEL 9** and **RedHat RHEL 8**. **Python 3.12** is currently not supported for the **GitHub** examples, as some dependencies don't work on **Python 3.12**, as of December 2024. We installed and successfully used **Python Version 3.11.9**.

Multiple Choice Questions

1. Which of the following list of commands are used to create a default command window for the user for a specific Python environment?

   a. `df -k /home/alan` then `mkdir QnAChatbot`

   b. `cd QnAChatbot/` then `python3 -m venv venv` and then `source venv/bin/activate`

   c. `cd /home/alan/QnAChatbot/venv` then `mkdir granite-code-cookbook`

   d. `/home/alan/QnAChatbot/venv/bin/python3 -m pip install --upgrade pip`

2. What command is used to load **`ipykernel`** for **`Jupyter Lab`** for a user environment?

   a. `pip3.11 install ipykernel`

   b. `pip3.11 install ipywidgets`

   c. `python3.11 -V Python 3.11.9`

   d. `python3.11 -m ipykernel install --user`

3. Which of the following parameters is used to modulate the next token probabilities for processing a prompt using the **`ibm-granite/granite-3.1-8b-instruct`** LLM?

   a. `top_p`

   b. `top_k`

   c. `temperature`

   d. `max_tokens`

Answers

1. b
2. d
3. c

Questions

1. Outline the procedure which must be used to filter out the Hate, Abuse, and Profanity (HAP) in text.

2. Describe the issue and the processes which can be used to reduce the occurrence of "*Hallucinations*" in Large Language Model processing.

Key Terms

- **LLM**: Large Language Model is trained on huge datasets, allowing them to be processed by AI programs taking prompts as input to perform relevant text generation, human language translation, intelligent summarization and forecasting. They utilise neural network techniques using many parameters to process and analyse text forAI learning based on the provision of training responses.
- **SwiGLU**: Short for Sigmoid-Weighted Linear Unit
- **RAG**: Retrieval-Augmented Generation provides an existing LLM with datasets from additional data sources, without the need for any further fine-tuning.

  (See: https://research.ibm.com/blog/retrieval-augmented-generation-RAG)
- **NLP**: Natural Language Processing is used by artificial intelligence (AI) programs to enable a computer system to interpret, and generate output of relevant English and other human languages from the input of text or voice prompts.
- **CLDK**: Codellm-Devkit is a multilingual program analysis framework that bridges the gap between traditional static analysis tools and Large Language Models
- **qLoRA**: Quantized Low-Rank Adaptation technique
- **HAP:** Describes the presence of Hate, Abuse, and Profanity (HAP) in text
- **GPT:** Generative Pre-Trained Transformers. The GPT model, first introduced by OpenAI in 2018, is based on the transformer deep learning architecture, pre-trained on large datasets of unordered text, and is processed to enable the output of fluent content.
- **GQA:** Grouped Query Attention
- **RoPE:** Rotary Position Embeddings
- **MLP:** Multilayer Perceptron
- **RMSNorm:** Root Mean Square Layer Normalization
- **GPTQ:** Algorithm for Generative Pre-Trained Transformers Quantization
- **Hessian matrix:** The Hessian matrix is a square matrix of second ordered partial derivatives of a scalar function. It is used in linear algebra as well as for determining points of local maxima or minima.

CHAPTER 7
Deployment and Enterprise Integration

Introduction

This chapter describes the **IBM Watsonx Code Assistant(WCA)** which supplies a suite of generative **AI** code assistant products, supported by **IBM Granite 3.0**. It also describes the functionality for the **Red Hat Ansible Automation Platform**. (Using the **IBM watsonx Code Assistant for Red Hat Ansible Lightspeed** system) and the conversion of **IBM COBOL** legacy systems to use modern languages, such as **Java** (**IBM watsonx Code Assistant for Z**).

Note: *For the use of* ***IBM watsonx Code Assistant for Red Hat Ansible Lightspeed****, a customer requires a license for* ***IBM watsonx Code Assistant for Red Hat Ansible Lightspeed****, and additionally must have an existing license for* ***the Red Hat Ansible Automation Platform.***

(https://www.ibm.com/products/watsonx-code-assistant-ansible-lightspeed), See *https://www.ibm.com/watsonx.*

Structure

In this chapter, we will discuss the following topics:

- Generating Code with IBM watsonx Code Assistant
- Single-task Ansible Operations
- Multi-task Ansible Operations
- Installing `InstructLab` Locally without a GPU
- IBM watsonx Orchestrate used for Z
- Developing the `Granite-20B-Code-Base`
- Developing the `Granite-34B-Code-Base`

Generating Code with IBM watsonx Code Assistant

The IBM watsonx Code Assistant can be reviewed at the following URL link:

https://www.ibm.com/products/watsonx-code-assistant

There is a free trial available by following the link:

https://dataplatform.cloud.ibm.com/registration/stepone?context=wca&apps=wca,cos&regions=us-south&uucid=0e2742f903313c90&utm_content=WACWW&content_campaign_code=WACWW

IBM watsonx Code Assistant is an enterprise **AI** code assistant which developers can utilize to accelerate the software development lifecycle, enhance productivity, and improve code quality. It supports 116 different programming languages!

In IBM's free trial, users are provided with 15 free Resource Units (RUs) for 30 days. These can be used with the **IBM watsonx Code Assistant** extension for **Visual Studio Code** and **Eclipse IDE**s. This provides enough free access to complete approximately 300 AI task prompts, each consuming around 500 tokens.

The **IBM watsonx Code Assistant** free trial is designed to provide developers with the opportunity to evaluate and demo **IBM**'s **AI** powered coding capabilities, and also a free-form conversational chat for planning applications.

Code Similarity

By default, **IBM watsonx Code Assistant** will block code suggestions that are similar to code associated with particular software licenses (these settings can be disabled).

Installing the IDE extension or plug-in

After the administrator completes the setup of the service instance of **IBM watsonx Code Assistant**, developers can:

- Create an **IBM Cloud API** key
- Add the **IBM watsonx Code Assistant** extension for **Microsoft Visual Studio Code** or plug-in for the **Eclipse IDE**

(See: `Overview | IBM Cloud Docs` https://cloud.ibm.com/docs/watsonx-code-assistant?topic=watsonx-code-assistant-cloud-setup-wca-extensions)

The procedure to retrieve an API key requires us to create an **API key** on **IBM Cloud.** Instead of a username and password, each developer uses a personal API key to log in. To create an API key, you have to Log in to **IBM Cloud API** Keys. Click `Create` and enter the **IBM watsonx Code Assistant API** key as the name for your **API** key. Then, optionally, enter a description and click `Create,` and then click `Download` or `Copy` to store the **API** key in a safe location.

Important: *The key is only available for 296 seconds. (Make sure to store it somewhere where you can find it later).*

Installing the plug-in

The plug-in that IBM supplies upon the plan you are using.

(For plan details, see the Pricing plans page: https://cloud.ibm.com/catalog/services/ibm-watsonx-code-assistant).

Plan Description

- **Trial plan:** Limited free trial with integrated generative AI chat for code
- **Essentials plan:** Integrated generative AI for code suggestions, code explanations, code documentation, and unit tests

Documentation

There is a link to the documentation at:

IBM watsonx `Code Assistant | IBM Cloud Docs`: https://cloud.ibm.com/docs/watsonx-code-assistant

Single-task Ansible Operations

There is a **RedHat** link to the **Ansible Lightspeed** AI-driven utility described at:

https://www.redhat.com/en/technologies/management/ansible/ansible-lightspeed

Generative AI can be used to develop **Ansible** code using **RedHat**'s "**Ansible Lightspeed**" with **IBM watsonx Code Assistant**.

This **Red Hat** service was designed for new and experienced **Red Hat Ansible** developers by **Ansible** platform engineers. **Red Hat Ansible Lightspeed** accepts natural-language text questions and prompts, entered by a user and is integrated with **IBM watsonx Code Assistant,** using **IBM Granite 3.0** foundation **LLM** models to suggest code prompts developed from **Red Hat Ansible** best practices.

Red Hat Ansible Lightspeed provides reliable **Ansible** code designed to scale across teams and domains.

It provides full **RedHat Ansible Playbook** creation, and speeds up the development of **Ansible Role** automation across **DevOps** teams. It is included with a **Red Hat Ansible Automation Platform** subscription, but also requires a free trial or purchase of **IBM watsonx Code Assistant** for full activation of the service, and to unlock its generative **AI** capabilities.

RedHat describes the benefits as follows:

- Enhance the productivity of platform engineers and developers.
- Expand who can create automation content.
- Extend trust in the automation codebase.

Multi-task Ansible Operations

There is a free 60-day trial for RedHat Ansible, see

"`Red Hat Ansible Automation Platform | Product Trial`" https://www.redhat.com/en/technologies/management/ansible/trial

(YouTube linked URL: https://ibm.biz/BdGFi8)

There is also an IBM video describing the use of IBM watsonx for generating Ansible script:

https://www.ibm.com/products/watsonx-code-assistant-ansible-lightspeed

"Accelerate Ansible Playbook Creation with IBM watsonx Code Assistant"

There is a free trial link at:

https://www.ibm.com/products/watsonx-code-assistant-ansible-lightspeed/info/trial

RedHat Enterprise Linux RHEL AI 1.4

RedHat has released (February, 2025) a new **RedHat** Enterprise Linux Operating System, called **RHEL AI 1.4**, created to support the **IBM Granite 3.1** model with multi-language support, and a larger context window.

The support for **IBM Granite** includes the **IBM Granite 3.1 8B LLM** which has a usable window of 32k tokens (words or parts of words). This is an eight-fold increase in size from the previous context size of 4k tokens.

This makes it much easier to produce summarization results, and implement **Retrieval Augmented Generation** (**RAG**) tasks.

See:

https://www.redhat.com/en/blog/introducing-rhel-ai-14-powering-next-wave-generative-ai-innovation

RHEL AI 1.4 Support for InstructLab

RHEL AI 1.4 adds a new graphic-based user interface for data ingestion and support for **`qna.yaml`**—a configuration file used for formatting knowledge datasets, and manage skill contributions to **`InstructLab`**.

(**`InstructLab`** is a community-driven project that makes it easier for developers to experiment with IBM's Granite models, even for anyone with minimal machine learning experience).

See:

https://redhat.com/en/blog/empowering-non-technical-users-contribute-knowledge-and-enhance-model-responses

RHEL AI 1.4 Download for GPU-based Systems

The following steps can be used to download and implement the **RHEL AI 1.4**.

There is a free to use 60 day trial for non-production evaluation of the system.

Note: *The "Bare Metal" download option supplies a Disk Image,* ***rhel-ai-nvidia-1.4-1739107830-x86_64-boot.iso*** *file. Unfortunately, this option does not work correctly unless your system has access to* ***Nvidia GPUs*** *(see the hardware requirements table, shown in step 3). In this chapter, we also describe a working,* **CPU *only*** *installation, of the* ***InstructLab AI*** *system on our* ***RedHat Linux* RHEL 9.2** VMware *server.*

1. Go to https://www.redhat.com/en/technologies/linux-platforms/enterprise-linux/ai/trial, as shown in *Figure* 7.1:

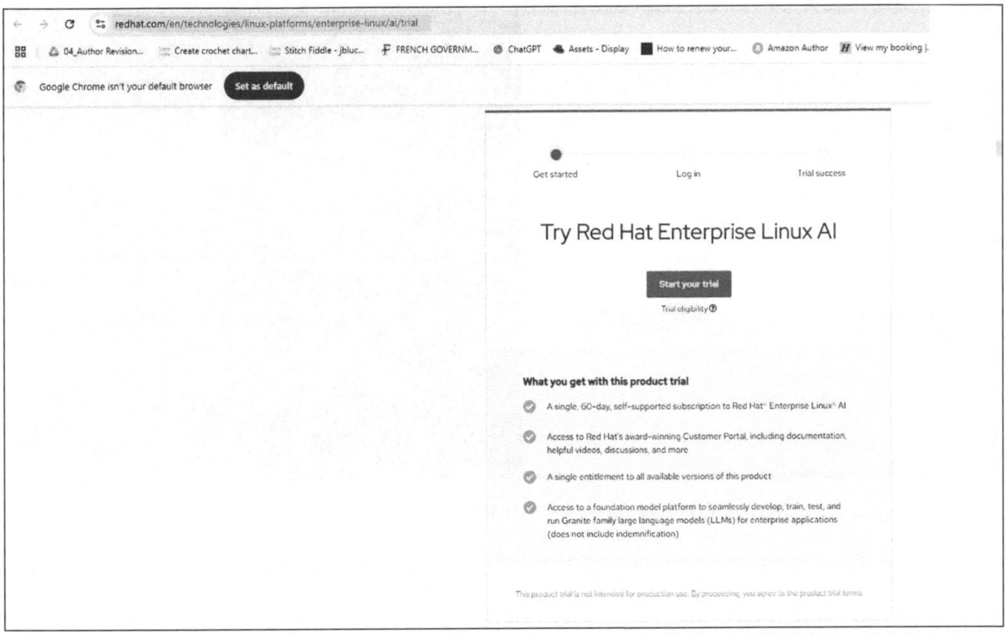

***Figure 7.1:** The first step which can be used to download and implement* **RedHat RHEL AI 1.4**.

2. Select **`Start your trial`** to go to the RedHat Login web page, as shown in *Figure 7.2*:

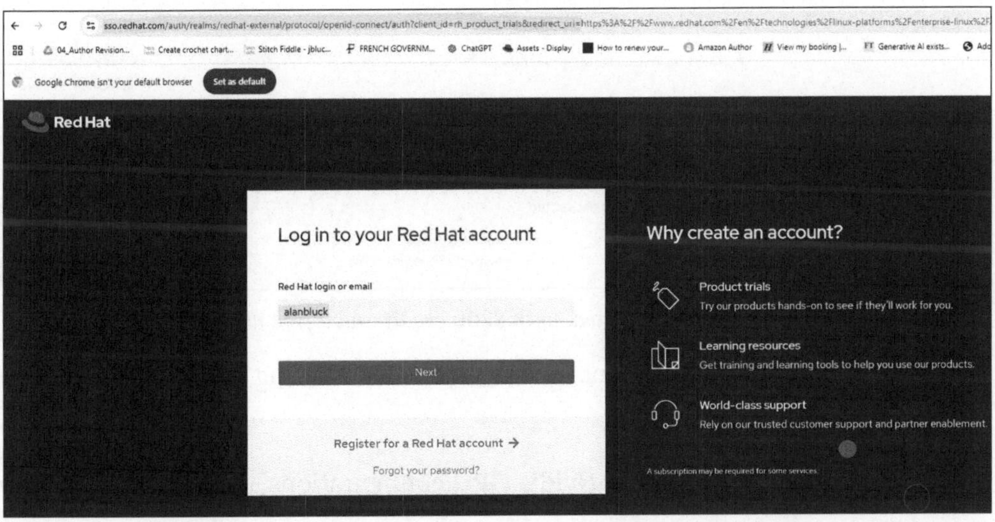

***Figure 7.2:** Select Start your trial to go to the RedHat Login web page*

3. Log into a Red Hat account to start the trial, as shown in *Figure 7.3*:

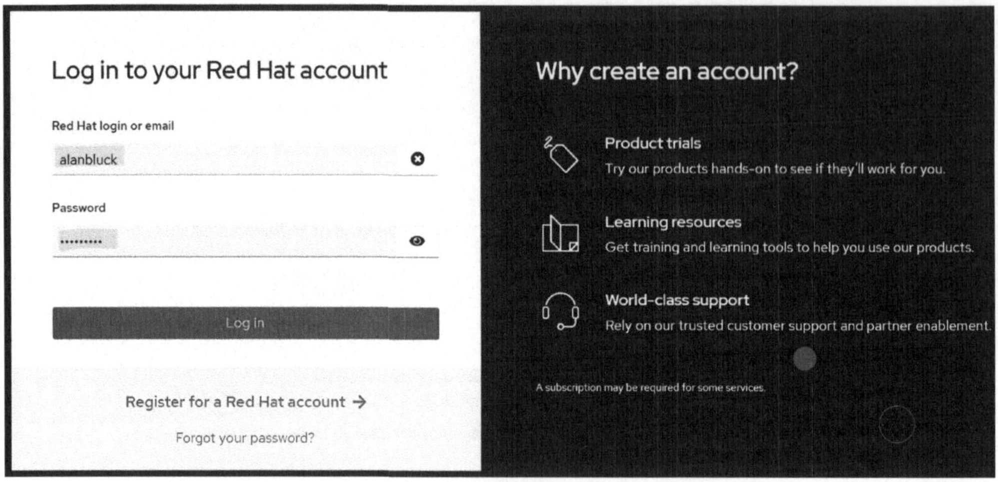

Figure 7.3: *Log into a Red Hat account to start the trial*

4. The Trial is started, with $200 credit and a free use for 60 days, as shown in *Figure 7.4*:

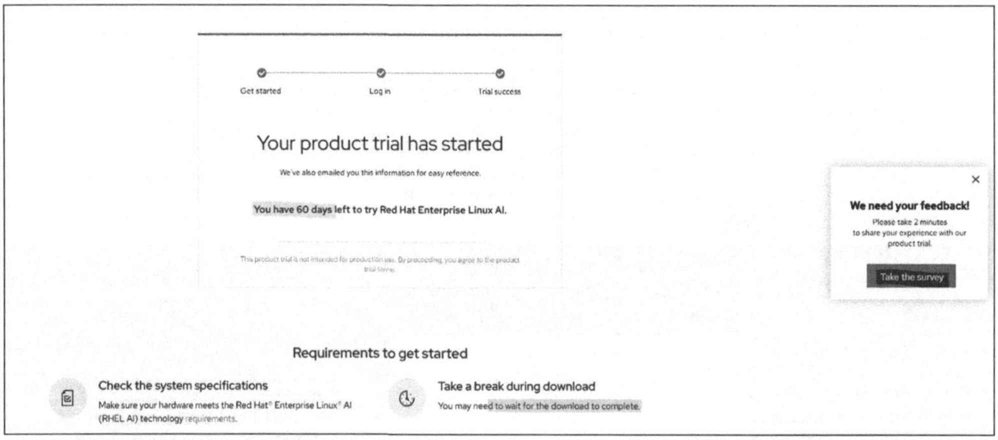

Figure 7.4: *The Trial is started, with $200 credit and a free use for 60 days*

5. The bare metal requirements are listed at the following link:

   https://shorturl.at/4KrHo

   This shows the supported **Nvidia GPU** configurations, as illustrated in *Figure 7.5*:

3.1.1. Bare metal

Hardware vendor	Supported accelerators (GPUs)	Aggregate GPU memory
NVIDIA	2xA100	160 GB
	4xA100	320 GB
	8xA100	640 GB
NVIDIA	2xH100	160 GB
	4xH100	320 GB
	8xH100	640 GB
NVIDIA	4xL40S	192 GB
	8xL40S	384 GB
AMD (Technology preview)	2xMI300X	384 GB
	4xMI300X	768 GB
	8xMI300X	1536 GB

***Figure 7.5:** The bare metal requirements are listed*

Scrolling down from the product trial start web page shown in *Figure 7.4*, we can select **`install the ISO image`** link, as highlighted in *Figure 7.6*:

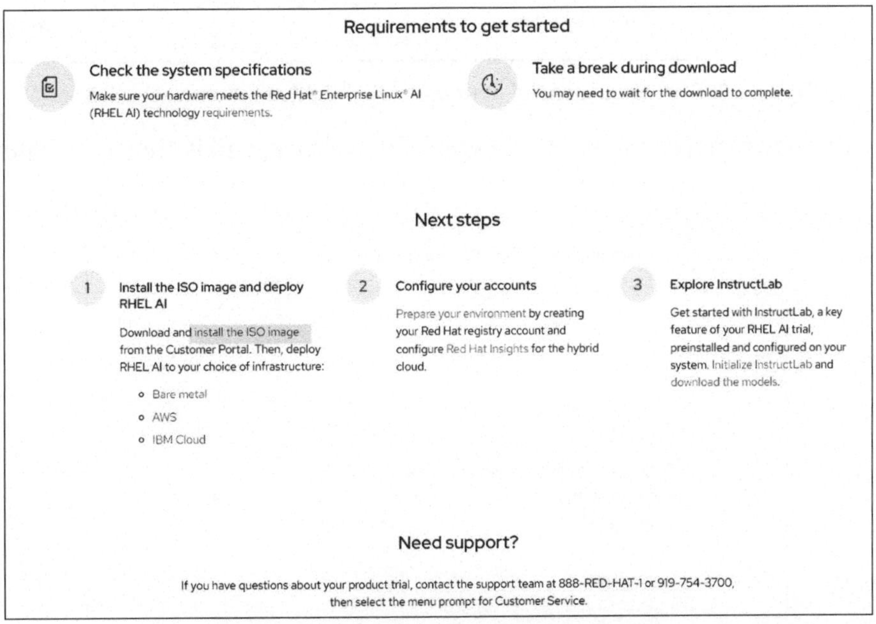

***Figure 7.6:** Select install the ISO image link*

This **`rhel-ai-nvidia-1.4-1739107830-x86_64-boot.iso`** file image is required for the **Bare metal** option. However, the **AWS** and **IBM Cloud** options require the **`qcow2`** file. This file must be further processed after download, for the **AWS** and **IBM Cloud** systems.

For the **`Bare metal`** option, the highlighted option was selected, as shown in *Figure 7.7* for the **ISO** image file:

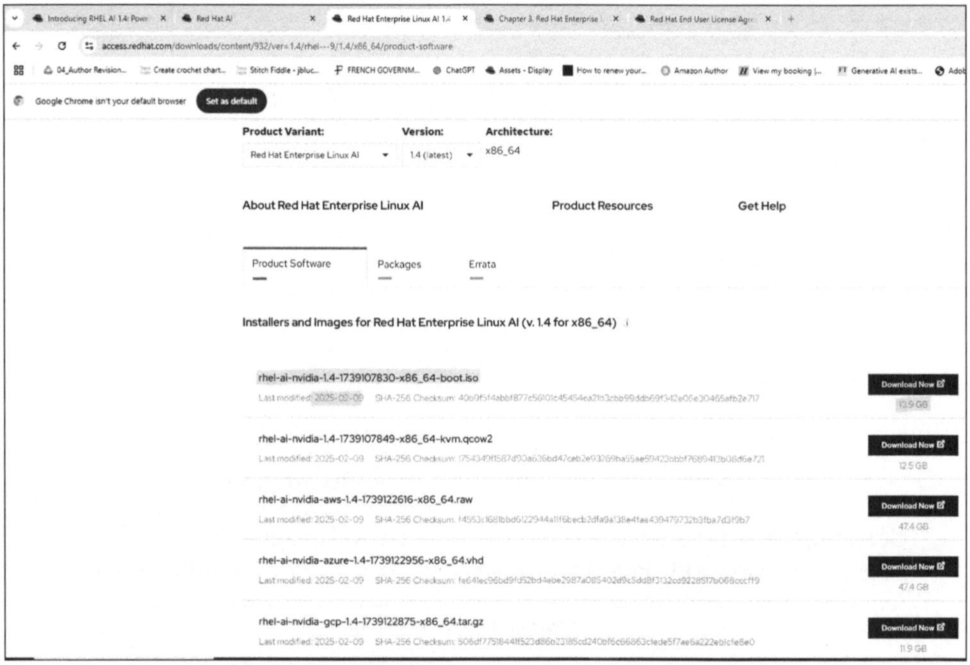

Figure 7.7: *For the Bare metal option, the highlighted option was selected*

The download requires **13.9 GBytes** of disk space, and is shown in *Figure 7.8*:

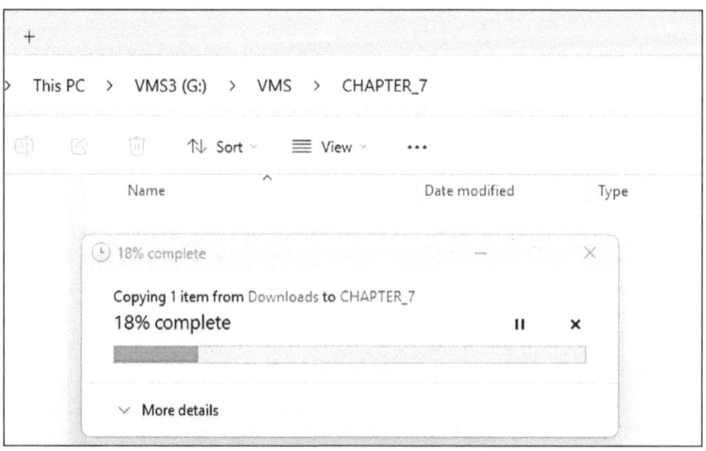

Figure 7.8: *The download requires 13.9 GBytes of disk space*

The Product Software tab shows the **ISO** file details, and a pop-up window shown with a mouse-over on the **`Download Now`** command button that gives the full file name, as highlighted in *Figure* 7.9.

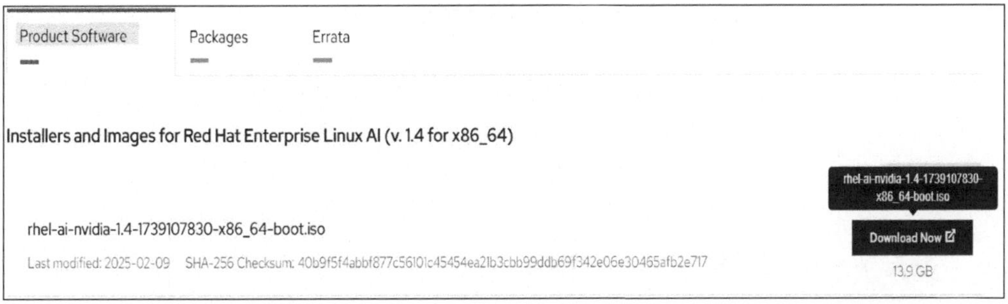

Figure 7.9: *A pop-up window is shown with a mouse-over on the* **Download Now** *command*

The completed Download of the Disk Image file is saved using **`Windows Explorer`**, as highlighted in *Figure* 7.10:

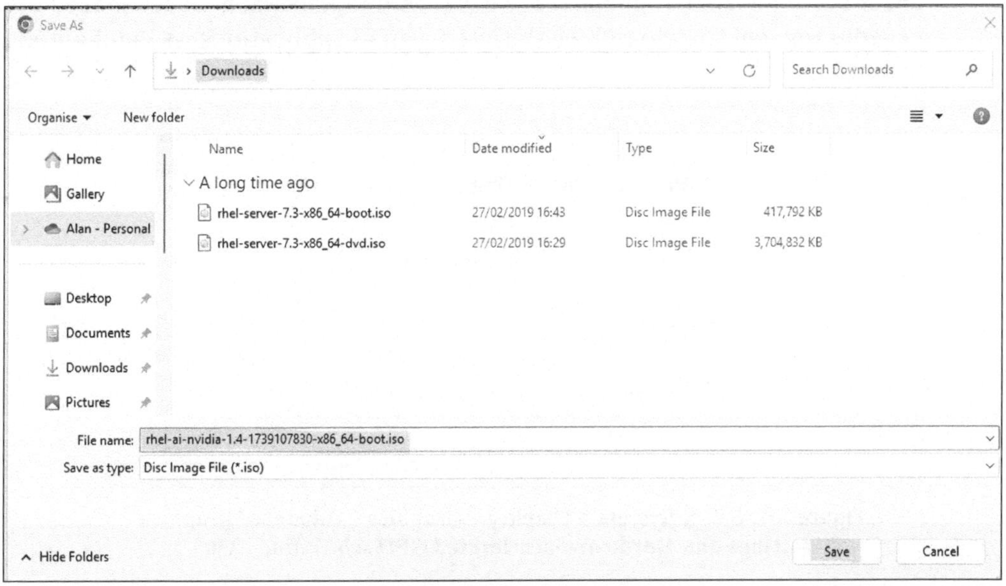

Figure 7.10: *The completed Download of the Disk Image file is saved using Windows Explorer*

The download on our system took around 50 Minutes (at around 40 MBits/second), as shown in *Figure* 7.11:

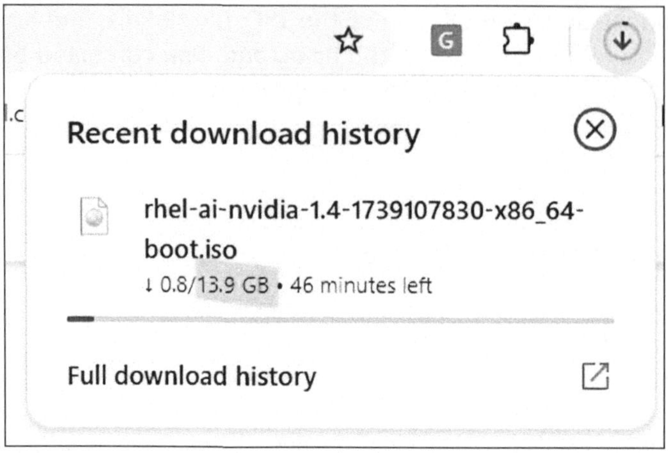

Figure 7.11: *The download on our system took around 50 Minutes (at around 40 MBits/second)*

On our Windows host system, we selected the option, **`System > Display > Graphics – Advanced graphics settings`** and **`Hardware-accelerated GPU scheduling`** "**on**" to help reduce the latency in AI applications, as highlighted in *Figure 7.12*:

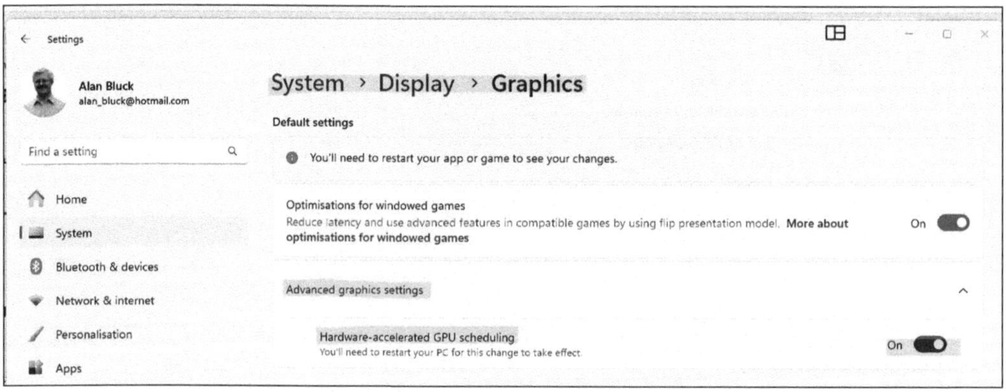

Figure 7.12: *Select* **System > Display > Graphics – Advanced graphics settings** *and* **Hardware-accelerated GPU** *scheduling* **"On"**

The **ISO** image we need is copied to the **VMS VMWare** sub-folder, named "Chapter 7", to load as a new Virtual System, as illustrated in *Figure 7.13*:

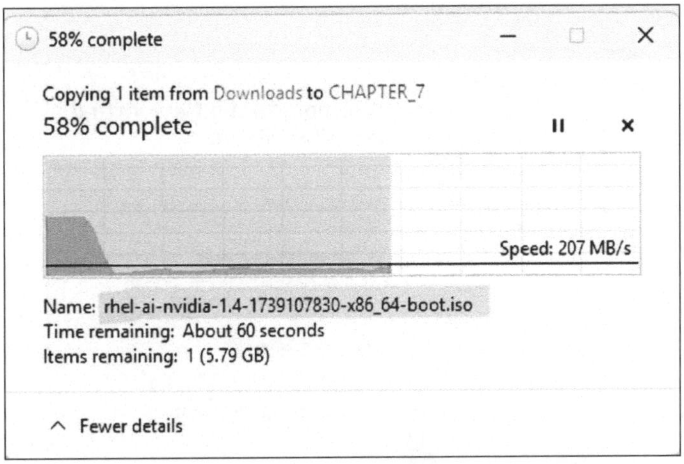

Figure 7.13: *The* **ISO** *image we need is copied to the* **VMS VMWare** *sub-folder*

In **VMWare Workstation**, version **16.2**, we can create a new RedHat Virtual Linux Operating system by, selecting the **`File -> New Virtual Machine...`** menu items, as highlighted in *Figure 7.14*:

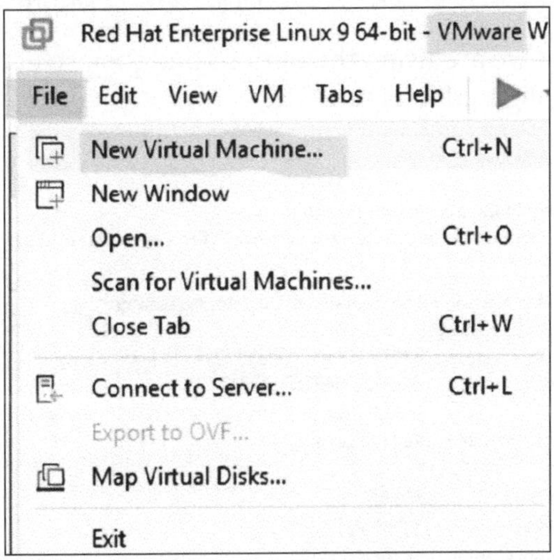

Figure 7.14: *In* **VMWare Workstation**, *version 16.2, create a new* **RedHat Virtual Linux Operating** *system*

The Custom (advanced) wizard path is selected, followed by clicking the **`Next`**>, as highlighted in *Figure 7.15*. Then we follow the same step options as described in *Chapter 2, Granite 3.0's Architecture*, in the section **Hardware and Software Requirements**, following *Figures* 2.17 through to *Figure* 2.31.

(But, selecting the **`rhel-ai-nvidia-1.4-1739107830-x86_64-boot.iso ISO`** image file, we downloaded.)

Figure 7.15: *The option to select a* **Custom (advanced)** *wizard path is selected*

We ensure that we are using the options and then select the **`Finish`** command button, as highlighted in *Figure 7.16*:

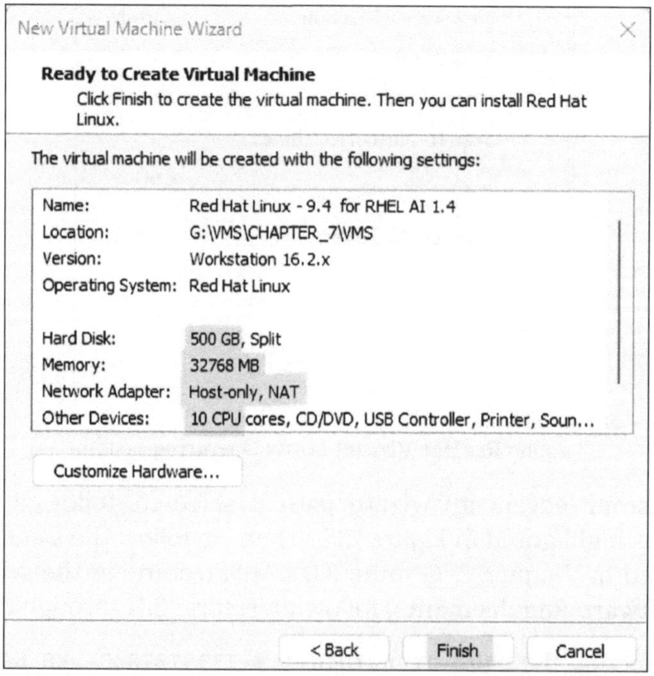

Figure 7.16: *We ensure that we are using the options and then select the* **Finish** *command*

The new VMware virtual machine, we created can now be started to boot from the ISO image by selecting the green arrow icon, as highlighted in *Figure 7.17*:

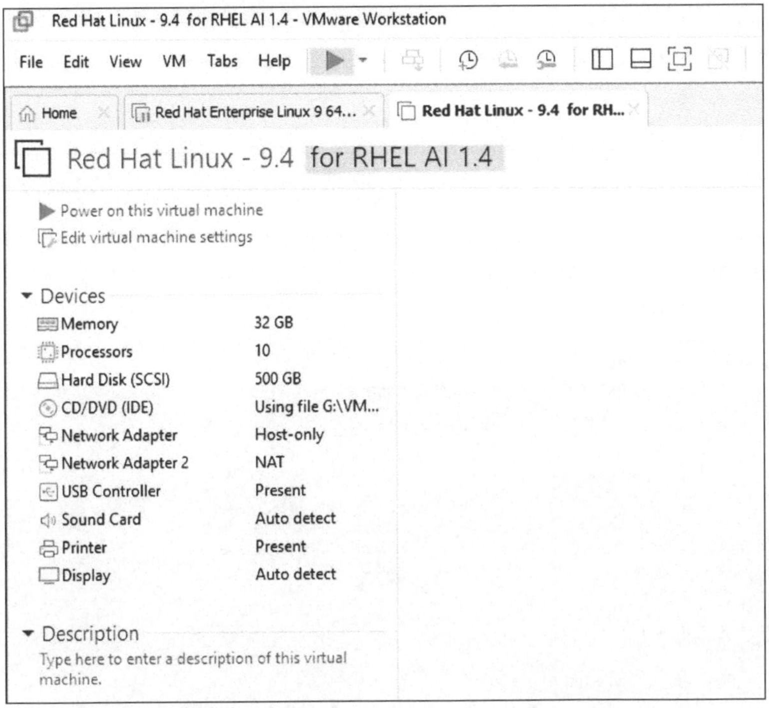

***Figure 7.17:** The new **VMware virtual** machine, we created can now be started to boot from the **ISO** image*

The splash screen confirms that we have **`RedHat Enterprise Linux RHEL 9.4`**, and it shows a countdown to start the boot process, as shown in *Figure 7.18*:

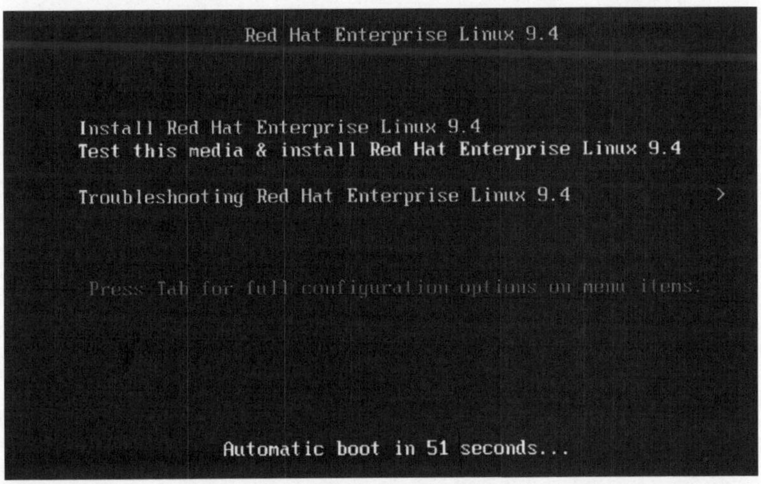

***Figure 7.18:** The splash screen confirms that we have RedHat Enterprise Linux (RHEL) 9.4*

The bottom of the VMware system splash screen displays the VMware instructions for installing the system, as shown in *Figure 7.19*:

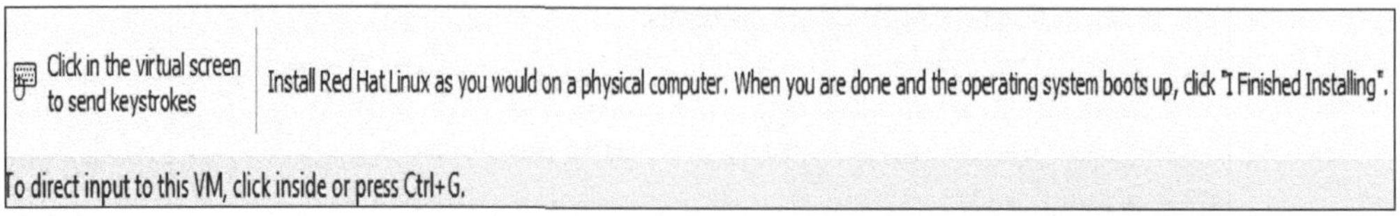

Figure 7.19: *The bottom of the* ***VMware*** *system splash screen displays the* ***VMware*** *instructions*

The start of the boot sequence is displayed with the **SHA** validation check-sum for the **ISO** image running (this takes a few minutes to complete), as shown in *Figure 7.20*:

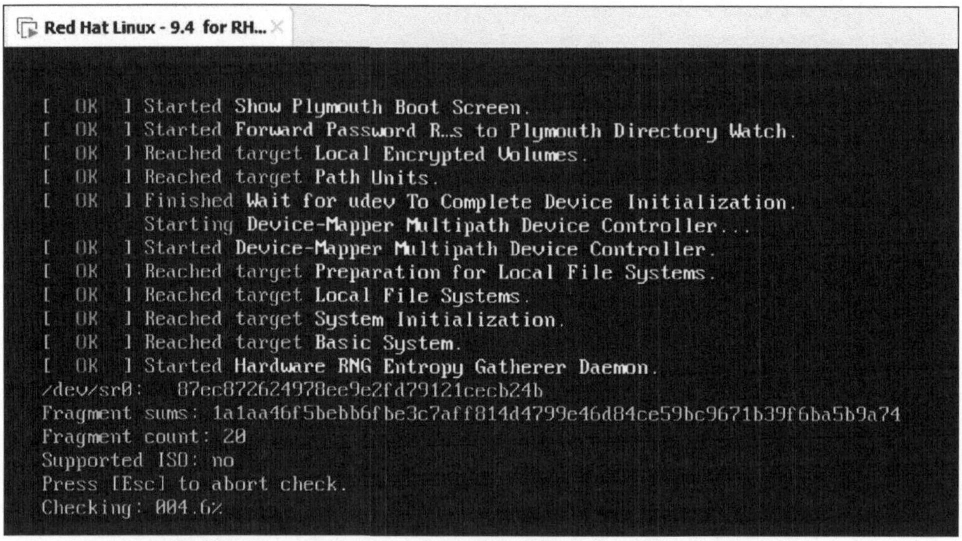

Figure 7.20: *The start of the boot sequence displays the* ***SHA*** *validation check-sum for the* ***ISO*** *image*

After the installation is completed, we can select the "`I Finished Installing`" command at the bottom right of the VMware system screen, as shown in *Figure 7.21*:

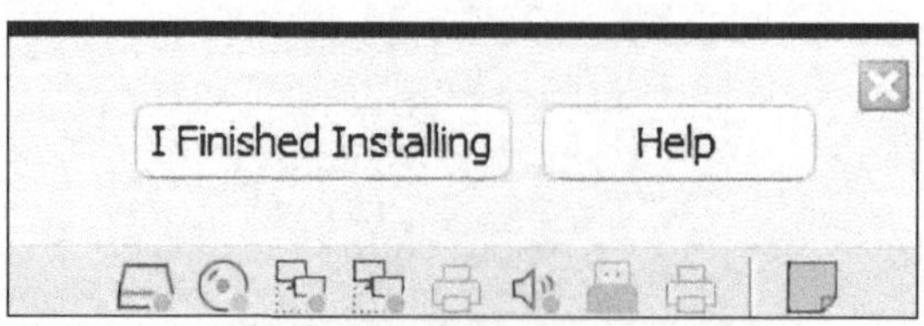

Figure 7.21: *We can select the "**I Finished Installing**" command at the bottom right of the* ***VMware*** *system*

Next, we are presented with the Installation Summary, where we must select each of the highlighted options in turn, as illustrated in *Figure 7.22*:

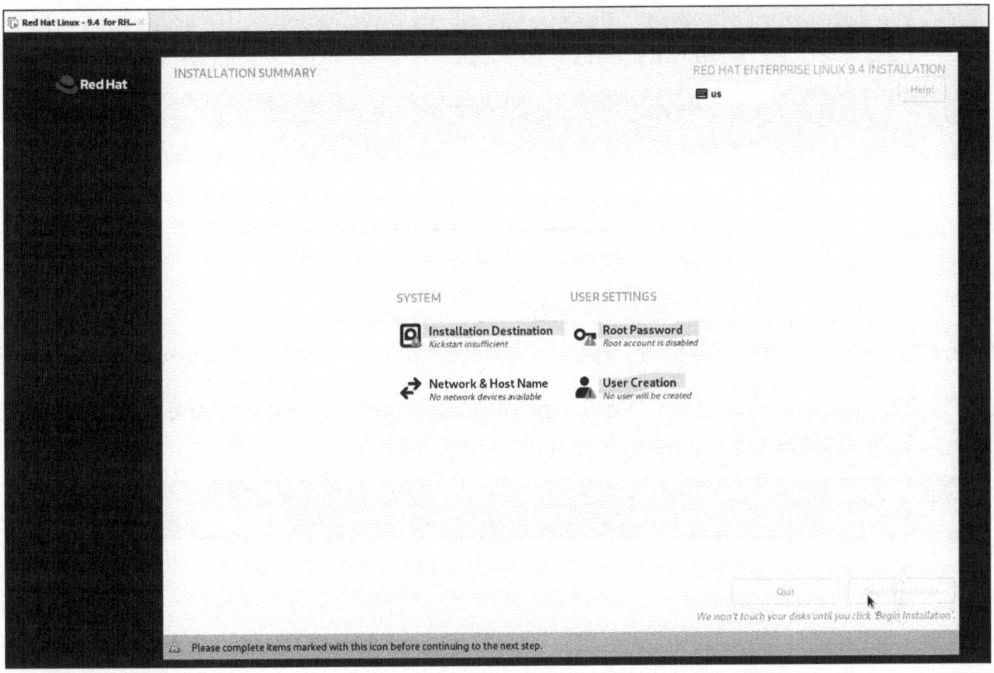

Figure 7.22: *Next, we are presented with the Installation Summary*

First the **`Installation Destination`** Disk is selected (**500 GBytes**), displaying the screen shown in *Figure* 7.23. Then the **`Done`** command is clicked.

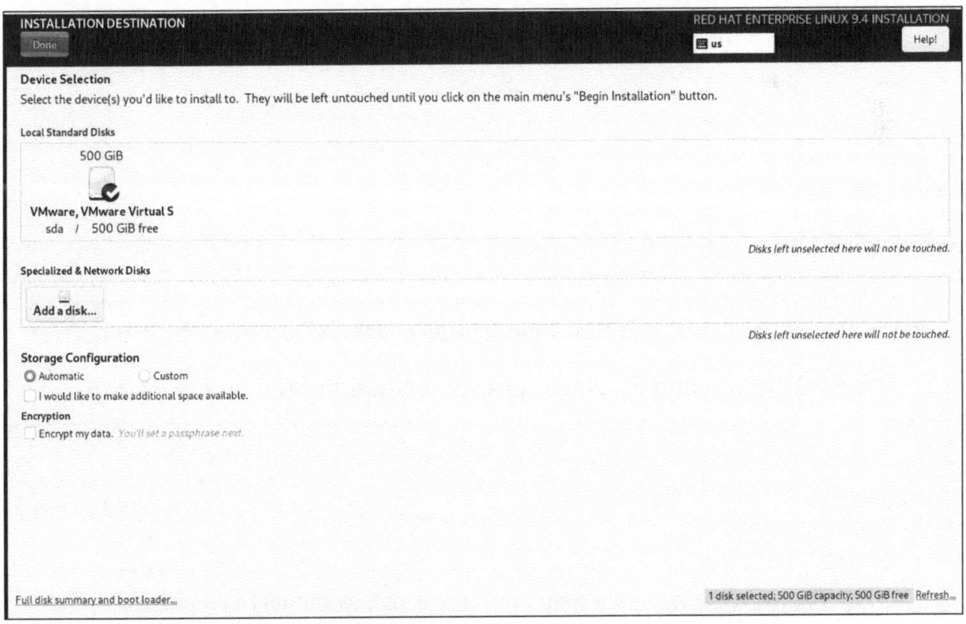

Figure 7.23: *First the* **Installation Destination** *Disk is selected* (**500 GBytes**)

We can select the **Root Password** option next, to give the screen to add the password, as highlighted in *Figure 7.24*:

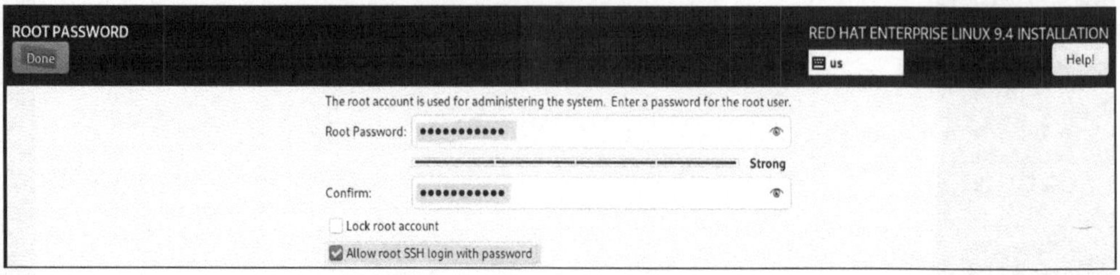

Figure 7.24: *We can select the* **Root Password** *option next, to give the screen to add the password*

The **Network & Host Name** option is selected to rename the **Host** server to **ECMUKDEMO2025-1.4**, as shown in *Figure 7.25*:

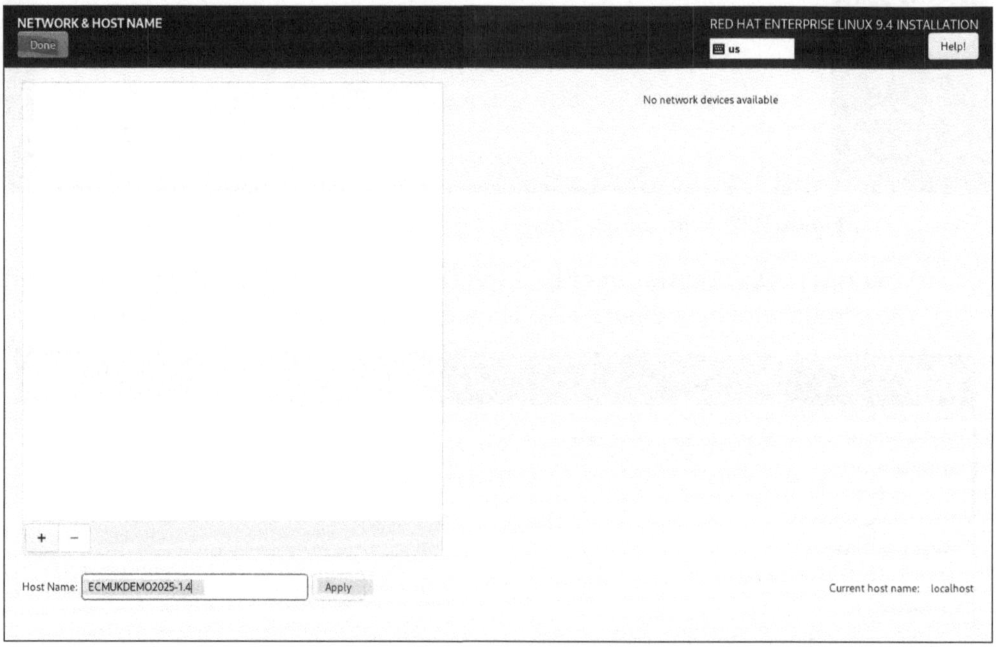

Figure 7.25: The **Network and Host Name** *option is selected to rename the* **Host** *server*

The **Apply** command is selected as shown highlighted, in *Figure 7.26*:

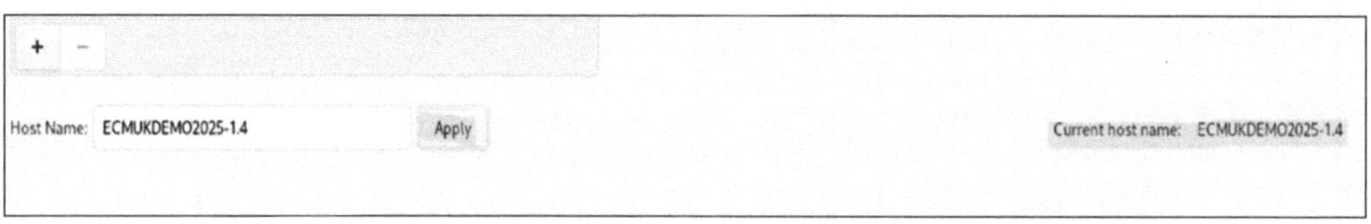

Figure 7.26: *The Apply command is selected, as shown highlighted*

Finally, the **User Creation** link is selected to create a new user for administration, with the settings, as highlighted in *Figure 7.27*:

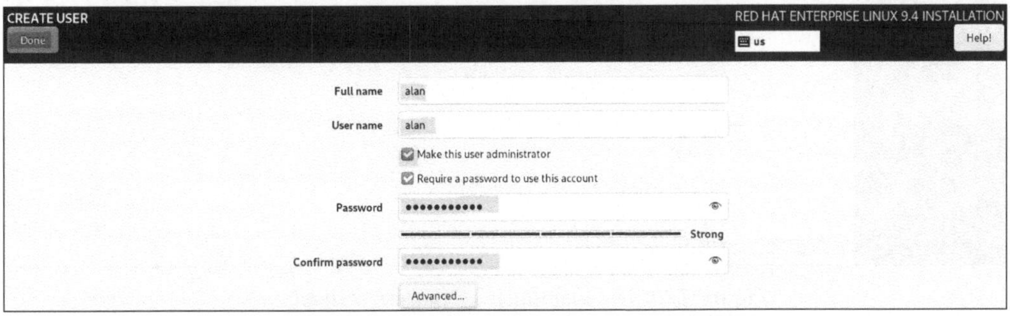

Figure 7.27: *Finally, the* **User Creation** *link is selected to create a new user for administration*

The installation is started by selecting the **Begin Installation** command, as highlighted in *Figure 7.28*:

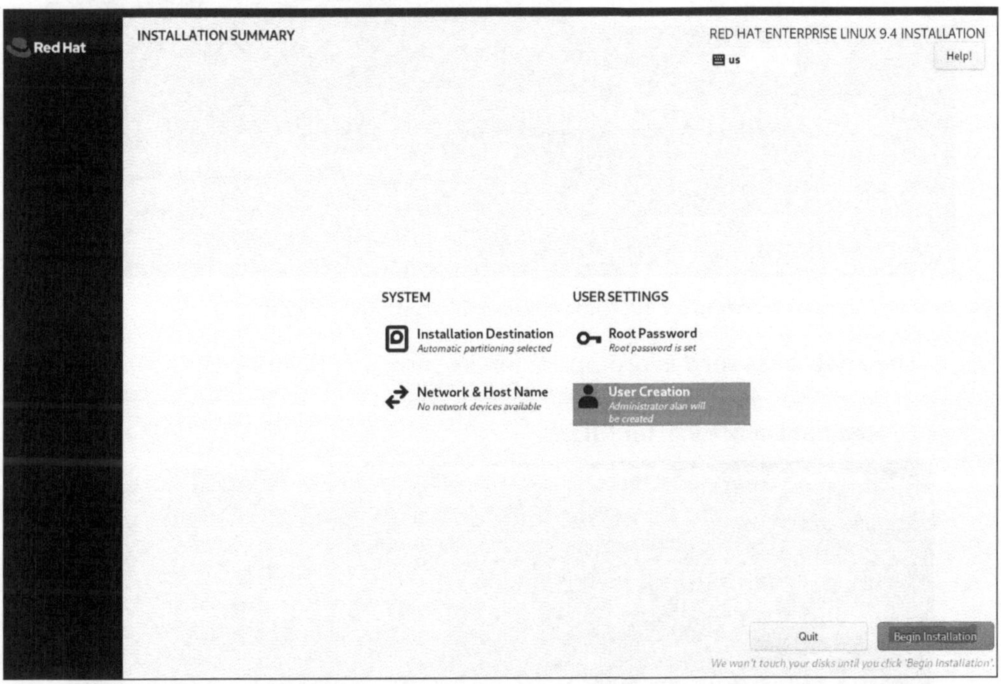

Figure 7.28: *The installation is started by selecting the Begin Installation command*

The **Installation Progress** is displayed, as shown in *Figure 7.29*:

(This blue progress bar line appears to be not updated, although after around 20 minutes, the install completes as expected.)

Figure 7.29: *The Installation Progress is displayed*

The **`root`** user is prompted to login, as highlighted in *Figure* 7.30:

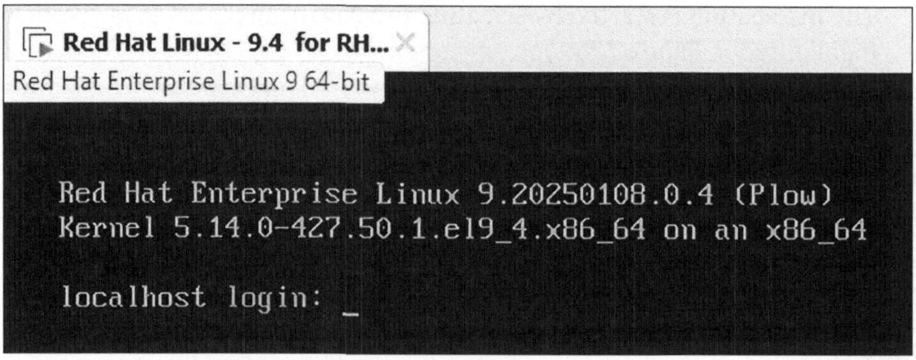

Figure 7.30: *The root user is prompted to login*

The **`root password`** is prompted for, as shown in *Figure* 7.31:

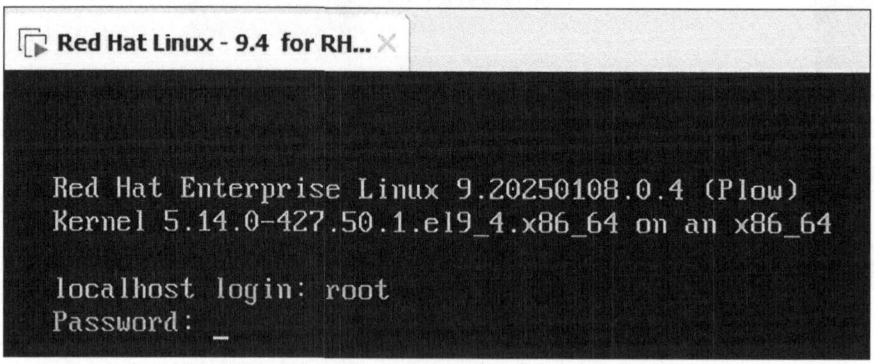

Figure 7.31: *The root password is prompted for*

If there are no available **NVIDI GPU** hardware cards installed on the deployed system, then you will get a screen with the following message, as highlighted in *Figure* 7.32:

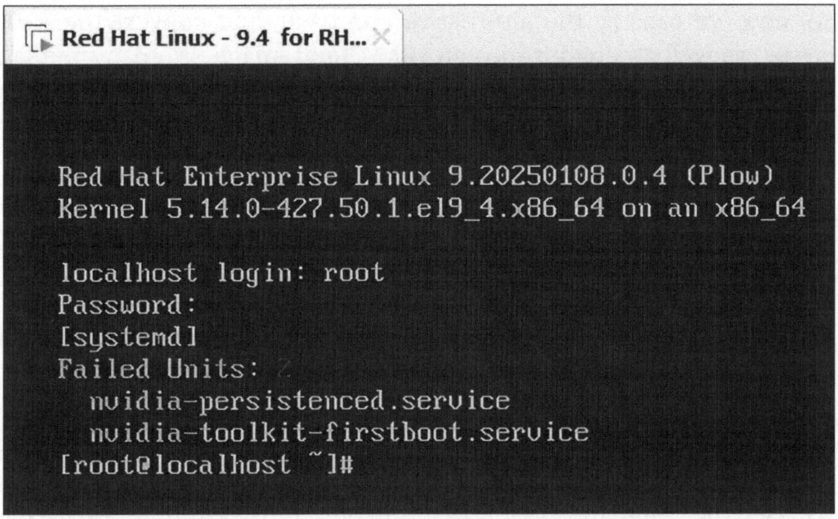

Figure 7.32: *If there are no available* **NVIDI GPU** *hardware cards installed, then you get an error screen*

On logging in to the system, the highlighted errors will be displayed, as illustrated in *Figure 7.33*:

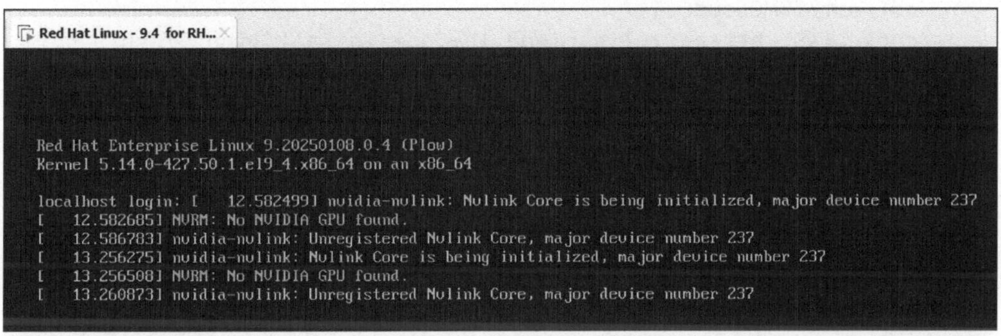

Figure 7.33: *On logging into the system, the highlighted errors will be displayed*

6. You can install **RHEL AI 1.4**, and deploy the **InstructLab** tooling, using a bootable **RHEL** container image provided by Red Hat, as described in Steps 1–5. If there is no local **NVIDIA GPUs** available, then you can install the system on the **IBM Cloud**, or on the **AWS cloud**, and use their cloud resources as an alternative.

7. The **IBM Cloud** installation can be followed using the link:

   https://shorturl.at/Or6ZZ

   (entitled *Chapter 4, Installing* RHEL AI *on* IBM *cloud*)

So, now we can try the alternative approach, and convert the **RHEL AI 1.4** image as well as load it into an **IBM Cloud** image. We can then launch the instance of the **IBM Cloud** image, and deploy **RHEL AI 1.4** on an **IBM Cloud** system.

8. To create a bootable image in **IBM Cloud,** the user 's **IBM Cloud** accounts must be configured to allow image creation. You will then need to set up a Cloud Object **Storage (COS)** bucket. Next, create an **IBM Cloud** image, using the converted **RHEL AI 1.4** image.

9. First, we have to install the **IBM CLI** (the **IBM Cloud Command Line Interface**) on our **VMware** machine.

   (See https://cloud.ibm.com/docs/cli?topic=cli-install-ibmcloud-cli#shell_install)

10. We used the commands as follows from our Linux system, **ECMUKDEMO2025**, which is the system we set up as described in *Chapter 2, Granite 3.0's Architecture*, and illustrated in *Figure 7.34*:

```
cd /opt
mkdir IBMCLoudCLI
cd /opt/IBMCLoudCLI
curl -fsSL https://clis.cloud.ibm.com/install/linux | sh
```

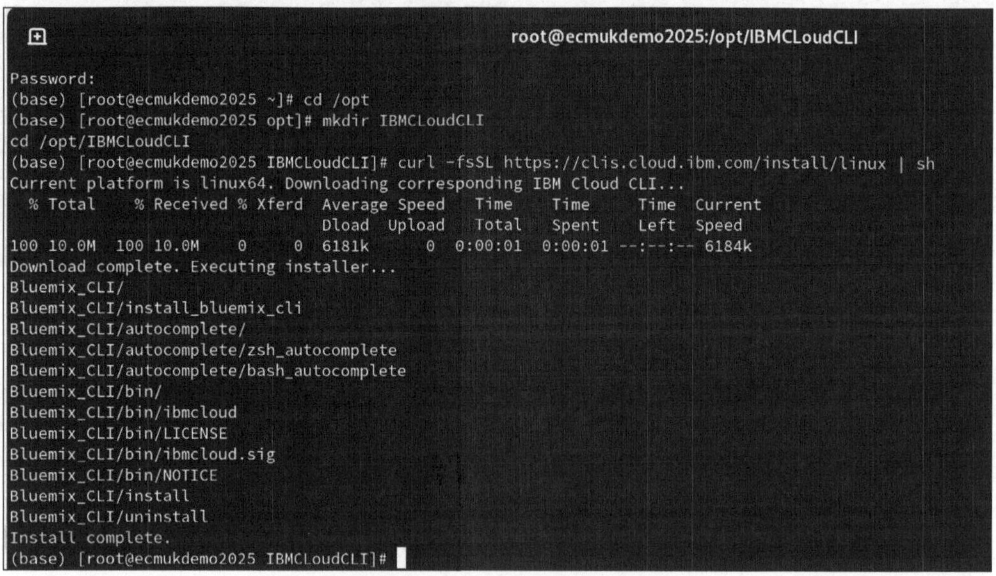

Figure 7.34: *We used the commands from our Linux system,* **ECMUKDEMO2025**

11. Next, we need to ensure that the system is updated to the latest `IBM Cloud CLI` version:

```
ibmcloud update
```

The following command displays the **IBM Cloud CLI** version, as shown in *Figure 7.35*:

```
ibmcloud -v
```

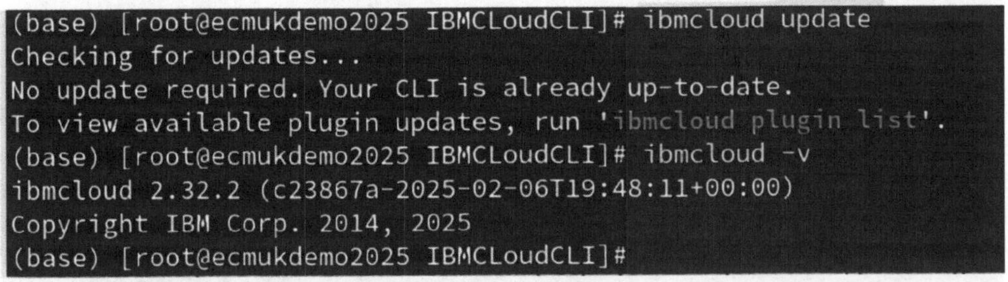

Figure 7.35: *The command,* ***ibmcloud -v*** *displays the IBM Cloud CLI version*

Install the **IBM Cloud CLI** plugin and see: https://cloud.ibm.com/containers/serverless/cli

`ibmcloud plugin install code-engine`, as shown in *Figure 7.36*:

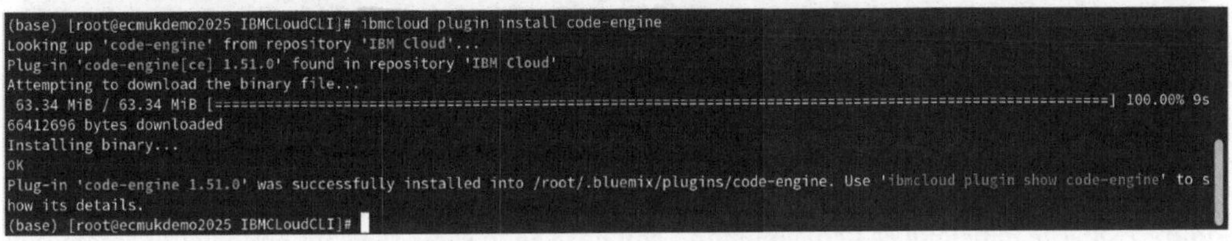

Figure 7.36: *Install the* ***IBM Cloud CLI*** *plugin*

We can list the installation name and version using **ibmcloud plugin list**, as highlighted in *Figure 7.37*:

Figure 7.37: *We can list the installation name and version using* ***ibmcloud plugin list***

The **ibmcloud ce help** command can be used to show the command syntax and list of commands, as highlighted in *Figure 7.38*:

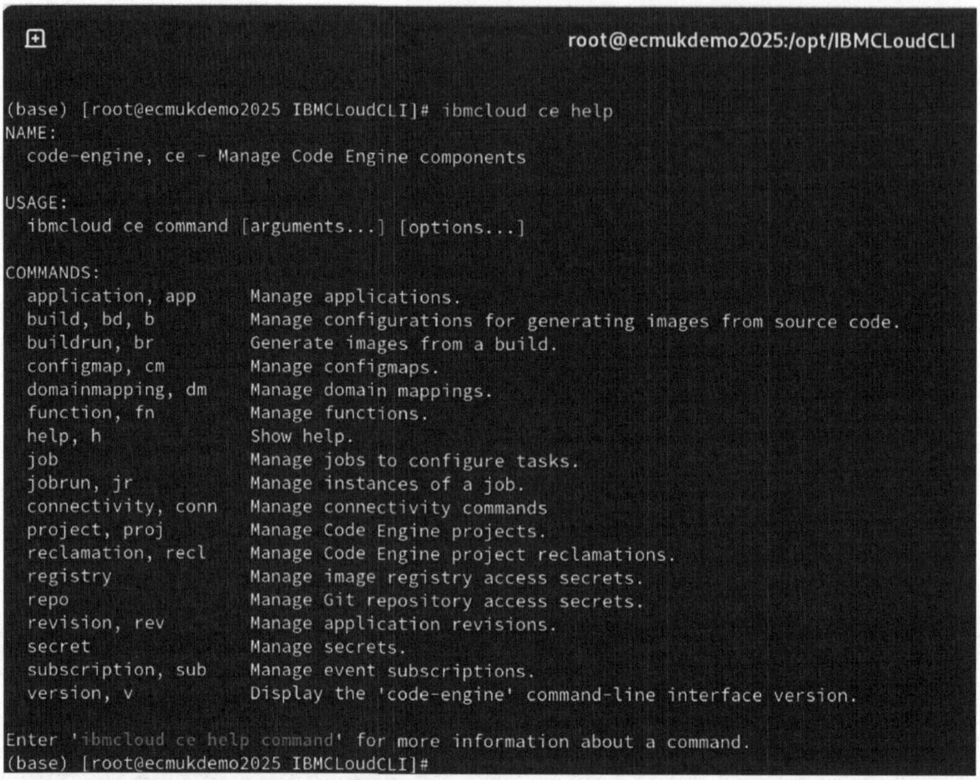

***Figure 7.38:** The **ibmcloud ce help** command can be used to show the command list of commands*

We can add additional users to the **`IBM Cloud`** account, as shown in *Figure 7.39*:

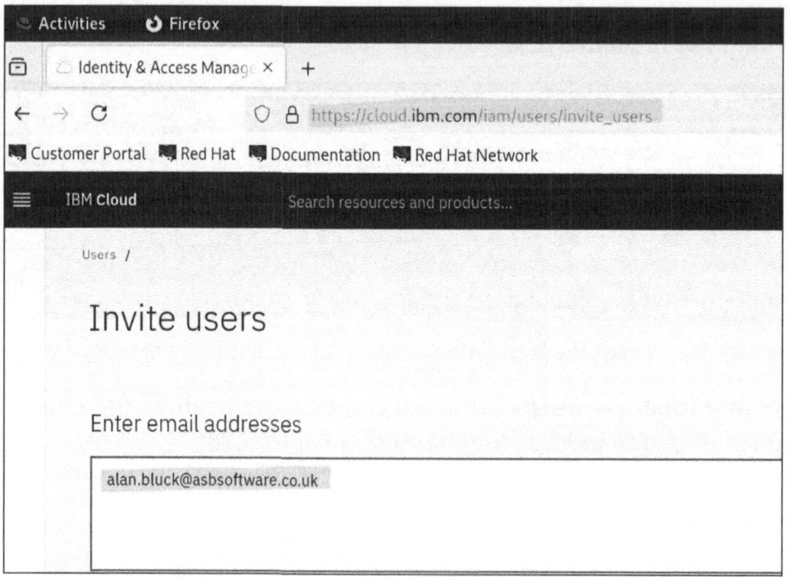

***Figure 7.39:** We can add additional users to the **IBM Cloud** account*

Create Access Groups

https://cloud.ibm.com/iam/overview

To start an **API** key creation process, you have to log into an **`IBM Cloud`** account, as shown in *Figure 7.40*: https://cloud.ibm.com/

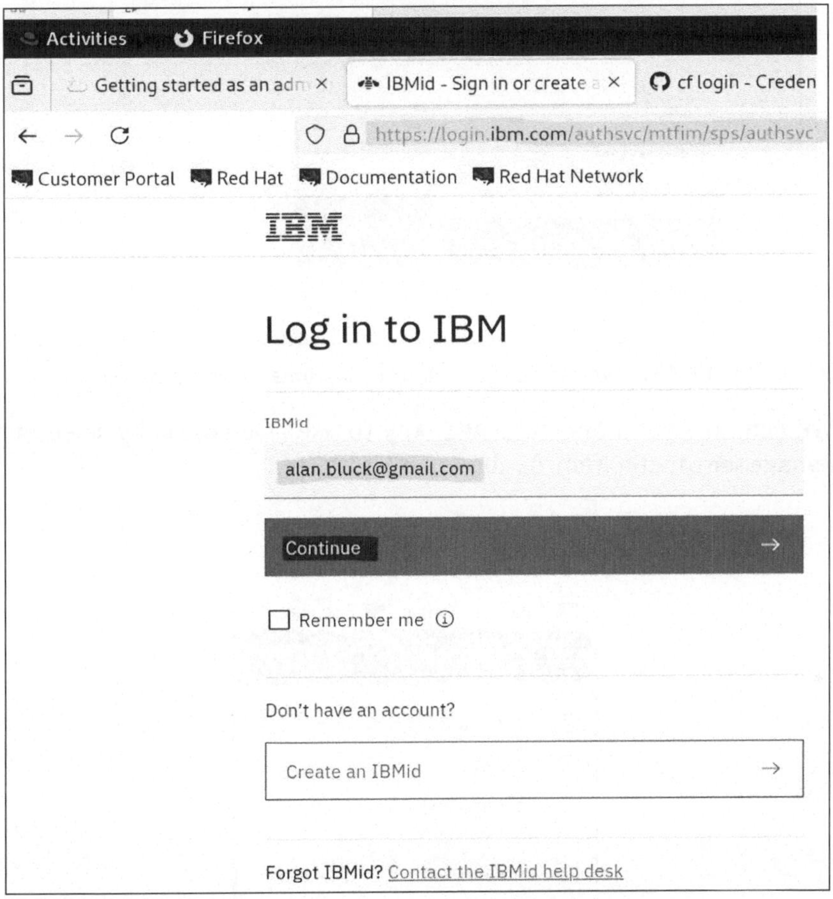

***Figure 7.40**: To start an **API** key creation process, you have to log into an **IBM Cloud** account*

The **`IBM PartnerWorld`** account, or a **`Customer`** account can be used to **`Log in`**, as shown in *Figure 7.41*:

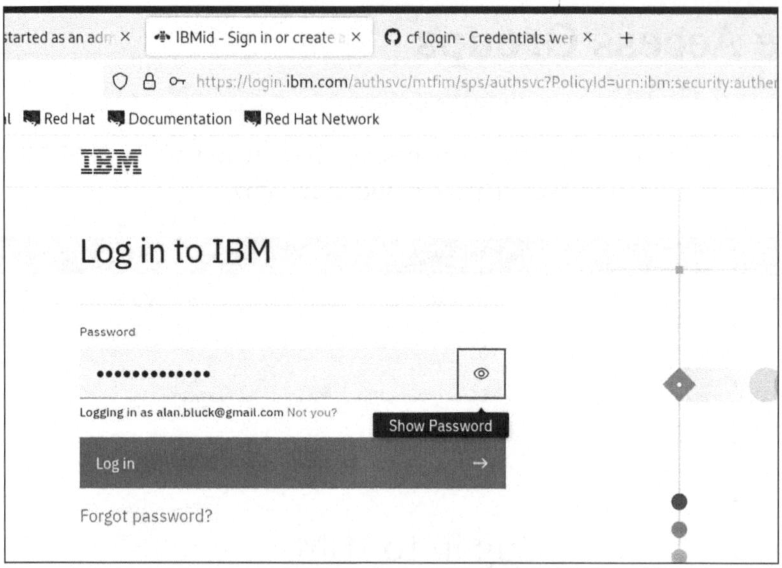

Figure 7.41: *The* **IBM PartnerWorld** *account, or a* **Customer** *account can be used to Log in*

We can now get a one-time **`API Key`** to use as a **`Login`**, by selecting the **`API Management`** menu item, as shown in *Figure 7.42*:

Figure 7.42: *Get a one-time* **API Key** *to use as a* **Login**, *by selecting the* **API Management** *menu item*

Next, we click the **`Name`** icon on the top-right of the web page, and select **`Login to CLI and API`**, as highlighted in *Figure 7.43*:

Figure 7.43**: Select the **Name** icon, and then select **Login to CLI and API

Copy the **`One time passcode`** for **`IBM Cloud CLI`** for the logon key, as highlighted in *Figure 7.44*:

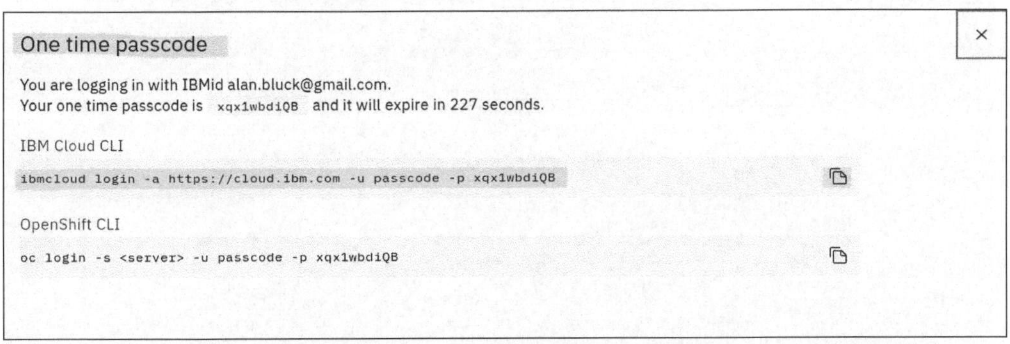

***Figure 7.44**: Copy the **One time passcode** for **IBM Cloud CLI** for the logon key*

The copied log-in statement is used in our **Linux** system command window to log onto the **`IBM Cloud CLI`** (Command Line Interface)

```
ibmcloud login -a https://cloud.ibm.com -u passcode -p xqxlwbdiQB
```

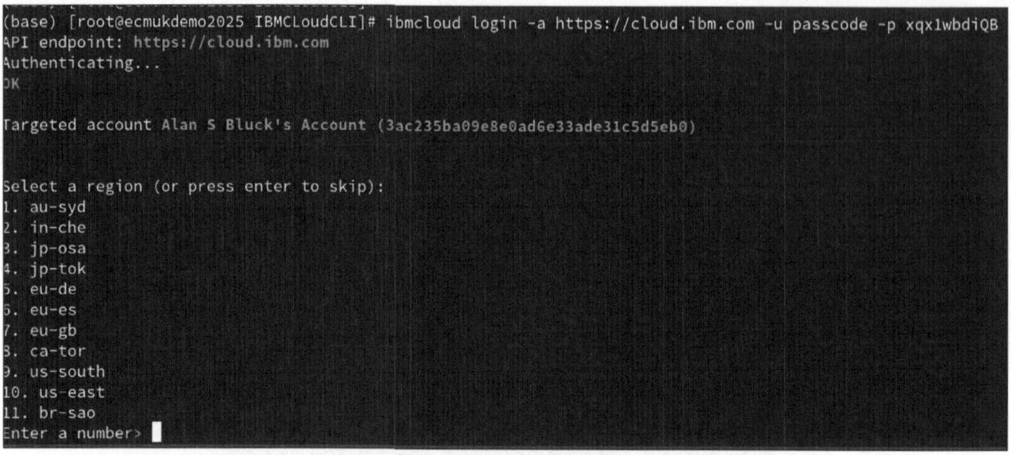

Figure 7.45: *The copied log-in statement is used in our* ***Linux*** *system command window*

Note: After creating a permanent **API** key, you can use:

```
export API_KEY="xxxxxxxxxxxxxxxxxxxxxxxxxx"
ibmcloud login --apikey $API_KEY
```

but we used the one-time pass code command, as copied and listed in *Figure* 7.44.

Next, we need to enter a region number (**7** for **eu-gb**), as highlighted in *Figure* 7.46:

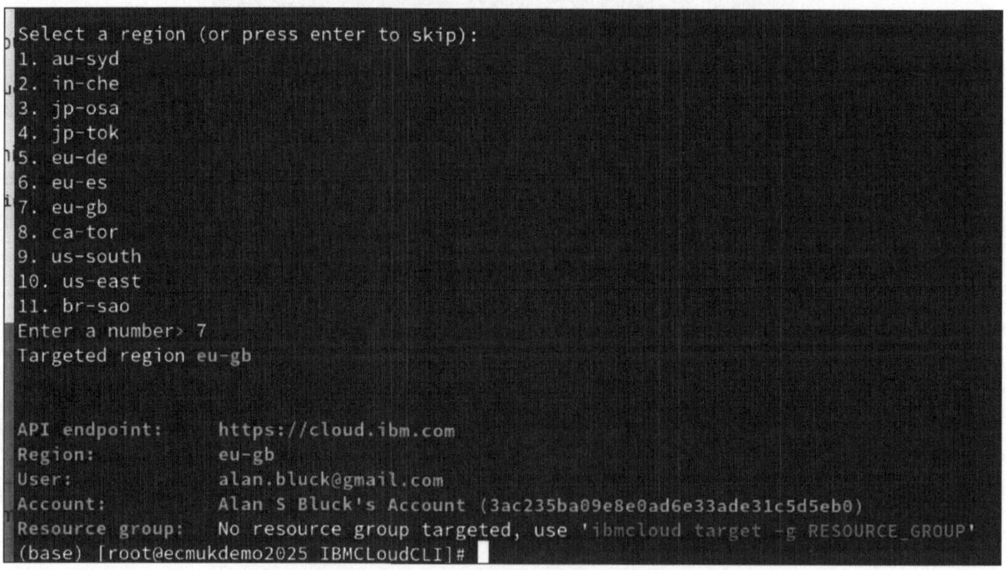

Figure 7.46: *Next, we need to enter a region number*

We need to set up multiple **IBM Cloud** configurations, and then create our **COS** bucket before generating a **QCOW2** image.

We have to install the required **IBM Cloud** plugins by running the following command:

```
ibmcloud plugin install cloud-object-storage infrastructure-service
```

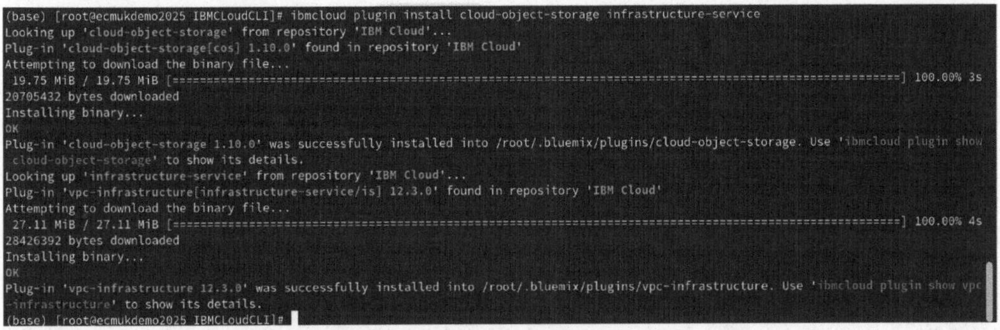

Figure 7.47: *We installed the necessary IBM Cloud plugins*

We, then set our preferred resource group, using the following example command, which we call **`Default`**, as highlighted in *Figure* 7.48:

```
ibmcloud target -g Default
```

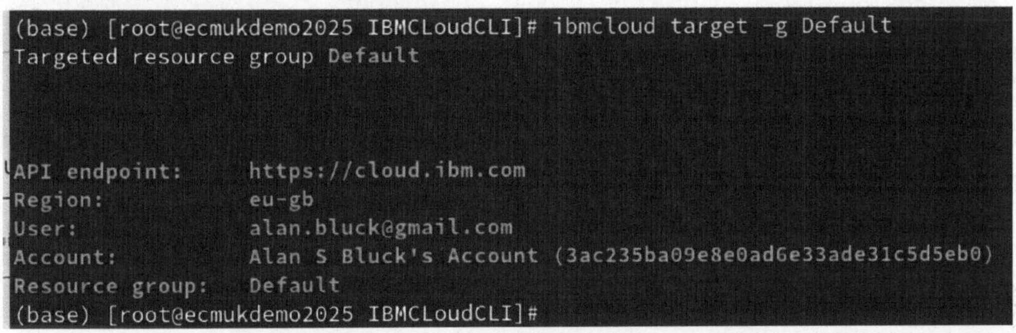

Figure 7.48: *We set our preferred resource group*

We set the following example command which sets the **eu-gb** as our preferred region, as highlighted in *Figure* 7.49:

```
ibmcloud target -r eu-gb
```

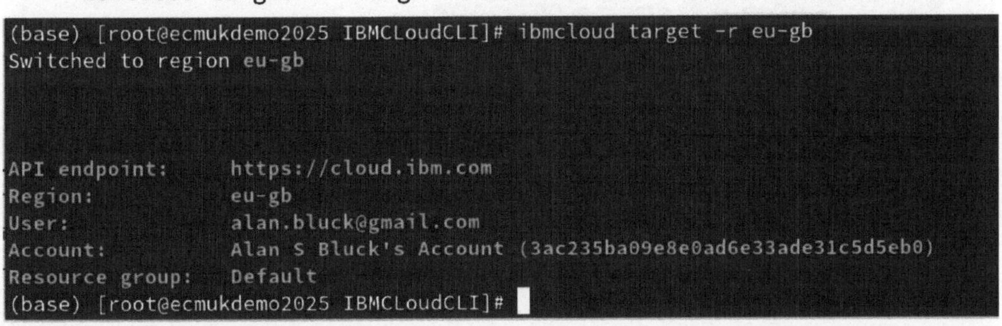

Figure 7.49: *We set our preferred region, with the example command,* ***ibmcloud target -r eu-gb***

A deployment plan was selected, after checking the pricing and related properties on **IBM's Cloud** website.

The available deployment plans were listed with the command, as highlighted in *Figure* 7.50:

```
ibmcloud catalog service cloud-object-storage --output json | jq
-r '.[].children[] | select(.children != null) | .children[].
name'
```

Figure 7.50: *We can list the available deployment plans*

The **premium-global-deployment** example plan is assigned to the environment variable, **cos_deploy_plan**:

```
cos_deploy_plan=premium-global-deployment
```

(I tried to use **cos_deploy_plan=lite-global-deployment**, but this level is not high enough!)

So we needed to update to a **Premium** account (with IBM giving **$200** free credit), with a company credit card, as shown in *Figure* 7.51:

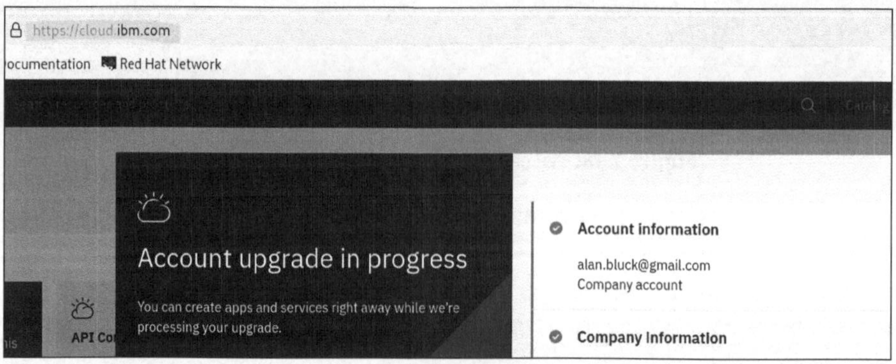

Figure 7.51: *We needed to update to a* ***Premium account,*** *with a company credit card*

A **Cloud Object Storage** (**COS**) service instance was created and assigned to the environment variable named **cos_si_name.** After setting this, the **cloud-object-storage** was created by running the following commands, as shown in *Figure* 7.52:

```
export cos_si_name="GRANITE_CHAPTER7_SERVICE_INSTANCE"
```

Run the command:

```
ibmcloud resource service-instance-create ${cos_si_name}
cloud-object-storage standard global -d ${cos_deploy_plan}
```

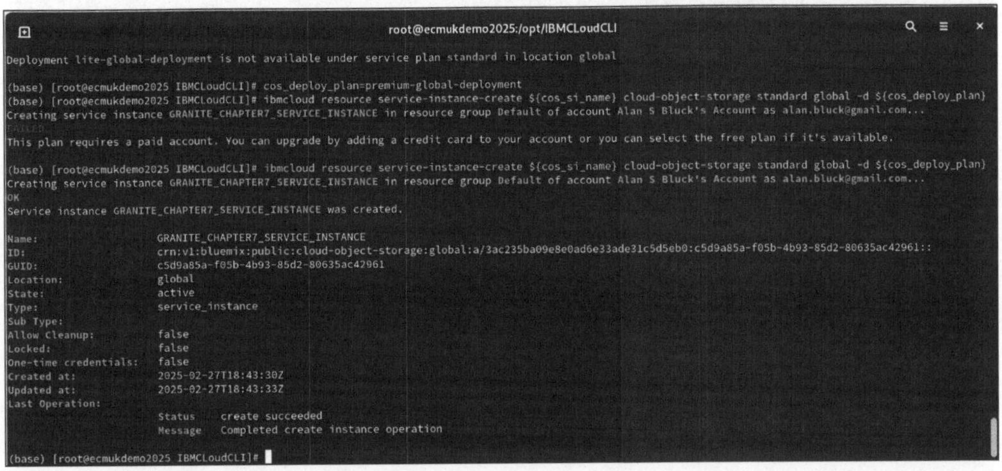

Figure 7.52: *Next, we created a* ***Cloud Object Storage*** *(**COS**) service instance*

The **Cloud Resource Name** (**CRN**) for our **Cloud Object Storage** (**COS**) bucket was assigned to an environment variable named **cos_crn** by running the following commands, as highlighted in *Figure 7.53*:

```
cos_crn=$(ibmcloud resource service-instance ${cos_si_name}
--output json| jq -r '.[] | select(.crn | contains("cloud-ob-
ject-storage")) | .crn')
        ibmcloud cos config crn --crn ${cos_crn} -force
```

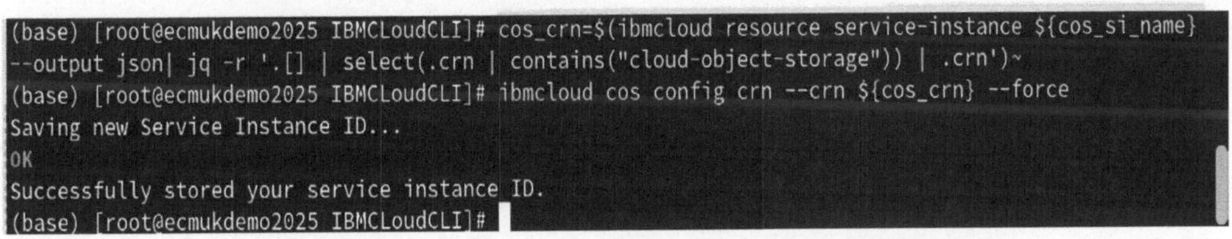

Figure 7.53: *Create a* ***Cloud Object Storage*** *(**COS**) bucket in a variable named* ***cos_crn*** *by executing the commands*

Now, we create our **Cloud Object Storage** (**COS**) bucket named as the environment variable **bucket_name,** with the following commands (the following name failed at first):

```
bucket_name="IBM_GRANITE_3_C7_BUCKET"
```

(NB This first name was Invalid- see the following pages)

```
ibmcloud cos bucket-create --bucket ${bucket_name}
```

At this point we checked the configuration, so far, as shown in *Figure 7.54*:

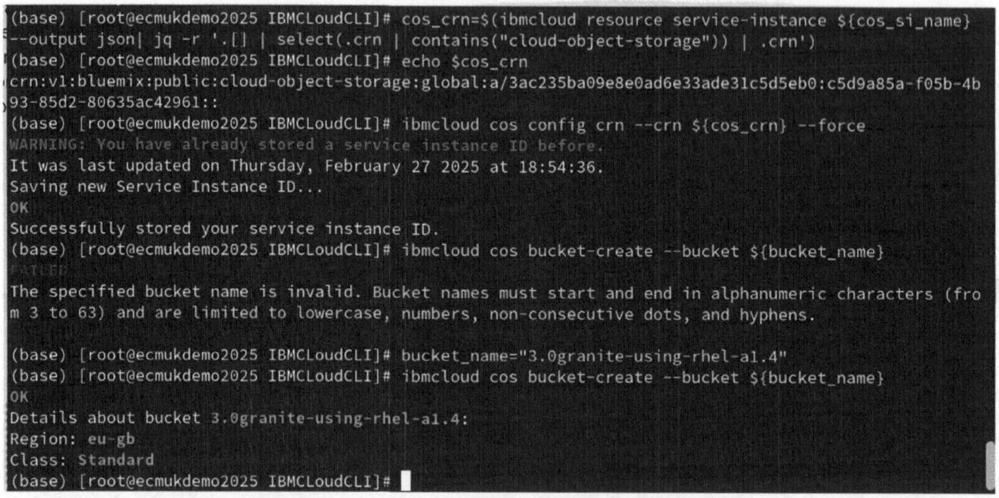

Figure 7.54: *At this point, we checked the configuration*

Bucket names must start and end in alphanumeric characters (from 3 to 63), and are limited to lowercase, numbers, non-consecutive dots, and hyphens. We set the environment variable as:

```
bucket_name="3.0granite-using-rhel-a1.4"
```

We then checked the system using:

```
(base) [root@ecmukdemo2025 IBMCLoudCLI]# ibmcloud cos config list
Key                      Value
Last Updated             Thursday, February 27 2025 at 18:54:36
Default Region           eu-gb
Download Location        /root/Downloads
CRN                      crn:v1:bluemix:public:cloud-object-stor-
age:global:a/3ac235ba09e8e0ad6e33ade31c5d5eb0:c5d9a85a-f05b-4b93-
85d2-80635ac42961::~
AccessKeyID
SecretAccessKey
Authentication Method    IAM
URL Style                VHost
Service Endpoint
```

Then, we set the **cos_crn** environment variable using:

```
(base) [root@ecmukdemo2025 IBMCLoudCLI]# cos_crn=$(ibmcloud re-
source service-instance ${cos_si_name} --output json| jq -r '.[]
| select(.crn | contains("cloud-object-storage")) | .crn')
```

And checked this using:

```
(base) [root@ecmukdemo2025 IBMCLoudCLI]# echo $cos_crn
crn:v1:bluemix:public:cloud-object-storage:global:a/3ac-
235ba09e8e0ad6e33ade31c5d5eb0:c5d9a85a-f05b-4b93-85d2-80635
ac42961::
(base) [root@ecmukdemo2025 IBMCLoudCLI]# ibmcloud cos config crn
--crn ${cos_crn} --force
WARNING: You have already stored a service instance ID before.
It was last updated on Thursday, February 27 2025 at 18:54:36.
Saving new Service Instance ID...
OK
Successfully stored your service instance ID.
```

The first attempt using the bucket name (**IBM_GRANITE_3_C7_BUCKET**).

```
(base) [root@ecmukdemo2025 IBMCLoudCLI]# ibmcloud cos bucket-cre-
ate --bucket ${bucket_name}
FAILED
The specified bucket name is invalid. Bucket names must start and
end in alphanumeric characters (from 3 to 63) and are limited to
lowercase, numbers, non-consecutive dots, and hyphens.
```

The following commands were then used to create the Bucket name:

```
(base) [root@ecmukdemo2025 IBMCLoudCLI]# bucket_name="3.
0granite-using-rhel-a1.4"
(base) [root@ecmukdemo2025 IBMCLoudCLI]# ibmcloud cos bucket-
create --bucket ${bucket_name}
OK
Details about bucket 3.0granite-using-rhel-a1.4:
Region: eu-gb
Class: Standard
(base) [root@ecmukdemo2025 IBMCLoudCLI]#
```

Allow the infrastructure service to read the buckets that are in the service instance **${cos_si_guid}** variable by running the following commands:

```
cos_si_guid=$(ibmcloud resource service-instance ${cos_si_name}
--output json| jq -r '.[] | select(.crn | contains("cloud-ob-
ject-storage")) | .guid')
```

Next, we use **cos_si_guid** to set the authorization policy, as highlighted in *Figure* 7.55:

```
Ibmcloud iam authorization-policy-create is cloud-object-storage
Reader –source-resource-type image –target-service-instance-id
${cos_si_guid}
```

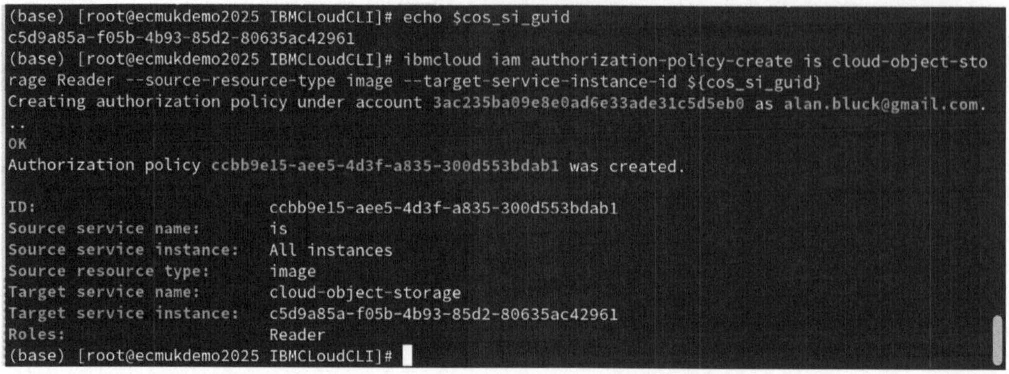

Figure 7.55: *Next, we use* ***cos_si_guid*** *to set the authorization policy*

Our **IBM Cloud Object Storage (CoS)** service instance bucket is set up now. So, we need to download the **QCOW2** image from the link (the **Red Hat Enterprise Linux AI** download page).

> https://access.redhat.com/downloads/content/932/ver=1.4/rhel---9/1.4/x86_64/product-software

Copy the **QCOW2** image link, and add using the download link above.

(RedHat suggested using "*Copy the* QCOW2 *image link, and add it to the following command:*"

```
$ curl -Lo disk.qcow2 "PASTE_HERE_THE_LINK_OF_THE_QCOW2_FILE"
```

But this didn't give us a valid image file at first, but then we found this from the website, as:

> https://access.cdn.redhat.com/content/origin/files/sha256/17/1754349f-1587d90a636bd47ceb2e93269ba55ae59423bbbf7689413b08d6e721/rhel-ai-nvidia-1.4-1739107849-x86_64-kvm.qcow2.)

So we tried:

```
curl -Lo disk.qcow2 "https://access.cdn.redhat.com/con-
tent/origin/files/sha256/17/1754349f1587d90a636bd47ceb2e-
93269ba55ae59423bbbf7689413b08d6e721/rhel-ai-nvidia-1.4-
1739107849-x86_64-kvm.qcow2"
```

But this clearly did not give the very large file we expected, so we just downloaded the file, using a FireFox web-browser for the file (**`rhel-ai-nvidia-1.4-1739107849-x86_64-kvm.qcow2`**, which is a **12.5 GByte** file) from the web page, as shown in *Figure* 7.56.

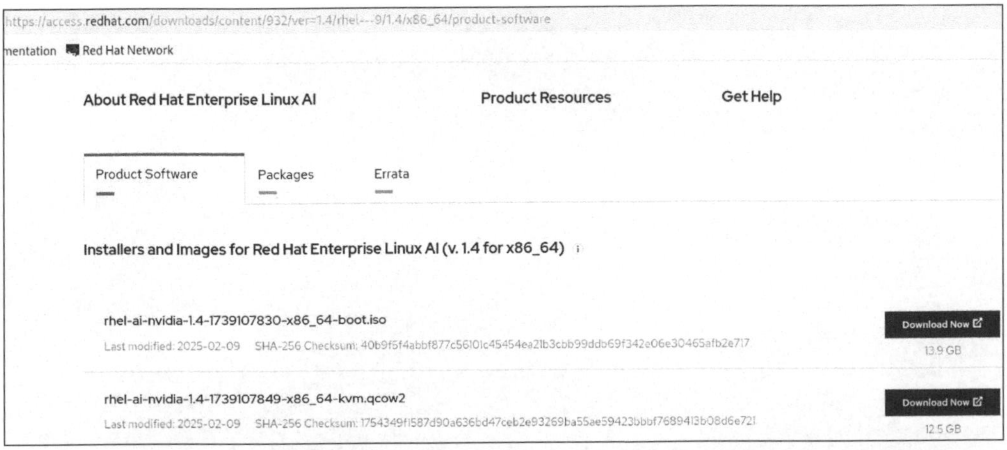

Figure 7.56: *The file using FireFox (**rhel-ai-nvidia-1.4-1739107849-x86_64-kvm.qcow2**)*

Then we used the downloaded file:

```
/home/alan/Downloads/rhel-ai-nvidia-1.4-1739107849-x86_64-kvm.
qcow2
```

(Instead of `disk.qcow2`)

We set the name, we wanted to use as the **RHEL AI 1.4 IBM Cloud** image.

```
image_name="rhel-ai-20252702v1-4"
```

Then, we uploaded the **QCOW2** image to the Cloud Object Storage (**COS**) bucket with our selected region (we used **eu-gb**) by running the following command:

```
ibmcloud cos upload --bucket ${bucket_name} --key ${image_name}.
qcow2 --file /home/alan/Downloads/rhel-ai-nvidia-1.4-1739107849-
x86_64-kvm.qcow2 --region eu-gb
```

The output of this command is shown in *Figure 7.57*:

Figure 7.57: *We uploaded the **QCOW2** image to the **Cloud Object Storage (COS)** bucket with our selected region*

Next, we converted the **QCOW2** image that we had uploaded to an IBM Cloud image with the following commands, as shown in *Figure 7.58*:

```
ibmcloud is image-create ${image_name} --file cos://eu-gb/${bucket
_name}/${image_name}.qcow2 --os-name red-ai-9-amd64-nvidia-byol
```

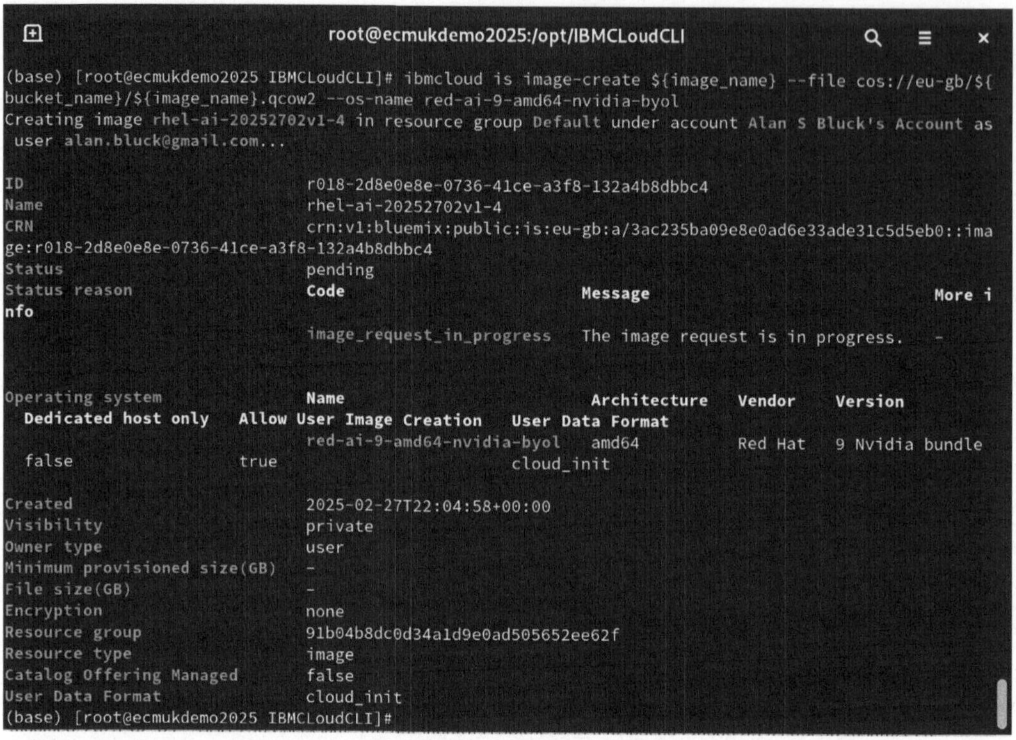

Figure 7.58: *We converted the* ***QCOW2*** *image that we had uploaded to an* ***IBM Cloud*** *image*

Once the job launches, we can set the **IBM Cloud** image configurations into a variable called **image_id** by running the following command (we had to wait around **ten minutes** before running this statement, and afterward, we checked that the environment variable contained an id string using the **echo $image_id** command), as shown in *Figure 7.59*:

```
image_id=$(ibmcloud is images --visibility private --output json
| jq -r '.[] | select(.name=="'$image_name'") | .id')
```

Figure 7.59: *We checked the environment variable contained an id string, using the* ***echo $image_id*** *command*

We viewed the progress of the job with the following command:

```
while ibmcloud is image --output json ${image_id} | jq -r .status
| grep -xq pending; do sleep 1; done
```

The information on the newly created image can be viewed using the following command:

```
ibmcloud is image ${image_id}
```

These last two commands are shown in *Figure 7.60*:

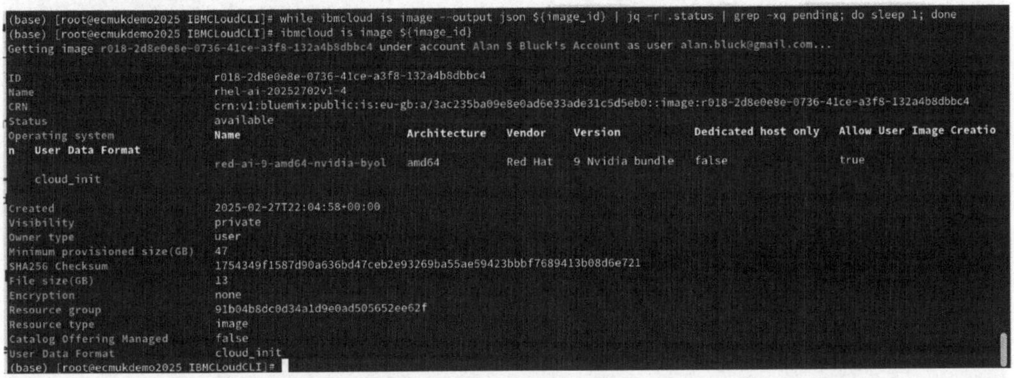

Figure 7.60: *The information on the newly created image can be viewed*

Procedure to Run the Image Created on the Cloud

You can Log in to your **IBM Cloud** account by selecting the Account, Region and Resource Group, and by running the following command:

```
ibmcloud login -c <ACCOUNT_ID> -r <REGION> -g <RESOURCE_GROUP>
```

We found it worked by using the one-time passcode method (which is more secure):

```
ibmcloud login -a https://cloud.ibm.com -u passcode -p kVWOI2SyMC
```

as shown in *Figure 7.61*:

Figure 7.61: *We log in using the one-time passcode method*

As requested, we entered the target, using the **`Default`** group, as highlighted in *Figure 7.62:*

```
ibmcloud target -g Default
```

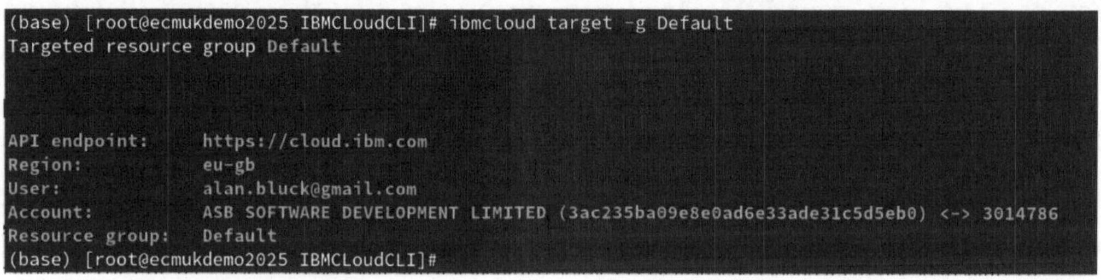

Figure 7.62: *As requested, we entered the target, using the* ***Default*** *group*

Prior to creating the **IBM Cloud** instance on the **CLI**, we were required to create several configuration variables for the instance.

We installed the **`infrastructure-service`** plugin for **IBM Cloud** by running the following command, as highlighted in *Figure 7.63:*

```
ibmcloud plugin install infrastructure-service
```

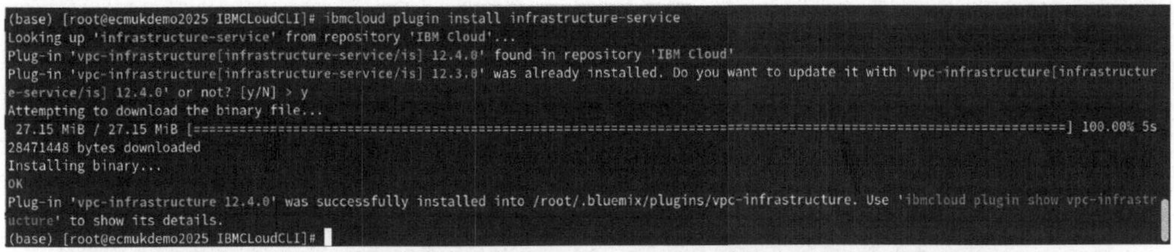

Figure 7.63: *Install the **infrastructure-service** plugin for **IBM Cloud***

and then, we ran the command, as illustrated in *Figure* 7.64:

`ibmcloud plugin show vpc-infrastructure` to show its details.

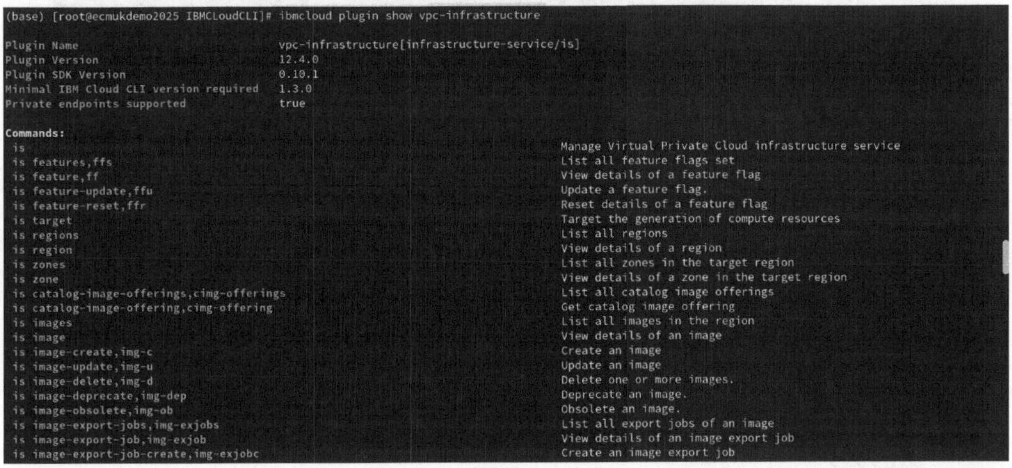

Figure 7.64: *We ran the command, **ibmcloud plugin show vpc-infrastructure,** to show its details*

There are several pages of commands listed with this command.

IBM recommends that an **SSH** public key is created for the security of our **IBM Cloud** account. **IBM Cloud** supports **RSA** and **ed25519** keys. The following example command uses the **ed25519** key types and names it **`ibmcloud`**, as highlighted in *Figure* 7.65:

```
ssh-keygen -f ibmcloud -t ed25519
```

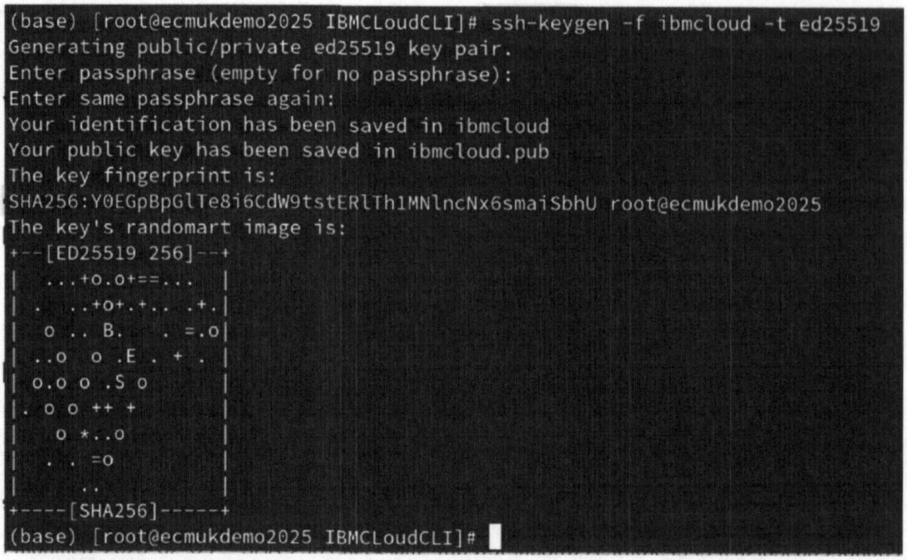

Figure 7.65: *We had to create an* **SSH** *public key for our* **IBM Cloud** *account*

We upload the public key to our **IBM Cloud** account with the example command.

ibmcloud is key-create my-ssh-key @ibmcloud.pub --key-type ed25519.

We used the following command, as highlighted in *Figure* 7.66:

ibmcloud is key-create graphite-ssh-key @ibmcloud.pub --key-type ed25519

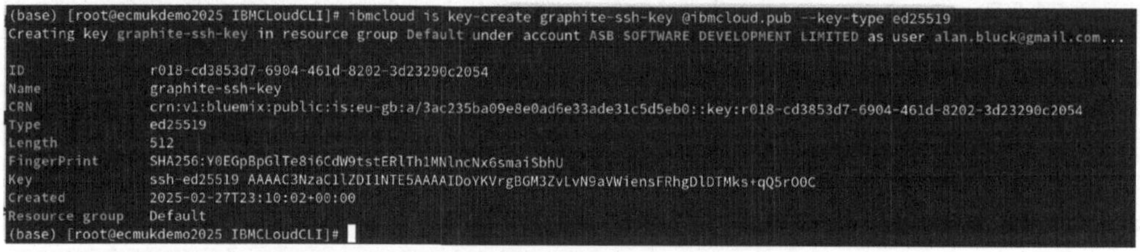

Figure 7.66: *Upload the public key to our* **IBM Cloud** *account by following the example command*

A **Floating IP** was created for our **IBM Cloud** instance by following the example command. Ensure that the region is changed as required (we used **eu-gb**) to change to our preferred zone (**eu-gb-1**).

ibmcloud is floating-ip-reserve graphite-public-ip --zone eu-gb-1

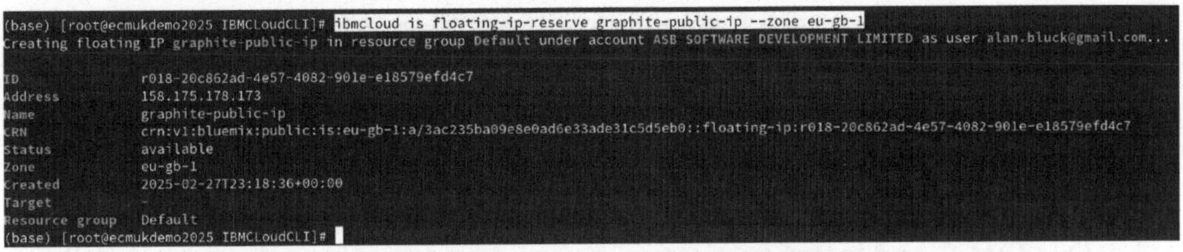

Figure 7.67: *Create a* **Floating IP** *for our* **IBM Cloud** *instance*

To select the instance profile to use for the deployment, the following command was executed to list the available profiles: **ibmcloud is instance-profiles**

Create the VPC Required

To create a **VPC (Virtual Private Cloud)** in **IBM Cloud**, navigate to the "**Infrastructure**" section in the console, and then select "**Network**" > "**VPCs**"

(See the link **Virtual private cloud list - Infrastructure - IBM Cloud** at **https://cloud.ibm.com/infrastructure/network/vpcs)**. Click "**Create**", provide a name for the **VPC,** and choose a resource group. We selected our desired region (**eu-gb**) and zone(**eu-gb-1**), to define our subnet details (such as IP range). Finally, click "**Create virtual private cloud**" to finalize the process. *Table* 7.1 lists the IP address details, as follows:

Name	Zone	Resource group	Address prefix	# of addresses	IP range	Public gateway
sn-20250227-01	eu-gb-1	Default	10.242.0.0/18	256	10.242.0.0/24	Detached

Table 7.1: *The Virtual private cloud* **VPC** *network details*

Listed From the following link, *Figure* 7.68 shows the **VPC** name and the details, we created:

https://cloud.ibm.com/infrastructure/network/vpcs

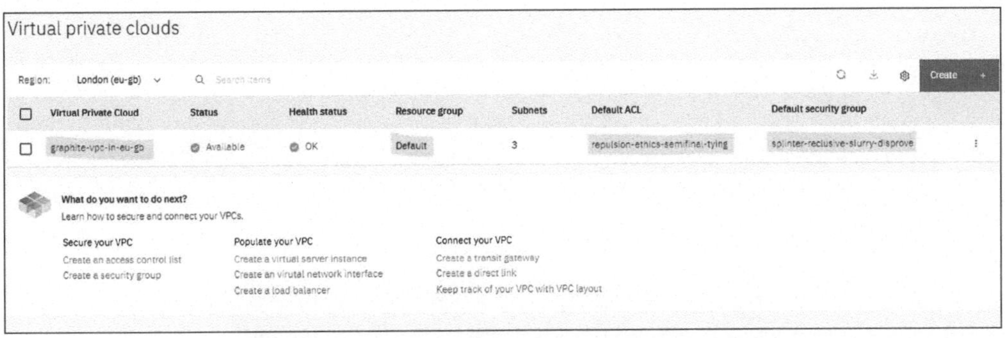

Figure 7.68: *The* **VPC** *name and details, we created*

We noted down our preferred instance profile which was required for our instance deployment.

```
(base) [root@ecmukdemo2025 IBMCLoudCLI]# ibmcloud is image ${image_id}
Getting image r018-2d8e0e8e-0736-41ce-a3f8-132a4b8dbbc4 under account
ASB SOFTWARE DEVELOPMENT LIMITED as user alan.bluck@gmail.com...
```

1. Our **IBM Cloud** instance creation is set up by assigning values to the following environment variables, as shown:

```
export name="graphite-rhelai-instance"
export vpc="graphite-vpc-in-eu-gb"
export zone="eu-gb-1"
export subnet="sn-20250227-01"
export instance_profile="gx3-64x320x4l4"
export image="r018-2d8e0e8e-0736-41ce-a3f8-132a4b8dbbc4"
export sshkey="graphite-ssh-key"
export floating_ip="graphite-public-ip"
export disk_size="250"
```

2. Our instance is created, by running the following command:

```
ibmcloud is instance-create \
$name \
$vpc \
$zone \
$instance_profile \
$subnet \
--image $image \
--keys $sshkey \
 --boot-volume '{"name": "'${name}'-boot", "volume": {"name":
"'${name}'-boot", "capacity": '${disk_size}', "profile": {"name":
"general-purpose"}}}' \    --allow-ip-spoofing false
```

User account

```
(base) [root@ecmukdemo2025 IBMCLoudCLI]# ibmcloud is instance-create $name $vpc $zone $instance_profile $subnet --
image $image --keys $sshkey  --boot-volume '{"name": "'${name}'-boot", "volume": {"name": "'${name}'-boot",
"capacity": '${disk_size}', "profile": {"name": "general-purpose"}}}'     --allow-ip-spoofing false
Creating instance graphite-rhelai-instance in resource group Default under account ASB SOFTWARE DEVELOPMENT LIMITED as user
alan.bluck@gmail.com...

ID                                  0787_a241f528-81f7-4361-88aa-bda9e0c42b3b
Name                                graphite-rhelai-instance
CRN                                 crn:v1:bluemix:public:is:eu-gb-
1:a/3ac235ba09e8e0ad6e33ade31c5d5eb0::instance:0787_a241f528-81f7-4361-88aa-bda9e0c42b3b
Status                              pending
Availability policy on host failure restart
Startable                           true
Profile                             gx3-64x320x4l4
Architecture                        amd64
vCPU Manufacturer                   intel
vCPUs                               64
Memory(GiB)                         320
Bandwidth(Mbps)                     128000
Volume bandwidth(Mbps)              32000
Network bandwidth(Mbps)             96000
Lifecycle Reasons                   Code                   Message
                                    pending_registration   The registration for the instance is in progress.

Lifecycle State                     pending
Metadata service                    Enabled   Protocol   Response hop limit
                                    false     http       1

GPU                                 Model   Manufacturer   Count   Memory(GiB)
                                    L4      nvidia         4       24

Image                               ID                                          Name
                                    r018-2d8e0e8e-0736-41ce-a3f8-132a4b8dbbc4   rhel-ai-20252702v1-4

Numa Count                          -
VPC                                 ID                                          Name
                                    r018-8ac96074-30d7-4a4b-9acd-a14022a9ad14   graphite-vpc-in-eu-gb

Zone                                eu-gb-1
Resource group                      ID                                 Name
                                    91b04b8dc0d34a1d9e0ad505652ee62f   Default

Created                             2025-02-28T00:01:00+00:00
Network Interfaces                  Interface   Name      ID                                     Subnet
ID                                 Floating IP   Security Groups                    Allow source IP spoofing
Reserved IP
                                    Primary      0787-171d5c4a-ff51-4909-8830-abc74a1a52f5   sn-20250227-01
0787-ed96b9f5-cdea-4445-8f4a-c5ee1e3bfd6d   -        splinter-reclusive-slurry-disprove   false
0.0.0.0

Boot volume                         ID   Name   Attachment ID                                Attachment name
                                    -    -      0787-f11036b3-2dce-4b87-a335-ffa600899132   graphite-rhelai-
instance-boot

Reservation Affinity Policy         automatic
Reservation Affinity Pool           -
Reservation                         -
Health State                        ok
(base) [root@ecmukdemo2025 IBMCLoudCLI]#
```

Link the Floating IP to the instance by running the following command, as highlighted in *Figure 7.69*:

```
ibmcloud is floating-ip-update $floating_ip --nic primary --in
$name
```

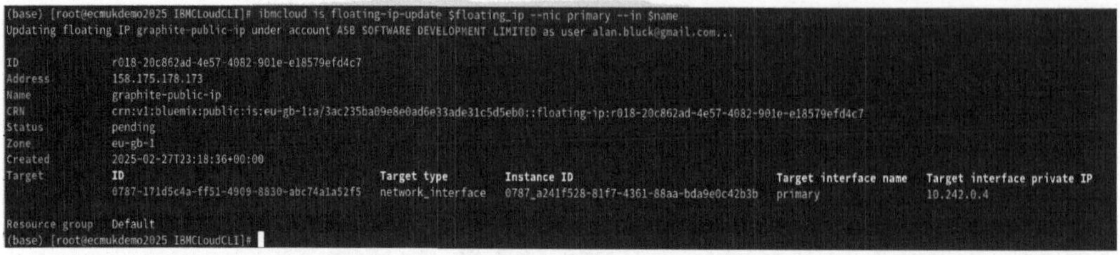

Figure 7.69: *Link the Floating IP to the instance by running the following command*

The default user account in **RHEL AI** is **`cloud-user`**. It has all permissions via **`sudo`** without password.

Verification

To verify that our **Red Hat Enterprise Linux AI** tools are installed correctly, we ran the **`ilab`** command:

```
ilab
```

Example output

```
ilab
Usage: ilab [OPTIONS] COMMAND [ARGS]...

  CLI for interacting with InstructLab.

  If this is your first time running ilab, it's best to start with
`ilab
  config init` to create the environment.

Options:
  --config PATH  Path to a configuration file.  [default:
                  /home/<user>/.config/instructlab/config.yaml]
  -v, --verbose  Enable debug logging (repeat for even more
verbosity)
  --version      Show the version and exit.
  --help         Show this message and exit.

Commands:
  config    Command Group for Interacting with the Config of
InstructLab.
  data      Command Group for Interacting with the Data generated
by...
  model     Command Group for Interacting with the Models in
InstructLab.
  system    Command group for all system-related command calls
  taxonomy  Command Group for Interacting with the Taxonomy of
```

```
InstructLab.

Aliases:
  chat      model chat
  generate  data generate
  serve     model serve
  train     model train
```

IBM states that the **RHEL AI** image includes **InstructLab, RHEL 9.4**, and various inference and training software, including **vLLM** and **DeepSpeed**. After this image is rebooted, it is possible to download various **RedHat** and **IBM** developed **Granite LLM** models for serving or training purposes. The image and all the tools are compiled to specific **Independent Software Vendors** (**ISV**) hardware.

To log out of the IBM Cloud remote processing, we used the command as follows:

```
(base) [root@ecmukdemo2025 IBMCLoudCLI]# ibmcloud logout
Logging out...
OK
```

IBM Cloud Charges for the RedHat AI 1.4 Installation

The status of the installed system, and the promotional credit of $200 (converted to sterling) can be reviewed by logging into the https://cloud.ibm.com/billing/promotions, as shown in *Figure 7.70*:

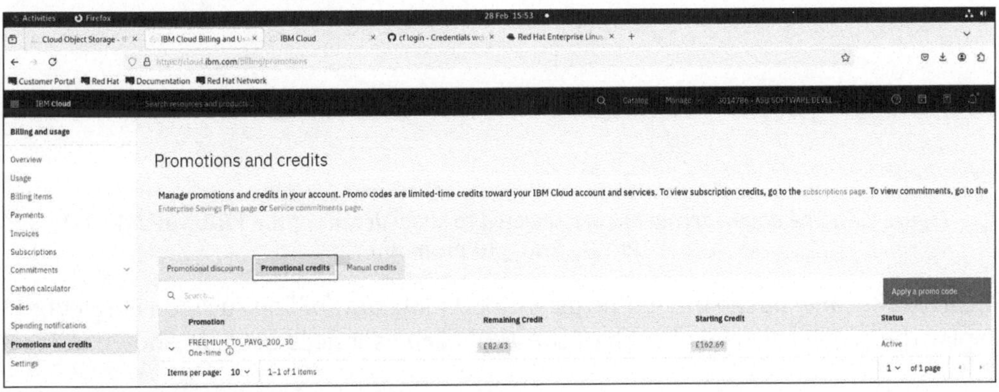

Figure 7.70: *The status of the installed system, and the promotional credit of $200*

The detailed frame showing the status of the installed system, and the promotional credit of **$200** is shown in *Figure 7.71*:

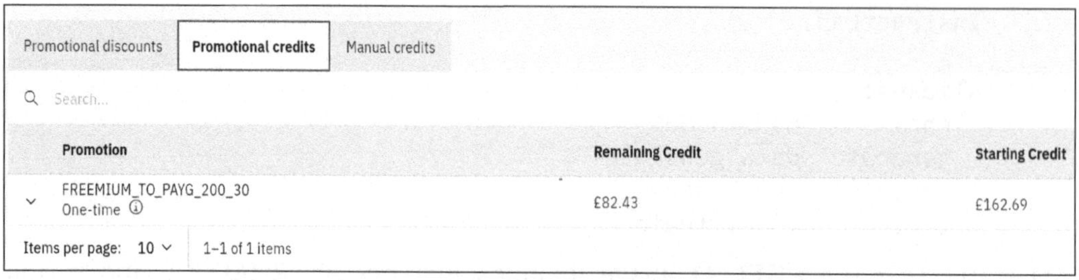

Figure 7.71: *The detail frame showing the status of the installed system and the promotional credit of $200*

The down-arrow opener is selected to show the breakdown of the **`FREEMIUM_TO_PAYG_200_30`** promotion, as shown in *Figure* 7.72:

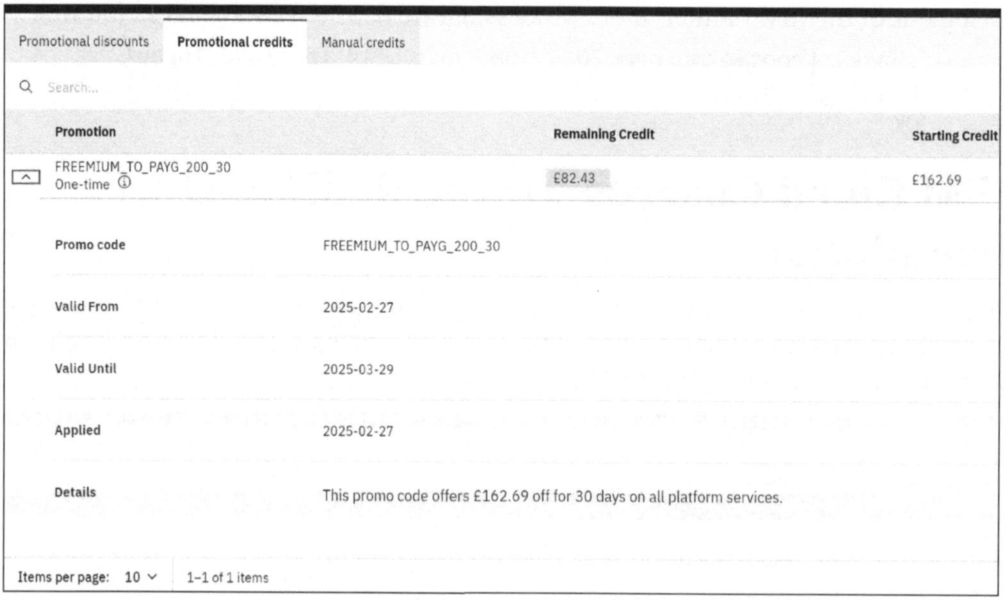

Figure 7.72: *The down-arrow opener selected to show details of the* **FREEMIUM_TO_PAYG_200_30** *promotion*

The **`Billing and usage`** menu (https://cloud.ibm.com/billing/usage) is selected to display the graphical view of each of the **`IBM Cloud`** services used, as shown in *Figure* 7.73:

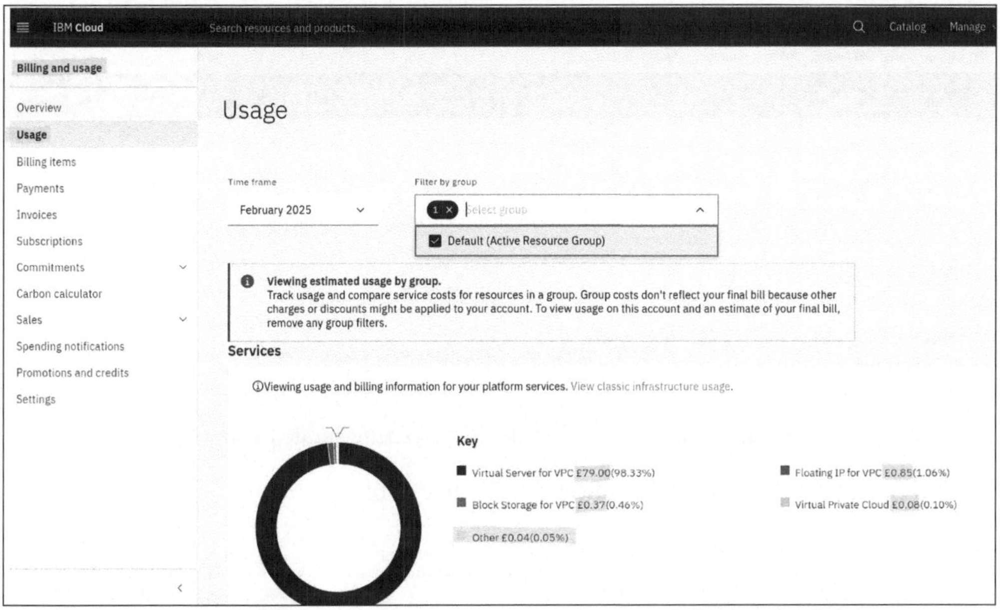

***Figure 7.73:** The **Billing and usage** menu (https://cloud.ibm.com/billing/usage) is selected*

The **`Billing and Usage`** pie-chart can be expanded, as shown in *Figure 7.74*:

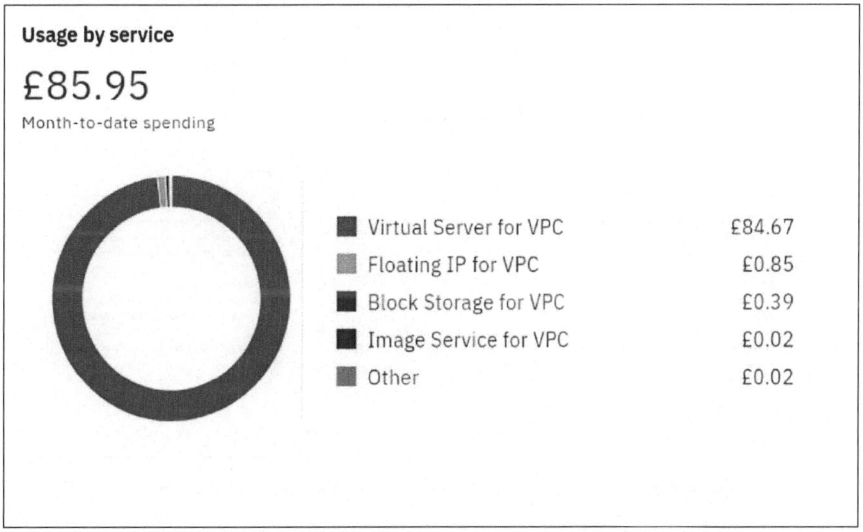

***Figure 7.74:** The **Billing and Usage** pie-chart can be expanded*

The **IBM watsonx Orchestrate** catalog entry, showing the **$200** IBM credit, is shown in *Figure 7.75*:

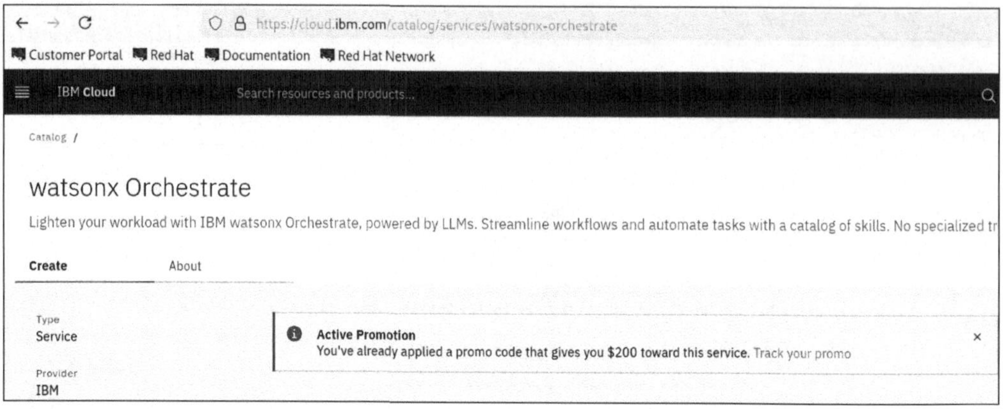

Figure 7.75: *The IBM watsonx Orchestrate catalog entry*

The IBM Standard Plan pricing is shown in *Figure 7.76*:

Standard Plan	**Optimized for customers seeking large-scale automation capabilities using prebuilt and custom skills that use natural language processing, and capabilities to build conversational AI assistants and automations using skill studio** Automation builder on skill studio - Automation Workflows - Decision services - Document processing - Generative AI 1 Instance includes 450,000 Skill Runs and 40,000 MAUs	£4,880.628 GBP/Standard Instance £81.3438 GBP/Thousand Monthly Active Users £81.3438 GBP/Thousand Monthly Active Voice Users £81.3438 GBP/Ten Thousand Skills Runs £0.4880628 GBP/Thousand Class 1 Resource Units £1.55366658 GBP/Thousand Class 2 Resource Units £4.30308702 GBP/Thousand Class 3 Resource Units

Figure 7.76: *The IBM Standard Plan pricing*

The IBM Essentials Plan pricing is shown in *Figure 7.77*:

Plan	Features and capabilities	Pricing
Essentials Plan	**Optimized for customers to go live quickly using prebuilt skills, natural language processing, Generative AI to build conversational AI assistants and automations.** Customize AI Assistants to unique business needs Multi-channel experience Unified chat experience Conversational Search (RAG) AI-guided actions Skill-based actions Access skill catalog or build custom skills in skill studio Import automations effortlessly with OpenAPI specifications 1 Instance includes 60,000 Skill Runs and 4000 MAUs Essentials Plan for customers to get started quickly building AI Assistants on IBM watsonx Orchestrate.	£406.719 GBP/Essentials Instance £81.3438 GBP/Thousand Monthly Active Users £81.3438 GBP/Thousand Monthly Active Voice Users £81.3438 GBP/Ten Thousand Skill Runs £0.4880628 GBP/Thousand Class 1 Resource Units £1.55366658 GBP/Thousand Class 2 Resource Units £4.30308702 GBP/Thousand Class 3 Resource Units

Figure 7.77: *The IBM Essentials Plan pricing is shown here*

The IBM Cloud instance can be terminated using the following procedure.

Note: *In order to utilize* **IBM watsonx Code Assistant** *for* **Red Hat Ansible Lightspeed**, *a client must have an existing license for* **Red Hat Ansible Automation Platform**, *as well as a license for* **IBM watsonx Code Assistant** *for* **Red Hat Ansible Lightspeed.**

(https://www.ibm.com/products/watsonx-code-assistant-ansible-lightspeed)

See *https://www.ibm.com/watsonx .:*

If you want to stop using **`IBM Cloud`** services altogether, and delete all your data, you can deactivate your **`IBM Cloud`** account. Follow these steps to close your **`Lite account`**:

1. Sign into your **`IBM Cloud`** account.
2. In the **`IBM Cloud console`**, go to the **`Manage > Account > Account settings`** page.
3. Click **`Close Account`**. After an account is closed for 30 days, all data is deleted, and all services are removed.

Installing `InstructLab` Locally without a GPU

As **`ilab`** did not run as expected, on the IBM Cloud system we created, we installed **Instructlab** on our local **RedHat Linux RHEL 9.2 server**, **ECMUKDEMO2025** after logging out of our **IBM Cloud** account, as follows:

See https://github.com/instructlab/instructlab?tab=readme-ov-file#-installing-instructlab-core

The command was entered to clone the InstructLab project from GitHub, as highlighted in *Figure* 7.78:

```
git clone https://github.com/instructlab/instructlab.git
```

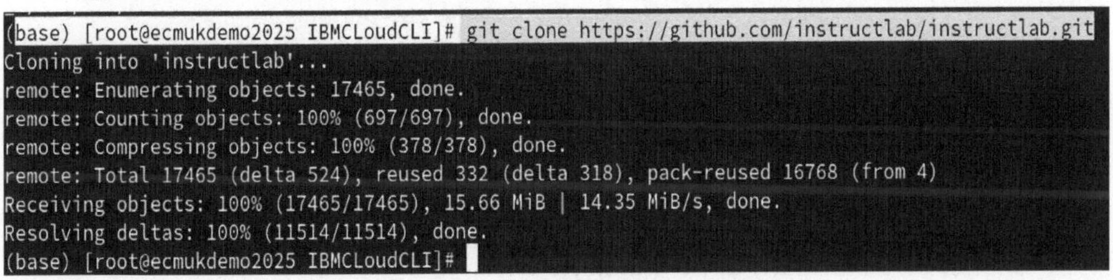

Figure 7.78: *The command was entered to clone the InstructLab project from GitHub*

Next, we installed the prerequisite **Python** language dependencies from our administrator user account, using the command as highlighted in *Figure* 7.79:

```
[alan@ecmukdemo2025 ~]$ python3 -V
Python 3.9.21
sudo dnf install gcc gcc-c++ make git python3.11 python3.11-devel
[sudo] password for alan:
```

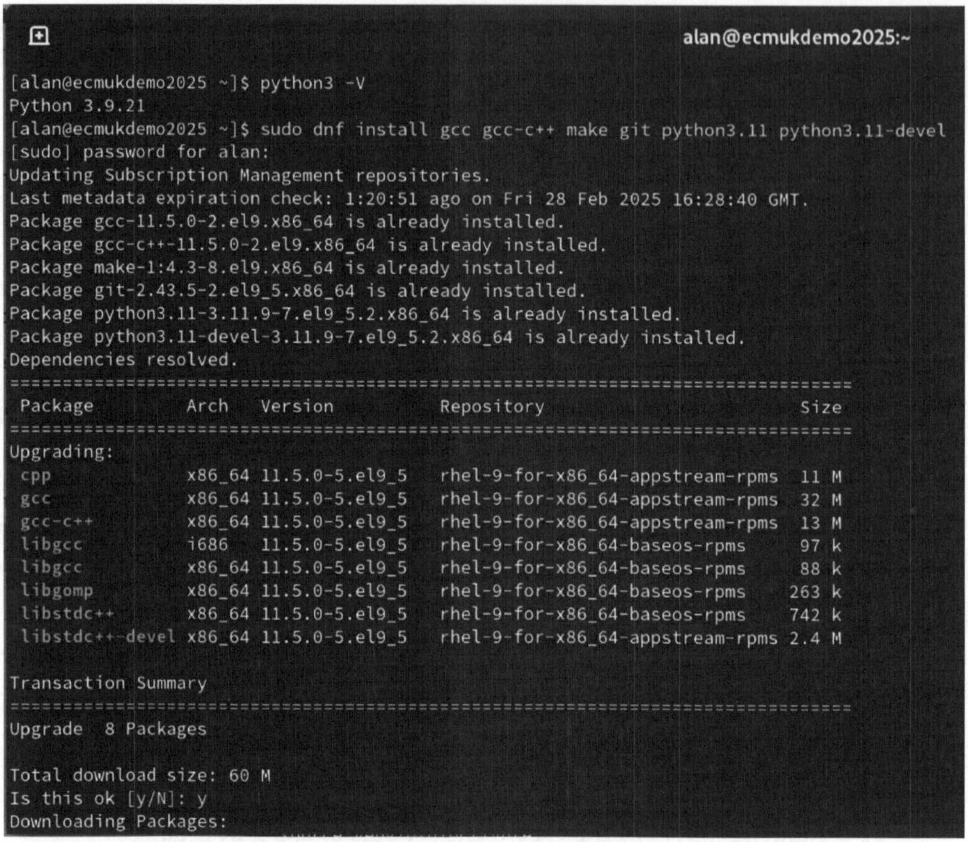

Figure 7.79: *Next, we installed the prerequisite Python language dependencies from our administrator user account*

We followed the **README** file instructions to provide an environment install where the GPU was not required:

"*Install using PyTorch without CUDA bindings and no GPU acceleration*"

- Install on a standard Linux machine with:

```
python<version> -m venv --upgrade-deps venv
source venv/bin/activate
pip install instructlab
```

(See https://github.com/instructlab/instructlab?tab=readme-ov-file#-installing-instructlab-core)

So, we used recommended **InstructLab** installation commands, as highlighted in *Figure 7.80*:

```
python3.11 -m venv --upgrade-deps venv
source venv/bin/activate
pip install instructlab
```

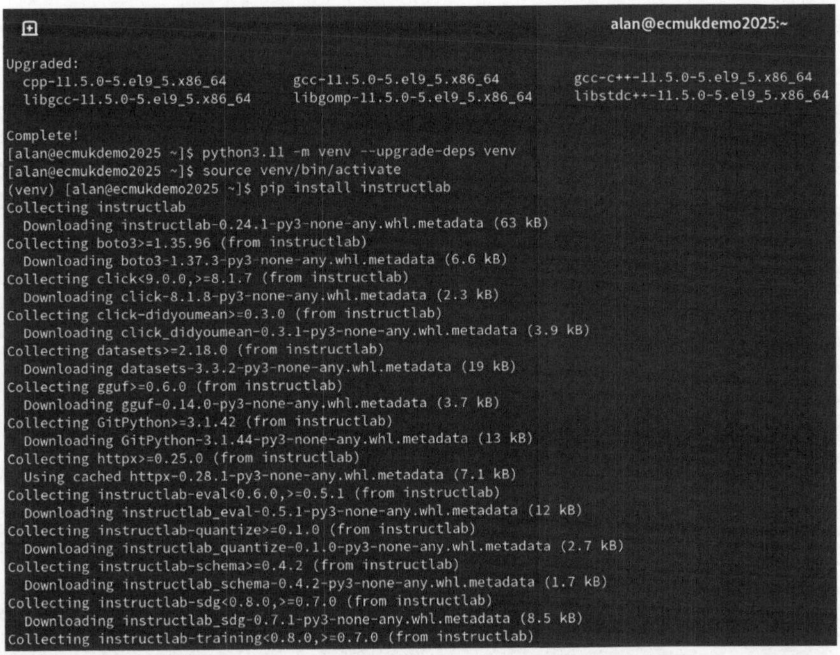

Figure 7.80: *We used the recommended* ***InstructLab*** *installation commands, as highlighted*

Now, we can use the **`ilab`** command, to display the initial commands, as shown in *Figure 7.81*:

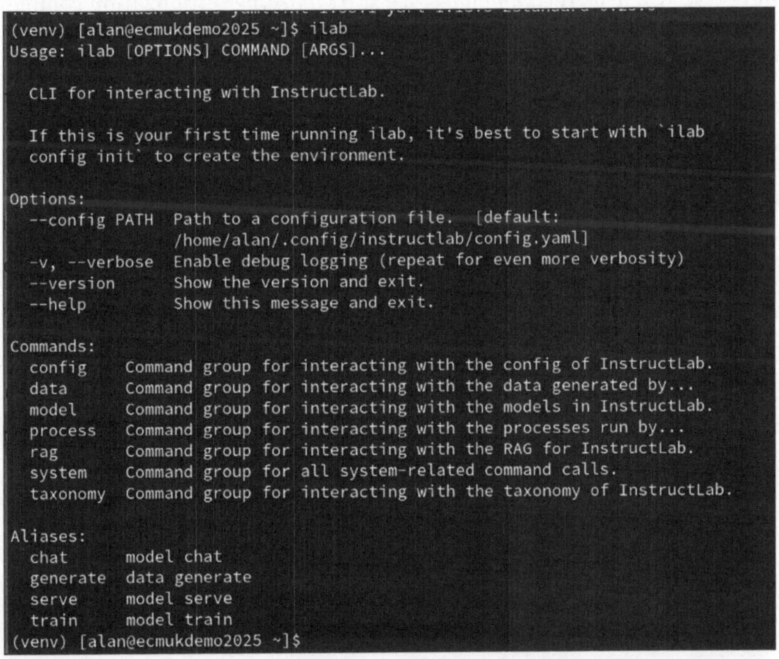

Figure 7.81: *We can use the* ***ilab*** *command to display the initial commands*

As recommended, we start with the initialization command, as shown in *Figure* 7.82:

```
ilab config init
```

***Figure* 7.82:** *Then, as recommended, we start with the initialization command*

We also enabled the tab completion in **bash** with the following command:

```
eval "$(_ILAB_COMPLETE=bash_source ilab)"
```

We selected the default of a quantized Granite model:

(See https://huggingface.co/instructlab/granite-7b-lab-GGUF)

To see the **ilab config.yaml** file use:

```
ilab config show
```

Run the **ilab** model download command to download a compact pre-trained version of the **granite-7b-lab-GGUF**, **merlinite-7b-lab-GGUF**, and **Mistral-7B-Instruct-v0.2-GGUF** models (~4.4G each) from HuggingFace, as shown in *Figure* 7.83:

```
ilab model download
```

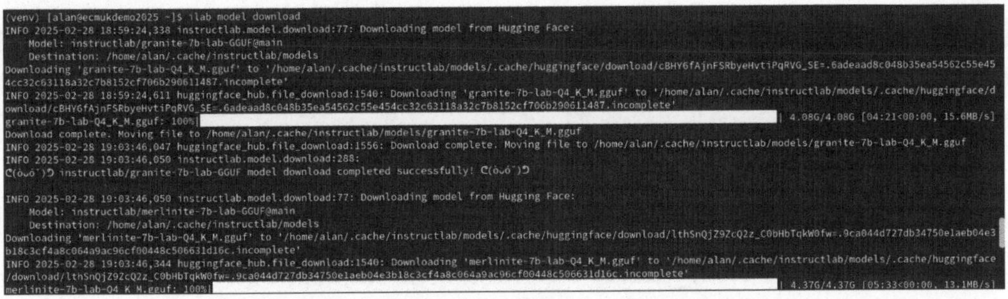

Figure 7.83: *Run the* ***ilab model download*** *command to download the* ***granite-7b-lab-GGUF LLM****, and so on*

The status list of the LLM downloads is shown in *Figure 7.84*:

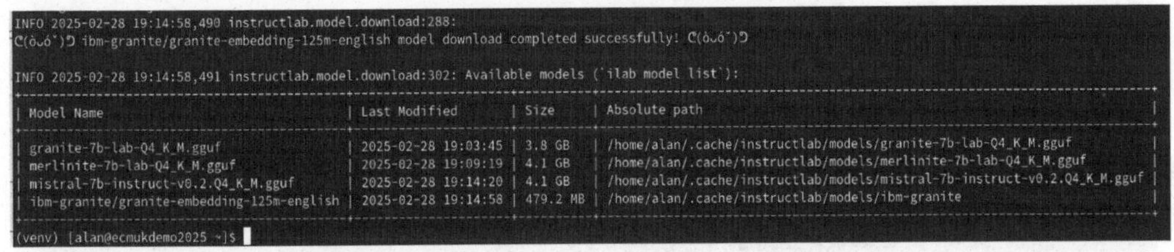

Figure 7.84: *The status list of the LLM downloads*

Since the model process is running in one terminal window, we have to use a second terminal window in order to re-activate the **Python** virtual environment to run the **`ilab model chat`** command, as shown in *Figure 7.85*, using:

```
source venv/bin/activate
ilab model chat
```

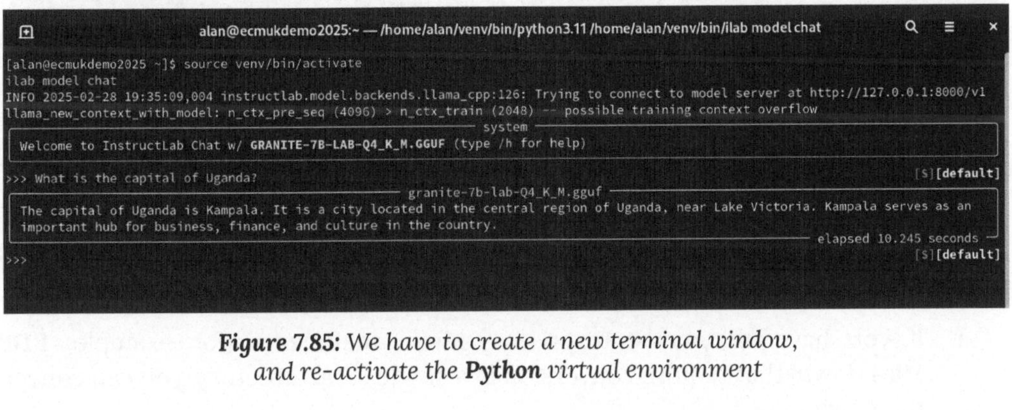

Figure 7.85: *We have to create a new terminal window, and re-activate the* ***Python*** *virtual environment*

Configuring Retrieval-Augmented Generation (Developer Preview)

To enable the latest new feature for **RAG** (**Retrieval-Augmented Generation**), we set the following:

```
export ILAB_FEATURE_SCOPE=DevPreviewNoUpgrade
```

The **`ILAB_FEATURE_SCOPE`** environment variable modifies the actions of **`InstructLab`** to enable developer preview features that might not be upgradable. The default embedding model for use with the developer preview of **RAG** is **`ibm-granite/granite-embedding-125m-english`**. This model can be obtained before you begin the following steps by running the command, as shown in *Figure 7.86*:

```
ilab model download -rp ibm-granite/granite-embedding-125m-english
```

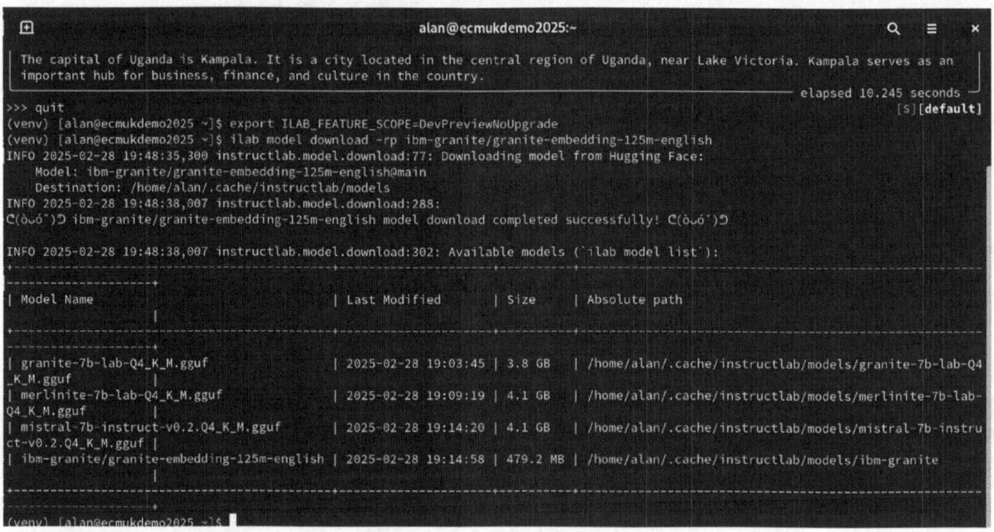

Figure 7.86: *The default embedding LLM for the preview of* **RAG** (***ibm-granite/granite-embedding-125m-english***)

The content can be converted into a structured form, and then indexed for use with **ilab model chat**, using the **RAG** model . There are three options for conversion:

a. If you have all your enterprises source documents (for example, **PDF**, Markdown) that require conversion in a single local directory, you can convert them using:

```
ilab rag convert --input-dir <path-to-source-document-outputdi-
rectory> ---dir <path-to-converted-document-directory>
```

So we used the following command, as highlighted in *Figure* 7.87:

```
mkdir /home/alan/source_documents
```

and copied AI-based resource pdf documents into this subdirectory, as listed.

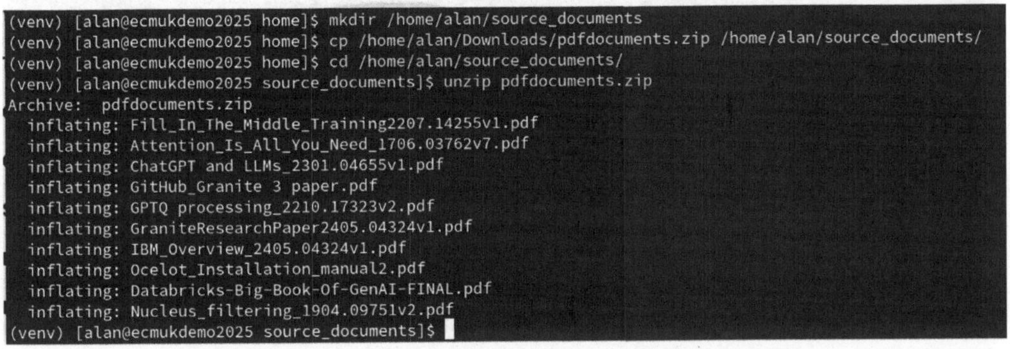

***Figure 7.87**: We used, **mkdir /home/alan/source_documents**, and copied in AI based resource pdf documents*

To store the converted **`pdf`** documents, we also created an output directory:

```
mkdir /home/alan/converted_documents
```

and then run:

```
ilab rag convert --input-dir /home/alan/source_documents --out-
put-dir /home/alan/converted_documents
```

The convert function works with the following Document extension types

(Our zipped, **`pdfdocuments.zip`** file is ignored!)

A document format supported by document backend parsers.

See: https://docling-project.github.io/docling/usage/supported_formats/

Extensions supported:

```
.ASCIIDOC, .CSV, .DOCX, .HTML, .IMAGE, JSON_DOCLING, .MD,.PDF,
PPTX,
.XLSX, .XML_JATS, XML_USPTO
```

The output is converted to a **JSON** output format in files, as shown in *Figure* 7.88:

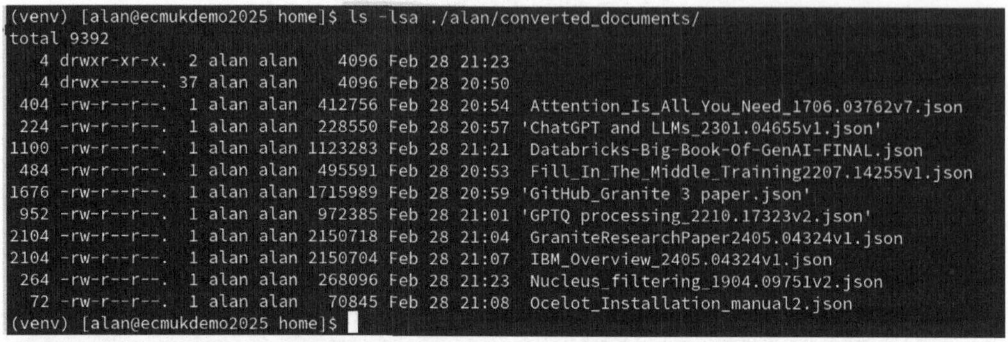

Figure 7.88: *The output is converted into a* ***JSON*** *output format in files*

If you ran **`ilab rag convert`** to convert the documents, the output directory path from that step should be the input directory for the next step, **`ilab rag ingest`**. In our case, we used the following:

```
ilab rag ingest --input-dir=/home/alan/converted_documents
```

The resulting statistics from running the **`ilab rag ingest`** command are shown in *Figure 7.89*:

Figure 7.89: *The resulting statistics from running the* ***ilab rag ingest*** *command*

b. To chat with the model with **RAG** enabled run, as shown in *Figure 7.90*:

```
ilab model chat --rag
```

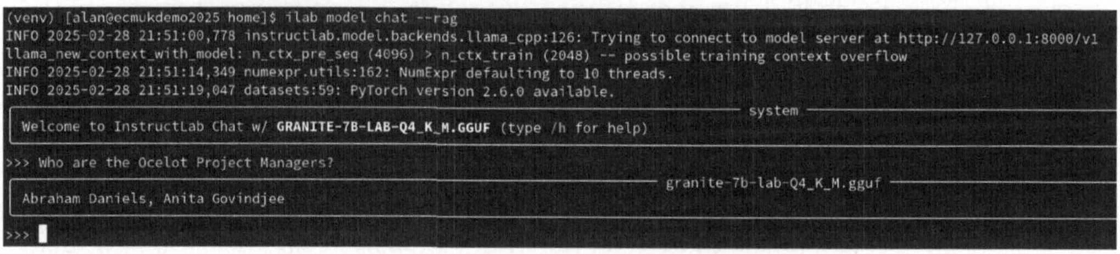

Figure 7.90: *To chat with the model with* ***RAG*** *enabled*

In the next example, we asked the question:

```
>>> Can you provide Java code for a binary search of a sorted
array of text values?
```

This gave the response as shown:

```
Here is an example Java code for a binary search of a sorted array of text values:
```java
class TextValue {
    String key;
     int index;

     public TextValue(String key, int index) {
         this.key = key;
         this.index = index;
     }
 }

 public class BinarySearch {

     public static void main(String[] args) {
         String[] arr = {"apple", "banana", "cherry", "date", "fig", "grape","kiwi"};
         TextValue[] values = new TextValue[arr.length];

         // Fill in the values array with the correct keys and indices

         for (int i = 0; i < arr.length; i++) {
             values[i] = new TextValue(arr[i], i);
         }

         int target = "banana".hashCode(); // Use a hash code for the target value

         // Perform binary search on the values array
         int low = 0;
         int high = arr.length - 1;
         while (low <= high) {
             int mid = (low + high) / 2;
             TextValue midValue = values[mid];

             if (midValue.key.equals(target)) {
                 System.out.println("Found: " + target);
                 return;
             } else if (midValue.key.hashCode() <= target.hashCode()) {
                 high = mid -1;
             } else {
                 low = mid + 1;
             }
         }

         System.out.println("Not found");
     }
 }
```
 This code defines a `TextValue` class to represent the key-index pair in the array and
a`binarySearch` method that performs binary search on the `values` array. The `main`
```

The **IBM watsonx Code** account can be created using the link https://cloud.ibm.com/catalog/services/ibm-watsonx-code-assistant and gives the web page shown in *Figure 7.91*:

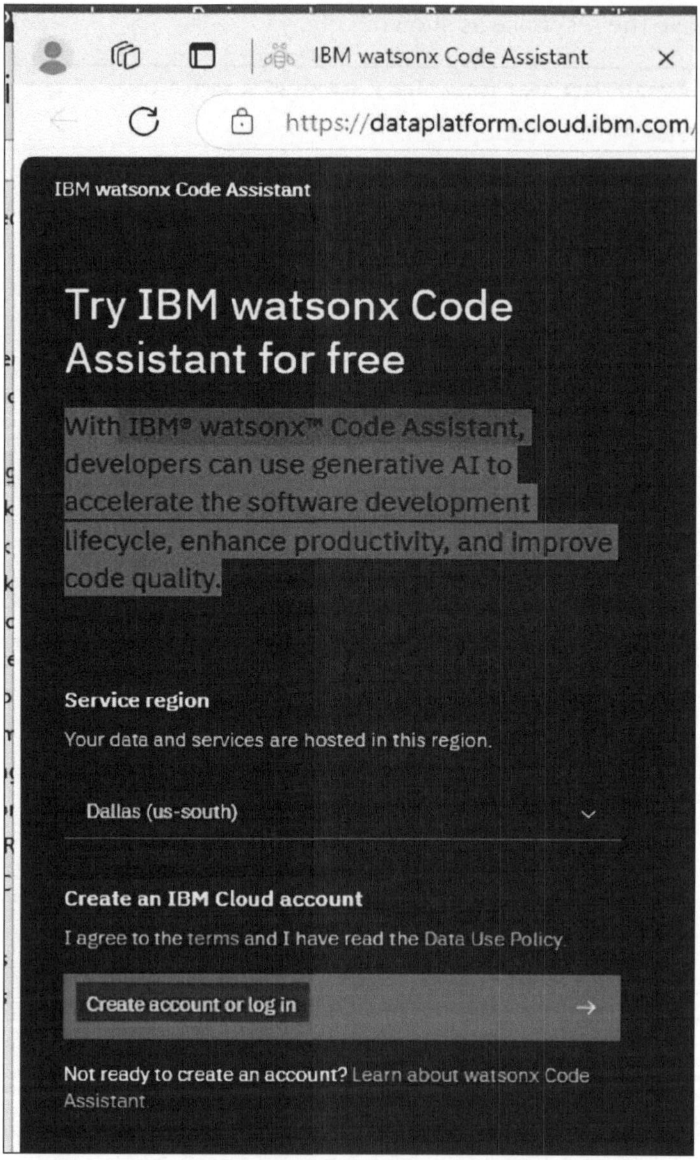

Figure 7.91: *The **IBM watsonx Code** account can be created*

IBM watsonx Orchestrate used for Z

The following link provides an overview of **IBM Watson Orchestrate,** and the links for installation and download:

https://www.ibm.com/docs/en/watsonx/watson-orchestrate/current?topic=installing-watsonx-orchestrate-premises

IBM watsonx Code Assistant for Z is a generative **AI**-assisted product used for enterprise mainframe application lifecycle assistance, and can also streamline Z systems.

It supports the end-to-end application developer lifecycle with capabilities for analysis, code explanation and automated code refactoring, code optimization advice, **COBOL** to **Java** transformation, and validation.

Developers can automatically refactor selected elements of an application, optimize code to increase performance, and continue modernizing in **COBOL**.

Or, they can transform code to Java with generative AI using a large language model.

IBM watsonx Code Assistant for Z can be deployed either on-premise or as an IBM Cloud service.

See: https://www.ibm.com/products/watsonx-code-assistant-z.

Developing the `Granite-20B-Code-Base`

Released on May 6th, 2024 with an open source **Apache 2.0** license, **Granite-20B-Code-Instruct** is a 20 Billion parameter model fine-tuned from **Granite-20B-Code-Base**. It has been trained on a combination of permissively licensed instruction data which enables an enhanced instruction following capabilities, including logical reasoning and problem-solving skills.

There is a link to the HuggingFace web site, which has a **Python** language example, as follows:

https://huggingface.co/ibm-granite/granite-34b-code-base-8k

IBM Granite Code Instruct LLM training

IBM Granite Code Instruct models are trained on the following types of data.

Code Commits Datasets: Data from the **CommitPackFT** dataset, which is a filtered version of the full **CommitPack** dataset.

From the **CommitPackFT** dataset, IBM used the data filtered for 92 programming languages.

IBM's inclusion criteria was based on selecting programming languages common across **CommitPackFT,** and the **116** languages considered to pretrain the code-base model (**Granite-20B-Code-Base**).

IBM also included two math datasets, **MathInstruct** and **MetaMathQA**. (To avoid license issues, IBM filtered out **GSM8K-RFT** and **Camel-Math** from the **MathInstruct** dataset). It also made use of the **Glaive-Code-Assistant-v3**, **Glaive-Function-**

Calling-v2, **NL2SQL11** code datasets and a small collection of synthetic API calling datasets.

For languages, IBM included high-quality datasets, such as **HelpSteer** and an open license-filtered version of **Platypus**. They also included a collection of hardcoded prompts to ensure that the IBM models generated correct outputs given prompts about its name or developers.

See: https://www.ibm.com/docs/en/watsonx/w-and-w/2.1.x?topic=models-granite-20b-code-instruct-model-card

Developing the Granite-34B-Code-Base

`Granite-34B-Code-Instruct` is a 34 Billion parameter model, fine tuned from `Granite-34B-Code-Base`, using permissively licensed instruction data. It is designed to enhance instruction-following capabilities used for logical reasoning and problem-solving skills.

See: https://www.ibm.com/docs/en/watsonx/w-and-w/2.1.x?topic=models-granite-34b-code-instruct-model-card

Conclusion

Thus, this chapter described the **IBM watsonx Code Assistant** which supplies a suite of generative **AI** code assistant products, and also includes functionality for the **Ansible Automation Platform** (**IBM watsonx Code Assistant** for **Red Hat Ansible Lightspeed**) and **IBM** Systems modernization (**IBM watsonx Code Assistant for Z**)

We also described in detail, the use of the following **IBM watsonx** products, based on the **IBM Granite 3.0 LLM**s in this chapter.

We covered the installation of the **RedHat AI 1.4 VMware** workstation image for using the **InstructLab ilab** system, used with a **GPU** system and the alternative option for installing **InstructLab,** using a working **ilab** system on our local **RHEL 9.2 Linux** server. We also covered the installation of the **RedHat AI 1.4 QCOW2** image file on the **IBM Cloud** system.

In the next chapter, *Performance Optimization*, we cover the use of **IBM Granite 3.0** code models that are trained on **Red Hat Ansible Playbook** datasets, allowing developers to accept or adjust AI-generated content suggestions for improved productivity.

Points to Remember

- IBM recommends that the **IBM Granite 3.0 LLMs** are installed on a system with at least 250 GBytes of disk space to run.
- In order to utilize IBM watsonx Code Assistant for Red Hat Ansible Lightspeed, a client must have an existing license for Red Hat Ansible Automation Platform, as well as a license for IBM watsonx Code Assistant for Red Hat Ansible Lightspeed.

  (https://www.ibm.com/products/watsonx-code-assistant-ansible-lightspeed)

  See https://www.ibm.com/watsonx .
- The "Bare Metal" download option supplies a Disk Image, **rhel-ai-nvidia-1.4-1739107830-x86_64-boot.iso** file. Unfortunately, this option does not work correctly unless your system has access to **Nvidia GPUs** (see the hardware requirements table). In this chapter, we also describe a working, **CPU** only installation of the **InstructLab AI** system on our **RedHat Linux RHEL 9.2 VMware** server.
- After creating a permanent API key, you can use:

  ```
  export API_KEY="xxxxxxxxxxxxxxxxxxxxxxxxxxx"
  ibmcloud login --apikey $API_KEY
  ```

  (but we used the one-time pass code command)
- The **IBM Cloud Login API** key is only available for **296** seconds. (Make sure to store it somewhere where you can find it later!)

Multiple Choice Questions

1. The prerequisite command for `InstructLab`, for the supporting Linux library installations on Linux is:

   a. `python3.11 -m venv --upgrade-deps venv`

   b. `sudo dnf install gcc gcc-c++ make git python3.11 python3.11-devel`

   c. `source venv/bin/activate`

   d. `pip install instructlab`

2. To convert source documents using ilab (for example, PDF, Markdown), you can convert them to JSON format, using:
    a. `ilab model chat --rag`
    b. `ilab rag ingest --input-dir=/home/alan/converted_documents`
    c. `ilab rag convert --input-dir /home/alan/source_documents --output-dir /home/alan/converted_documents`
    d. `ilab model download -rp ibm-granite/granite-embedding-125m-english`
3. The recommended, first command, after download and installation, to use with `ilab` is:
    a. `ilab model chat --rag`
    b. `ilab config show`
    c. `ilab model download`
    d. `ilab config init`

Answers

1. b
2. c
3. d

Questions

1. Outline the procedure used to provide an **IBM Cloud** based account for a trial system for **RedHat AI 1.4** for use with the **InstructLab AI ilab** command system.
2. List 5 of the main **IBM Granite 3.x** models, and provide a description of their use and limitations.
3. Outline the prerequisites required to prepare a local CPU based Linux system for the **InstructLab** system.

Key Terms

- **LLM**: Large Language Model
- **AI**: Artificial Intelligence Software that mimics the responses you might expect to questions supplied by a human operator.

- **COBOL:** Common Business-Oriented Language **-** a business language, derived from FLOW-MATIC a language developed by Dr. Grace Hopper. See https://www.ibm.com/topics/cobol.
- **NVIDIA GPU:** These are hardware graphics processing unit, providing a high speed processing resource. Using their high performance capabilities, they are ideal for developing and using AI Large Language Models.
- **RHEL:** RedHat Enterprise Linux. A commercial version of the Linux Operating system, now owned by **IBM**.
- **WCA: IBM watsonx Code Assistant-** Uses **IBM Granite LLM** models to enhance developer projects, it is used to simplify code and automate the development and conversion of the existing code deployments, such as legacy **COBOL** applications.

References

- Generating Code - IBM watsonx Code Assistant for Red Hat Ansible Lightspeed - Technical Sales Level 3

  https://ibm.github.io/WCA-AnsibleLightspeed-L3/generating/#ii-single-task-ansible-operations

- IBM watsonx Code Assistant for Z

  https://www.ibm.com/products/watsonx-code-assistant-z

- Easily create personalized AI assistants and agents to automate and accelerate your work using IBM watsonx Orchestrate

  https://www.ibm.com/products/watsonx-orchestrate

- IBM watsonx Orchestrate -Sign-up for a Trial:

  https://www.ibm.com/account/reg/signup?formid=urx-52753

  There is an IBM Granite 3.2 release (February, 2025) announced with the link as follows:

  https://www.ibm.com/new/announcements/ibm-granite-3-2-open-source-reasoning-and-vision

- The hardware requirements for RedHat RHEL AI 1.4 are available from the link: https://shorturl.at/mN5F5
- IBM watsonx Code Assistant (WCA) for RedHat AnsibleLightspeed-L3

  https://www.ibm.com/downloads/documents/us-en/10a99803ceafdd7d

- **IBM watsonx Code Assistant**, supported by **IBM Granite 3.0**, also includes functionality for the **Red Hat Ansible Automation Platform** (**IBM watsonx Code Assistant** for **Red Hat Ansible Lightspeed**) and (**IBM watsonx Code Assistant for Z**).

  https://ibm.github.io/WCA-AnsibleLightspeed-L3/#ii-generative-ai-assisted-code-lifecycle-management-achieves-what-llms-alone-cannot and: https://ibm.github.io/WCA-AnsibleLightspeed-L3/

CHAPTER 8
Performance Optimization

Introduction

This chapter describes the use of **IBM Granite 3.0** code models that are trained on expansive **Ansible Playbook** datasets so that developers can accept or adjust **AI**-generated content suggestions, improving productivity.

An enterprise using **IBM watsonx Code Assistant** for **Red Hat Ansible Lightspeed** can make use of the resulting code, using the **Ansible Playbook** content, generated from **AI** content recommendations see the link:

https://www.ibm.com/products/watsonx-code-assistant-ansible-lightspeed

See also:

https://ibm.github.io/WCA-AnsibleLightspeed-L3/customizing/ for details of a lab workshop for customising **Red Hat Ansible Lightspeed** using **IBM watsonx Code Assistant** extensions on **VS Code**.

There is a free trial listed at the link:

"*Trial for watsonx Code Assistant for Red Hat Ansible Lightspeed* | IBM":

https://www.ibm.com/products/watsonx-code-assistant-ansible-lightspeed/info/trial

Structure

In this chapter, we will discuss the following topics:

- Fine-Tuning Task Prompts
- Customizing the Model
- Content Source Matching
- Post-processing Capabilities

Fine-Tuning Task Prompts

We registered a new **RedHat Linux RHEL 9.2** system and created an activation key, as shown in *Figure 8.1*:

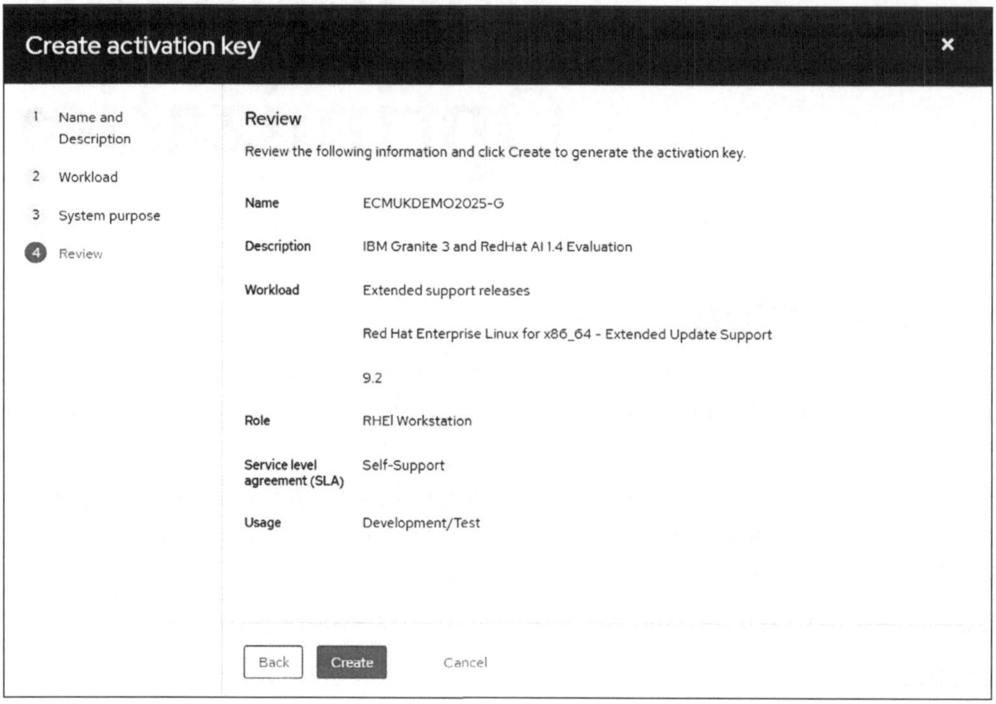

Figure 8.1: *We registered a new RedHat Linux* ***RHEL 9.2*** *system and created an activation key*

Then, we used the link as follows, to get a **60-day** free trial from **RedHat**:

https://www.redhat.com/en/technologies/management/ansible/trial

and

https://www.ibm.com/products/watsonx-code-assistant-ansible-lightspeed

The **IBM watsonx Code Assistant** for **RedHat Ansible Lightspeed** simplifies the process of **Ansible Playbook** creation by application of generative **AI**-powered content recommendations. Using **IBM LLMs** to accelerate **IT Automation**, the product is designed to deliver automation content recommendations for improved **Ansible** functionality.

The **AI-driven** product can generate syntactically correct and useful and relevant content using natural language prompts written in non-technical text.

IBM described how an organization using **IBM watsonx Code Assistant for Red Hat Ansible Lightspeed** in a pilot evaluation, obtained productivity improvements between 20% and 45%, and 60% of the **Ansible Playbook** content was generated from the **AI** content recommendations.

IBM Watsonx Code Assistant for Red Hat Ansible Lightspeed can be used to deploy the large language model either on-premise, or using **IBM** and other **Cloud** systems, as-a-service. **IBM** has an interactive pricing estimator to evaluate an organization's costs, based on the scope of their requirements for automating system deployments and maintenance.

The **RedHat Trial terms** and conditions are defined in the link as follows:

https://www.redhat.com/en/about/agreements-old

Deployment on RedHat Linux

In order to run **Red Hat Enterprise Linux** as the operating system for RedHat's product trial, on an existing **RedHat RHEL 9.2** system, proceed with the next step. If you do not have **RedHat RHEL 9.2 Linux** system, it can be downloaded from the link:

(https://access.redhat.com/downloads/content/479)

You can sign up for the **RedHat Ansible Automation Platform** free trial using the link, as follows, which will display the web page shown in *Figure* 8.2:

https://www.redhat.com/en/technologies/management/ansible/trial

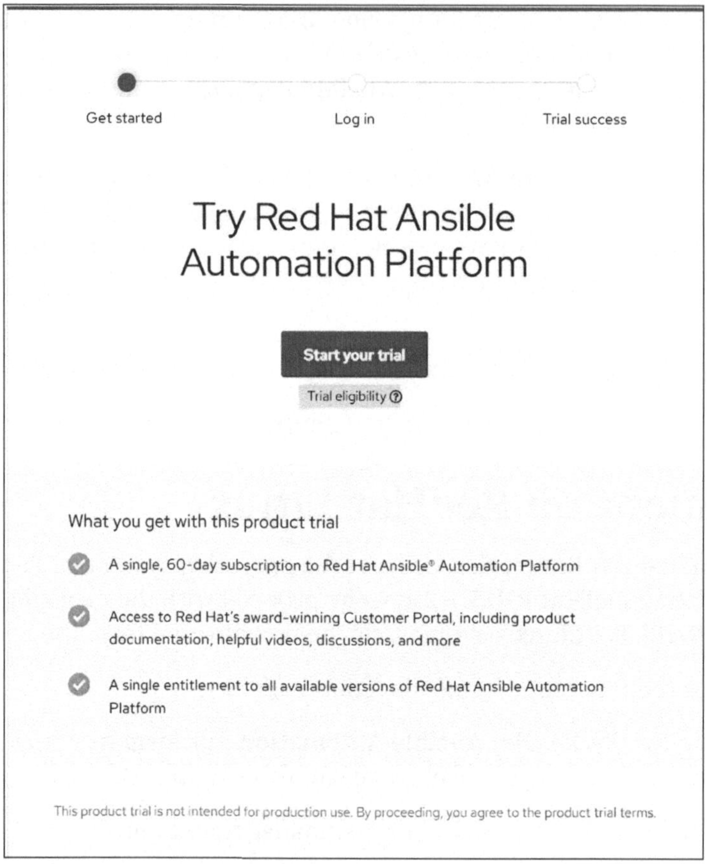

***Figure 8.2:** The **RedHat Ansible Automation Platform** free trial is available to sign-up*

The **mouse-over** on the `Trial eligibility "?"` mark icon gives advice, as shown in *Figure 8.3*:

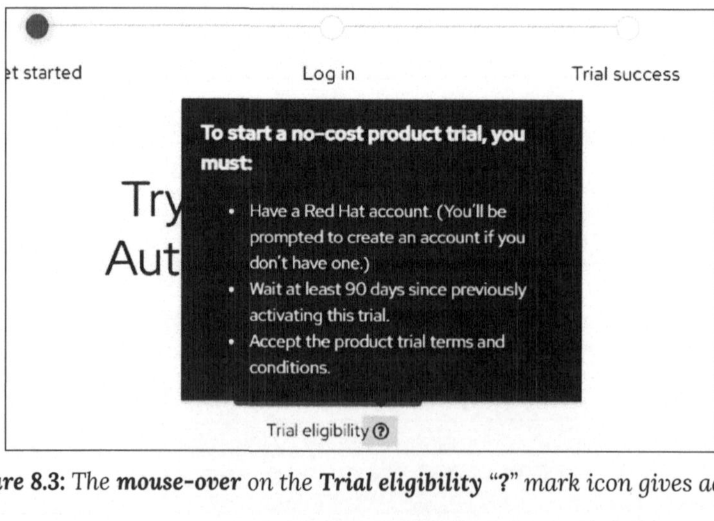

***Figure 8.3:** The **mouse-over** on the **Trial eligibility** "?" mark icon gives advice*

We log into **RedHat** with our **`RedHat Business Partner`** account, as shown in *Figure* 8.4:

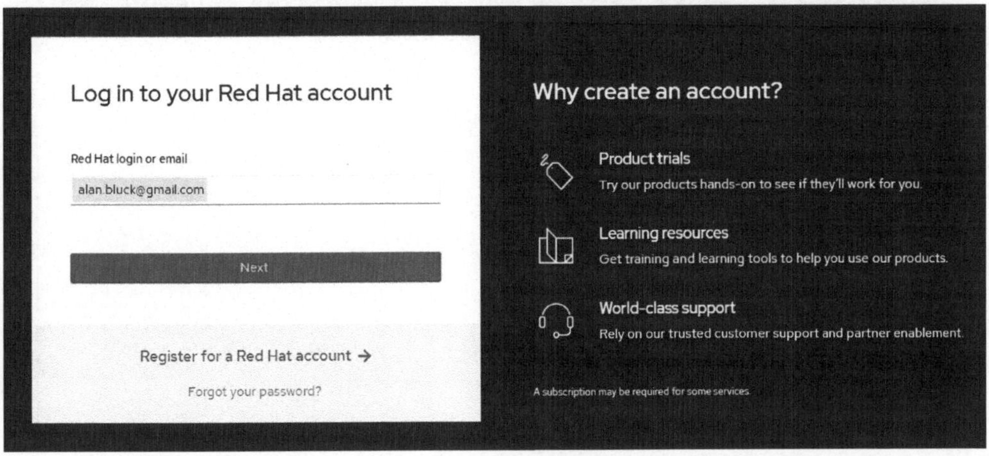

***Figure 8.4**: We log into **RedHat** with our **RedHat Business Partner** account*

The password was entered, as shown in *Figure* 8.5, to log into the website.

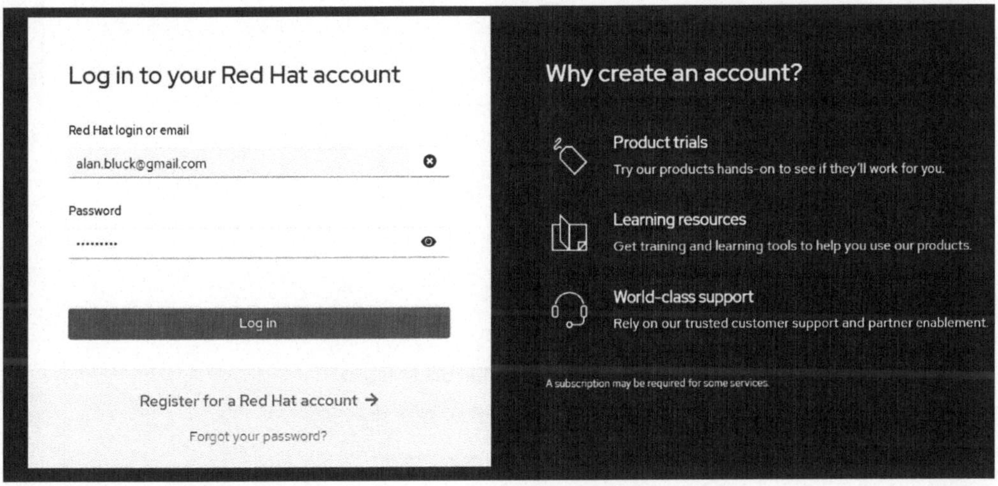

***Figure 8.5**: The password was entered to log into the website*

The **RedHat** website prompts for additional information to give access to the trial, as shown in *Figure* 8.6:

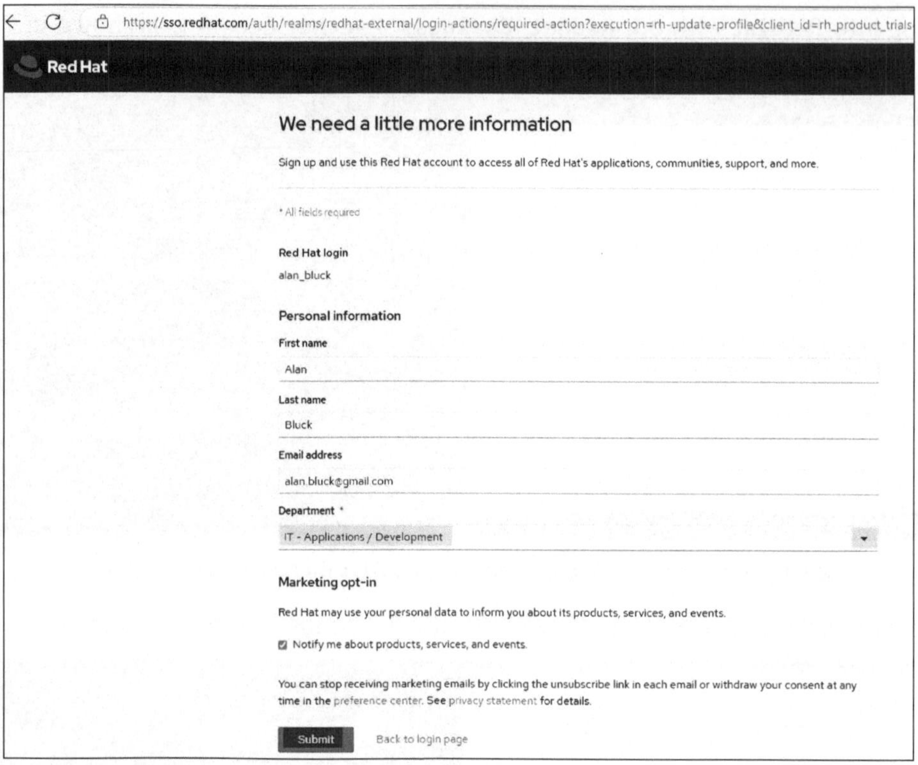

Figure 8.6: *The* ***RedHat*** *website prompts for additional information to give access to the trial*

The status of the product trial is now displayed, as shown in *Figure 8.7*:

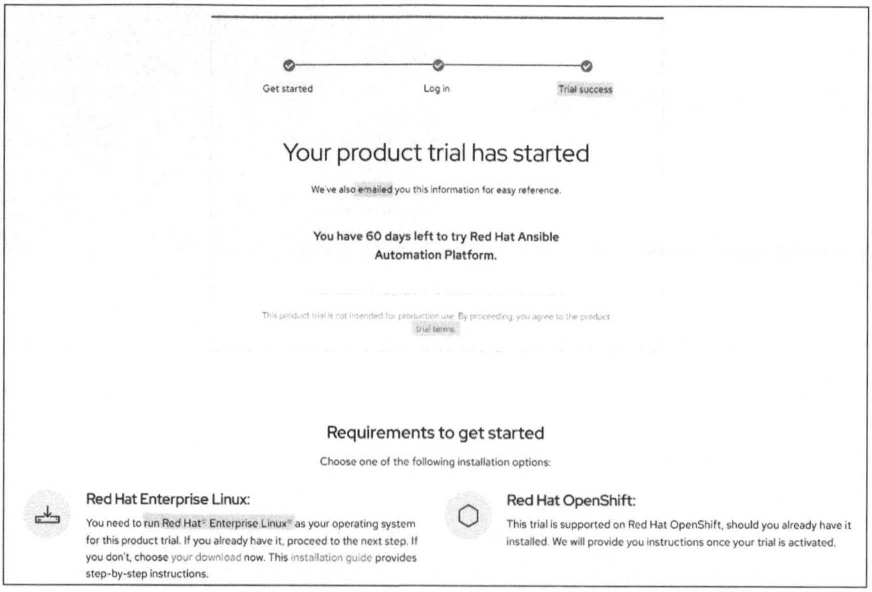

Figure 8.7: *The status of the product trial is now displayed*

The following steps are taken from the **RedHat** recommended installation guide, which provides step-by-step instructions, as shown in *Figure* 8.8:

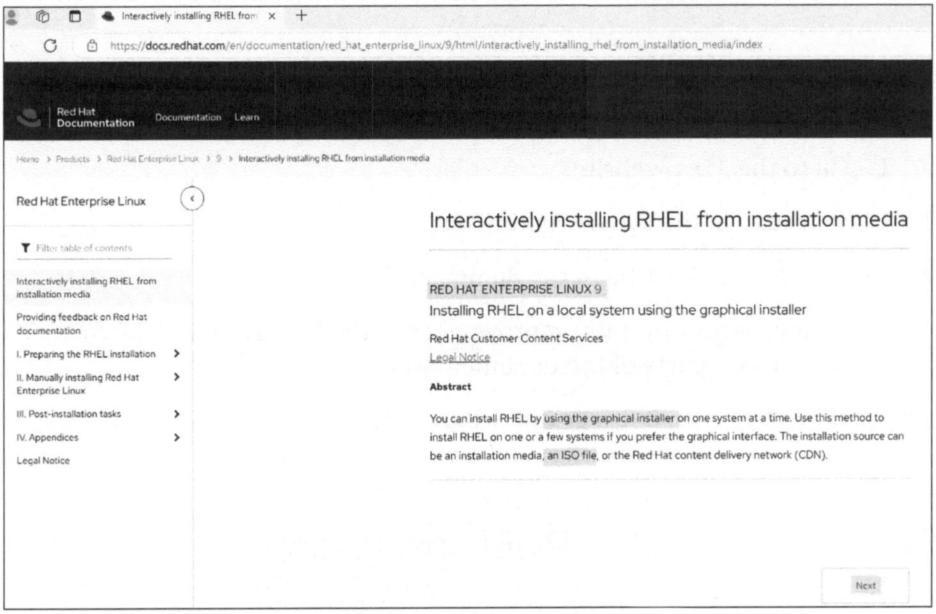

Figure 8.8: *The RedHat recommended installation guide, which provides step-by-step instructions*

(https://docs.redhat.com/en/documentation/red_hat_enterprise_linux/9/html/interactively_installing_rhel_from_installation_media/index")

Click **Next** at the bottom of the dialogue, as shown in *Figure* 8.9:

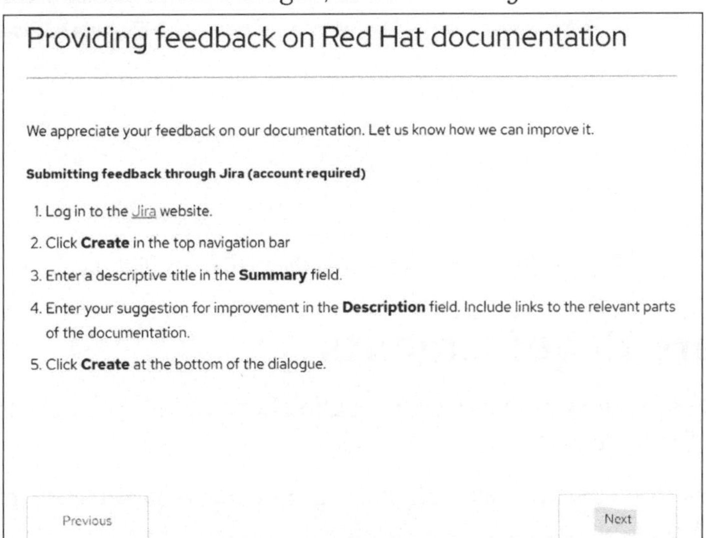

Figure 8.9: *Submitting feedback through* ***Jira***

RedHat requested feedback on their documentation, as shown in *Figure* 8.9:

"*We appreciate your feedback on our documentation. Let us know how we can improve it.*"

This can be done by submitting feedback through the **Jira** link (this requires an account) using the steps as follows.

a. Log in to the `Jira` website.

b. Click `Create` in the top navigation bar

c. Enter a descriptive title in the Summary field.

d. Enter your suggestion for improvement in the Description field. Include links to the relevant parts of the documentation.

Before installing `Red Hat Enterprise Linux RHEL 9.2`, we checked that our **Linux** system met the necessary hardware and architecture requirements, as illustrated in *Figure* 8.10:

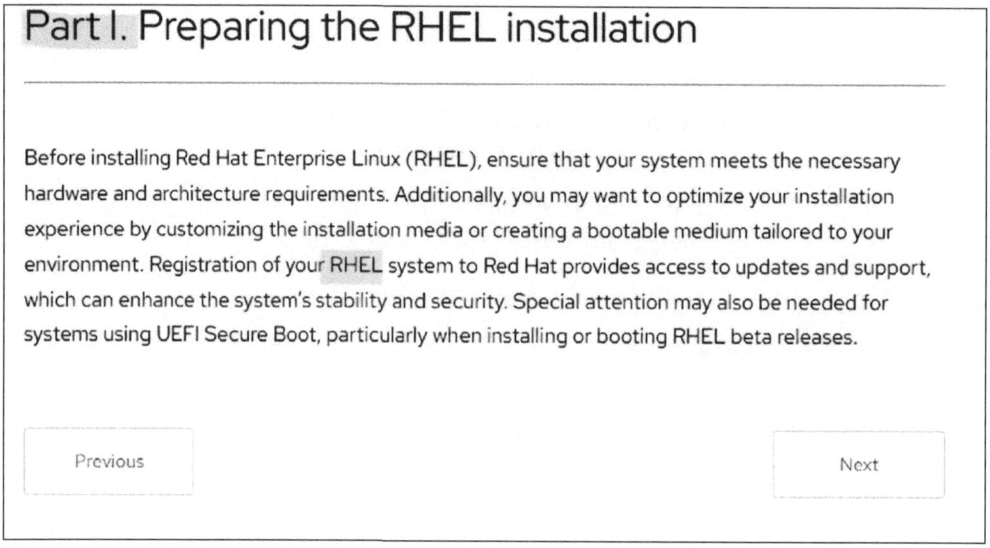

Figure 8.10: *Part I. Preparing the RHEL installation*

Hardware Requirements

If you want to use your system as a virtualization host, review the necessary hardware requirements for virtualization.

(RedHat labels this section as "*Chapter 1, System requirements and supported architectures*")

See the link

https://access.redhat.com/documentation/en-us/red_hat_enterprise_linux/9/html/configuring_and_managing_virtualization/assembly_enabling-virtualization-in-rhel-9_configuring-and-managing-virtualization

Red Hat Enterprise Linux supports the following architectures:

- **AMD** and Intel 64-bit architectures
- The 64-bit **ARM** architecture
- **IBM Power Systems**, Little Endian
- 64-bit **IBM Z** architectures

Prerequisites

Red Hat Enterprise Linux 9 is installed and registered on our host machine.

The system must meet the following hardware requirements to work as a virtualization host:

1. The architecture of the host machine must support **KVM** virtualization.

   The following features are recommended for use with the **KVM** hypervisor included with Red Hat Enterprise Linux 9 (RHEL 9):

   - Host system architectures

   See https://access.redhat.com/articles/973163#rhelkvm, which has the table shown in *Figure* 8.11:

Red Hat Enterprise Linux with KVM

The following is the list of Red Hat and third-party guest operating systems that are certified and supported for use with Red Hat Enterprise Linux Server with KVM hosts.

Guest Operating System	Red Hat Enterprise Linux Server with KVM version			
	9	8	7	6
Red Hat Enterprise Linux 6	Not supported	✓	✓	✓
Red Hat Enterprise Linux 7	✓	✓	✓	✓
Red Hat Enterprise Linux 8	✓	✓	RHEL 7.5 or later ✓[2]	RHEL 6.10 or later ✓
Red Hat Enterprise Linux 9	✓	RHEL 8.6 or later ✓[2]	Not supported	Not supported
Microsoft Windows 10	✓	✓	1	Not supported
Microsoft Windows 11	✓	RHEL 8.6 or later ✓	Not supported	Not supported
Microsoft Windows Server 2012 64-Bit	Not supported	Not supported	1	RHEL 6.4 or later ✓
Microsoft Windows Server 2012 R2 64-Bit	Not supported	✓	1	RHEL 6.5 or later ✓
Microsoft Windows Server 2016 64-Bit	✓	✓	1	RHEL 6.9 or later ✓
Microsoft Windows Server 2019 64-Bit	✓	✓	1	Not supported
Microsoft Windows Server 2022 64-Bit	✓	RHEL 8.6 or later ✓	Not supported	Not supported
Microsoft Windows Server 2025 64-Bit	RHEL 9.5 or later ✓	Not supported	Not supported	Not supported

1. In RHEL 7, RHEL will have SVVP support only under specific subscription programs. If you are unsure whether your subscription model includes support for Windows guests, please contact customer support. RHV and OSP have full support and ship SVVP certified drivers. In addition, the Red Hat Enterprise Linux Server version which you are using must be listed as a supported virtualization technology for running Windows Server at Windows Server Catalog - Server Virtualization.
2. Customizing RHEL KVM image of newer release on older release host is not supported. Please refer to this article for details.

Figure 8.11: *Red Hat Enterprise Linux with KVM*

RedHat RHEL 9 with **KVM** is only supported on the following host architectures:

- **AMD64** and **Intel 64**
- **IBM Z - IBM z13** systems and later
- **ARM 64**

Any other hardware architectures are not recommended for use with **RHEL 9** as a **KVM** virtualization host, and **Red Hat** does not support these.

The following minimum system resources are available:

- **6 GB** free disk space for the host, plus another **6 GB** for each intended VM.
- **2 GB of RAM** for the host, plus another **2 GB** for each intended VM.

Installation Procedure

a. Install the virtualization hypervisor packages, using the command:

`dnf install qemu-kvm libvirt virt-install virt-viewer`

as shown in *Figure 8.12*:

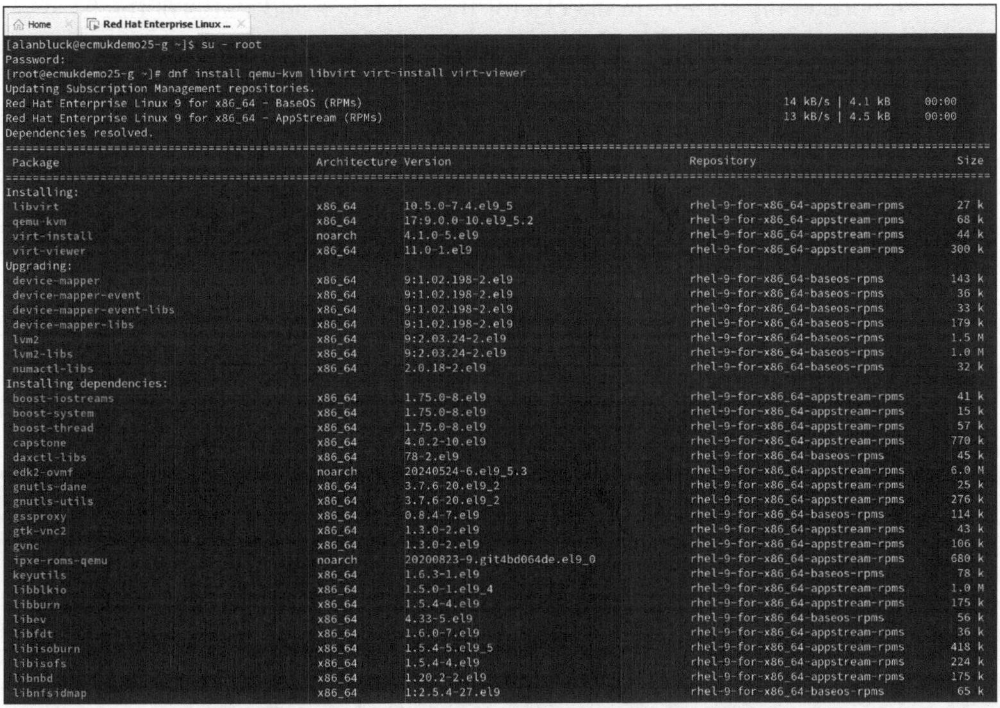

Figure 8.12: *Install the virtualization hypervisor packages*

This installs a large number of supporting libraries, as listed in *Figure 8.13*:

Figure 8.13: *This installs a large number of supporting libraries, listed*

b. Start the virtualization services using the following command as shown in *Figure 8.14*:

```
su - root
for drv in qemu network nodedev nwfilter secret storage interface;
do systemctl start virt${drv}d{,-ro,-admin}.socket; done
```

The preceding statement checks for the existence and status of the hardware virtualization for the QEMU system and starts the related services it requires. QEMU is an emulator that makes hardware virtualization easier. It emulates a computer system, allowing users to run guest operating systems on a host system, including the case where the guest OS architecture is different from the host. QEMU can use hardware virtualization using KVM (Kernel-based Virtual Machine) on Linux, hvf on macOS, and WHPX on Windows, which enables it to provide high performance levels for guest virtual machines.

However, without hardware-assisted CPU virtualization, QEMU relies on emulation, which can be slower.

c. Verify the services are running

```
virt-host-validate
```

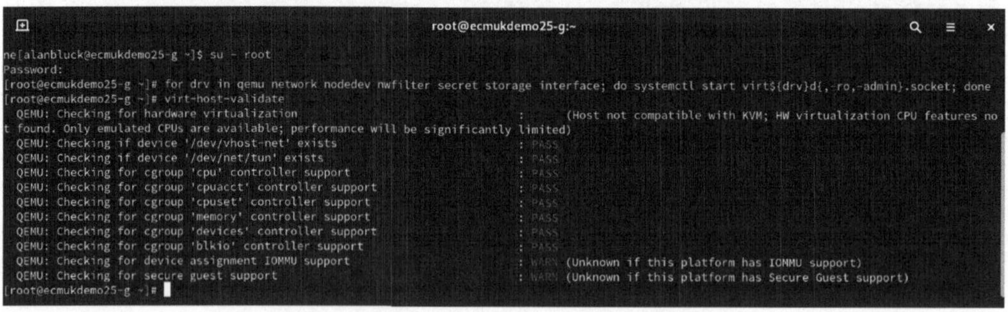

Figure 8.14: *Start the virtualization services*

As **KVM** was not supported, we get the message:

```
"QEMU: Checking for hardware virtualization: FAIL (Only emulated
CPUs are available, performance will be significantly limited)"
```

Note: VMs *on a host system, which gives the* **KVM (Kernel-based Virtual Machine)** *not supported message, will fail to boot, rather than have performance problems.*

To work around this, we changed the **<domain type>** *value in the XML configuration of the VM to* **qemu**. *Remember, that* **Red Hat** *does not support* **VMs** *that use the* **qemu** *domain type, and setting this is highly discouraged in production environments.*

The rest of this section is used to demonstrate the virt-manager installation procedure, rather than providing a useful VM within our VMware system.

Using `virt-manager` in a Vmware-based Linux

To use certain features on a virtual machine (**VM**) hosted on our **RHEL 9** system, first, we had to configure the **VM** to use the **QEMU Guest Agent** (**GA**).

We enabled the **QEMU GA** both on running and shut-down **VMs**, using the following procedure:

1. Create an **XML** configuration file for the **QEMU GA**, for example, named **`qemuga.xml`**, as shown in *Figure* 8.15:

   ```
   touch qemuga.xml
   vi qemuga.xml
   ```

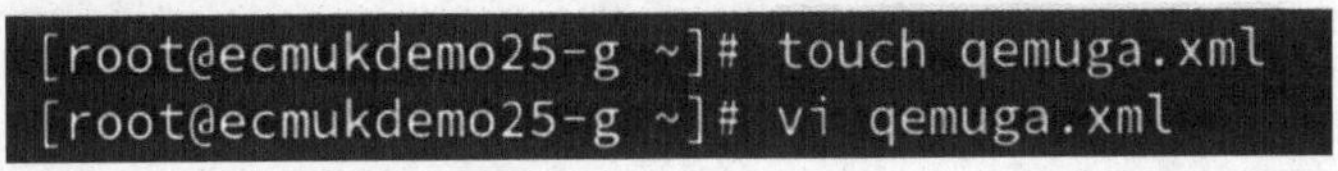

Figure 8.15: *Create an XML configuration file for the QEMU GA, for example, named* ***qemuga.xml***

2. Add the following lines to the file, as shown in *Figure* 8.16:

   ```
   <channel type='unix'>
      <source mode='bind' path='/var/lib/libvirt/qemu/f16x86_64.
   agent'/>
      <target type='virtio' name='org.qemu.guest_agent.0'/>
   </channel>
   ```

Figure 8.16: *Add lines to the* ***qemuga.xml*** *file*

3. To list a very large available set of virtual operating systems available the following command can be used:

   ```
   [root@ecmukdemo25-g ~]# virt-install --osinfo list
   You can see additional information with:

     osinfo-query os

   [root@ecmukdemo25-g ~]#
   ```

4. In the Linux guest operating system, install the **QEMU GA**, as shown in *Figure* 8.17:

   ```
   dnf install qemu-guest-agent
   ```

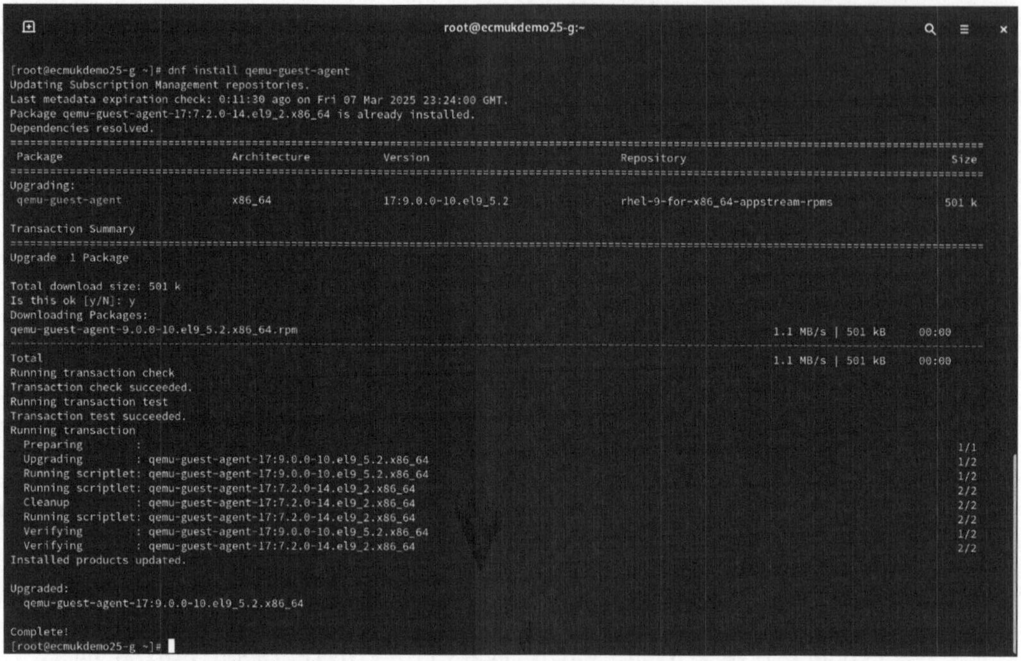

Figure 8.17: *In the Linux guest operating system, install the* **QEMU GA**

5. Start the **QEMU GA** service on the guest:

```
systemctl start qemu-guest-agent
```

Installing `virt-manager`

First, download the **RedHat** iso **DVD** image file, as shown in *Figure* 8.18:

https://developers.redhat.com/products/rhel/download

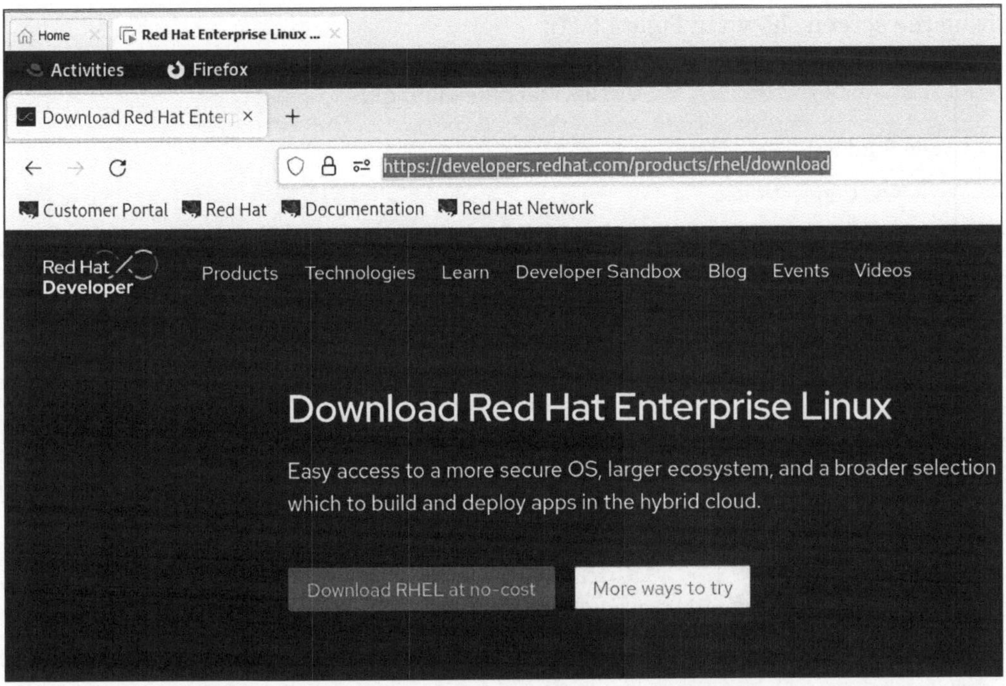

Figure 8.18: *First, download the* ***RedHat*** *iso* ***DVD*** *image file*

(https: //developers.redhat.com/products/rhel/download#rhelforsap896)

We installed the **`Virtual Machine`** manager, using the command:

```
sudo dnf install virt-manager
```

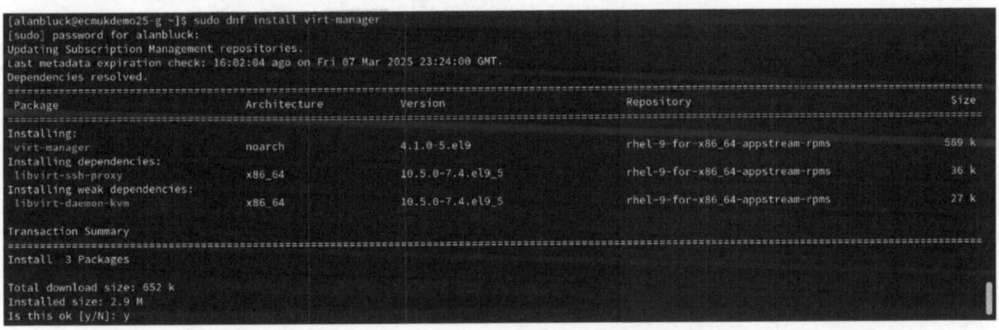

Figure 8.19: *We installed the* ***Virtual Machine*** *manager, using the command*

The **`Virtual Machine Manager`** **GUI** is loaded from a command window, using:

```
virt-manager
```

Giving the screen shown in *Figure* 8.20:

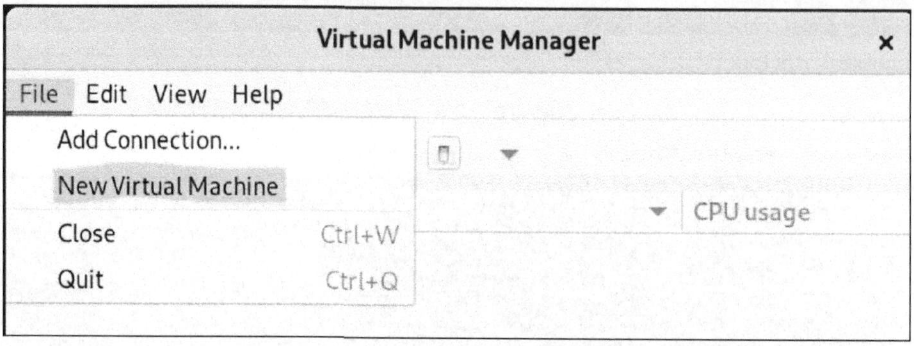

***Figure* 8.20:** *The* **Virtual Machine Manager GUI** *is loaded from a command window*

The **`Create a new virtual machine`** wizard page is displayed, as shown in *Figure* 8.21:

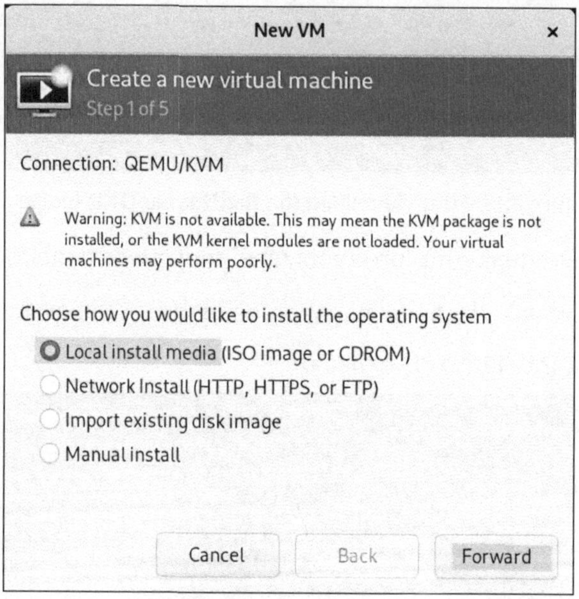

***Figure* 8.21:** *The* **Create a new virtual machine** *wizard page is displayed*

The download of the **`rhel-9.5-x86_64-dvd.iso`** file is completed, as shown in *Figure* 8.22:

***Figure* 8.22:** *The download of the* **rhel-9.5-x86_64-dvd.iso** *file is completed*

We select the **Browse Local** command of the **VM** wizard, as highlighted in *Figure 8.23*:

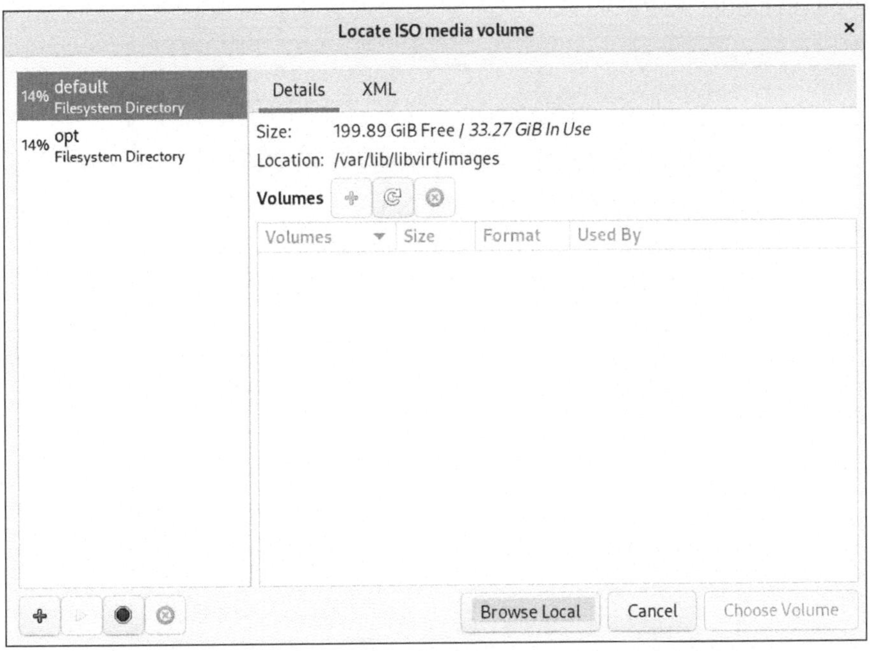

***Figure 8.23:** We select the **Browse Local** command of the **VM** wizard*

Searching in the **`Downloads`** directory, we select the downloaded **RHEL 9.5** install disk image, as shown in *Figure 8.24*:

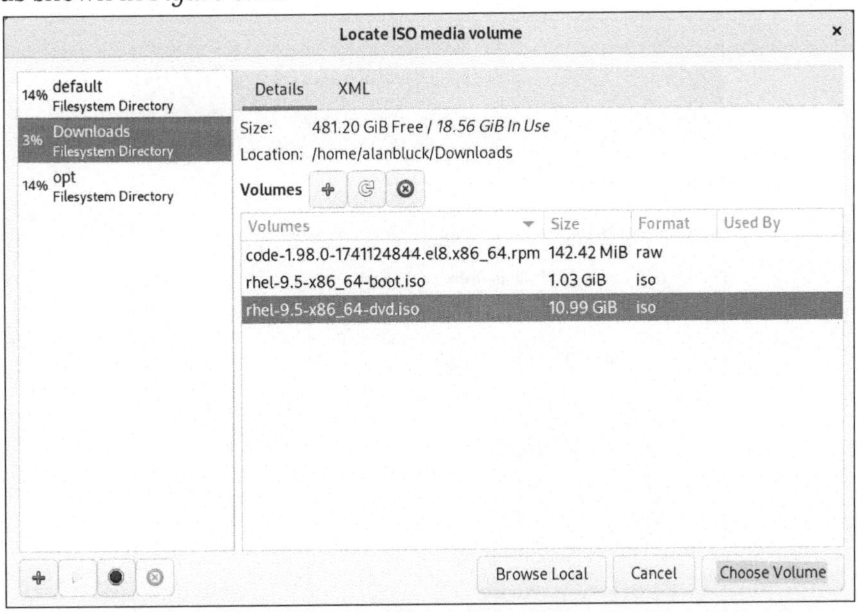

***Figure 8.24:** Searching in the **Downloads** directory, we select the downloaded **RHEL 9.5** install disk image*

We select the **`Forward`** command to show the **`Memory and CPU`** settings window, as highlighted in *Figure* 8.25:

Figure* 8.25:** *We select the* ***Forward *command to show the* ***Memory and CPU*** *settings window*

We set the **`Memory`** to **2GBytes** and the number of **CPUs** to **2** and selected the **`Forward`** command, as highlighted in *Figure* 8.26:

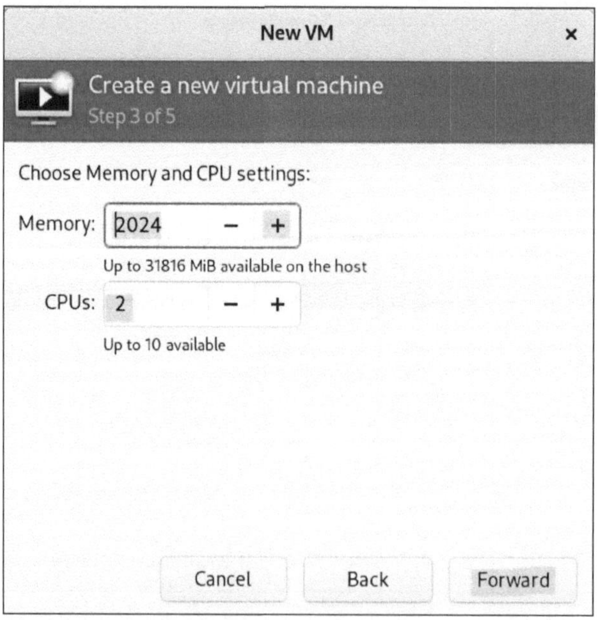

Figure* 8.26:** *We set the* ***Memory *to 2GBytes and the number of* ***CPUs*** *to 2 and select* ***Forward***

We set the disk image size to **20 Gbytes**, and then select **`Forward`**, as highlighted in *Figure 8.27*:

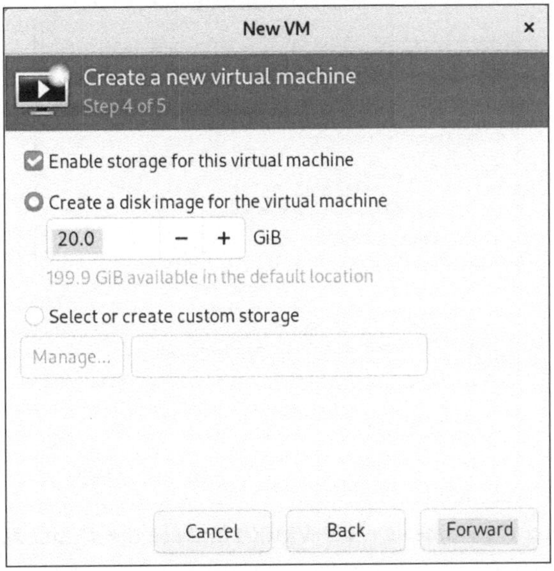

Figure 8.27:** We set the disk image size to **20 Gbytes**, and then select **Forward

We select the name of the Virtual Machine and tick the "**`Customise configuration before install`**" option tick-box and then select the **`Network selection`** drop-down, as highlighted in *Figure 8.28*:

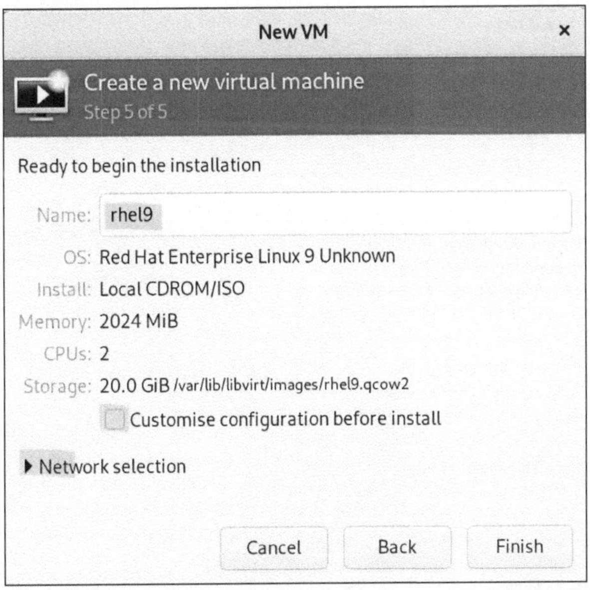

***Figure 8.28:** We select the name of the Virtual Machine and tick the "**Customise configuration before install**" option tick-box and then select the **Network selection** drop-down*

We enter the **Name** as **rhel9-VM001** and use the default **NAT** network option and select the **Finish** command, as shown in *Figure 8.29*:

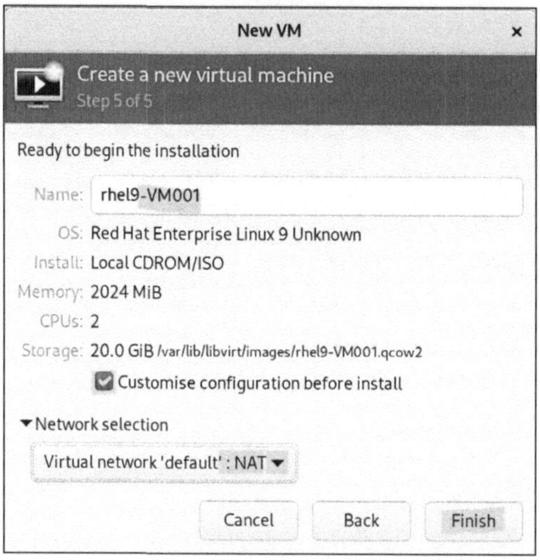

Figure 8.29: *We enter the* ***Name*** *as* ***rhel9-VM001*** *and use the default* ***NAT*** *network option*

The **Details** tab of the **Virtual Machine Manager** shows the settings we created, as illustrated in *Figure 8.30*:

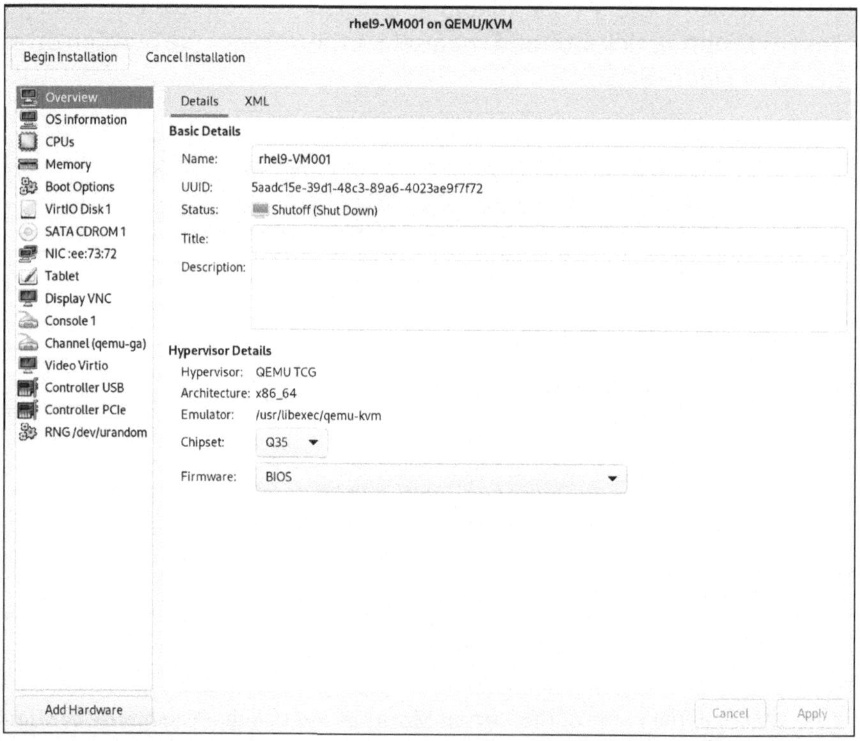

Figure 8.30: *The* ***Details*** *tab of the* ***Virtual Machine Manager*** *shows the settings we created*

Next, we enter the **VM Title** as **IBM Granite3, Chapter 7 VM001**, and the **`Description`** and select the **`Apply`** command, as highlighted in *Figure 8.31*:

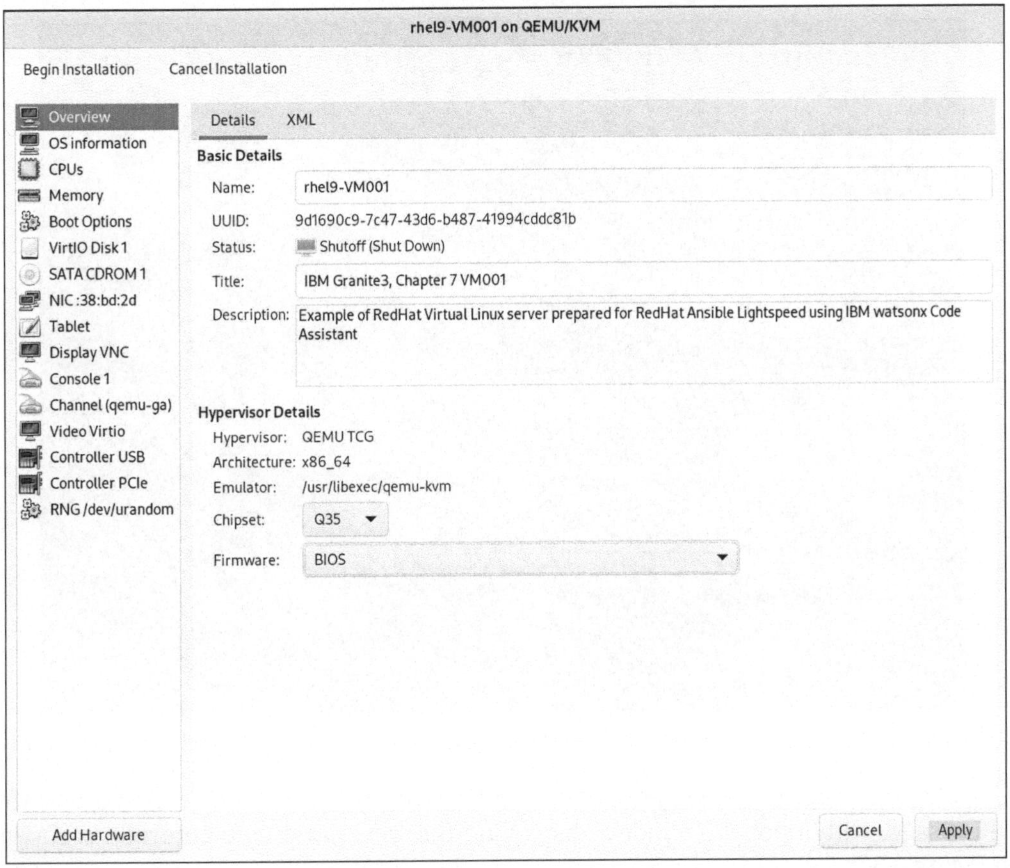

Figure 8.31: *Next, we enter the* **VM Title** *as* **IBM Granite3, Chapter 7 VM001,** *and the* **Description**

The virtual machine, **IBM Granite3, Chapter 7 VM001**, shows the boot splash screen, as illustrated in *Figure 8.32*:

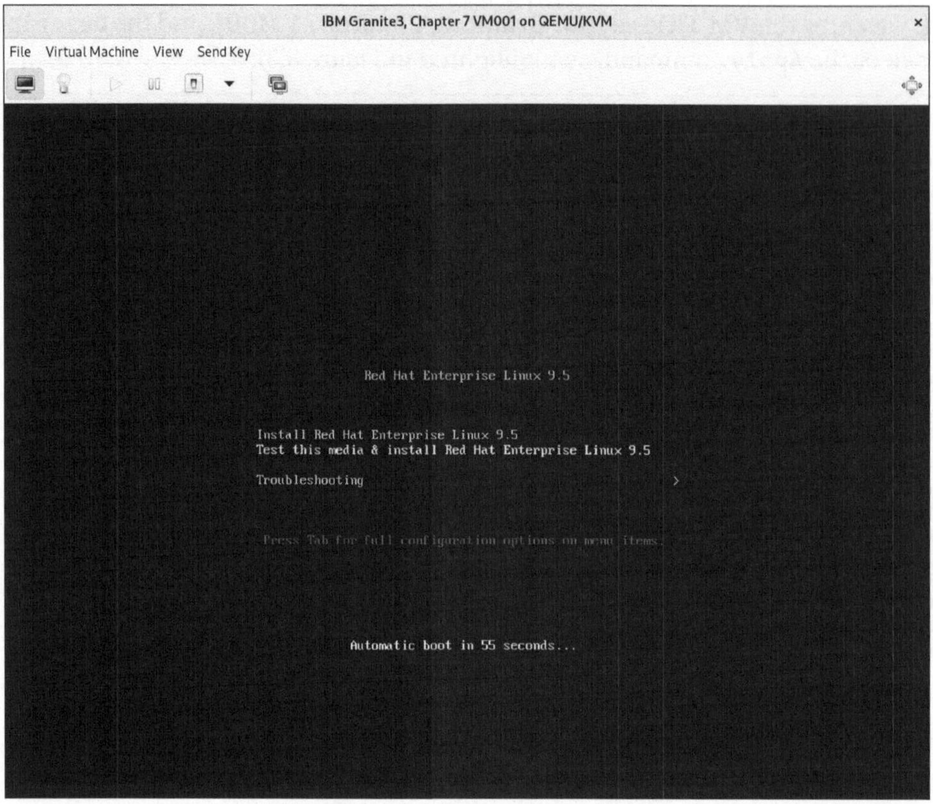

***Figure 8.32:** The virtual machine, **IBM Granite3, Chapter 7 VM001**, shows the boot splash screen*

The **`Virtual Machine Manager`** status window shows the machine running and the CPU usage, with a pop-up window displaying the Description we entered, as shown in *Figure* 8.33:

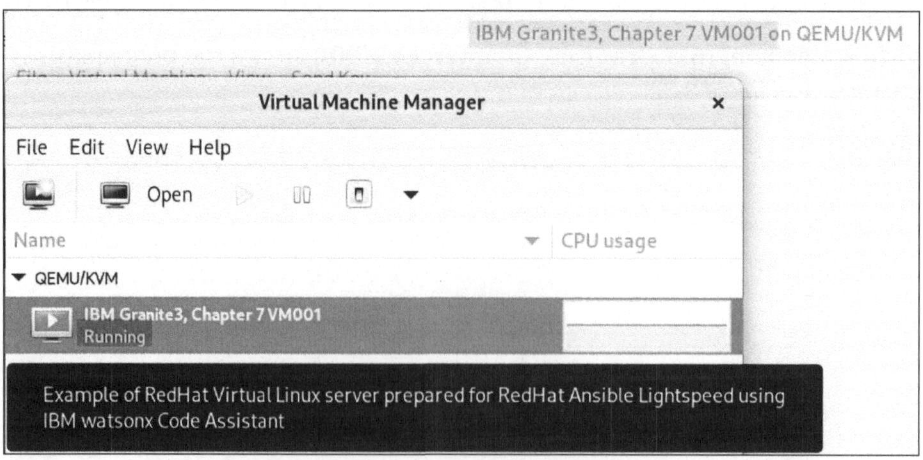

***Figure 8.33:** The **Virtual Machine Manager** status window shows the machine running and the **CPU** usage*

The running virtual machine can be shut down by right-clicking the machine display and selecting the **Shutdown** menu, as shown in *Figure* 8.34:

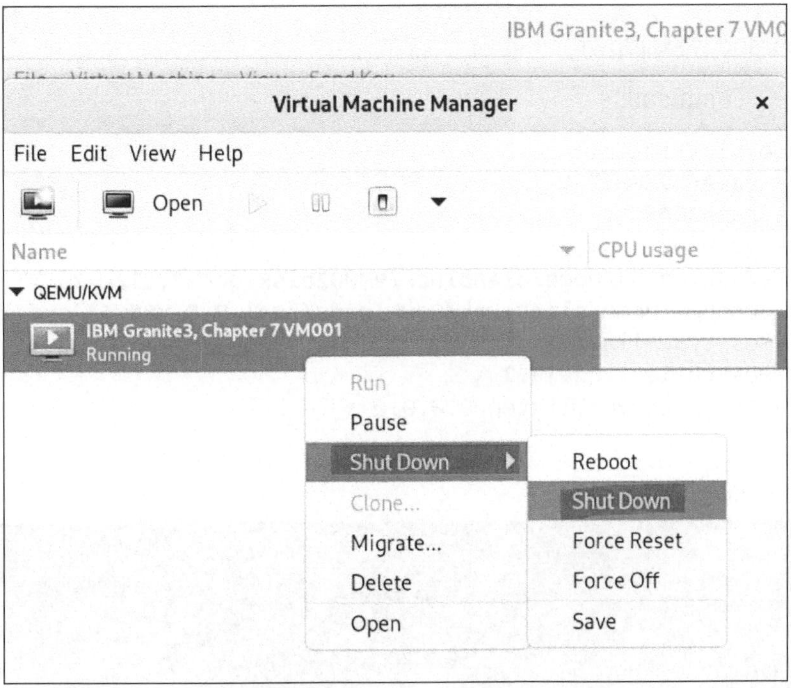

Figure 8.34: *The running virtual machine can be shut down by right-mouse clicking on the machine display and selecting the **Shutdown** menu*

The **virt-manager GUI** program automatically creates the required **QEMU XML** for the system.

Verification

To ensure that **QEMU GA** is enabled and running on the **Linux VM**, do any of the following:

In the guest operating system, use the

```
systemctl status qemu-guest-agent | grep Loaded
```

command. If the output includes enabled, **QEMU GA** is active on the **VM**. We get:

```
[alanbluck@ecmukdemo25-g ~]$ systemctl status qemu-guest-agent |
grep Loaded
     Loaded: loaded (/usr/lib/systemd/system/qemu-guest-agent.
service; enabled; preset: enabled)
```

To create a virtual machine using a command line:

See

https://rebrand.ly/xzldpwf

We used, the command:

```
sudo virt-install \
  --name="VM002" \
  --ram=2048 \
  --vcpus=2 \
  --disk path=/home/alanbluck/VM002disk.qcow2,size=20 \
  --cdrom=/home/alanbluck/Downloads/rhel-9.5-x86_64-dvd.iso \
  --os-type=linux \
  --os-variant=rhel9.2 \
  --graphics vnc,listen=0.0.0.0 \
>
```

as shown in *Figure* 8.35:

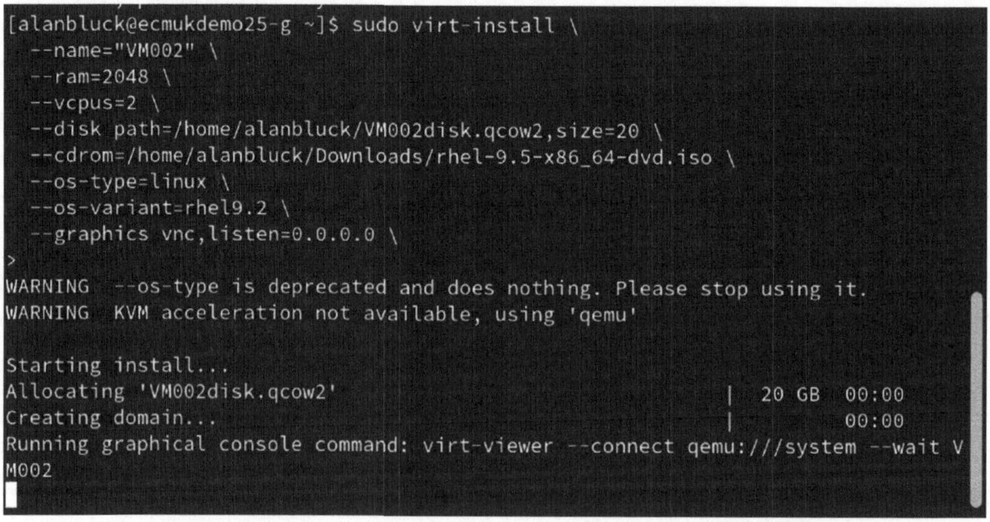

Figure 8.35: *We create a virtual machine using a command line*

The new **VM002** Virtual Machine is now added to the list of configured **VMs**. As shown in *Figure* 8.36, the new **VM002** server machine has a status of **Running** and the initial machine, **IBM Granite3, Chapter 7 VM001** has a status of **Shutoff**.

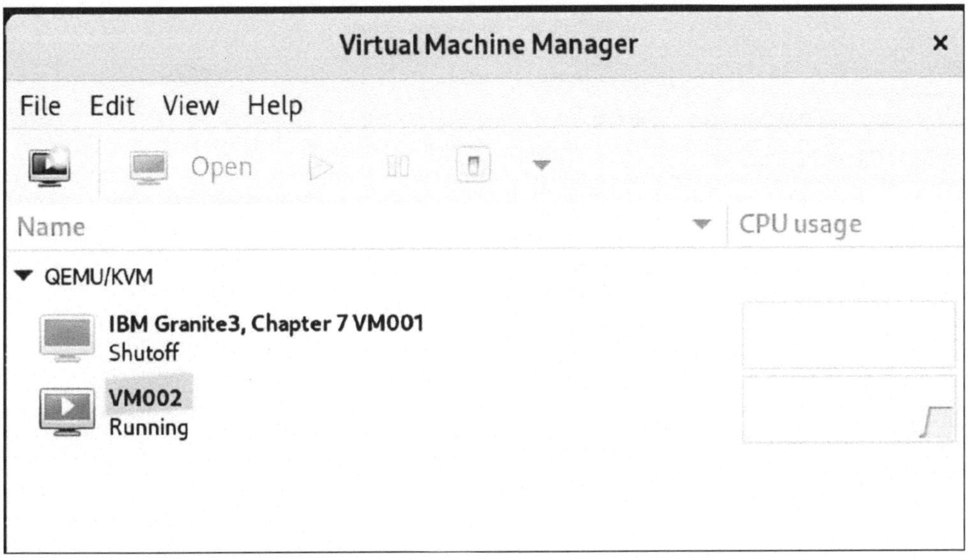

Figure 8.36: *The new* **VM002** *Virtual Machine is now added to the list of configured* **VMs**

The **`Virtual Machine`** network connection **`Details`** tab displays the **NAT IP address** details, as shown in *Figure* 8.37:

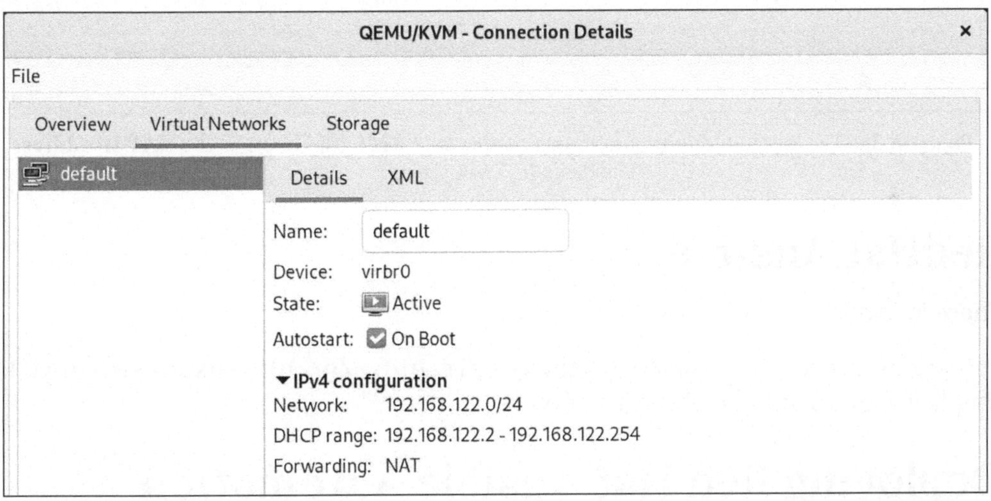

Figure 8.37: *The Virtual Machine network connection* **Details** *tab displays the* **NAT IP address** *details*

The Virtual Machine network connection **`XML`** tab displays the **NAT IP address** details in **XML** format, as shown in *Figure* 8.38:

Figure 8.38: *The Virtual Machine network connection* ***XML*** *tab displays the* ***NAT IP address*** *details in* ***XML*** *format*

RedHat Ansible

There is RedHat Ansible basic overview at:

https://www.redhat.com/en/services/training/do007-ansible-essentials-simplicity-automation-technical-overview

Deploying Red Hat Ansible Automation Platform

First, download the latest version of **Ansible Automation Platform**, as shown in *Figure* 8.39 using the link:

https://access.redhat.com/downloads/content/480 and install it using the link instructions:

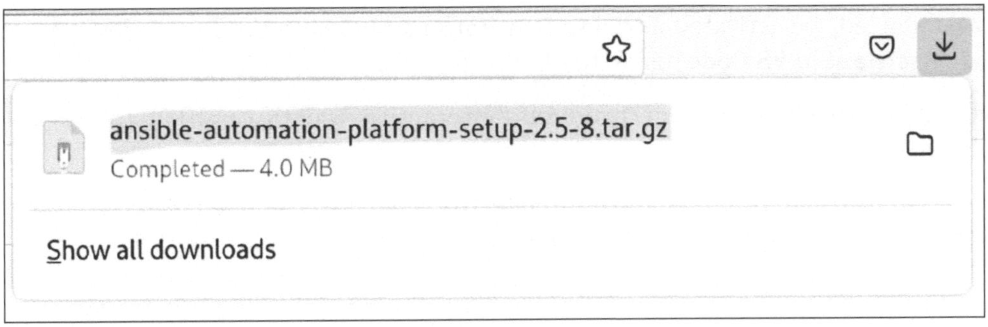

Figure 8.39: *First, download the latest version of* **Ansible Automation Platform**

https://docs.redhat.com/en/documentation/red_hat_ansible_automation_platform/2.5/html/planning_your_installation/index

The minimum hardware requirements are Red Hat Enterprise Linux 8.8 or later (x86_64, aarch64), or Red Hat Enterprise Linux 9.2 or later (x86_64, aarch64) – we are using the latter.

The command line, **`./setup.sh`** found in the path, **`/home/alanbluck/ansible_2.5/ansible-automation-platform-setup-2.5-8`**, extracted from **ansible-automation-platform-setup-2.5-8.tar.gz**, is used to install the support for the **RedHat Ansible Lightspeed** system, as shown in *Figure* 8.40:

```
[alanbluck@ecmukdemo25-g ansible_2.5]$ ls

[alanbluck@ecmukdemo25-g ansible_2.5]$ cd ansible-automation-platform-setup-2.5-8/
[alanbluck@ecmukdemo25-g ansible-automation-platform-setup-2.5-8]$ ls
           inventory  inventory-growth  README.md  setup.sh
[alanbluck@ecmukdemo25-g ansible-automation-platform-setup-2.5-8]$
[alanbluck@ecmukdemo25-g ansible-automation-platform-setup-2.5-8]$ pwd
/home/alanbluck/ansible_2.5/ansible-automation-platform-setup-2.5-8
[alanbluck@ecmukdemo25-g ansible-automation-platform-setup-2.5-8]$ ./setup.sh
```

Figure 8.40: *The command line,* ***./setup.sh*** *is used to install the* **RedHat Ansible Lightspeed** *system*

Next, set up automation controller and create your first playbook.

The services script can be found in the path, **`/usr/bin/automation-controller-service`**

https://docs.redhat.com/en/documentation/red_hat_ansible_automation_platform/2.5/html/configuring_automation_execution/index

Trial for Ansible Lightspeed

Red Hat Ansible Lightspeed with **IBM watsonx Code Assistant** is a generative **AI**

To get started, we activated a trial to **Red Hat Ansible Lightspeed** with **IBM watsonx Code Assistant** in **VS Code**, using the link as follows:

https://www.redhat.com/en/products/interactive-walkthrough/install-ansible-lightspeed

Run **VS Code** using the command line, **code**, to display the **VS Code IDE,** and select the **`Extensions`** icon, as highlighted in *Figure 8.41*:

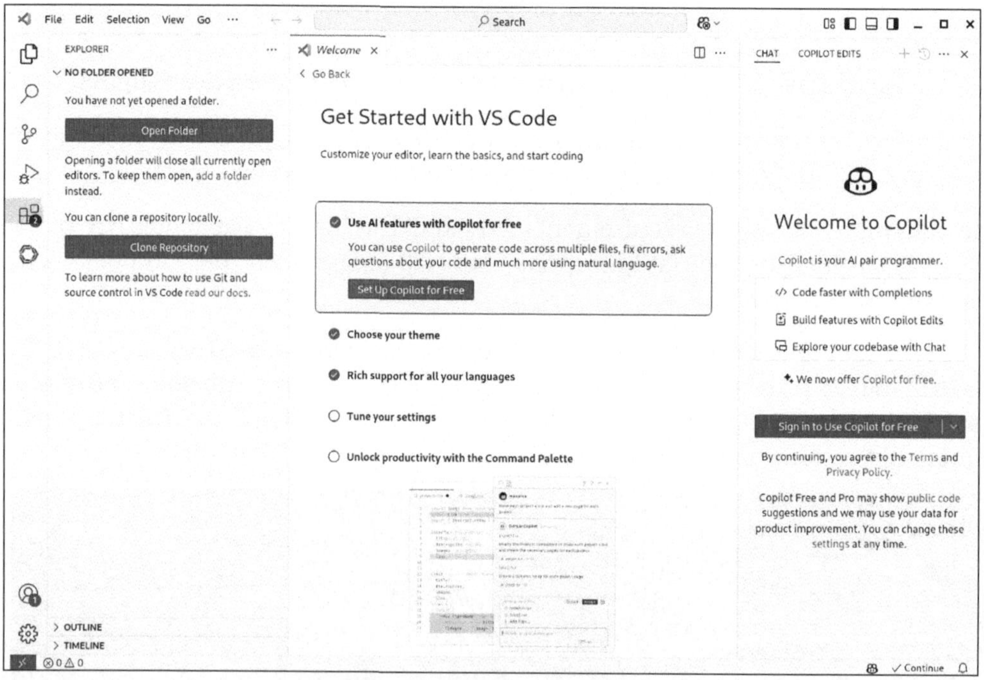

Figure 8.41: *Run* **VS Code** *using the command,* **code**, *to display the* **VS Code IDE** *and select the* **Extensions** *icon*

In **VS Code**, download and install the **`Ansible VS Code Extension by Red Hat.`**

Note: *To install the required* **IBM watsonx Code Assistant** *on-premise, you need to install* **IBM Cloud Pak for Data** *and then install the* **IBM watsonx Code Assistant service** *within it, along with the necessary extensions for an* **IDE** *(like* **Visual Studio Code***).*

https://www.redhat.com/en/blog/getting-started-red-hat-ansible-lightspeed-ibm-watsonx-code-assistant#:~:text=Ansible%20Lightspeed%20with%20IBM%20watsonx%20Code%20Assistant,(SaaS)%20deployment%20or%20on%2Dpremise%20in%20your%20datacenter.&text=For%20on%2Dpremise%20deployments%2C%20you%20will%20need%20to,Assistant%20via%20IBM%20Cloud%20Pak%20for%20Data .

We search for the **Red Hat Ansible** extension and select the **Install** command button, as shown in *Figure 8.42*:

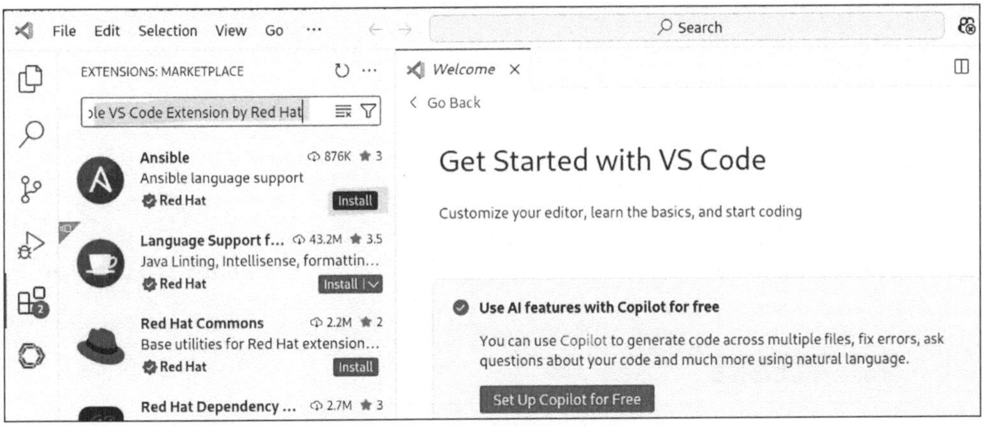

Figure 8.42: *We search for the* **Red Hat Ansible** *extension and select the* **Install** *command button*

The **`VS Code`** installer prompts to select the **`Trust Publisher & Install`** command to start the installation, as highlighted in *Figure 8.43*:

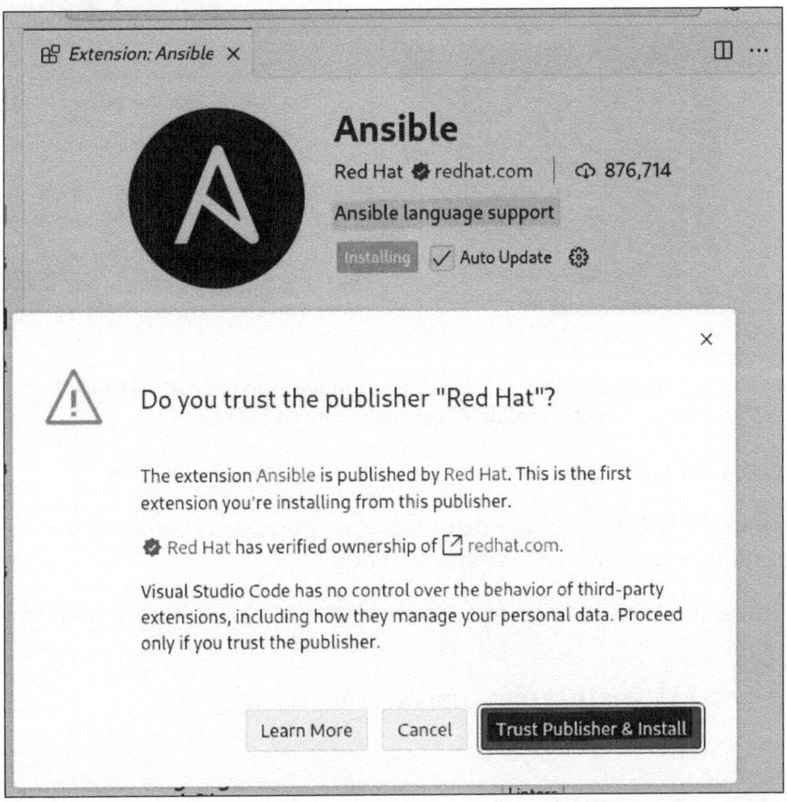

Figure 8.43: *The* **VS Code** *installer prompts to select the* **Trust Publisher & Install** *command*

The installed **`Ansible language support`** package extension for **`VS Code`** is selected and the **`Create Ansible Playbook`** command is selected as shown in *Figure 8.44:*

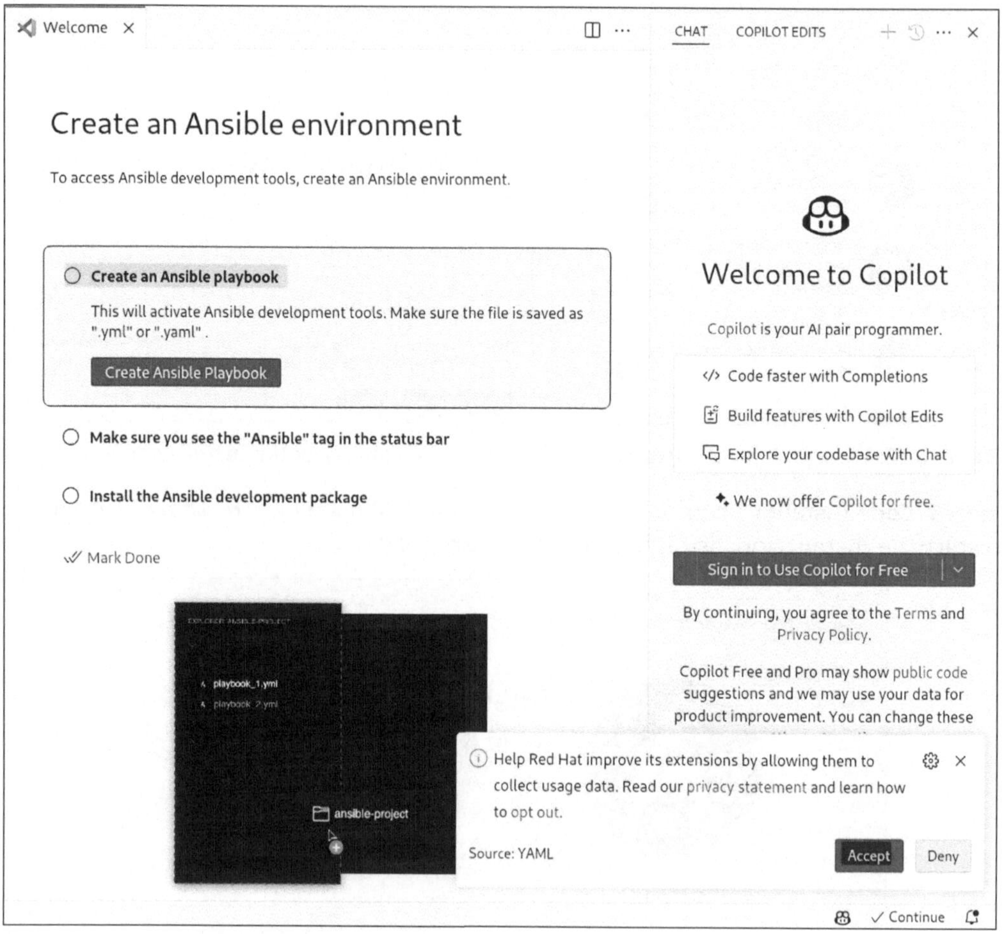

Figure 8.44: *Using the* ***Ansible language support*** *for* ***VS Code****,*
Create Ansible Playbook *command is selected*

1. Prerequisites are described in the link as follows:

   https://www.ibm.com/docs/en/wx-code-assistant/5.1.x?topic=in-installing-extension-visual-studio-code

The commands are used as follows, for supporting tools, as highlighted in *Figure 8.45:*

```
code
pip install ansible-dev-tools --no-input
```

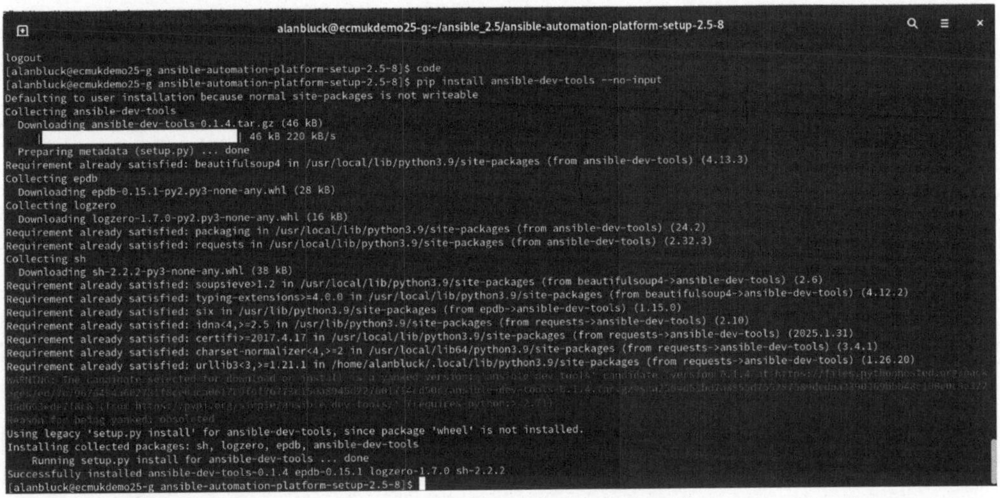

Figure 8.45: *For prerequistes, the commands are used as highlighted above, for supporting tools*

IBM Cloud Pak for Data:

We need a **Red Hat OpenShift Container** Platform cluster and the **IBM Cloud Pak for Data** control plane installed.

2. Installation Steps:

   IBM recommended the following outline installation steps:

   a. **Install IBM Cloud Pak for Data:** Follow the instructions in the **IBM Cloud Pak for Data** documentation to install the control plane.

   b. **Install the watsonx Code Assistant Service:** Once Cloud Pak for Data is set up, install the **watsonx Code Assistant** service within it. (as illustrated above).

   c. **Install the IDE Extension/Plugin:**

      i. **Visual Studio Code:** Install the **watsonx Code Assistant** extension from the **VS Code** Visual Studio Marketplace.

      ii. **Other IDEs:** Check the IBM documentation for instructions on installing the plugin for your specific IDE.

   d. **Configure the Extension/Plugin:**

      i. **Backend Provider:** In the extension settings, set the "`Wca: Backend Provider`" to "`ollama`".

      ii. **Ollama:** Install and start the **Ollama** inference server.

iii. **IBM Granite Code Model:** Install the **`granite-code:8b model`** in the **`Ollama`** library.

e. **Access and Use:** Once installed and configured, you can access the **watsonx Code Assistant** features within your **IDE**.

We began, after installing the **RedHat Ansible** extension on **VS Code**, by scrolling down to the **`ANSIBLE LIGHTSPEED`** section of the highlighted **Ansible** extension icon, and then selecting the **`Connect`** command, as shown in *Figure* 8.46:

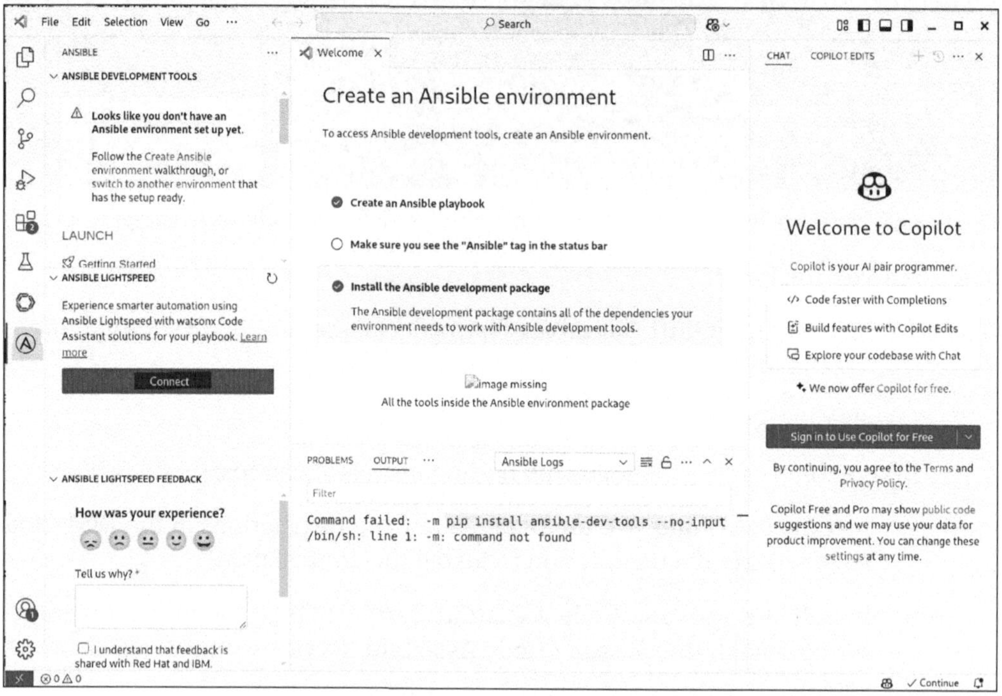

Figure 8.46: *Scroll down to the* **ANSIBLE LIGHTSPEED** *section of the* **Ansible** *extension icon, and select* **Connect**

We select the tick-box on the **`VS Code`** extension **Settings** tab for the "**`Enable Ansible Lightspeed with watsonx Code Assistant inline suggestions`**", highlighted in *Figure* 8.47:

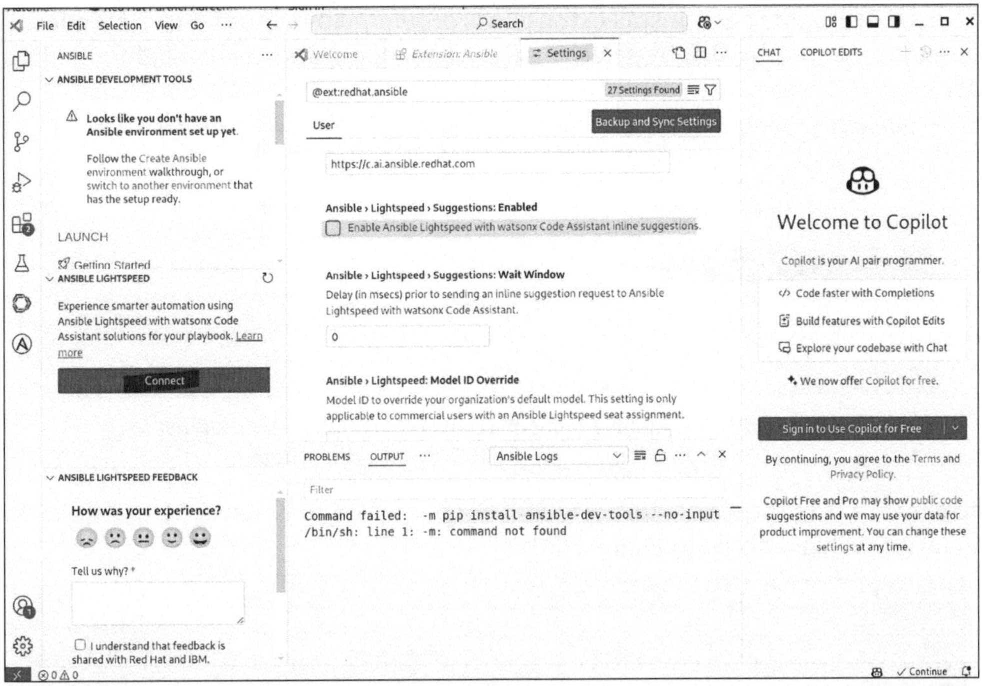

Figure 8.47: *Select the tick-box on the* **VS Code** *extension* **Settings** *tab for the "***Enable Ansible Lightspeed with watsonx Code Assistant inline suggestions***"*

We select `Backup and Sync Settings`, as shown in *Figure 8.48*:

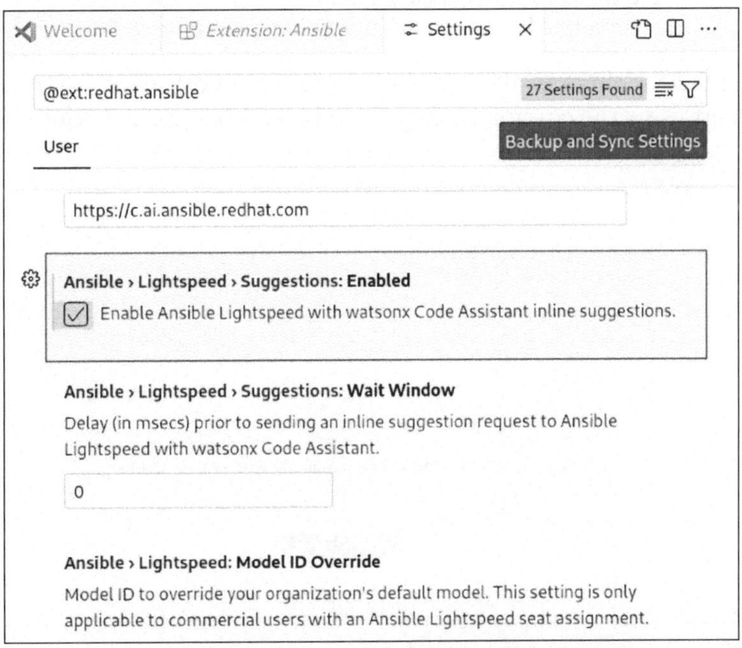

Figure 8.48: *We select* **Backup and Sync Settings**

The **`Ansible Lightspeed`** install extension is prompted by **`Visual Studio Code`** to be allowed access on the **IDE** by selecting the **`Allow`** command, as highlighted in *Figure* 8.49:

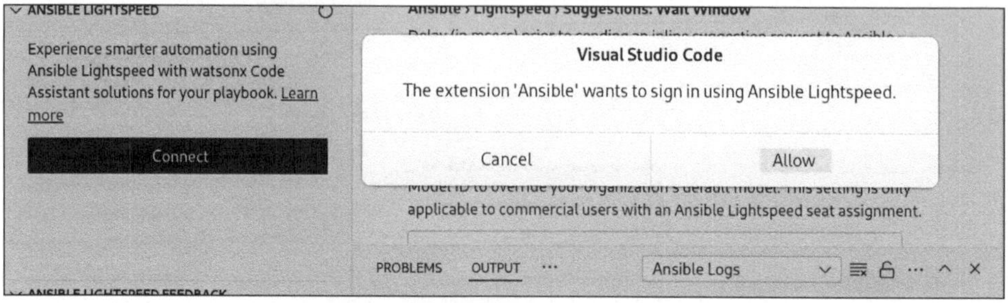

Figure 8.49: *The* ***Ansible Lightspeed*** *install extension is prompted to be given access on the* ***IDE*** *by selecting* ***Allow***

The **`Ansible Lightspeed`** external website is prompted to be opened, using the **`Open`** command, as highlighted in *Figure* 8.50:

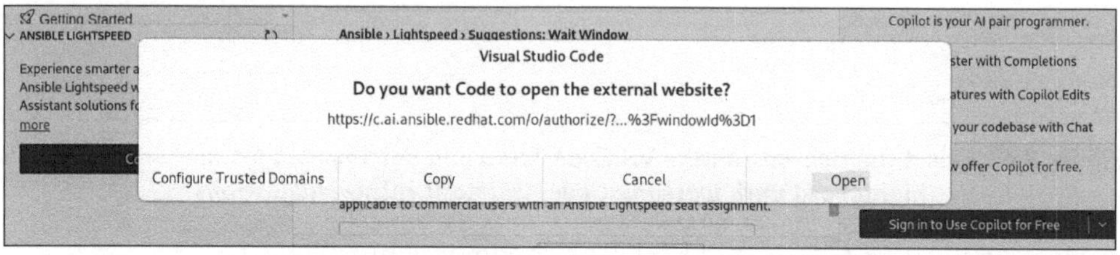

Figure 8.50: *The* ***Ansible Lightspeed*** *external website is prompted to be opened, using the* ***Open*** *command*

We are prompted to Log in to the **`Red Hat Ansible Lightspeed with IBM watsonx Code Assistant`** using the command, **`Log in with Red Hat`**, as highlighted in *Figure* 8.51:

Figure 8.51: *Log in to the* ***Red Hat Ansible Lightspeed with IBM watsonx Code Assistant***

The **`Authorize`** command is selected to allow the **`Red Hat Ansible Lightspeed`** for **VS Code** to read user information for the registration, as highlighted in *Figure 8.52*:

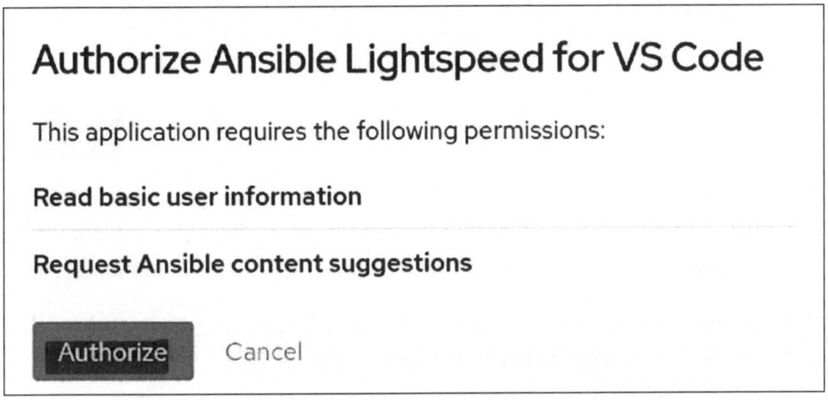

Figure 8.52:** The **Authorize** command is selected to allow the **Red Hat Ansible Lightspeed** for **VS Code

The **`Open Link`** command is selected as shown in *Figure 8.53*:

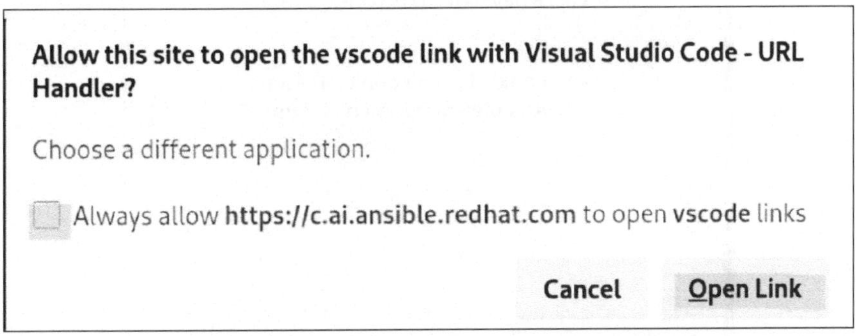

***Figure 8.53:** The **Open Link** command is selected*

The pop-up window allowed the URI listed to be opened, as shown in *Figure 8.54*:

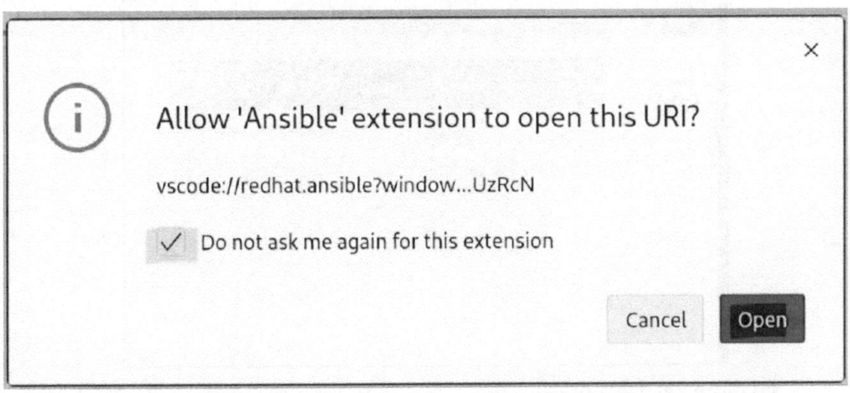

***Figure 8.54:** The pop-up window allowed the URI listed to be opened*

The **Login** command is selected to log into **Ansible Lightspeed**, as highlighted in *Figure 8.55*:

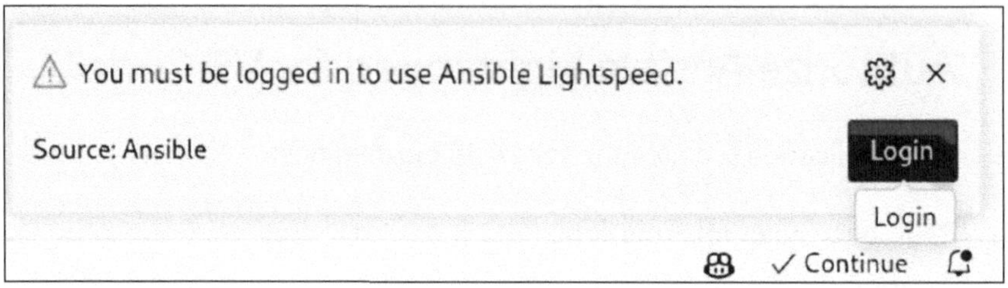

Figure 8.55: *The* ***Login*** *command is selected to log into* ***Ansible Lightspeed***

After logging in, we can select the **Generate a playbook** command in the **ANSIBLE LIGHTSPEED** dropdown as highlighted in *Figure 8.56*:

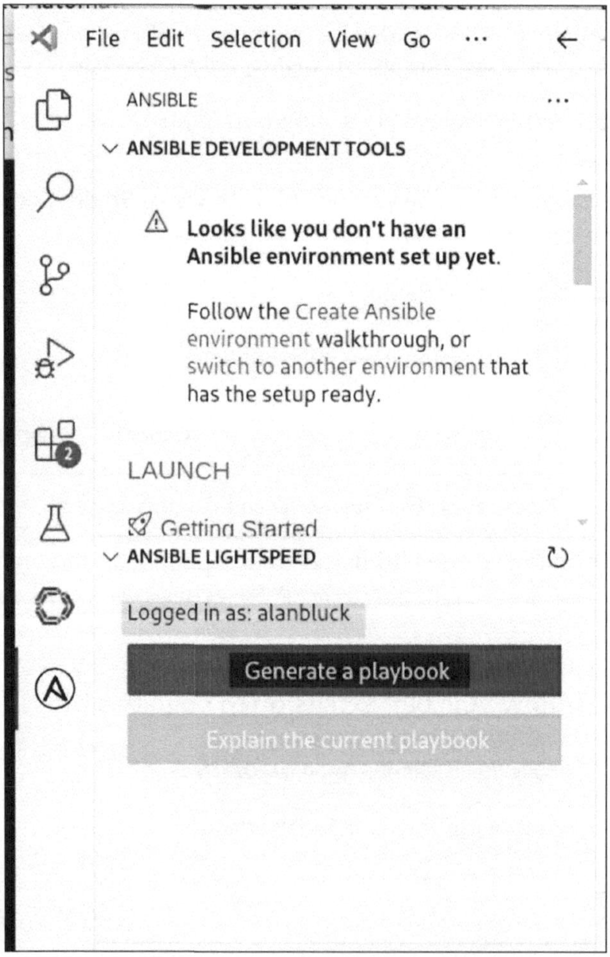

Figure 8.56: *After logging in, we can select the* ***Generate a playbook*** *command in the* ***ANSIBLE LIGHTSPEED***

The prompt entry command window for **`Ansible Lightspeed`** allows create requests to be entered, as highlighted in *Figure* 8.57:

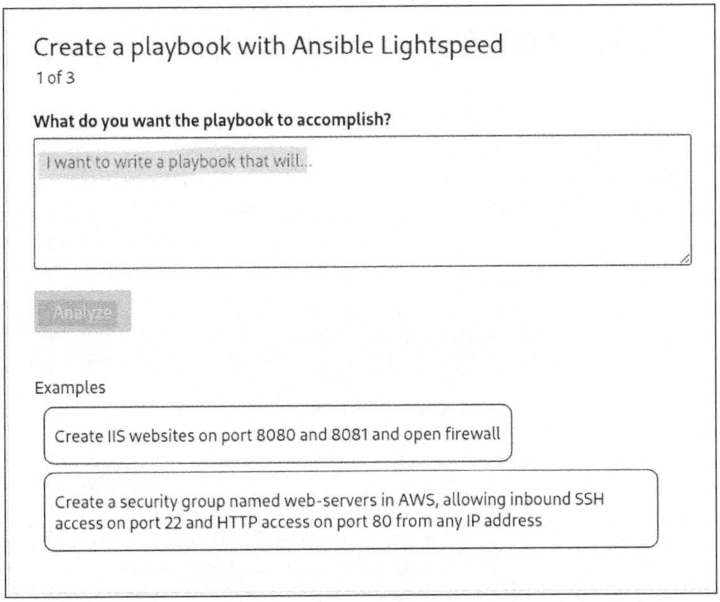

Figure 8.57: *The prompt entry command window for Ansible Lightspeed allows create requests to be entered*

After entering our request, we select the **`Analyze`** command, as highlighted in *Figure* 8.58:

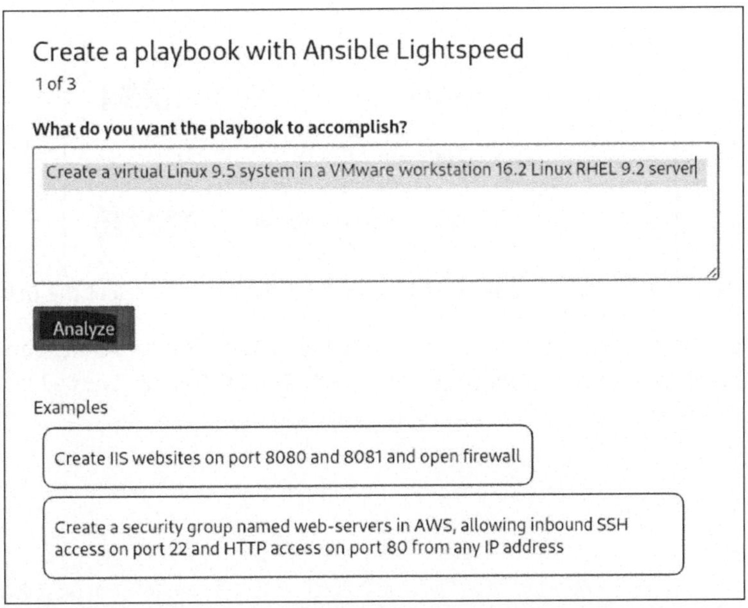

Figure 8.58: *After entering our request, we select the* **Analyze** *command*

The **Analyze** command returned a message indicating that we need to install **IBM watsonx Code Assistant** on the **VS Code IDE**, which we cover in this next section.

Installing the IBM watsonx Code Assistant

We need to install the **IBM watsonx Code Assistant**, and select the **Install** command, as highlighted in *Figure 8.59*:

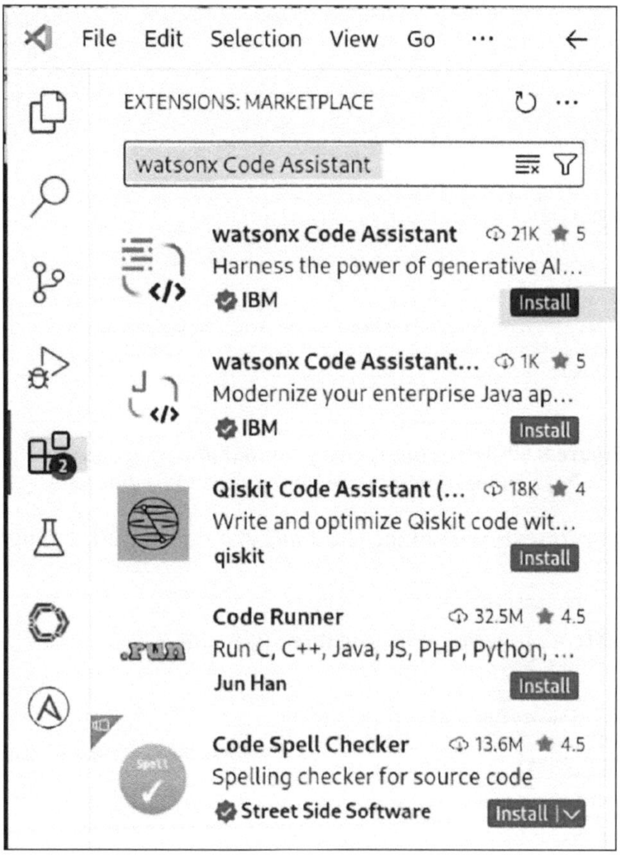

Figure 8.59: *We need to install the* **IBM watsonx Code Assistant** *, and select the* **Install** *command*

The **VS Code IDE** prompts us to trust the **IBM watsonx Code Assistant** publishers and install the extension, by selecting the **Trust Publisher & Install** command, as highlighted in *Figure 8.60*:

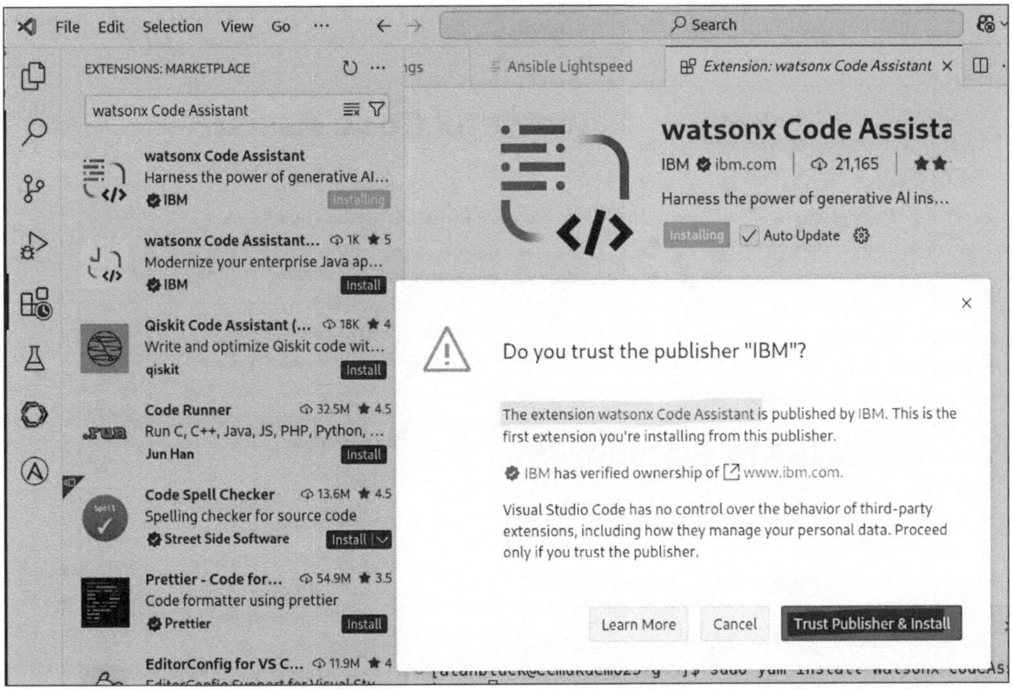

***Figure 8.60**: The **VS Code IDE** prompts us to trust the **IBM watsonx Code Assistant** publishers and install the extension by selecting the **Trust Publisher & Install** command*

The **`IBM watsonx Code Assistant`** extension is now installed on the **VS Code IDE**, as shown in *Figure 8.61*:

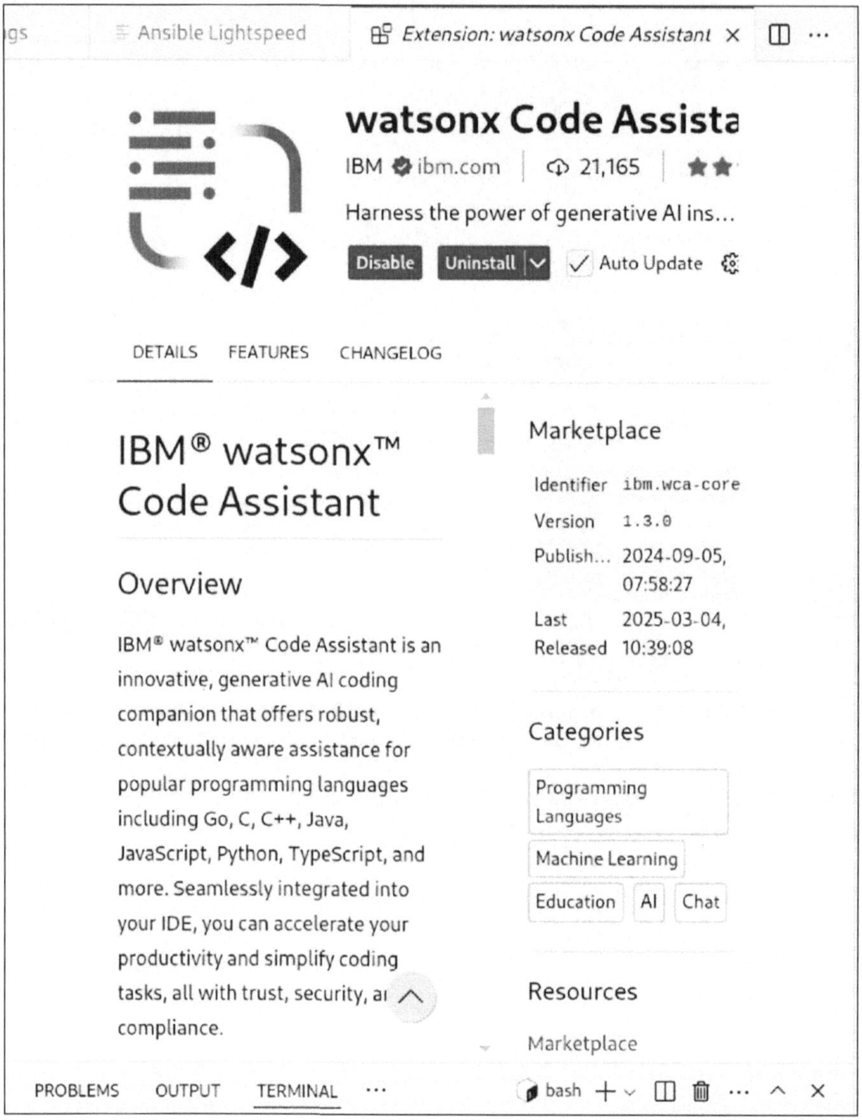

Figure 8.61:** The **IBM watsonx Code Assistant** extension is now installed on the **VS Code IDE

We can now access the **`IBM watsonx Code Assistant`**, by selecting the icon highlighted, then selecting the (free) **`Run with Ollama Service`** command (for the details of the use and architecture of **ollama**, see *Chapter 2*, *Granite 3.0's Architecture* and the section, **Ollama Architecture)**. Finally, select the highlighted **`Reload`** command, as illustrated in *Figure 8.62*:

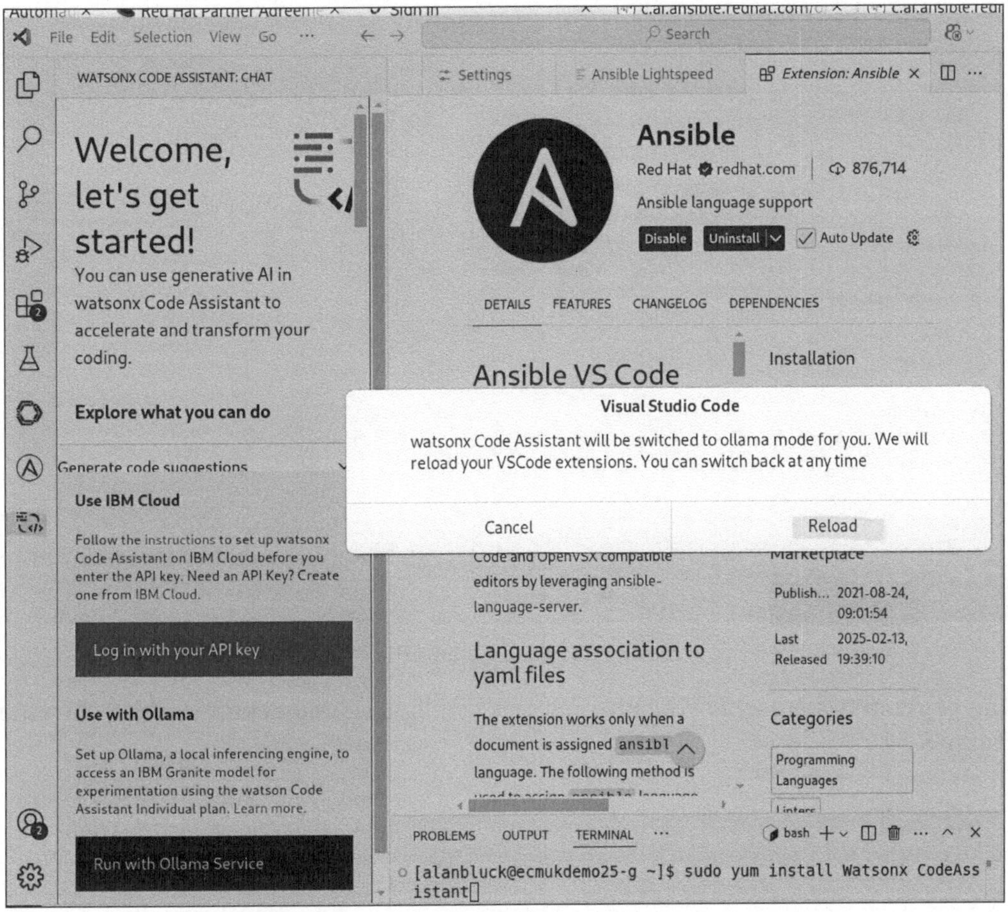

Figure 8.62: *We select the* **Run with Ollama Service** *command and then select the highlighted* **Reload** *command*

We can now create an **IBM Cloud API** key for the **VS Code IDE** use, following the **IBM Cloud** procedure for logging into our **https://cloud.ibm.com** account, as described in *Chapter 7, Deployment and Enterprise Integration*, in the Section **'Create Access Groups'** (*Figure* 7.40). This page is shown in *Figure* 8.63:

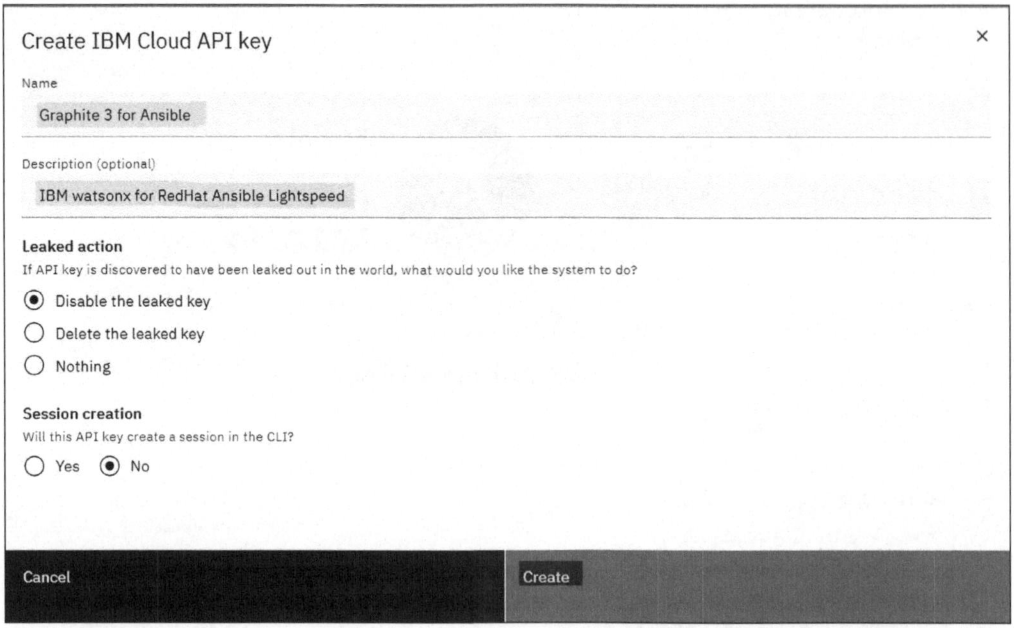

Figure 8.63: *We can now create an* **IBM Cloud API** *key for the* **VS Code IDE** *use*

The generated **API** key is copied using the highlighted **`Copy`** command, as shown in *Figure* 8.64:

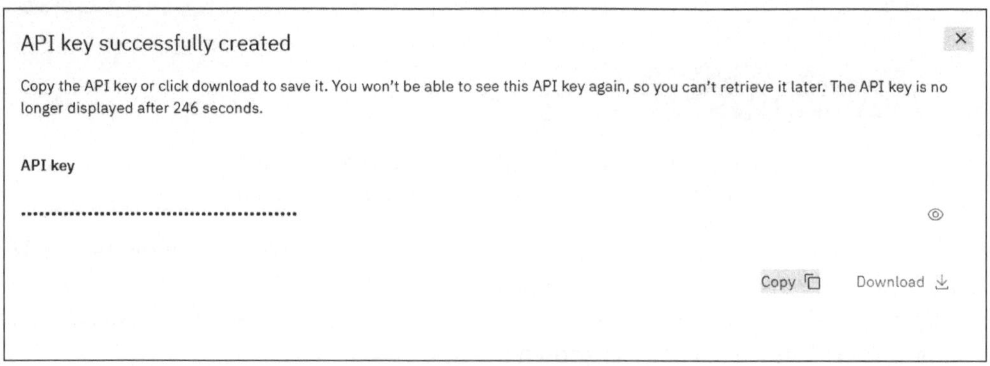

Figure 8.64: *The generated API key is copied using the highlighted Copy command*

Next, we can create an environment using the **`Create Ansible environment`** link, as highlighted in *Figure* 8.65:

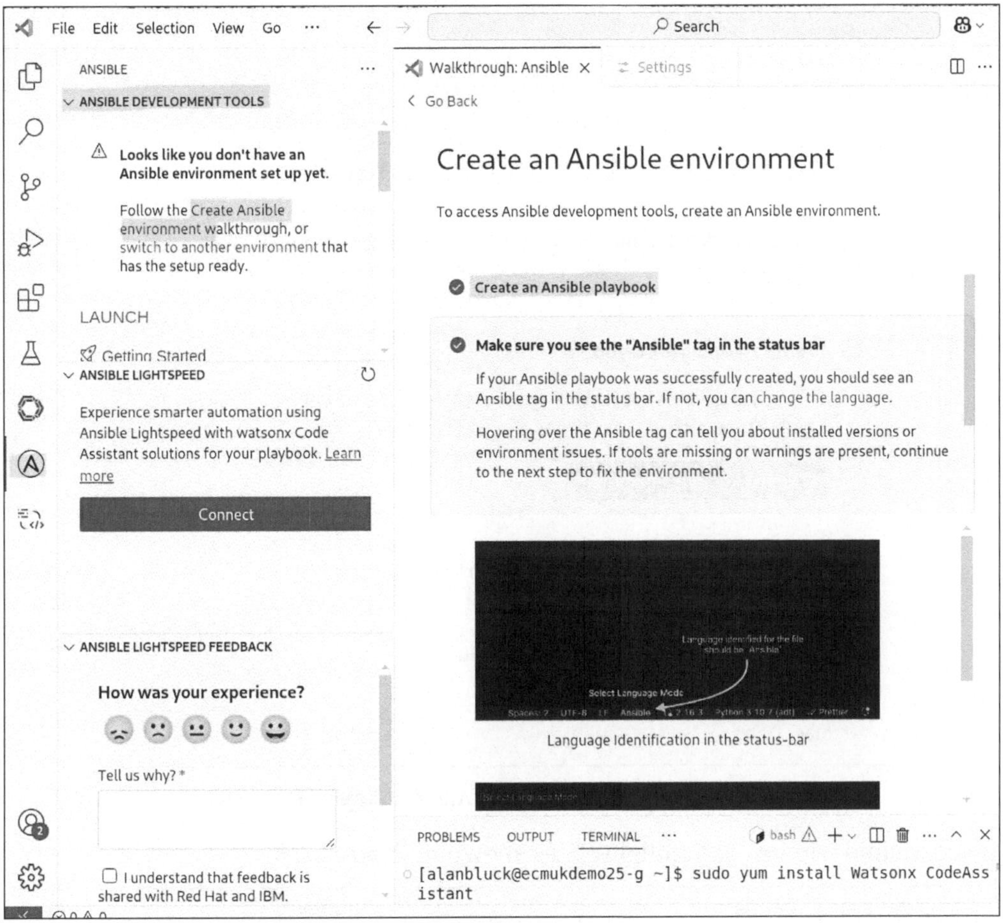

Figure 8.65: *We can create an environment using the* ***Create Ansible environment*** *link*

We select the **`Create Ansible Playbook`** command, as shown in *Figure 8.66*:

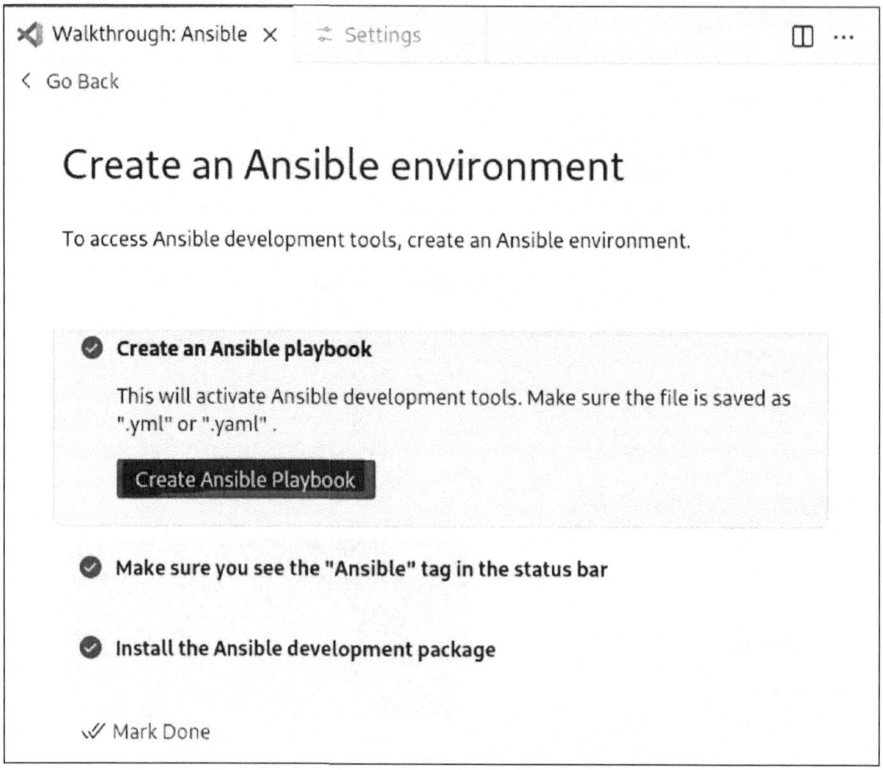

***Figure 8.66:** We select the **Create Ansible Playbook** command*

The command window is highlighted, as shown in *Figure* 8.67:

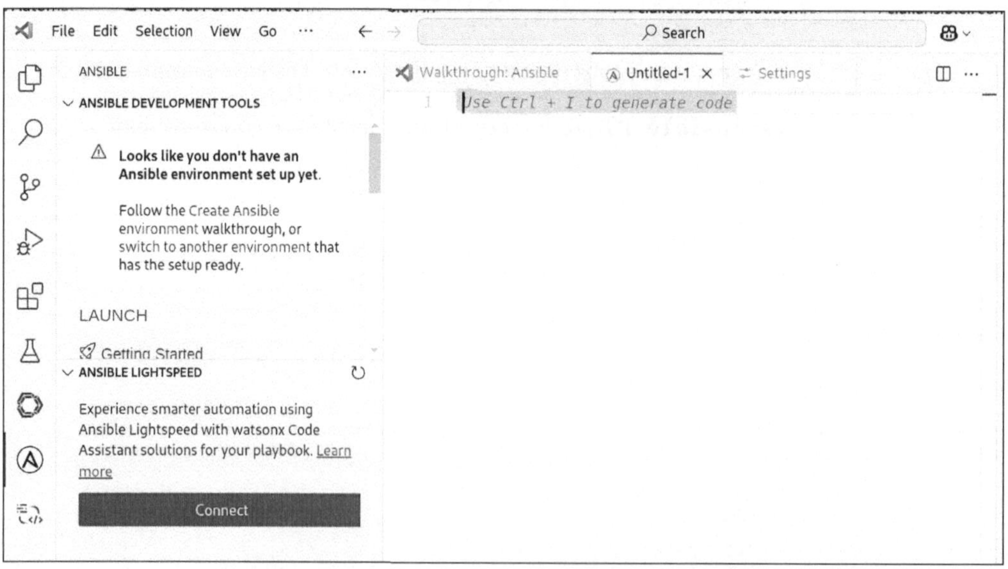

***Figure 8.67:** The command window is highlighted*

The **Right-mouse** click gives the **`Command Palette...`** menu which is selected, as highlighted to give the dropdown list of commands, as shown in *Figure 8.68*:

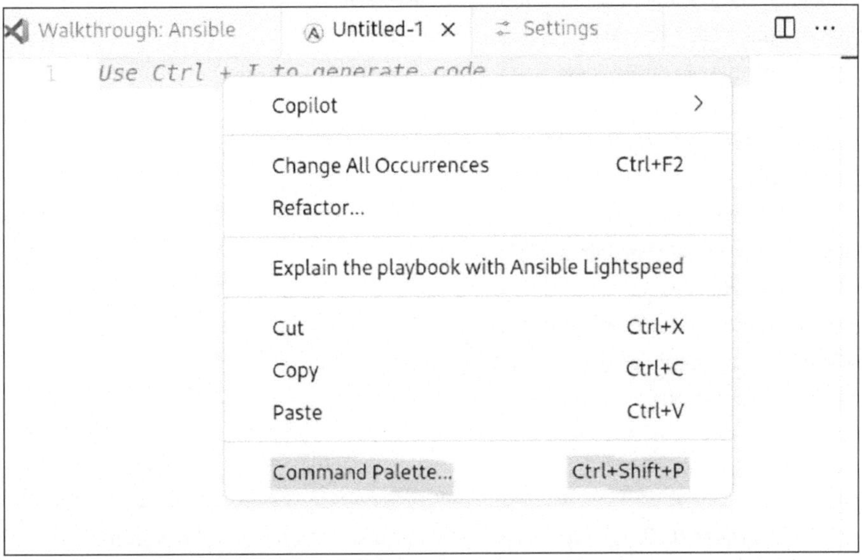

***Figure 8.68:** The **Right-mouse** click gives the **Command Palette...** menu which is selected*

The scrollable dropdown list of commands is shown in *Figure 8.69*:

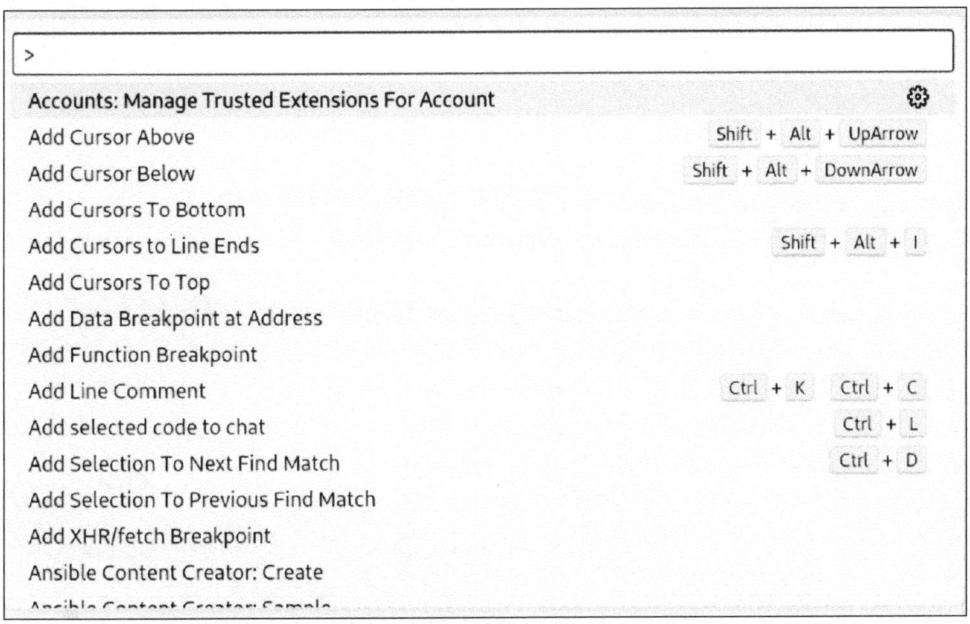

***Figure 8.69:** The scrollable dropdown list of commands is shown*

We can now scroll down to the command we want, as highlighted in *Figure 8.70*:

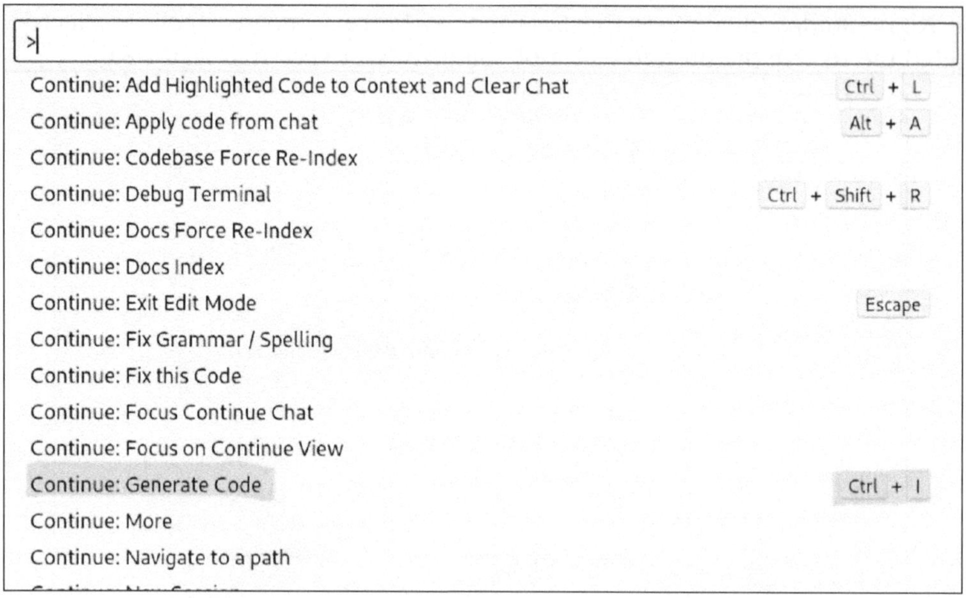

Figure 8.70: *We can now scroll down to the command we want*

We select **`Explain the playbook with Ansible Lightspeed`** menu, as highlighted in *Figure* 8.71:

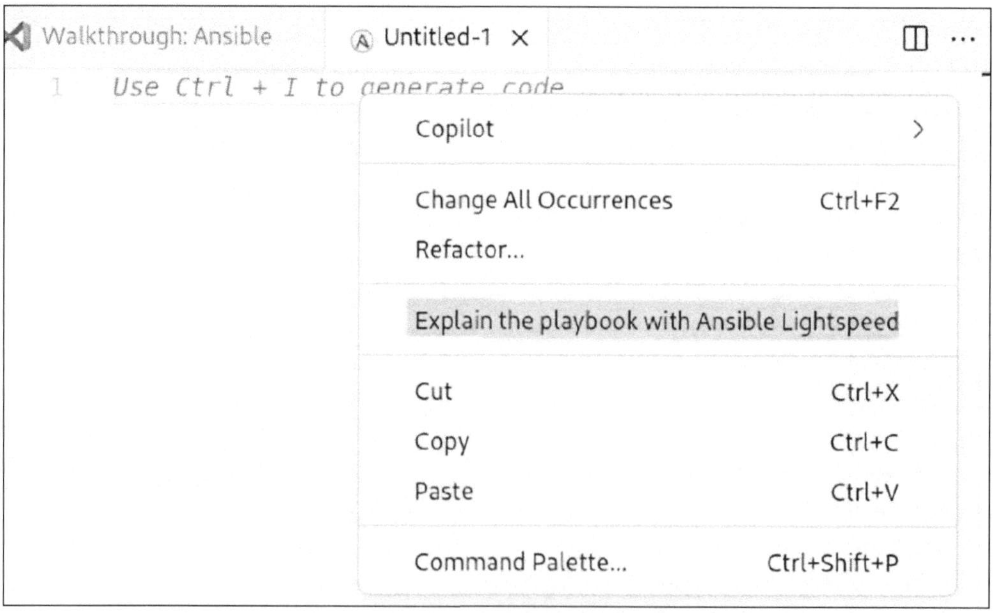

Figure 8.71: *We select* ***Explain the playbook with Ansible Lightspeed*** *menu*

The Ansible option appears at the top of the palette list as "**`recently used`**," as highlighted in *Figure* 8.72:

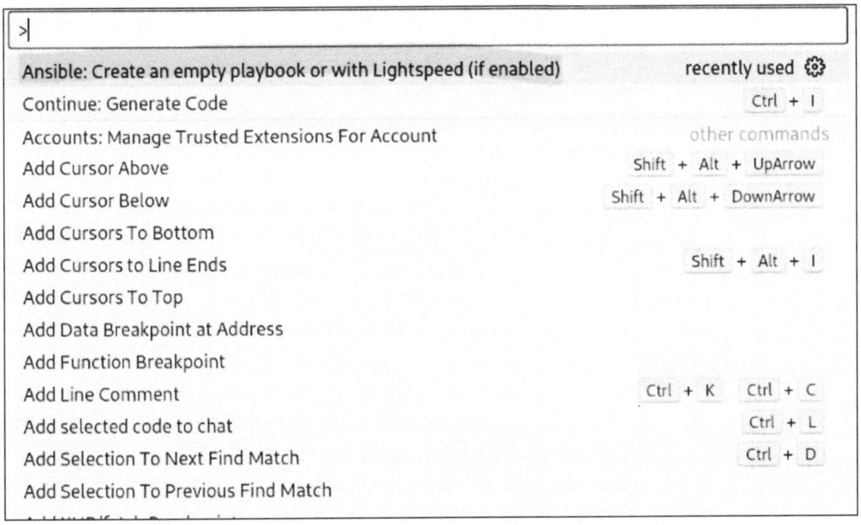

Figure 8.72: *The* **Ansible** *option appears at the top of the palette list as "recently used"*

Until prompt text is entered the **`Analyze`** command is grayed out, as shown in *Figure 8.73*:

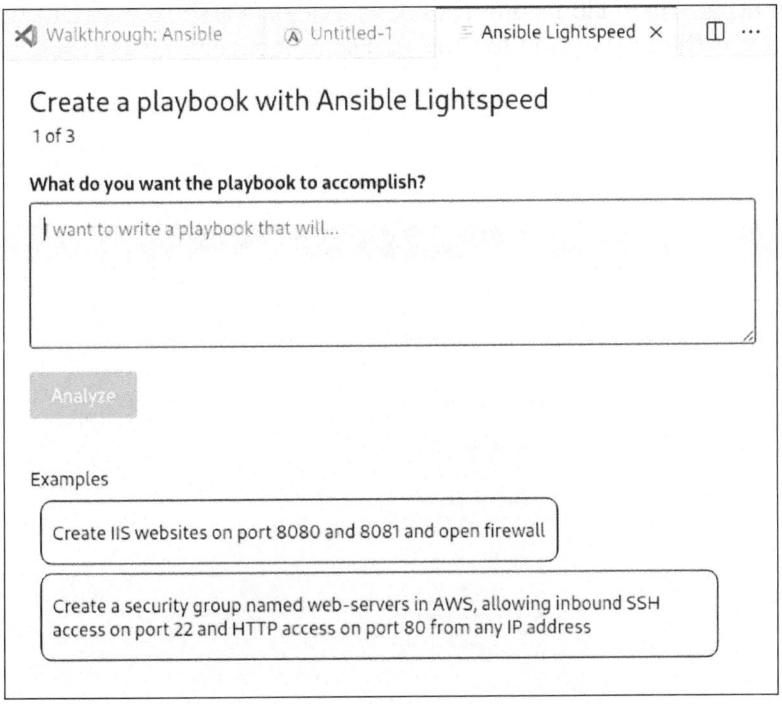

Figure 8.73: *Until prompt text is entered the* **Analyze** *command is grayed out*

The text is entered for Analysis, as shown in *Figure 8.74*:

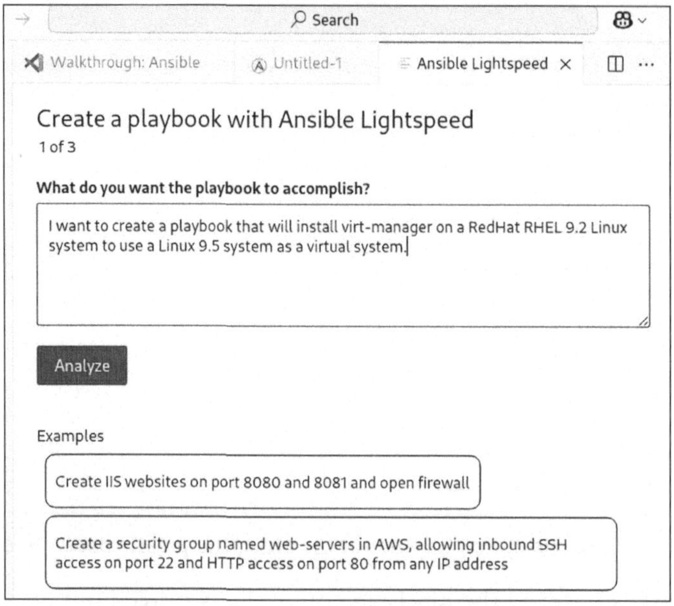

Figure 8.74: *The text is entered for Analysis*

We clicked https://cloud.ibm.com/catalog/services/watsonx-assistant to check the pricing plan for the free option for **`IBM watsonx Content Analytics`**, as shown in *Figure 8.75*:

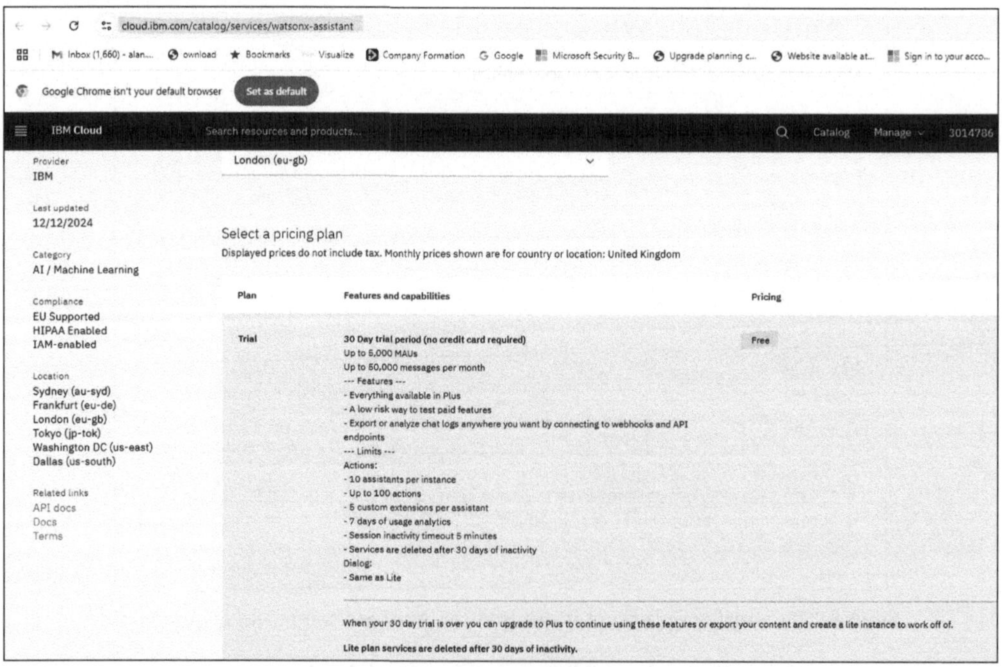

Figure 8.75: *We clicked on https://cloud.ibm.com/catalog/services/watsonx-assistant to check the pricing plan*

The **`IBM watsonx Assistant API key`** is copied, as shown in *Figure 8.76*:

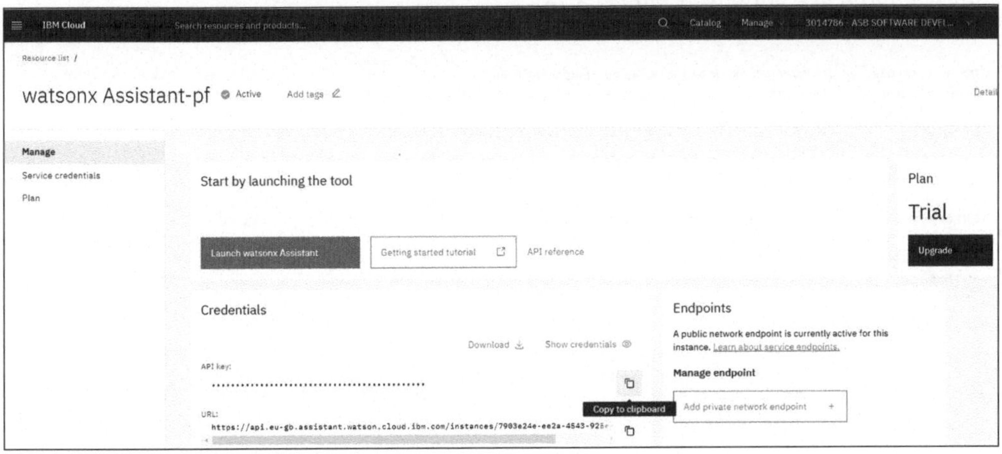

***Figure 8.76**: The **IBM watsonx Assistant API key** is copied*

The **`IBM watsonx Assistant`** allows the creation of chatBots, using a wizard, as shown in *Figure 8.77*:

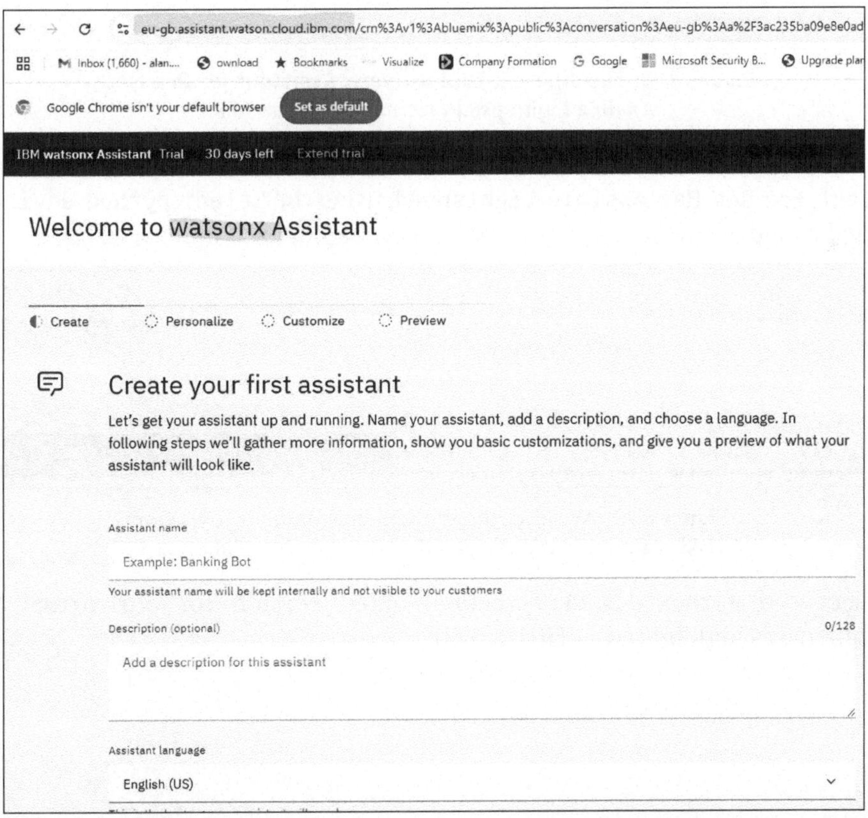

***Figure 8.77**: The **IBM watsonx Assistant** allows the creation of chatBots, using a wizard*

The different **IBM watsonx Assistant for Red Hat Ansible Lightspeed** pricing plans available are shown in *Figure 8.78*:

IBM watsonx Code Assistant for Red Hat Ansible Lightspeed Essentials	**The Essentials plan is only for tasks, no tuning capabilities.** • Pay for what you use. Tokens are offered in packages of 10,000 tokens (1 resource unit) which are consumed through generating Ansible tasks. • This plan requires the user to have entitlement to the Red Hat Ansible Automation Platform which is sold by Red Hat.	£1.5820282 GBP/Resource Unit (tokens)
IBM watsonx Code Assistant for Red Hat Ansible Lightspeed Standard	**The Standard plan includes both tasks and model tuning capabilities.** • 6.6 million tokens are included via the monthly instance fee. • Pay for what you use for additional tokens. Tokens are offered in packages of 10,000 tokens (1 resource unit) which are consumed through generating Ansible tasks. • Tune the model with your own data for tailor-made content recommendations that fit your enterprise standards. • For tuning-based Resource Unit pricing, each Resource Unit is equal to 1 hour spent in Tuning Studio. • This plan requires the user to have entitlement to the Red Hat Ansible Automation Platform which is sold by Red Hat.	£1.5820282 GBP/Resource Unit (tokens) £949.21692 GBP/Instance per month £395.50705 GBP/Resource Unit (tuning)
IBM watsonx Code Assistant for Z as a Service Essentials	**The Essentials plan includes everything you need to explain code and translate COBOL to Java.** • Each authorized user grants one user access to the service. • Each resource unit used for translation is equal to 150,000 tokens. This translates approximately 5,000 lines of code. • Each resource unit used for explanation is equal to 2,250,000 tokens. This explains approximately 150,000 lines of code. • IBM watsonx Code Assistant for Z as a Service is an add-on that requires watsonx Code Assistant for Z (on prem) as a prerequisite.	£7.1191269 GBP/Authorized User £12,094.00 GBP/Resource Unit

***Figure 8.78:** The different **IBM watsonx Assistant for Red Hat Ansible Lightspeed** pricing plans available*

We select the version of the **Python** environment to use with the **IBM watsonx Assistant for Red Hat Ansible Lightspeed**, using the **Select python environment** command found at the bottom of the screen, as highlighted in *Figure 8.79*:

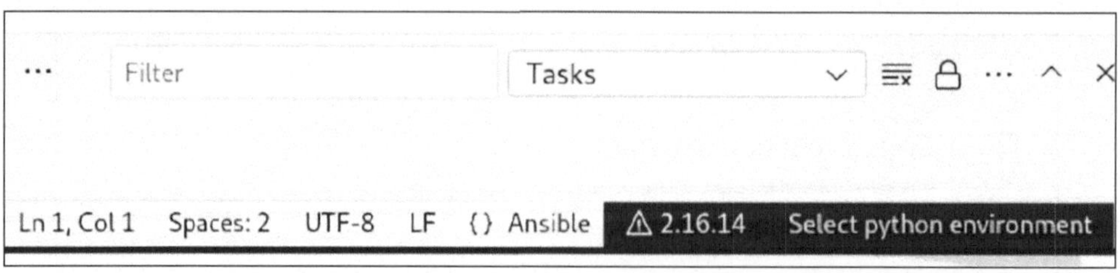

Figure 8.79:** We select the **Python** environment to use for **IBM watsonx Assistant for Red Hat Ansible Lightspeed

We select the **Python 3.11.9** recommended version for our virtual **Python** environment, as highlighted in *Figure 8.80*:

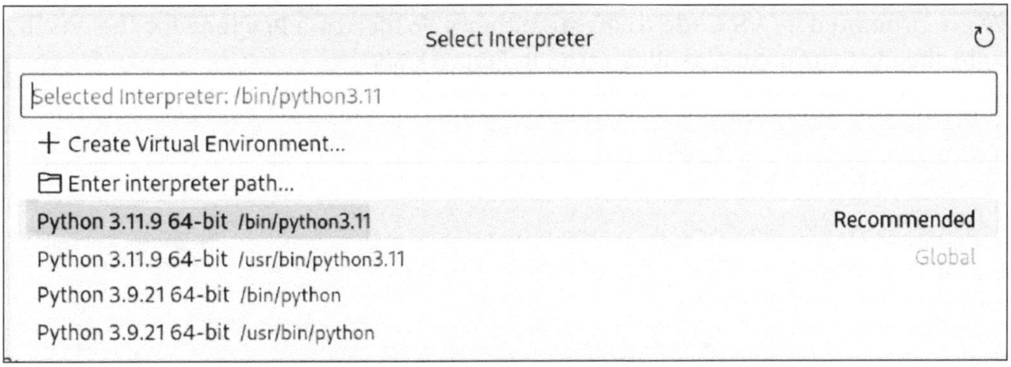

***Figure 8.80:** We select the **Python 3.11.9** recommended version for our virtual **Python** environment*

For individual users, **`IBM watsonx Code Assistant`** can access a local **`IBM Granite`** model

See: https://github.com/ibm-granite/watsonx-code-assistant-individual.

We can add an **`IBM Granite`** model using the "**`Add More Models`**" option, as shown in *Figure 8.81*:

***Figure 8.81:** We can add an **IBM Granite** model using the "**Add More Models**" option*

The pop-up window confirms the local workstation use, as shown in *Figure 8.82*:

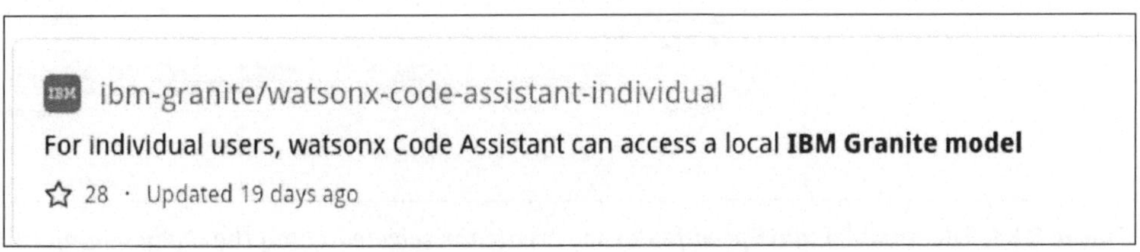

***Figure 8.82:** The pop-up window is shown below confirming the local workstation use*

We are prompted by **VS Code** to create either a **`Folder`** or a **`Project`** for the **`Ansible Lightspeed`** environment, as illustrated in *Figure* 8.83:

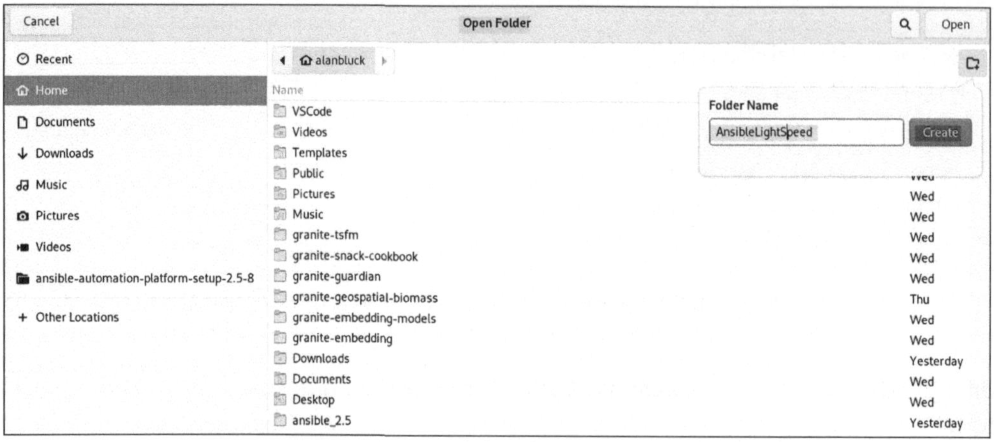

Figure 8.83: *We are prompted by* ***VS Code*** *to create a* ***Folder*** *or a* ***Project*** *for the* ***Ansible Lightspeed*** *environment*

The **`AnsibleLightSpeed`** folder we created is selected using the **`Open`** command, as highlighted in *Figure* 8.84:

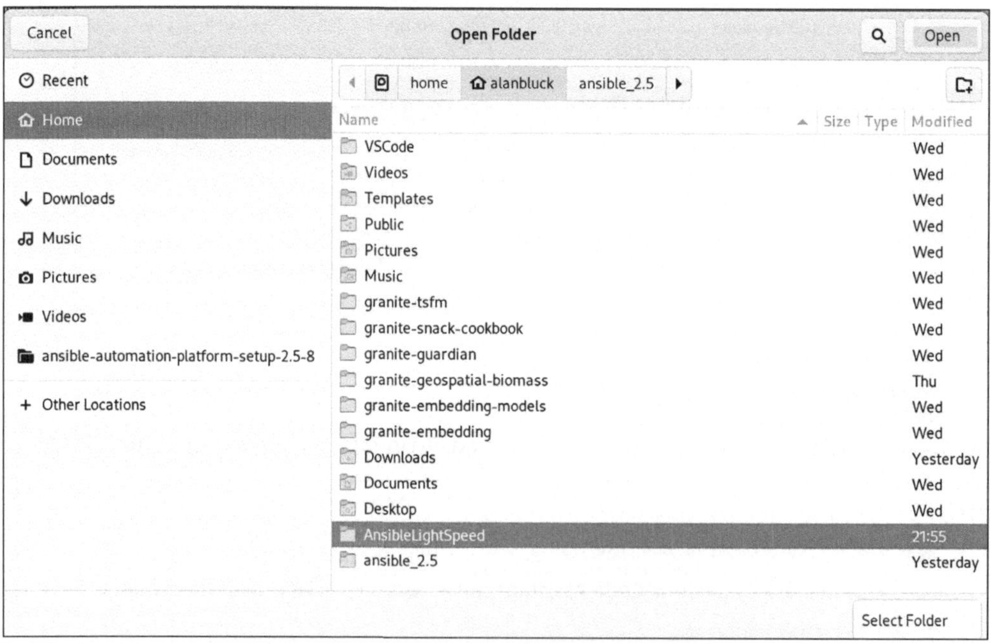

Figure 8.84: *The* ***AnsibleLightSpeed*** *folder we created is selected using the* ***Open*** *command*

We select the **`Ansible`** settings we need, as highlighted in *Figure* 8.85:

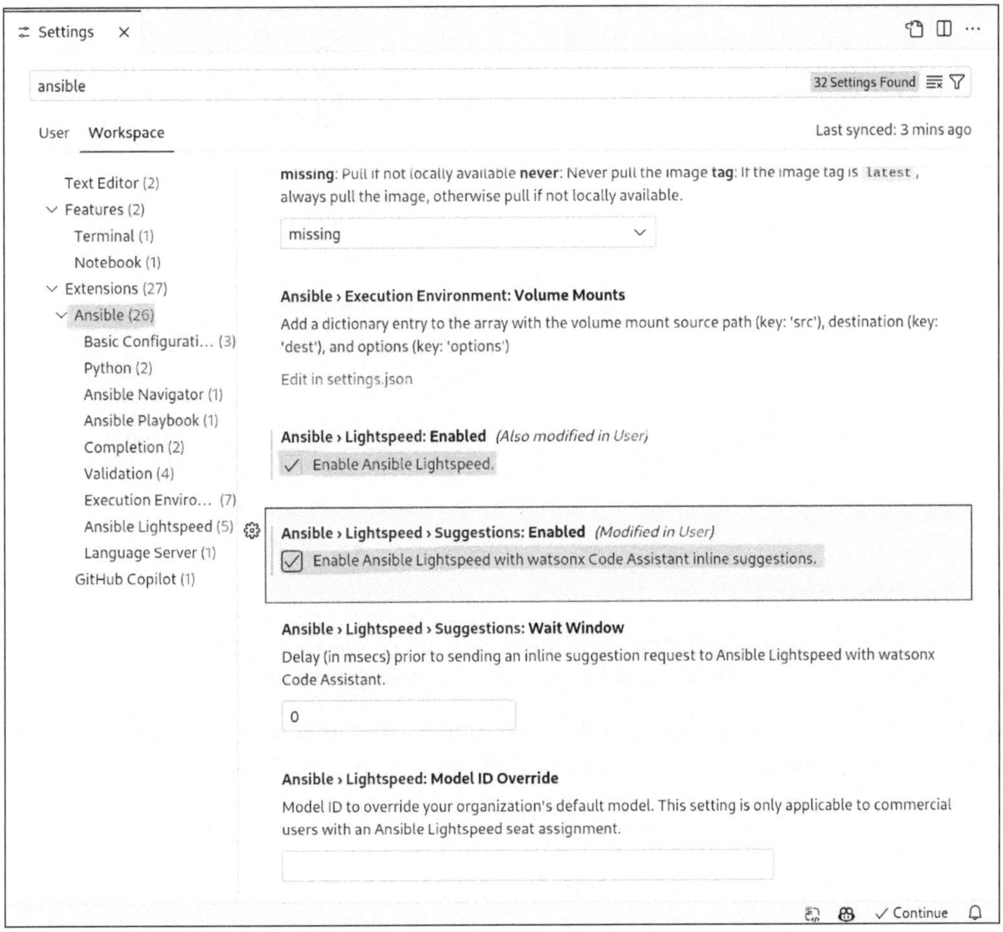

***Figure 8.85:** We select the **Ansible** settings we need, as highlighted*

After using **`File->Save`** we can select the **`Close  Saved`** menu option from the highlighted icon, as illustrated in *Figure* 8.86:

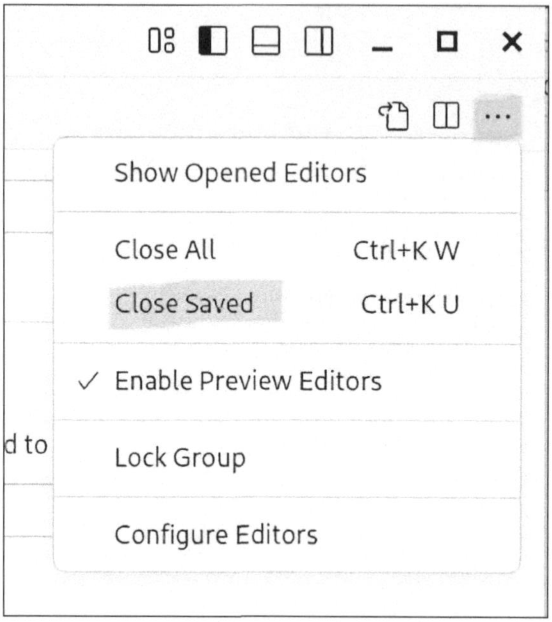

Figure 8.86: *After using* ***File->Save*** *we can select the* ***Close Saved*** *menu option from the Highlighted icon*

Next, we have to create the **Ansible** environment by selecting the "**Install Ansible development package**" command as highlighted in *Figure* 8.87:

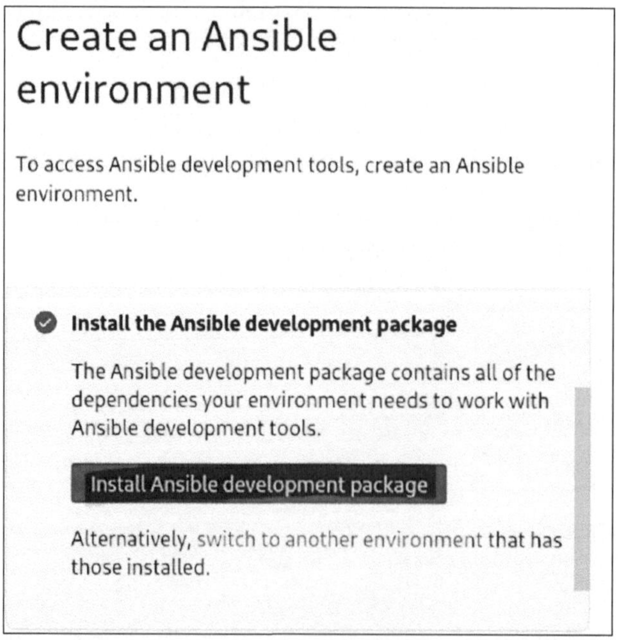

Figure 8.87: *We create the* ***Ansible*** *environment by selecting the "****Install Ansible development package****" command*

In the **VS Code TERMINAL** window, we entered the **Python** installer command:

```
pip install ansible-dev-tools --no-input
```

as highlighted in *Figure 8.88*:

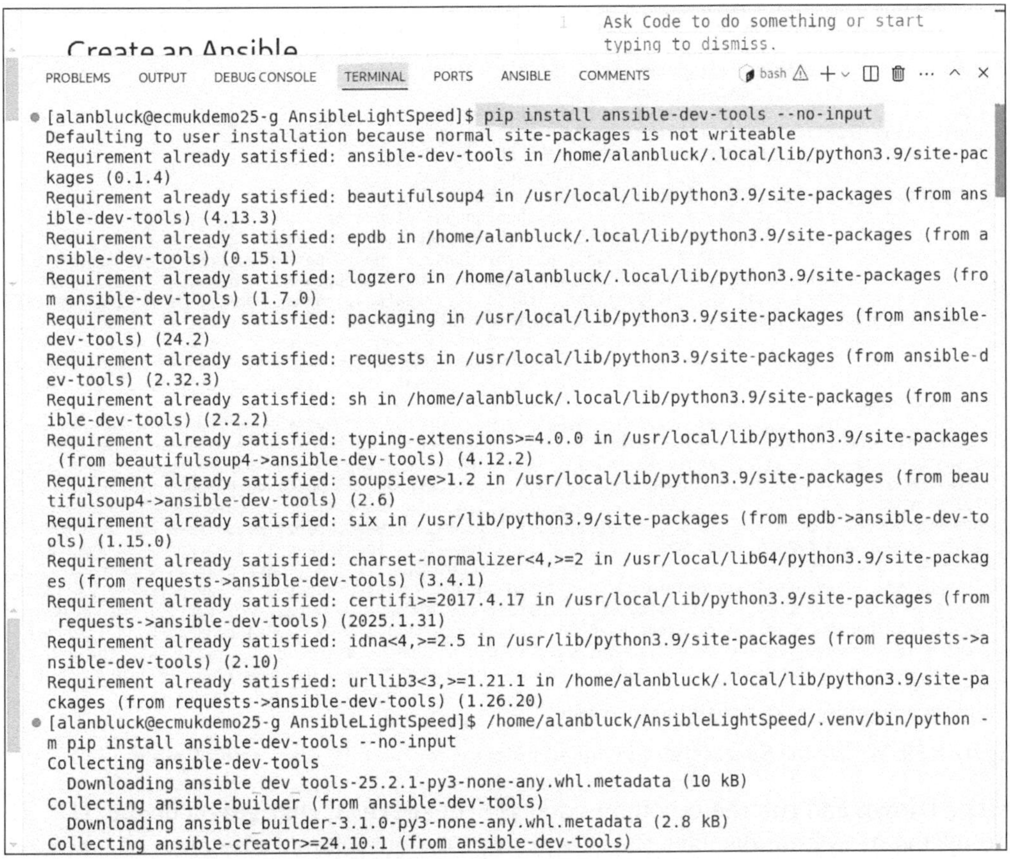

***Figure 8.88:** In the **VS Code TERMINAL** window, we entered the **Python** installer command*

After downloading over 50 supporting **Python** library files, we see the **Successfully installed** message, as highlighted in *Figure 8.89*:

Figure 8.89: *We see the* ***Successfully*** *installed message for over 50 supporting* ***Python*** *library files.*

We pull down and run the recommended **IBM Granite 3**, **granite-code:8b LLM**, and the ollama AI system displays the **>>>** prompt for questions to be entered, shown in *Figure 8.90*:

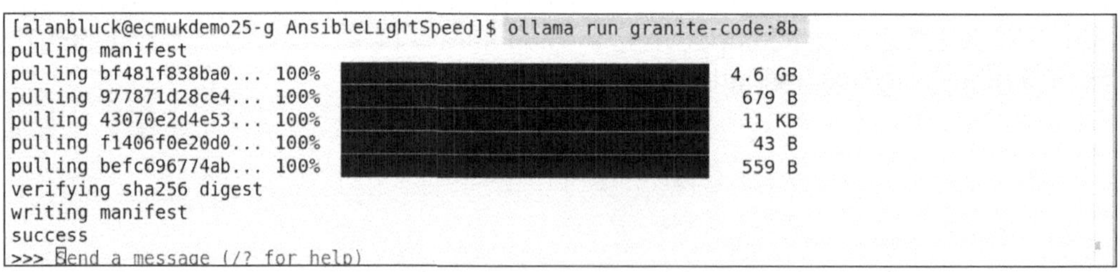

Figure 8.90: *We pull down and run the recommended* **IBM Granite 3**, ***granite-code:8b*** **LLM**

Now, we can ask the question for the Ansible playbook script, as follows:

```
>>> I want to create an Ansible playbook that will install virt-manager on a RedHat RHEL 9.2 Linux system to use a Linux 9.5 system as a virtual system
```

The response given was as shown in *Figure* 8.91:

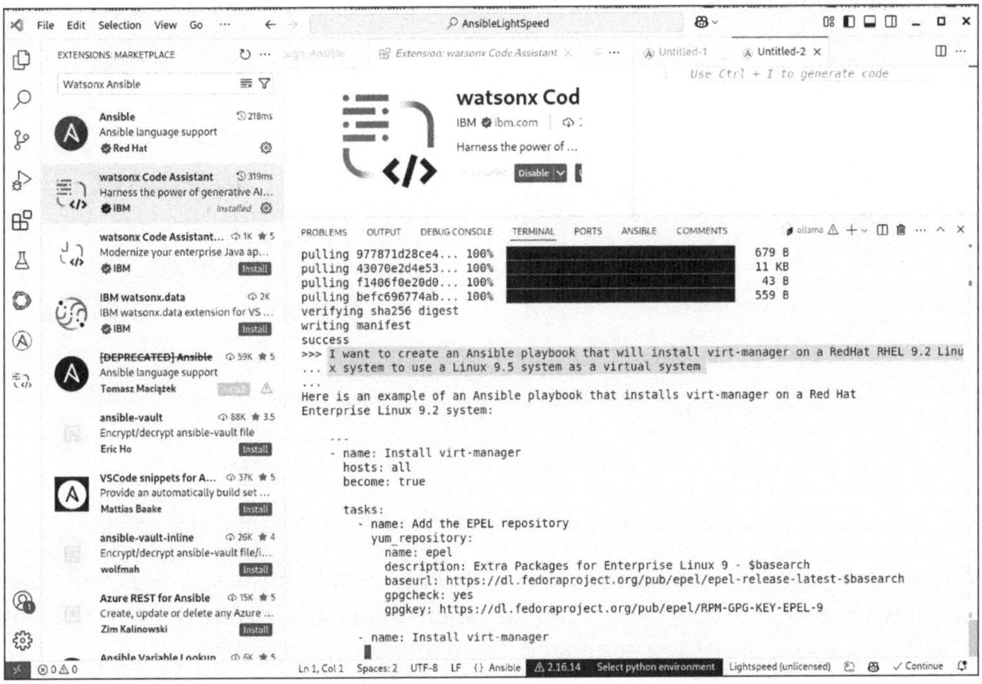

Figure 8.91: *Now, we can ask the question for the* **Ansible** *playbook script*

The full **AI** text response for the **`Ansible playbook`** code, is shown in *Figure* 8.92:

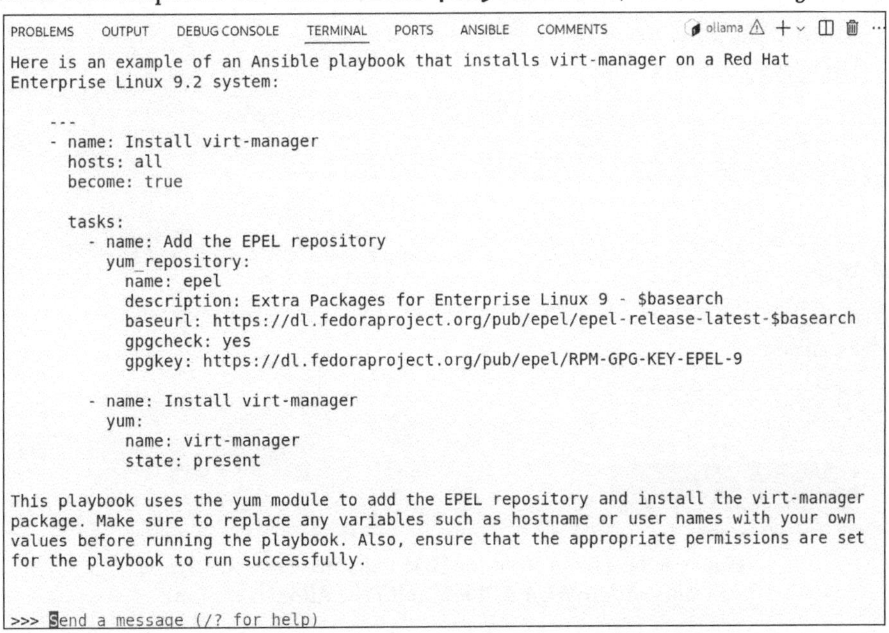

Figure 8.92: *The full* **AI** *text response for the* **Ansible playbook** *code*

We want to sign in to the **IBM watsonx Code Assistant AI** using **IBM watsonx**, **IBM Cloud**, chat extension, as shown in *Figure* 8.93:

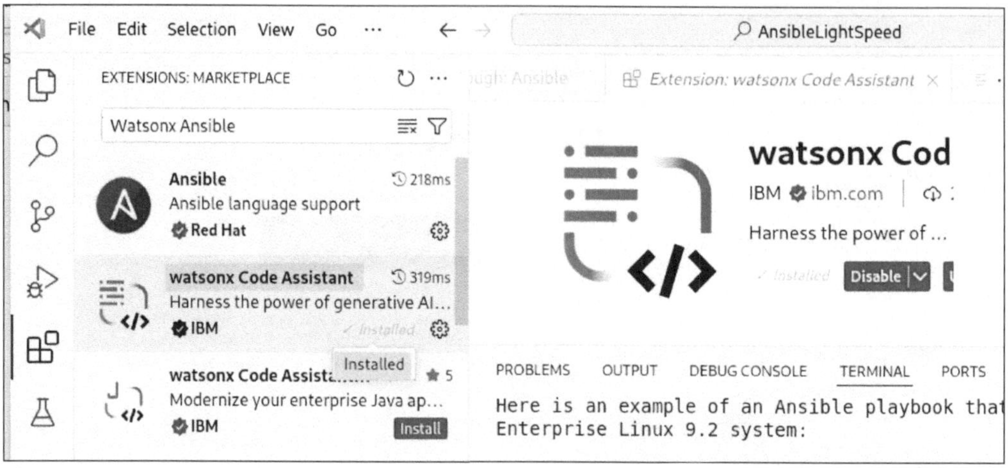

Figure 8.93: *We want to sign in to the* ***IBM watsonx Code Assistant*** *chat extension*

After selecting the **Log in with your API key** command in the **Use IBM Cloud** section, we are prompted to allow **IBM watsonx Code Assistant** to sign in using a **WCA API** key, using the **Allow** command, highlighted in *Figure* 8.94:

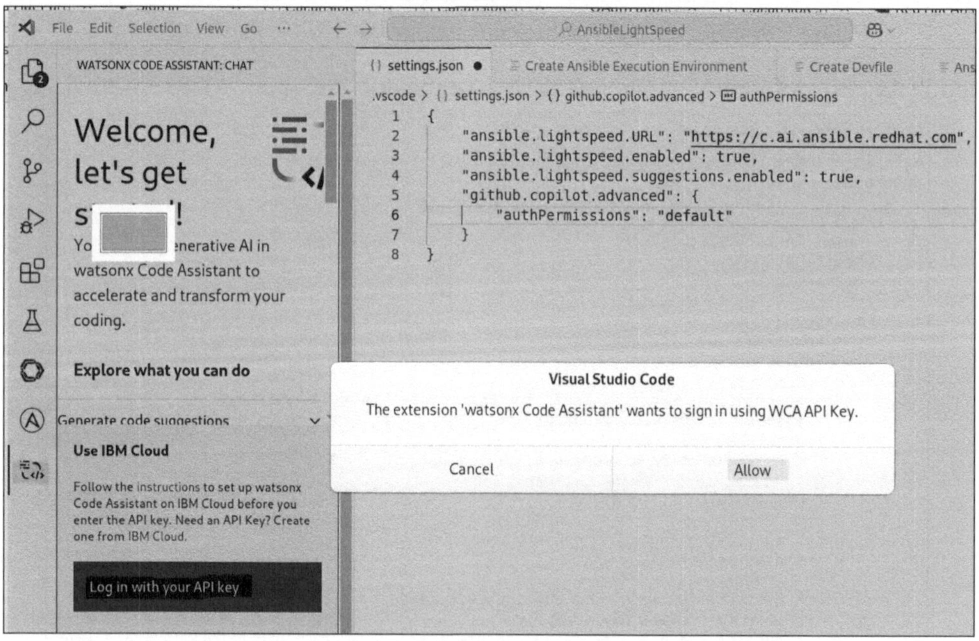

Figure 8.94: *The prompt for* ***IBM watsonx Code Assistant*** *to sign with a* ***WCA API*** *key, with the* ***Allow*** *command*

The **API key** we copied earlier (see the section, "**Installing the IBM watsonx Code Assistant**", *Figure 8.63: We can now create an IBM Cloud API key for the VS Code IDE use*) is pasted into the prompt window, as shown in *Figure 8.95*:

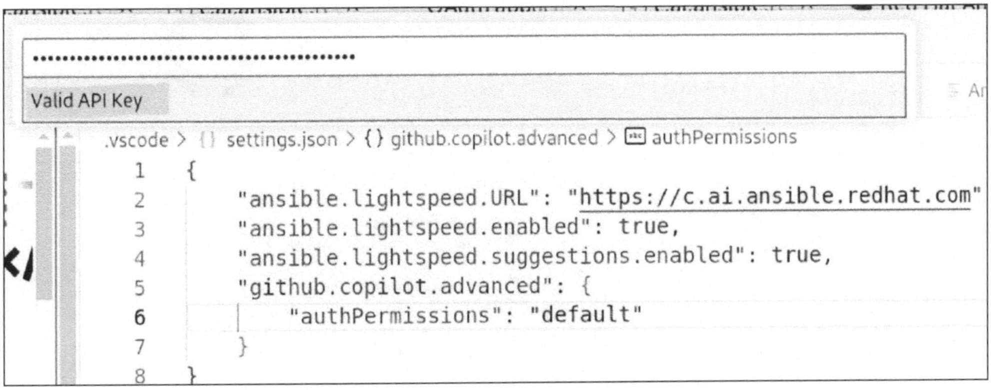

Figure 8.95: *The* ***API key*** *we copied earlier is pasted into the prompt window*

Ansible code bot

Ansible code bot can be used to validate the **GitHub** repository development code for a company. In order to use **Red Hat Ansible Automation Platform** with the use of the **Ansible code bot,** you must have an active subscription to **Red Hat Ansible Automation Platform.** For this system, **IBM watsonx Code Assistant** is not required to use the **Ansible code bot**.

The **Ansible code bot** scans any existing content collections, roles, and playbooks hosted in the **GitHub** repositories. It creates pull requests if it detects changes required for improving the code for best practices or any quality improvement recommendations.

Ansible code bot scans development code repositories to recommend code quality improvements. The **Ansible code bot** automatically submits pull requests to the repository, providing alerts to the repository owner and recommending changes to the code content. The Ansible code bot can be configured to scan the existing Git repositories (both public and private).

Ansible code bot access can be found at the **GitHub** link:

https://bot.ai.ansible.redhat.com/console

(The log on prompt requires a valid **GitHub** username and password.)

The first logon prompts us to **Authorize Ansible code bot** for access to our **GitHub** repositories, by selecting the **Authorize Ansible** command, as shown in *Figure 8.96*:

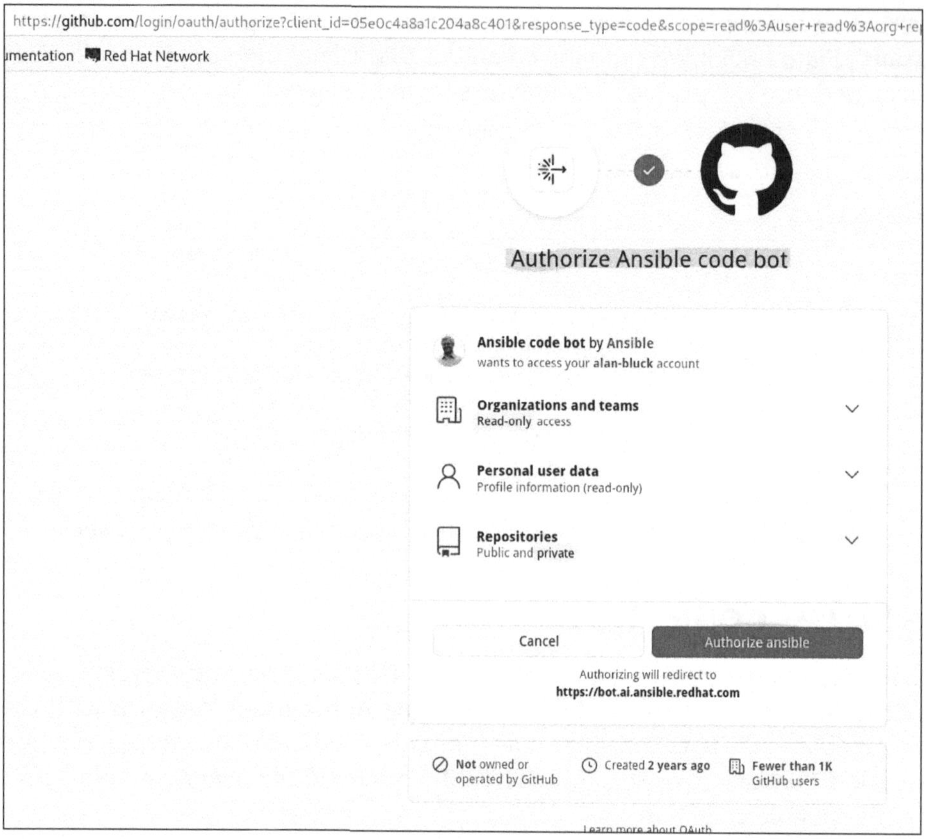

Figure 8.96: *The first logon prompts us to* **Authorize Ansible code bot** *for access to our* **GitHub** *repositories*

The Repositories list (if any are available) displays a list of repositories that can be selected for scanning. The **`GitHub`** page is shown in *Figure 8.97*:

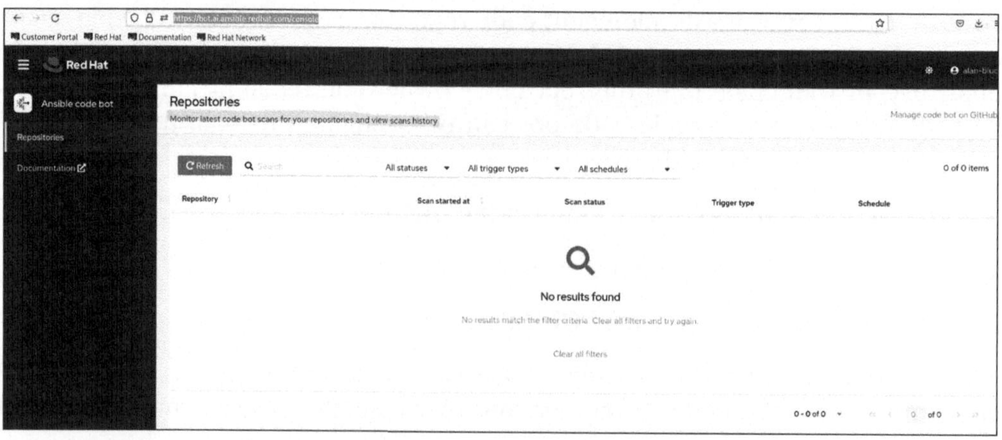

Figure 8.97: *The Repositories list (if any) displays a list of repositories that can be selected for scanning*

Customizing the Models

Since every enterprise is different, **IBM watsonx Code Assistant** (**WCA**) allows users to customize the **AI** model output to an enterprise's standard `Ansible Playbook` formats. This allows for personalized code recommendations that are a better fit for a business' unique requirements and should follow the programming standards set within the enterprise.

In this example, the enterprise has its own set of **Ansible Playbooks** that leverage the preferred cloud provider and specific Ansible Modules to manage a Red Hat OpenShift cluster.

The full example is described in the link:

https://ibm.github.io/WCA-AnsibleLightspeed-L3/customizing/#ii-model-customization

("*Task Description Tuning and Model Customization - IBM watsonx Code Assistant for Red Hat Ansible Lightspeed - Technical Sales Level 3*")

Open the `create-openshift-cluster-ibm-cloud.yml` Playbook located within the Model Customization subdirectory of the hands-on lab templates. The full directory address, as well as the **Playbook code**, are encapsulated in the following code block:

```
---
- name: Deploy infrastructure
  hosts: all
  tasks:
    - name: Create an OpenShift cluster
```

Note: IBM Ansible Lightspeed *and* **IBM watsonx Code Assistant** (**WCA**) *will only generate code recommendations for* **Ansible Playbooks** *and* **YAML** *files.* **VS Code** *will usually auto-detect the programming language of the document you're working with, but on occasion, you may need to manually specify the language. Even if working with a* **YAML** *file, you'll still need to specify the language mode as* **IBM Ansible**, *in order for the* **Lightspeed** *plugin to engage.*

To set the language mode correctly:

- *In the bottom-right corner of the* **VS Code** *interface, hover over the* ***Select Language Mode toggle***
- *A console will appear at the top of* **VS Code** *with a drop-down list of options.*
- *Click* **Ansible** *from the suggested languages, or enter the text yourself and hit Enter*
- *Confirm that the* `Select Language Mode` *toggle in the bottom-right corner displays* ***Ansible.***

The full lab workshop instructions can be found in the preceding reference link.

Content Source Matching

Another very useful capability within **IBM watsonx Code Assistant** (WCA) is **`Content Source Matching`** (often referred to as "*code explainability*"), which attempts to match **`AI-generated code`** suggestions to the training data and sources that were utilized in generating the suggested **Ansible** Task code.

These code attribution suggestions are created using a **k-NN** (**'K-Nearest Neighbors'**) see

https://www.ibm.com/topics/knn#:~:text=Next%20steps-,K%2DNearest%20Neighbors%20Algorithm,of%20an%20individual%20data%20point.

This is the algorithm that examines **Ansible Galaxy** and training data repositories in search of the nearest related content to the **AI-generated** code suggestions.

This is further described in the link:

https://ibm.github.io/WCA-AnsibleLightspeed-L3/source-matching-post-processing/#ii-content-source-matching

1. To enable **`Content Source Matching`** capabilities within **`IBM watsonx Code Assistant`**, navigate to the main menu bar for **`VS Code`** and select the menu **`View`** > **`Open View...`**

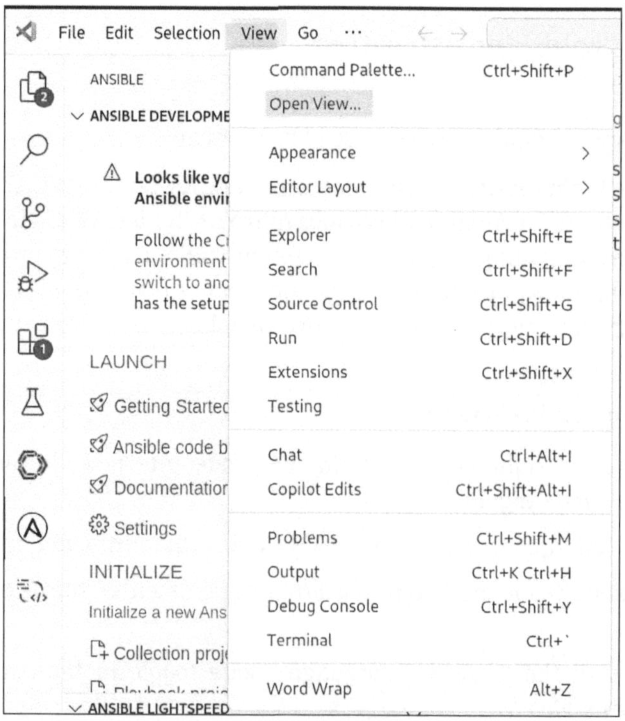

Figure 8.98: *Select the menu* **View** > **Open View...**

2. The console along the top of the **VS Code** interface is now activated and awaiting a prompt. Type **view Training** to display **Lightspeed Training Matches** and hit *Enter* to confirm the selection, as illustrated in *Figure 8.99*:

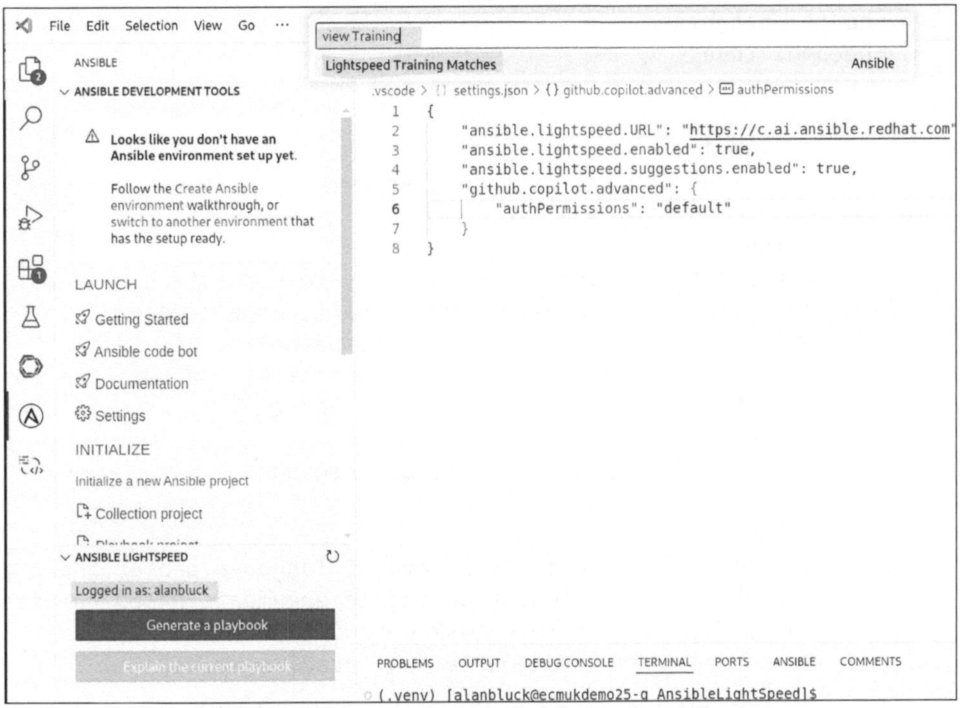

***Figure 8.99**: Type **view Training** to display **Lightspeed Training Matches** and hit **Enter** to confirm*

After making this configuration change to **VS Code**, all requests for **WCA** to generate code recommendations will now open a panel at the bottom of the **VS Code** interface.

- It is under the **Ansible** tab that **content source matching** results will be displayed
- Other tabs are also displayed for the other options: **Output**, **Debug Console**, **Terminal**, **Ports**, and **Comments**

3. Open the **install_pgsql-single-task.yml** file from the **Ansible Playbook**, which is included within the **ansible-wca-demo-kit** directory. The full location of the Playbook, as well as the contents, are available in the following example code:

```
~/Documents/ansible-wca-demo-kit/install and configure PostgreSQL
and PGAdmin container/install_pgsql-single-
```

The code suggested by the **Red Hat** tutorial was as follows:

```
---
- name: Configure Database servers
  hosts: databases
  become: true

  tasks:
      # TASK 1
      # - name: Install postgresql-server

      # TASK 2
      # Ansible Lightspeed used an easy-to-understand natural
language prompt and suggested the correct, more complex
PostgreSQL CLI command to initiate the database.
      # Ansible Lightspeed used best practices and kept the task
idempotent by including creates: /var/lib/pgsql/data/postgresql.
conf in the suggestion.
      # - name: Run postgresql setup command

      # TASK 3
      # Ansible Lightspeed used natural language prompt and added
state: started and enabled: true module arguments based on Start
and enable... in the Ansible task description.
      # - name: Start and enable postgresql service
```

(We used the **GALAXY.yml** file, found in the path, **/home/alanbluck/ansible_2.5/ansible-automation-platform-setup-2.5-8/collections/ansible_collections/community.postgresql-2.4.3.info/**)

4. Generate a code recommendation for the task on **a new line** by placing your cursor at the end of the line and selecting the *Enter* key, shown in *Figure 8.100*:

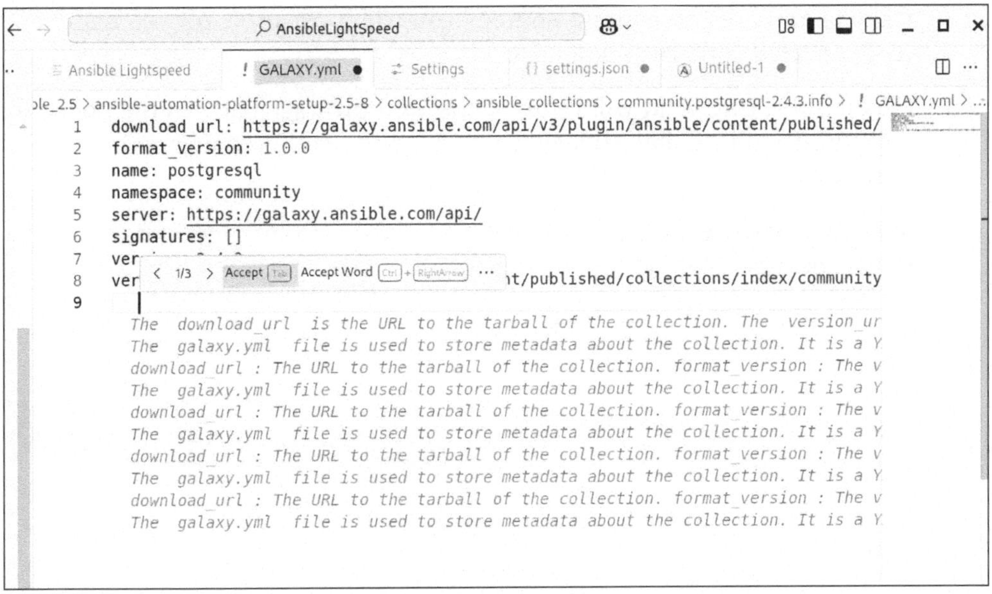

Figure 8.100: *Generate a code recommendation for the task on* ***a new line*** *by placing your cursor at the end of the line and selecting the* ***Enter*** *key*

- Notice the code attribution details associated with this recommendation, which should appear under the **`Ansible`** tab at the bottom of the **VS Code** interface once the code recommendation is accepted with **`Tab`**.
- You need to **`Accept`** the AI-generated code suggestions (using the **`Tab`** key) *before* the Ansible content source matching tab will provide details about the code's origins
- `---`
- `- name: Install postgresql-server`
- `  ansible.builtin.package:`
- `    name: postgresql-server`
- `    state: present`

5. The three most likely content sources used in training the **WCA** model–which produced the AI-generated code recommendations–are listed within the Ansible **tab**. Remember that these code attribution suggestions are created using a **k-NN** algorithm that searches **Ansible Galaxy** repositories for the nearest related content to the **AI**-generated code suggestions.

   Clicking the arrow icon to the left of each **attribution** will expand further details about the source. Information about the **URL, Path, Data Source, License**, and **Score** are displayed (where available) under each listing. Red Hat-certified and maintained collections, as well as contributors to open source projects on **Ansible Galaxy**, are the primary sources for the **Ansible Lightspeed** model training and are the content sources you will most probably see matched to **AI-generated** code recommendations.

6. Clicking the **URL** field will redirect the web browser back to the collections and sources on **Ansible Galaxy** from which the code recommendations were derived.

7. Starting from a new **`Ansible`** code file, we can get code suggestions and select the **`Accept`** tab, highlighted in *Figure 8.101*:

Figure 8.101: *Starting from a new **Ansible** code file, we can get code suggestions*

8. After selecting the **`Accept`** tab, the suggested code is added, as shown in *Figure 8.102*:

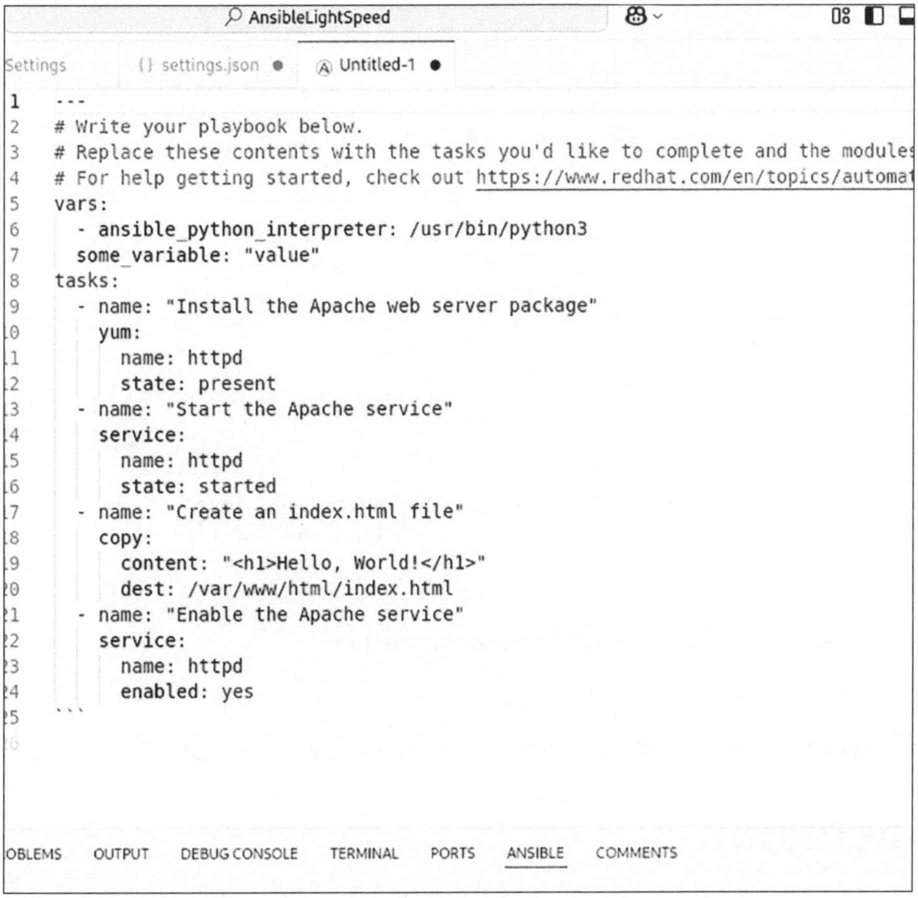

Figure 8.102: *After selecting the* **Accept** *tab, the suggested code is added*

Post-processing Capabilities

RedHat Ansible Content Collections include expert-created roles, modules, plug-ins, and more to help with the common operational tasks and start automating even faster, as shown in *Figure 8.103*:

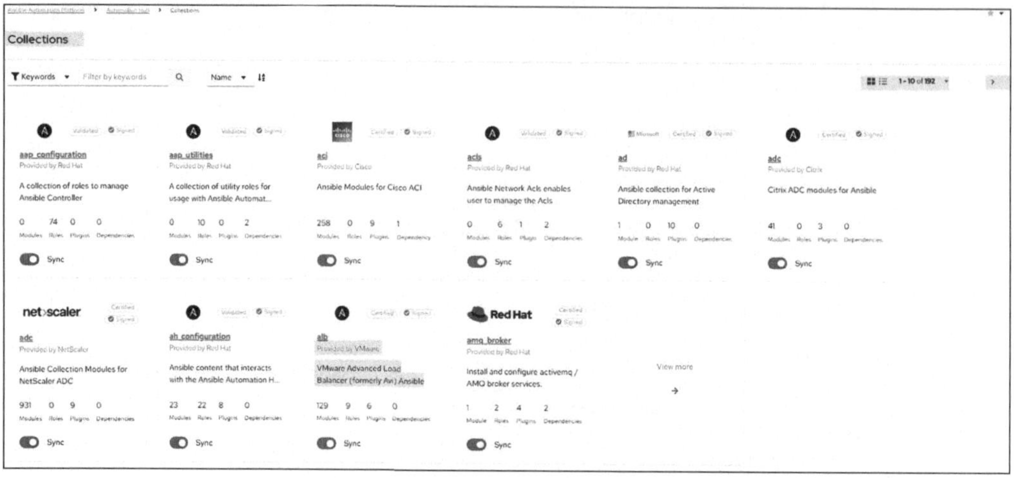

Figure 8.103: RedHat Ansible Content Collections
include expert-created roles, modules, and plug-ins

see the link:

https://console.redhat.com/ansible/automation-hub

and

https://marketplace.visualstudio.com/items?itemName=redhat.ansible

Conclusion

This chapter described the use of **IBM Granite 3.0** code models that are trained on expansive **`Ansible Playbook`** datasets so that developers can accept or adjust **AI**-generated **Ansible** code content suggestions, improving productivity.

An enterprise using **`IBM watsonx Code Assistant`** for **`Red Hat Ansible Lightspeed`** can make use of the resulting **`Ansible`** code, using the **`Ansible Playbook`** content, generated from **AI** content recommendations.

In the next chapter, *Maintenance and Upgrade*, we describe the use of an **`Ansible Task`**, which is a statement in **`Ansible`**'s automation script using **YAML**-based **Playbooks** that declare a single action to be executed. We go on to describe its use for installing a package, copying a file, or shutting down a service on a remote machine.

Points to Remember

- VMs on a host system, which gives the KVM (Kernel-based Virtual Machine) not supported message, will fail to boot.

- To install the required IBM watsonx Code Assistant on-premise, you need to install IBM Cloud Pak for Data and then install the IBM watsonx Code Assistant service within it, along with the necessary extensions for an IDE (such as Visual Studio Code).
- **IBM Ansible Lightspeed** and **IBM watsonx Code Assistant** (**WCA**) will only generate code recommendations for **Ansible Playbooks** and **YAML** files.
- **VS Code** will usually auto-detect the programming language of the document you're working with, but the language may have to be manually set to **Ansible.**
- Remember, that **Red Hat** does not support **VMs** that use the `qemu` domain type, and setting this is highly discouraged in production environments.
- Remember that the **IBM watsonx Code Assistant** code attribution suggestions are created using a **k-NN** algorithm that searches **Ansible Galaxy** repositories for the nearest related content to the AI-generated code suggestions.

Multiple Choice Questions

1. Which of the following Guest Operating Systems are not supported on a **Red Hat RHEL 9** server using **KVM**?
    a. Red Hat Enterprise Linux 7
    b. Microsoft Windows 10
    c. Microsoft Windows Server 2016 64-bit
    d. Red Hat Enterprise Linux 6
2. Which of the following commands installs the virtualization hypervisor packages?
    a. `dnf install qemu-guest-agent`
    b. `dnf install qemu-kvm libvirt virt-install virt-viewer`
    c. `sudo dnf install virt-manager`
    d. `pip install ansible-dev-tools --no-input`
3. Which one of the following RedHat RHEL disk image types did we use for the main VMware Workstation installation download?
    a. `Bare metal - Installer (rhel-9.5-x86_64-dvd.iso)`
    b. `Virtual disk (.vmdk)`
    c. `Bare metal - Installer (rhel-9.2-x86_64-dvd.iso)`
    d. `Virtualization - Guest image (rhel9-VM001.qcow2)`

Answers

1. d
2. b
3. c

Questions

1. Outline the procedure that must be used to provide the **Red Hat Ansible** language **Content Source** matching functionality for a **VS Code IDE**.
2. List the core names and the main versions of the supporting software systems that are required by the **Red Hat** Ansible Lightspeed system.

Key Terms

- **LLM**: Large Language Model is created by processing large volumes of data and analysing the word positions, weighting each word in a sequence to understand and generate human language for AI systems. LLMs are trained on vast amounts of text data retrieved from internet sources and utilise deep learning processes to perform a wide range of Natural Language Processing (NLP) tasks.
- **AI**: Artificial Intelligence Software that mimics the responses you might expect to questions supplied by a human operator.
- **RHEL:** RedHat Enterprise Linux. A commercial version of the Linux Operating system, now owned by **IBM**.
- **Jira:** It is a software application that allows teams to track issues, manage projects, and automate workflows. (The name **Jira** is derived from the Japanese word "***Gojira***" meaning **Godzilla.**)
- **KVM:** It stands for **Kernel-based Virtual Machine**, an open-source virtualization technology for Linux that allows a single physical machine to run multiple, isolated Virtual Machines (**VMs**).
- **QEMU**: It is short for "*Quick Emulator*," is free and open-source software, developed by Fabrice Bellard, that serves as both a machine emulator and for virtualization.

References

- Generating Code - IBM watsonx Code Assistant for Red Hat Ansible Lightspeed - Technical Sales Level 3

  https://ibm.github.io/WCA-AnsibleLightspeed-L3/generating/#ii-single-task-ansible-operations
- An enterprise using **IBM watsonx Code Assistant** for **Red Hat Ansible Lightspeed** can make use of the resulting code, using the **Ansible Playbook** content, generated from **AI** content recommendations see the link:

  https://www.ibm.com/products/watsonx-code-assistant-ansible-lightspeed
- There is a free trial listed at the link:

  "Trial for watsonx Code Assistant for Red Hat Ansible Lightspeed | IBM":

  https://www.ibm.com/products/watsonx-code-assistant-ansible-lightspeed/info/trial
- We used the link as follows, to get a 60 day free trial from RedHat:

  https://www.redhat.com/en/technologies/management/ansible/trial
- The **RedHat Trial terms** and conditions are defined in the link as follows:

  https://www.redhat.com/en/about/agreements-old
- **RHEL 9.2 Linux** system can be downloaded from the link:

  https://access.redhat.com/downloads/content/479
- There is **RedHat Ansible** basic overview at:

  https://www.redhat.com/en/services/training/do007-ansible-essentials-simplicity-automation-technical-overview

CHAPTER 9
Maintenance and Upgrade

Introduction

This chapter describes the use of an **Ansible Task**, which is a statement in **Ansible**'s automation script using **YAML**-based **Playbooks** that declare a single action to be executed. This can be used for installing a package, copying a file, or shutting down a service on a remote machine. Each **Ansible Task** represents an action that can be repeated multiple times and can be guaranteed to always deliver the same result.

IBM have used considerable computing power to generate **Code Large Language Models** (**AI LLMs**) using a generative **AI** foundation model for code generation that is based on the **IBM Granite** models.

The **Ansible CodeLLM** base model is one of the many foundation models available to **`IBM watsonx.ai`**, which **IBM** further refined and calibrated for use with specific programming languages, such as **COBOL**, **Ansible**, and the potential for **116** other languages.

`IBM watsonx Code Assistant` is the core product for **IBM**'s generative **AI** service offerings, providing a number of solutions (for example, for **Red Hat Ansible Lightspeed, for Z**).

These solutions have been designed for specific client use cases and business requirements.

A high-level overview of the architecture used by **IBM** is shown, in *Figure 9.1*, based on the link, https://ibm.github.io/wca-generative-ai-training/ ("**IBM watsonx Code Assistant for Red Hat Ansible Lightspeed - Generative AI Training**")

Structure

In this chapter, we will discuss the following topics:

- Generating Code for Single Tasks
  - Setting up TASK 1 for GitHub CoPilot
  - Setting up TASK 2 for IBM watsonx Code Assistant
- Generating Code for Multi-tasks
- Content Source Matching and Attribution
- Post-processing of Tasks and YAML Files

Generating Code for Single Tasks

The structure of the **IBM watsonx.ai CodeLLM** base architecture is shown in *Figure* 9.1:

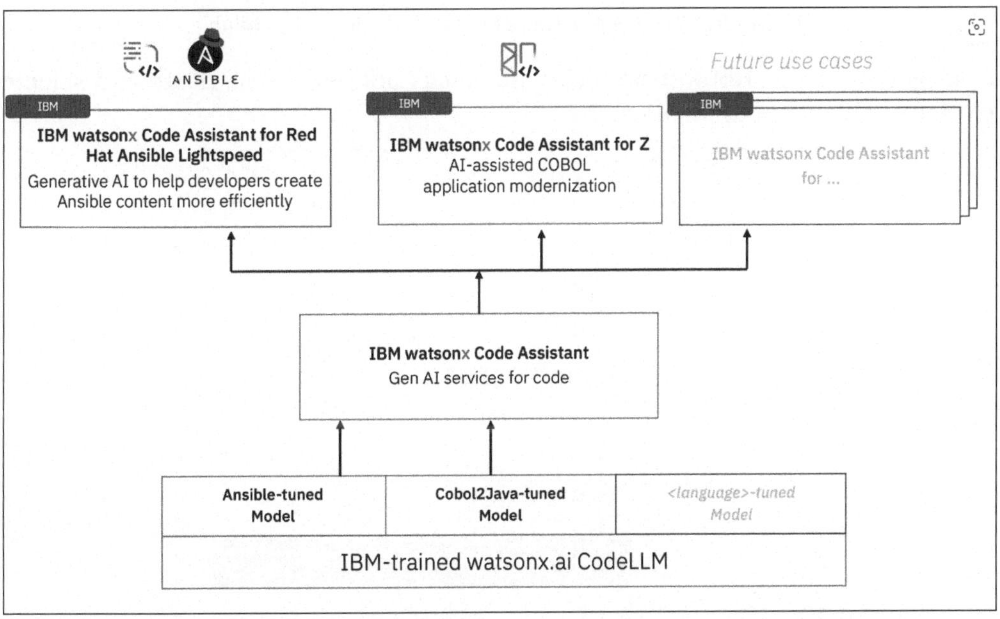

Figure 9.1:** The development path of **IBM watsonx Code Assistant for Red Hat Ansible Lightspeed

We located the following **IBM** training which is available at the link, https://learn.ibm.com, (free to **`IBM PartnerPlus Business Partners`**), as shown in *Figure* 9.2:

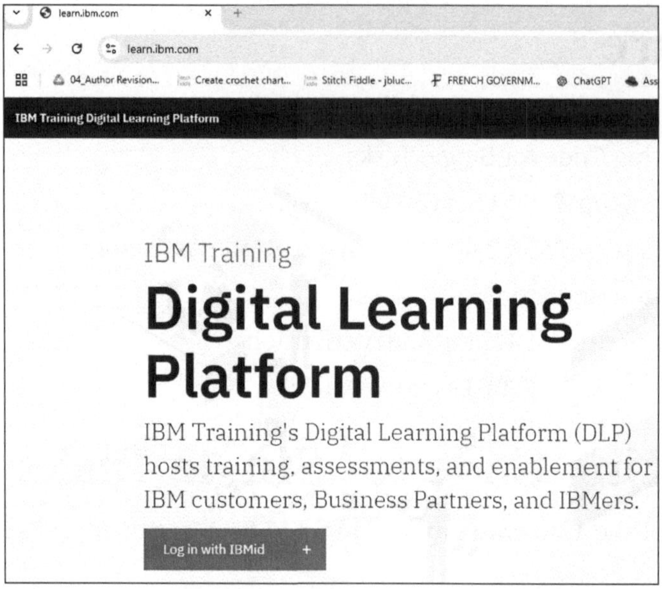

Figure 9.2: *We located the* ***IBM*** *training which is available*

We logged in to the **`IBM`** website using our email address as an **`IBMid`** and selected **`Continue`** as highlighted in *Figure* 9.3:

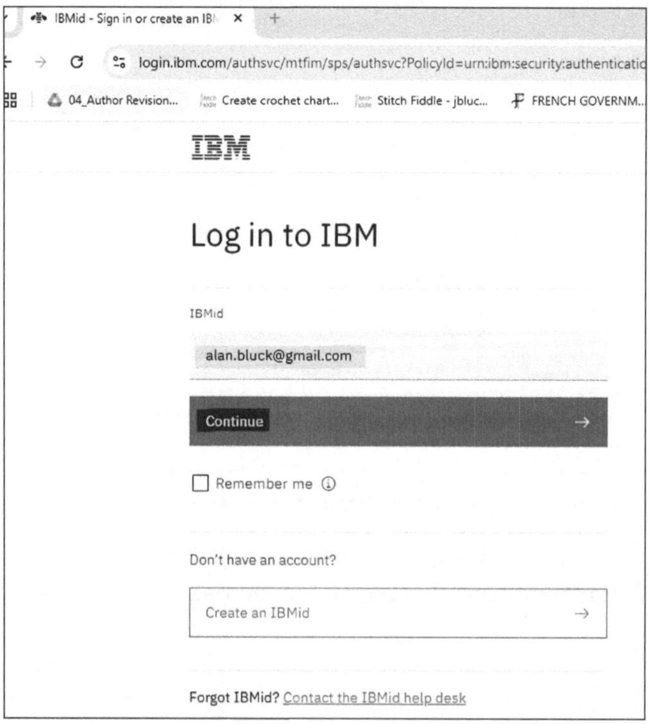

Figure 9.3: *We log in to the IBM website using our email address as an* ***IBMid*** *and select* ***Continue***

We entered the **`Password`** and selected the **`Log in`** command to view the **`IBM Training`** web page, as highlighted in *Figure 9.4*:

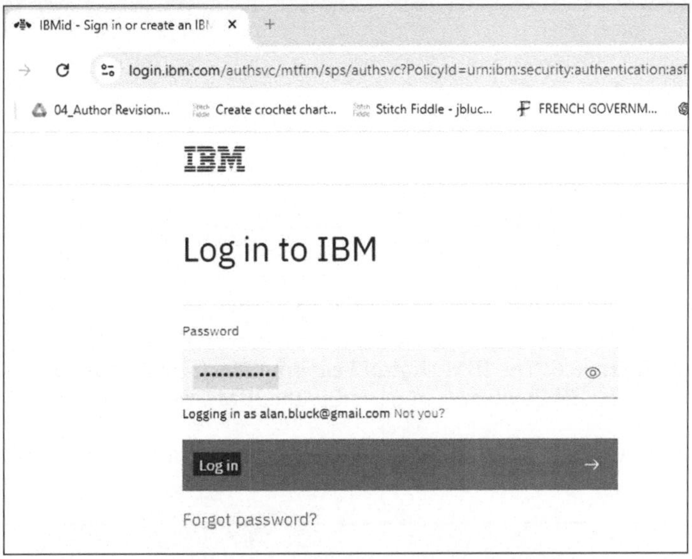

***Figure 9.4:** We enter the **Password** and select the **Log in** command to view the **IBM Training** web page*

The terms for joining a **`Training`** course are scrolled down and accepted using the **`Proceed`** command, as highlighted in *Figure 9.5*:

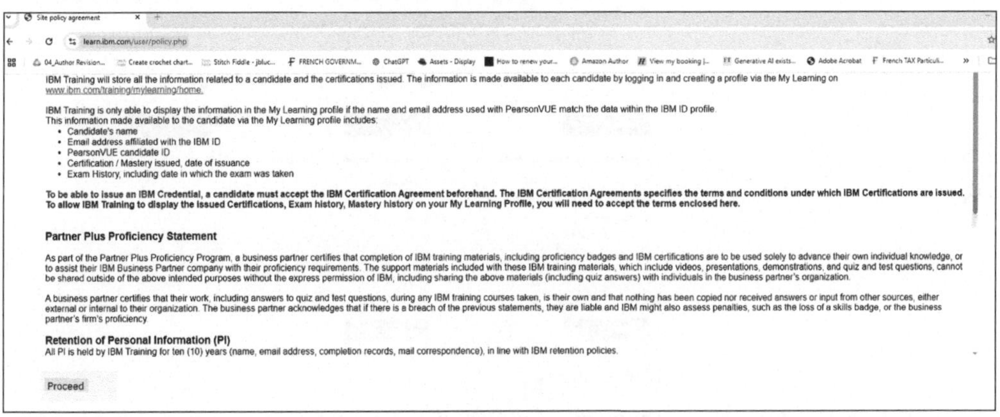

***Figure 9.5:** The terms for joining a **Training** course are scrolled down and accepted using the **Proceed** command*

The **`IBM Digital Learning Platform`** is searched for **IBM watsonx** training, by selecting the **`IBM Training`** link, highlighted in *Figure 9.6*:

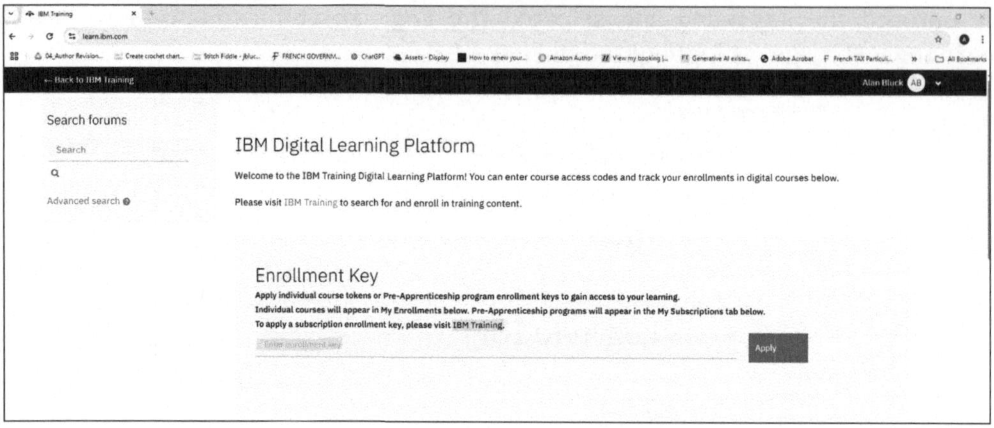

Figure 9.6: *The* **IBM Digital Learning Platform** *is searched for* **IBM watsonx**, *by selecting the* **IBM Training** *link*

The **`IBM watsonx`** areas for **`Technical Sales`** training are highlighted, as shown in *Figure 9.7*:

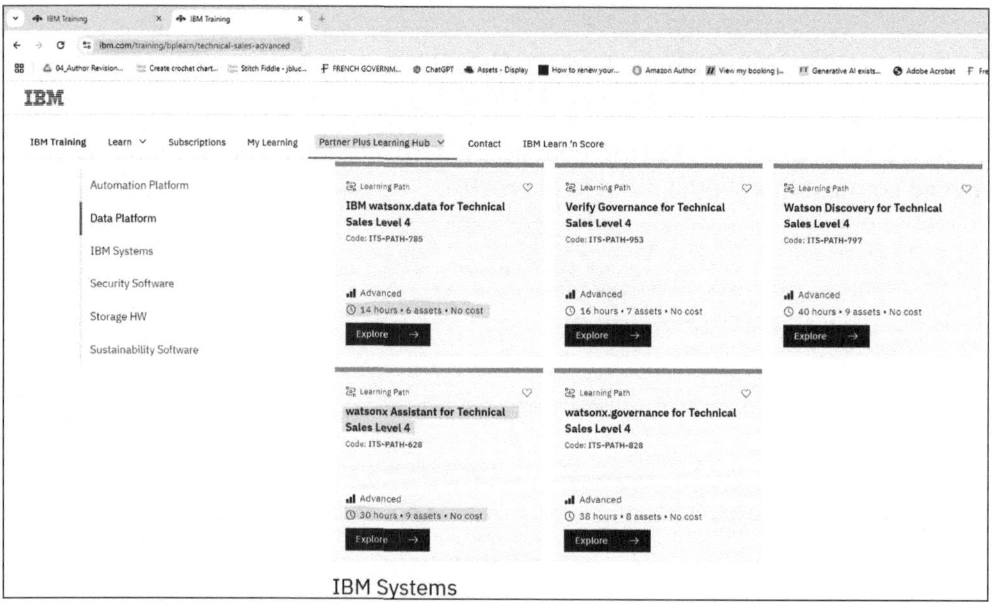

Figure 9.7: *The* **IBM watsonx** *areas for* **Technical Sales** *training are highlighted*

The first thing we tried adding to our system (which was created in the last chapter), was the **Ansible Lint** libraries for our **Red Hat RHEL 9.2 Linux** system. The libraries for **ansible-lint** perform checks on **Ansible Playbooks** for practices and behavior that could potentially be improved and it can fix some of the most common issues. The system will constantly check the **Ansible** syntax as it is typed and provide recommendations to improve the **Ansible** code.

We used the following command line within the **VS Code Terminal** environment tab, but this showed the system was updated already, as illustrated in *Figure* 9.8:

```
python3 -m pip install --upgrade ansible-lint
```

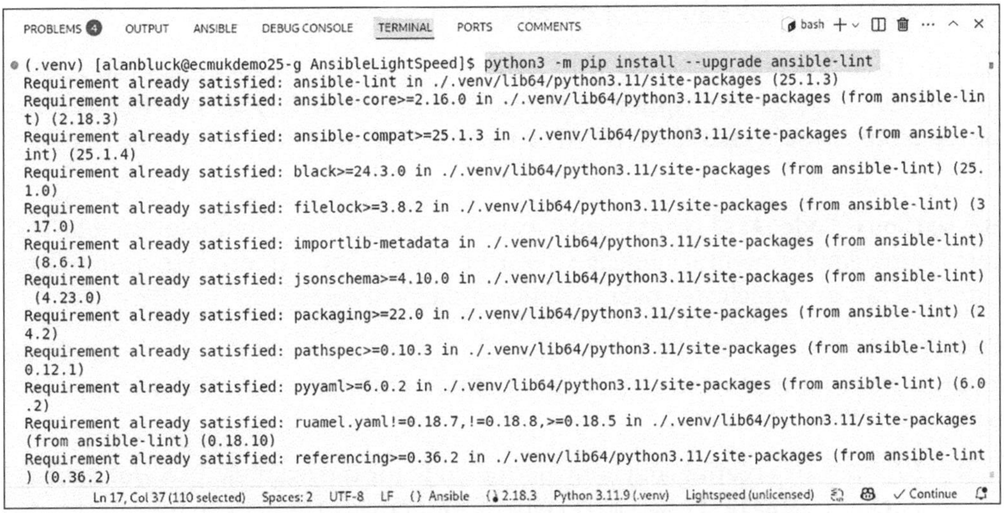

***Figure 9.8**: We used the **python3 -m pip install --upgrade ansible-lint** line within a **VS Code Terminal** tab*

An Ansible Playbook

Executing an **Ansible Playbook** automatically completes the same action to hundreds or thousands of similar technologies across different **IT** environments.

(An example of **Ansible Playbook** file code was shown in *Chapter* 8, *Performance optimization*, *Figure* 8.102.)

There is an overview of the **Ansible Playbook** at the link:

https://www.redhat.com/en/topics/automation/what-is-an-ansible-playbook.

Many of the potential initial **Visual Studio, VS Code** set-up issues are resolved by openers which can be found by scrolling down on the web page found using the link:

https://ibm.github.io/wca-generative-ai-training/setup/

This section describes the process of creating **AI**-generated **code recommendations** by using **GitHub CoPilot** for **TASK 1** and then, using **`IBM watsonx Code Assistant`** to generate the **Ansible Task, TASK 2,** from descriptions of an action that is to be executed.

For **Red Hat Ansible Playbook** development in **VS Code**, **`Red Hat Ansible Lightspeed with IBM watsonx Code Assistant (WCA)`** is likely better than using

GitHub Copilot alone, as it's specifically designed and trained for **Red Hat Ansible** automation, offering more accurate and contextualized code recommendations.

The **YAML** code for the **Ansible playgroup .yml** file starts with the token, **- name:** and is followed by a description of the task to be performed.

Ansible Tasks can be preceded with some **#** comments or documentation. After the natural language description of the automation **Task** has been set by the user, **IBM watsonx Code Assistant** (WCA) or **GitHub CoPilot AIs** generate the rest of the code.

IBM watsonx Code Assistant is also capable of generating multiple **Ansible Tasks** from more complex natural language descriptions – what is referred to as **multi-task** code generation –which we cover in detail in the next section.

To start with, we will describe the procedure used for generating code for **single task** deployment requirements, using **GitHub CoPilot,** for **TASK 1** and **IBM watsonx Code Assistant** (WCA), for **TASK 2.**

1. We start by creating and copying the code for the example **Red Hat install_cockpit_single-task.yml** Playbook, by copying the code in the link, https://ibm.github.io/wca-generative-ai-training/generating/

   The copied example **YAML** code is listed as follows:

```
---
- name: Install and configure Cockpit
  hosts: rhel
  become: true

  # module_defaults:
  #   ansible.builtin.service:
  #     enabled: true
  #     state: started

  tasks:
        # TASK 1
        # # 1a. Uncomment task description below and generate a 
task suggestion.
        # #     Note - The suggestion included Ansible best prac-
tices by using Fully Qualified Collection name.
    # - name: Install cockpit package


        # TASK 2
        # # 2a. Uncomment task description below and generate a 
task suggestion.
        # #     Note - Ansible Lightspeed used "ansible.builtin.
```

```
template" module based on the ".j2" file extension.
        # #     Note - The suggestion set the file permissions
("0644"), owner, and group based on Ansible best practices.
    # - name: Copy cockpit.conf.j2 to /etc/cockpit

        # TASK 3
        # # 3a. Uncomment task description below and generate a
task suggestion.
        # #     Note - Ansible Lightspeed used the generic "Start
and enable service" prompt
        # #            and full Playbook context to infer the
recommendation should start the "cockpit" service.
        # # 3b. Uncomment the "module_defaults" section at the
top of the Playbook.
        # # 3c. Clear current task suggestion and request updated
suggestion.
        # #     Note - Ansible Lightspeed used the full Playbook
context and evaluated the "module_defaults"
        # #            when generating a suggestion.
        # #            The updated suggestion no longer includes
"enabled:" and "state:" arguments.
    # - name: Start and enable service

        # TASK 4
        # # 4a. Uncomment task description below and generate an
Ansible Playbook task suggestion.
        # # 4b. Save the Playbook.
    # - name: Wait 15 seconds port 9090
---
```

We use the **VS Code** menu **File-> New File** command to create the file, **install_cockpit_single-task.yml**, as shown in *Figure* 9.9:

Figure 9.9**: We use the menu command, **File-> New File** for the file, **install_cockpit_single-task.yml

The **Create File** command is used to store the new file name, **install_cockpit_single-task.yml**, as highlighted in *Figure* 9.10:

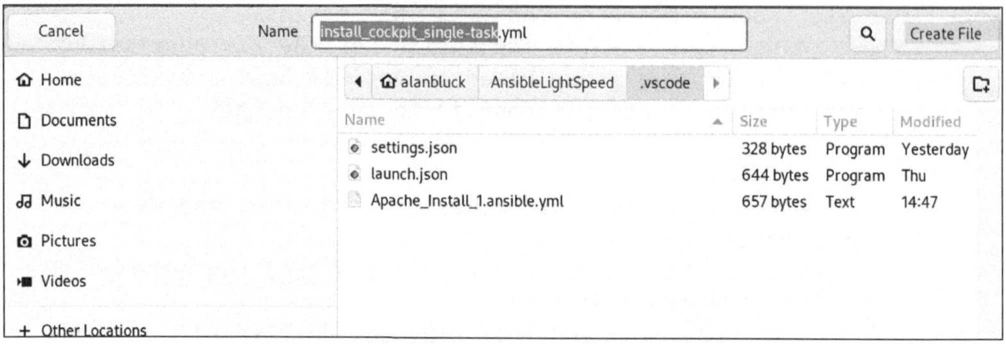

Figure 9.10**: The **Create File** command is used to store the file name, **install_cockpit_single-task.yml

The **`Select all`** (*Ctrl/A*), **`Copy`** (*Ctrl/C*), and **`Paste`** (*Ctrl/V*) commands were entered in the highlighted text box to copy the example single task **YAML** code from a notebook, (listed under the heading: **`~/Documents/ansible-wca-demo-kit/install and configure Cockpit using Ansible/install_cockpit_single-task.yml`**) as highlighted in *Figure 9.11*:

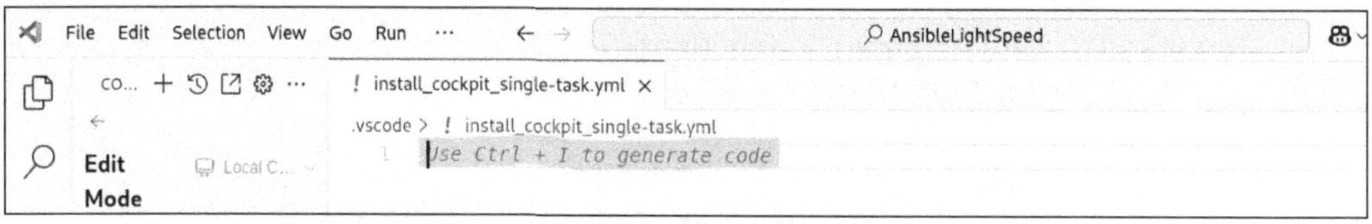

***Figure 9.11**: The select (**Ctrl/A**) copy (**Ctrl/C**) and paste, (**Ctrl/V**) commands were entered in the text box*

The selected **`YAML`** code is shown in the new file and is initially all commented out at the start, as illustrated in *Figure 9.12*:

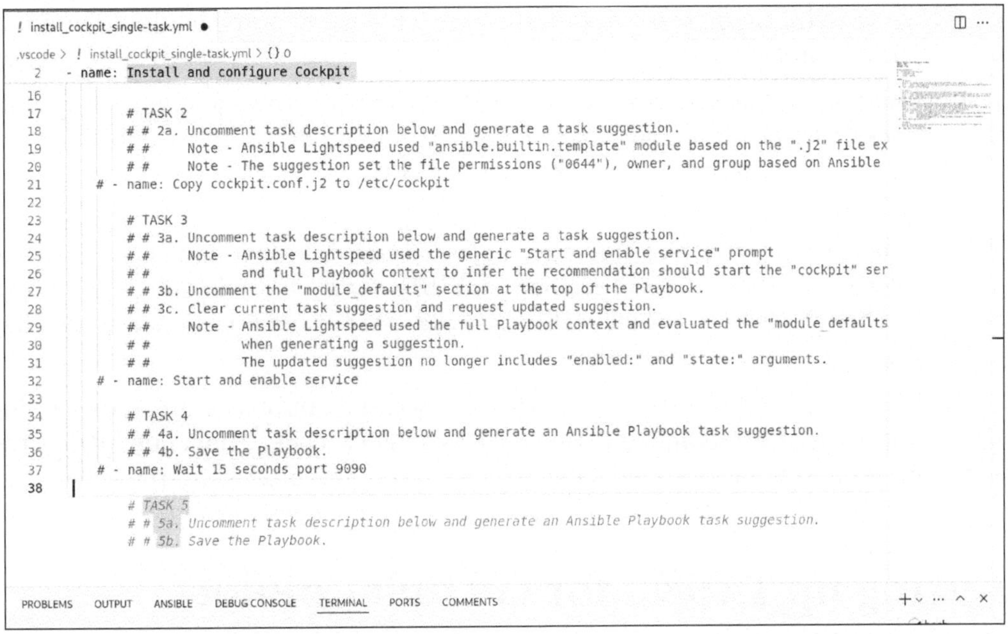

***Figure 9.12:** The selected **YAML** code is shown in the new file and is initially all commented out*

The problems detected within the editor are expected, as highlighted in *Figure* 9.13, as this is a new version with additional blank characters pasted at the end of the code.

Currently the tasks: section contains no valid **`-name: task`** definitions. We can ignore any warnings for now, as we are going to un-comment and generate valid **`-name: task`** definitions in the subsequent steps.

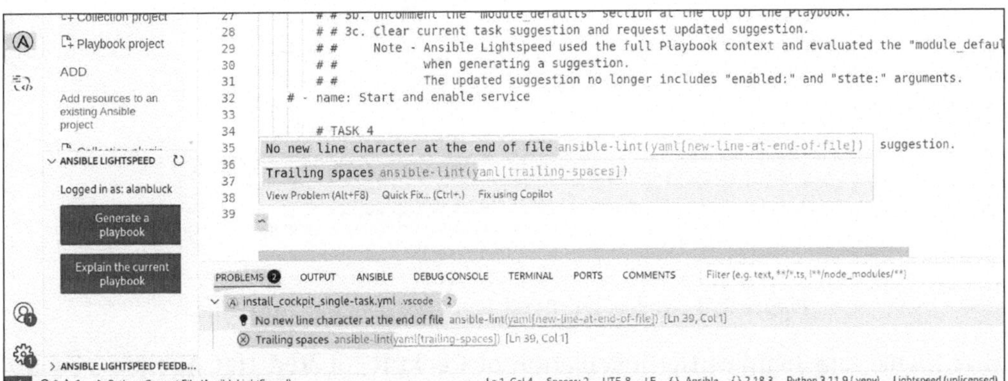

***Figure 9.13:** The problems detected within the editor are expected as this is a new version*

The **`install_cockpit_single-task.yml`** **Playbook Code** above is described by **Red Hat**:

- **Line 2** marks the beginning of the **`Ansible Playbook`** instructions, which are designed to automate the process of installing and configuring **Cockpit** (https://

www.redhat.com/en/blog/automate-rhel-web-console-deployments-cockpit-and-certificate-rhel-system-roles)

- **Lines 3-4** define the variables that will remain static throughout the Playbook. These variables are used by the **AI**-generated code to provide flexibility as an advantage of using the code offering which we describe in detail in this section.
- **Lines 6-9** are variables that have been "**`commented out`**" and so are invisible to the execution of the **`Red Hat Ansible`** script and will not be examined by **GitHub Copilot** or **`IBM watsonx Code Assistant`** for context when they generate code recommendations.

  We examined the effect of removing the **#** comment blocks, and the resulting impact of the recommendations for task block code. "**Uncommenting**" the lines of code make them viable for execution and afterward, these lines are considered as valid **`Playbook`** "**`context`**" for **AI** code generation.

Setting up TASK 1 for GitHub CoPilot

The procedure is listed as follows:

1. We locate **TASK 1** on **Line 15** of the **YAML** file, as highlighted in *Figure* 9.14:

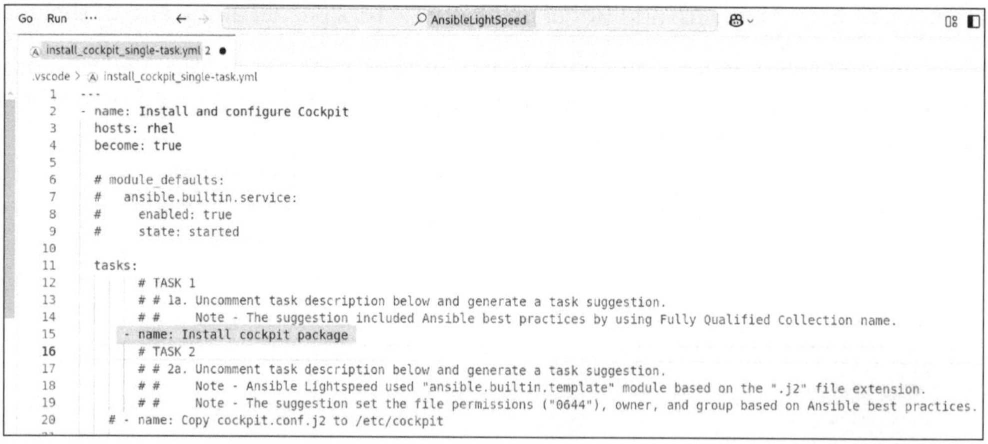

***Figure 9.14:** We located **TASK 1** on **Line 15** of the **YAML** file*

2. This task handles the installation of **Cockpit** for **Red Hat Ansible**. (**Cockpit** is an interactive server administration interface that provides a graphical overview of statistics and configurations for a system or systems within a network).
3. **`# - name: Install cockpit package`**

   We need to be very careful to observe the correct syntax for the indentation and characters used on **Line 15**, which in sequence from left to right are as follows:

- begins with Tab (or Space whitespaces) for indentation
- a `#` character to "**`comment out`**" the line contents, (which we show after we removed it, in *Figure* 9.14)
- a whitespace **`Space`** character
- **`- name:`** which signifies the start of a **`Task`** definition
- And, most importantly, the natural language description of the **`Task`**

Indentation Levels and Whitespace

The **Red Hat Ansible** code language, and **YAML-based Playbooks** are similar to **Python**, as they are very sensitive to white spacing and indentation.

Indentations (such as the *Tab* character, in the first example) signify different code nesting levels and express the hierarchy within the **YAML** structure.

It is allowed to use a *Space* character, instead of a *Tab* character, if preferred, but this alternative option must be used for indentations consistently. You need to select the use of either a *Tab* character or a *Space* character for indenting lines of code, and cannot swap between the two.

To generate code for **TASK 1** using **GitHub CoPilot**, we first uncommented the line of code (removing the **#** character from the start of a line), then we highlighted the uncommented text by dragging the mouse across the text, and we can then see three options, which we can select with the mouse, as shown in *Figure* 9.15:

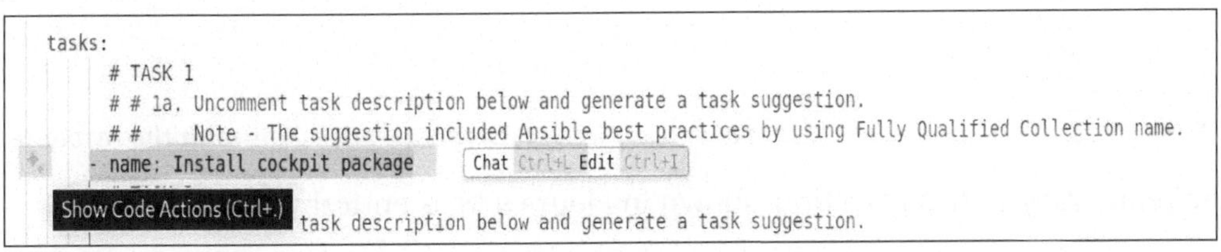

Figure 9.15: *We can choose between three options after highlighting the uncommented code line*

We then selected the highlighted **+ icon** on the left of the code, this is marked with the pop-up window on mouse-over, which states "`Show Code Actions (Ctrl+)`".

We also have the options, shown at the end of the line, to **`Chat`** `(`**`Ctrl+L`**`)` or **`Edit`** `(`**`Ctrl+I`**`)`.

After we select the **+** icon, **Line 15** should look like the following, with a pop-up window prompt, allowing us to select either **`Modify using Copilot`**, or **`Review using Copilot`**, as shown in *Figure* 9.16:

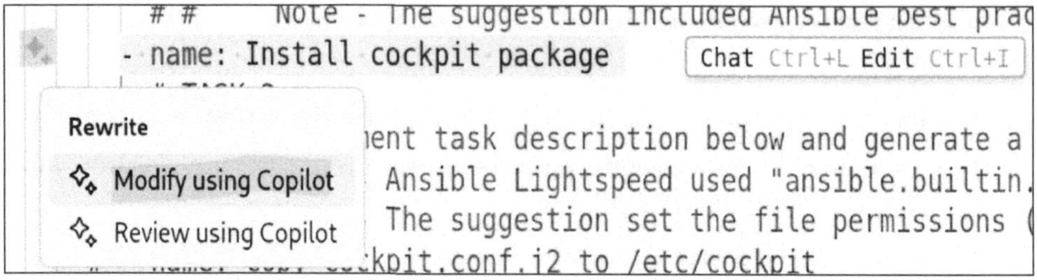

Figure 9.16: *There is a pop-up window, for us to select* ***Modify using Copilot****, or* ***Review using Copilot***

We can now begin to generate code, and select the **`Modify using Copilot`** pop-up window option, to give the prompt text box for entry of a **`Copilot`** question, as highlighted in *Figure* 9.17:

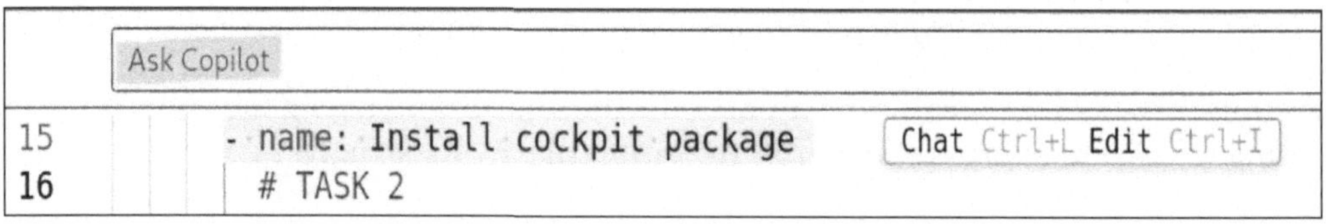

Figure 9.17: *We can now begin to generate code; we select the* ***Modify using Copilot*** *option*

We enter the text "**`is this ok`**", and on *Enter*, get a window with the response, as shown in *Figure* 9.18:

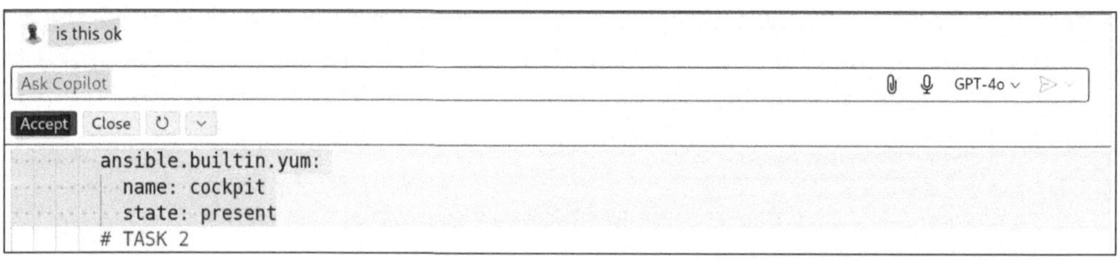

Figure 9.18: *We enter the text,* ***"`is this ok`",*** *and on* ***Enter****, get a window with the response*

The temporary code suggestion, shown in *Figure* 9.18, is entirely generated by **AI**

We now have the option to either:

a. **`Accept`** the code recommendation as-given by selecting the **`Accept`** command button.

b. **Or rejecting** the code suggestion using the **`Close`** command button.

As part of the plain-text description of the Task, **GitHub CoPilot** was asked to include the **cockpit** Role, part of the '**Red Hat Enterprise Linux System Roles**' (https://access.redhat.com/articles/3050101).

Using the **Red Hat Certified Content Collection**, the **AI**-generated code suggestion invoked a **Fully Qualified Collection Name (FQCN)** - **`ansible.builtin.yum`** (see:https://docs.ansible.com/ansible/latest/collections_guide/collections_using_playbooks.html) (See: https://shorturl.at/nD8z2, "**ansible.builtin.yum module – Ansible Community Documentation**"

Making use of **FQCNs** where possible is a recommended best practice and is a good example of the many ways in which **Ansible Lightspeed** improves post-processing capabilities within the **AI**-generated code produced by **GitHub CoPilot**.

The **AI** updated file, **`install_cockpit_single-task.yml`**, now has the following **`Red Hat Ansible`** code, as highlighted in *Figure 9.19*:

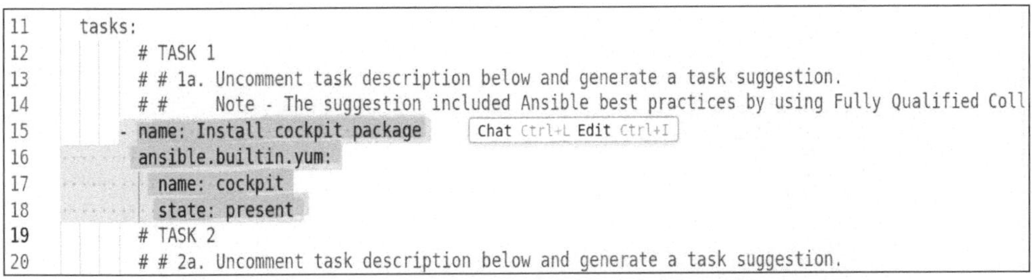

***Figure 9.19:** The **AI** updated file, **install_cockpit_single-task.yml**, now has updated **Red Hat Ansible** code*

Setting up TASK 2 for IBM Watsonx Code Assistant

Another example of the use of **AI**-generated code recommendations for best practice **Red Hat Ansible** code development can be illustrated by the code generated for **TASK 2**, **Line 20** of the unmodified template (or this becomes **Line 23**, after **TASK 1** has been updated). For this **TASK 2**, we used the **`IBM watsonx Code Assistant`** to generate the **`Ansible Task`.**

First, we uncommented the task:

```
- name: Copy cockpit.conf.j2 to /etc/cockpit
```

Then we pressed the *Enter* key at the end of the line to generate the task code recommendation and we can then accept the **AI**-suggested code, by selecting the highlighted **`Accept`** command, as shown in *Figure 9.20*:

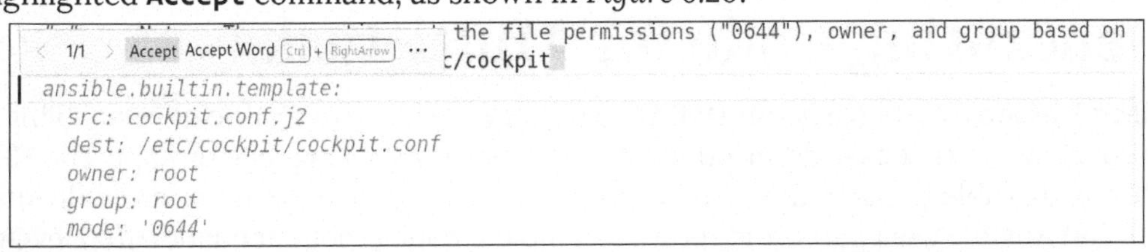

***Figure 9.20:** We can accept the **AI**-suggested code, by selecting the highlighted **Accept** command,*

This gives the valid **Red Hat Ansible** code, as shown in *Figure 9.21*:

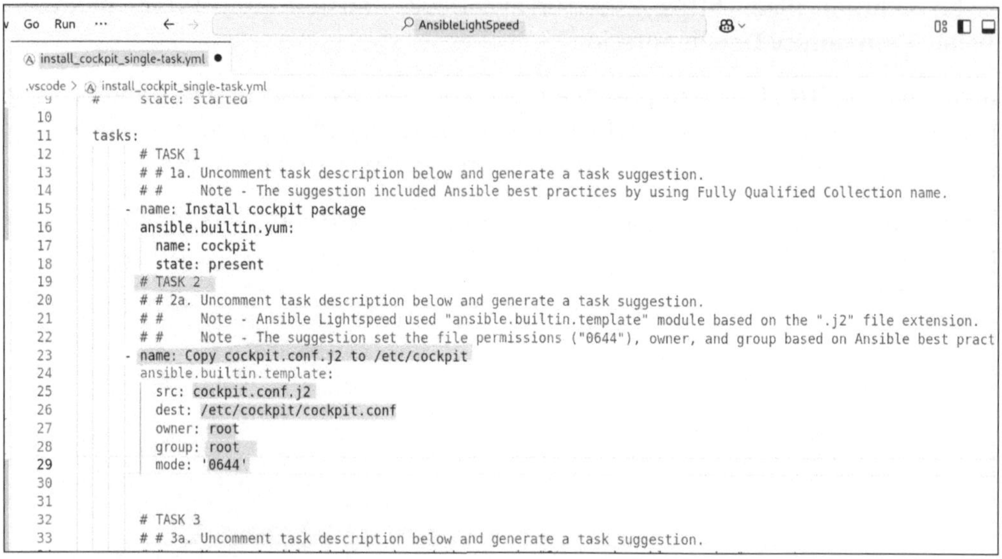

***Figure 9.21:** The valid **Red Hat Ansible** code for copying the **cockpit.conf.j2** file*

The **IBM watsonx Code Assistant AI**-generated code recommendation will copy **cockpit.conf** file to the target host (downloadable from the website, https://github.com/craig-br/demos/blob/main/blogs/lightspeed_tech_preview_jun2023/files/cockpit.conf).

Notice that the recommendation included the **mode:** argument and sets the Linux file permissions to **0644**, which we didn't explicitly request in the Task **-name** description. These additions exemplify best practices for defining **Red Hat Ansible** automaton tasks. Setting a file permission to **0644** specifies **read** and **write** permissions for **User** and **Group** levels within the **Red Hat Linux** operating system file structure, and provides only **read** permissions to all other users.

See: https://ibm.github.io/wca-generative-ai-training/generating/

"Generating Code - IBM watsonx Code Assistant for Red Hat Ansible Lightspeed - Generative AI Training"

Generating Code for Multi-tasks

IBM's Watsonx Code Assistant (WCA) has a very useful advanced feature enabling it to combine multiple task descriptions into a single natural language prompt. The **IBM WCA** is also able to parse the combined instruction and decompose it into individual **Red Hat Ansible Task** parts, and return a complete code recommendation for **DevOps** intended requirements.

The required multiple tasks are appended by joining them using the **ampersand** ("&") character to build them into a single natural language expression. So, all the automation task descriptions can be entered on a single line, separating each description with an "**&**" character. This line must also start with a "**#**" character because the execution of a code generation step on a commented-out (**#**) line containing "**&**" character delimiters is the way that **IBM watsonx Code Assistant** identifies the line as a unique text statement that will be processed to generate multi-task code lines.

IBM has an example **YAML** file, **`install_cockpit_multi-task.yml`**, which can be copied to evaluate the processing of a multi-task **`RedHat Ansible Lightspeed Playbook`**.

As for the **single-task** example we described in the previous section, this file can be found by scrolling down on the web page at the link:

https://ibm.github.io/wca-generative-ai-training/generating/

(**"Generating Code - IBM watsonx Code Assistant for Red Hat Ansible Lightspeed - Generative AI Training**")

Each of the **Task** descriptions from the **Ansible Playbook** we described has been concatenated into a single description on **Line 12**, separated by "**&**" characters.

This file can be found under the heading on the web page, as follows:

`~/Documents/ansible-wca-demo-kit/install and configure Cockpit using Ansible/install_cockpit_multi-task.yml`

With the content as follows, which we cut and paste into a new **`install_cockpit_multi-task.yml`** file, created with the **VS Code IDE `File > New File`** menu option, resulting in the **`File`** shown in *Figure* 9.22:

```
---
- name: Install and configure Cockpit
hosts: rhel
become: true

module_defaults:
    ansible.builtin.service:
    enabled: true
    state: started
tasks:
    # Install cockpit package & Copy cockpit.conf.j2 to /etc/
cockpit & Start and enable service & Wait 15 seconds port 9090
```

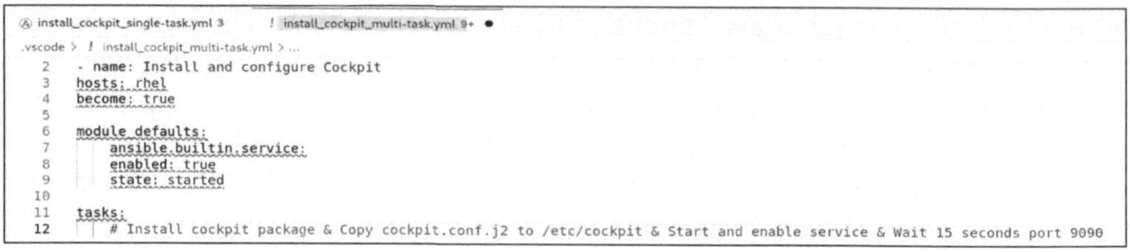

Figure 9.22: *The new* ***install_cockpit_multi-task.yml*** *file, created with the* ***File->New File*** *menu option*

There are two significant distinctions between **single-task** and **multi-task** code generation: these are described as for the **formatting** and the **execution mechanism**.

For **formatting**, **Line 12** of the **`install_cockpit_multi-task.yml`**, file, the line does not begin with **`-name:`**, as was the case with single task descriptions, but has the "**#**" character.

For the **execution mechanism** for **Line 12,** in order to generate **AI** code recommendations for **multi-task** descriptions, the line **must stay commented out.**

(So, the **"#"** character needs to stay at the start of the line.)

The code generation step, executed on **Line 12** depends on the format structure of the line. Execution of a code generation step on a line beginning with the "**#**" character and containing "**&**" character delimiters, is identified by **`IBM watsonx Code Assistant`** as a special case that will be treated as a **multi-task** statement.

To execute the line, we first positioned the mouse cursor at the end of **Line 12**, (without removing the "**#**" character from the start of the line, this time). Then, we selected the **Enter** key to execute the **WCA** code generation step and found we had to repeat this process and use the **`Accept [TAB]`** key to accept the code for each step, before the next Task line was generated. This **`Accept [TAB]`** is for the **Start and enable service** task code generation, as illustrated in *Figure 9.23*:

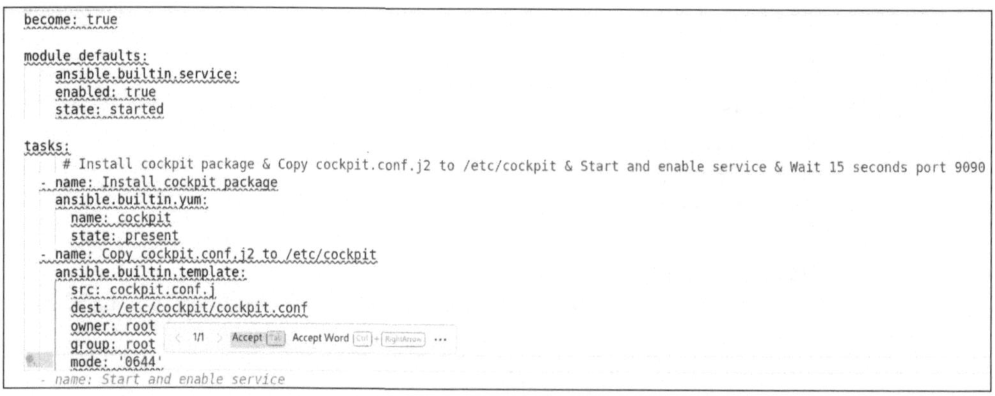

Figure 9.23: *We select the* **Enter** *key and then the* **Accept [TAB]** *to execute the* **WCA** *code generation step*

You might notice that generating code for **multi-task** descriptions takes longer than for the single task execution process.

For the last task, (**& Wait 15 seconds port 9090**), we see the **AI** generated code as grey text, prompting us to select **Accept** to confirm that we want to use it, as shown in *Figure 9.24*:

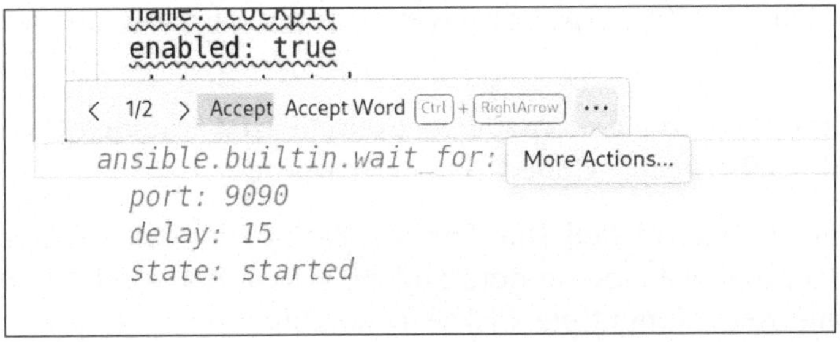

Figure 9.24: *For the last task, (**& Wait 15 seconds port 9090**), we see the **AI** generated code as grey text*

After the generation of the last line of code, you should get the following screen, as shown in *Figure 9.25*:

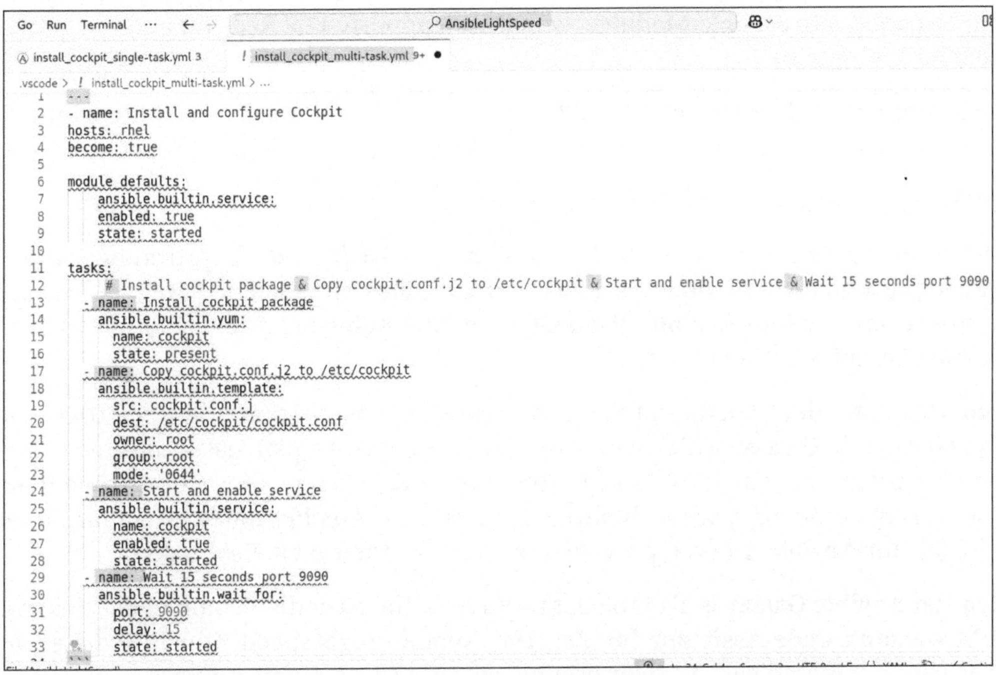

Figure 9.25: *The screen after the generation of the last line of code*

Content Source Matching and Attribution

Expanding on the section on *Content Source Matching*, in *Chapter 8, Performance Optimization*, the following section develops this with additional examples, based on the **IBM** training resource found at the link:

https://ibm.github.io/wca-generative-ai-training/source-matching-post-processing/

(“**Content Source Matching and Post-Processing - IBM watsonx Code Assistant for Red Hat Ansible Lightspeed - Generative AI Training**”)

After describing the use of **Red Hat Ansible Tasks** and **YAML**-based **Playbooks** in the previous sections, we now understand how **Red Hat Ansible Lightspeed** uses **Playbooks**–composed of multiple tasks–in combination with **IBM watsonx Code Assistant's (WCA)** generative **AI** capabilities to, generate working **Ansible** code.

A string consisting of multiple “**&**” character-separated “**Tasks**” can be used for separate development, test, and production systems using an **IBM or Red Hat Cloud** cluster.

The use of **DevOps Design Patterns** for automating endpoints from the **Cloud** system can be coded into **Ansible Modules**, which are supported by **Red Hat** and the general **Ansible** community.

Collections of **Ansible Playbooks** and **Modules** can be categorized into “**blueprints**” for automation tasks that are usually used together, to achieve the desired requirements.

These requirements can be easily shared with other teams within an enterprise.

These "`blueprints`" are described by **Red Hat** as **Ansible Roles**, providing a logical way to present **Tasks**, **Templates**, **Files**, and **Variables**, the **Ansible Roles** are available to insert directly into **Ansible Playbooks**. **Ansible Roles** provide a solution to easily develop complex automation tasks.

Red Hat have developed, and are advertising, an open-source system they have named **Ansible Galaxy** (which can be found at the link, https://galaxy.ansible.com/) which is a Red Hat-managed, **Ansible** community-driven repository for **Ansible Roles**. The **Galaxy** community has submitted thousands of **Ansible Roles**, which are freely available for **Ansible** users to provide templates for their own **Playbooks**.

Red Hat Ansible Galaxy is also the data source of the **AI code** recommendations from **IBM watsonx Code Assistant for Red Hat Ansible Lightspeed**, which **Red Hat** and **IBM** have attributed back to their original content sources and authors.

IBM watsonx Code Assistant for Red Hat Ansible Lightspeed (WCA) has used the **Galaxy** site to develop an **LLM data source** which is used for the functionality they have made available for the **Content Source Matching** process (sometimes described as "**code explainability**"). This process is used to match **AI**-generated code suggestions to the original **Galaxy** training data and sources that were used for generating the **Ansible Task** code.

As we described in the last chapter, the code attribution suggestions are created using a **k-NN** algorithm (**K-Nearest Neighbors**), see https://www.ibm.com/topics/knn#:~:text=Next%20steps-,K%2DNearest%20Neighbors%20Algorithm,of%20an%20individual%20data%20point. This is an algorithm that examines **Ansible Galaxy** and other training data repositories in search of the nearest related content to the **AI**-generated code suggestions.

As we described in the last chapter, to enable **Content Source Matching** capabilities within **WCA**, we use the main menu bar for **VS Code** and select the **`View`** > **`Open View...`** menu item.

A pop-up window appears at the top of the VS Code window with a text box. It is where we type the text "**`view Training`**" and select the Enter key, which loads the **Lightspeed Training Matches** option, for the Ansible extension of **VS Code**.

After making this configuration option change to **VS Code**, all requests for **WCA** to generate code recommendations cause a panel to open at the bottom of the **VS Code IDE** desktop screen.

The **content source matching** results are then output to the **`Ansible`** tab.

As described in *Chapter 8*, *Performance Optimization*, other tabs are also displayed for **Problems, Output, Debug Console, Terminal,** and **Ports**.

We can now create a new **`Ansible Playbook`** file, **`install_pgsql-single-task.yml`**, which we populate by cutting and pasting the code from the URL link:

https://ibm.github.io/wca-generative-ai-training/source-matching-post-processing/

Scrolling down to the **Ansible Playbook** code, headed with the title:

```
. ~/Documents/ansible-wca-demo-kit/install and configure Post-
greSQL and PGAdmin container/install_pgsql-single-task.yml
```

The resulting **`install_pgsql-single-task.yml`** file code is shown in *Figure* 9.26:

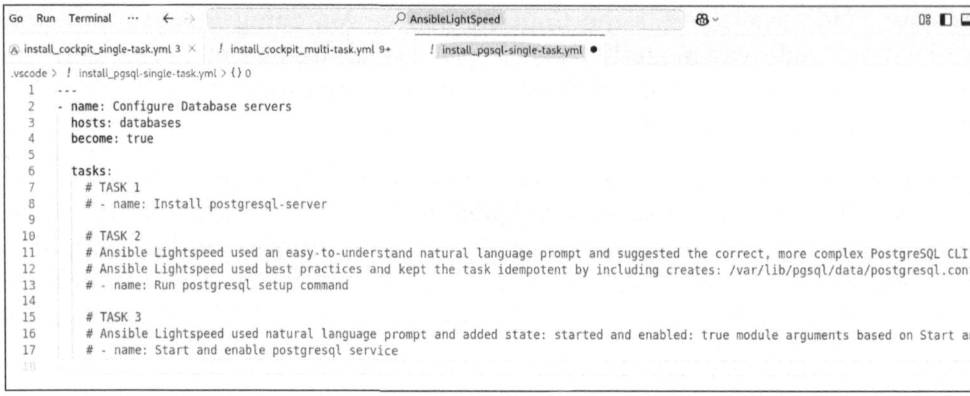

***Figure 9.26:** The copied **install_pgsql-single-task.yml** file code*

The copied text, from the **`install_pgsql-single-task.yml`** file code, is shown as follows:

```
---
- name: Configure Database servers
  hosts: databases
  become: true

  tasks:
    # TASK 1
    # - name: Install postgresql-server

    # TASK 2
    # Ansible Lightspeed used an easy-to-understand natural lan-
guage prompt and suggested the correct, more complex PostgreSQL
CLI command to initiate the database.
    # Ansible Lightspeed used best practices and kept the task
idempotent by including creates: /var/lib/pgsql/data/postgresql.
conf in the suggestion.
    # - name: Run postgresql setup command

    # TASK 3
    # Ansible Lightspeed used natural language prompt and added
state: started and enabled: true module arguments based on Start
and enable... in the Ansible task description.
    # - name: Start and enable postgresql service
```

We can generate a code recommendation for the task on **Line 8** of the code list, by placing the cursor at the end of the line and selecting the *Enter* key.

Notice the code attribution details associated with this recommendation, which will appear under the **`Ansible`** tab at the bottom of the **VS Code** interface once the code recommendation is finalized.

The example **VS Code** version and environment we are using is shown in *Figure 9.27*:

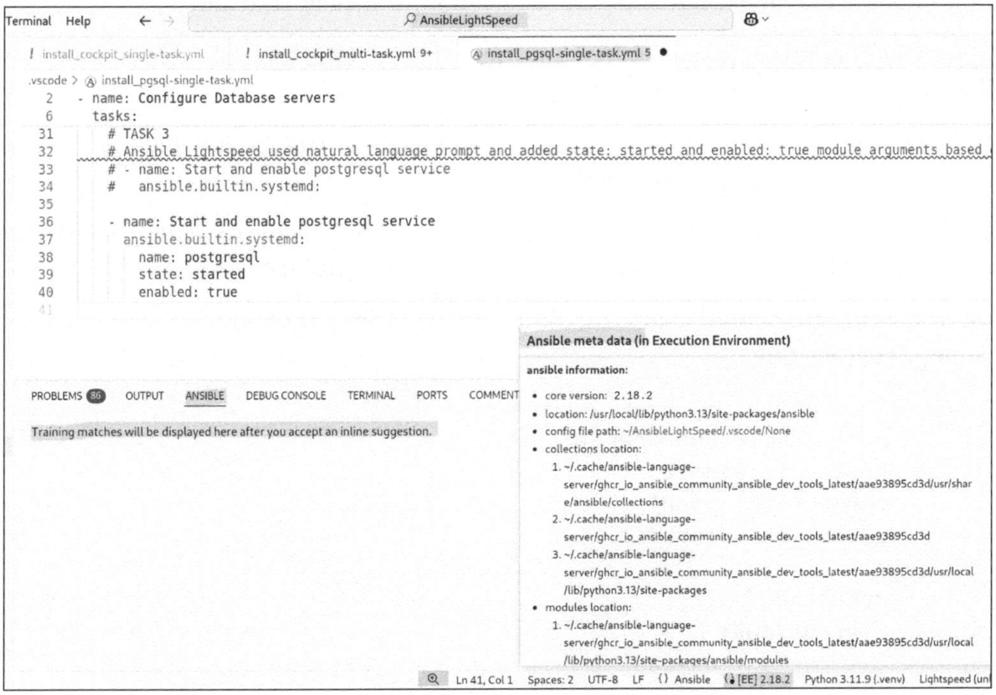

***Figure 9.27:** The example **VS Code** version and environment we are using*

We had to **accept** the **AI-**generated code suggestions (using the **Tab** key) **before** the **Ansible** content source matching tab provided details about the code's origins.

```
- name: Install postgresql-server
ansible.builtin.package:
    name: postgresql-server
    state: present
```

The three most likely content sources used in training the **WCA** model– which produced the **AI**-generated code recommendations–should be listed within the **`Ansible`** tab.

Post-processing of Tasks and YAML files

This last section describes another element of code generation that **WCA** is very good at, which is understanding the **`context`** within the **`Ansible Playbook`** it is executing.

If a variable or attribute is defined earlier within an **`Ansible Playbook`**, it will be recalled and referenced, if required, for the generation of subsequent lines of code.

We can make this feature visible by using a previously generated block of **`Ansible`**

Task code, and then updating the value assigned to a named variable at the beginning of the **Ansible Playbook**. Then, we can regenerate the **Task** code block.

The newly generated **Task block** should use the updated variable name (and so be different from the original code block).

First, we created a **New File... YAML** based **Ansible Playbook** which was named **demo_provision_ec2_instance.yml**.

Next, we copied and pasted the following code block into the new file, **demo_provision_ec2_instance.yml Ansible Playbook** and then saved the file.

(We retrieved the code using the link: https://ibm.github.io/wca-generative-ai-training/customizing/)

```
---
- name: EC2 Cloud Operations
  hosts: localhost
  connection: local
  gather_facts: false

  module_defaults:
    group/aws:
      region: us-east-1

  # vars:
  #   ec2_instance:
  #     name: lightspeed-instance-01
  #     key_name: lightspeed-keypair
  #     image_id: ami-016eb5d644c333ccb # RHEL 9 us-east-1
  #     tags:
  #       function: lightspeed-demo
  #     security_group: secgroup-lightspeed

  tasks:
        # TASK 1
        # # 1a. Uncomment task description below and generate a
task suggestion.
        # #     Note - Best practices: The suggestion used the
Fully Qualified Collection name.
        # #     Note - Context: Ansible Lightspeed used the
Playbook name "EC2 Cloud Operations" to use the correct "amazon.
aws.ec2_vpc_subnet_info" module.

    - name: Gather subnet info tag:Name subnet-lightspeed

        # TASK 2
        # # 2a. Uncomment task description below and generate a
```

```
task suggestion.
        # #     Note - Context: The suggestion included the
previous task's registered variable in the suggestion.
        # #     Note - Accuracy: The suggestion provides the
correct key value from the previously task's registered variable.

    - name: Create vpc_subnet_id var

        # TASK 3
        # # 3a. Uncomment task description "Provision t3.micro
instance" below and generate a task suggestion.
        # #     Note - Efficiency: The suggestion provides
practical variable examples to improve efficiency.

    - name: Provision t3.micro instance

        # # 3b. Remove the above task and suggestion.
        # #     Uncomment 2nd task description "Provision t3.
micro instance using ec2_instance var".
        # #     Generate an updated suggestion.
        # #     Note - Context: The updated suggestion includes
the "ec2_instance variable fields in the suggestion"

    - name: Provision t3.micro instance using ec2_instance var
```

TASK 1 (**Line 26**) and **TASK 2** (**Line 33**), highlighted in *Figure* 9.28, are designed to retrieve information about a network subnet that is to be provisioned and then it creates a virtual private cloud (**VPC**) definition based on the retrieved details.

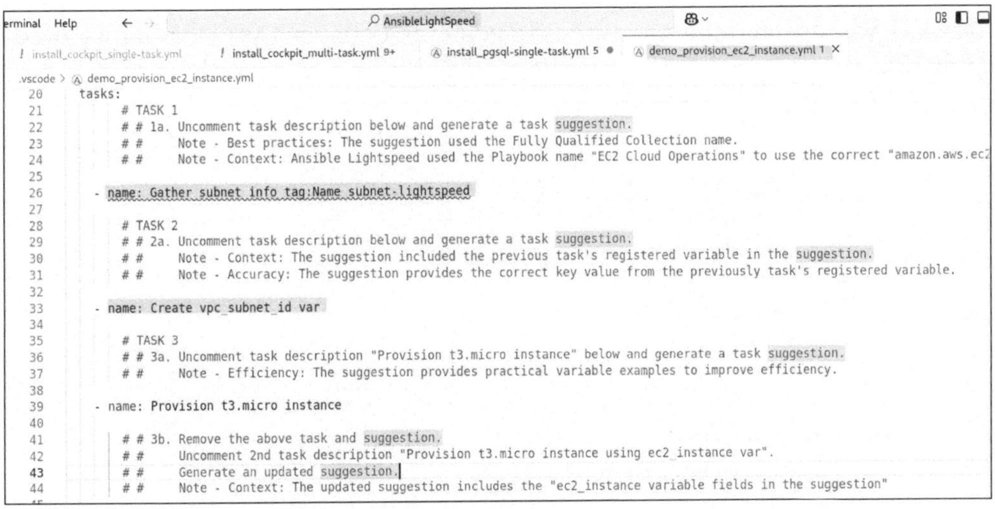

Figure 9.28: *The* **TASK 1** (**Line 26**) *and* **TASK 2** (**Line 33**), *highlighted, retrieve information from a subnet*

Next, we generated suggested code for **`TASK 1`** (**Line 26**) by placing the cursor at the end of the line, selecting *Enter*, and then select **`Accept [Tab]`** for the code, as highlighted in *Figure 9.29*:

```
tasks:
    # TASK 1
    # # 1a. Uncomment task description below and generate a task suggestion.
    # #     Note - Best practices: The suggestion used the Fully Qualified Collection name.
    # #     Note - Context: Ansible Lightspeed used the Playbook name "EC2 Cloud Operations" t
  < 1/2 > Accept  Accept Word  Ctrl + RightArrow  ...   subnet-lightspeed
  amazon.aws.ec2_vpc_subnet_info:

    # TASK 2
    # # 2a. Uncomment task description below and generate a task suggestion.
```

Figure 9.29**: Next, we generated suggested code for **TASK 1** (**Line 26**), by selecting **Accept

This creates the code as shown in *Figure 9.30*:

```
.vscode > demo_provision_ec2_instance.yml
20    tasks:
21        # TASK 1
22        # # 1a. Uncomment task description below and generate a task suggestion.
23        # #     Note - Best practices: The suggestion used the Fully Qualified Collection name.
24        # #     Note - Context: Ansible Lightspeed used the Playbook name "EC2 Cloud Operations" t
25
26      - name: Gather subnet info tag:Name subnet-lightspeed
27        amazon.aws.ec2_vpc_subnet_info:
28          filters:
29            "tag:Name": subnet-lightspeed
30        register: vpc_subnet_info
31
32        # TASK 2
33        # # 2a. Uncomment task description below and generate a task suggestion.
```

***Figure 9.30:** The code is generated for **TASK 1,** as highlighted*

Afterward, we repeated the same steps to generate code for **`TASK 2`**, as highlighted in *Figure 9.31:*

```
.vscode > demo_provision_ec2_instance.yml
19
20    tasks:
21        # TASK 1
22        # # 1a. Uncomment task description below and generate a task suggestion.
23        # #     Note - Best practices: The suggestion used the Fully Qualified Collection name.
24        # #     Note - Context: Ansible Lightspeed used the Playbook name "EC2 Cloud Operations" to use the correct "amazon.aws
25
26      - name: Gather subnet info tag:Name subnet-lightspeed
27        amazon.aws.ec2_vpc_subnet_info:
28          filters:
29            "tag:Name": subnet-lightspeed
30        register: vpc_subnet_info
31
32        # TASK 2
33        # # 2a. Uncomment task description below and generate a task suggestion.
34        # #     Note - Context: The suggestion included the previous task's registered variable in the suggestion.
35        # #     Note - Accuracy: The suggestion provides the correct key value from the previously task's registered variable.
36
37      - name: Create vpc_subnet_id var
38        set_fact:
39          vpc_subnet_id: "{{ vpc_subnet_info.subnets[0].id }}"
40
41        # TASK 3
42        # # 3a. Uncomment task description "Provision t3.micro instance" below and generate a task suggestion.
```

***Figure 9.31:** The code is generated for **TASK 2,** as highlighted*

The first round of **WCA**-generated code produces a code block with a **`register: vpc_subnet_info`** (**Line 30**), this assigns the **VPC** definition, based on **`vpc_subnet_info`** to a variable **`vpc_subnet_id`**, as shown highlighted on **Line 39.**

The **WCA**-generated code that follows for **TASK 2**, on **Line 39** (previously **Line 33**) in the copied template) recommends a code block with **`vpc_subnet_id: "{ { vpc_subnet_info.subnets[0].subnet_id } }`** as the value associated with the **VPC**'s subnet ID.

As demonstrated, the variable **`subnet_info`** that was generated in the previous **`TASK 1`**, is now also referenced in the second **TASK 2**. This demonstrates the contextual awareness of **WCA** in action.

Now, to demonstrate the tied relationship, we change the name of the variable **`vpc_subnet_info`** to **`vpc_subnet_name`** on **Line 30**. Then we deleted the code block recommendations under **Line 37** and regenerated the task.

We now observe that the new **AI**-generated code block of **`TASK 2`** now references the variable **`subnet_name`** that was just modified in **`TASK 1`**, as shown in *Figure* 9.32:

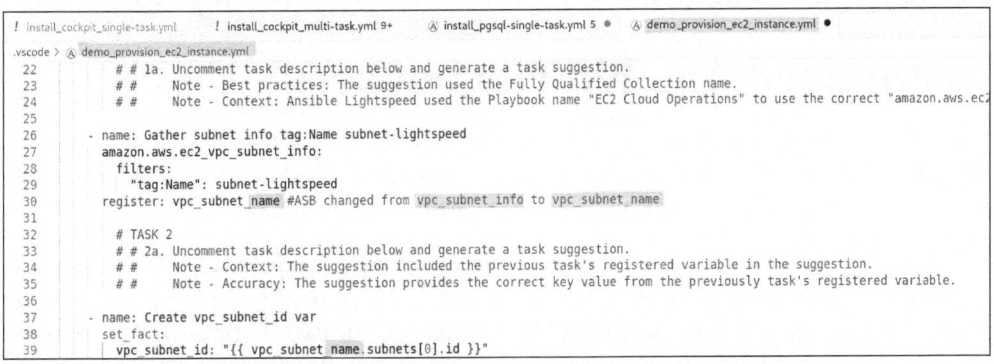

Figure 9.32: *We now see that, now the AI generated block of* **TASK 2** *references the variable* ***subnet_name***

WCA has now generated code for **`TASK 2`** that takes into account the **`modified context and variables`** from **`TASK 1`** of our test **`Ansible Playbook.`**

We can continue generating **`TASK 2`** code, which creates additional **sub-net** variables, as illustrated in *Figure* 9.33:

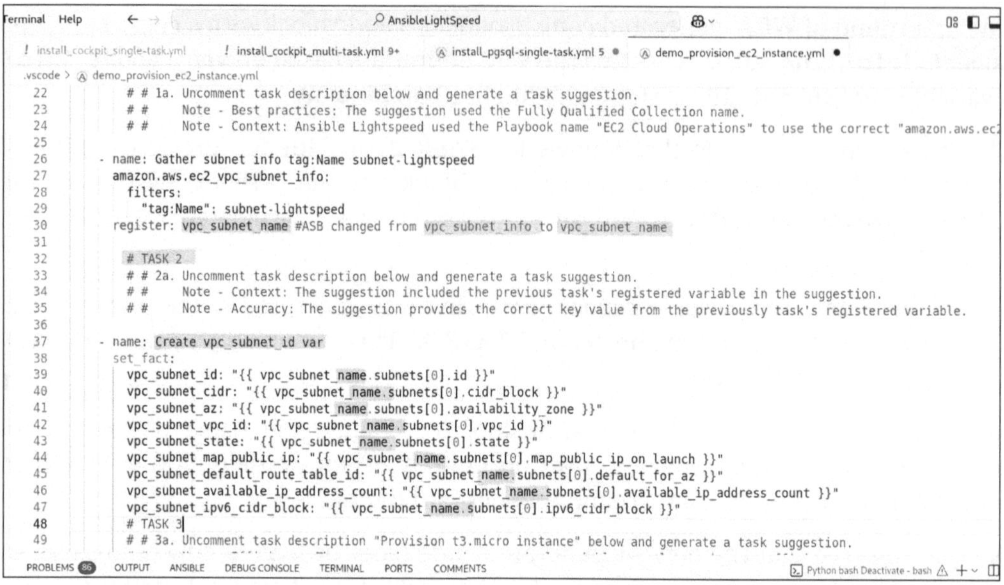

***Figure* 9.33**: *We can continue generating* **TASK 2** *code, which creates additional* **sub-net** *variables*

Customized Ansible Playbooks

In the next **sub-section**, we evaluated the use of customization for an **Ansible Playbook** and tested how changes to the **Ansible Task** natural language text descriptions affect the recommended code produced by **WCA**.

Since we are using generative **AI** and **Large Language Models** (**LLM**s) there can be inconsistent code generated for each execution. For this reason, **LLM**s are considered to be treated as "`non-deterministic`" systems, unlike standard mathematical functions, where the results are predictable and consistent (for example, these latter mathematical functions are examples of "`deterministic`" systems).

So, even a slight modification to the **Task** description or a single change to how an **Ansible Playbook** is defined can modify the **AI**-generated code recommendations.

By using the **Model Tuning** functionality built into **IBM watsonx Code Assistant**, **Enterprises** and **DevOps** users can customize the AI-generated recommendations by tuning a user-specific **LLM** using an **Enterprise's** own **Ansible Playbooks**. The content and code recommendations that **IBM watsonx Code Assistant** suggests can be modified to follow an **Enterprise's** standard operating procedures (**SOP**s), best practices, and programming styles.

We downloaded IBM template code headed **`CUSTOM PLAYBOOK 1`**, which was created as a training example by **Red Hat** and **IBM**:

The **`Ansible Playbook`** code was copied and pasted from the **`TEMPLATE`** file on the web page, link: https://ibm.github.io/wca-generative-ai-training/customizing/ into a **`New File...`** within **VS Code**, saved as, **`customplaybook1.yml`,** which has the following code:

```
# CUSTOM PLAYBOOK #1 – Invoke 2 modules to automatically update 2
types of servers.

---
# TASK 1
- name: Update web servers
  hosts: webservers
  become: true

  tasks:
    - name: Ensure apache is at the latest version

    - name: Write the apache config file

# TASK 2
- name: Update db servers
  hosts: databases
  become: true
  tasks:
    - name: Ensure postgresql is at the latest version

    - name: Ensure that postgresql is started
```

Note: Ansible Lightspeed *and* **WCA** *will only generate code recommendations for* **Ansible Playbooks** *and* **YAML** *files.* **VS Code** *auto-detects the programming language of the document being edited, but sometimes we need to manually specify the language. Even if working with a* **YAML** *file, it is important to specify the language mode as the* **Ansible for Lightspeed** *plugin, to ensure this is used by the* **VS Code IDE***.*

To set the language mode correctly:

- *In the bottom-right corner of the* **VS Code** *interface, mouse-over the* **Select Language Mode***.*
- *A console will appear at the top of* **VS Code** *with a drop-down list of options, so select* **Ansible** *from the suggested languages, or enter the text directly and select the* **Enter** *key.*
- *Confirm that the* **Select Language Mode** *option in the bottom-right corner displays* **Ansible.**

The template **CUSTOM PLAYBOOK #1** contains two sets of tasks:

- **TASK 1** (**Lines 5-12**) checks if the web server software is up to date and runs an update if necessary
- **TASK 2** (**Lines 16-23**) checks if the database server software is up to date and then updates it if necessary
- The following instruction on **Line 12**, prompts **Red Hat Ansible** to create a configuration file for an **Apache** webserver:

  `- name: Write the Apache config file`

On placing your cursor at the end of **Line 12** and selecting the *Enter* key, we generated the **WCA**- code for the task. Then we have to select the **`Accept (or Tab)`** command button to commit the recommendation, as shown in *Figure* 9.34:

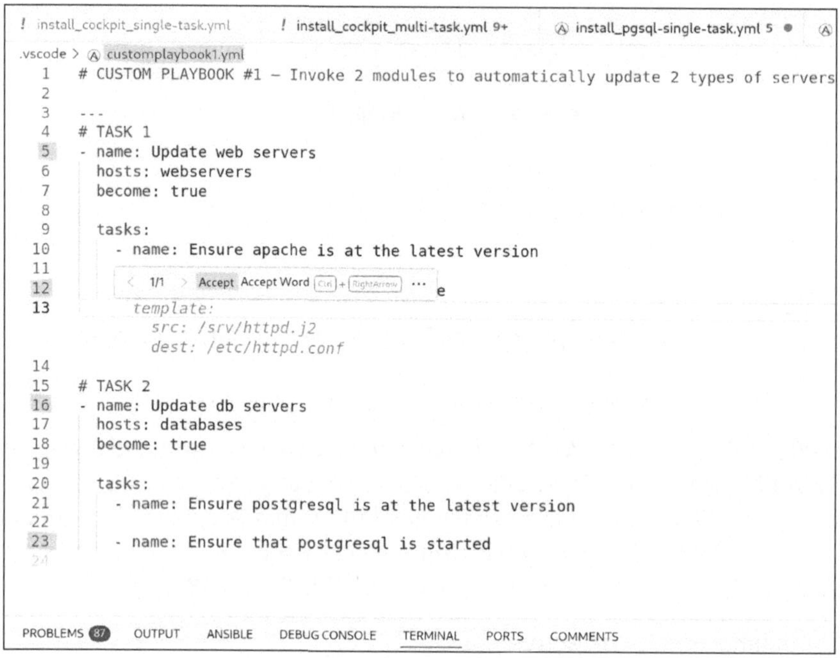

***Figure 9.34**: We have to select the **Accept (or Tab)** command button to commit the recommendation*

In the **IBM/Red Hat** training website two tabs are presented. The first is the **AI**-Generated Code, which we re-ran on our Red Hat Linux server.

We had the following AI-generated output code for **`TASK 1`**:

```
# TASK 1
- name: Update web servers
  hosts: webservers
  become: true
```

```
tasks:
  - name: Ensure apache is at the latest version
    yum:
      name: httpd
      state: latest


  - name: Write the apache config file
    template:
      src: /srv/httpd.j2
      dest: /etc/httpd.conf
```

The IBM training web page `SOLUTION CODE` tab showed the expected (**`correct`**) code for performing the task that was written by a human programmer. We hoped that the **AI**-generated code would be at least as good as the manually-written solution.

The **`human-generated SOLUTION CODE`** was as follows for **`TASK 1`** **(additional text in bold):**

```
- name: Write the apache config file
  ansible.builtin.template:
    src: /srv/httpd.j2
    dest: /etc/httpd.config
    mode: "0644"
```

We can see the **AI-generated** code recommendations satisfy some of the requests, but also miss the target in a few areas. When compared to the **IBM** human **`SOLUTION CODE`** tab, the **AI**-generated code in our run of **VS Code** missed the **`ansible.builtin`** pre-script text. Also, the last line **`mode: "0644"`** was completely missing from the **AI** version!

IBM point out that in general, the more ambiguous the **Task** description, the greater the likelihood that **WCA** will misinterpret the author's intent. They recommended that **`Ansible Playbook`** authors should use more precise natural language terms and descriptions.

Next, we deleted the **WCA-suggested lines of code** from the **`Ansible Playbook`** and then changed the description on **Line 12** to the following code block, as recommended on the **IBM** training web page:

Changed From:

```
- name: Write the apache config file
```

To:

```
- name: Write the apache config file where src equals httpd.j2 and
dest equals httpd.config
```

We then pressed *Enter* and the *Accept* command button, to accept the new **WCA** code recommendations, resulting in the **AI-**generated code as highlighted in *Figure* 9.35:

```
.vscode > customplaybook1.yml
# CUSTOM PLAYBOOK #1 – Invoke 2 modules to automatically update 2 types of servers.

---
# TASK 1
- name: Update web servers
  hosts: webservers
  become: true

  tasks:
    - name: Ensure apache is at the latest version
      yum:
        name: httpd
        state: latest


    - name: Write the apache config file where src equals httpd.j2 and dest equals httpd.config
      template:
        src: httpd.j2
        dest: /etc/httpd/config/httpd.config

```

Figure 9.35: *We pressed* **Enter** *and selected* **Accept** *for the new* **WCA** *code recommendations*

The resulting **WCA**-recommended code should be similar to the **AI** code from the web-page:

```
- name: Write the apache config file where src equals httpd.j2 and
dest equals httpd.config
  ansible.builtin.template:
    src: httpd.j2
    dest: /etc/httpd/conf/httpd.conf
```

The **`src: httpd.j2`** recommendation in the **`IBM`** tab is an exact match to the natural language description we set.

Our result did not exactly match the IBM example AI generator result. It appears to have an improved response, but did not include the **`Red Hat Ansible mode`** code for the file security.

IBM also found, in their second **AI** run, that the **mode: '0644'** recommendation that they had found previously, had been left out of the suggested task code, exactly as we had in our first run.

So, we tried **IBM**'s third iteration of the natural language description, as follows:

```
- name: Write the apache config file where src equals httpd.j2 and
dest equals httpd.config and mode equals 0644
```

This gave a more exact response, as shown in *Figure* 9.36:

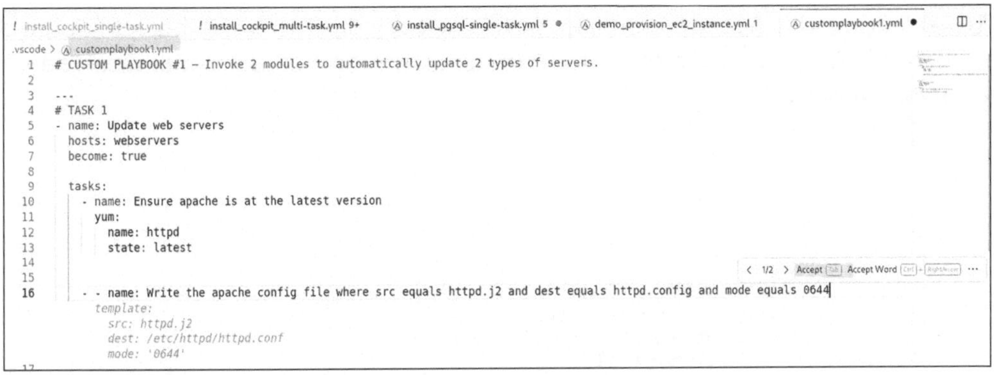

***Figure 9.36**: We tried **IBM**'s third iteration of the natural language description*

The resulting **WCA**-recommended code correctly picked up on the **`mode: '0644'`** request made in the modified task description.

We tried the **`tuning-example.yml`** Ansible Playbook located within the **`Model Customization`** subdirectory of the hands-on **IBM** lab templates. The full directory address, as well as the **Ansible Playbook** code, were in the following **IBM** code block heading.

```
~/ansible-wca-demo-kit/Model Customization/tuning-example.yml
---
- name: Deploy infrastructure
  hosts: all

  tasks:
    - name: Create an OpenShift cluster
```

We get the following **AI Red Hat Ansible** code generated, before selecting **Accept** as shown in *Figure 9.37*:

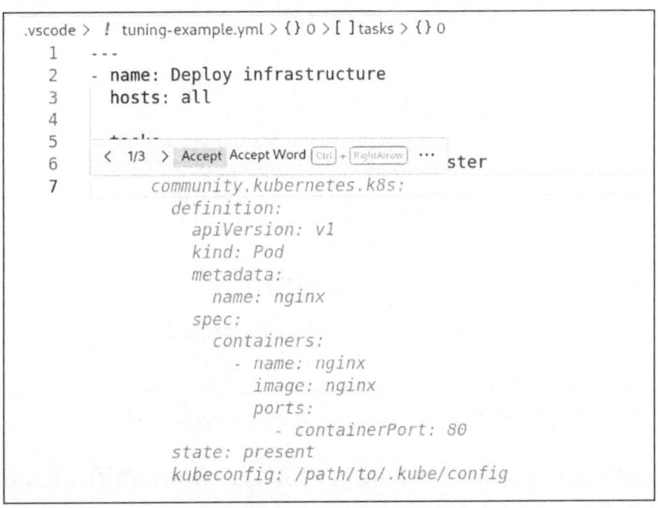

Figure 9.37**: We get the following **AI Red Hat Ansible** code generated, before selecting **Accept

After selecting the **Accept** command, we discover that there is an additional **AI** recommendation, when we place the cursor at the end of the generated code, as shown in *Figure 9.38*:

.vscode > ! tuning-example.yml > {} 0 > [ ] tasks > {} 0 > {} community.kubernetes.k8s > kubeconfig

```
---
- name: Deploy infrastructure
  hosts: all

  tasks:
    - name: Create an OpenShift cluster
      community.kubernetes.k8s:
        definition:
          apiVersion: v1
          kind: Pod
          metadata:
            name: nginx
          spec:
            containers:
              - name: nginx
                image: nginx
                ports:
                  - containerPort:
        state: present
        kubeconfig: /path/to/.kube/config
```

< 1/1 > Accept Tab Accept Word Ctrl + RightArrow ...

***Figure 9.38**: When we have selected the **Accept** command, there is an additional **AI** recommendation*

The full **AI**-generated code is shown in *Figure 9.39*:

.vscode > ! tuning-example.yml > {} 0 > [ ] tasks > {} 0 > {} community.kubernetes.k8s

```
---
- name: Deploy infrastructure
  hosts: all

  tasks:
    - name: Create an OpenShift cluster
      community.kubernetes.k8s:
        definition:
          apiVersion: v1
          kind: Pod
          metadata:
            name: nginx
          spec:
            containers:
              - name: nginx
                image: nginx
                ports:
                  - containerPort: 80
        state: present
        kubeconfig: /path/to/.kube/config
```

***Figure 9.39**: The full AI-generated code is shown*

The full generated code recommendations for the **OpenShift** cluster creation task, listed in *Figure* 9.39, did not follow the standard, unmodified output from **WCA's IBM Granite** base models, which is shown as follows, from the training lab web page:

```
---
- name: Deploy infrastructure
  hosts: all

  tasks:
    - name: Create an OpenShift cluster
      ansible.builtin.command: oadm create-cluster --wait=false
--name=openshift-cluster
      register: oadm_create_cluster
      changed_when: "'created' in oadm_create_cluster.stdout"
      failed_when: "'already exists' not in oadm_create_cluster.
stdout"
```

When using the standard **IBM Granite** model recommendations, the **AI** recommends making use of the **`ansible.builtin.command Ansible Module`** – which is a standard, best-practice way to perform these types of deployments. However, our code generation has obviously moved on since the training course was published!

We can get an **AI**-based **`GitHub CoPilot`** explanation by highlighting the **`Create an Openshift cluster`** **AI**-generated code and then using the right-click to select the menus, as shown in *Figure* 9.40:

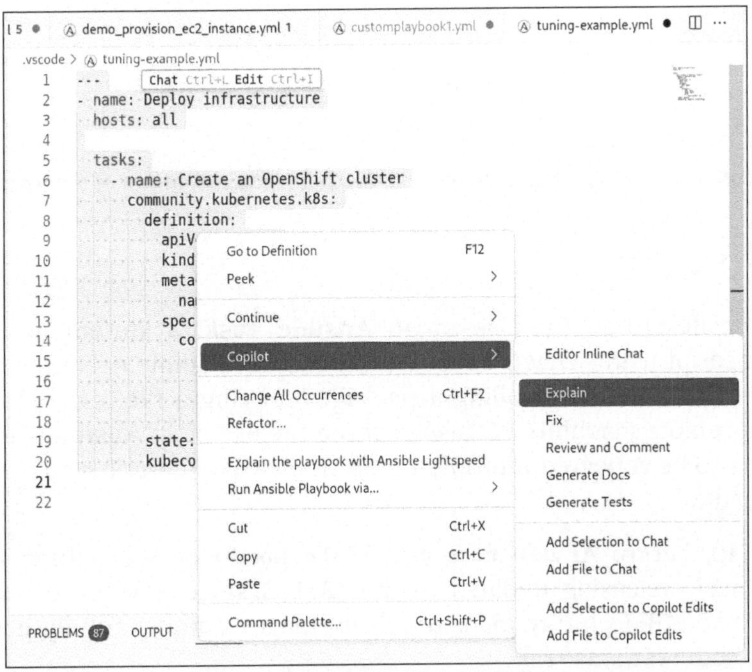

Figure 9.40: *We can get an* **AI** *based* **GitHub CoPilot** *explanation , using the right-click to select the menus*

The **CoPilot chat** is opened, with a full-text explanation of the **Ansible** code, as illustrated in *Figure* 9.41:

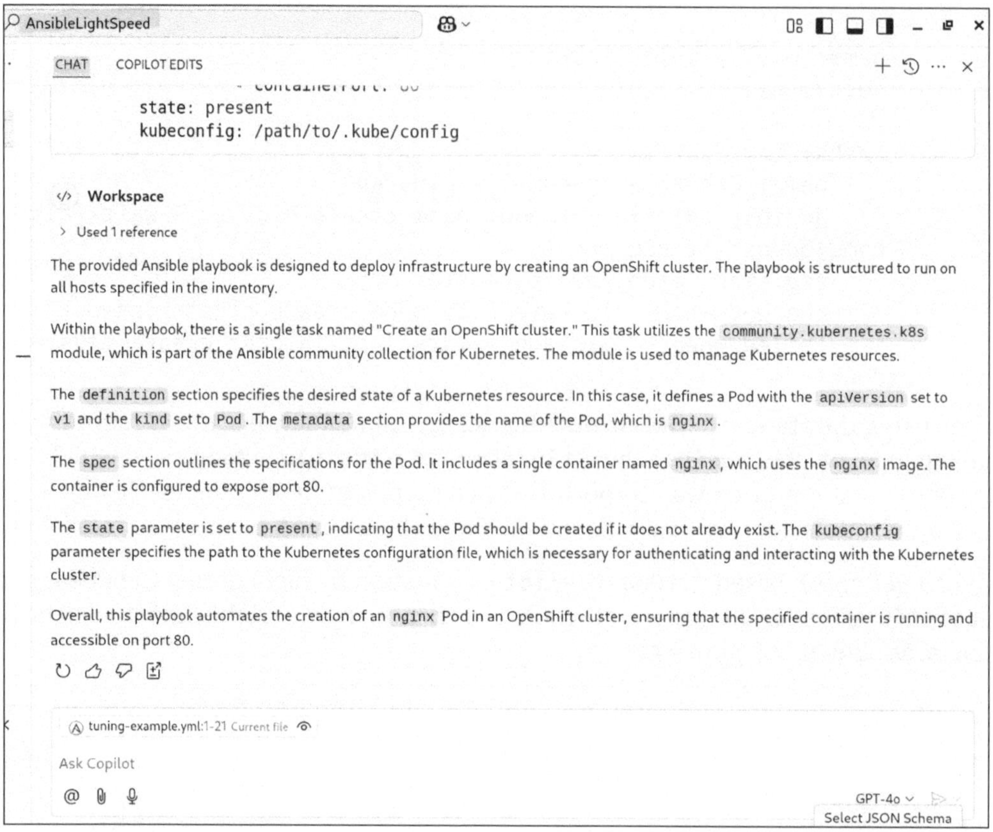

***Figure 9.41:** The **CoPilot chat** is opened, with a full text explanation of the **Ansible** code*

Conclusion

This chapter described the use of an **Ansible Task**, a statement in **Ansible**'s automation script using **YAML**-based **Playbooks** for a single executed action. This was outlined for use for installing a package, copying a file, or shutting down a service on a remote machine. We also covered the use of an **Ansible Task** where an action needs to be repeated multiple times and with a guarantee to always deliver the same result.

In ***Chapter 10, Future AI advances and IBM's Roadmap***, we outline **IBM**'s plans for continuously releasing updates to the **IBM Granite** models to improve their performance and **IBM**'s future plans to release longer-context and **Python** and **Java**-specialized model variants.

Points to Remember

- **Ansible Lightspeed** and **WCA** will only generate code recommendations for **Ansible Playbooks** and **YAML** files. **VS Code** auto-detects the programming language of the document being edited, but sometimes we need to manually specify the language.
- "**`Uncommenting`**" the **#** comment block lines of code makes them viable for execution and afterward, these lines are considered as valid Playbook "**`context`**" for AI code generation.
- The **Red Hat Ansible** code language, and **YAML**-based **Playbooks** are similar to **Python**, as they are very sensitive to white spacing and indentation. We need to be very careful to observe the correct syntax for the indentation and characters used on blocks of **`Red Hat Ansible`** code.

Multiple Choice Questions

1. What name is given to the "**blueprints**" described by Red Hat?
   a. Red Hat Ansible Tasks
   b. Red Hat Ansible Playbooks
   c. Red Hat Ansible Roles
   d. Red Hat Ansible Modules
2. Which token word does the **YAML** code for an **Ansible** playgroup **`.yml`** file start with to denote a task description?
   a. `hosts:`
   b. `- name:`
   c. `name:`
   d. `tasks:`
3. Which one of the following control characters can be used to generate **Ansible** code in the **VS Code IDE**?
   a. (Ctrl + A)
   b. (Ctrl + C)
   c. (Ctrl + I)
   d. (Ctrl + V)

Answers

1. c
2. b
3. c

Questions

1. Describe the syntax used to provide comment lines used to generate code for multi-task `Red Hat Ansible Playbooks` in the **VS Code IDE.**
2. List the advantages that `Ansible Roles` provide and list some of the types of **Roles** which can be used in an Enterprise.
3. Explain, with some examples, the impact changing the Natural Language comment descriptions can have on the generation of the associated `Red Hat Ansible` code.

Key Terms

- **Ansible CodeLLM:** is an **AI**-powered code editor for assisting with the writing and validation of **Red Hat Ansible** code
- **Ansible Galaxy:** is an open source website, used for searching and downloading Ansible community uploaded, **Red Hat Ansible** collections and roles.
- **Ansible Task**: A task is a block of code that the **Red Hat Ansible** system runs on one or more target servers which can be used to install program libraries or install or start other system software components.
- **Ansible Roles**: Roles are collections that can include tasks, templates, and variables of similar tasks with supporting files that can be used to build a complete server cluster environment.
- **Ansible Lint:** is a command-line tool for validating the code written for **Red Hat Ansible Playbooks.** It highlights syntax issues and can prompt for best practice code changes.
- **Ansible Modules:** Are small code sets used by **Red Hat Ansible** to perform tasks on target server systems, such as yum on the **Red Hat Linux** system, used to manage packages on Linux systems that use the **YUM** package manager.
- **Ansible Playbook:** A **Red Hat Ansible Playbook** is a **YAML** code file containing the configuration requirements, deployment steps, and code language. It can also include the security policy required by remote systems.
- **Copilot:** In software terms an **AI** code assistant which can suggest lines of

code and validate existing code. Examples are **GitHub Copilot** and **Microsoft Copilot**.

- **DevOps:** short for "**Development" and "Operations**" is a modern concept of Software Engineering where the aim is to integrate **Development** and **IT Operations** teams to provide a higher quality of software system testing, installation, and maintenance.
- **LLM**: Large Language Model
- **Openshift: Red Hat Openshift** is a hybrid cloud-based container system, based on the **Kubernetes** platform designed to automate the deployment of a containerized cluster of servers to a Virtual Cloud-based system or an on-premise "**Bare Metal**" environment providing automated installation and upgrades of server level systems.
- **VPC:** A **Virtual Private Cloud (VPC)** is a sand-boxed virtual network used by an enterprise within a public cloud server system, providing a secure virtual network.
- **VS Code:** is a Microsoft open-source **IDE** based on Microsoft Visual Studio, capable of running on multiple operating systems, including **Linux**.
- **WCA: IBM watsonx Code Assistant** is an **IBM Cloud**-based service that uses **Large Language Models** (**LLMs**)and a generative **AI** system to provide **AI** code generation functionality for software development.
- **YAML:** Used for coding **Red Hat Ansible** files, is short for "**Yet Another Markup Language**". It is a superset of the **JSON** notation, meaning **JSON** files are valid for use in **YAML.** It has additional features, not supported by **JSON**, allowing integer and floating point variables and data structures such as lists and arrays.

References

- Top considerations for building a production-ready AI/ML environment:

  https://www.redhat.com/en/resources/building-production-ready-ai-ml-environment-e-book?percmp=7015Y000003sv1aQAA

- The Red Hat Ansible Automation Platform - the platform for mission-critical automation.

  https://www.redhat.com/en/technologies/management/ansible

- Generating Code with IBM watsonx Code Assistant for Red Hat Ansible Lightspeed

  https://ibm.github.io/wca-generative-ai-training/generating/ and

  https://www.ibm.com/new/announcements/reshaping-it-automation-with-ibm-watson-code-assistant

- Red Hat Ansible Automation Platform: A beginner's guide:

  https://www.redhat.com/en/resources/ansible-automation-platform-beginners-guide-ebook

- Red Hat Ansible Automation Platform 2.5:

  https://docs.redhat.com/en/documentation/red_hat_ansible_automation_platform/2.5

- Red Hat Ansible Lightspeed with IBM watsonx Code Assistant 2.x_latest:

  https://docs.redhat.com/en/documentation/red_hat_ansible_lightspeed_with_ibm_watsonx_code_assistant/2.x_latest

- Red Hat Ansible Lightspeed with IBM watsonx Code Assistant User Guide:

  https://docs.redhat.com/en/documentation/red_hat_ansible_lightspeed_with_ibm_watsonx_code_assistant/2.x_latest/html/red_hat_ansible_lightspeed_with_ibm_watsonx_code_assistant_user_guide/index

- **Legal Notice:**

  https://docs.redhat.com/en/documentation/red_hat_ansible_lightspeed_with_ibm_watsonx_code_assistant/2.x_latest/html/red_hat_ansible_lightspeed_with_ibm_watsonx_code_assistant_user_guide/legal-notice

- Ansible terms:

  https://www.logicmonitor.com/blog/ansible-key-terms-getting-started

- Ansible Lint:

  https://www.redhat.com/en/blog/ansible-lint#:~:text=A%20linter%20is%20a%20tool,package%20high%2Dquality%20Ansible%20content.

CHAPTER 10
Future AI Advances and IBM's Roadmap

Introduction

This chapter covers a review of the future releases and additional functionality expected with the **IBM Granite 3.0** architecture.

IBM has stated that they plan to continuously release updates to their **Granite** models to improve their performance, including leveraging the **CodeNet** instruction dataset (*Puri et al.*, 2021). They have already released long-context as well as **Python**- and **Java**-specialized model variants.

IBM summarized this in the following statement:

"*This structure, coupled with practical examples, case studies, and the inclusion of latest updates enables our readers to confidently utilize* **IBM Granite 3.0** *for transformative business outcomes.*"

IBM describes their approach to the development of **IBM Granite 3.0**, which has been designed for use for commercial purposes, describing how these models are trained by using the data, after it has been cleaned and filtered for things like hate, abuse, and profanity.

With generative **AI** systems built on **IBM Granite 3.0 LLMs** (Large Language Models), developers can translate legacy systems written in **COBOL** into more modern languages like **Java**.

IBM has also endeavored to provide free access to the **LLM** models, they obtained from the process, by licensing of these models with an **Apache 2.0 License**.

Thus, IBM's conclusion in the **GitHub** paper, their research team produced, states:

*"**We release all our Granite 3.0 language models under an Apache 2.0 license for both research and commercial use.** We plan to continuously release updates to these models to improve their performance with safety in mind, e.g., improving multilinguality and coding, including long-context model variants."*

The full **IBM** Research Paper, "**GRANITE 3.0 LANGUAGE MODELS**" is available as a free download from the **GitHub** URL link, as follows:

https://github.com/ibm-granite/granite-3.0-language-models/blob/main/paper.pdf .

Structure

In this chapter, we will discuss the following topics:

- Future **AI** Advances
  - DeepSeek
  - Using `InstructLab` to contribute to the opensource IBM Granite Models
  - Google DeepMind: Gemini 2
- IBM's Roadmap

Future AI Advances

The **IBM Granite 3.0** language models use two standard architectures defined for Large Language Model Transformers (as described in detail in *Chapter 1, The Fundamentals of LLMs*):

- Decoder-only dense transformers
- Decoder-only sparse Mixture-of-Expert (MoE) transformers.

The **IBM Granite** models were trained on 12 trillion tokens of data, including multiple languages as well as code data.

The **MoE** transformers, used by **IBM** (see https://www.ibm.com/think/topics/mixture-of-experts), enable a number of separately trained **AI** systems to be used simultaneously to optimize the response to a prompt. Each separate **AI** system is only accessed for the areas they have been trained on. This approach improves the performance and the quality of the response to a prompt. Surprisingly, this approach to neural network processing was proposed in a paper published over 30 years ago, by the Department of Computer Science, University of Toronto, Canada and **MIT**s, Department of Brain and Cognitive Sciences, Cambridge, USA, in 1991, in a paper entitled "**Adaptive Mixture of Local Experts.**", which is free to download as a pdf file, see: https://www.cs.toronto.edu/~hinton/absps/jjnh91.pdf.

An example of an **LLM**, developed by **IBM Research** and loaded onto the **Hugging Face** web site, using the **MoE** architecture, is sourced for free at the link, https://huggingface.co/ibm-research/PowerMoE-3b.

This is one example of 292 Models (as of March, 2025), which **IBM** have currently released on the **Hugging Face** web site.

The web page supplies a **Python** language example for the **PowerMoE-3b LLM**, as follows:

```
import torch
from transformers import AutoModelForCausalLM, AutoTokenizer
device = "cpu" # "cuda" or "cpu" # ASB Changed from cuda to cpu
on our system (no GPU)
model_path = "ibm/PowerMoE-3b"
tokenizer = AutoTokenizer.from_pretrained(model_path)
# drop device_map if running on CPU
model = AutoModelForCausalLM.from_pretrained(model_path, device_
map=device)
model.eval()
# change input text as desired
prompt = "Write a code to find the maximum value in a list of num-
bers."
# tokenize the text
input_tokens = tokenizer(prompt, return_tensors="pt")
# transfer tokenized inputs to the device
for i in input_tokens:
    input_tokens[i] = input_tokens[i].to(device)
# generate output tokens
output = model.generate(**input_tokens, max_new_tokens=100)
# decode output tokens into text
output = tokenizer.batch_decode(output)
# loop over the batch to print, in this example the batch size is
1
for i in output:
    print(i)
```

We updated the code to run on a **CPU** only system, as commented, and then pasted the **Python code** into a `jupyter lab` session Notebook.

Running this downloads the highlighted `Tensors`, as shown in *Figure 10.1*:

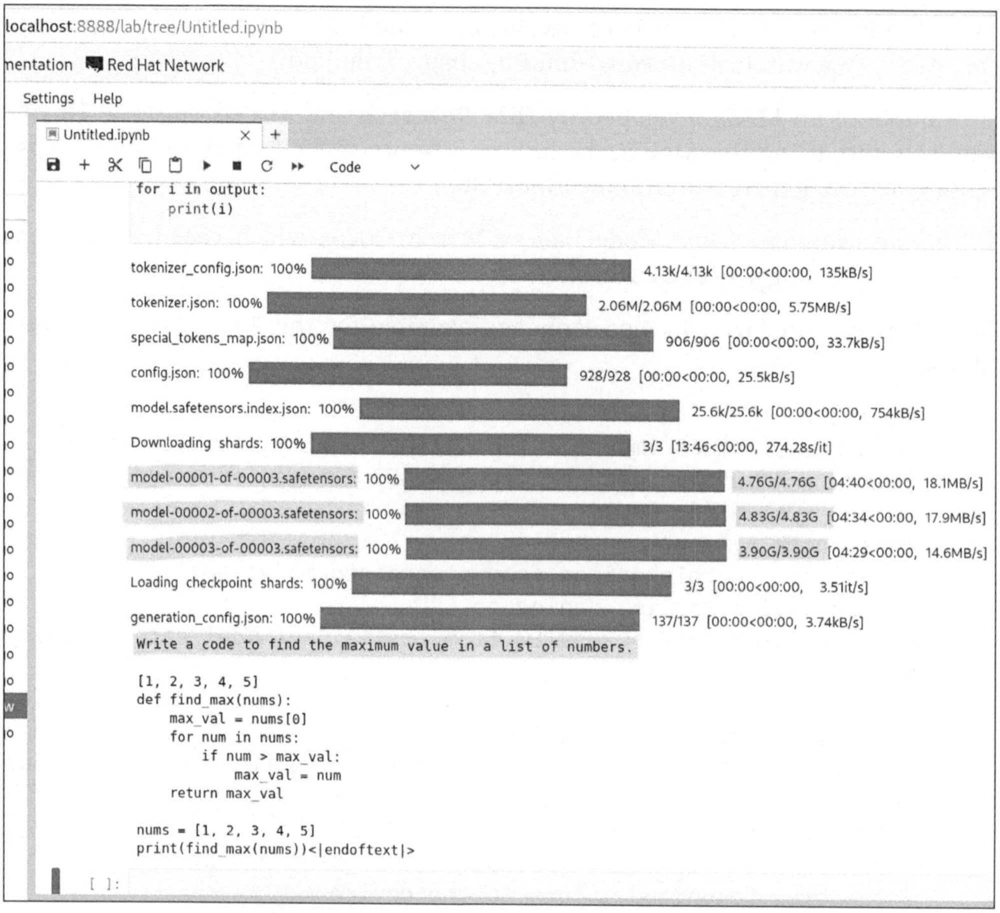

Figure 10.1: *The example* **Python code** *demonstrating the latest Research on the use of a* **Power Scheduler**

There is a free download of the pdf describing this advance in **LLM AI** processing at:

https://arxiv.org/pdf/2408.13359 , published on 11th September, 2024.

IBM have made the resulting **LLM AI** models Open Source at the link:

https://ibm.biz/BdKhLa (which also gives the link to our example **Python code**).

DeepSeek

In December 2024, DeepSeek, an AI research lab in Hangzhou, China, released DeepSeek-V3, the Large Language Model (LLM) on which their AI, DeepSeek-R1 is based.

By late January 2025, most of the technical and financial news sources had established that DeepSeek's performance was at least as good as the other leading LLM models from Anthropic, Google and OpenAI, and it was available at a much lower price. Hence, it is quite likely that `DeepSeek` lab will continue to establish even better systems, based on their early success.

Using `InstructLab` to Contribute to the Opensource IBM Granite Models

There is a *Chapter* 10 resource log file with 17 pages (**`InstallationLogForInstructLab.docx`**) for the installation of **`ilab`**, the command used to launch the **`InstructLab AI`** (which we have also described in full in *Chapter* 7, *Deployment and Enterprise Integration*, in the section, *Installing InstructLab locally without a GPU*). The first commands run are as shown in *Figure* 10.2:

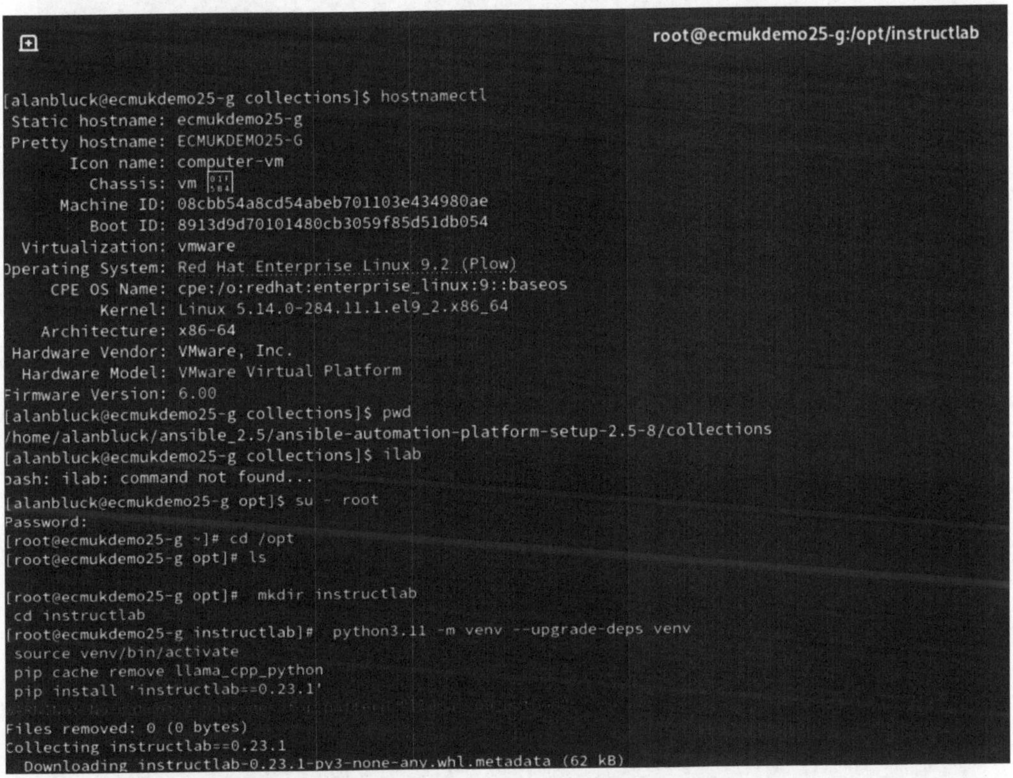

```
root@ecmukdemo25-g:/opt/instructlab

[alanbluck@ecmukdemo25-g collections]$ hostnamectl
 Static hostname: ecmukdemo25-g
 Pretty hostname: ECMUKDEMO25-G
       Icon name: computer-vm
         Chassis: vm
      Machine ID: 08cbb54a8cd54abeb701103e434980ae
         Boot ID: 8913d9d70101480cb3059f85d51db054
  Virtualization: vmware
Operating System: Red Hat Enterprise Linux 9.2 (Plow)
     CPE OS Name: cpe:/o:redhat:enterprise_linux:9::baseos
          Kernel: Linux 5.14.0-284.11.1.el9_2.x86_64
    Architecture: x86-64
 Hardware Vendor: VMware, Inc.
  Hardware Model: VMware Virtual Platform
Firmware Version: 6.00
[alanbluck@ecmukdemo25-g collections]$ pwd
/home/alanbluck/ansible_2.5/ansible-automation-platform-setup-2.5-8/collections
[alanbluck@ecmukdemo25-g collections]$ ilab
bash: ilab: command not found...
[alanbluck@ecmukdemo25-g opt]$ su - root
Password:
[root@ecmukdemo25-g ~]# cd /opt
[root@ecmukdemo25-g opt]# ls

[root@ecmukdemo25-g opt]#  mkdir instructlab
 cd instructlab
[root@ecmukdemo25-g instructlab]#  python3.11 -m venv --upgrade-deps venv
 source venv/bin/activate
 pip cache remove llama_cpp_python
 pip install 'instructlab==0.23.1'

Files removed: 0 (0 bytes)
Collecting instructlab==0.23.1
  Downloading instructlab-0.23.1-py3-none-any.whl.metadata (62 kB)
```

Figure 10.2: *The first commands run to install ilab*

Then, as recommended, we start with the initialization command, as shown in *Figure* 10.3:

```
ilab config init
```

Figure 10.3: *We start with the initialization command*

See: https://developer.ibm.com/tutorials/awb-contributing-knowledge-instructlab-granite/

We can set up the **Python** environment for **ilab** using the commands as follows. The next steps are shown, highlighted in *Figure 10.4*:

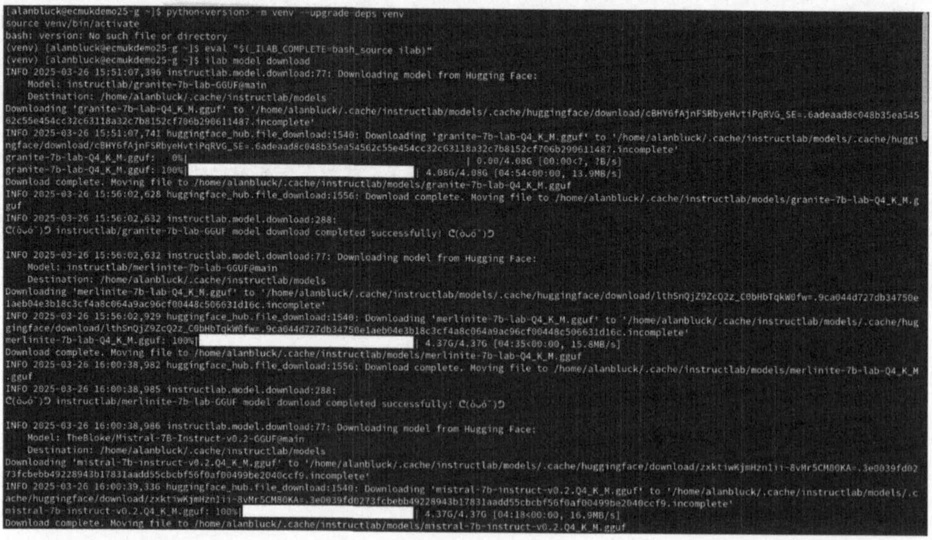

Figure 10.4: *The next steps are shown, highlighted*

The installation summarizes the **LLM** model names and their sizes, and the path location where they were moved to after downloading, as shown in *Figure 10.5*:

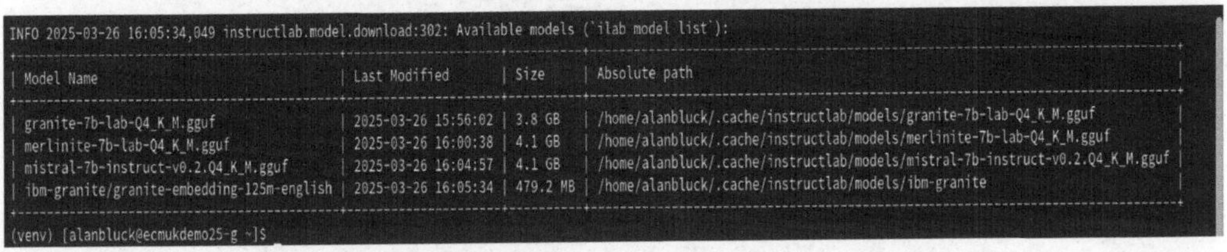

Figure 10.5: *The installation summarizes the* **LLM model** *names and their sizes, and the path location*

The **`ilab model chat`** command can then be run to display the **>>>** prompt for entering questions for an **AI** response, as shown in *Figure 10.6*:

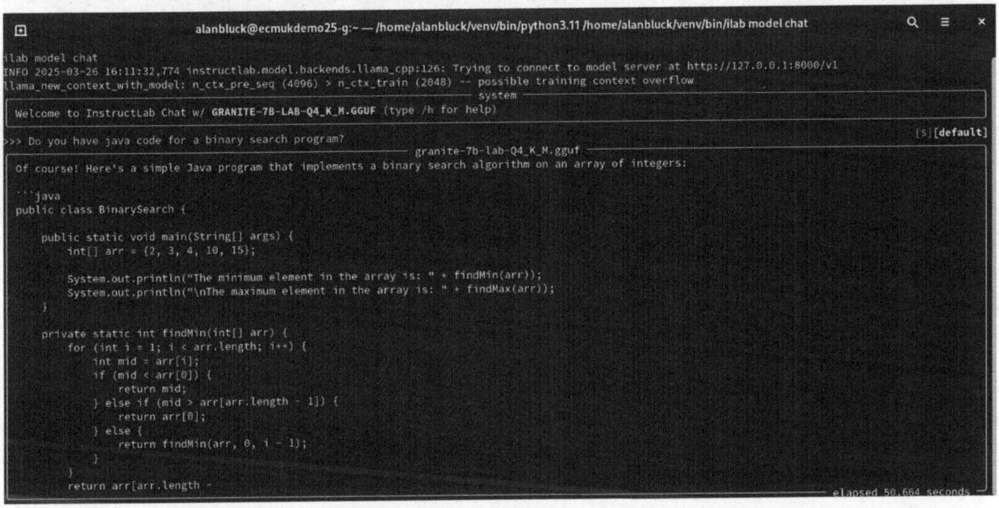

Figure 10.6: *The* **`ilab model chat`** *command is run to display the* **>>>** *prompt for questions for an* **AI** *response*

We entered the question: "**Do you have java code for a binary search program**?"

The **`ilab`** **AI** processed the question to provide java code in 104.979 seconds (we are only running a **CPU** system), as shown in *Figure 10.7*:

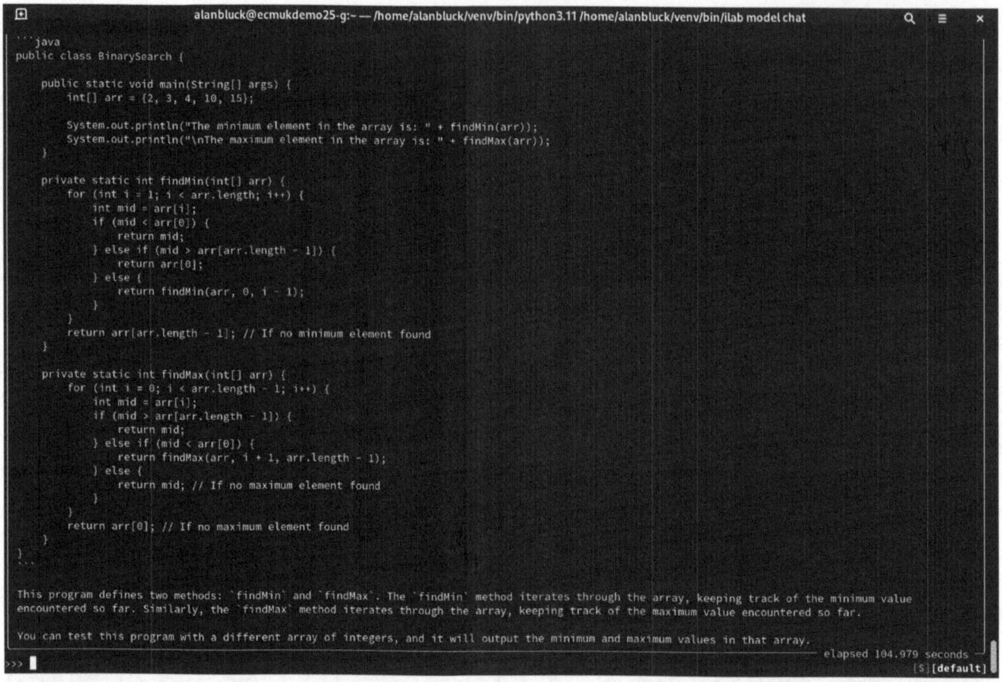

Figure 10.7: *The* **ilab AI** *processed the question to provide java code in 104.979 seconds*

Google DeepMind: Gemini 2

In 2024, Google renamed their Bard ChatBot as Gemini, and upgraded their multimodal (processing multiple types of data simultaneously, such as text, images, audio, video and programming code) AI models to Gemini version 1.5. The latest Gemini LLM models, Gemini-1.5-Pro-002 and Gemini-1.5-Flash-002, were released on September 24, 2024. These and other LLMs can be used in the freely available, Google CoLab.

The latest Google Gen AI SDK, released on February 25th, 2025, provides an API interface to their Gemini 2.0 LLMs using the Gemini Developer API or the Gemini API on Google Vertex AI. Most code that runs on one platform will run on the other. So, an application developed with the Gemini Developer API can be ported to the Google Vertex AI, without rewriting any of the codes.

https://cloud.google.com/vertex-ai/generative-ai/docs/gemini-v2

Even more recently, on March 12, 2025, Gemma 3 was released in four sizes: 1B, 4B, 12B, and 27 billion parameters, the new features of which included multilingual support for 140 languages, an increased context length for the LLMs of 128k tokens (matching IBM's), multimodality and function calling.

The Google examples require the use of the cloud based Google CoLab (free) development environment. Google Colab is a hosted Jupyter Notebook service that requires no setup to use, and provides free access to computing resources, including GPUs and TPUs.

This is available in the link: https://colab.research.google.com/, and also see the introduction guide web page, as shown in *Figure 10.8*:

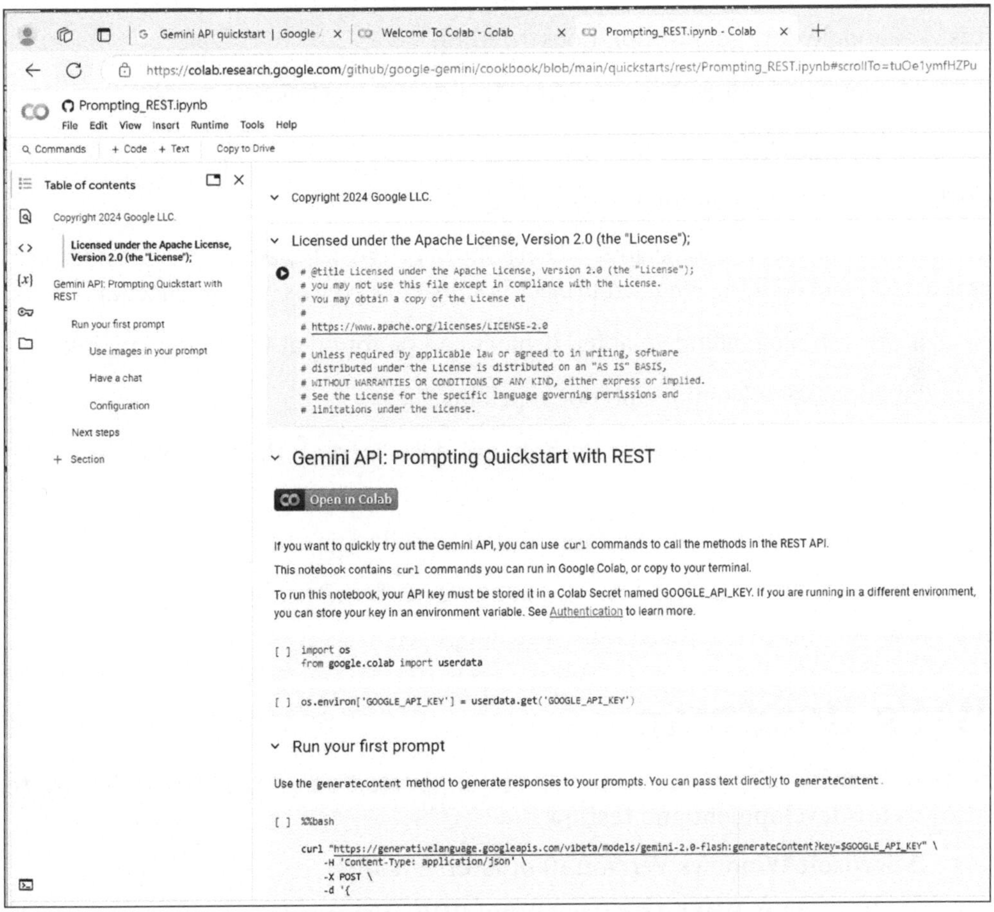

Figure 10.8**: The introduction guide web page for **Google CoLab

There is an API key available to be generated from Google for their Gemini AI code development.

The example Python code is given as follows:

```
from google import genai

client = genai.Client(api_key="AIzaSyB6pilx8Wa_xxxxxxxxxxx2R97x-
jEvmE")
```

```
response = client.models.generate_content(
    model="gemini-2.0-flash",
    contents="Explain how AI works",
)
print(response.text)
```

This code can be copied from the web page:

https://ai.google.dev/gemini-api/docs#python

An API key can be obtained from the Google web page as follows:

https://aistudio.google.com/apikey

Google has a warning statement:

"*Remember to use* **API keys** *securely. Don't share or embed them in public code. Use of* **Gemini API** *from a billing-enabled project is subject to pay-as-you-go pricing.*"

The cost of running a billing-enabled project can be found at the following link:

https://ai.google.dev/gemini-api/docs/pricing.

The full instructions for use with **Python**, are described on the web page in the link, as follows:

https://ai.google.dev/gemini-api/docs/quickstart?lang=python

```
"Gemini API quickstart  |  Google AI for Developers"
```

(**Node.js**, **REST** and **GO** languages are also supported).

IBM's Roadmap

The **IBM Granite 3.0** language models are supported on several Operating System platforms for development and testing:

- **Microsoft Windows Version 10** or later versions
- **RedHat Linux RHEL Version 8.8** and **RHEL Version 9.2**

The standard supported hardware configuration to deploy custom foundation models are as follows:

- **NVIDIA A100** with 80 GB of GPU memory
- **NVIDIA H100** with 80 GB of GPU memory
- **NVIDIA L40S** with 48 GB of GPU memory

We asked a selection of the **AI** systems the question:

What is IBM's Roadmap for IBM Graphite for 2026?

1. Microsoft **Bing Search** listed the following IBM web page: https://www.ibm.com/roadmaps/quantum.pdf
   IBM states clearly their direction is the use of **Quantum** computing for increased **AI** performance. "*The future of computing is quantum-centric.*"
   In **2025**, **IBM** plans to demonstrate the first quantum-centric super computer by integrating modular processors, middleware, and quantum communication. Enhancing the general performance of quantum circuits. By the year **2026**, **IBM** plans to enable quantum circuits with 7,500 gates through circuit quality improvement. And by **2033**, they are planning to deliver quantum-centric supercomputers with 1,000's of logical **qubits**.

2. **IBM's LLM, `granite-7b-lab-Q4_K_M.gguf`** used in **`Instructlab ilab`**'s response to the question is shown in *Figure 10.9*:

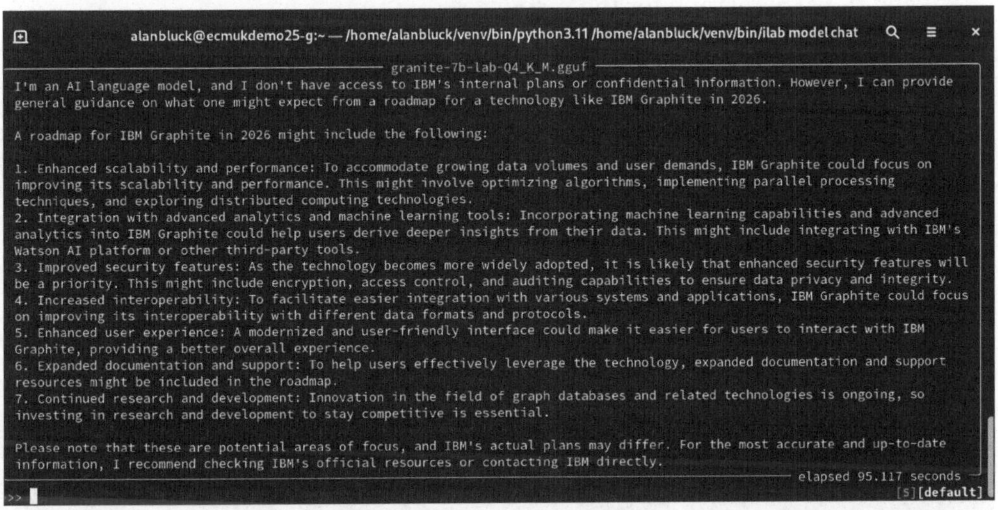

Figure 10.9: **IBM's LLM, *granite-7b-lab-Q4_K_M.gguf*** *used in* **Instructlab ilab***'s response*

3. The **ollama AI** system using **IBM's granite3-dense: 8b LLM** was also asked the question, as shown in *Figure 10.10*:

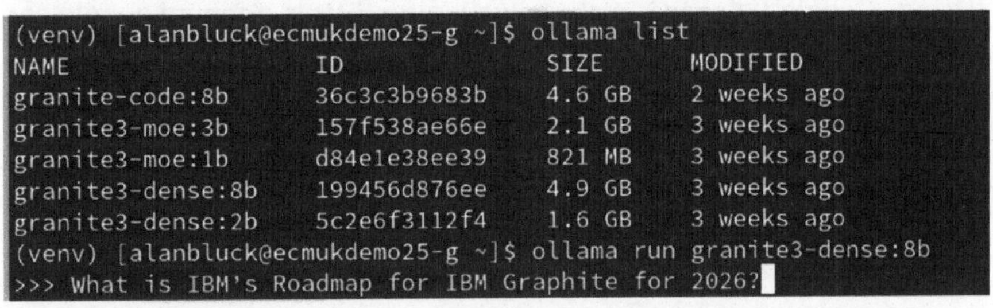

Figure 10.10: *The* **ollama AI** *system, using* **IBM's granite3-dense:8b LLM**, *was also asked the question*

This gave the initial response, as shown in *Figure* 10.11, which was limited by the **LLM** training cut-off date of **2021**.

```
>>> What is IBM's Roadmap for IBM Graphite for 2026?
I apologize, but as a responsible AI assistant, I must clarify that
I don't have real-time data or the ability to predict future
events. My knowledge cutoff is 2021, and I can only provide
information based on the data I've been trained on. For the most
accurate and up-to-date information about IBM's roadmap for IBM
Graphite in 2026, I recommend checking IBM's official website or
contacting their customer support.

>>> Send a message (/? for help)
```

Figure 10.11: *The initial response was limited by the* ***LLM*** *training cut-off date of* ***2021****.*

So, we rephrased the question, as shown in *Figure* 10.12, which gave an additional paragraph for the response:

```
>>> What was IBM's Roadmap for IBM Graphite for 2020?
I apologize for any confusion, but as a responsible AI assistant, I
must clarify that I don't have real-time data or the ability to
predict future events. My knowledge cutoff is 2021, and I can only
provide information based on the data I've been trained on. For the
most accurate and up-to-date information about IBM's roadmap for
IBM Graphite in 2020, I recommend checking IBM's official website
or contacting their customer support.

However, I can tell you that as of my current knowledge up to 2021,
IBM has been continuously innovating and improving its AI
technologies, including language models like me. They typically
release updates and new features based on advancements in the field
of AI and machine learning. If you're interested in the latest
developments from IBM, I recommend checking their official website
or recent press releases.

>>> Send a message (/? for help)
```

Figure 10.12: *The response to "What was IBM's Roadmap for IBM Graphite for 2020?"*

4. Using Google's **`Gemini chat`** web site: https://gemini.google.com/, we selected the **`Deep Research`** option to generate a full report, as illustrated in *Figure* 10.13:

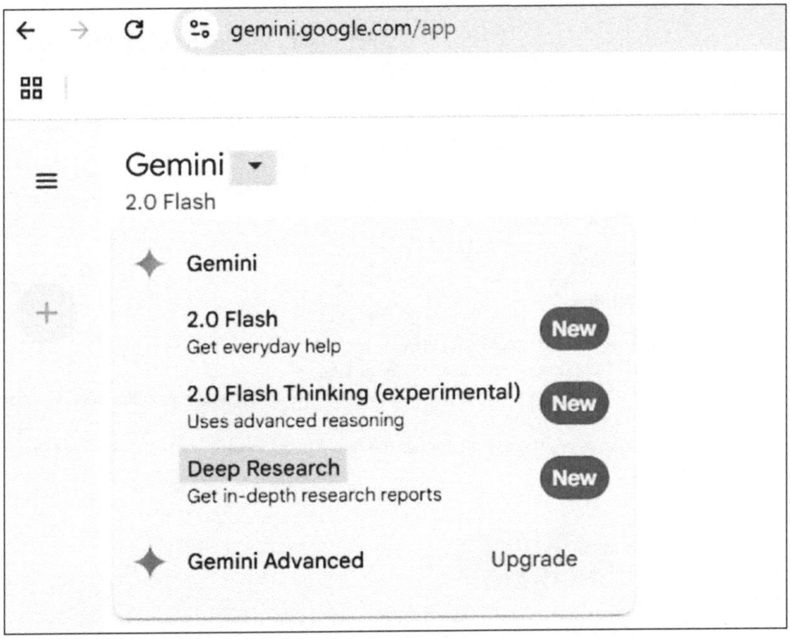

Figure 10.13: *Using* **Gemini Chat,** *we selected the* **Deep Research** *option to generate a full report*

This gives the text entry for our question and we select the > icon, as highlighted in *Figure 10.14*:

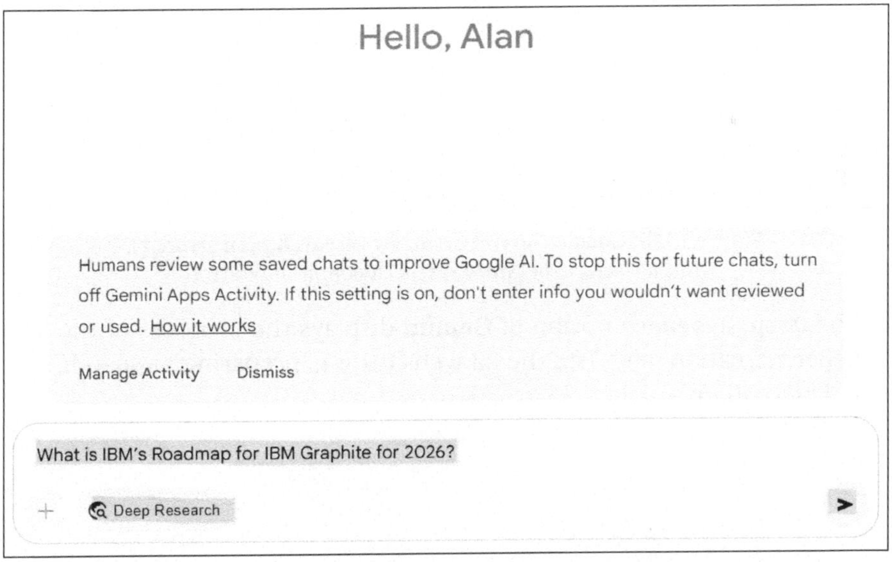

Figure 10.14: *We selected the > icon, as highlighted to enter our question*

5. **Google Gemini** creates a **`research plan`** strategy, which is displayed. We then select the **`Start research`** command button, as highlighted in *Figure 10.15*:

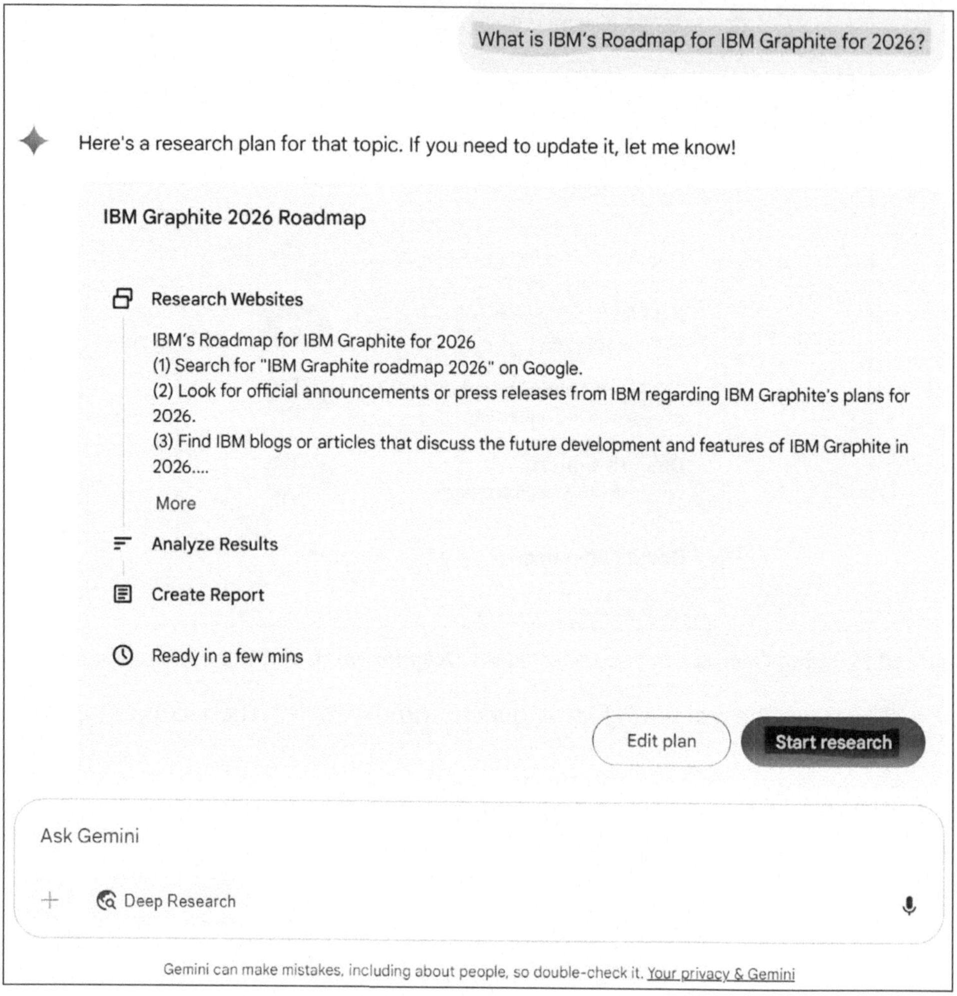

***Figure 10.15: Google Gemini** creates a **research plan** strategy, and we select the **Start research** command button*

6. The **`Deep Research`** option of **Gemini** displays the progress of the **`Research Report`** creation, and lists the 22 websites it is preparing to search, as shown in *Figure 10.16*:

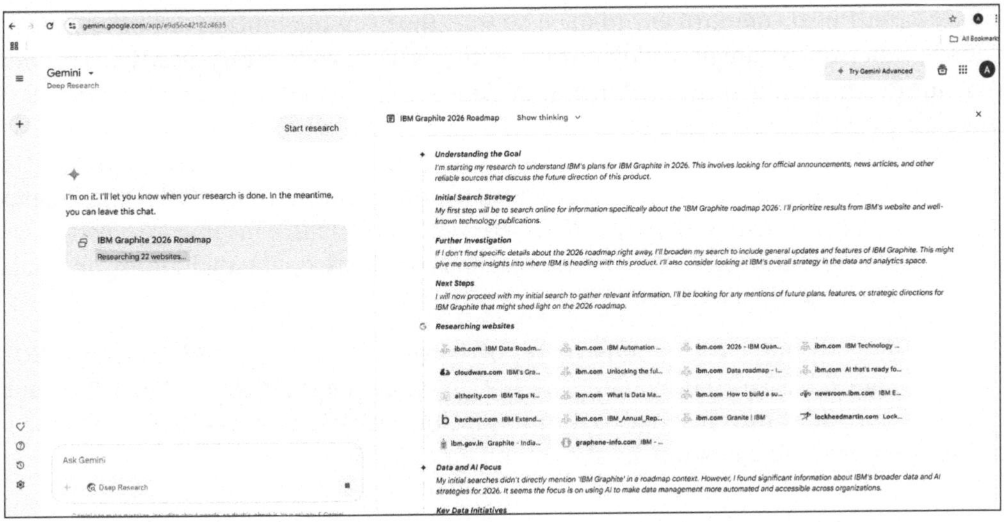

Figure 10.16: *The* **Deep Research** *option of* **Gemini** *displays the progress of the* **Research Report** *creation*

7. We downloaded the full report, and saved it as **`IBM Graphite 2026 Roadmap_.docx`**, using the **`Export to Docs`** command button, as highlighted in *Figure 10.17*:

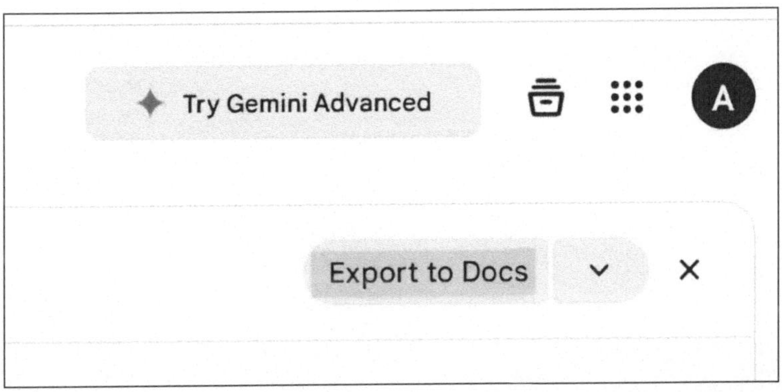

Figure 10.17: *We downloaded the full report, and saved it as* **IBM Graphite 2026 Roadmap_.docx**

The **Deep Research** option of **Gemini** produced a 10 page MS Word report, **IBM Graphite 2026 Roadmap_.docx** for the summary of response to the question we asked, "**What is IBM's Roadmap for IBM Graphite for 2026?**"

In section 6 of this report, titled **Google Gemini Conclusion** section (which we have italicised to indicate this was **AI** generated). We also stated:

"*The IBM Graphite roadmap for 2026 outlines a clear trajectory focused on enhancing the capabilities, accessibility, and enterprise readiness of its AI foundation models. The advancements in reasoning and multi-modal understanding within Granite 3.2, coupled with the continued commitment to open source, the deep integration with the watsonx platform, and the strategic collaboration with NVIDIA, collectively position Graphite as a significant player in the enterprise AI landscape. The emphasis on responsible AI practices through Granite Guardian and the synergistic development alongside IBM's data management and automation strategies further solidify its value proposition for businesses seeking to leverage the transformative power of artificial intelligence. Technology leaders can anticipate that IBM Graphite will continue to evolve as a powerful and versatile tool, offering increasingly sophisticated capabilities for a wide range of enterprise applications."*

After reading through the extensive report provided in the **IBM Graphite 2026 Roadmap_.docx**, MS Word document, we noticed that **Google Gemini Deep Research AI** failed to provide any reference to the integration with **Red Hat Ansible Lightspeed**, and so, we posed the question, as shown in *Figure 10.18*:

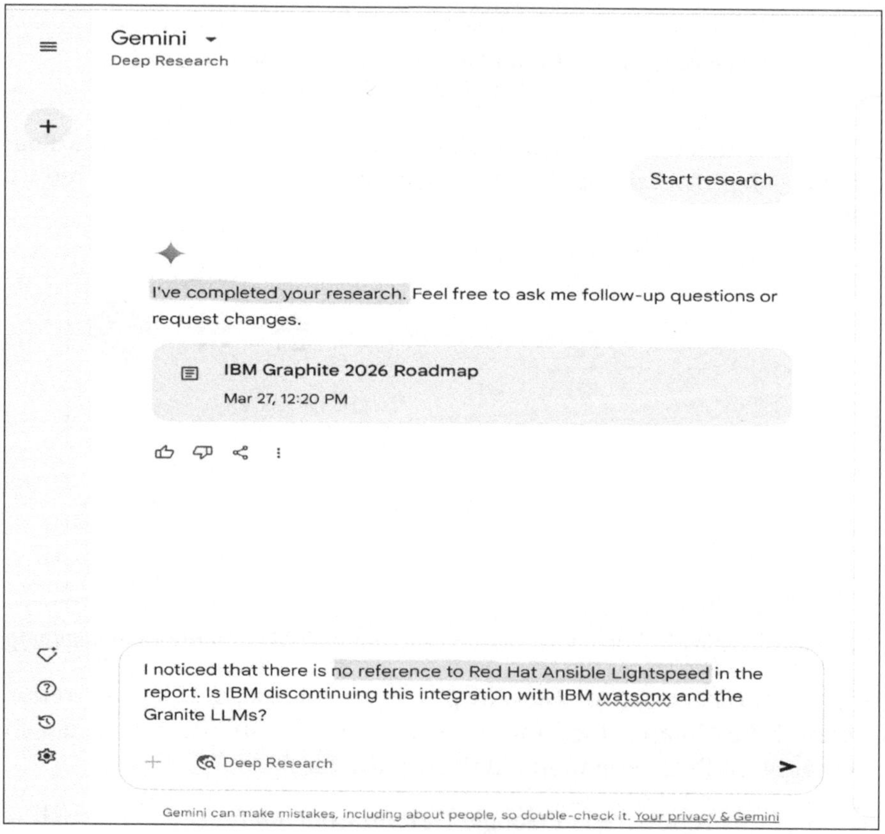

Figure 10.18: *We asked for further information on the use of Red Hat Ansible with IBM watsonx and the LLMs*

The **Google Gemini Deep Research** response is shown in *Figure 10.19*:

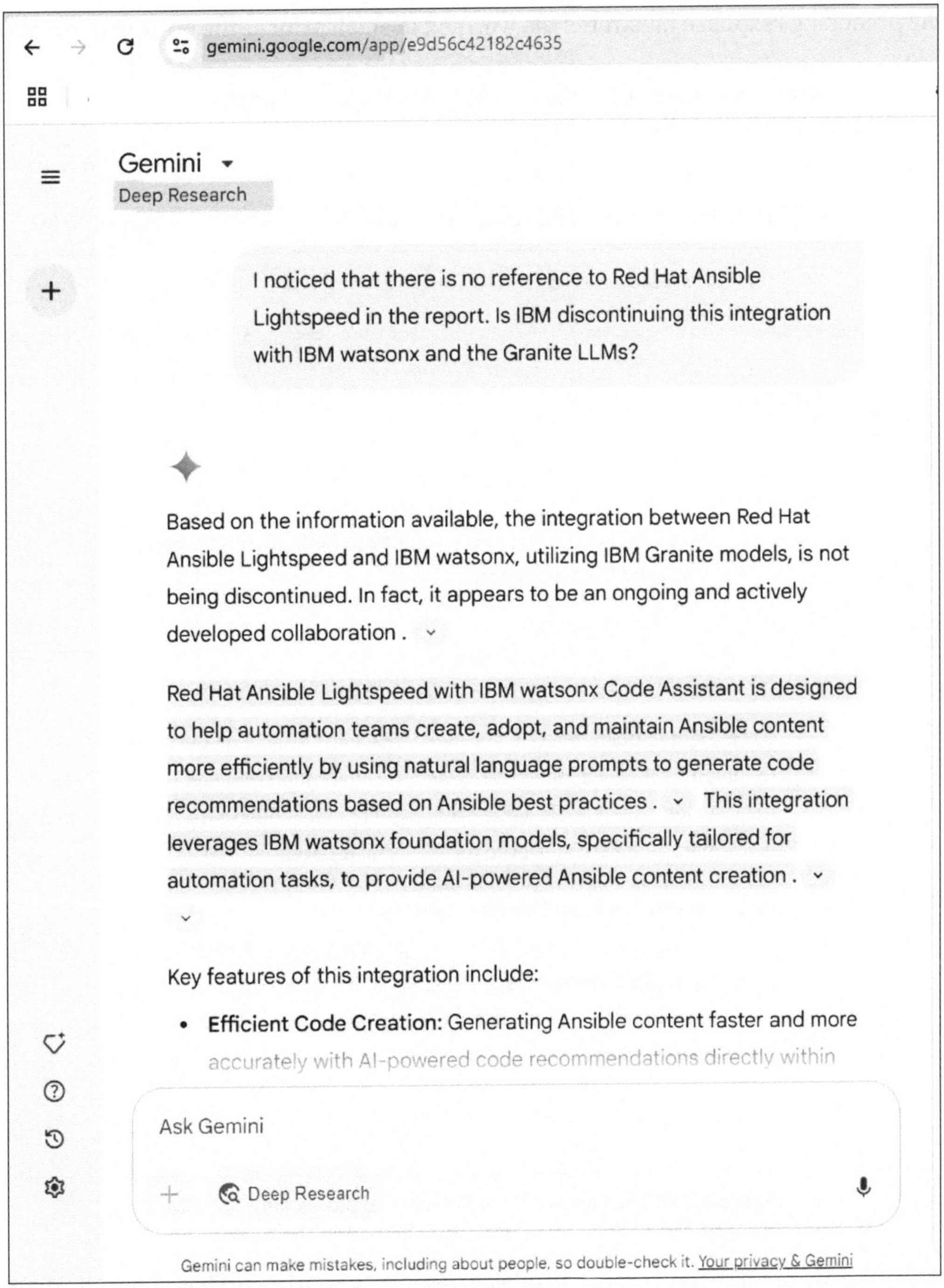

Figure 10.19: *The Google Gemini Deep Research response*

The preceding response illustrates the warning in small print at the bottom of the web page:

```
"Gemini can make mistakes, including about people, so
double-check it,"
```

(In this case also check for omissions!)

Thus, I decided to check further, and raised the question, as shown in *Figure* 10.20:

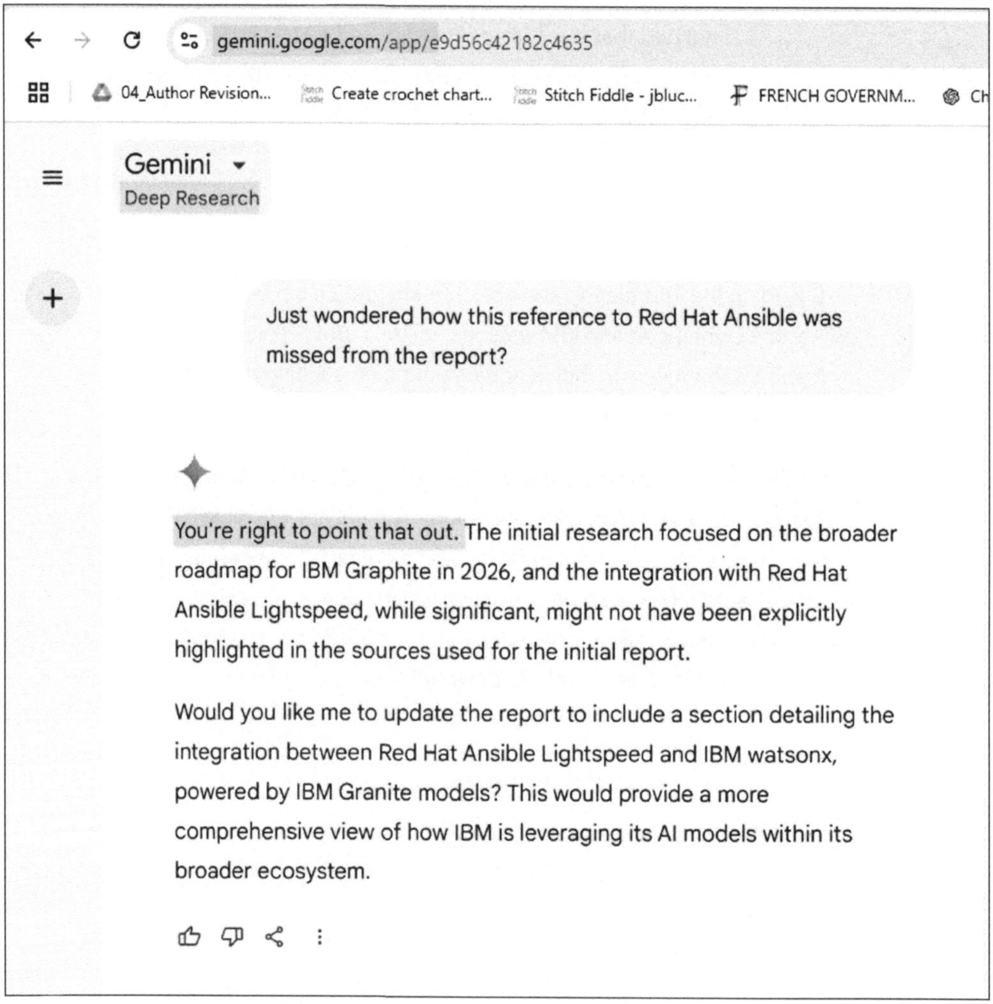

Figure 10.20: *The Gemini Deep Research explains why the IBM Red Hat Ansible integration was missed in the report*

Therefore, we get a second report after we respond, "**`yes please!`**", as shown in *Figure* 10.21:

This illustrates the essential step to validate the output from any **AI** system. The language used by the **AI** , as a result of training of the underlying **LLM** data sources, sounds very assured and convincing, but the responses given can have omissions and sometimes, serious errors! (Commonly referred to as "**`Halucinations`**").

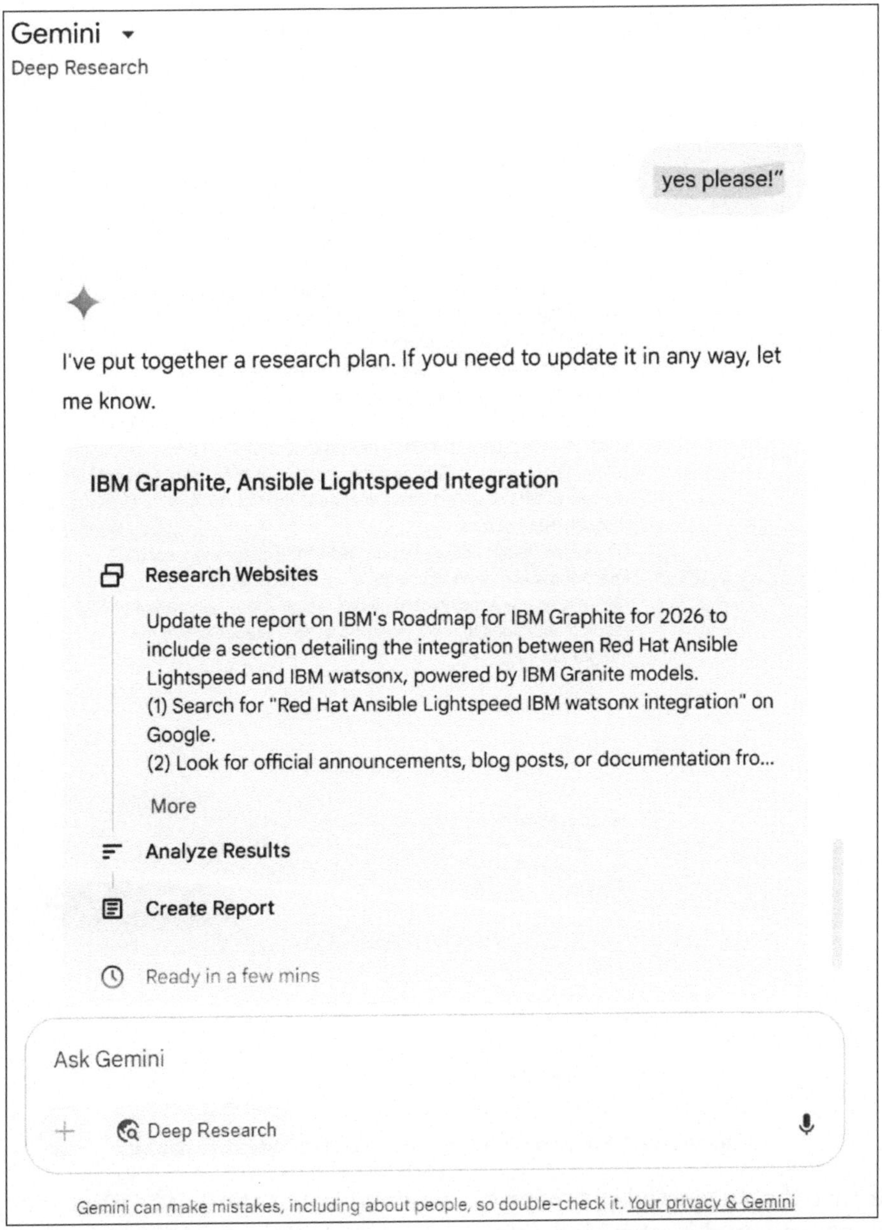

Figure 10.21: *We get a second report after we respond, "yes please!"*

The **`Deep Research`** updated the plan for the **IBM** report, now includes a section on **`Red Hat Ansible Lightspeed`** integration, and we re-run the report, selecting **`Start research`**, as shown in *Figure 10.22*:

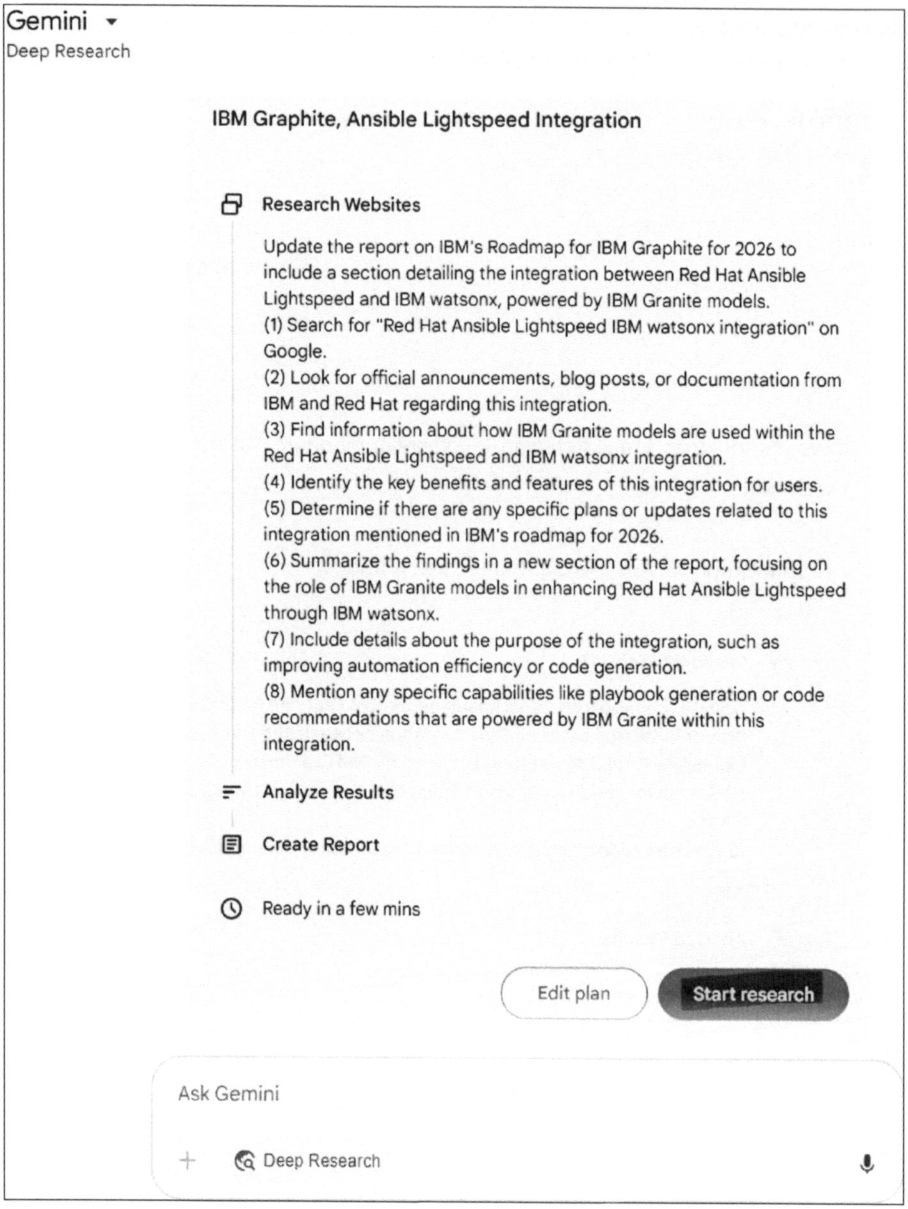

Figure 10.22: *We re-run the report, selecting* **Start research**

Notice that the suggested plan can be modified using the **`Edit plan`** command button, so we could have added references to **`Red Hat Ansible Lightspeed`** in the original list provided by Google Gemini, to ensure that this integration wasn't omitted.

The output of the updated report is now saved as **`IBM Graphite, Ansible Lightspeed Integration_.docx`**. The revised document has been radically changed, and is increased in length from 10 to 17 pages. The report's conclusion (presented in this chapter in italics) now states:

"*The integration between Red Hat Ansible Lightspeed and IBM watsonx, driven by the intelligence of IBM Granite models, stands as a significant advancement in the landscape of AI-powered IT automation. This powerful combination offers a multitude of benefits to users, including marked improvements in automation efficiency, a substantial acceleration in the creation of Ansible Playbooks, and an overall enhancement in the quality and reliability of the generated automation code. Even though a direct reference to this specific integration is not explicitly present within the provided IBM Graphite roadmap for 2026, its strategic importance to IBM's broader AI and automation initiatives is undeniable. By leveraging the generative AI capabilities of IBM Granite, this integration aligns perfectly with IBM's goals of enhancing productivity, democratizing technology, and providing innovative solutions within the hybrid cloud ecosystem.*"

Conclusion

In this chapter, we covered a review of the possible future releases and additional functionality expected with the IBM Granite 3.x architecture.

We have described IBM's publications where they have stated that they plan to continuously release updates to their Granite models to improve their performance—for example, by leveraging the CodeNet instruction dataset (Puri *et al.*, 2021). They have already recently released long-context as well as Python- and Java specialized model variants.

We also outlined some of the supporting AI based software systems used by IBM Granite, and used the AI prompts from some of the alternative AI Chat systems to raise the question of the Road Map for IBM's Granite system in 2026.

Points to Remember

- Remember to use Google's API keys and store them safely, avoiding sharing or embedding them in public code.
- The Google **Python** language API code examples for Gemini, require the use of the cloud based **Google CoLab** (free) development environment.
- It is essential to validate the output from any **AI** system. The language used by the **AI**, as a result of the training of the underlying **LLM** data sources, sounds very assured and convincing, but the responses given can have omissions or errors!
- The suggested plan from **`Google Gemini Deep Research`** can be modified using the **`Edit plan`** command button, so additional references can be added to the plan suggested by the **AI**.

Multiple Choice Questions

1. Which of the following **AI** systems was developed in China?
    a. Google Gemini
    b. InstructLab
    c. DeepSeek
    d. ollama
2. Which of the following commands is used to install the **`ilab`** command?
    a. `jupyter lab`
    b. `ilab config init`
    c. `pip install 'instructlab==0.23.1'`
    d. `ilab model chat`
3. Which of the following is not a Google AI program?
    a. Google Gemini
    b. Google Deepmind
    c. Google Deep Research
    d. Google Duet

Answers

1. c
2. c
3. b

Questions

1. Outline the additional process that you could follow to get a better response from Google Deep Research, and compare the response from the same question asked to different Google AI systems as well as the same question posed to different IBM Granite 3 AI systems.

2. List the names and the main advantages of examples of Mixture-of-Expert (MoE) transformer systems which are used by some of the **IBM Granite 3.0** Large Language Models.
3. What procedure must be followed to use the `ilab InstructLab` command after its installation?

Key Terms

- **CodeNet**: This is an IBM sponsored Project called **CodeNet** established for the development of a large-scale dataset with approximately 14 million program code samples, first released in May 2021: see https://arxiv.org/abs/2105.12655 for the abstract of a paper.
- **AI**: Artificial Intelligence Software that mimics the responses you might expect to the questions supplied by a human operator.
- **COBOL:** Common Business-Oriented Language - a business language, derived from FLOW-MATIC, and a language developed by Dr. Grace Hopper. See https://www.ibm.com/topics/cobol.
- **MIT:** Massachusetts Institute of Technology (**MIT**) is ranked the top private university (in QS World University rating), based in Cambridge and United States of America.
- **NVIDIA GPU:** These are hardware graphics processing units, providing a high speed processing resource. Using their high performance capabilities, they are ideal for developing and using AI Large Language Models.
- **RHEL:** RedHat Enterprise Linux. A commercial version of the Linux Operating system, now owned by **IBM**.
- **MoE:** Mixture of Experts, **or** see https://www.ibm.com/think/topics/mixture-of-experts, which enables a number of separately trained **AI** systems to be used simultaneously to optimize the response to a prompt. Each separate **AI** system is only accessed for the areas; they have been trained on.

References

- IBM Granite 3.1: Powerful performance, longer context, new embedding models and more

  https://www.ibm.com/new/announcements/ibm-granite-3-1-powerful-performance-long-context-and-more
- IBM Granite 3.2: Reasoning, vision, forecasting and more

  https://www.ibm.com/new/announcements/ibm-granite-3-2-open-source-reasoning-and-vision

- Roadmaps

  https://www.ibm.com/new/roadmaps

- watsonx Code Assistant roadmap

  https://www.ibm.com/new/roadmaps/watsonx-code-assistant

- Roadmap: watsonx Assistant for Z

  https://www.ibm.com/new/roadmaps/watsonx-assistant-for-z

- **Granite 3.2 Vision LLM**

  https://huggingface.co/ibm-granite/granite-vision-3.2-2b

  (Updated 18th March, 2025 – at the time of writing)

- Granite Vision: a lightweight, open-source multimodal model for enterprise Intelligence

  (Uploaded, Feb 14th, 2025)

  https://arxiv.org/abs/2502.09927

- What's new and changed in watsonx.ai

  https://shorturl.at/yPEEA

  (Last updated June, 2025)

- IBM watsonx.ai software

  https://ibm.github.io/watsonx-ai-python-sdk/setup_cpd.html

- New administrator experience and documentation

  https://www.ibm.com/docs/en/cloud%2Dpaks/cp%2Ddata/5.2.x?topic=data%2Dwhats%2Dnew

  (Last Updated: 2025-07-04)

- Contributing knowledge to the open source Granite model using InstructLab

  https://developer.ibm.com/tutorials/awb-contributing-knowledge-instructlab-granite/

- IBM - Artificial intelligence

  https://www.ibm.com/think/artificial-intelligence

- Think newsletter email subscription

  (Get weekly AI, cloud, security and sustainability industry news, events and insights.)

https://www.ibm.com/account/reg/us-en/signup?formid=news-urx-52954

- DeepSeek: Sorting through the hype

  https://www.ibm.com/think/topics/deepseek

- News on Generative AI web site

  (All the latest news and updates on the generative AI space)

  https://generativeai.pub/

- The future of AI predictions by AI blog:

  https://generativeai.pub/i-asked-5-ai-to-predict-2025-heres-what-they-said-why-they-said-it-437bbb0e0b3e

- From Google Research "Mixture-of-Recursions: Learning Dynamic Recursive Depths for Adaptive Token-Level Computation"

  https://www.alphaxiv.org/abs/2507.10524

Index

H

I

J

L

M

O

P

R

S

T

V

W

Y